Contents

KT-362-129

Welcome to Tibet

Tibet offers fabulous monasteries, breathtaking high-altitude treks, stunning views of the world's highest mountains and one of the most likeable peoples you will ever meet.

A Higher Plain

For many people, the highlights of Tibet will be of a spiritual nature – magnificent monasteries, prayer halls of chanting monks and remote cliffside retreats. Tibet's pilgrims are an essential part of this appeal, from the local grannies mumbling mantras in temples heavy with the aroma of juniper incense and yak butter, to the hard-core pilgrims walking or prostrating themselves around Mt Kailash. Tibet has a level of devotion and faith that seems to belong to an earlier age.

The Roof of the World

For travellers nonplussed by Tibet's religious significance, the big draw is likely to be the elemental beauty of the highest plateau on earth. Geography here is on a humbling scale and every view is lit with spectacular mountain light. Your trip will take you past glittering turquoise lakes, across huge plains dotted with yaks and nomads' tents and over high passes draped with colourful prayer flags. Hike past the ruins of remote hermitages, stare up open-mouthed at the north face of Everest or make an epic overland trip along some of the world's wildest roads. The scope for adventure is limited only by your ability to get permits.

Politics & Permits

There's no getting away from politics in modern Tibet. Whether you see Tibet as an oppressed, occupied nation or simply an underdeveloped province of China, the normal rules for travel in China simply don't apply.

Travel restrictions mean that independent travel is currently not possible, as foreign travellers need to prearrange a tour with a guide and transportation for their time in Tibet. On the plus side, new airports, boutique hotels and paved roads offer a level of travel comfort unheard of just a few years ago. If the rigours of high-altitude Tibet travel have deterred you in the past, now might just be the time to take the plunge.

The Tibetan People

Whatever your interests, your lasting memories of Tibet are likely to be of the bottle of Lhasa Beer you shared in a Lhasa teahouse, the yak-butter tea offered by a monk in a remote monastery or the picnic shared with a herder's family on the shores of a remote lake. Always ready with a smile and with a great tolerance and openness of heart despite decades of political turmoil and hardship, it is the Tibetan people that truly make travelling in Tibet such a profound joy.

Why I Love Tibet

By Bradley Mayhew, Author

For me Tibet is a uniquely spiritual place. Those moments of peace, fleeting and precious, when everything seems to be in its proper place, just seem to come more frequently here. Despite the overpowering pace of change and a sobering political situation, underpinning everything for me are the Tibetan people, whose joy and devotion remain deeply inspiring. Tibet is a place that will likely change the way you see the world and remain with you for years to come. And that for me is the definition of the very best kind of travel.

For more about our authors, see page 352

Above: Monks walking outside a monastery

Tibet

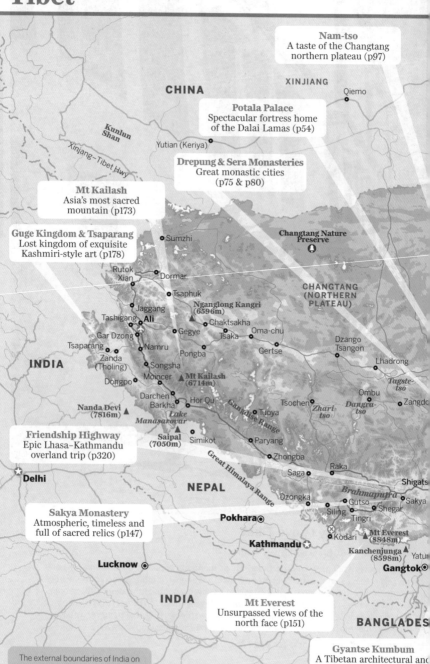

Nam-tso
A taste of the Changtang northern plateau (p97)

CHINA

XINJIANG

Qiemo

Potala Palace
Spectacular fortress home of the Dalai Lamas (p54)

Kunlun Shan

Xinjiang–Tibet Hwy

Yutian (Keriya)

Drepung & Sera Monasteries
Great monastic cities (p75 & p80)

Mt Kailash
Asia's most sacred mountain (p173)

Guge Kingdom & Tsaparang
Lost kingdom of exquisite Kashmiri-style art (p178)

Sumzhi

Changtang Nature Preserve

Rutok Xian
Dormar

Tsaphuk

Nganglong Kangri (6596m)

CHANGTANG (NORTHERN PLATEAU)

Jaggang

Tashigang
Ali
Gegye
Chaktsakha
Oma-chu

Gar Dzong
Tsaka

Dzango Tsangon

Tsaparang
Namru
Pongba
Gertse

Lhadrong

Zanda (Tholing)
Songsha

INDIA
Dongpo
Moincer
Mt Kailash (6714m)

Tagste-tso

Darchen
Hor Qu
Ombu
Zangdc

Barkha
Gangdise Range
Tsochen
Zhari-tso
Dangra-tso

Nanda Devi (7816m)
Lake Manasarovar
Tuoya

Saipal (7050m)
Simikot
Paryang

Friendship Highway
Epic Lhasa–Kathmandu overland trip (p320)

Zhongba

Raka

Delhi

NEPAL
Saga

Shigats

Dzongka
Brahmaputra
Sakya

Sakya Monastery
Atmospheric, timeless and full of sacred relics (p147)

Pokhara
Gutso
Shegar

Siling
Tingri

Kathmandu
Kodari
Mt Everest (8848m)

Lucknow
Kanchenjunga (8598m)
Yatur

Gangtok

INDIA
Mt Everest
Unsurpassed views of the north face (p151)

BANGLADES

The external boundaries of India on this map have not been authenticated and may not be correct.

Gyantse Kumbum
A Tibetan architectural and artistic masterpiece (p129)

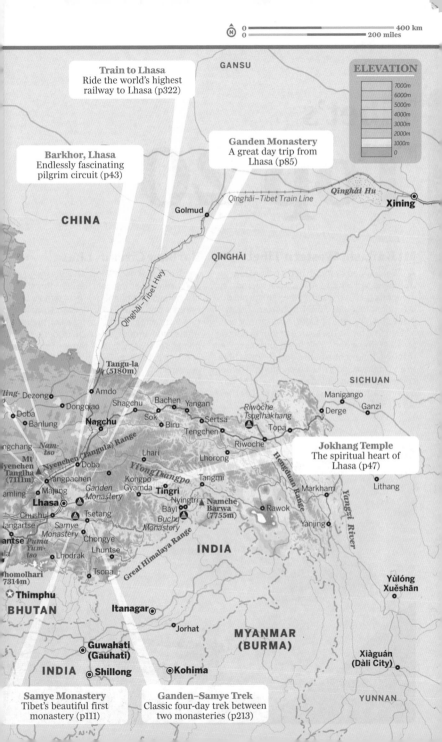

0 ⟨————⟩ **400 km**
0 ⟨————⟩ **200 miles**

GANSU

Train to Lhasa
Ride the world's highest
railway to Lhasa (p322)

Ganden Monastery
A great day trip from
Lhasa (p85)

Barkhor, Lhasa
Endlessly fascinating
pilgrim circuit (p43)

ELEVATION

7000m
6000m
5000m
4000m
3000m
2000m
1000m
0

Qīnghǎi–Tibet Train Line

Qīnghǎi Hu

CHINA

Golmud

Xining

QĪNGHǍI

Qīnghǎi–Tibet Hwy

Tangu-la
(5180m)

SICHUAN

Manigango

ling- Dezong

Amdo

Shagchu

Bachen

Yangan

*Riwoche
Tsuglhakhang*

Derge

Ganzi

Doba

Dongqiao

Sok

Biru

Sertsa

Topa

Nagchu

Tengchen

Riwoche

Banlung

*ngchang Nam-
tso*

Lhari

Lhorong

Jokhang Temple
The spiritual heart of
Lhasa (p47)

**Mt
yenchen
Tanglha**
(7111m)

Nyenchen Tanglha Range

Doba

YlongTsangpo

Tangmi

Markham

Lithang

amling Yangpachen

Kongpo

Gyamda

Tingri

Hengduan Range

Majang

*Ganden
Monastery*

Nyingtri

Yangzi River

Lhasa

Bayi

Namche
Barwa
(7755m)

Rawok

Chushul

Tsetang

*Buchu
Monastery*

Yanjing

angartse

*Samye
Monastery*

Chongye

antse

*Puma
Yum-
tso*

Lhodrak

Lhuntse

Great Himalaya Range

INDIA

la

Tsona

*homolhari
7314m)*

☼ Thimphu

Itanagar

**Yùlóng
Xuěshān**

BHUTAN

Jorhat

**MYANMAR
(BURMA)**

**Guwahati
(Gauhati)**

**Xiàguán
(Dàli City)**

INDIA

Shillong

Kohima

YUNNAN

Samye Monastery
Tibet's beautiful first
monastery (p111)

Ganden–Samye Trek
Classic four-day trek between
two monasteries (p213)

Tibet's
Top 20

Mt Kailash, Western Tibet

1 Worshipped by more than a billion Buddhists and Hindus, Asia's most sacred mountain (p173) rises from the Barkha plain like a giant four-sided 6714m chörten. Throw in the stunning nearby Lake Manasarovar and a basin that forms the source of four of Asia's greatest rivers, and who's to say this place really isn't the centre of the world? Travel here to one of the world's most beautiful and remote corners brings an added bonus: the three-day pilgrim path around the mountain erases the sins of a lifetime.

Barkhor Circuit, Lhasa

2 You never quite know what you're going to find when you join the centrifugal tide of Tibetans circling the Jokhang temple on the Barkhor circuit (p45). Pilgrims and prostrators from across Tibet, stalls selling prayer wheels and turquoise, Muslim traders, Khampa nomads in shaggy cloaks, women from Amdo sporting 108 braids, thangka artists and Chinese military patrols are all par for the course. It's a fascinating microcosm of Tibet and a place you'll want to come back to again and again. Right: Barkhor Square (p43)

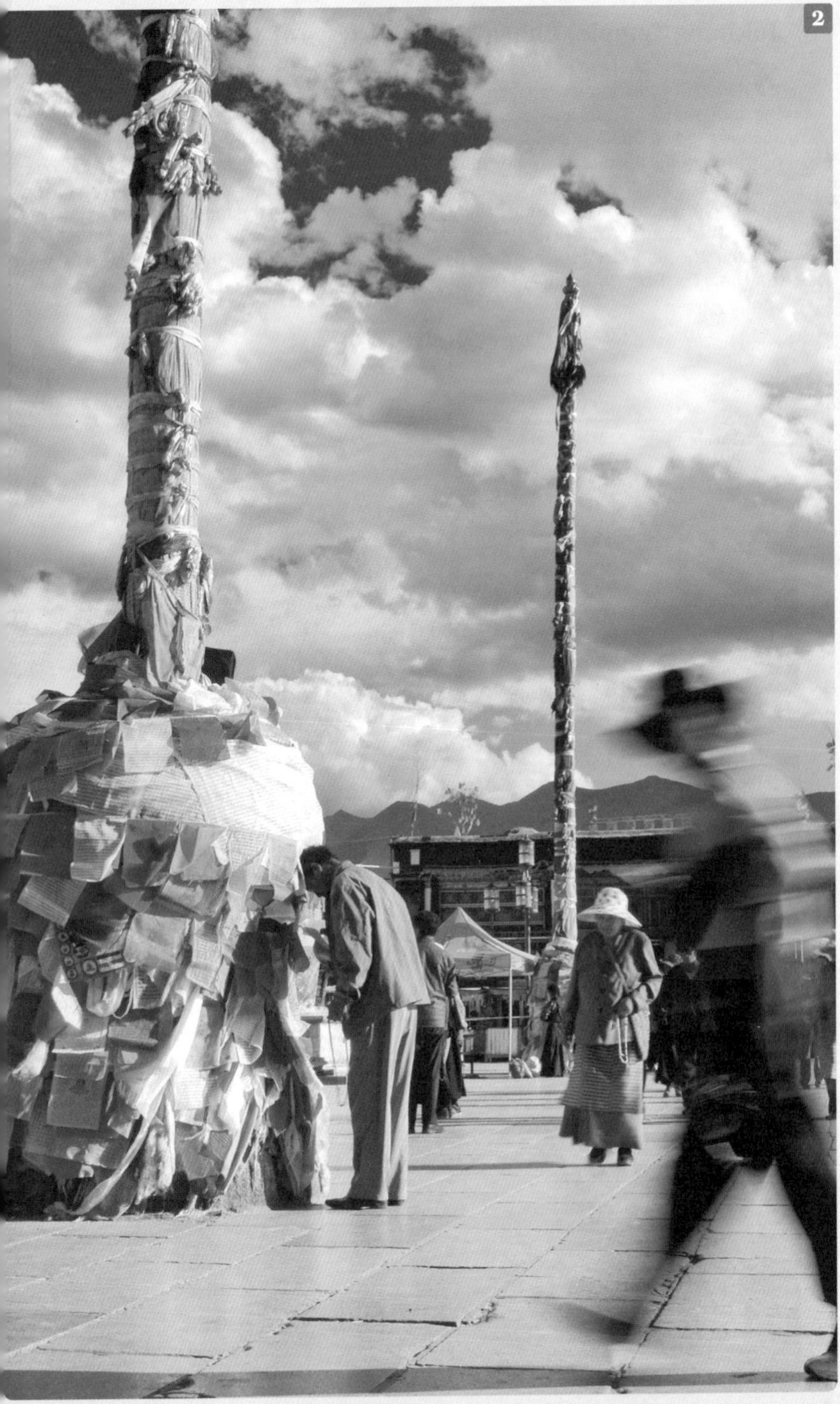

Jokhang Temple, Lhasa

3 The atmosphere of hushed awe is what hits you first as you inch through the dark, medieval passageways of the Jokhang (p47). Queues of wide-eyed pilgrims shuffle up and down the stairways, past medieval doorways and millennium-old murals, pausing briefly to top up the hundreds of butter lamps that flicker in the gloom. It's the beating spiritual heart of Tibet. Welcome to the 14th century.

Views of Mt Everest

4 Don't tell the Nepal Tourism Board, but Tibet has easily the best views of the world's most famous mountain (p151). While two-week-long trekking routes on the Nepal side offer up only occasional fleeting glimpses of the peak, the view of Mt Everest's unobstructed north face framed in the prayer flags of Rongphu Monastery or from a tent at the Base Camp will stop you in your tracks. Bottom: View from Everest Base Camp (p153)

TIM HUGHES / GETTY IMAGES ©

MERTEN SNIJDERS / GETTY IMAGES ©

Saga Dawa Festival

5 The line between tourist and pilgrim can be a fine one in Tibet, none more so than during the Saga Dawa Festival (p24), when thousands of pilgrims pour into Lhasa to visit the city and make a ritual procession around the 8km Lingkhor path. Load up on small bills and juniper incense before joining the pilgrims past chapels and prostration points, or travel west to Mt Kailash for the mountain's biggest annual party.

Samye Monastery

6 Tibet's first monastery (p111) is a heavily symbolic collection of chapels, chörtens and shrines arranged around a medieval Tibetan-, Chinese- and Indian-style temple. The 1200-year-old site is where Guru Rinpoche battled demons to introduce Buddhism to Tibet and where the future course of Tibetan Buddhism was sealed in a great debate. The dreamy location on the desert-like banks of the Yarlung Tsangpo is just superb.

Train Ride to Lhasa

7 For all its faults, China's railway to Tibet (the world's highest) is an engineering wonder and a delightful way to reach the holy city. Pull up a window seat to view huge salt lakes, plains dotted with yaks and herders' tents, and hundreds of miles of desolate nothing, as you inch slowly up onto the high plateau. Peaking at 5072m may send you diving for the piped oxygen, but it's still a classic rail trip (p322).

KEREN SU / GETTY IMAGES ©

Drepung & Sera Monasteries, Lhasa

8 Lhasa's great religious institutions of Sera (p80) and Drepung (p75) are more than just monasteries – they are self-contained towns. A web of whitewashed alleyways climbs past medieval kitchens, printing presses and colleges to reach giant prayer halls full of chanting, tea-sipping, red-robed monks. Don't miss the afternoon debating, an extravagant spectator sport of Buddhist dialectics and hand slapping. Top left: Monk worshipping at Drepung Monastery (p75)

Potala Palace, Lhasa

9 There are moments in travel that will long stay with you – your first view of Lhasa's iconic Potala Palace (p54) is one such moment. A visit to the former home of the Dalai Lamas is a spiralling descent past gold-tombed chapels, opulent reception rooms and huge prayer halls into the bowels of a medieval castle. It's nothing less than the concentrated spiritual and material wealth of a nation.

Yak-Butter Tea

10 Some people prefer to call it 'soup', others liken it to brewed socks and sump oil. However you describe it, your first mouthful of yak-butter tea (p309) is the signal that you have finally reached Tibet. Our favourite thing about the Tibetan national drink is the view from the rim: a monk's quarters, a herder's yak-hair tent or a teahouse full of card-playing Tibetan cowboys. Definitely our cup of tea...

Gyantse Kumbum

11 The giant chörten at Gyantse (p129) is unique in the Himalayas. As you spiral around and up the snail-shell-shaped building, you pass dozens of alcoves full of serene painted buddhas, bloodthirsty demons and unrivalled Tibetan art. Finally you pop out onto the golden eaves, underneath all-seeing eyes, for fabulous views of Gyantse fort and old town.

Ganden Monastery

12 A two-hour drive from Lhasa takes you to the stunning location of Ganden (p85), set in a natural bowl high above the braided Kyi-chu Valley. Brought back to life after nearly total destruction in the Cultural Revolution, the collection of restored chapels centres on Tsongkhapa's tomb and offers a delightful kora path that will soon have you breathing hard from the altitude.

JULIET COOMBE / GETTY IMAGES ©

Koras & Pilgrims

13 All over Tibet you'll see wizened old pilgrims twirling prayer wheels, rubbing sacred rocks and walking around temples, monasteries and sometimes even entire mountains. It's a fantastic fusion of the spiritual and physical, and there are few better ways of spending an hour than joining a merry band of pilgrims on a monastery kora. En route you'll pass rock paintings, sacred spots and probably be invited to an impromptu picnic. Our favourite? Shigatse's Tashilhunpo Kora (p137). Top left: A pilgrim holding a prayer wheel and beads

Adding Your Prayer Flags to a High Pass

14 Crossing a spectacular high pass, fluttering with prayer flags, to view an awesome line of Himalayan peaks is an almost daily experience in Tibet. Join your driver in crying a breathless 'so, so, so' and throwing colourful squares of paper into the air like good-luck confetti, as the surrounding multicoloured flags flap and crackle in the wind. Better still, bring your own string of flags to a pass and add them to the collection for some super-good karma.

Sakya Monastery

15 A 25km detour off the main Friendship Hwy takes you to this brooding, massive grey-walled fortresslike building (p147). In a land of magnificent monasteries, Sakya's main prayer halls are among the most impressive, lined with towering Buddhas, tree-trunk-sized pillars, sacred relics, a threestorey library and a fine kora path. Pilgrims come here from across western Tibet, adding to the colour and charm. This is the real Tibet.

Nam-tso

16 Just a few hours north of Lhasa, spectacular Nam-tso (p97) epitomises the dramatic but harsh scenery of northern Tibet. This deep blue lake is fringed by prayer-flag-draped hills, craggy cliffs and nesting migratory birds, all framed by a horizon of snowcapped 7000m peaks. Walking the kora path at dusk with a band of pilgrims is superb. It's cold, increasingly developed and devastatingly beautiful.

NICHOLAS REUSS / GETTY IMAGES ©

Guge Kingdom, Western Tibet

17 The spectacular lost kingdom of Guge (p178) at Tsaparang is quite unlike anything you'll see in central Tibet; it feels more like Ladakh than Lhasa. There comes a point when you are lowering yourself down a hidden sandstone staircase or crawling through an interconnected cave complex that you stop and think: 'This is incredible!' What's really amazing is that you'll likely have the half-forgotten ruins to yourself. Rank this as one of Asia's great travel secrets.

Ngan-tso & Rawok-tso

18 Tibet is not short on spectacular, remote, turquoise lakes. Of these, none surpasses the crystal-clear waters, sandy beaches and snowcapped peaks of these twin lakes (p201), more reminiscent of the Canadian Rockies than anything on the high plateau. Stay overnight at a hotel on stilts above the lake and explore nearby glaciers during the day.

ALEX LINGHORN / GETTY IMAGES ©

YVAN COHEN / CONTRIBUTOR / GETTY IMAGES ©

Ganden–Samye Trek

19 Tibet is one of those places you really should experience at the pace of one foot in front of the other. This classic four-day trek (p213) between two of Tibet's best monasteries takes you past herders' camps, high alpine lakes and a Guru Rinpoche hermitage, as well as over three 5000m-plus passes. Hire a horse for a wonderful wilderness trek, with just the marmots for company.

Friendship Highway: Lhasa to Kathmandu

20 Organising a 4WD trip across Tibet is the quintessential traveller experience (p34). You'll have to overcome the labyrinthine permit system and some terrible toilets but the rewards are ample: the visually stunning Tibetan countryside, little-visited monasteries, a satisfying sense of journey and a giant slice of adventure. At the end of the trip you finally drop like a stone off the plateau into the green oxygen-rich and curry-scented jungles bordering Nepal.

Need to Know

For more information, see Survival Guide (p303)

Currency
Renminbi, or yuán (¥)

Language
Tibetan and Chinese

Visas
Valid Chinese visa required. Tibet Tourism Bureau (TTB) permit required to enter Tibet.

Money
ATMs available in Lhasa, Shigatse and a couple of other towns. Credit cards can be used in Lhasa. Otherwise bring cash.

Mobile Phones
Buy an inexpensive local pay-as-you-go SIM call or data card for cheap local calls. Buying a mobile phone in China is cheap and easy.

Time
China Time (GMT/UTC plus eight hours)

When to Go

Mt Kailash
GO May–Sep

Nagchu
GO Jun–Aug

Lhasa
GO Apr–Oct

Bayi
GO Feb–Nov

Everest Base Camp
GO May–Sep

Desert, dry climate
Warm to hot summers, mild winters
Mild to hot summers, cold winters
Cold climate

High Season
(May–Sep)

➡ The warmest weather makes travel, trekking and transport easiest.

➡ Prices are at their highest, peaking in July and August.

➡ Book ahead during the 1 May and 1 October national holidays.

Shoulder
(Apr, Oct–Nov)

➡ The slightly colder weather means fewer travellers and a better range of 4WDs.

➡ Prices are 20% cheaper than during the high season.

Low Season
(Dec–Feb)

➡ Very few people visit Tibet in winter, so you'll have the place largely to yourself.

➡ Hotel prices and many entry tickets are discounted by up to 50%, but some restaurants close.

Useful Websites

Land of Snows (www.theland ofsnows.com) Inspirational and practical travel advice, including on Tibetan areas outside the Tibet Autonomous Region (TAR).

Phayul (www.phayul.com) Good for Tibet-related news.

Central Tibetan Administration (www.tibet.net) The view from Dharamsala.

China Tibet Information Center (http://eng.tibet.cn) News from the Chinese perspective.

Lonely Planet (www.lonely-planet.com/china/tibet) Great for pre-planning.

Important Numbers

Country code	☏86
International access code	☏00
Ambulance	☏120
Fire	☏119
Police	☏110

Exchange Rates

Australia	A$1	¥5.3
Canada	C$1	¥5.5
Europe	€1	¥7.7
Japan	Y100	¥5.7
Nepal	Rs100	¥6.1
New Zealand	NZ$1	¥4.8
UK	UK£1	¥9.9
US	US$1	¥6.1

For current exchange rates see www.xe.com

Daily Costs

**Budget:
Less than US$75**

➡ One-way hard sleeper Xīníng–Lhasa train and permits: US$130

➡ Rooms without bathroom: US$5–US$12

➡ Meal in local restaurant: US$5

➡ Join a small group and stay in Lhasa to keep costs lowest

**Midrange:
US$75–US$150**

➡ One-way flight to Lhasa from Kathmandu/Chéngdū: US$410/$270

➡ Daily shared 4WD rental per person: US$50–US$60

➡ Double room with bathroom US$25–US$50

**Top End:
Over US$150**

➡ Boutique or four-star hotel in Lhasa: US$90–US$150

➡ Main course in a top restaurant in Lhasa: US$8–US$10

Warning

Travellers flying into Lhasa from Kathmandu should be aware that customs officials at Lhasa airport often confiscate Lonely Planet guides to Tibet. The best way to avoid this is to travel with an e-book or PDF preloaded on your tablet or smartphone. Travellers flying into Lhasa from airports in China report no such problems. PDFs are available for download at http://shop. lonelyplanet.com.

Arriving in Tibet

Gongkar Airport (p74) Your tour guide will most likely meet you in your rented 4WD vehicle. Taxis are ¥300 to Lhasa.

Train station (p74) Your tour guide will likely pick you up in your rented 4WD vehicle. Taxis cost around ¥30 to Lhasa's old town.

Tours & Permits

➡ To board a plane or train to Tibet you need a TTB permit, and to get this you must book a guide for your entire trip and pre-arrange private transport for trips outside of Lhasa.

➡ Travel outside Lhasa requires additional permits, arranged in advance by your tour company, so you need to decide your itinerary beforehand.

➡ Foreigners are not allowed to take public transport outside Lhasa.

➡ Tour companies need 10 to 14 days to arrange permits and post you the TTB permit (the original permit is required if flying).

➡ Entering Tibet from Nepal you have to travel on a short-term group visa, which can make it tricky to continue into the rest of China.

PLAN YOUR TRIP NEED TO KNOW

For much more on **getting around**, see p322

If You Like...

Off-the-Beaten-Track Monasteries

Beyond Lhasa's famous monastic cities there are hundreds of smaller, lesser-visited places, each holding their own treasures and with more local pilgrims than tour-group hordes. The following are a few of our favourites.

Sakya Monastery Towering golden buddhas and sacred relics reveal an important past that ties Tibet to the Mongols. (p147)

Phuntsoling Monastery Remote, little-visited and with a spectacular location. (p146)

Dorje Drak Monastery A dramatic location and great kora path surrounded by sand dunes and the braided Yarlung Tsangpo river. (p109)

Keru Lhakhang A 1200-year-old temple, haunting monastery ruins and a Tsongkhapa meditation cave make the Ön Valley a great detour between Samye and Tsetang. (p115)

Korjak Monastery Delightful and quirky monastery at the far end of Tibet. (p184)

Thöling Monastery The frescoes hidden here, in the remote far west, offer a sublime fusion of Kashmiri and Tibetan styles found almost nowhere else. (p180)

Trekking & Hiking

Trekking 'the roof of the world' isn't easy. The altitude, weather and rugged terrain present significant challenges but the following trails take hardy walkers into some timeless corners of Tibet.

Ganden to Samye A classic three- or four-day walk between two of Tibet's most important monasteries. (p213)

Dode Valley hike It's hard to imagine a better way to spend half a day in Lhasa, with the best views in the city. (p81)

Tsurphu to Yangpachen Get a taste of the wild northern plateau on this high three-day trek past herding camps and black-haired nomads' tents. (p217)

Samding Monastery An hour's hike up the ridge behind Samding reveals 360-degree views of three lakes and snowcapped Himalayan giants as far off as Bhutan. (p127)

Palaces, Forts & Temples

There's more to Tibet than just monasteries. This mix of spectacular buildings represents a millennium of Tibetan history.

Potala Palace Towering home to the Dalai Lamas, full of priceless Tibetan art and jewel-studded tombs. (p54)

Gyantse Dzong Pack your pith helmet and grow your best Younghusband moustache for this ruined fort with views over Gyantse's old town. (p131)

Tsaparang Your inner Indiana Jones will love the caves, tunnels and hidden stairways of this ruined cliffside fort. (p181)

Gyantse Kumbum One of the great repositories of Tibetan art and a masterpiece of Himalayan architecture. (p129)

Jampaling Kumbum The impressive ruins of Tibet's largest stupa stand as silent testament to the destructive insanity of the Cultural Revolution. (p107)

Incredible Scenery

Whether it's the rolling grasslands of the north, Mars-like deserts of the west, snowcapped Himalayan views to the south or the huge valleys and gigantic lakes of the centre, all of Tibet is blessed with amazing high-altitude colours.

Everest Base Camp Jaw-dropping views of the north face that are *so* much better than from the Nepal side. (p153) visit. Tibet sees half of its (minimal) rainfall in July and August.

⭐ Shötun (Yoghurt Festival)

This major festival in the first week of the seventh lunar month starts with the dramatic unveiling of a giant thangka at Drepung Monastery before moving to Sera and then down to the Norbulingka for performances of *lhamo* (Tibetan opera) and some epic picnics.

🏃 Horse-Racing Festival

Thousands of nomads head to summer pastures around Damxung and Nam-tso for a week of horse racing, archery and other traditional nomad sports. A similar and even larger event is held in Nagchu a few weeks earlier.

⭐ Bathing Festival

The end of the seventh and beginning of the eighth lunar months sees locals washing away the grime of the previous year in an act of purification that coincides with the weeklong appearance of the constellation Pleiades in the night sky.

⭐ Onkor

In the first week of the eighth lunar month, Tibetans in central Tibet get together and party in celebration of the upcoming harvest.

⭐ Tashilhunpo

More *cham* dances, from the ninth to 11th days of the eighth month, at Shigatse's Tashilhunpo Monastery.

October

Clear Himalayan skies and good driving conditions in eastern and western Tibet make this a good off-peak time to visit before the winter cold arrives, as the trekking season comes to a close.

⭐ 1 October

Many people take a week off for National Day so expect flights and hotels to be full and rates higher than normal.

November

Temperatures are still pleasant during the day in Lhasa and Shigatse, but cold in the higher elevations of the north and west.

⭐ Lhabab Düchen

Commemorating Buddha's descent from heaven, the 22nd day of the ninth lunar month sees large numbers of pilgrims in Lhasa. Ladders are painted afresh on rocks around many monasteries to symbolise the event.

⭐ Palden Lhamo

The 15th day of the 10th lunar month sees a procession in Lhasa around the Barkhor bearing Palden Lhamo (Shri Devi), the protective deity of the Jokhang.

December

By December temperatures are starting to get seriously cold everywhere and some high passes start to close, but there's still surprisingly little snow in the Land of Snows.

⭐ Tsongkhapa Festival

Much respect is shown to Tsongkhapa, the founder of the Gelugpa order, on the anniversary of his death on the 25th of the 10th lunar month. Monasteries light fires and carry images of Tsongkhapa in procession. Check for *cham* dances at the monasteries at Ganden, Sera and Drepung.

Itineraries

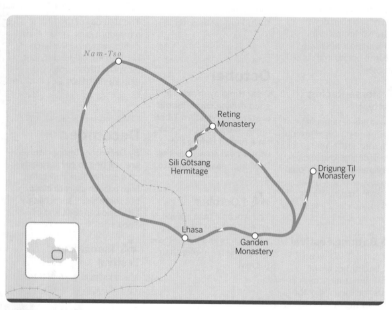

 10 DAYS **Lhasa & Around**

There's enough to see in and around **Lhasa** to occupy at least a week. Highlights include the Potala Palace (a Unesco World Heritage Site), the Jokhang temple and the Barkhor pilgrimage circuit. The huge monastic institutions of Drepung and Sera lie on the edge of town.

Plenty of excursions can be made from Lhasa. An overnight return trip to stunning **Nam-tso** offers a break from peering at Buddhist deities, though allow a few days in Lhasa to acclimatise before heading out here. If you add three days you can loop back to Lhasa via the timeless and little-visited **Reting Monastery**, the amazing cliffside **Sili Götsang Hermitage** and the atmospheric **Drigung Til Monastery**, visiting **Ganden Monastery** en route to Lhasa.

To get way off the beaten track, explore the monasteries between Reting and Drigung Til, or around Nyima Jiangre.

can fit four people fairly comfortably (including the guide). For a long overland trip, eg to Kailash, it's well worth paying a little extra to have more space.

Note that the agency that arranges your TTB permit is legally responsible for you in Tibet. Should you get caught talking politics with the wrong person, or staying in Tibet after the date on your TTB permit, the agency will likely be questioned by the authorities and perhaps fined. This is one reason why some guides can appear overprotective.

Tours from Nepal

Arranging a tour to Tibet from Nepal makes sense geographically but there are several complications to bear in mind, primarily visas. In general, the same rules of Tibet travel apply – you have to pre-arrange a guide and transport in order to get the requisite permits.

Instead of posting your TTB permit to a city in China your Tibet travel agency will send the permit details to the Chinese embassy in Kathmandu. You then need to pay a Nepali travel agency to obtain your visa. This can take up to a week.

Note that the Chinese embassy in Kathmandu does not give individual Chinese visas to travellers headed to Tibet, only group visas. If you already have a valid individual China visa (p315) in your passport it will be cancelled. A group visa is a separate sheet of paper with all the names and passport numbers of the group members. It's useful to get your own individual 'group' visa (a 'group' can be as small as one person!) because, otherwise, come the end of your tour in Lhasa, you will have to exit China with your fellow group members.

Group visas are generally issued for 15 days, though 30 days or more is possible, especially for trips to Kailash or if you want to travel through China at the end of your Tibet trip. Note that it is very difficult, if not impossible, to extend the duration of a group visa or to split from your group visa, regardless of what agents in Kathmandu may tell you.

Once your trip is arranged and your permits secured, your Tibetan agent will send your Tibetan guide and driver to meet you on the Chinese side of the border at Kodari. At customs on the Chinese side of the Friendship Bridge you will be asked to present your TTB permit.

If you are flying in to Lhasa you will need to show your group visa and TTB permit at check-in in Kathmandu. Your Tibetan guide will meet you at Lhasa airport.

A simpler option is to join an organised tour from Kathmandu. Travel agents there offer 'budget' tours of Tibet from around US$350 per person for a basic seven-day trip stopping in Zhāngmù/Nyalam, Lhatse, Shigatse, Gyantse and then Lhasa for two days. These trips generally run every Tuesday and Saturday. A nine-day trip that adds a visit to Everest Base Camp costs up to double this and will be harder to find. Prices include transport, permits, a Chinese group visa, dormitory accommodation for the first two nights and then shared twin rooms, a fairly useless guide and admission fees.

Bear in mind that most agencies are just subcontractors and normally pool clients, so you could find yourself travelling in a larger group than expected and probably on a bus instead of the promised 4WD. Other potential inconsistencies may include having to share a room when you were told you would be given a single, or paying a double-room supplement and ending up in a dorm. We do get a fair number of complaints about the service of some of these tours; it's best just to view it as the cheapest way to get to Tibet.

Tour Agencies in Tibet

In general, Tibetan tour agencies are not as professional as agencies in neighbouring Nepal. The following companies in Lhasa are experienced in arranging customised trips.

For good information on responsible tour companies and ecotourism initiatives in Tibet, visit www.tibetecotravel.com and www.tibetgreenmap.

Explore Tibet (☎0891-632 9441, 158 8909 0408; www.tibetexploretour.com; 4-5 House, Namsel No 3, Doudi Rd) Contact Jamphel.

FIT Banak Shol Hotel (☎189 0899 0100; tibetanintibet@yahoo.cn; 8 Beijing Donglu) Contact Xiaojin. Connected with Tibet Highland Tours.

Namchen Tours (☎634 5009; www.tibetnamchen.com) At Barkhor Namchen Guest House. Contact Dhoko.

Road to Tibet (☎133 0898 1522; www.roadtotibet.com) Contact Woeser Phel.

Shigatse Travel Agency (☎683 5735; cits841@vip.163.com; 3-070 Gyatso Juweihui,

Beijing Zhonglu, near the Norbulinka) Contact Yonghong. Strong on art tours.

Shigatse Travels (☑633 0489; www.shigatsetravels.com; Yak Hotel, 100 Beijing Donglu) Top-end tours from a large agency that uses European trip managers.

Spinn Café (☑136 5952 3997; www.cafespinn.com; 135 Beijing Donglu) Contact Kong or Pazu.

Tibet FIT Travel (☑634 9239; www.tibetfit.com; Zangyiyuan Lu) Contact Lhakpa Tsering; also goes under the name Chang Tang.

Tibet Highland Tours (☑634 8144, 139 0898 5060; www.tibethighlandtours.com; Zangyiyuan Lu) Contact Tenzin or Dechen.

Tibet Roof of World International Travel (☑679 1995; www.budgettibettour.com; Kailash Hotel, 143 Beijing Donglu) Offers scheduled budget tours across Tibet.

Tibet Songtsan International Travel Company (☑136 3890 1182; www.songtsantravel.com; 2nd fl next to Dico's restaurant, Jokhang Temple Sq; ☎) Run by Tenzin, this up-and-coming outfit is eager to serve new clients.

Tibet Tsolha Garbo Travel (☑633 3871, 139 0891 5618; www.tibetgtravel.com) Contact David Migmar or Sonam Yergye.

Tibetan Guide (☑635 1657, 136 2898 0074; www.tibetanguide.com) Contact Mima Dhondup.

Visit Tibet Travel and Tours (☑8325 7742; www.visittibet.com; Jiaji Lu, Lhasa) Can arrange Nepal add-ons.

Wind Horse Adventure (☑683 3009; www.windhorsetibet.com; B32 Shenzheng Huayuan, Sera Beilu) Top-end trips, strong on trekking and rafting.

Tour Agencies Elsewhere in China

There are several good companies outside the TAR that can arrange tours in Tibet. Many are based in the Tibetan areas of China and operate through local contacts in Lhasa. Depending on your itinerary it can be useful to arrange your tour through one of these outfits; if catching the train from Xīníng, for example, it's handy to use an agency there to help arrange hard-to-find train tickets and permit pick-up.

Access Tibet (☑028-8618 3638; www.accesstibettour.com; Room 178-188, 4F, Yuanheng Trade Bldg, 235 Shuhan Lu, Chéngdū) Also with an office in Lhasa.

China Yak (☑028-8551 3102; www.chinayak.com; A904-906 Xinhua Yuan, No 51, 4th Block, Renmin Nanlu, Chéngdū) Part of CITS, with an office in Lhasa.

Gesar Tours (☑139 0976 9192; www.gesar-tour.com; Shan Xiao Tai, Shenti Wei Bldg No 5, Room 261, Xīníng) Strong on tours to Amdo.

Khampa Caravan (☑0887-828 8648; www.khampacaravan.com; 117 Beimen Jie, Zhōngdiàn) Overland trips from Yúnnán to Lhasa when possible, and strong on Kham, with an emphasis on sustainable tourism and local communities. Contact Dakpa.

Leo Hostel (☑10-8660 8923; www.leohostel.com; 52 Dazhalan Xijie, Qiánmēn, Běijīng) Popular backpacker hostel that books tours through an agency in Tibet.

Mix Hostel (☑028-8322 2271; www.mixhostel.com; 23 Renjiawan, Xinghui Xilu, Chéngdū) Popular backpacker hostel.

Snow Lion Tours (☑971-816 3350, 134 3932 9243; www.snowliontours.com; Office 1212, Chenglin Mansion, 7 Dongdajie Lu, Xīníng) Contact Wangden Tsering.

Tibet Caravan Tours (☑151 0973 2251; www.tibetancaravan.com; 12 Rujing Yuan, Bayi Lu, Xīníng) Contact Pema Gyatso. Strong on Amdo.

Tibetan Connections (☑135 1973 7734; www.tibetanconnections.com; Jiancai Xiang, 16th fl, International Village Apts, Bldg 5, Xīníng) This friendly tour company focuses on remoter parts of Amdo and Kham but can arrange trips into Tibet. Prices may be a little higher than local travel agencies but staff speak English and are good to deal with.

Tibetan Trekking (☑028-8597 6082; www.tibetantrekking.com; Room 1035, Yu Lin Feng Shang, 47 Yong Feng Lu, Chéngdū) Contact Gao Liqiang for treks and 4WD trips, especially in Tibetan areas of western Sìchuān.

Travel Wild Tibet (☑0971-6313 188, 139 9712 4471; www.travelwildtibet.com; Qinghai International Business Centre, 12th fl, 37 Kunlun Zhonglu, Xīníng) Contact Tashi Phuntsok.

Wild China (☑010-6465 6602; www.wildchina.com; Room 803, Oriental Place, 9 Dongfang Donglu, North Dongsanhuan Rd, Chaoyang District, Běijīng) Professionally run and top-end private trips.

Windhorse Tour (☑028-8559 3923; www.windhorsetour.com; Suite 904, Wanheyuan, Bldg C, 1 Babao Lu, Chéngdū) Chinese agency, not connected to Wind Horse Adventure in Lhasa. Contact Helen.

wall was formerly used by the Dalai Lamas. You'll see a line of pilgrims filing past the main Jokhang entrance as they walk the pilgrim circuit around the temple.

The inner prayer hall of the Jokhang houses the most important images and chapels. Most prominent are six larger-than-life statues that dominate the central prayer hall. In the foreground and to the left is a 6m statue of Guru Rinpoche. The statue to the right is of Jampa (Maitreya), the Future Buddha, with an ornate crown. At the centre of the hall, between and to the rear of these two statues, is a thousand-armed Chenresig (Avalokiteshvara). At the far right are two more Jampa statues, one behind the other, and to the far rear, behind Chenresig and facing the main Jowo statue (you'll see it later), is another statue of Guru Rinpoche, encased in a cabinet.

Encircling this enclosed area of statues is a collection of chapels, which Tibetan pilgrims visit in a clockwise direction. There are generally long queues for the holiest chapels, particularly the Chapel of Jowo Sakyamuni. Pilgrims rub the doorways and chain-mail curtains, touch their heads to re-vered statues, throw seeds as offerings and pour molten yak butter into the heat of a thousand prayer lamps. The atmosphere of hushed sanctity is broken only by the occasional mobile-phone ringtone.

The chapels, following a clockwise route, are as follows. The numbers listed here refer to those marked on the Jokhang map (p50).

Tsongkhapa was the founder of the Gelugpa order, and you can see him seated in the centre of the Chapel of Tsongkhapa & His Disciples (1), flanked by his eight disciples. Just outside is the large Tagba chörten. The eight medicine buddhas in the Chapel of the Eight Medicine Buddhas (2) are recent and not of special interest.

The Chapel of Chenresig (3) contains the Jokhang's most important image after the Jowo Sakyamuni. Legend has it that the statue of Chenresig here sprang spontaneously into being and combines aspects of King Songtsen Gampo, his wives and two wrathful protective deities. The doors of the chapel are among the few remnants still visible of the Jokhang's 7th-century origins and were fashioned by Nepali artisans. This and

DEMONESS-SUBDUING TEMPLES

Buddhism's interaction with the pre-existing Bön – a shamanistic folk religion of spirits, ghosts and demons – combined with the wild and inhospitable nature of the Tibetan terrain has led to many metaphoric fables about Buddhism's taming of Tibet. The story of the early introduction of Buddhism to Tibet is represented by the story of a vast, supine demoness whose body straddled the entire plateau.

It was Princess Wencheng, the Chinese wife of King Songtsen Gampo, who divined the presence of this demoness. Through Chinese geomantic calculations she established that the heart of the demoness lay beneath a lake in the centre of Lhasa, while her torso and limbs lay far away in the outer dominions of the high plateau. As in all such fables, the demoness can be seen as a symbol, of both the physical hardships of Tibet and the existing Bön clergy's hostility towards Buddhism; both had to be tamed before Buddhism could take root here. It was decided that the demoness would have to be pinned down.

The first task was to drain the lake in Lhasa of its water (read lifeblood of the demoness) and build a central temple that would replace the heart of the demoness with a Buddhist heart. The temple built there was the Jokhang. A stake through the heart was not enough to put a demoness of this size out of action, however, and a series of lesser temples, in three concentric rings, were conceived to pin the extremities of the demoness.

There were four temples in each of these rings. The first are known as the *runo* temples and form a protective circle around Lhasa, pinning down the demoness' hips and shoulders. Two of these are Trandruk Monastery (p118) in the Yarlung Valley and Katsel Monastery (p103) on the way to Drigung. The second group, known as the *tandrul* temples, pin the knees and elbows of the demoness. Buchu Monastery (p197) near Bayi in eastern Tibet is one of these. And the final group, known as *yandrul* temples, pin the hands and feet. These last temples are found as far away as Bhutan (Paro and Bumthang) and Sìchuān, though the location of two of them is unknown. You can see a representative image of the demoness and the temples that pin her down in the Tibet Museum (p64).

The Jokhang

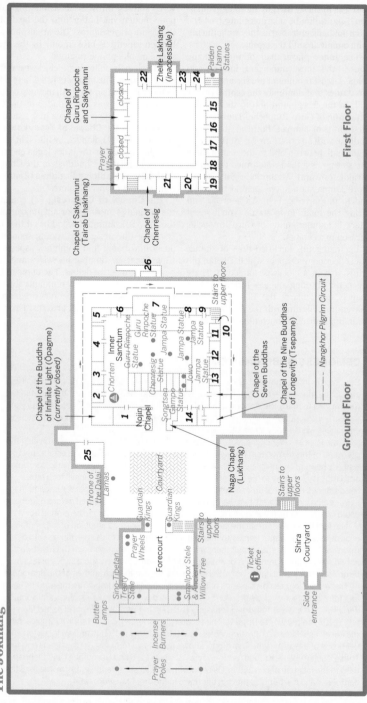

First Floor

Chapel of Guru Rinpoche and Sakyamuni

Zhelre Lakhang (inaccessible)

Palden Lhamo Statues

22 23 24

15 16 17 18 19

20 21

Prayer Wheel

Chapel of Sakyamuni (Tairab Lhakhang)

Chapel of Chenresig

26

Ground Floor

Chapel of the Buddha of Infinite Light (Opagme) (currently closed)

Inner Sanctum

Chorten

2 3 4 5 6

Guru Rinpoche Statue

Guru Rinpoche Statue

Chenresig Statue

Jampa Statue

7

Nojin Chapel

1

Songtsen Gampo Statue

Jowo Statue

Jampa Statue

8

Jampa Statue

9

Jampa Statue

13 12 11 10

14

Stairs to upper floors

Chapel of the Seven Buddhas

Chapel of the Nine Buddhas of Longevity (Tsepame)

Naga Chapel (Lukhang)

25

Throne of the Dalai Lamas

Guardian Kings

Guardian Kings

Courtyard

Forecourt

Prayer Wheels

Sino-Tibetan Treaty Stele

Butter Lamps

Smallpox Stele & Ancient Willow Tree

Incense Burners

Prayer Poles

Stairs to upper floors

Ticket office

Stairs to upper floors

Shira Courtyard

Side entrance

----- *Nangkhor Pilgrim Circuit*

the next four chapels are the most popular with pilgrims and lines can be long.

In the **Chapel of Jampa (4)** are statues of Jampa as well as four smaller bodhisattvas: Jampelyang (Manjushri), Chenresig (to the left), Chana Dorje (Vajrapani) and Drölma (Tara). Öpagme (Amitabha) and Tsongkhapa are also present here, as are two chörtens, one of which holds the remains of the original sculptor.

The image of Tsongkhapa in the **Chapel of Tsongkhapa (5)** was commissioned by the subject himself and is said to be a precise resemblance. It is the central image on top of the steps of the wooden alcove.

The **Chapel of the Buddha of Infinite Light (6)** is the second of the chapels consecrated to Öpagme (Amitabha), the Buddha of Infinite Light. The outer entrance, with its wonderful carved doors, is protected by two fierce deities, red Tamdrin (Hayagriva; right) and blue Chana Dorje (Vajrapani; left). There are also statues of the eight bodhisattvas. Pilgrims generally pray here for the elimination of impediments to viewing the most sacred image of the Jokhang, that of Jowo Sakyamuni, which awaits in the next chapel.

To the right as you leave the chapel are statues of King Songtsen Gampo with his two wives, and of Guru Rinpoche (at the back).

The most important shrine in Tibet, the **Chapel of Jowo Sakyamuni (7)** houses the image of Sakyamuni Buddha at the age of 12 years, brought to Tibet by Princess Wencheng. You enter via an anteroom containing the Four Guardian Kings, smiling on the left and frowning to the right. Inside are statues of the protectors Miyowa (Achala) and Chana Dorje (Vajrapani, blue). Several large bells hang from the anteroom's Newari-style roof. The carved doorway has been rubbed smooth by generations of pilgrims.

The 1.5m statue of Sakyamuni is embedded with precious stones, covered in silks and jewellery, and surrounded by silver pillars with dragon motifs. The silver canopy above was financed by a Mongolian khan. Pilgrims touch their forehead to the statue's left leg or are blessed with some brocade before being tapped on the back by a monk 'bouncer' when it's time to move on.

To the rear of Sakyamuni are statues of the seventh and 13th Dalai Lamas (with a moustache), Tsongkhapa and 12 standing bodhisattvas. Look for the 7th-century pillars on the way out.

The Jampa (Maitreya, or Future Buddha) enshrined in the **Chapel of Jampa (8)** is a replica of a statue that came to Tibet as a part

THE SACRED GOAT

When Princess Wencheng chose the site of the Jokhang, she chose Lake Wothang (perhaps because she was still upset at having to live in barbarian Tibet). The lake was eventually filled in, but it is said that a well in the precincts of the Jokhang still draws its waters from those of the old lake. Over the years, many legends have emerged around the task of filling in Lake Wothang. The most prominent of these is the story of how the lake was filled by a sacred white goat (the Tibetan word for goat, *ra*, is etymologically connected with the original name for Lhasa – Rasa). Look for a small image of the goat peeking out from the Chapel of Jampa on the south wall of the Jokhang's ground-floor inner sanctum.

of the dowry of Princess Bhrikuti, King Songtsen Gampo's Nepali wife. Around the statue are eight images of Drölma, a goddess seen as an embodiment of the enlightened mind of buddhahood and who protects against the eight fears – hence the eight statues. There are some fine door carvings here. As you exit the chapel look for the unexpected statues of the Hindu gods Indra and Brahma.

In the **Chapel of Chenresig Riding a Lion (9)**, the statue of Chenresig on the back of a *sengye* (snow lion) is first on the left (it's not the largest of the icons within). Most of the other statues are aspects of Chenresig.

Some pilgrims exit this chapel and then follow a flight of stairs up to the next floor, while others complete the circuit on the ground floor. Unless you're chapelled out (you've seen the important ones already), continue on upstairs, but look out first for a small hole in the wall on the left as you exit the chapel, against which pilgrims place their ear to hear either the beating wings of a mythical bird or the lapping waters of Lake Wothang on which the Jokhang was built.

The **Guru Rinpoche Shrine (10)** contains two statues of Guru Rinpoche and one of King Trisong Detsen next to the stairs. Beside the shrine is a self-arising golden rock painting of the medicine buddha protected by a glass plate. Inside the **Chapel of Tsepame (11)** are nine statues of Tsepame (Amitayus), the red Buddha of Longevity, in *yabyum* (sexual and spiritual union) pose.

The **Chapel of Jampa (12)** holds the Jampa statue that was traditionally borne around the Barkhor on the 25th day of the first lunar month for the Mönlam festival. This yearly excursion was designed to hasten the arrival of the Future Buddha. Jampelyang and Chenresig flank the Buddha.

The chapel is also named Ramo Gyalmo (Chapel of the Sacred Goat), after the rough 'self-arisen' (ie not human-made) image of the goat emerging from the wall in the first corner, beside the god of wealth Zhambhala.

The **Chapel of the Hidden Jowo (13)** is where Princess Wencheng is said to have hidden the Jowo Sakyamuni for safe keeping after the death of her husband and the ensuing anti-Buddhism backlash. You can see the cavity on the eastern wall. Inside is a statue of Öpagme (Amitabha) and the eight medicine buddhas with characteristic blue hair.

The last of the ground-floor chapels is the **Chapel of the Kings (14)**, with some original statues of Tibet's earliest kings. The central figure is Songtsen Gampo, flanked by images of King Trisong Detsen and King Ralpachen. Pilgrims touch their head to the central pillar. On the wall outside the chapel is a fine mural depicting the original construction of the Jokhang and the Potala, alongside performances of Tibetan opera, yak dances, wrestling, stone weightlifting and horse racing.

First Floor

At this point you should return clockwise to the rear of the ground floor (if you did not do so earlier) and climb the stairs to the upper floor of the Jokhang. The upper floor of the Jokhang's inner sanctum is also ringed with chapels, though some of them are closed.

As you begin the circuit, you will pass by several newly restored rooms that feature **Sakyamuni (15, 18)** accompanied by his two main disciples, and one featuring the **eight medicine buddhas (17)**. The **Lamrin Chapel (16)** near the southeast corner features Pabonka Rinpoche, Sakyamuni, Tsongkhapa and Atisha (Jowo-je). The chapel in the southwest corner is the **Chapel of Five Protectors (19)** and has some fearsome statues of Tamdrin (Hayagriva) and other protector deities, attended by deep Tantric drumming in the atmospheric anteroom.

Next is the **Chapel of the Three Kings (20)**, dedicated to Songtsen Gampo, Trisong Detsen and Tri Ralpachen. Also featured in the room are the statues of Songtsen Gampo's

Town Walk
Old Town

START BARKHOR SQ
END BARKHOR SQ
LENGTH 3KM; THREE HOURS

The fragile Tibetan old town shelters the soul of Lhasa, far from Chinese influence. This walk takes in craft workshops, backstreet chapels and pilgrim paths, passing en route some of Lhasa's last remaining traditional architecture.

At the first turn of the ❶ **Barkhor circuit** (p45) take a left and then quick right, past strips of dried yak meat and yellow bags of yak butter to the bustling ❷ **Tromsikhang Market** (p72). After a quick look around the modern market (the original Tibetan-style building was demolished in 1997), head north to the main road, Beijing Donglu, and then right to visit the ❸ **Gyüme Tratsang** (p62), Lhasa's Lower Tantric College. It's easy to miss this working temple; look for an imposing entrance set back from the road.

About 50m further down the road are the deceptively long white walls of the small but active ❹ **Meru Sarpa Monastery** (p62).

Cross Beijing Donglu, take the alley into the old town and follow the winding branch to the right, past the yellow walls of the House of Shambhala, which has a nice rooftop restaurant if you need a break. As you continue south you'll pass Tibetan craftspeople making statues, embroidery, cabinets, prayer wheels and Tibetan banners. At the junction there's the ❺ **Eizhi Thangka Shop** to the left; you want to take a left at this junction but first look down the alleyway to the right to see the brassware shop and monk's clothing store.

As you head southeast from the thangka shop, past statue makers and a small market, curve right to the quiet but interesting yellow-walled ❻ **Karmashar Temple**, once the home of the Karmashar, Lhasa's main oracle. Look for the Karmashar statue in the far right corner of the back chapel and for the spooky faded icon painted on a pigskin bag in the main hall, pacified with offerings of tsampa and barley beer. Enter from the right (southwest) side.

➡ Third Floor

On the 3rd floor, the first room is the **Chapel of Jampa** (Jamkhang), which contains an exquisite image of Jampa (Maitreya, or the Future Buddha) commissioned by the eighth Dalai Lama; it stands opposite the Dalai Lama's throne. To the right of the throne, in the corner, is a wooden Kalachakra mandala. The walls are stacked with the collected works of Tsongkhapa and the fifth Dalai Lama. The chapel was unfortunately damaged in a fire in 1984 (caused by an electrical fault) and many valuable thangkas were lost.

Next, the **Chapel of Three-Dimensional Mandalas** (Loilang Khang) houses spectacular jewel-encrusted mandalas of the three principal Tantric deities of the Gelugpa order. These are essentially three-dimensional versions of the mandalas you see painted on thangkas everywhere and act as meditation maps for the mind.

The **Chapel of the Victory over the Three Worlds** (Sasum Namgyal) houses a library and displays of Manchu texts. The main statue is a golden thousand-armed Chenresig, while the main thangka is of the Manchu Chinese emperor Qianlong dressed in monk's robes, with accompanying inscriptions in Tibetan, Chinese, Mongolian and Manchurian.

Next, the **Chapel of Immortal Happiness** (Chimey Dedan Kyil) was once the residence of the sixth Dalai Lama, Tsangyang Gyatso, whose throne remains; it is now dedicated to Tsepame, the Buddha of Longevity, who sits by the window. Next to him in the corner is the Dzogchen deity Ekajati (Tsechigma), with an ostrich-feather hat and a single fang.

In the northwest corner is the **Lamo Lhakhang** and the golden **tomb of the Seventh Dalai Lama** (Serdung Tashi Obar Khang), constructed in 1757 and encased in half a tonne of gold. To the right stands a statue of Kalsang Gyatso, the seventh Dalai Lama.

In the northwest corner, steps lead up into the small but important **Chapel of Arya Lokeshvara** (Phagpa Lhakhang). Allegedly this is one of the few corners of the Potala that dates from the time of Songtsen Gampo's 7th-century palace. It is the most sacred of the Potala's chapels, and the sandalwood image of Arya Lokeshvara inside is the most revered image housed in the Potala. The statue is accompanied on the left by the seventh Dalai Lama and Tsongkhapa, and on the right by the fifth, eighth and ninth Dalai Lamas. Relics include stone footprints of Guru Rinpoche and Tsongkhapa.

The last two rooms on this floor are the towering, jewel-encrusted **tombs of the Eighth and Ninth Dalai Lamas**, the former built in 1805 and over 9m tall.

If you're exhausted already (not even halfway!), you can rest your legs at a reception area in the middle of the 2nd floor.

➡ Second Floor

The first of the chapels you come to on the 2nd floor is the **Chapel of Kalachakra** (Dukhor Lhakhang), also known as the Wheel of Time. It is noted for its stunning three-dimensional mandala, which is over 6m in diameter and finely detailed with over 170 statues. Access to the room is limited.

The **Chapel of Sakyamuni** (Thubwang Lhakhang) houses a library, the throne of the seventh Dalai Lama, eight bodhisattvas and some fine examples of gold painted calligraphy. It is often closed.

In the **Chapel of the Nine Buddhas of Longevity** (Tsepak Lhakhang), look for the murals by the left window; the left side depicts Tangtong Gyelpo and his celebrated bridge (now destroyed) over the Yarlung Tsangpo near Chushul. The images of coracle rafts halfway up the wall add an intimate touch. There are also nine statues of Tsepame here, as well as green and white Drölma.

Passing the closed Chapel of Sakyamuni (Zegya Lhakhang), continue to the northwestern corner where you'll find a small corridor that leads to **King Songtsen Gampo's Meditation Chamber** (Chogyal Drupuk), which, along with the Chapel of Arya Lokeshvara on the 3rd floor, is one of the oldest rooms in the Potala. The most important statue is of Songtsen Gampo himself, to the left of the pillar. To the left is his minister Tonmi Sambhota (said to have invented the Tibetan script) and to the right are his Chinese and Nepali wives. A statue of the king's Tibetan wife Mongsa Tricham (the only one to bear a son) is in a cabinet by the door. The fifth Dalai Lama lurks behind (and also on) the central pillar. Also here is Gar Tsongtsen, the Tibetan prime minister (and Songtsen Gampo's right-hand man) who travelled to the Tang court to escort Princess Wencheng back to Lhasa. Queues for this chapel can be long.

The last three rooms are all linked and are chock-a-block full of 3000 pieces of statuary, many donated by a Khampa businessman in 1995.

Red Palace of the Potala

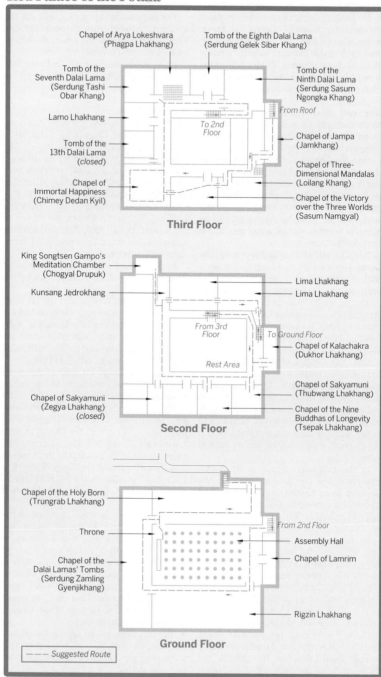

Chapel of Arya Lokeshvara
(Phagpa Lhakhang)

Tomb of the Eighth Dalai Lama
(Serdung Gelek Siber Khang)

Tomb of the
Seventh Dalai Lama
(Serdung Tashi
Obar Khang)

Tomb of the
Ninth Dalai Lama
(Serdung Sasum
Ngongka Khang)

Lamo Lhakhang

From Roof

*To 2nd
Floor*

Chapel of Jampa
(Jamkhang)

Tomb of the
13th Dalai Lama
(closed)

Chapel of Three-
Dimensional Mandalas
(Loilang Khang)

Chapel of
Immortal Happiness
(Chimey Dedan Kyil)

Chapel of the Victory
over the Three Worlds
(Sasum Namgyal)

Third Floor

King Songtsen Gampo's
Meditation Chamber
(Chogyal Drupuk)

Lima Lhakhang

Kunsang Jedrokhang

Lima Lhakhang

*From 3rd
Floor*

To Ground Floor

Chapel of Kalachakra
(Dukhor Lhakhang)

Rest Area

Chapel of Sakyamuni
(Thubwang Lhakhang)

Chapel of Sakyamuni
(Zegya Lhakhang)
(closed)

Chapel of the Nine
Buddhas of Longevity
(Tsepak Lhakhang)

Second Floor

Chapel of the Holy Born
(Trungrab Lhakhang)

From 2nd Floor

Throne

Assembly Hall

Chapel of Lamrim

Chapel of the
Dalai Lamas' Tombs
(Serdung Zamling
Gyenjikhang)

Rigzin Lhakhang

Ground Floor

--- *Suggested Route*

The 1st floor has been closed to visitors for years and is unlikely to reopen soon.

➡ Ground Floor

As you round the steps on the ground floor, enter the beautiful **assembly hall**, which is the largest hall in the Potala and is its physical centre. Note the fine carved pillar heads. The large throne that dominates one end of the hall was the throne of the sixth Dalai Lama. Four important chapels frame the hall.

The first chapel on this floor is the **Chapel of Lamrim**. *Lamrim* means literally 'the graduated path', and refers to the graduated stages that mark the path to enlightenment. The central figure in the chapel is Tsongkhapa, with whom *lamrim* texts are usually associated. Outside the chapel to the left a fine mural depicts the Forbidden City, commemorating the fifth Dalai Lama's visit to the court of Emperor Shunzhi in 1652.

The next chapel, the long **Rigzin Lhakhang**, is dedicated to eight Indian teachers who brought various Tantric practices and rituals to Tibet. The central figure is a silver statue of Guru Rinpoche (one of the eight), who is flanked by his consorts Mandarava and Yeshe Tsogyel (with a turquoise headdress), as well as statues of the eight teachers to the left and a further eight statues of him in different manifestations on the right. As you exit the chapel, take an up-close look at the fine wall murals.

In the west wing of the assembly hall is one of the highlights of the Potala, the awe-inspiring **Chapel of the Dalai Lamas' Tombs** (Serdung Zamling Gyenjikhang). The hall is dominated by the huge 12.6m-high chörten of the great fifth Dalai Lama, gilded with some 3.7kg of gold. Flanking it are two smaller chörtens containing the 10th and 12th Dalai Lamas, who both died as children. Richly embossed, the chörtens represent the concentrated wealth of an entire nation. One of the precious stones is a pearl said to have been discovered in an elephant's brains and thus, in a wonderful piece of understatement, 'considered a rarity'. Eight other chörtens represent the eight major events in the life of the Buddha.

The last chapel is the **Chapel of the Holy Born** (Trungrab Lhakhang). Firstly, in the corner, is the statue and chörten of the 11th Dalai Lama, who died at the age of 17. There are also statues of the eight medicine buddhas with their characteristic blue hair, a central golden Sakyamuni and the fifth Dalai Lama (silver), and then Chenresig, Songtsen Gampo, Dromtönpa (founder of the Kadampa order) and the first four Dalai Lamas.

Around the Potala

A morning visit to the Potala can easily be combined with a circuit of the Potala kora and an afternoon excursion to some of the temples nearby.

Potala Kora   PILGRIM CIRCUIT

(Map p56) The pilgrim path that encircles the foot of the Potala Palace makes for a nice walk before or after the main event. Budget around half an hour; longer if you stop for tea. The exit from the Potala conveniently deposits you on the northern side of the kora path.

From the large western chörten (formerly the west gate to the city), follow the prayer wheels to the northwest corner, marked by three large chörtens. There's a particularly nice teahouse (p71) here.

The northeast corner is home to several rock paintings and a delightful prayer hall alive with the murmurs of chanting nuns. Just past here, spin the large prayer wheel of the recently rebuilt **Phurbu Chok Hermitage Mani Lhakhang** (Map p56) and then swing past the Chinese-style square, where pilgrims prostrate in front of the Potala on auspicious dates.

Look out for the three 18th-century *doring* (stele); the two to the north side of the road commemorate victories over the Central Asian Dzungars (1721) and Nepali Gorkhas (1788 and 1791). King Trisong Detsen is said to have erected the single southern obelisk in the eighth century.

Drubthub Nunnery   BUDDHIST, NUNNERY

(Map p56) Southwest of the Potala an unmarked road leads around the eastern side of Chagpo Ri, the hill that faces Marpo Ri, site of the Potala. Take this road past stone carvers and rock paintings to Drubthub Nunnery. The nunnery is dedicated to Tangtong Gyelpo, the 15th-century bridge-maker, medic and inventor of Tibetan opera, who established the original nunnery on the top of Chagpo Ri. Gyelpo's white-haired statue graces the nunnery's main hall.

Palha Lu-puk   BUDDHIST, TEMPLE

(查拉鲁普寺, Zhālālǔpǔ Sì; Map p56; admission ¥20; ⊙9am-7pm) Palha Lu-puk (next to Drubthub Nunnery) is an atmospheric cave temple said to have been the 7th-century meditational retreat of King Songtsen Gampo. The main attraction of the

LHASA SIGHTS

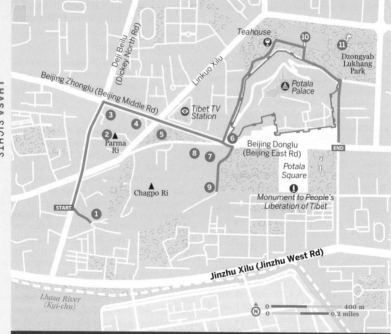

City Walk
Lingkhor

START DEJI ZHONGLU (DEKYI LAM)
END POTALA PALACE
LENGTH 3KM TO 4KM; TWO TO THREE HOURS

This walk follows the most interesting section of the city's main pilgrimage circuit, the Lingkhor. It's best walked in the morning, when you'll be joined by hundreds of Tibetan pilgrims.

To start the walk, take a taxi to Deji Zhonglu (德吉中路; Dickey Lam in Tibetan). An alley branches east of here to reach one of the city's real gems: the painted ①**Chagpo Ri rock carvings** (p61), centred on a huge image of Tsepame.

From here, return along the alley back to Deji Zhonglu and head north. Just before you hit Beijing Zhonglu (the second crossroads) follow the alleyway to the right to visit the friendly ②**Kunde Ling** (p61). Back at the intersection with Beijing Zhonglu, watch the pilgrims as they rub their backs, shoulders and hips against a series of polished ③**holy stones**. Head east

along Beijing Zhonglu to the yellow walls of the Chinese-style ④**Gesar Ling** (p61).

Continue east to the ⑤**Golden Yaks statue**, erected for the 40th anniversary of the 'liberation' of Tibet, before reaching the former western ⑥**city gate** (Daggo Kani), in the shape of a large white chörten. B&W photos displayed in the Brahmaputra Grand Hotel show British Army troops entering the city through the original gate during the invasion of 1903–04.

Climb up to the ⑦**viewpoint** just above the white chörten for one of Lhasa's classic photo-ops. The hilltop behind you is Chagpo Ri (Iron Mountain), the site of Lhasa's principal Tibetan medical college from 1413 until its destruction in the 1959 uprising.

Head down the nearby alley, past ⑧**Drubthub Nunnery** (p59), to visit ⑨**Palha Lupuk** (p59), the site of Lhasa's earliest religious icons. If you have the energy, finish with a quick circuit of the Potala kora, stopping in at the ⑩**Lukhang Temple** (p61). Finish up with a well-deserved thermos of sweet tea at either of two nearby ⑪**teahouses** (p71) in the pleasant park.

cave is its relief rock carvings, some of which are over a thousand years old, making them the oldest religious images in Lhasa. Altogether there are over 70 carvings of bodhisattvas here; the oldest images are generally the ones lowest on the cave walls. Songtsen Gampo is depicted on the west side.

The yellow building above the Palha Lupuk is a chapel that gives access to the less interesting meditation cave (*drub-puk*) of King Songtsen Gampo's Chinese wife, Princess Wencheng.

Lukhang Temple BUDDHIST, TEMPLE

(禄康寺, Lùkāng Sì; Map p56; admission ¥10, photos ¥50; ☉9am-5pm) The Lukhang is a little-visited temple on a small island in a lake, behind the Potala in the pleasant Dzongyab Lukhang Park. The Lukhang is celebrated for its 2nd- and 3rd-floor murals, which date from the 18th century. Bring a torch (flashlight).

The lake was created during the construction of the Potala. Earth used for mortar was excavated from here, leaving a depression that was later filled with water. *Lu* (also known as *naga*) are subterranean dragonlike spirits that were thought to inhabit the area, and the Lukhang, or Chapel of the Dragon King, was built by the sixth Dalai Lama to appease them (and also to use as a retreat). You can see Luyi Gyalpo, the *naga* king, at the rear of the ground floor of the Lukhang. He is riding an elephant, and protective snakes rise from behind his head. The *naga* spirits were finally interred in the nearby Palha Lu-puk.

The 2nd-floor murals tell a story made famous by a Tibetan opera, while the murals on the 3rd floor depict different themes on each of the walls – Indian yogis demonstrating yogic positions (west), 84 *mahisaddhas* or masters of Buddhism (east), and the life cycle as perceived by Tibetan Buddhists (north), with the gods of Bardo, the Tibetan underworld, occupying its centre. Look for the wonderful attention to detail, down to the hairy legs of the sadhus and the patterns on the clothes.

The 3rd floor contains a statue of an 11-headed Chenresig and a meditation room used by the Dalai Lamas. To reach the 3rd floor, walk clockwise around the outside of the building and enter from the back via a flight of stairs (access was closed during our last visit). Finish off a visit with a kora of the island.

For a detailed commentary on the murals check out Ian Baker and Thomas Laird's coffee-table book *The Dalai Lama's Secret Temple: Tantric Wall Paintings from Tibet.*

Kunde Ling BUDDHIST, MONASTERY

(贡德林, Gòngdélín; Map p56; Deji Zhonglu; admission ¥10; ☉9am-7pm) At the foot of Parma Ri, close to Beijing Zhonglu, is one of Lhasa's four former royal temples. The *ling* (royal) temples were appointed by the fifth Dalai Lama, and it was from one of them that regents of Tibet were generally appointed. There are only a couple of restored chapels open, but it's a friendly place with around 60 monks and worth a visit. Look for the upstairs mural of the original Kunde Ling, 80% of which has been destroyed.

There's normally debating here between 2pm and 4pm.

Gesar Ling BUDDHIST, TEMPLE

(关帝格萨尔拉康, Guāndì Gésà'ěr Lākāng; Map p56; Beijing Zhonglu; ☉9.30am-7.30pm) On the north side of Parma Ri is the Gesar Ling, a Chinese construction dating back to 1793 that was recently renovated. It is the only Chinese-style temple in Lhasa. The main red-walled temple has a Chinese-style statue of Guandi, the Chinese God of War, while a separate yellow chapel holds the Tibetan equivalent, the mythical warrior Gesar, along with statues of Jampelyang, Chana Dorje (Vajrapani) and Chenresig.

★Chagpo Ri Rock Carvings HISTORIC SITE

(药王山; Yàowáng Shān; Map p56; Deji Zhonglu; admission ¥10; ☉dawn-dusk) This hidden corner of Lhasa features over 5000 painted rock carvings that were created on the back side of Chagpo Ri over the course of a millennium. Throughout the day pilgrims perform full body prostrations in front of the images, while stonecarvers at the far end of the courtyard contribute to a large chörten built entirely of the carvers' mani stones. The best way to visit the area is as part of the Lingkhor pilgrim route (p60).

Ramoche Temple & Around ར་མོ་ཆེ 小昭寺

The sister temple to the Jokhang, the Ramoche was constructed around the same time as its more famous sibling. It was originally built to house the Jowo Sakyamuni image brought to Tibet by Princess Wencheng. Sometime in the 8th century the Sakyamuni image was moved to the Jokhang and

BRAHMAPUTRA GRAND HOTEL

Even if you're not in the market for showy five-star digs, it's worth investing ¥10 in a cab ride out to the opulent **Brahmaputra Grand Hotel** (雅鲁藏布大酒店, Yǎlǔzàngbù Dàjiǔdiàn; Map p44; www.tibethotel.cn; Section B, Yangcheng Plaza, Zangda Xilu, Gongbutang) in the east of town. It occupies a space somewhere between Vegas theme hotel and ethnographic museum, and you could easily spend an hour wandering the hundreds of exhibits in the free 2nd-floor museum, from antique opera masks to armour and historic B&W photographs. Amazingly, it's all for sale. Pick up a floor plan from the lobby.

replaced with the image of Jowo Mikyöba (Akshobhya), brought to Tibet in the 7th century by King Songtsen Gampo's Nepali wife, Princess Bhrikuti. By the mid-15th century the temple had become Lhasa's Upper Tantric College.

The pedestrian street **Ramoche Lam** (Xiaozhaosi Lu) that leads from Beijing Donglu to the Ramoche is one of the most interesting streets in Lhasa, jam-packed with teahouses, restaurants and stalls selling everything from traditional jackets and Tibetan-style tents to handmade potato chips, Amdo breads, top-grade tsampa (roasted-barley flour) and Tibetan scriptures. It's well worth a stroll.

Ramoche Temple BUDDHIST, TEMPLE
(ར་མོ་ཆེ, 小昭寺; Xiǎozhāo Sì; Map p44; admission ¥20; ⊙ 7.30am-8pm) The main image here is the fabulously ornate Jowo Mikyöba (Akshobhya) image, which represents Sakyamuni at the age of eight. The statue is in the inner Tsangkhang, protected by the four guardian kings and a curtain of chain mail, which pilgrims rub for good luck. The lower half of the statue was discovered in 1983 in a Lhasa rubbish tip and the head was discovered in Beïjing's Forbidden City and brought back to Lhasa by the 10th Panchen Lama.

As you enter the temple, past pilgrims doing full-body prostrations and the first of two inner koras, you'll see a protector chapel to the left, featuring masks and puppets on the ancient pillars and an encased image of the divination deity Dorje Yudronma cov-

ered in beads on a horse. The main chapel is full of fearsome protector deities in *yab-yum* pose, as befitting a Tantric temple. The Ramoche was badly damaged by Red Guards during the Cultural Revolution, but the complex has since been restored with Swiss assistance.

Tsepak Lhakhang BUDDHIST, CHAPEL
(Map p44; Ramoche Lam/Xiaozhaosi Lu) As you exit the Ramoche, a doorway to the right by a collection of yak-butter and juniper-incense stalls leads to one of Lhasa's hidden gems, the Tsepak Lhakhang. The central image is Tsepame, flanked by Jampa and Sakyamuni, and there's a wonderful kora path. The site is very popular with pilgrims.

Gyüme Tratsang BUDDHIST, TEMPLE
(下密寺, Xiàmì Sì; Map p46; Bejing Donglu) Gyüme was founded in the mid-15th century as one of Tibet's foremost Tantric training colleges, second only in Lhasa to the monasteries of Sera and Drepung. More than 500 monks were once in residence, and students of the college underwent a physically and intellectually gruelling course of study. It's easy to miss the surprisingly impressive temple; look for an imposing entrance set back from Beijing Donglu.

The main *dukhang* has statues of Tsongkhapa, Chenresig and Sakyamuni. Look for the monks' alms bowls encased in crafted leather, hanging from the pillars. Behind are huge two-storey statues of Tsongkhapa and his two main disciples, and next door is a fearsome statue of Dorje Jigje (Yamantaka). Upstairs is a famous speaking rock image of Drölma. The college was desecrated during the Cultural Revolution, but a growing number of monks are now in residence.

Meru Sarpa Monastery BUDDHIST, MONASTERY
(Map p46; Beijing Donglu) The traditional woodblock printing press in the middle of this traditional housing compound doesn't really welcome visitors, so head instead to the atmospheric chapel in the northwest corner. Look for the statue of thousand-armed Chenresig, an unusual 'frog-faced' Palden Lhamo and the preserved jaws of a crocodile-like gharial. It's about 50m east of the Gyüme Tratsang.

Other Old Town Sights

Down the alleys off Beijing Donglu is an active nunnery and five obscure temples which can be visited if you've seen everything else.

Ani Sangkhung Nunnery BUDDHIST, NUNNERY
(仓姑寺, Cānggū Sì; Map p46; 29 Linkuo Nanlu; admission ¥40; ⌚8am-6pm) This small and politically active nunnery is the only one within the precincts of the old Tibetan quarter. The site of the nunnery probably dates back to the 7th century, but it housed a monastery until at least the 15th century. The principal image, upstairs on the 2nd floor, is a thousand-armed Chenresig. A small alley to the side of the main chapel leads down to the former meditation chamber of Songtsen Gampo, the 7th-century king of Tibet.

The busy nuns run a great teahouse (p70) in the courtyard, as well as a popular shop selling prayer beads and jewellery.

Tsome Ling BUDDHIST, TEMPLE
(Map p46) The small but interesting Tsome Ling is one of the four *ling* temples of Lhasa (along with Kunde Ling and Tengye Ling). To the east of the residential courtyard is the Kharpo Podrang (White Palace), built in 1777, and to the west is the Marpo Podrang (Red Palace), built at the beginning of the 19th century. Both buildings have fine murals and are well frequented by pilgrims.

Tengye Ling BUDDHIST, TEMPLE
(Map p46) This obscure and little-visited Nyingmapa-sect temple is dedicated to the central red-faced deity Tseumar, as well as Pehar (a protector linked to Samye) and Tamdrin (Hayagriva). The crates of *báijiǔ* (rice wine) stacked in the corner are there to refill the silver cup in Tseumar's hand; apparently he's in a better mood if constantly plastered. The entire chapel smells like a distillery. Look for the wonderful old photo of the Dalai Lama's pet elephant, stabled in the Lukhang behind the Potala. The chapel is hidden in the backstreets west of the Shangbala Hotel and is hard to find; enter through the gateway marked by juniper and *báijiǔ*-sellers, just south of the Tsen Bar.

Shide Tratsang BUDDHIST, TEMPLE
(Map p46) Once one of the six principal temples encircling the Jokhang, this badly ruined temple is connected to Reting Monastery. It's in a housing courtyard, down a back alley near Tashi I restaurant, and remains a rare example of what Lhasa looked like before the renovation teams moved in. Look for the brown walls.

Rigsum Lhakhang BUDDHIST, TEMPLE
(Map p46) One of four chapels surrounding the Jokhang at cardinal points, this lovely small chapel hidden in a housing courtyard southwest of Barkhor Sq is dedicated to the Rigsum Gonpo trinity of Jampelyang, Chenresig and Chana Dorje (Vajrapani). Look for the line of prayer wheels disappearing down the alley.

Pode Kangtsang BUDDHIST, TEMPLE
(Map p46) Diehards can track down this hard-to-find chapel with old murals in the south of the old town. It's accessed from the south.

The Norbulingka ནོར་བུ་གླིང་ཀ་ 罗布林卡

The summer palace of the Dalai Lamas, the **Norbulingka** (Luóbùlínkǎ; Map p44; Minzu Lu; admission ¥60; ⌚9am-6pm) is in the western part of town. The lifeless templelike buildings rank well behind the other points of interest in and around Lhasa, since most rooms are closed to the public. This said, the Norbulingka is worth a visit if you don't mind the entry fee, and the park is a great place to be during festival times and public holidays. In the seventh lunar month of every year, the Norbulingka is crowded with picnickers for the **Shötun** festival, when traditional Tibetan opera performances are held here.

As you leave the palace after your visit, pop into the charming yellow-walled **mani lhakhang** (Map p44) to the south of the Norbulingka entrance.

History

The seventh Dalai Lama founded the first summer palace in the Norbulingka (whose name literally means 'jewel park') in 1755. Rather than use the palace simply as a retreat, he decided to use the wooded environs as a summer base from which to administer the country, a practice that was repeated by each of the succeeding Dalai Lamas. The grand procession of the Dalai Lama's entourage relocating from the Potala to the Norbulingka became one of the highlights of the Lhasa year.

The eighth Dalai Lama (1758–1804) initiated more work on the Norbulingka, expanding the gardens and digging the lake, which can be found south of the New Summer Palace. The 13th Dalai Lama (1876–1933) was responsible for the three palaces in the northwest corner of the park, and the 14th (present) Dalai Lama built the New Summer Palace.

In 1959 the 14th Dalai Lama made his escape from the Norbulingka disguised as a Tibetan soldier. All the palaces of the Norbulingka were damaged by Chinese artillery fire in the popular uprising that followed. At the time, the compound was surrounded by some 30,000 Tibetans determined to defend the life of their spiritual leader. Repairs have been undertaken but have failed to restore the palaces to their full former glory.

Sights

Palace of the Eighth Dalai Lama   PALACE
(Map p44) This palace (also known as Kelsang Podrang) is the first you come to and also the oldest. Every Dalai Lama from the eighth to the 13th has used it as a summer palace. Only the main audience hall is open; it features 65 hanging thangkas and some lovely painted wood.

New Summer Palace   PALACE
(Map p44) The New Summer Palace (Takten Migyü Podrang) in the centre of the park was built by the present Dalai Lama between 1954 and 1956 and is the most interesting of the Norbulingka palaces. You can only enter the walled complex from its east side.

The first of the rooms is the Dalai Lama's audience chamber. Note the wall murals, which depict the history of Tibet in 301 scenes that flow in rows from left to right. As you stand with your back to the window, the murals start on the left wall with Sakyamuni and show the mythical beginnings of the Tibetan people (from the union of a bodhisattva and a monkey in the Sheldrak Cave), as well as the first field in Tibet (representing the introduction of agriculture). The wall in front of you depicts the building of the circular monastery of Samye, as well as Ganden, Drepung and other monasteries to the right. The right wall depicts the construction of the Potala and Norbulingka.

Next come the Dalai Lama's private quarters, which consist of a meditation chamber and a bedroom. The rooms have been maintained almost exactly as the Dalai Lama left them, and apart from the usual Buddhist images they contain the occasional surprise (a Soviet radio, among other things).

The assembly hall, where the Dalai Lama would address heads of state, is home to a gold throne backed by wonderful cartoon-style murals of the Dalai Lama's court (left, at the back). Look out for British representative Hugh Richardson in a trilby hat, and several Mongolian ambassadors. The right wall depicts the Dalai Lamas. The first five lack the Wheel of Law, symbolising their lack of governmental authority. Last are the suites of the Dalai Lama's

mother, whose bathroom sink overflows with offerings of one-máo notes.

South of the New Summer Palace is the artificial lake commissioned by the eighth Dalai Lama. The only pavilion open here at the time of research was the personal retreat of the 13th Dalai Lama (Map p44) in the southwestern corner, featuring a library, a thousand-armed Chenresig statue, and a stuffed tiger in the corner! Pilgrims walk around the Mongolian-style cairn of stones to the left of the building. The seats overlooking the duck pond offer a wonderful spot for a picnic.

Summer Palace of the
13th Dalai Lama   PALACE
(Map p44) The summer palace of the 13th Dalai Lama (Chensek Podrang) is in the western section of the Norbulingka northwest of the awful zoo (Map p44; admission ¥10). The ground-floor assembly hall is stuffed full of various buggies, palanquins and bicycles. The fine murals depicting the life of Sakyamuni are hard to see without a torch.

Nearby, the smaller Kelsang Dekyi Palace was also built by the 13th Dalai Lama, in 1926, as a Tantric temple. The fine murals depict Ganden and Potala; not the buildings but the Buddhist paradises of the same name.

Tibet Museum
西藏博物馆

This grand-looking museum (Xīzàng Bówùguǎn; Map p44; Minzu Nanlu; ⊙10am-5pm Tue-Sun) FREE, in the west of town just opposite the Norbulingka, isn't too bad as long as you can filter out the heavy Communist Party propaganda. A useful audio tour (¥5) is available with a ¥200 deposit.

The halls start logically with prehistory, highlighting the Neolithic sites around Chamdo and rock paintings at Rutok and Nam-tso, mixed in with a few oddities (5000-year-old grain; 4000-year-old musk deer teeth…). The 'Tibet is Inalienable in History' hall is full of boring seals and Chinese political spin, but it's worth seeking out the Guge kingdom shields and the 18th-century gold urn and ivory slips (exhibit No 310) that were used by the Chinese to recognise their version of the Panchen Lama.

The more interesting third hall covers Tibetan script, opera masks, musical instruments, astrological and divination guides, medical thangkas and statuary. Look for the terrifiying set of medical instruments and the hat worn by Khampa bards as they recited the Tibetan epic *Gesar of Ling*. The next hall concentrates on thangkas.

The final hall has a good display of folk handicrafts, ranging from coracle boats to nomad tents. Photos are allowed.

🏃 Activities

Tenzin Blind Massage Centre　　MASSAGE
(Map p46; ☏135 4901 5532; Danjielin Lu; ⏰9.30am-11pm) There's no better way to recover from an overland trip than with a massage from this graduate of the Braille Without Borders organisation (www.braillewithoutborders. org). Choose between hour-long Chinese (¥100 per hour) or Tibetan oil massage (¥150), the former clothed, the latter naked (don't be self-conscious, they're blind).

Lightness Blind Massage Centre　　MASSAGE
(光明盲人按摩中心, Guāngmíng Mángrén Ànmó Zhōngxīn; Map p46; ☏632 0681; Yak Hotel, 100 Beijing Donglu; massage ¥120-150; ⏰10am-10pm) Blind masseurs Dawa and Tenzin offer Tibetan or Chinese styles at this conveniently located massage centre.

✺ Festivals & Events

If at all possible, try to time your visit to Lhasa with one of the city's main festivals. The **Saga Dawa** festival (in May/June) in particular sees huge numbers of pilgrims making circuits around the Barkhor late into the night. Follow the locals' cue and change ¥10 into a fat wad of one-máo notes to hand out as alms during the walk.

A couple of months later, during the **Chökor Düchen** festival, Lhasa residents trek up to the summit of Gambo Ütse Ri, the high peak behind Drepung Monastery. In the olden days even the Dalai Lama would ascend the peak, riding atop a white yak.

🛏 Sleeping

The Tibetan eastern end of town is easily the most interesting place to be based, with accommodation options in all budgets. Apart from the hotels listed here there are dozens of shiny, characterless Chinese-style hotels scattered around town. You might find yourself in one of these if you arrive on a tour or book a hotel online.

Prices given here (and throughout this guide) apply to the high season from May to October. We have listed the full rack rate but if things are quiet you can expect discounts of up to 25% even in high season. Between mid-October and April you can expect still deeper discounts. Your agency may arrange your hotels for you (and will indeed often get specially discounted rates) but you can always request a specific hotel. Note that most of the budget places don't accept reservations.

Rama Kharpo Hotel　　HOTEL $
(热玛嘎布宾馆, Rèmǎ Ábù Bīnguǎn; Map p46; ☏634 6963; www.lhasabarkhor.com; 15 Ongto Shingka Lam; dm ¥40, d/tr incl breakfast ¥180/260; ❋ 🛜) Named the 'White Goat' after the legendary founder of the city, this easily missed lodge is hidden deep in the old town near the Muslim quarter. Both dorm and en-suite rooms are comfortable (though check for barking dogs) and the dark but pleasant cafe is a great meeting place. Bathrooms are en suite but simple. Vehicles can't reach this part of the old town.

Barkhor Namchen House　　GUESTHOUSE $
(八廓龙乾家庭旅馆, Bākuò Lónggān Jiātíng Lǚguǎn; Map p46; ☏679 0125; www.tibetnamchen.com; 2 Barkhor North St; dm/d without bathroom ¥40/100; @🛜) This backstreet Tibetan-style guesthouse is a good budget choice. The old-town location just off the Barkhor is near perfect, the staff are friendly, and the (squat) bathrooms and hot showers are super-clean. Rooms are fairly small with hard beds and some have limited natural light (ask for an upper-floor room) but you can head to the rooftop for fine views.

Dōngcuò International Youth Hostel　　HOSTEL $
(东措国际青年旅社, Dōngcuò Guójì Qīngnián Lǚshè; Map p46; ☏627 3388; www.yhalasa.com; 10 Beijing Donglu; dm ¥40-60, r without bathroom ¥80-120, s/d/tr ¥160/180/210; @🛜) Lhasa's best Chinese-run hostel attracts mainly Chinese backpackers, though a few foreign travellers find their way here. Rooms are smallish but well maintained, with wooden floors and crisp white sheets, though a few don't have any exterior windows. Bike rental (¥30) and free laundry are bonuses. Prices rise in July and August.

Banak Shol　　HOTEL $
(八郎学宾馆, Bālángxué Bīnguǎn; Map p46; ☏632 3829; 8 Beijing Donglu; dm ¥50, d/tr without bathroom ¥100/150, d with bathroom ¥230; 🛜) It's a mixed picture at this old backpacker stalwart. The newest triple rooms without bathroom are spacious, fresh and carpeted and the shared shower blocks are sparkling. Unfortunately the older roadside doubles and

LHASA'S BOUTIQUE HOTELS

A welcome recent trend in the Lhasa hotel scene has been the restoration and conversion of several of Lhasa's crumbling historic courtyards into stylish, atmospheric luxury lodgings. The following places ooze historic charm and traditional Tibetan decor, though to be honest you often pay for this with dark rooms.

Gorkha Hotel (郭尔喀饭店, Guò'ěrkā Fàndiàn; Map p46; ☏ 634 7000; gorkhahotel@yahoo.com; 47 Linkuo Nanlu, 林廓南路47号; r/ste ¥380/450; @) This atmospheric Nepali-Tibetan venture is a nice blend of cultures, from the Tibetan-style entry murals and traditional architecture to the photographs of Nepali royalty and Nepali-style restaurant on the roof. The creaking back block housed the Nepali consulate in the 1950s. Other rooms vary considerably, with some dark and small and others modern, so take a look at a few. The hotel is in the south of the old town, near several lovely old temples.

Trichang Labrang Hotel (志江拉让宾馆, Chìjiāng Lāràng Bīnguǎn; Map p46; ☏ 630 9555; 11 Lugu Wu Xiang; r ¥288-440, ste ¥588-988; @) This new hotel occupies the former residence of Trijang Rinpoche, former tutor to the current Dalai Lama. Rooms are set around a charming Nepali-run courtyard restaurant and there is pleasant rooftop and verandah seating. The building is certainly charming, but the rooms are dim and the crummy carpets and bathrooms are a bit out of place.

House of Shambhala (桌玛拉宫, Zhuōmǎlā Gōng; Map p46; ☏ 632 6533; www.shambhalaserai.com; 7 Jiri Erxiang, 吉日二巷7号; d incl breakfast ¥675-1015; ☉ closed mid-Jan to end Apr; @) Hidden in the old town in a historic Tibetan building, the romantic, boutique-style Shambhala mixes the earthy charm of the old town with a great rooftop lounge and spa treatments, making it perfect for couples who prefer atmosphere over mod cons. The nine rooms, decorated in natural wood and slate with antique Tibetan furniture, vary only in size. The spa offers a herbal bath in holy water blessed by a local lama (!), and the hotel's soft furnishings are made in an on-site workshop by disadvantaged Tibetans. The fabulous rooftop terrace is a great place to relax over a Baileys-and-masala-chai cocktail and pet the resident husky. Just don't take it as seriously as the owners seem to. Off-season discounts of 20%.

Shambhala Palace (香巴拉宫, Xiāngbālā Gōng; Map p46; ☏ 630 7779; www.shambhalaserai.com; 16 Taibeng Gang; r incl breakfast ¥450-720; ☉ closed mid-Jan to end Apr; @ ☎) The House of Shambhala's quiet 17-room annex is hidden deeper in the old town, offering identical styling but no spa. Avoid the smallest rooms here. Off-season discounts of 20%.

Yabshi Phunkhang (尧西平康, Yáoxī Píngkāng; Map p46; ☏ 632 8885; www.yabshi-phunkhang.com; 68 Beijing Donglu; r ¥799-880, ste ¥1808; ❖ ☎) Architectural integrity is rare in Lhasa these days, which makes the four-year restoration of this mid-19th-century mansion all the more remarkable. The collection of 21 large but fairly simple rooms linked by lovely courtyards and sitting areas is both stylish and atmospheric. The complex was built for the parents of the 11th Dalai Lama (*yabshi* is the title given to the parents of a Dalai Lama).

Lingtsang Boutique Hotel (林仓酒店, Líncāng Jiǔdiàn; Map p46; ☏ 689 9991; lingtsanghotel@163.com; No 38, No 1 Alley, Lugu; 鲁固一巷38号; s/d/ste ¥980/880/1680) There are just nine rooms in this traditional and intimate courtyard, the former residence of Nyi Rinpoche, a tutor of the Dalai Lama. The decor is a mixture of authentic architecture and modern stylish elements, with an open-plan wooden bathroom and dressed stone floors that add to the monastic feel. The suite occupies the former throne room of the *rinpoche* and has the atmosphere of a monastery chapel. Avoid the jarringly modern ground-floor restaurant and bar and instead soak up the views of the Jokhang from the rooftop restaurant.

singles are still small, noisy and overpriced. The recently renovated standard rooms with bathroom are normally the cheapest such options in town.

Bonuses include free access to a washing machine and pleasant wooden verandahs. The majority of guests nowadays are Chinese backpackers.

Kailash Hotel
HOTEL **$**

(凯拉斯酒店, Kǎilāsī Dàjiǔdiàn; Map p46; ☎693 9888; www.kailash.com.cn; 143 Beijing Donglu; r ¥160-180; ❄ @ ☎) A good location and some of the cheapest prices in town make this place worth looking at. Rooms are smallish and a tad dated but come with hot-water bathroom and a computer. The lobby is hidden behind a shopping-mall entrance.

★ Kyichu Hotel
HOTEL **$$**

(吉曲饭店, Jíqǔ Fàndiàn; Map p46; ☎633 1541; www.kyichuhotel.com; 18 Beijing Donglu; r standard/ deluxe from ¥400/500; ❄ @ ☎) The renovated Kyichu is a friendly and well-run choice that's very popular with repeat travellers to Tibet. Rooms are comfortable and pleasant, with wooden floors, Tibetan carpets and private bathrooms, but the real selling points are the location, the excellent service and – that rarest of Lhasa commodities – a peaceful garden courtyard (with espresso coffee). Reservations recommended.

Rates generally include a fine buffet breakfast in the excellent restaurant. The only grumbles we hear are related to the occasional issues with hot water. Credit cards accepted.

Yak Hotel
HOTEL **$$**

(亚宾馆, Yà Bīnguǎn; Map p46; ☎630 0195; 100 Beijing Donglu; dm ¥50, d ¥450-650, r VIP ¥880; ❄ @ ☎) The ever-popular Yak has matured in recent years from backpacker hang-out to tour-group favourite, eschewing the cramped dorm rooms (there are three left) for a range of comfortable en-suite rooms. Reservations are recommended. The 5th-floor breakfast bar offers great views of the Potala. Discounts of 30% are standard. Room options include the colourful Tibetan-style decor of the quiet back block; the larger but noisier deluxe rooms overlooking the main street, which have better bathrooms; or the plush VIP rooms (guìbīnlóu).

Dékāng Hotel
HOTEL **$$**

(德康酒店, Dékāng Jiǔdiàn; Map p44; ☎630 6555; De.kang@yahoo.com; 2 Shengtai Lu; d/tr ¥380/500; ❄ @ ☎) A well-run, modern mid-range choice, with easy vehicle access but walking distance from the old town, offering fresh and modern Tibetan-style rooms. Highlights include the friendly staff, pleasant rooftop cafe and Nepali restaurant.

Dhood Gu Hotel
HOTEL **$$**

(敦固宾馆, Dūngù Bīnguǎn; Map p46; ☎632 2555; www.dhodgu-hotel.com; 19 Shasasu Lu, 冲赛康夏

莎苏19号; s/d/ste incl breakfast ¥450/530/1050; @ ☎) If you're looking for a dash of style, this comfortable Nepali-run three-star place near the Tromsikhang market is a good choice, with ornate Tibetan-style decor, a decent restaurant and a superb location in the old town. Rooms are dark and on the small side but all come with modern bathrooms. Upper-floor rooms are brighter but there's no lift. A room tip: skip the pricier Potala-view rooms and grab a beer on the rooftop for even better views. Credit cards are accepted.

Tashi Choeta Hotel
HOTEL **$$**

(扎西曲塔酒店; Zhāxī Qūtǎ Jiǔdiàn; Map p46; ☎633 3028; losang1989@gmail.com; d/ tr ¥298/398) Travellers from Taiwan and Hong Kong love this reliable option in the old town. The four floors of rooms are set around a pleasant inner courtyard, which means they suffer from a lack of natural light, but rooms are clean and fresh and bathrooms are spotless. There are great Potala views from the rooftop.

Heritage Hotel
HOTEL **$$**

(古艺酒店, Gǔyì Jiǔdiàn; Map p46; ☎691 1333; heritagehotel@hotmail.com; 11 Chaktsalgang Lu; r ¥300-420; ❄ ☎) Located inside the artsy courtyard holding the Dropenling (p71) craft centre, the friendly Heritage offers 21 stylish rooms featuring stone-walled showers, wooden floors and Tibetan wall hangings. The old-town location is atmospheric if you don't mind a 10-minute walk to most restaurants.

Cool Yak Hotel
HOTEL **$$**

(酷牦牛酒店; Kùmáoniú Jiǔdiàn; Map p46; ☎685 6777; coolyak@gmail.com; r ¥160-260; ❄ ☎) The great old-town location and the giant Tibetan thangka in the central courtyard are the most eye-catching things about this modern place. The rooms are fresh and comfortable, though there's a definite lack of natural light. It's hidden down an alley off Danjielin Lu.

Flora Hotel
HOTEL **$$**

(哈达花神旅馆; Hǎdáhuāshén Lǚguǎn; Map p46; ☎632 4491; www.florahtl.piczo.com; Hebalin Lu; d incl breakfast ¥250-280; @ ☎) The Flora is a well-run and reliable hotel in the interesting Muslim quarter (it's run by a Nepali Muslim). Nice touches include a minibar at local-shop prices and a laundry service. Rooms are clean and spacious, though the bathrooms are a bit crummy. Credit cards accepted.

Shangbala Hotel
HOTEL **$$**

(香巴拉酒店, Xiāngbālā Jiǔdiàn; Map p46; ☑632 3888; www.tibetshangbalahotel.com; 1 Danjielin Lu; ❋🛜) This tour-group blockhouse was under major renovation in 2014. Expect upgraded facilities and the same superbly convenient location.

Mandala Hotel
HOTEL **$$**

(满斋饭店, Mǎnzhāi Fàndiàn; Map p44; ☑636 7666; Jiangsu Lu; d/tr ¥280/400; ❋@🛜) This newish Tibetan-run three-star place, just south of the old town, is a modern hotel with a few Tibetan touches. Rooms are comfortable but the wi-fi currently only works in the lobby.

Shangri-La Hotel
LUXURY HOTEL **$$$**

(香格里拉大酒店, Xiānggélǐlā Dàjiǔdiàn; Map p44; ☑655 8888; www.shangri-la.com; 19 Norbulingka Lu; r from ¥2488; 🛁) It was really only a question of time before the Shangri-La brand opened their first hotel in Tibet. The decor is modern and tasteful and there are fine restaurants, including an excellent buffet and a 'Tibetan tapas bar' serving Yúnnánese snacks. Five-star facilities include a gym, oxygen lounge and clinic, most likely in that order. Other perks include a large swimming pool and spa, plus free magazines via an e-reader.

St Regis Lhasa
LUXURY HOTEL **$$$**

(瑞吉度酒店, Ruìjídù Jiǔdiàn; Map p44; ☑630 8888; www.stregis.com/lhasa; 22 Jiangsu Lu; r from ¥3000; ❋@🛁) Six-star travellers accustomed to uberluxury, 24-hour butler service and, yes, a gold-plated pool, can finally consider a trip to the plateau. If you have to ask the price, you can't afford it. Proximity to the old town is an unexpected bonus. At least Richard Gere has a place to stay, if he's ever allowed back into Tibet.

The fortresslike main building has three restaurants, a spa, tearoom and the largest selection of wines in Tibet (although any collection of more than 10 bottles qualifies as this). An expansion is scheduled for 2015.

Four Points
HOTEL **$$$**

(福朋喜来登酒店, Fúpéng Xǐláidēng Jiǔdiàn; Map p44; ☑634 8888; www.fourpoints.com/lhasa; 10 Bolinka Lu; r¥935; ❋@🛜) After only a couple of years under the Tibetan sun the paint is starting to peel off this four-star Sheraton property. It's functional rather than luxurious (no gym, no pool) but there's pleasant courtyard seating and some nice touches, like a room humidifier for Lhasa's dry climate.

InterContinental Resort Lhasa Paradise
LUXURY HOTEL **$$$**

(圣地天堂洲际大酒店, Shèngdì Tiāntáng Zhōují Dàjiǔdiàn; ☑656 9999; 1 Jiangsu Donglu; r from ¥2000; ❋🛜🛁) This new monstrosity of glass pyramids in Lhasa's far eastern suburbs is so architecturally out of place that it feels more like a science experiment than a hotel. It plans to eventually operate an amazing 2000 rooms and 10 restaurants. The hotel has been the focus of a vocal Free Tibet campaign, run under the biting slogan 'all rooms occupied'.

Lhasa Gang-Gyen Hotel
HOTEL **$$$**

(刚坚饭店, Gāngjiān Fàndiàn; Map p46; ☑630 5555; 83 Beijing Donglu; d incl breakfast ¥680; ❋🛜) Modern and quiet four-star place popular with groups, with spacious, modern and clean rooms. Discounted agency rates as low as ¥300 can make this place a steal.

Thangka Hotel
HOTEL **$$$**

(康卡酒店, Kāngkǎ Jiǔdiàn; Map p46; ☑636 7322; 38 Yuthok Lam/Yutuo Lu; r¥480-680, ste ¥880; 🛜) A modern, friendly and comfortable four-star place with some Tibetan touches and a super-convenient location near Barkhor Sq. Standard rooms are best value, as superior and 'palace view' rooms don't offer much extra.

✖ Eating

As with accommodation, the best Tibetan, Nepali and Western restaurants are in the Tibetan quarter around the Barkhor Sq area. Almost all places offer decent breakfasts, perhaps the best being at the Lhasa Kitchen and Snowland restaurants. All the eateries listed serve lunch and dinner, but you will struggle to find a meal after about 10pm. For the flashiest Chinese restaurants you'll have to head to the western districts.

With the arrival of half-a-dozen Nepali restaurants, Lhasa now rivals Kathmandu in its range of foreign foods (though prices are a bit higher). All offer a mix of Indian, pseudo-Chinese and Western dishes for about ¥40, with Indian vegie dishes cheaper. If you're hankering for a *dal bhat* (lentils and rice), masala chai or banana lassi, make a beeline for these places.

There are several simple hole-in-the-wall Chinese places down the alleys off Beijing Donglu.

haunt of the licentious sixth Dalai Lama, who met the famed Tibetan beauty Makye Amye here and composed a famous poem about her. Chinese tourists are drawn to the absorbing views of the Barkhor from the corner tables and fine rooftop terrace, but the food (mains ¥25 to ¥60) is just so-so.

Dzongyab Lukhang
Park Teahouse
TEAHOUSE

(Map p56; Dzongyab Lukhang Park; tea ¥2-6) One of two good teahouse restaurants in pleasant Dzongyab Lukhang Park. Grab a thermos of sweet tea or try a cheap lunch of *shemdre* or curried potatoes (mains ¥8 to ¥15). There's a second **teahouse** (Map p56; tea ¥2-6) in the northeast corner of the park.

☆ Entertainment

Unfortunately there is little in the way of cultural entertainment in Lhasa. For authentic performances of Tibetan opera and dancing you'll probably have to wait for one of Lhasa's festivals.

For something a bit earthier there are several Tibetan *nangma* dance halls around town, which offer a mildly nationalistic mix of disco, traditional Tibetan line dancing, lots of beer and a bit of Chinese karaoke thrown in for good measure. Ask a Tibetan friend or your guide for the latest places.

Shöl Opera Troupe
PERFORMING ARTS

(雪巴拉姆, Xuěbā Lāmǔ; Map p44; ☏632 1111; 6 Linkuo Donglu) Performs a selection of Tibetan operas nightly at 6.30pm at the Himalaya Hotel. Tickets for the 90-minute show cost ¥180 with dinner and drinks, and there's a small museum on site. It was under renovation in 2014.

Gyelpo's Nangma
KARAOKE

(雪域杰布, Xuěyù Jiébù; Map p44; Beijing Donglu; ⊙7pm-2am) Gyelpo's is a local favourite *nangma* place, with a good floor show and singers. Gyelpo was a famous dancer on Tibet TV. It's a great place to meet local Tibetans, but be sure to secure a table before 9pm.

🔒 Shopping

You can get most things in Lhasa these days, though water-purifying tablets, deodorant and English-language books and magazines are still not easy to find.

For souvenirs, the Barkhor circuit is lined with shops. Expect to be asked an outrageous initial price and then settle down for some serious and persistent haggling. Popular purchases include prayer wheels, rings, prayer scarves and prayer flags, all of which are fairly portable. Most of the stuff on offer is actually made in Nepal and sold by Chinese or Hui Muslim traders.

Items of Tibetan clothing, such as *chubas* (long-sleeved sheepskin cloaks), cowboy hats, Tibetan brocade and fur hats, are good buys. There are several Tibetan dress shops on Beijing Donglu where you can get a formal Tibetan dress made or buy off the rack. Several good places are near the Kyichu Hotel.

The majority of shops around the Barkhor sell jewellery, most of it turquoise and coral (Tibetans believe that turquoise is good for the liver, and coral for the heart), but almost all of it is fake. The fake stuff is bluer and is flawless; beware of a string of identically shaped and rounded beads – nature did not intend them to be this way. The final test is to scratch the surface with a sharp metal object; the fake turquoise will leave a white line, the real stuff won't show a thing. Take a close look at the stone to make sure it's all in one piece. Unscrupulous traders glue together tiny bits of turquoise to make larger pieces of stone.

You'll also see 'Buddha eye' beads, known as *dzi* – black or brown oblong beads with white eye symbols. These are replicas of natural fossils found in rocks in the mountains containing auspicious eye symbols thought to represent the eyes of the Buddha. The real things pass hands for tens of thousands of dollars.

To find basic items, such as thermoses and water canisters, the best places are the lanes that run from the Tromsikhang Market down to the Barkhor circuit. Cheap pots and pans (ideal for instant noodles) are available at the stalls on the east side of the Potala. For hard-to-find items such as sunscreen and deodorant, dig around in Nepali-stocked shops dotted around the Barkhor circuit.

Cheese-heads desperate for a lactose fix can try the Dunya restaurant for Nepali-made 'yak' (actually *dri,* or female yak) cheese by the half-kilo.

There are now dozens of trekking shops on Beijing Donglu and Danjielin Lu, though make sure you can tell the difference between the real McCoy and the Chinese-made knock-offs.

★ Dropenling
HANDICRAFTS

(Map p46; ☏633 0898; www.tibetcraft.com; 11 Chaktsalgang Lam; ⊙10am-8pm) 🌱 This impressive nonprofit enterprise aims to bolster traditional Tibetan handicrafts in the face of rising Chinese and Nepali imports. There are two shops; a main showroom in the old town and a smaller but more convenient **branch** (Map p46; ☑632 2443; Danjielin Lu; ☺10am-7pm) 🖉 next to Lhasa Kitchen restaurant. Ask about the 90-minute artisan walking tour of Lhasa's old town (¥150 minimum for up to five people).

Products are unique, of high quality and employ traditional techniques (natural dyes, wool not acrylic etc) updated with contemporary designs. Artefacts for sale include woolly carpets (US$300) from the Wangden region of southern Tsang, Tibetan aprons, leather appliqué bags, cuddly toys and impossibly soft yak cashmere scarves. Prices are fixed, with proceeds going back to artisans in the form of wages and social funds. Foreign currency and credit cards are accepted (the latter with a 4.2% fee) and it can arrange international shipping.

Snow Leopard Carpet Industries CARPETS
(雪豹毯业, Xuěbào Tǎnyè; Map p46; ☑139 8901 0068; snowleopardcarpet@yahoo.com; 2 Danjielin Lu) This tiny place sells a collection of high-quality carpets and yak-wool blankets at fixed prices. At around ¥160 per sq ft, a 4ft by 6ft carpet costs around US$600. Credit cards are accepted and staff can arrange delivery abroad. Ask for friendly English-speaking Phurbu. The company uses some profits to fund a local orphanage. If you are serious, ask to see the warehouse a short drive away.

Tibet Lhasa Carpet Company CARPETS
(拉萨地毯公司, Lāsà Dìtǎn Gōngsī; Map p44; ☑632 6225; www.tibetzt.com; 24 Jiangsu Lu) If you are in the market for a handmade Tibetan carpet, head to this showroom opposite the St Regis hotel. Prices are fixed, at around ¥2500 to ¥3600 (US$400 to US$600) for a 1m by 2m carpet.

Barkhor Supermarket HANDICRAFTS
(八廓商城, Bākuò Shāngchéng; Map p46; Beijing Donglu; ☺9.30am-7.30pm) The souvenir stalls that once clogged the Barkhor Circuit were recently shepherded into this three-storey concrete building with a Tibetan facade. It's quite charmless but there's a surprisingly good range of products here, from butter lamps and prayer flags to monk's clothes.

Băiyì Supermarket FOOD
(百益超市, Băiyì Chāoshì; Map p56; Beijing Donglu; ☺10am-9pm) Next to Lhasa Department Store and boasting a wide range of food-

stuffs from frozen squid to ripe pineapples to a bewildering array of dried yak meat. The **branch** (Map p46; cnr Zhisenge Lu & Beijing Donglu; ☺9am-10pm) on the corner of Zhisenge Lu is the closest supermarket to the old town.

Tromsikhang Market MARKET
(冲赛康市场, Chōngsàikāng Shìchǎng; Map p46) This bazaar-style area in the old town has the widest selection of dried fruits and nuts (imported from Xīnjiāng) and is the place to buy such Tibetan specialities as tsampa, *churpi* (dried yak cheese) and yak butter. Khampa-style cowboy hats are for sale in the streets outside.

Norling Supermarket FOOD
(罗林超市, Luólín Chāoshì; Map p46; 20 Linkuo Donglu) Located near the Muslim quarter, this Tibetan-run Nepali import shop sells everything from muesli and Digestive biscuits to Indian spices, sunscreen and rolling tobacco, though at prices higher than in Nepal.

Outlook Outdoor Equipment OUTDOOR EQUIPMENT
(看风云便换远镜; Map p46; ☑633 8990; 11 Beijing Donglu) This reliable trekking shop has Western-quality sleeping bags (¥350 to ¥600), Gore-Tex jackets and tents, plus hard-to-find imported knick-knacks like altimeters, trekking socks and Primus cook sets. Gear is also available for rent.

Rental rates are ¥20 for a stove, ¥30 for a tent or ¥20 for a sleeping bag per day, with a deposit of ¥500 to ¥700. There's currently no English sign.

❶ Information

INTERNET ACCESS

Most public internet cafes won't accept foreigners without a local identity card. Almost all hotels and some cafes such as the Summit Café (p70) offer free wi-fi to patrons.

MEDICAL SERVICES

Several hotels and pharmacies around town sell Tibetan herbal medicine recommended by locals for easing symptoms of altitude sickness. The most common medicine is known as *solomano* in Tibetan and *hóngjīngtiān* (红景天) in Chinese, though locals also recommend *gāoyuánníng* (高原宁) and *gāoyuánkāng* (高原康). A box of vials will cost you ¥35 to ¥50; take three vials a day.

120 Emergency Centre (急救中心, Jíjiù Zhōngxīn; Map p44; ☑633 2462; 16 Linkuo Beilu) Part of People's Hospital. Consultations cost around ¥150.

BICYCLE

Bicycles are a reasonably good way to get around Lhasa once you have acclimatised to the altitude. The Dōngcuò International Youth Hostel (p65) rents mountain bikes for ¥30 per day with a ¥200 deposit, or try the **Bike Hostel** (风马飞扬旅舍, Fēngmǎ Fēiyáng Lûshě; Map p46), behind the Yak Hotel, which is a meeting place for long-distance Chinese cyclists.

Bicycle theft is a problem in Lhasa, so be sure to park your bike in designated areas. A lock and chain are essential.

CITY BUSES

Buses (¥1) are frequent on Beijing Donglu, and if you need to get up to western Lhasa this is the cheapest way to do it. That said, route maps are in Chinese only so if you aren't with your guide it's easiest to just take an inexpensive taxi.

PEDICAB

There is no shortage of pedicabs plying the streets of Lhasa, but they require endless haggling and are only really useful for short trips (around ¥5). At least most are Tibetan owned. *Always* fix the price before getting in.

TAXI

Taxis charge a standard fare of ¥10 for the first 5km (then ¥2 per subsequent kilometre), resulting in a ¥10 ride almost anywhere within the city.

AROUND LHASA

Within a short bus or taxi ride or easy cycling distance of central Lhasa are the impressive Gelugpa monasteries of Sera and Drepung. Both are must-sees, even if you have only a brief stay in Lhasa. Current regulations require foreign tourists to visit Drepung, Sera and Ganden Monasteries in the company of a registered guide.

Drepung Monastery འབྲས་སྤུངས་
哲蚌寺

About 8km west of central Lhasa, **Drepung** (Zhébàng Sì; admission ¥50; ☺9.30am-5.30pm, smaller chapels close at 2pm) was once one of the world's largest monasteries. The word Drepung literally translates as 'rice heap', a reference to the huge numbers of white monastic buildings that once piled up on the hillside.

Drepung was founded in 1416 by a charismatic monk and disciple of Tsongkhapa called Jamyang Chöje. Within just a year of

ⓘ PUBLIC TRANSPORT

At the time of research, foreigners were not allowed to travel on public transport out of Lhasa, with the possible exception of buses to the airport and the pilgrim bus to Ganden. Basic information is included here in case the situation changes.

completion the monastery had attracted a population of some 2000 monks.

It suffered through the ages with assaults by the kings of Tsang and the Mongols, but was left relatively unscathed during the Cultural Revolution and there is still much of interest intact. Rebuilding and resettlement continue at a pace unmatched elsewhere in Tibet and the site once again resembles a small village, with around 450 monks resident out of a pre-Liberation total of around 7000.

The best way to visit the chapels is to follow the pilgrims or, failing that, the yellow signs. Interior photography costs ¥10 to ¥20 per chapel. Try to visit in the morning as many chapels close at 2pm.

East of the main central grouping of sights is a cluster of friendly colleges that the tour groups never reach, including the **Lamba Mitze**, **Lumbum Kangtsang** and **Jurche Mitze**, once home to students from Inner Mongolia, and the **Khardung Kangtsang**, the upstairs back hallway of which is defaced with faded Mao slogans and images.

A restaurant near the bus stop serves reviving tea by the glass, as well as bowls of *shemdre* and *momos*.

⊙ Sights

Ganden Palace PALACE
In 1530 the second Dalai Lama established the Ganden Palace, the palace that was home to the Dalai Lamas until the fifth built the Potala. It was from here that the early Dalai Lamas exercised their political as well as religious control over central Tibet, and the second, third and fourth Dalai Lamas are all entombed here.

To reach the palace from the monastery's car park, pass the woodblock and juniper stalls and follow the kora clockwise around the outside of the monastery until you reach the steps.

Around Lhasa

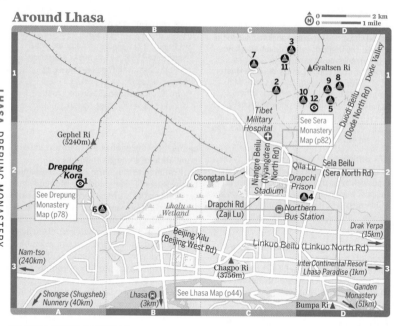

Around Lhasa

The first hall on the left is the **Sanga Tratsang**, a recently renovated chapel housing statues of the protectors Namtöse (Vaishravana), Nagpo Chenpo (Mahakala), Dorje Jigje (Vajra Bhairavo), Chögyel (Dharmaraja), Palden Lhamo (Shri Devi; on a horse) and Dorje Drakden (the Nechung oracle), all arranged around a central statue of the fifth Dalai Lama.

Head up the stairs and then across the main courtyard, where performances of *cham* (a ritual dance) are traditionally performed during the Shötun festival. Tibetan pilgrims stop to buy amulets and traditional sacred threads here. The upper floor of the main building has three chapels that make up the apartments of the early Dalai Lamas. The second of the three chapels, to the right, is an audience room with wonderfully detailed murals and the throne of the fifth Dalai Lama, next to a thousand-armed statue of Chenresig. The third is a simple living room.

From here descend and cross over to a final chapel, the entrance of which is defaced by a Cultural Revolution–era political slogan (Mao's image was only recently removed). Signs lead past a refreshment stand and a corner rock shrine to Drölma to the exit to the north.

★ **Main Assembly Hall**   BUDDHIST

The main assembly hall, or Tsogchen, is the principal structure in the Drepung complex. The hall is reached through an entrance on the west side, just past a **kitchen**, whose medieval-looking giant cauldrons and ladles look like a set from the film *The Name of the Rose*.

The huge interior is very atmospheric, draped with thangkas, covered in monks' robes and yellow hats and supported by over 180 columns – the ones near the western protector chapel dedicated to goddess Palden Lhamo are decorated with ancient chainmail and bows.

The back-room chapel features the protector deities Chana Dorje (Vajrapani, blue) and Tamdrin (Hayagriva, red) on either side of the door, and contains statues of Sakyamuni with his two disciples, the Buddhas of the Three Ages, and nine chörtens above. The walls and pillars are lined with statues of eight standing bodhisattvas. To the front centre there is also a youthful-looking statue of Lamdrin Rinpoche (a former abbot of Drepung recognisable by his black-rimmed glasses); next to it is his chörten. To the east is Tsongkhapa, the founder of the Gelugpa sect.

Sculptures of interest in the main hall include a two-storey Jampelyang (Manjushri), accompanied by the moustached 13th Dalai Lama; Sakyamuni; a statue of Tsongkhapa that is said to have spoken; Jamyang Chöje, in a cabinet to the right; the seventh Dalai Lama; and to the right Sakyamuni, flanked by five of the Dalai Lamas. At either end of the altar you will find a group of eight *arhats* (literally 'worthy ones'). Look for the two-storey statue of Jampa in the back room to the right. Pilgrims walk under the long cabinet on the eastern wall, which holds a huge building-sized thangka that is unveiled during the **Shötun** festival (there's a photo of it at one end).

Back by the main entrance, steps lead up to the 1st and 2nd floors. At the top of the stairs is the **Hall of the Kings of Tibet**, featuring statues of Tibet's early kings, as well as Lobsang Gyatso (the fifth Dalai Lama), and a chapel containing the head of a two-storey Jampa statue. Pilgrims prostrate themselves here and drink from a sacred conch shell.

Continue moving clockwise through the Sakyamuni Chapel, stuffed with chörtens, and then descend to the **Miwang Lhakhang**.

This chapel contains the assembly hall's most revered image, a massive statue of Jampa, the Future Buddha, at the age of 12. The statue rises through three floors of the building from the ground-floor chapel you saw earlier, and it is flanked by Tsongkhapa to the left and Jamyang Chöje to the right.

Next is the **Drölma Lhakhang**. Drölma is a protective deity, and in this case the three Drölma images in the chapel are responsible for protecting Drepung's drinking water, wealth and authority respectively. There are also some fine examples of gold-inked Tibetan Kangyur scriptures here. The central statue is a form of Sakyamuni, whose amulet encases one of Tsongkhapa's teeth.

Exit the building from the western side of the 2nd floor.

Ngagpa College
BUDDHIST, CHAPEL

Ngagpa is one of Drepung's four *tratsang* (colleges), and was devoted to Tantric study. The chapel is dedicated to bull-headed Dorje Jigje (Yamantaka), a Tantric meditational deity who serves as an opponent to the forces of impermanence. The cartoon-style Dorje Jigje image in the inner sanctum is said to have been fashioned by Tsongkhapa himself.

Walking clockwise, other statues include Palden Lhamo (first clockwise, riding a horse), Nagpo Chenpo (third), Drölma (fourth), Tsongkhapa (fifth), the fifth Dalai Lama (seventh) and, by the door, the Nechung oracle. Look for bull-headed Chögyel to the side, his hand almost thrusting out of the expanded glass cabinet.

To get a feel for what Drepung was like before the renovation teams arrived, detour briefly up to the **Samlo Kangtsang**, unrestored and surrounded by melancholic ruins.

As you follow the pilgrim path (clockwise) around the back of the assembly hall

---

THE BUMPA RI TREK

The demanding but excellent five-hour return trek up imposing Bumpa Ri, the holy peak to the southeast of Lhasa, is worth attempting if you're fit and acclimatised. It's straight up and then straight down, but offers unparalleled views over the Holy City, either from the top or just part of the way. Some travellers have been told the hill is off limits, so check with your guide and keep a low profile if hiking here.

From just south of the Lhasa Bridge a path ascends the base of the hill to a chörten and incense-burning site. From here faint trails head straight up the hillside to the third small ridge, where a faint trail branches to the right. In general, aim for the pylon, to meet up with the main trail. After an hour you reach a ridge with views of the summit spires ahead. It's another hour's climb from here to the summit, following the trail to the right of the spires, over a spur and then up a gully to the two main summits, festooned in prayer flags. From the top it's a two-hour descent back down the way you came.

Drepung Monastery

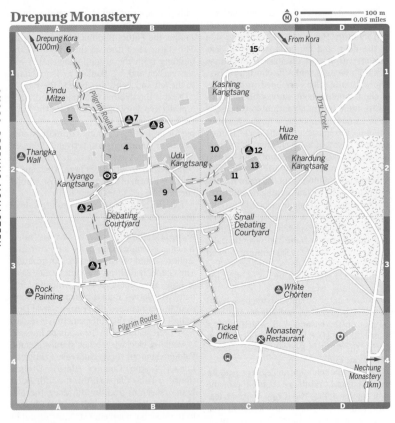

Drepung Monastery

◉ Sights

you will pass the small **Jampelyang Temple**, where pilgrims pour yak butter on the wall and then peer in to glimpse holy rock images of Jampelyang and Drölma and get hit on the back with a holy iron rod. Just a little further, tucked in on the right, is the tiny **meditation cave** of Jamyang Chöje, with some fine rock paintings.

Loseling College   BUDDHIST, CHAPEL
Loseling is the largest of Drepung's colleges, and studies here were devoted to logic. If you have time, pop into the small debating courtyard west of Loseling College. Monks sometimes practise their music in the garden here, blowing huge horns and crashing cymbals.

The **main hall** houses a throne used by the Dalai Lamas, an extensive library, and a long altar decorated with statues of the fifth, seventh and eighth Dalai Lamas, Tsongkhapa and former Drepung abbots. The two chörtens of Loseling's earlier abbots are covered with offerings. There are three chapels to the rear of the hall. The one to the left houses 16 *arhats*. The central chapel has a large statue of Jampa and a self-arisen stone painting of the Nechung oracle on the opposite wall; the chapel to the right has a small but beautiful statue of Sakyamuni.

On the 2nd floor you'll pass a small printing press to enter a small chapel full of angry deities, and then you pass under the body of a stuffed goat draped with one-máo notes before entering the spooky *gönkhang* (protector chapel). There are more protective deities here, including the main Dorje Jigje (Yamantaka), plus Nagpo Chenpo (six-armed Mahakala), Dorje Drakden and Dorje Lekpa.

Gomang College   BUDDHIST, CHAPEL

Gomang is the second-largest of Drepung's colleges and follows the same layout as Loseling. The main hall has a whole row of images, including Jampa, Tsepame and the seventh Dalai Lama. Again, there are three chapels to the rear: the one to the left houses three deities of longevity, but more important is the central chapel, chock-a-block with images. As at Loseling, there is a single protector chapel on the upper floor. Women are not allowed into this chapel.

Deyang College   BUDDHIST, CHAPEL

The smallest of Drepung's colleges, this one can safely be missed if you've had enough. The principal image in the main hall is Jampa, flanked by Jampelyang, Drölma, the fifth Dalai Lama and others. Upstairs are some fine puppet-like standing protector deities.

★ Main Debating Courtyard   BUDDHIST

If you're here in the afternoon, save some time to watch the monk-debating (lots of shouting, hand slapping and gesticulation) between 2.30pm and 4.30pm in the main debating courtyard in the northeast corner of the monastery (photos ¥15).

★ Drepung Kora   PILGRIM CIRCUIT

(Map p76) This lovely kora climbs up to around 3900m and probably should not be attempted until you've had four or five days to acclimatise in Lhasa. The path passes several rock paintings, climbs up past a high wall used to hang a giant thangka during the Shötun festival, peaks at a valley of prayer flags, and then descends to the east via an encased Drölma (Tara) statue and several more rock carvings. There are excellent views along the way.

The walk takes about an hour at a leisurely pace (it is possible to do it more quickly at hiking speed). Look for the path that continues uphill from the turn-off to the Ganden Palace.

ℹ️ **Getting There & Away**

The easy way to get out to Drepung is by bus 18, 25 or 16, which run from Beijing Donglu to the foot of the Drepung hill. From here minivans run up to the monastery (¥3). A taxi from the Barkhor is ¥30.

Nechung Monastery གནས་ཆུང་ དགོན་ 乃琼寺

Only 10 minutes' walk downhill from Drepung Monastery, **Nechung** (Map p76; admission ¥10; ☉8.30am-5pm) is worth a visit for its historical role as the seat of the Tibetan State Oracle until 1959. The oracle was the medium of Dorje Drakden, an aspect of Pehar, the Gelugpa protector of Buddhist state, and the Dalai Lamas would make no important decision without first consulting him. The oracle was not infallible, however; in 1904 the oracle resigned in

---

THE NECHUNG ORACLE

Every New Year in Lhasa until 1959, the Dalai Lama consulted the Nechung oracle on important matters of state. In preparation for the ordeal, the oracle would strap on eye-shaped bracelets and an elaborate headdress of feathers, so heavy that it had to be lifted onto his head by two men.

The oracle would then whip himself into a trance in an attempt to dislodge his spirit from his body. Eyewitness accounts describe how his eyeballs swelled and rolled up into his sockets, and how his mouth opened wide, his tongue curling upward as his face reddened. As he began to discern the future in a steel mirror, the oracle would answer questions in an anguished, tortured, hissing voice, and the answers would be interpreted and written on a small blackboard. After the trance the oracle would faint from the ordeal and have to be carried away.

disgrace after failing to predict the invasion of the British under Younghusband. In 1959 the State Oracle fled to India with the Dalai Lama.

Nechung is an eerie place associated with possession, exorcism and other pre-Buddhist rites. The blood-red **doors** at the entrance are painted with flayed human skins, and scenes of torture line the top of the outer courtyard. Tantric drumming booms from the depths of the building like a demonic heartbeat.

For images of Dorje Drakden, the protective spirit manifested in the State Oracle, see the back-room chapel to the left of the main hall. The statue in the left corner shows Dorje Drakden in his wrathful aspect, so terrible that his face must be covered; the version on the right has him in a slightly more conciliatory frame of mind. The *la-shing* (sacred tree) in between the two is the home of Pehar.

The far right chapel has an amazing **spirit trap** and a statue of the Dzogchen deity Ekajati, recognisable by her single fang and eye and representing the power of concentration. On the 1st floor is an audience chamber, whose throne was used by the Dalai Lamas when they consulted with the State Oracle. The 2nd floor features a huge new statue of Guru Rinpoche. Don't miss the fine murals in the exterior courtyard.

Nechung is easily reached on foot after visiting Drepung, en route to the main road. A scenic path leads past mani-stone carvers to the monastery (10 minutes).

Sera Monastery ᠱᩮ᠋ᠵᠭᠣᠨᠫᠠ
色拉寺

Approximately 5km north of central Lhasa, **Sera Monastery** (Sèlā Sì; admission ¥50; ⊙ 9am-5pm) was one of Lhasa's two great Gelugpa monasteries, second only to Drepung. Its once-huge monastic population of around 5000 monks has now been reduced by 90% and building repairs are still continuing. Nevertheless the monastery is worth a visit, particularly in the morning when the monastery is at its most active, but also between 3pm and 5pm (not weekends), when debating is usually held in the monastery's debating courtyard. Chapels start to close at 3pm, so it makes sense to see the monastery chapels before heading to the debating.

Interior photography costs ¥15 to ¥30 per chapel; video fees are an outrageous ¥850.

Near the entrance there is a simple but pleasant monastery restaurant.

History

Sera was founded in 1419 by Sakya Yeshe, a disciple of Tsongkhapa also known by the honorific title Jamchen Chöje. In its heyday, Sera hosted five colleges of instruction, but at the time of the Chinese invasion in 1959 there were just three: Sera Me specialised in the fundamental precepts of Buddhism; Sera Je in the instruction of itinerant monks from outside central Tibet; and Sera Ngagpa in Tantric studies.

Sera survived the ravages of the Cultural Revolution with light damage, although many of the lesser colleges were destroyed.

⊙ Sights

Sera Me College   BUDDHIST, CHAPEL

Follow the pilgrims clockwise, past the **Tsangba Kangtsang** and **Tsowa Kangtsang** residential halls and several minor buildings, to the Sera Me College. This college dates back to the original founding of the monastery.

The central image of the impressive main hall is a copper Sakyamuni, flanked by Jampa and Jampelyang. To the rear of the hall are four chapels. To the left is a dark chapel dedicated to the dharma protector of the east, Ta-og (in an ornate brass case and wearing a hat), alongside Dorje Jigje. Look for the masks, iron thunderbolts and mirrors hanging from the ceiling. Women cannot enter this chapel. To the left of the entrance is a three-dimensional wooden mandala used to invoke the Medicine Buddha.

Continue to the central chapel, which contains statues of the Past, Present and Future Buddhas, as well as 16 *arhats* depicted in their mountain grottoes.

The next chapel is home to Dagtse Jowo, a central Sakyamuni statue that dates from the 15th century and is the most sacred of the college's statues. At the back are Tsepame and eight bodhisattvas. The entrance to the chapel is guarded by the protectors Tamdrin (Hayagriva; red) and Miyowa (Achala; blue). The last chapel is dedicated to Tsongkhapa and there are also images of several Dalai Lamas, as well as of Sakya Yeshe (in the left corner with a black hat), Sera's founder and first abbot.

There are two chapels on the upper floor. The first, after you mount the stairs, is dedicated to Sakyamuni, depicted in an unusual standing form known as Thuwang. The second is a Drölma chapel with 1000 statues of this protective deity. The third has 1000 statues of Chenresig, as well as a huge brass pot in the corner.

Sera Ngagpa College
BUDDHIST, CHAPEL

A Tantric college, Ngagpa is also the oldest structure at Sera. The main hall is dominated by a statue of Sakya Yeshe (wearing a black hat), behind the throne, surrounded by other famous Sera lamas.

There are three chapels to the rear of the hall, the first featuring Jampa and thousand-armed Chenresig, the second with 16 *arhats* and a large Sakyamuni statue, and the third with a statue of the protective deity Dorje Jigje, as well as Namtöse (Vaishravana), the guardian of the north, to the right, who rides a snow lion and holds a mongoose that vomits jewels. There are also a couple of rooms upstairs featuring Tsepame, the eight medicine buddhas (Menlha) and the funeral chörtens of several past abbots.

After exiting, most pilgrims pay a visit to the nearby **Jarung Kangtsang** residential college.

★ Sera Je College
BUDDHIST, CHAPEL

This is the largest of Sera's colleges, generally accessed from a western side entrance. It has a breathtaking main hall, hung with thangkas and lit by shafts of light from high windows. Several chörtens hold the remains of Sera's most famous lamas. To the left of the hall is a passage leading, via a chapel dedicated to the Past, Present and Future Buddhas, to the most sacred of Sera Monastery's chapels, the Chapel of Tamdrin.

DIY: TREKKING THE DODE VALLEY

From the Sera Monastery kora you can make a great half-day trek up to the Sera Ütse retreat above the monastery and then around the ridge to the little-visited retreats of the Dode Valley. You shouldn't attempt the trek until you are well acclimatised to the altitude.

From Sera the steep relentless 400m vertical climb up to the yellow-walled **Sera Ütse** (Map p76) retreat takes at least an hour (look up and see it high on the cliff above Sera; if that doesn't put you off, you'll be fine!). Take the path towards the Chöding hermitage and branch off to the left before you get there, climbing the ridge via a switchback path until you reach the yellow building perched high above the valley. Sera Ütse (4140m) was a retreat used by Tsongkhapa (his *drub-puk*, or meditation cave, can be visited) and is currently home to two monks. You can also reach the retreat directly from Pabonka's Tashi Chöling hermitage, which makes for a stunning day-long hike.

From the Ütse continue east along a level trail for 10 minutes to a superb **viewpoint** (Map p76), probably Lhasa's most scenic picnic spot. From here the main trail continues east down into the Dode Valley, though it's possible for fit climbers to detour straight up the hillside to the summit, a knob of rock covered in prayer flags.

The main trail descends to the small **Rakadrak** (Map p76) hermitage, where you can visit three simple caves associated with Tsongkhapa. Five minutes' walk below Rakadrak is the larger **Keutsang Ritrö** (Map p76), a retreat complex home to 23 monks. The original hermitage lies in ruins in an incredible location on the side of the sheer cliff-face to the east. A painting inside the main chapel (to the right) depicts the original. As you leave the complex a path to the left leads to the dramatic ruins, but the trail is dangerous and ends in a sheer drop. The far section of the ruins can only be reached from the other side of the cliff.

From the Keutsang Ritrö follow the dirt road downhill and after 10 minutes branch left for the short uphill hike to the **Phurbu Chok Monastery** (Map p76) and its hilltop Rigsum Gonpo Lhakhang (an hour detour in total from the road). You can spot two nunneries from here; Negodong to the east and Mechungri to the southeast. Back at the junction, descend to the main road to flag down bus 14 or 15, which terminate at Linkuo Beilu, just north of the Ramoche Temple.

On the ride back it's worth getting off at Zaji (Drapchi) Lu to visit **Drapchi Monastery** (扎基寺, Zājī Sì; Map p76), an active and unusual monastery that is located near Lhasa's most notorious political prison. Huge amounts of rice wine and *chang* (barley beer) are offered continuously to the local protectress Drapchi Lhamo and the site has an almost animist feel to it.

Sera Monastery

Sera Monastery

◉ **Sights**

Tamdrin (Hayagriva) is a wrathful meditational deity whose name means 'horse headed'. He is the chief protective deity of Sera, and there is often a long line of shuffling pilgrims waiting to touch their – and especially their children's – foreheads to his feet in respect. Monks sell holy threads, protective amulets and sacred pills here, as well as red slips of inscribed paper, which pilgrims buy to burn for the recently deceased. The ornate brass shrine recalls the temples of the Kathmandu Valley. Take a look at the weapons, hats and masks hanging from the ceiling. There is a second chapel for him on the upper floor, but there he is in another aspect with nine heads.

The first chapel to the rear of the hall is devoted to a lovely statue of Sakyamuni, seated below a fine canopy and ceiling mandala. Pilgrims climb steps to the right to touch his left leg. The next two chapels are dedicated to Tsongkhapa, with Sakyamuni and

Öpagme (Amitabha); and to Jampelyang, flanked by Jampa and another Jampelyang. From here head to the upstairs chapels.

To the northeast of Sera Je is Sera's **debating courtyard**. There is usually debating practise here on weekday afternoons from around 3pm to 5pm, which provides a welcome relief from peering at Buddhist iconography. You will hear it (with much clapping of hands to emphasise points) as you approach Sera Je. Foreign photographers circle the site like vultures at a sky burial.

Hardong Kangtsang   BUDDHIST, CHAPEL
Hardong served as a residence for monks studying at Sera Je College. At the entry of the chapel look for three photos of Ekai Kawaguchi, the Japanese monk who studied here in disguise in 1901. As you walk downhill, note the wonderful **rock paintings** depicting Jampelyang, Chenresig, Chana Dorje (Vajrapani) and Green Tara.

★ **Main Assembly Hall**   BUDDHIST, CHAPEL
The main assembly hall, or Tsogchen, is the largest of Sera's buildings and dates back to 1710. The central hall is particularly impressive and is noted for its wall-length thangkas and two-storey statue of Jampa. He is surrounded by other figures, including Dalai Lamas on the right, while to the left is the large throne of the 13th Dalai Lama. Left of the throne is a figure of Sakya Yeshe. There are some incredibly ornate yak-butter sculptures in this hall.

Of the three chapels to the rear of the hall, the central is the most important, with its 6m-high Jampa statue. The statue rises up to the upper floor, where it can also be viewed from a central chapel.

Also on the upper floor (to the far left of the central chapel) is a highly revered statue of a thousand-armed Chenresig. Pilgrims put their forehead to a walking stick that connects them directly and literally to the heart of compassion. The pilgrim path enters the building from the back so this may be the first chapel you come across, before descending to the prayer hall.

The atmospheric monastery **kitchen** on the east side of the Tsogchen is worth a visit.

Printing Press   BUDDHIST, CHAPEL
Before leaving the monastery it's worth having a look at the printing blocks in this new hall. Photos are ¥5. Prints made on-site are for sale (¥25). A small building to the side holds three **sand mandalas**.

Sera Kora   PILGRIM CIRCUIT
The Sera kora takes less than an hour and is well worth the time. It starts outside the entrance and heads west, following an arc around the monastery walls. On the eastern descent, look out for several brightly coloured **rock paintings**. The largest ones on the eastern side of the monastery are of Dorje Jigje, Tsongkhapa and others. Next to the rock paintings is a support wall used to hang a giant thangka during festivals.

Chöding Hermitage   BUDDHIST, CHAPEL
A path branches off the kora up side steps beside the **thangka wall** to the Chöding hermitage. The hermitage was a retreat of Tsongkhapa, and predates Sera. There is not a great deal to see, but it is a short walk and the views from the hermitage are worthwhile. A path continues south around the hillside past a holy spring to a **viewpoint** that has fine views of Sera and Lhasa beyond.

ℹ **Getting There & Away**
Sera is only a half-hour bicycle ride from the Barkhor area of Lhasa, or take bus 20 from Beijing Donglu, or bus 22 or 23 from Niangre Lu. A taxi costs ¥15.

Pabonka Monastery པ་བོང་ཁ་
དགོན་པ་ 帕邦喀寺
One of the most ancient Buddhist sites in the Lhasa region, **Pabonka Monastery** (Pàbāngkǎ Sì; Map p76; ⊙dawn-dusk) **FREE** is infrequently visited, but is only a short detour from the Sera Monastery turn-off and is worth the effort.

Built on a flat-topped granite boulder said to resemble a tortoise, Pabonka may even predate the Jokhang and Ramoche. King Songtsen Gampo built the monastery in the 7th century and he, his Chinese wife Princess Wencheng, Tibetan King Trisong Detsen, Guru Rinpoche and Tibet's first seven monks all meditated here at various times. The nine-storey tower was destroyed in 841 by the anti-Buddhist King Langdharma and rebuilt in the 11th century. The fifth Dalai Lama added an extra floor to the two-storey building. It suffered damage in the Cultural Revolution and has undergone repairs in recent years.

The first building you come across, below the road, is the **Rigsum Gonpo Temple**, jam-packed with shrines, whose most famous relic is the blue and gold carved mantra '*Om mani padme hum*' ('hail to the

MONASTERIES IN TIBET

The great Gelugpa monasteries of Drepung, Sera and Ganden, collectively known as the *densa chenmo sum,* once operated like self-contained worlds. Drepung alone, the largest of these monasteries, was home to around 10,000 monks at the time of the Chinese takeover in 1951. Like the other major Gelugpa institutions, Drepung operated less as a single unit than as an assembly of colleges, each with its own interests, resources and administration.

The colleges, known as *tratsang* or *dratsang,* were (and still are) in turn made up of *kangtsang* (residences). A monk joining a monastic college was assigned to a *kangtsang* according to the region in which he was born. For example, it is thought that 60% of monks at Drepung's Loseling College were from Kham, while Gomang College was dominated by monks from Amdo and Mongolia. This gave the monastic colleges a distinctive regional flavour and meant that loyalties were generally grounded much deeper in the colleges than in the monastery itself.

At the head of a college was the *khenpo* (abbot), a position that was filled by contenders who had completed the highest degrees of monastic studies. The successful applicant was chosen by the Dalai Lama. Beneath the abbot was a group of religious leaders who supervised prayer meetings and festivals, and a group of economic managers who controlled the various *kangtsang* estates and funds. There was also a squad of huge monks known as *dob-dobs,* who were in charge of discipline and administering punishments.

In the case of the larger colleges, estates and funds were often extensive. Loseling College had over 180 estates and 20,000 serfs who worked the land and paid taxes to the monastery. Monasteries were involved in many forms of trade. For the most part, these holdings were not used to support monks – who were often forced to do private business to sustain themselves – but to maintain an endless cycle of prayer meetings and festivals that were deemed necessary for the spiritual good of the nation.

jewel in the lotus') that faces the entrance on the far side of the hall. The central shrine contains a 1300-year-old 'self-arising' carving depicting Chenresig, Jampelyang and Chana Dorje (Vajrapani) – the Rigsum Gonpo trinity after which the chapel is named. The stone carvings were buried during the Cultural Revolution and only dug up in 1985.

Continue uphill, turn left at the row of chörtens, and follow the road clockwise around the Pabonka rock (said to represent a female tortoise) to the **Palden Lhamo Cave** on the west side, where King Songtsen Gampo once meditated. Images inside are of Songtsen Gampo (with a turban), his two wives, Guru Rinpoche, Trisong Detsen (in the corner) and a *rangjung* (self-arising) rock carving of the protectress Palden Lhamo.

Pabonka Podrang sits atop the ancient rock. There is nothing to see on the ground floor, but the upper floor has an intimate assembly hall with a 'self-arising' Chenresig statue hidden behind a pillar to the right. The inner protector chapel has a statue of red-faced local protector Gonpo Dashey Marpo (second from the right). The four-pillared Kashima Lhakhang next door is lined with various lamas, ministers, three kings and

their wives. The cosy rooftop quarters of the Dalai Lama have a statue of the meditational deity Demchok (Chakrasamvara), along with fine views back towards Lhasa.

Further above the Pabonka Podrang are the remains of 108 chörtens and the yellow **Gyasa Podrang** (temple of Princess Wencheng). The two ground-floor rooms are dedicated to different manifestations of Tsongkhapa and the medicine buddhas, and an upper-floor chapel has a small statue of Wencheng herself in the far right, near an image of Thonmi Sambhota, who reputedly invented the Tibetan alphabet here. Songtsen Gampo's Nepali wife Bhrikuti is also present, as are images on the other side of the room of Green and White Drölma, of whom the two wives are thought to be emanations. Also present (but hard to see) is Gar Tongtsen, the Tibetan minister who travelled to the Tang Chinese court to escort Princess Wencheng back to Tibet.

Walks Around Pabonka

A few intrepid (and fit) travellers use Pabonka as a base for walks further afield. The half-day kora around Pabonka, Tashi

Chöling hermitage and Chupsang Nunnery makes a nice addition to a visit to Sera Monastery. Noontime can be hot here, so bring water.

An easy 20-minute walk from Pabonka leads up to **Tashi Chöling hermitage** (Map p76). There's not a lot left to see at the hermitage, but it offers good views. Pilgrims drink holy spring water from the upper chapel before making a kora of the hermitage. To get here from the back of the Pabonka kora, follow the path diagonally up the hillside, following the electricity poles.

From Tashi Chöling, the trail drops into a ravine and follows this down for 30 minutes to **Chupsang Nunnery** (Map p76). There are some 136 nuns residing at Chupsang and it's a very friendly place. A ¥5 minivan ride takes you back to the main road to Lhasa.

An alternative route from Tashi Chöling is to hike for 30 minutes northeast up the ravine to the cliffside hermitage of 4200m **Dadren Ritrö** (Map p76). You can see the hermitage from the trail. From here, trekkers can follow trails across two ridges for an hour to Sera Ütse and on to the Dode Valley for Lhasa's best day hike.

❶ Getting There & Away

To get to Pabonka, take bus 20, 22 or 23 to the Sera Monastery turn-off on Nangre Beilu. A paved road branches left before the military hospital and leads all the way to Pabonka and Chupsang. You'll soon see Pabonka up ahead to the left, perched on its granite boulder. The 'monastery' to the right is actually Chupsang Nunnery. A ride from the junction in a motor rickshaw costs ¥5 per person, or ¥20/30 for a van/taxi.

Ganden Monastery དགའ་ལྡན་
甘丹寺
ELEV 4300M

Just 50km northeast of Lhasa, **Ganden** (Gāndān Sì; admission ¥50; ⊙ dawn-dusk) was the first Gelugpa monastery and has been the main seat of this major Buddhist order ever since. If you only have time for one monastery excursion outside Lhasa, Ganden would probably be the best choice. With its stupendous views of the surrounding Kyichu Valley and fascinating kora, Ganden is an experience unlike the other major Gelugpa monasteries in the Lhasa area.

The monastery was founded in 1409 by Tsongkhapa, the revered reformer of the Ge-

lugpa order, after the first Mönlam festival was performed here. Images of Tsongkhapa flanked by his first two disciples, Kedrub Je and Gyaltsab Je, are found throughout the monastery. When Tsongkhapa died in 1411, the abbotship of the monastery passed to these disciples. The post came to be known as the Ganden Tripa and was earned through scholarly merit, not reincarnation. It is the Ganden Tripa, not, as one might expect, the Dalai Lama, who is the head of the Gelugpa order.

Ganden means 'joyous' in Tibetan and is the name of the Western Paradise (also known as Tushita) that is home to Jampa, the Future Buddha. There is a certain irony in this because, of all the great monasteries of Tibet, Ganden suffered most at the hands of the Red Guards, possibly because of its political influence.

Today it is the scene of extensive rebuilding, but this does not disguise the ruin that surrounds the new structures. In 1959 there were 2000 monks at Ganden; today there are just 300. The destruction was caused by artillery fire and bombing in 1959 and 1966. New chapels and residences are being opened all the time, so even pilgrims are sometimes unsure in which order to visit the chapels.

Ganden was temporarily closed to tourists in 1996 after violent demonstrations against the government's banning of Dalai Lama photos. There were further scuffles in 2006 when monks smashed a statue of the controversial deity Dorje Shugden. A new police station and military barracks were built at the monastery following the riots of 2008.

Interior photography fees are ¥20 per chapel; video fees are an amazing ¥1500. Make sure you visit the monastery in the morning as many chapels are closed in the afternoon.

Ganden is also the start of the popular wilderness trek to Samye Monastery (p213).

❍ Sights

Ngam Chö Khang   BUDDHIST, CHAPEL

The first chapel you reach from the parking area is Ngam Chö Khang, one of Ganden's oldest. It is built on the site of Tsongkhapa's original *dukhang*, and has a small shrine with images of Tsongkhapa. On the left is a *gönkhang* that houses four protective deities, including the local deity Genin.

Ganden Monastery

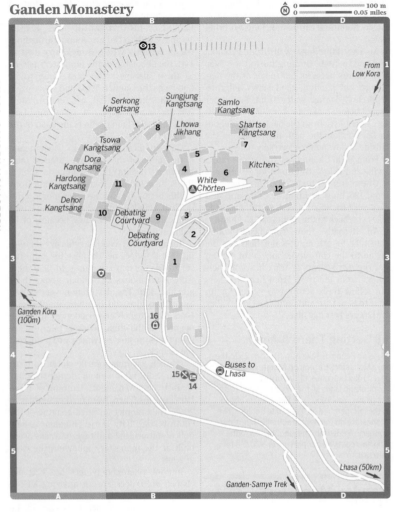

Ganden Monastery

Debating Courtyard BUDDHIST
Southeast of the **Gomde Khang** residence is the debating courtyard. You should be able to hear the clapping of hands as you pass if there is a debate in progress.

★**Tomb of Tsongkhapa** BUDDHIST, CHAPEL
The red fortresslike structure of Tsong-khapa's mausoleum, also known as the Serkhang, is probably the most impressive of the reconstructed buildings at Ganden. It's above the prominent white chörten. Red Guards destroyed both the original tomb and the preserved body of Tsongkhapa inside it. The new silver-and-gold chörten was built to house salvaged fragments of Tsong-khapa's skull.

The main entrance leads to a new prayer hall with a small sand mandala and an inner Sakyamuni chapel. The protector chapel to the right is the domain of the three main Gelugpa protectors: Chögyel (far right), Dorje Jigje and Palden Lhamo. Women are not allowed into this chapel.

Stairs lead to the upper floors and the holy Yangpachen Khang (or Serdung) chapel, which houses Tsongkhapa's funeral chörten. The chapel is named after the stone in the back left (covered in offerings of yak butter), which is said to have flown from India. The images seated in front of the chörten are of Tsongkhapa flanked by his two principal disciples. The room also holds several holy relics attributed to Tsongkhapa. Pilgrims line up to buy votive inscriptions written in gold ink by the monks. Protective amulets and high-quality incense are sold outside the chapel.

You can sometimes climb up to the roof for good views.

Chapel of Jampa BUDDHIST, CHAPEL
This small chapel (Jampa Lhakhang), just across from the exit of the Tomb of Tsong-khapa, holds two large images of the Future Buddha, plus the eight bodhisattvas.

★**Assembly Hall** BUDDHIST, CHAPEL
The recently renovated assembly hall has statues of the 16 *arhats* and two huge statues of Tsongkhapa (only visible from upstairs). Stairs lead up to the inner sanctum, the Golden Throne Room (Ser Trikhang), which houses the throne of Tsongkhapa. Pilgrims get thumped on the head here with the yellow hat of Tsongkhapa and the shoes of the 13th Dalai Lama.

On exiting the assembly hall there are two entrances on the north side of the building. The west one gives access to a 2nd-floor view of two Tsongkhapa statues, and the east one houses a library (Tengyur Lhakhang).

Residence of the Ganden Tripa BUDDHIST, CHAPEL
To the east of the Golden Throne Room and slightly uphill, this residence (also known as Zimchung Tridok Khang) contains the living quarters and throne of the Ganden Tripa.

Other rooms include a protector chapel, with statues of Demchok, Gonpo Gur (Mahakala) and Dorje Naljorma (Vajrayogini); a Tsongkhapa chapel; and a room with the living quarters of the Dalai Lama. To the right is the 'Nirvana Room', which has a large shrine to Kurt Cobain (only kidding, it's Tsongkhapa again, who is said to have died in this room). The upper-floor library has a round platform used for creating sand mandalas.

Lumbung Kangtsang BUDDHIST, CHAPEL
Lumbung Kangtsang is also known as the Amdo Kangtsang. Tsongkhapa himself was from Amdo (modern-day Qīnghǎi), and many monks came from the province to study here. Look for the *rangjung* (self-arisen) and *sumjung* (with the power of speech) stone representation of Drölma.

Shartse Tratsang BUDDHIST, CHAPEL
Shartse Tratsang is one of several renovated *kangtsang* (residences) that offer the opportunity to meet the local monks away from the tourist trail. In the early afternoon (1.30pm to 3pm) listen out for debating in the enclosed courtyard to the south. Nearby is the interesting **Barkhang (printing press)**, as well as the **Changtse Tratsang**, with its impressive main prayer hall.

Nyare Kangtsang BUDDHIST, CHAPEL
Below the main assembly hall, the rather innocuous-looking Nyare Kangtsang houses a controversial statue of the deity Dorje Shugden, worship of which has been outlawed by the Dalai Lama for its alleged dangerous Tantric practices. The statue is in the third chapel, in the far right corner, with a red face and third eye, wearing a bronze hat and riding a snow lion.

In 2006 monks stormed the building and smashed the statue, leading to the arrest of two monks. The statue was replaced in 2007 with the support of the Chinese government, seemingly more than happy to fan the flames of a sectarian split between local monks and the Dalai Lama. The stand-off remains tense and around two dozen Chinese soldiers remain barracked in the main chapel.

★ **Ganden Kora** PILGRIM CIRCUIT

The Ganden kora is a simply stunning walk and should not be missed. There are superb views over the braided Kyi-chu Valley along the way and there are usually large numbers of pilgrims and monks offering prayers, rubbing holy rocks and prostrating themselves along the path. There are actually two parts to the walk: the high kora and the low kora. The high kora climbs Angkor Ri south of Ganden and then drops down the ridge to join up with the lower kora.

To walk the **high kora**, follow the path southeast of the car park, away from the monastery. After a while the track splits – the left path leads to Hepu village on the Ganden–Samye trek; the right path zigzags up the ridge to a collection of prayer flags. Try to follow other pilgrims up. It's a tough 40-minute climb to the top of the ridge, so don't try this one unless you're well acclimatised. Here, at two peaks, pilgrims burn juniper incense and give offerings of tsampa before heading west down the ridge in the direction of the monastery, stopping at several other shrines en route.

The **low kora** is an easier walk of around 45 minutes. From the car park the trail heads west up past the new police station and then around the back of the ridge behind the monastery. The trail winds past several isolated shrines and rocks that are rubbed for their healing properties or squeezed through as a karmic test. At one point, pilgrims all peer at a rock through a clenched fist in order to see visions.

A *dürtro* (sky-burial site) is reached shortly before the high point of the trail. Some pilgrims undertake a ritual simulated death and rebirth at this point, rolling around on the ground.

Towards the end of the kora, on the eastern side of the ridge, is Tsongkhapa's hermitage, a small building with relief images of Atisha, Sakyamuni, Tsepame and Palden Lhamo. These images are believed to have the power of speech. Above the hermitage is a coloured rock painting that is reached by a narrow, precipitous path. From the hermitage, the kora drops down to rejoin the monastery.

🛏 Sleeping & Eating

Monastery Guesthouse GUESTHOUSE $

(dm ¥20-45, d without bathroom ¥200) The simple Monastery Guesthouse at Ganden is occasionally used by trekkers headed to Samye. The better-quality double rooms are above the well-stocked monastery shop just down from the car park.

Monastery Restaurant TIBETAN $

(dishes ¥3-8) The monastery restaurant has low-grade *thugpa* (Tibetan noodles) and some fried dishes.

❶ Getting There & Away

Pilgrim buses run to Ganden in the early morning from Barkhor Sq; tourists are currently not allowed to take them but you could ask your agency. A paved road switchbacks the steep final 12km to the monastery.

On the way back to Lhasa, pilgrims traditionally stop for a visit at Sanga Monastery, set at the foot of the ruined Dagtse Dzong (or Dechen Dzong; *dzong* means 'fort').

A 4WD for a day trip out to Ganden costs around ¥500.

Drak Yerpa བྲག་ཡེར་པ་
扎叶巴寺
ELEV 4885M

For those with an interest in Tibetan Buddhism, **Drak Yerpa** (Zhā Yèbā Sì; admission ¥30) hermitage, about 30km northeast of central Lhasa, is one of the holiest cave retreats in Ü. Among the many ascetics who have sojourned here are Guru Rinpoche and Atisha (Jowo-je), the Bengali Buddhist who spent 12 years proselytising in Tibet. King Songtsen Gampo also meditated in a cave, after his Tibetan wife established the first of Yerpa's chapels. The peaceful site offers lovely views and is a great day trip from Lhasa.

At one time the hill at the base of the cave-dotted cliffs was home to Yerpa Drubde Monastery, the summer residence of Lhasa's Gyutö College at the Ramoche Temple. The monastery was destroyed in 1959. Monks have begun to return to Yerpa but numbers are strictly controlled by the government, which carries out regular patriotic study sessions.

◉ Sights & Activities

From the car park, take the left branch of the stairway to visit the caves in clockwise fashion. The first caves are the **Rigsum**

Gompo Cave and the Demdril Drubpuk, the cave where Atisha (shown in a red hat) meditated. Look for the stone footprints of Yeshe Tsogyel in the former and the fifth Dalai Lama in the latter. At one nearby cave pilgrims squeeze through a hole in the rock wall; at another they take a sip of holy water.

The yellow Jamkhang has an impressive two-storey statue of Jampa flanked by Chana Dorje (Vajrapani) to the left and Namse (Vairocana) and Tamdrin (Hayagriva) to the right. Other statues are of Atisha (Jowo-je) flanked by the fifth Dalai Lama and Tsongkhapa. The upper cave is the Drubthub-puk, recognisable by its black yak-hair curtain. Continuing east along the ridge a detour leads up to a chörten that offers fine views of the valley.

Climb to the Chögyal-puk, the Cave of Songtsen Gampo. The interior chapel has a central thousand-armed Chenresig (Avalokiteshvara) statue known as Chaktong Chentong. Pilgrims circle the central rock pillar continually. A small cave and statue of Songtsen Gampo are in the right-hand corner.

The next chapel surrounds the Lhalung-puk, the cave where the monk Lhalung Pelde meditated after assassinating the anti-Buddhist King Langdharma in 842. A statue of the monk wearing his black hat occupies the back room.

The most atmospheric chapel is the Dawa-puk (Moon Cave), where Guru Rinpoche (the main statue) is said to have meditated for seven years. Look for the rock carvings in the left corner of the ante-room and the stone footprint of Guru Rinpoche in the inner room, to the right.

Below the main caves and to the east is the yellow-walled Neten Lhakhang, where the practice of worshipping the 16 *arhats* was first introduced. Below here is where Atisha is said to have taught. A 15-minute walk takes you around the holy mountain of Yerpa Lhari, topped by prayer flags and encircled by a kora.

There are several caves and retreats higher up the cliff-face and some fine hiking possibilities in the hills if you have time, including a half-day high kora. A very basic pilgrim guesthouse and simple food is available.

ⓘ Getting There & Away

The paved road from Lhasa crosses the prayer-flag-draped 3980m Ngachen-la before turning into the side valley at Yerpa village and passing two ruined *dzongs* and a large disused dam en route to the caves, 10km from the main road. Drak Yerpa makes for a good biking destination.

A daily pilgrim bus leaves from Barkhor Sq but foreigners currently can't take it. Drivers often call the site 'Drayab'.

Drölma Lhakhang 卓玛拉康

This significant although small monastery (Zhuómǎlākāng; admission ¥30; ⊙ dawn-dusk) is jam-packed with ancient relics and hidden treasures. It's only 30 minutes' drive southwest of Lhasa and is worth a stop for those interested in Tibetan Buddhism.

As you take the Lhasa–Tsetang road out of Lhasa, you'll pass a blue rock carving of Sakyamuni Buddha at the base of a cliff about 11km southwest of town (it's easily missed coming from the south). Netang village and the monastery are about 6km further on, between kilometre markers 4662 and 4663.

Drölma Lhakhang is associated with the Bengali scholar Atisha (982–1054). Atisha came to Tibet at the age of 53 at the invitation of the king of the Guge kingdom in western Tibet and his teachings were instrumental in the so-called second diffusion of Buddhism in the 11th century. Drölma Lhakhang was established at this time by one of Atisha's foremost disciples, Dromtönpa, who also founded the Kadampa order, to which the monastery belongs. It was here at Netang that Atisha died aged 72.

The 11th-century monastery was spared desecration by the Red Guards during the Cultural Revolution after a direct request from Bangladesh (which now encompasses Atisha's homeland). Apparently, Chinese premier Zhou Enlai intervened on its behalf.

The first chapel to the left is a *gönkhang*, decorated with severed stags' heads and arrow holders. As you enter and exit the main monastery building look for the two ancient guardian deities, which may even date back to the 11th-century founding of the monastery. An inner kora surrounds the main chapels.

From the entry, pass into the first chapel, the Namgyel Lhakhang, which contains a number of chörtens. The black-metal Kadampa-style chörten to the right reputedly holds the staff of Atisha and the skull of Naropa, Atisha's teacher. Statuary includes Atisha and the eight medicine buddhas.

The eponymous middle **Drölma Lhakhang** houses a number of relics associated with Atisha. The statues at the top include an 11th-century statue of Jowo Sakyamuni and statues of the 13th Dalai Lama, Green Tara, and Serlingpa (right, with a red hat), another teacher of Atisha. The lower central statue behind the grill is an image of Jampa that was reputedly saved from Mongol destruction when it shouted 'Ouch!'. There are also 21 statues of Drölma, after whom the monastery and the chapel are named.

The final **Tsepame Lhakhang** has original statues of Tsepame, cast with the ashes of Atisha, flanked by Marmedze (Dipamkara, the Past Buddha), Jampa (the Future Buddha) and the eight bodhisattvas. The small central statue of Atisha in a glass case is backed by his original clay throne. As you leave the chapel, look out for two sunken white chörtens, which hold Atisha's robes.

Upstairs is the throne room and living room of the Dalai Lamas, and to the right a library.

❶ Getting There & Away

Drölma Lhakhang is 16km southwest of Lhasa on the old road to Shigatse but is bypassed by the main airport expressway that connects the capital to the Yarlung Tsangpo Valley.

Shongse (Shugsheb) Nunnery

雄色尼姑寺

ཤུག་གསེབ་ཨ་ནེ་དགོན་པ་

ELEV 4410M

Hikers and anyone who likes to get well off the beaten track will enjoy this excursion to Tibet's largest **nunnery** (Xióngsè Nígū Sì; admission free), set in a large natural bowl about 55km south of Lhasa and home to over 160 nuns. The region is a favourite of birdwatchers.

The newly paved road leads right up to the village-like nunnery. The central **assembly hall** contains statues of Guru Rinpoche and several old lamas of the Nyingma and Dzogchen schools. Stairs to the right lead upstairs to a chapel with a statue of Machik Labdronma (holding a double drum), the famous 11th-century adept who opened up the valley and is considered an emination of Yeshe Tsogyel (the consort of Guru Rinpoche). The assembly hall contains a B&W photo and wall mural of one of Labdronma's subsequent reincarnations.

You can hike up the hill, following the electric poles, for about 45 minutes to the **Gangri Tokar shrine** (Drubkhang), where Longchenpa, an important 14th-century Dzogchen lama, once meditated. The chapel has a cave shrine and a sacred tree stump in front of a rock image of the Dzogchen deity Rahulla.

From here fit and acclimatised hikers can climb for a couple of hours up past meditation caves (marked by prayer flags) to the ridgeline behind. The views of the Kyi-chu Valley are fantastic from here and if the weather is clear you'll get views of snow-capped 7191m Nojin Kangtsang and other Himalayan peaks to the south. From the ridgeline you can continue northwest across a boulder field for 15 minutes to a small hill (5160m) topped by a chörten that offers epic views northwards as far as Lhasa. Alternatively you can continue east along the ridge to summit the bowl's main peak.

❶ Getting There & Away

The road to Shongse branches off the main airport expressway at Tsena village, 40km south of Lhasa, and diverts 13km up a side valley, passing the picturesque cliffside Samanga Monastery and small Öshang Lhakhang en route.

A nunnery bus runs here from Lhasa's Barkhor Sq three times a week but foreigners are not able to take it under current travel restrictions.

Ü དབུས་

Why Go?

Ü is Tibet's heartland and has almost all the landscapes you'll find across the plateau, from sand dunes and meandering rivers to soaring peaks and juniper forests. Due to its proximity to Lhasa, Ü is the first taste of rural Tibet that most visitors experience, and fine walking opportunities abound, from day hikes and monastery koras to overnight treks.

Ü is also the traditional power centre of Tibet, and home to its oldest buildings and most historic monasteries. The big sights, such as Samye, are unmissable but consider also heading off the beaten path to places like the Drak and Ön Valleys, or to smaller monasteries like Dranang and Gongkar Chöde. Make it to these hidden gems and you'll feel like you have Tibet all to yourself.

Best Monastery Koras

➡ Tsurphu Monastery kora (p95)

➡ Tashi Dor Kora (p97)

➡ Reting Monastery Kora (p101)

Best off the Beaten Track

➡ Sili Götsang Hermitage (p100)

➡ Samtenling Nunnery (p101)

➡ Drak Yangdzong Caves (p110)

➡ Gongkar Chöde Monastery (p106)

When to Go

➡ Nam-tso gets very busy in July and August so consider visiting in late April or May. The lake remains frozen from November until May.

➡ Pilgrims converge on Tsurphu in May/June to take part in a festival of *cham* dancing, the unfurling of a huge thangka and epic bouts of Tibetan-style drinking games.

➡ Festival season at Samye Monastery is in June/July. Time your trek from Ganden to end in the middle of the festivities.

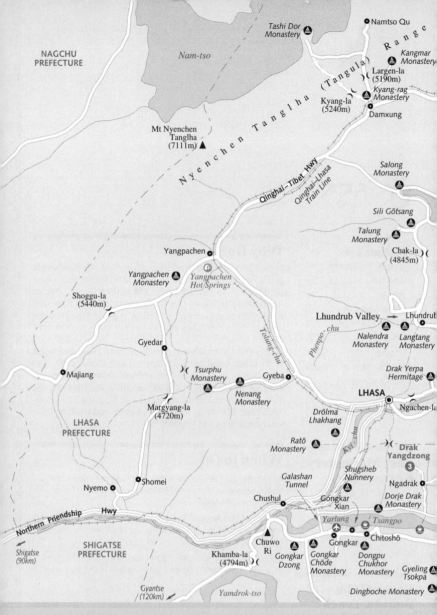

Ü Highlights

1 Taking a scenic river journey across the Yarlung Tsangpo to the spectacular circular complex of **Samye** (p111), Tibet's first monastery.

2 Visiting Yarlung Valley, the cradle of Tibetan civilisation, stopping at the iconic **Yumbulagang** (p119), ancient **Trandruk Monastery** (p118) and the ruins of **Rechung-puk** (p121).

3 Squeezing, dragging and pushing yourself through the sacred cave complexes of **Drak Yangdzong** (p110), an

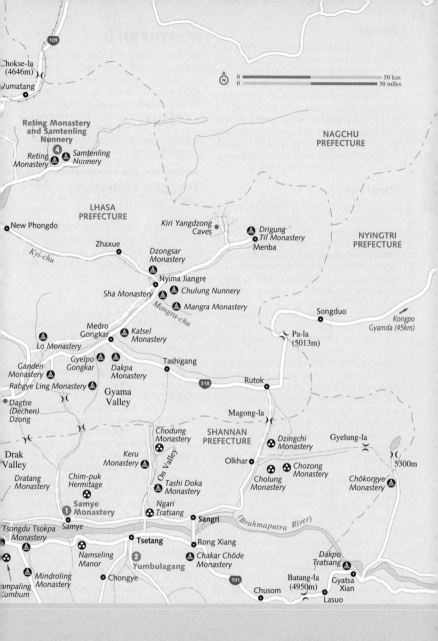

Chokse-la
(4646m)

Vumatang

109

N

0   50 km
0   30 miles

NAGCHU
PREFECTURE

**Reting Monastery
and Samtenling
Nunnery**

Reting   4   Samtenling
Monastery   Nunnery

LHASA
PREFECTURE

New Phongdo

*Kiri Yangdzong
Caves*

Drigung
Til Monastery
Menba

NYINGTRI
PREFECTURE

Kyi-chu

Zhaxue

*Dzongsar
Monastery*

Nyima Jiangre

Songduo

*Kongpo
Gyamda (45km)*

Sha Monastery   Chulung Nunnery

Mangra Monastery

Mangra-chu

Pa-la
(5013m)

Medro
Gongkar   *Katsel
Monastery*

Lo Monastery

*Ganden
Monastery*

*Gyelpo
Gongkar*

*Dakpa
Monastery*

Tashigang

Rutok

318

Rabgye Ling Monastery

**Gyama
Valley**

Magong-la

Dagtse
(Dechen)
Dzong

**Drak
Valley**

*Chodung
Monastery*

**SHANNAN
PREFECTURE**

*Dzingchi
Monastery*

Gyelung-la

*Keru
Monastery*

On Valley

Olkhar

*Chozong
Monastery*

5300m

*Dratang
Monastery*

*Chim-puk
Hermitage*

*Tashi Doka
Monastery*

*Cholung
Monastery*

*Chökorgye
Monastery*

1   **Samye
Monastery**

*Ngari
Tratsang*

Sangri

(Brahmaputra River)

*Tsongdu Tsokpa
Monastery*

Samye

Rong Xiang

*Dakpo
Tratsang*

*Namseling
Manor*

Tsetang

2   **Yumbulagang**

*Chakar Chöde
Monastery*

Batang-la
(4950m)

Gyatsa
Xian

*Mindroling
Monastery*

Chongye

101

Chusom

Lasuo

*ampaling
Kumbum*

adventurous overnight pilgrim
destination.

4 Exploring the renovated
prayer halls, juniper-scented
kora path and meditation
retreat of Tsongkhapa at

Reting Monastery (p101),
before making the lovely walk
to **Samtenling Nunnery**
(p101).

Permits

Travel in Lhasa prefecture (central and northern Ü) requires only the standard Tibet Tourism Bureau (TTB) permit but you still need to prearrange a guide and transport to receive this. Most of the Yarlung Tsangpo Valley (Shānnán prefecture) requires an additional alien's travel permit, which your agency will need to arrange in Lhasa or Tsetang. Lhamo La-tso requires five permits which need to be organised at least 15 days in advance of your trip.

Itineraries

Ü is a relatively small region compared to other areas of Tibet, resulting in shorter drives and fewer days on the road. The exception is Lhamo La-tso – well off the beaten track. Some sights, including Tsurphu Monastery and Lhundrub, could be visited as day trips from Lhasa, although spending nights out of the city allows for a slower pace and reduces backtracking.

Ü is tackled in three stages, usually broken up with stops in Lhasa. If time is short your priority should be the Yarlung Valley (four to six days), which houses the highest concentration of historic and religious sites.

With two or three more days at your disposal, head north of Lhasa to Drigung Til Monastery and Tidrum Nunnery for an overnight trip, or continue along the back roads to overnight at Reting, Nam-tso and Tsurphu Monastery, before heading back to Lhasa.

Keep in mind that at no part of this journey do you actually have to go back to Lhasa – roads from Ü connect with Tsang and eastern Tibet. From Nam-tso you can connect with the Friendship Hwy via the Shoggu-la or Margyang-la. From Drigung Til you can head back to Medro Gongkar and then continue east to Draksum-tso before returning via Samye Monastery. From Gongkar (the airport), you can get onto the southern Friendship Hwy and head west to Gyantse.

For more itineraries in this area, see p26 and p28.

PUBLIC TRANSPORT

At the time of research, foreigners were not allowed to travel on public transport in Tibet. We've included basic information in case the situation changes.

NORTHERN Ü   དབུས་བྱང་

The featured sights in this section are best visited as part of a loop; first north to Tsurphu and the Nam-tso, then east to Reting and Talung and then further east to Drigung Til. Drigung, Reting and Lhundrub can also be broken off to make a separate four-day trip. If you are not acclimatised, consider first exploring the Yarlung Valley, which is at a lower elevation.

Tsurphu Monastery   མཚུར་ཕུ་
མཚུར་ཕུ་ 楚布寺
ELEV 4480M

Around 65km west of Lhasa, **Tsurphu Monastery** (楚布寺, Chǔbù Sì; admission ¥40) is the seat of the Karma branch of the Kagyu order of Tibetan Buddhism. The Karma Kagyu (or Karmapa) are also known as the Black Hats, a title referring to a crown given to the fifth Karmapa by the Chinese emperor Yongle in 1407. Said to be made from the hair of 100,000 *dakinis* (celestial beings, known as *khandroma* in Tibetan), the black hat, embellished with gold, is now kept at Rumtek Monastery in Sikkim, India. You'll see images of the 16th Karmapa wearing the hat, holding it down with his hand to stop it flying away.

It was the first Karmapa, Dusum Khyenpa (1110–93), who instigated the concept of reincarnation and the Karmapa lineage has been maintained this way ever since.

The respected 16th Karmapa fled to Sikkim in 1959 after the popular uprising in Lhasa and founded a new centre at Rumtek. He died in 1981 and his reincarnation, Ogyen Trinley Dorje, an eight-year-old Tibetan boy from Kham, was announced amid great controversy by the Dalai Lama and other religious leaders in 1992. More than 20,000 Tibetans came to Tsurphu to watch the Karmapa's coronation that year. In December 1999 the 17th Karmapa undertook a dramatic escape from Tibet into India via Mustang and the Annapurna region.

Tsurphu has an annual **festival** around the time of the Saga Dawa festival, on the ninth, 10th and 11th days of the fourth Tibetan month (around May). There is plenty of free-flowing *chang* (Tibetan barley beer), as well as ritual *cham* dancing and the unfurling of a great thangka on the platform across the river from the monastery.

History

Tsurphu was founded in 1187 by Dusum Khyenpa, some 40 years after he established the Karma Kagyu order in Kham, his birthplace. It was the third Karma Kagyu monastery to be built and, after the death of the first Karmapa, it became the head monastery for the order.

The Karma Kagyu order traditionally enjoyed strong ties with the kings and monasteries of Tsang, a legacy that proved a liability when conflict broke out between the kings of Tsang and the Gelugpa order. When the fifth Dalai Lama invited the Mongolian army of Gushri Khan to do away with his opponents in Tsang, Tsurphu was sacked (in 1642) and the Karmapa's political clout effectively came to an end. Shorn of its political influence, Tsurphu nevertheless bounced back as an important spiritual centre and is one of the few Kagyud institutions still functioning in the Ü region. When Chinese forces invaded in 1950, around 1000 monks were in residence, and now there are about 330 monks.

Viewing the Monastery

If you are short on time, concentrate on the assembly hall and the upstairs former living quarters of the Karmapa. The latter still has some of the 17th Karmapa's boyhood possessions, including a globe, a toy car and an eyebrow-raising collection of books that includes *Peter Pan, The Fantastic Four* and *Star Wars: The Empire Strikes Back.*

The large **assembly hall** in the main courtyard houses a chörten (stupa) containing relics of the 16th Karmapa, as well as statues of Öpagme (Amitabha), Sakyamuni (Sakya Thukpa), and the eighth and 16th Karmapas.

Scamper up the ladder to the right of the main entrance to visit the private quarters of the Karmapa. First up is the Karmapa's classroom, complete with a jigsaw puzzle of a Buddhist thangka. The small Audience Hall contains a footprint of the 14th Karmapa as well as a picture of the 16th Karmapa wearing his holy headgear.

Across the upper courtyard is the 17th Karmapa's **bedroom**, where an attendant monk will pat you on the back with a shoe once worn by the man himself. A quick look at the Karmapa's bookshelves reveals an interest in birdwatching and astronomy.

Walking west (clockwise) around the monastery complex you pass a large *darchen*

(prayer pole) covered in yak hide and prayer flags before coming to the main **protector chapel** (*gönkhang*). There are five rooms here, all stuffed to the brim with wrathful deities. A row of severed animal heads, including ibex and Marco Polo sheep, lines the entry portico.

The first room is dedicated to Tsurphu's protector deity, an aspect of blue Nagpo Chenpo (Mahakala) called Bernakchen. There are also statues of Palden Lhamo (Shri Devi) and Tamdrin (Hayagriva), as well as a spirit trap and several dead birds. The third room features Dorje Drolo, a wrathful form of Guru Rinpoche astride a tiger, and the fourth room features the Kagyud protector Dorje Phurba holding a ritual dagger. The fifth room contains a silver statue of Tseringma, a protector associated with Mt Everest, riding a snow lion.

The large building behind the *gönkhang* is the Serdung Chanpo, which once served as the residence of the Karmapa. The side chapel features new statues of all 16 previous Karmapas.

The Lhakhang Chenmo, which is to the right of the Serdung Chanpo, houses a new 20m-high statue of Sakyamuni that rises through three storeys; this replaced a celebrated 13th-century image destroyed during the Cultural Revolution.

Behind the Serdung Chanpo and Lhakhang Chenmo is the sprawling Chökang Gang Monastery, the residence of the exiled regent of Tsurphu. Newly renovated chapels to explore include the Suri Lhundrup Phodrang and a new *shedra* (college).

The outer walls of the monastery are marked at four corners by four coloured chörtens.

Tsurphu Kora

The Tsurphu kora, a walk of around 4km (two hours), is quite taxing if you are not acclimatised to the altitude. It ascends 150m, past springs, shrines and meditation retreats, providing splendid views of Tsurphu below.

To follow the kora take the track west of Tsurphu that leads up past walls of mani stones to a walled garden. Bear right here up to a *dürtro* (sky-burial site) and follow the cairns that snake up the hill to a small pass marked by prayer flags. The kora then winds in and out of the ridges above the monastery and detours up to the Samtenling retreat, before descending eastward into a gully to

THE KARMAPA CONUNDRUM

Reincarnation is an integral part of Buddhist doctrine and Tibetan political culture but it is by no means an exact science. The controversy over the selection of the 17th Karmapa is a fine example of how things can go horribly wrong when opinions differ on the legitimacy of a newly chosen *trulku* (incarnate lama).

In 1981 the 16th Karmapa died in Chicago. Administration of the Karmapa sect in Sikkim was passed down to four regents, who in 1992 announced the discovery of a letter written by the 16th Karmapa that provided critical clues as to the whereabouts of his reincarnation, eight-year-old Ogyen Trinley Dorje.

Two weeks after one of the regents was killed in a road accident, one of the four, Shamar Rinpoche, announced that the mystery letter was a fraud, but it was too late. By early June clues from the letter had been deciphered, Ogyen Trinley Dorje had been found in eastern Tibet and the Dalai Lama had made a formal announcement supporting the boy's candidature.

Shamar Rinpoche opposed the Dalai Lama's decision and began a letter-writing campaign. Meanwhile, the Chinese authorities formally enthroned the 17th Karmapa at Tsurphu in front of a crowd of 20,000, using the occasion to announce that they had a 'historical and legal right to appoint religious leaders in Tibet'. In March 1994, Shamar Rinpoche announced that he had discovered the rightful reincarnation, a boy named Tenzin Chentse (also known as Thaye Dorje), who had been spirited out of China to Delhi.

In December 1999 the then 14-year-old 17th Karmapa dramatically fled Tibet into India via Nepal's Mustang region. In a letter left behind at Tsurphu he told the Chinese he was going to collect the black hat of the Karmapa (originally given to the 5th Karmapa by Chinese Emperor Yongle and taken to India by the 16th Karmapa when he fled Tibet in 1959), as well as several relics, including a human skull encased in silver.

The flight of the Karmapa was a particular blow for the Chinese. The Karmapa ranks as the third-most important lama in Tibet after the Panchen Lama and the Dalai Lama and is the only high-level reincarnation recognised by both the Chinese and Tibetan authorities. China's fury over the escape was levelled at the Karmapa's tutor Yongzin Nyima, who spent 15 months in jail for his alleged involvement.

For now the rivalry between the Karmapas is at a stalemate. Ogyen Trinley Dorje has been granted refugee status and residence at the Gyuto Monastery in Dharamsala, but the Indian authorities, in an attempt to avoid a political dispute with China, have not allowed him to travel to Rumtek (the black hat is kept at Rumtek Monastery in Sikkim; until recently China did not recognise India's claim to Sikkim). The other Karmapa, Tenzin Chentse, has established his base at Kalimpong, West Bengal. The rival Karmapas have never met, although both have indicated they are open to the idea.

For more on the starkly differing viewpoints, see the websites www.rumtek.org, www.karmapa.org and www.karmapa-issue.org. Mick Brown's book *The Dance of 17 Lives* is a good investigation into the controversy.

the chörten at the northeastern corner of the monastery.

🛏 Sleeping

Tsurphu Monastery
Guesthouse   GUESTHOUSE $
(寺庙旅馆, Simiào Lüguǎn; ☑ 136 2898 8393; dm ¥40-50, r ¥150-250) This recently revamped guesthouse, beside the parking lot, has good-quality mattresses and a pleasant Tibetan-style restaurant, making it a nice place to stay if you want to experience the monastery at a more relaxed pace. The upper-floor rooms are best.

ⓘ Getting There & Away

About 40km west of Lhasa, the road to Tsurphu crosses the Tolung-chu near the railroad bridge. From here it's another 25km to the monastery, passing Nenang Monastery en route.

Most travellers visit Tsurphu as a side trip on the way to Nam-tso. The road to Tsurphu passes Nenang Monastery, home to the young 11th Powa Rinpoche, an important Karma Kagyud reincarnation. It's worth a quick stop, although you will probably need to have this listed on your itinerary.

A pilgrim minibus runs between Lhasa's Barkhor Sq and Tsurphu but is currently off limits to foreigners.

Nam-tso গ্রন্থ'মর্ক্ত 纳木错

ELEV 4730M

Approximately 240km northwest of Lhasa, **Nam-tso** (Nàmùcuò; admission May-Oct ¥120, Nov-Apr ¥60) is the second-largest saltwater lake in China and one of the most beautiful natural sights in Tibet. It is over 70km long, reaches a width of 30km and is 35m at its deepest point. When the ice melts in late April, the lake is a miraculous shade of turquoise and there are magnificent views of the nearby mountains.

The Nyenchen Tanglha (Tangula) range, with peaks of over 7000m, towers over the lake to the south – it was these mountains that Heinrich Harrer and Peter Aufschnaiter crossed on their incredible journey to Lhasa (their expedition is documented in the book *Seven Years in Tibet*).

The lake is at 4730m so you'll need to acclimatise in and around Lhasa for a few days before heading this way. It is not unusual for visitors to get symptoms of altitude sickness on an overnight stay out at the lake.

Almost all travellers head for Tashi Dor, situated on a hammerhead of land that juts into the southeastern corner of the lake. Here at the foot of two wedge-shaped hills are a couple of small chapels with views back across the clear turquoise waters to the huge snowy Nyenchen Tanglha massif (7111m).

Your initial experience of Tashi Dor is unlikely to inspire visions of Shangri La. The poorly planned tourist base is an unsightly mess, ringed with barking dogs, litter and overflowing toilets. Food is overpriced and day-tripping crowds of Chinese tourists can be heavy during summer lunchtimes. Try to ignore all this and push ahead to the monastery and kora.

On the eastern edge of the peninsula is a bird sanctuary populated with migratory birds between April and November. Species to look out for include bar-headed geese and black-necked cranes.

◎ Sights

★ Tashi Dor Kora PILGRIM CIRCUIT

The short kora takes less than an hour (roughly 4km) and is unmissable. Try to tag along with some pilgrims and do one circuit at dusk, when the light on the lake is magical. If you have enough time, it's well worth

also hiking up to the top of the western hill for good views, especially at sunset.

The main kora path leads off west from the accommodation area to a hermit's cave hidden behind a large splinter of rock. The trail (now a jeep track) continues round to a rocky promontory of cairns and prayer flags, where pilgrims undertake a ritual washing, and then continues past several caves and a *chaktsal gang* (prostration point). The twin rock towers here look like two hands in the *namaste* greeting and are connected to the male and female attributes of the meditational deity Demchok (Chakrasamvara). Pilgrims squeeze into the deep slices of the nearby cliff face as a means of sin detection. They also drink water dripping from cave roofs and some swallow 'holy dirt'.

From here the path curves around the shoreline and passes a group of ancient rock paintings, where pilgrims test their merit by attempting to place a finger in a small hole with their eyes closed. At the northeastern corner of the hill is the Mani Ringmo, a large mani wall at the end of which is a chörten with a *chakje* (handprint) of the third Karmapa.

There are several other great hikes around Tashi Dor. If you have time it's worth walking to the top of the larger and less visited of the two hills to the east (two hours return). There are superb views to the northeast of the Tanglha range, which marks the modern border between Tibet and Qīnghǎi (Amdo).

For the seriously devout there is a pilgrim route that circles the entire lake. It takes around 18 days to make a full lap,

Ü NAM-TSO

DON'T MISS

STRETCHING YOUR LEGS

Tightly planned 4WD tours sometimes leave your legs itchin' for a walk and some exploration. One sure way of shaking things up is to embed the following day hikes and koras into your itinerary.

➡ Tsurphu kora (p95)

➡ Drak Yangdzong (p110)

➡ Chim-puk Hermitage (p115)

➡ Dorje Drak kora (p109)

➡ Tashi Dor kora

NOMADS

If you get off the beaten track around Nam-tso you might get a peek at the otherwise inaccessible life of Tibet's *drokpas*, seminomadic herders who make their home in the Changtang, Tibet's vast and remote northern plateau. In the Changtang, the *drokpas* are known as Changpa. You will also get the chance to visit a *drokpa* camp on the trek from Ganden to Samye.

Nomad camps are centred on spider-like brown or black yak-hair tents. Each tent is usually shared by one family, though a smaller subsidiary tent may be used when a son marries and has children of his own. The interior of a nomad tent holds all the family's possessions. There will be a stove for cooking and also a family altar dedicated to Buddhist deities and various local protectors, including those of the livestock, tent pole and hearth. The principal diet of nomads is tsampa (roasted-barley flour) and yak butter (mixed together with tea), *churpi* (dried yak cheese) and *sha gambo* (dried yak meat).

Tending the herds of yaks and sheep is carried out by the men during the day. Women and children stay together in the camp, where they are guarded by one of the men and the ferocious Tibetan mastiffs that are the constant companions of Tibet's nomads. The women and children usually spend the day weaving blankets and tanning sheepskins.

With the onset of winter it is time to go to the markets of an urban centre. The farmers of Tibet do the same, and trade between nomads and farmers provides the former with tsampa and the latter with meat and butter. Most nomads these days have a winter home base and only make established moves to distant pastures during the rest of the year.

The nomads of Tibet have also traditionally traded in salt, which for generations was collected from the Changtang and transported south in bricks, often to the border with Nepal, where it was traded for grain (as documented in the film *The Saltmen of Tibet*). These annual caravans are fast dying out. Traditional life suffered its greatest setback during the Cultural Revolution, when nomads were collectivised and forcibly settled by the government. In 1981 the communes were dissolved and the collectivised livestock divided equally, with everyone getting five yaks, 25 sheep and seven goats.

Until recently *drokpas* numbered around 500,000 across the plateau. Government incentives are forcing the settlement of nomads, further reducing their numbers and grazing grounds. The black 'nomads' tents' you see along the road to Nam-tso are now little more than facades for the nomads' new homes – prefabricated white shacks. The introduction of the motorbike has further transformed nomad life. Pressure also comes in the form of enforced migration dates and winter housing, as well as attitude changes among the *drokpas* themselves, as young people move from the grasslands in search of a 'better life' in urban centres. How far into the 21st century their way of life will persist is a matter for debate among Tibetologists.

staying at small chapels and hermitages along the way.

Tashi Dor Monastery   BUDDHIST, MONASTERY
(扎西岛寺, Zhāxīdǎo Sì) There are two separate monastery buildings. The first is smaller but more atmospheric and features a statue of Luwang Gyelpo, the king of the *naga* (snake spirits). Pilgrims test their sin by lifting the heavy stone of Nyenchen Tanglha, the mountain deity who resides in the nearby peak of the same name.

The second, main chapel features a central Guru Rinpoche statue and the trinity of Öpagme, Chenresig and Pema Jigme, known collectively as the Cholong Dusom. Protectors include Nyenchen Tanglha on a horse and the blue-faced Nam-tso, the god of the lake, who rides a water serpent. Both gods are rooted deep in Bön belief. Several other chapels and retreats are honeycombed into the surrounding cliffs.

🛏 Sleeping & Eating

There are now a dozen places to stay at Tashi Dor, which these days resembles a sort of Wild West mining camp, with lots of ugly prefabricated shacks that serve as hotels, restaurants and shops.

Bedding is provided at all places but nights can get very cold, so it's a good idea to bring a sleeping bag and warm clothes.

Between the altitude, cold and the barking dogs, most people sleep fitfully at best. None of the hotels have indoor toilets or running water – in fact the whole site is an E coli outbreak waiting to happen. Most accommodation is only available between April and October, with prices peaking in July, August and September.

There are plenty of decent camping spots far away from the hubbub if you are prepared for the cold.

The guesthouses and tent restaurants offer pricey Sichuanese dishes (¥30 to ¥70 per dish). Several places sell delicious locally made yoghurt.

Damxung is a popular lunch spot en route to Nam-tso and there are several good Muslim noodle joints as you enter the town from the south.

Namtso Sheep Hotel GUESTHOUSE $
(羊宾馆, Yáng Bīnguǎn; ☑139 0890 0990; dm ¥40-80, r ¥160-260; 🛜) This is one of the better-run camps at Nam-tso. The metal cabins aren't pretty, but there's a wide range of rooms with proper beds, electric blankets and clean sheets. Rooms have electrical outlets and the walk to the toilets is shorter than at any other guesthouse. The nicest part about the place is its cosy restaurant warmed by a dung-fuelled stove. It's the only place run by locals and so is open year-round.

Holy Lake Namtso Guesthouse GUESTHOUSE $
(神湖纳木措客栈, Shénhú Nàmùcuò Kèzhàn; ☑0891-611 0388; dm ¥60, d ¥150-280; @🛜) While most places at Nam-tso look like glorified toolsheds, this one is an actual structure. The cheapest rooms surround a comfortable sitting area where you can get Chinese or Tibetan meals. The better rooms are in a side building and offer proper mattresses with electric blankets.

ℹ Getting There & Away

By road it's 9km from Damxung to the checkpost where you pay the entry fee, a further 16km winding uphill journey to the 5190m Largen-la, 7km to a junction and then a circuitous 30km to Tashi Dor.

Around 4km before the checkpost, just past the horse-racing stadium near Najia village, a paved road branches 3km to Kyang-rag (also spelled Jangra or Gyara) Monastery, a possible detour. Another road leads north from the ticket gate for 12km to Kangmar Monastery.

Some Chinese tourists visit Nam-tso as an exhausting day trip from Lhasa. It's much better to make this a two- or three-day trip, stopping off at Tsurphu en route, or to combine Nam-tso with Reting and Talung monasteries.

For details of the three-day trek to Nam-tso see p229.

Lhundrub ལྷུན་གྲུབ་གཞུང་
林周
☑0894 / ELEV 3800M

Peaceful Lhundrub county, around 70km from Lhasa, is dotted with small monasteries and temples that rarely get a foreign visitor. Most of the sites here are spread across the lush and fertile Phenyul Valley. If you are on a 4WD tour you can easily visit Lhundrub while travelling between Lhasa and Reting Monastery.

The main town in the valley is Lhundrub (Línzhōu), whose northwestern section has several hotels and restaurants, as well as Ganden Chökhorling Monastery.

◉ Sights

Nalendra Monastery BUDDHIST, MONASTERY
(那仁扎寺, Nàrénzhá Sì) Ruins dwarf the rebuilding work at Nalendra Monastery but it's still an impressive place. Founded in 1435 by the lama Rongtonpa (1367–1449; a contemporary of Tsongkhapa), it was largely destroyed in 1959. Where there were once 4000 monks, now only 100 remain. To get an idea of the original layout, look closely at the mural on the immediate left as you enter the main assembly hall.

As you enter Nalendra's main building, the impressive *gönkhang* (women cannot enter) has a central Gompo Gur, a form of Mahakala and protector of the Sakyapa school, as well as statues of Pehar (on an elephant) and Namse (Vairocana, on a snow lion), both in the left corner. Look for the three huge wild-yak heads and the stuffed mountain goat, in varying states of decay.

The main hall has a statue of Rongtonpa in a glass case, while the inner sanctum features Rongtonpa in the front centre, flanked by two Sakyapa lamas. The same room contains the silver funeral stupa of Khenpo Tsultrim Gyeltsen, who is credited with rebuilding Nalendra after its destruction during the Cultural Revolution.

The chapel to the left contains hundreds of statues of Buddha Sakyamuni, which pilgrims crawl under to receive a blessing. In the centre is an unusual statue of Nampar Namse (Vairocana) with four faces.

Other chapels worth popping into include the Tsar Kangtsang, still under renovation, the *shedra* (monastic college), the Jampa Kangtsang (with its interesting statue of skeletons in a *yabyum* pose), and the ruins of the *dzong* (fort) outside the monastery gate to the west.

You can get a great overview of the monastery from ascending to the top of the new white chörten just below the monastery's main buildings.

Nalendra is 12km west of Lhundrub. En route you can pop into Langtang Monastery, with its impressive Kadampa-style chörtens.

🛏 Sleeping

Government Hotel   HOTEL $
(政府接待中心, Zhèngfǔ Jiēdài Zhōngxīn; ☑139 8901 4873; 9 Suzhou Zhonglu; d with bathroom ¥120-150, tr without bathroom ¥120) The best-value rooms in Lhundrub town, though there is a distinct lack of hot water. You'll only get a room if it's not booked out by visiting party officials. Make your way through the Soviet-like compound to find the lobby.

Nalendra Monastery
Guesthouse   GUESTHOUSE $
(dm ¥20) If you prefer atmosphere over mod cons you can overnight at the monastery. The four-bed rooms with a shared pit toilet are simple but comfortable enough and a teahouse below the monastery offers simple meals.

Talung   སྟག་ལུང་དགོན་པ་ 达龙寺
ELEV 4150M

Dynamited by Red Guards and now in ruins in the green fields of the Pak-chu Valley, the sprawling monastic complex of Talung (or Taglung) is around 120km north of Lhasa. Rebuilding is currently underway, but not on the scale of other, more important, monasteries in the area.

Talung was founded in 1180 by Tangpa Tashipel as the seat of the Talung school of the Kagyupa order. At one time it may have housed some 7000 monks (it currently has 70) but was eventually eclipsed in importance and grandeur by its former branch, the Riwoche Tsuglhakhang in eastern Tibet.

Talung Monastery   BUDDHIST, MONASTERY
(达龙寺, Dálóng Sì) Talung's most important structure was its **Tsuglhakhang** (grand temple), also known as the Red Palace. The building was reduced to rubble but its impressively thick stone walls remain.

To the south of the Tsuglhakhang is the main assembly hall, the **Targyeling Lhakhang**. Look out for the destroyed set of three chörtens behind the building, one of which contained the remains of the monastery's founder.

To the west in the main monastery building, the **Choning (Tsenyi) Lhakhang** is used as a debating hall and has a statue of the bearded Tashipel to the right. The fine *cham* masks are traditionally worn during a festival on the eighth day of the fourth month (the festival clothes are in a metal box in the corner) but there are currently not enough monks to hold the celebrations. Snarling stuffed wolves hang from the ceiling of the protector chapel next door. Just behind here is the Jagji Lhakhang.

Down in the centre of the village is the renovated **Tashikang Tsar**, the residence of the local reincarnation Tsedru Rinpoche, who died in 2007 and whose body was laid to dry for three years under a pile of salt before being entombed in a chörten in the monastery's Kumbun Lhakhang.

Talung Monastery is 60km north of Lhundrub, over the 4845m Chak-la. It's a 4km detour west of the main road.

⭐**Sili Götsang**   BUDDHIST, MONASTERY
A 4km drive north of the turn-off to Talung brings you to Sili Götsang, an amazing eagle's-nest hermitage perched high above the main road. The monks at Talung have recently renovated the hermitage.

Many of the chapels have murals of the main Kagyud teachers – Tiropa, Naropa, Milarepa and Marpa. In the assembly hall ask to see the giant arrow said to have belonged to medieval trader Tsongpon Norbu Tsangpo. Also here is the meditation cave of the site's founder, Tangbu Rinpoche, as well as several sacred rocks.

A new road climbs for 2km to the base of the hermitage, from where it's a 20-minute walk. The village at the base of the hill was moved here after old Phondo village was flooded by the new dam and reservoir.

Reting Monastery རྭ་སྒྲེང་དགོན་པ་
热振寺
ELEV 4100M

Pre-1950 photographs show **Reting Monastery** (Rèzhèn Sì; admission ¥30) sprawled gracefully across the flank of a juniper-clad hill in the Rong-chu Valley. Like Ganden Monastery, it was devastated by Red Guards and its remains hammer home the tragic waste caused by the ideological zeal of the Cultural Revolution. Still, the site is one of the most beautiful in the region. The Dalai Lama has stated that should he ever return to Tibet it is at Reting, not Lhasa, that he would like to reside.

The monastery dates back to 1056. It was initially associated with Atisha (Jowo-je) but in its later years it had an important connection with the Gelugpa order and the Dalai Lamas. Two regents – the de facto rulers of Tibet for the interregnum between the death of a Dalai Lama and the majority of his next reincarnation – were chosen from the Reting abbots. The fifth Reting Rinpoche was regent from 1933 to 1947 and played a key role in the search for the current Dalai Lama, serving as his senior tutor. He was later accused of collusion with the Chinese and died in a Tibetan prison.

The sixth Reting Rinpoche (Tenzin Jigne) died in 1997. In January 2001 the Chinese announced that a boy named Sonam Phuntsog had been identified out of 700 candidates as the seventh Reting Rinpoche; the Dalai Lama opposes the choice.

⦿ Sights

Tsogchen
BUDDHIST, CHAPEL

The current main assembly hall, or Tsogchen, had been completely gutted at the time of research as part of a huge renovation project. Things were due to return to normal from 2015.

The main inner shrine, the Ütse, has a central statue of Jampai Dorje, an unusual amalgam of the gods Jampelyang (Manjushri), Chana Dorje (Vajrapani) and Chenresig (Avalokiteshvara). To the left is an ancient thangka of Drölma that, according to the resident monks, was brought here by Atisha himself. A wooden box beside the altar holds the giant molar of Sangye Wösong, the Buddha before Sakyamuni.

To the left of the Ütse entrance are some interesting photos of the monastery that date to 1948. To the right of the entrance is a picture of the current Reting Rinpoche and a footprint and photo of the fifth Reting Rinpoche. In front of the entrance is a platform used for creating sand mandalas. Behind the Ütse is a storeroom stuffed with Tantric drums and Buddha statues.

As you leave the chapel look for a second hall to your right. The hall contains a gold chörten with the remains of the sixth Reting Rinpoche. Lining the back wall are statues of all six previous Reting Rinpoches. The metal box in the right corner holds a giant thangka (known as a *thongdrol*), unveiled once a year.

Reting Kora
PILGRIM CIRCUIT

The monastery is still graced by surrounding juniper forest, said to have sprouted from the hairs of its founder Dromtompa. A pleasant 40-minute kora leads up from the old guesthouse around the monastery ruins, passing several stone carvings, a series of eight chörtens and an active sky-burial site.

At the kora's highest point a side trail branches 25 minutes up the hillside to the *drubkhang* (meditation retreat) where Tsongkhapa composed the Lamrim Chenmo (Graduated Path), a key Gelugpa text.

Samtenling Nunnery
BUDDHIST, NUNNERY

A pleasant hour-long (2.5km) walk northeast of Reting leads to the village-like Samtenling Nunnery, home to more than 140 nuns. The main chapel houses a meditation cave used by Tsongkhapa; to the right is his stone footprint and a hoofprint belonging to the horse of the protector Pelden Lhamo. The trail branches off to the nunnery from the sky-burial site to the northeast of the monastery.

🛏 Sleeping

Reting Monastery Guesthouse
GUESTHOUSE $

(dm new/old bldg ¥70/40) The monastery actually operates two guesthouses. The new building has overpriced concrete rooms arranged around an often-noisy teahouse-bar where construction workers go to watch TV after their shift. The old guesthouse offers simple mud-walled rooms and basic meals but is actually more pleasant, despite the fact there's only one squat toilet (which doesn't even have a door!).

Ü RETING MONASTERY

❶ Getting There & Away

Getting to Reting has been made considerably more difficult in recent years by the construction of the huge Phongdo reservoir. Vehicles now have to make a 50km detour by heading west along the road to Damxung, doubling back at the Rinphu Bridge along the north side of the reservoir and then swinging north into the Reting Valley.

From Reting it is 74km to Talung and 100km to Damxung. A dirt road leads north over the mountains from a signed junction 11km southwest of Reting, to join the main Lhasa–Nagchu highway near Womatang. Check conditions with locals before attempting this short cut.

Road to Drigung Til Monastery

Drigung Til Monastery and Tidrum Nunnery, around 120km northeast of Lhasa, are popular destinations for travellers looking for a short trip near the Tibetan capital. The steep-sided valleys are only a few hours' drive from the capital but offer a glimpse into rural life in Tibet. But change is coming to the region: towns are being developed, rivers dammed and hillsides mined. Despite these intrusions many locals carry on as usual and there are plenty of opportunities to stop off at remote villages as you monastery-hop your way through the region.

Gyama Valley 　　　　རྒྱ་མ་ཤོང་ 甲玛

This valley (Jiǎmǎ in Chinese), 60km east of Lhasa, is famed as the birthplace of Tibet's greatest king, Songtsen Gampo, who lived here until he became king at the age of 15. In recent years the valley has been targeted for tourism development, with new hotels and museums aimed mostly at Chinese tourists, and a hefty ¥100 entry fee planned. The sights aren't unmissable but it's an easy detour if you are headed to Drigung Til.

From the main highway it's 2km south to the **Songtsen Gampo Lhakhang (Gyelpo Gongkar)**, a chapel just east of the tarmac road that's dedicated to Songtsen Gampo and his two wives. The original building dates from the 7th century and resembles a small Yumbulagang.

From here it's 5km up the valley to the heavily renovated **Rabgye Ling Monastery** and, in the compound behind, the huge Kadam-style funeral **chörten** of Sangye On (1251–96), a master of the Talung school and founder of the Riwoche Tsuglhakhang in eastern Tibet. The small monastery boasts some fine black murals and a golden stone mantra that is said to have appeared naturally at the moment of Songtsen Gampo's birth. The chapel is cared for by two nuns from nearby Tekchen Shedrubling Nunnery.

From the monastery, head back down the main road and turn left towards the new **Songtsen Gampo Memorial Hall**, a Tibetan-style building recognisable by its red tower. Just behind this are three **Dumburi chörtens** and the shrine and natural springs that mark the birthplace of Songtsen Gampo. Archaeologists have linked the nearby ruins of Gyama Mingyur Ling to the palace that Songtsen Gampo's father, Namri Songtsen, built after moving his capital here from the Chongye Valley in the 7th century. A new yellow-walled **museum** is under construction nearby.

To get to the valley turn off the main highway at kilometre marker 4572, 8km before Medro Gongkar.

KILOMETRE MARKERS ALONG THE KYI-CHU

MARKER	FEATURE
4632	Lhasa bridge
4611	Dagtse/Dechen Dzong and Sanga Monastery
4610/09	Dagtse bridge, turn-off to Lhundrub
4592/1	turn-off to Ganden Monastery
4587	large chörten surrounded by three others
4584/3	Lhamo Monastery
4572	Gyama village and valley
4569	roadside chörten
4564	Medro Gongkar

Medro Gongkar མལ་གྲོ་གུང་དཀར

墨竹工卡

📞 0891 / POP 2000 / ELEV 3600M

On the wide banks of the Kyi-chu, 75km northeast of Lhasa, Medro Gongkar (Mòzhú Gōngkǎ) is just a pit stop en route to Drigung. If you have time it's worth stopping at **Katsel Monastery**, 3km from town on the road to Drigung. Legend has it that this Kagyupa-order monastery was founded by the 7th-century King Songtsen Gampo, who was led here by the Buddha disguised as a doe with antlers. The temple is also significant as one of the original demoness-subduing temples – it pinned the monster's right shoulder. The monastery was under heavy renovation in 2014.

The rabidly unfriendly local PSB office refuses to allow foreigners to stay overnight in Medro Gongkar, despite the fact that there are several decent hotels. Overnight at Ganden or Drigung Til instead.

Nyima Jiangre (Drigung Qu)
འབྲི་གུང་ཆུ 尼玛江热

📞 0891 / POP 1900 / ELEV 3850M

The one-yak town of Nyima Jiangre (Nímǎ Jiāngrè in Chinese), halfway between Medro Gongkar and Drigung Til, is a Tibetan Wild West town, with wild-haired traders strolling the streets and rocky escarpments forming the town's backdrop.

It's set at the auspicious confluence of three rivers and Chinese engineers have not overlooked the strategic location; an ugly dam has been stretched across the valley floor, forming a shallow reservoir.

Most travellers blow through in a rush to reach Drigung Til but the intrepid may want to stop off and explore some little-visited monasteries near the town. Places to explore include the Nyingmapa-sect Chulung Nunnery, a short drive northeast up the side valley from Sha Monastery, and the Gelugpa-school Mangra Monastery, around 5km up the main Mangra-chu valley behind Sha.

◎ Sights

Dzongsar Monastery   BUDDHIST, MONASTERY

About 1km northwest of town is the Drigungpa-school Dzongsar Monastery. A short but steep climb brings you up to a monastery located on a jagged slope; the name of the place soon becomes clear – the monastery is a converted *dzong*. It's home

to 30 friendly monks, and if they're not too busy they may invite you into their quarters for a spot of Tibetan tea.

Apart from the usual statues of Guru Rinpoche and Sakyamuni inside the main assembly hall, there is a two-armed standing Chenresig, as well as the founder of the Drigung school, Jikten Sumgon (and his golden footprints). On the left side of the hall, look out for the picture of the 13th Dalai Lama with his dog resting by his feet.

Below the hall in a protector chapel is an icon of Abchi, the white female protector of the region.

Sha Monastery   BUDDHIST, MONASTERY

Just 2km southeast of Nyima Jiangre, Sha is dedicated to the Dzogchen suborder. A highlight of the monastery is the pair of 9th-century *doring* (inscribed pillars) that flank the entrance gate. These have inscriptions that detail the estates given to Nyangben Tengzin Zangpo, a boyhood chum of King Tritsug Detsen, who ruled Tibet and much of Central Asia. It was Nyangben Tenzin Zangpo who founded the monastery. Only one of the pillars remains intact.

Once inside the temple, look out for the remains of a stuffed snow leopard. To the right is a side protector chapel with the Dzogchen trinity of Dorje Lekpa, Rahulla and Ekajati, and a mask depicting the mountain deity Tseringma. This chapel contains the hoofprints of the goat that allegedly carried both Dorje Lekpa and the inscribed pillars to the monastery. Continue through an unusual courtyard encircling a huge chörten to an upstairs chapel above the entrance.

⌂ Sleeping & Eating

Níjiāng Zhāodàisuǒ   GUESTHOUSE $

(尼江招待所; 📞 158 8909 6198; dm ¥30) If you need a place to crash in Nyima Jiangre this is probably your best bet. It was closed during our visit but it should have reopened by now. It has simple four-bed dorms in clean rooms with concrete floors. It also boasts the town's only real toilet.

Chulong Nunnery Teahouse   TIBETAN $

(曲龙寺藏餐馆, Qūlóngsì Zàng Cānguǎn; dishes ¥15) Super-friendly place on the main street run by nuns from nearby Chulong Nunnery. Grab a flask of sweet milk tea and choose from *momos* (dumplings), noodles and fried vegetable dishes.

❶ Getting There & Away

From Nyima Jiangre it's 30km to Drigung Til, 36km to Medro Gongkar and 100km to new Phongdo.

If you are headed to Reting Monastery you can take the direct route along the Kyi-chu valley via new Phongdo (the old town and *dzong* of Phongdo now lie at the bottom of the Phongdo reservoir). En route you'll pass the hillside Trakto Monastery (with fine views), partially rebuilt Yu Monastery (in Zashu village), ruined Nyong Dzong and the impressive Karma Monastery (across the Kyi-chu and accessed by a bridge). Several other monastery ruins line the scenic route.

Drigung Til Monastery

འབྲི་གུང་མཐིལ་ 直贡梯寺

ELEV 4150M

Although it suffered some damage in the Cultural Revolution, **Drigung Til Monastery** (Zhígòngtī Sì; admission ¥30) is in better shape than most of the other monastic centres in this part of Ü. First established in 1167, it is the head monastery of the Drigungpa school of the Kagyupa order and the most famous sky-burial site in central Tibet. By 1250 it was already vying with Sakya for political power – as it happened, not a particularly good move because the Sakya forces joined with the Mongol army to sack Drigung Til in 1290. Thus chastened, the monastery subsequently devoted itself to the instruction of contemplative meditation. There are around 205 monks at Drigung Til these days.

Drigung Til sprouts from a high, steep ridge overlooking the Zhorong-chu Valley. The 180-degree views from the main courtyard are impressive and a serene stillness pervades the site. It's a joy just to hang out in the courtyard by the monastery to take in the view with the monks after their morning prayer or during afternoon debates.

Every 12 years, in the year of the monkey, Drigung Til stages the massive Powa Chenmo festival, which brings pilgrims from all over Tibet. The festival was banned by the Chinese in 1959 but allowed to resume in 1992 and 2004, when it attracted more than 100,000 people. The next Powa Chenmo is scheduled for 2016, if the authorities allow it to go ahead.

◉ Sights

Assembly Hall   BUDDHIST, MONASTERY

The main assembly hall is the most impressive of Drigung's buildings. The central figure inside is Jigten Sumgon, the founder of

the monastery. Look for the statue of local protector Abchi on a pillar to the side.

Upstairs on the 1st-floor Serkhang (golden chapel) you can see statues of Jigten Sumgon and his two successors, all wearing red hats. Jigten's footprint is set in a slab of rock to the side of the statue, as is his silver funeral chörten.

From the 1st floor you can go upstairs to a balcony and a circuit of prayer wheels. Steps lead up from here to the chörtens of two previous abbots.

Abchi Lhakhang   BUDDHIST, MONASTERY

Back in the lower courtyard is the monastery's main protector chapel, which houses an impressive bronze statue of the protector Abchi Chudu next to the pelt of a snow leopard. Also look out for the pair of yak horns on the pillar, after which Drigung is said to be named (a *dri* is a female yak and *gung* means 'camp'). The name may also derive from the hillside, which is said to be in the shape of a yak.

In the rear chapel of this building is a photo of Bachung (Agu) Rinpoche, a hermit who lived in the caves above Drigung Til for 65 years. The monks of Drigung Til still praise Bachung Rinpoche for his efforts in helping to rebuild the monastery.

Kora Path   PILGRIM CIRCUIT

Drigung's hour-long monastery kora is worth a stroll for its fine valley views. A side trail leads from a gate to the *dürtro*. This is the holiest sky-burial site in the Lhasa region – people travel hundreds of kilometres to bring their deceased relatives here.

Tourists are no longer welcome to view the sky burials, though monks say that it's normally fine to hike up to the site when no sky burials are taking place. It's possible to see the circular platform of stones where the bodies are cut up and the adjacent buildings where the shaved hair of the dead is stored (the site is purified once a year in the sixth lunar month and the hair is disposed of). If the birds are circling, don't go up to the site.

⛏ Sleeping

Kham Renjung Dromkhang   GUESTHOUSE **$**

(☏152 8918 8077; Men village; dm ¥25) The pleasant and clean pair of Tibetan-style dorm rooms here are your best bet. The squat toilet out in the courtyard is clean, though the walls are only waist high. The rooms are above a shop opposite the Monastery Hotel in Men village, below Drigung Til Monastery.

Drigung Til Monastery Guesthouse
GUESTHOUSE $

(dm ¥40) Foreigners are allowed to stay in this scruffy guesthouse in the main monastery courtyard but the cleanliness and quality of the mattresses varies greatly by room. You can get simple meals at the monastery kitchen and there's a small shop. You can't beat the location.

ⓘ Getting There & Away

The trip from Lhasa to Drigung Til takes around three hours but you could easily spend a full day, with stops. It's worth spending at least one night in Tidrum or Drigung Til, more if you want to do any hiking.

The daily public bus from Lhasa's Eastern Bus Station to Drigung Til is currently off limits to foreigners.

Tidrum Nunnery གཏེར་སྒྲོམ་བཙུན་
དགོན་ 德仲寺
ELEV 4325M

⦿ Sights & Activities

Just 3km northwest of Drigung Til, an 8km road leads up the side valley to **Tidrum Nunnery** (Dézhòng Sì; admission ¥25). Tidrum, with its medicinal hot springs, has a great location in a narrow gorge at the confluence of two streams. The entire valley is festooned with prayer flags. The small nunnery has strong connections to Yeshe Tsogyal, the wife of King Trisong Detsen and consort of Guru Rinpoche. The Kandro-la, the resident spiritual leader of the nunnery, is considered a reincarnation of Yeshe Tsogyal.

The nunnery's main **assembly hall** is worth a visit. A cabinet holds a selection of self-arising rock images found in the hot springs.

The **hot springs** (free with admission to the nunnery) are popular with convalescing Tibetans, who soak in the mineral-rich waters to cure everything from rheumatism to paralysis. There are separate men's and women's pools and everyone bathes buck naked despite little privacy. Bring a towel and flip-flops. Photography is forbidden, even if no one is in the pool.

At the time of research Tidrum was undergoing major renovations and resembled a refugee camp – not really conducive to an enjoyable soak. Far more relaxing is a visit to the *chu semye* (lower springs) resort of Shambhala Source, where staff will let you soak in the clean hotel pools for ¥10 or rent you a room with private tub for ¥50.

If you have the time and are well acclimatised, you could do a tough day hike up to the **Kiri Yangdzong caves**, associated with Guru Rinpoche and Yeshe Tsogyal. The kora trail heads west from Tidrum to Tengyer Monastery and then ascends to a 5180m pass to visit the caves, before descending steeply down a scree slope to the Dronger Sumdong Monastery, where a road leads back to Tidrum. Take a guide from the nunnery because the trail can be hard to find.

🛏 Sleeping & Eating

There are four simple guesthouses at the nunnery, mostly catering to Tibetan pilgrims and patients – none have toilets or running water.

Dingjie Temple Limin Hotel
GUESTHOUSE $

(dm ¥25-30) The new guesthouse run by Tengyer Nunnery is probably the nicest place to stay at Tidrum proper. Riverside rooms have four beds and are arranged around a sunny glass-roofed atrium. Upper rooms are best. It's on the kora path behind the nunnery's main assembly hall.

Zhigong Dedrong Hot Spring Hotel
HOTEL $

(直孔得仲温泉宾馆, Zhíkǒng Dézhòng Wēnquán Bīnguǎn; ☏ 180 7690 1113; dm/d ¥40/120) This privately run concrete place offers clean rooms and the best mattresses in Tidrum. The sunny back doubles are easily the best options, and the ground-floor restaurant is the best pick for lunch or dinner.

Shambhala Source
HOTEL $$$

(得仲下温泉和宾馆, Dézhòng Xià Wēnquán Hé Bīnguǎn; ☏ 180 0899 7315; www.shambhalaserai. com; d with/without shower ¥320/200, d with private tub ¥450; ☒) Easily the most comfortable place to stay is this chic resort run by Lhasa's Shambhala Serai group. The hotel has its own riverside hot springs, 5km before Tidrum, and the best split-level suites boast their own private hot-water tubs. Simple food is available but don't expect much in the way of spa service. Towels and flip-flops are provided, that's about it.

YARLUNG TSANGPO VALLEY

ཡར་ཀླུང་གཙང་པོའི་ལུང་ 雅鲁流域

The serene waters of the braided Yarlung Tsangpo meander through a swath of land flanked by dramatic sand dunes and rich in Tibetan history. It's only a couple of hours from Lhasa and the numerous attractions are relatively near one another, allowing you to see the main sights in two or three days. With more time you could spend days exploring the various side valleys on foot or by mountain bike.

Gongkar

གོང་དཀར་ 贡嘎

☑ 0891 / ELEV 3600M

Gongkar's main claim to fame is its airport, but there are also a couple of interesting monasteries west of the airport. Note that there are three places called Gongkar: the airport, the Gongkar Chöde Monastery 10km to the west and the county town of Gònggā Xiàn (རྫི་གོང་དཀར་, 贡嘎县), about 10km to the east.

◉ Sights

★ Gongkar Chöde Monastery   BUDDHIST, MONASTERY

(གོང་དཀར་ཆོས་སྡེ་དགོན་, 贡嘎曲德寺, Gònggā Qūdé Sì; admission ¥20, photos ¥15) Surprisingly large, the Sakyapa-school Gongkar Chöde Monastery, founded in 1464, is famous for its 16th-century Kyenri-style murals. It lies 400m south of the highway, around 10km from the airport, along the road to Gyantse. The monastery has been renovated with the help of the **Shalu Foundation** (www.asianart.com/shalu).

The **assembly hall** has statues of Sakya Pandita, Drölma, Guru Rinpoche and the monastery founder, Dorje Denpa (1432–96). To the left of the hall is the *gönkhang*, whose outer rooms have black murals depicting a sky burial. The inner hall has a statue of the Sakyapa protector Gonpo Gur (Mahakala Panjaranatha) and some elaborate spirit traps (in a case to the right). The inner sanctum has fine murals of the Sakyapa founders by the entrance, and an inner kora *(nangkhor)*. Art specialists say the Khyenri-style murals show a marked Chinese influence,

KILOMETRE MARKERS ALONG THE YARLUNG TSANGPO

MARKER	FEATURE
72	Chuwo Ri, one of Ü's four holy mountains
73	Tsechu Drubdey monastery on side of Chuwo Ri
80/1	Shedruling Monastery and ruins of Gongkar Dzong
84	Gongkar Chöde Monastery
90	Gālá Shān bridge and tunnel to/from Lhasa
93/4	Gongkar airport
100	Dakpo Tratsang Monastery
102/3	Gongkar Xian town, Mao statue and Rame Monastery
112	ferry to Dorje Drak Monastery
117/18	Chitoshö village, ruined *dzong* and Dongphu Chukhor Monastery
138	ferry to Drak Valley, for Drak Yangdzong Caves
142	Dranang Xian and turn-off to Dranang Monastery (2km)
144	new bridge to Samye Monastery
147	road to Mindroling Monastery (8km)
148/9	Tsongdu Tsokpa Monastery
155	old Samye ferry
161	Namseling Manor turn-off
165	photo-op of the Yarlung Tsangpo river
170	sand dunes
173	police checkpost
190	Tsetang town

most noticeable in the cloud and landscape motifs. Bring a powerful torch (flashlight). The chapel to the right of the assembly hall has particularly fine images of the Past, Present and Future Buddhas.

The upper floor has more lovely old murals, including some showing the original monastery layout. On either side of the roof is the Kyedhor Lhakhang, which has fine protector murals in *yabyum* (Tantric sexual union) pose, and the Kangyur Lhakhang.

As you walk clockwise around the main monastery building, look for the *shedra* on the northern side. The monks practice debating here around 6pm.

Shedruling Monastery   BUDDHIST, MONASTERY
Around 13km west of Gongkar airport, 3km west of Gongkar Chöde Monastery, the impressive Shedruling Monastery rises from the main road like a miniature Potala. The recently renovated monastery is less impressive close up but the views over the valley are fine in afternoon light. A road leads right up to the monastery gates. Just below the monastery are the ruins of Gongkar Dzong, which was bombed by the Chinese military in 1959.

Chairman Mao Statue   STATUE
The county town of Gongkar Xian is of note for hosting Tibet's only public Chairman Mao statue, located next to a school west of the town centre. The 12m-tall icon, erected in 2006, has more to do with the town's economic connections to Mao's home province of Húnán than with a major ideological statement. It's 9km east of the airport.

🛌 Sleeping & Eating

There are a couple of decent spots to stay near the airport if you want to use Gongkar as a base from which to explore the valley.

Xīnchuānyuán Bīnguǎn   HOTEL $
(鑫川源宾馆; d ¥150-200; 🛜) Decent budget place at the main crossroads to the airport, above the Bank of Tibet. Choose from small but quiet back rooms with a double bed, or noisier roadside twin rooms. All have attached hot-water bathrooms. Traffic noise is a problem during the day but quietens at night. Staff are Chinese-speaking only.

Háodí Dàjiǔdiàn   HOTEL $$$
(豪迪大酒店; 📞618 5555; d ¥500, discounted to ¥340; ❀@🛜) New in 2014, this spotless four-star hotel is easily the most comforta-

ble place to stay. Rooms are bright, fresh and immaculate. Prices will likely rise after the initial opening discounts wear off.

ℹ️ Information

Bank of China (中国银行, Zhōngguó Yínháng; ⊙9.30am-5pm Mon-Fri, 11am-3pm Sat & Sun) The bank is 300m south of the airport; it changes cash and travellers cheques into yuán and has a 24-hour ATM but, inconveniently for an airport bank, it cannot change yuán back into foreign currency.

ℹ️ Getting There & Away

Airport buses run from the office of the Civil Aviation Authority of China (CAAC) in Lhasa to Gongkar seven times a day (60 minutes, ¥25). Return buses to Lhasa are timed to coincide with the arrival of flights. Taxis to Lhasa cost around ¥300.

Dranang Monastery གྲ་ནང་
གྲ་ནང་ 扎塘寺

About 48km east of Gongkar airport is the turn-off to the 11th-century **Dranang Monastery** (Zhātáng Sì; admission ¥25, photos ¥75), located 2km off the main road in the Dranang Valley. This small Sakyapa monastery of 22 monks is of interest mainly to art specialists for its rare murals, which combine Indian (Pala) and inner Asian (Western Xia) styles. Bring a torch to see the murals.

The assembly hall has central statues of Dorje Chang (Vajradhara; with crossed arms) and the monastery's founder, Drapa Ngonshe, who helped establish Tibet's earliest medical canon. Look for the interesting oracle costume and mirror (to the left of Dorje Chang) in which the oracle would discern his visions. The inner sanctum holds all that remains of the murals, the best of which are on the back (western) wall.

A side protector chapel is accessed by steps outside and to the left of the main entrance. The chapel (whose central image is that of a yak's head) has a hidden passage at the back that leads to a rooftop chapel and kora.

Also worth visiting are the ruins of the **Jampaling Kumbum**, on the hillside a 2km walk or drive southeast of Dranang. The 13-storey chörten, built in 1472, was one of the largest in Tibet with an attendant monastery of 200 monks before it was dynamited by the Chinese in 1963. Rebuilding efforts are limited to a two-storey Jampa chapel. Check out the little brass toe on the throne – all that remains of the original Jampa statue after which the complex was named. Old B&W photos show the chörten in its original glory. Hike up amongst the ruins for the sobering views.

To get to Jampaling, head south from Dranang Monastery and after a couple of minutes turn left, following a path to the base of the ruins visible on the hillside above.

Gāodì Xiāngcūn Jiǔdiàn HOTEL $

(高地乡村酒店; ☑ 0893-736 3888; Zhemu Lukou, Dranang Xian; d ¥160-180, without bathroom ¥120; @) Your best option is this hotel on the main highway by the junction to Dranang. The best rooms come with hot showers, though some have just a toilet (there are no shared hot showers). You can watch the traffic from the pleasant lawn and pavilions in front of the rooms.

Zhūzhōu Bīnguǎn HOTEL $

(株洲宾馆; ☑ 0893-736 3333; dm/d ¥50/150) A back-up option, this clean modern place has dorms in spacious triples with stinky squat toilets down the hall. It's 250m south of the main highway.

Mindroling Monastery
 སྨིན་གྲོལ་གླིང་དགོན་པ། 敏珠林寺

A worthwhile detour from the Lhasa–Tsetang road, between the Dranang turn-off and the Samye ferry crossing, is **Mindroling Monastery** (敏珠林寺, Mǐnzhūlín Sì; admission ¥25). It is the largest and most important Nyingmapa monastery in Ü.

Although a small monastery was founded at the present site of Mindroling as early as the 10th century, the date usually given for the founding of Mindroling is the mid-1670s. The founding lama, Terdak Lingpa (1646–1714), was highly esteemed as a *terton* (treasure finder) and scholar, and counted among his students the fifth Dalai Lama. Subsequent heads of the monastery were given the title Minling Trichen, a title that passed from father to son. The monastery was razed in the Dzungar Mongol invasion of 1718 and later restored.

Mindroling has *cham* dancing on the 10th day of the fifth Tibetan lunar month and the fourth day of the fourth lunar month. The latter festival features the creation of a sand mandala nine days later.

Nice walks lead off the **kora** around the Tsuglhakhang, west up the valley through the village to the ruins of what used to be a nunnery.

◎ Sights

Mindroling Tsuglhakhang BUDDHIST, CHAPEL

The central Tsuglhakhang is an elegant brown stone structure on the west side of the courtyard. As you walk clockwise, the first chapel you'll see is the Zheye Lhakhang, with statues of Guru Rinpoche and Terdak Lingpa (with a white beard and excellent hat). The bare main hall itself has another statue of Terdak Lingpa, along with Dorje Chang and a row of seven Kadam-style chörtens – the monastery originally belonged to the Kadampa school.

The inner chapel has a large Sakyamuni statue. Only the statue's head is original; the body was ripped apart by Chinese troops for its relics.

Upstairs, the **Tresor Lhakhang** houses several treasures, including a stone hoofprint, a mirror that reputedly takes away disease, and a famed old thangka with the gold footprints and handprints of Terdak Lingpa, which was given to the fifth Dalai Lama.

The top floor holds the Lama Lhakhang, with some fine ancient murals of the Nyingma lineages, plus a central statue of Kuntu Zangpo (Samantabhadri). The Dalai Lama's quarters remain empty.

Sangok Podrang BUDDHIST, CHAPEL

The other main building, to the right, is the Sangok Podrang, used for Tantric practices. To the left of the main entrance is a famous 'speaking' mural of Guru Rinpoche. Flanking the left wall is a huge thangka that is unfurled once a year on the 18th day of the fourth lunar month.

Kumbum Tongdrol Chenmo BUDDHIST, CHÖRTEN

This new white chörten just outside the monastery was constructed in 2000 with Taiwanese funds. It replaces an original 13-storey chörten destroyed in the Cultural Revolution. It's possible to climb past the ground-floor statue of Jampa to its upper floors.

🛏 Sleeping & Eating

Mindroling Monastery Guesthouse GUESTHOUSE $

(dm/d/tr ¥20/100/120) Staying overnight at a Tibetan monastery sounds romantic but there are some significant drawbacks at this one, including ropey mattresses, doors that don't lock and basic shared squat toilets (without doors) that are a long hike from the rooms. The unhelpful staff don't make things any easier. On the plus side, there's a decent restaurant and you are just 20m from the monastery's eastern gate.

ℹ Getting There & Away

Mindroling is 8km south of the Gongkar–Tsetang road, up the Drachi Valley. Foreigners are not allowed to take the daily monastery bus to or from Tsetang.

Namseling Manor ནམ་སྲས་གླིང་
朗色林庄园

Perhaps the only building of its type still standing in Tibet, **Namseling Manor** (Lǎngsèlín Zhuāngyuán; ☏ caretaker 133 9803 5933) is a seven-storey family mansion dating from the 17th century. It's a minor site with just a few murals left but it's worth a scramble around if you can track down the caretaker. The moat and bridge are a recent addition.

The building is 3km south of the main highway near kilometre marker 161.

Dorje Drak Monastery
རྡོ་རྗེ་བྲག་དགོན་པ་ 多吉扎寺

ELEV 3550M

Along with Mindroling Monastery, **Dorje Drak** (Duōjízhá Sì) is one of the two most important Nyingmapa monasteries in Ü. With a remote and romantic location, it is less accessible than Mindroling and consequently gets few Western visitors. It's currently under expansion.

Dorje Drak was forcibly relocated to its present site in 1632 by the kings in Tsang. A line of hereditary lamas known as the Rigdzins leads the monastery. The title is named after the first Rigdzin Godemachen, thought to be a reincarnation of Guru Rinpoche. The fourth Rigdzin, Pema Trinley, was responsible for expanding the monastery in the early 18th century, though his efforts were for naught as the Dzungar Mongols sacked the place in 1717; Pema Trinley did not survive the onslaught. The 10th Rigdzin Lama currently resides in Lhasa.

Dorje Drak's main assembly hall has statues of the first and second Rigdzins and the 5th Dalai Lama, while the inner room features Pema Trinley, the fourth Rigdzin, next to Sakyamuni. The old B&W photo by the entryway shows the extents of the original monastery.

The Samsum Namgyel Gönkhang to the right has five butter sculptures representing the chapel's five protectors. A cabinet holds the monastery's treasures, including a fragment of a staff belonging to Milarepa that was smashed in the Cultural Revolution.

A demanding 1½ hour **kora** leads around the back of the *dorje*-shaped rock (*dorje* means 'thunderbolt') behind the monastery, up to the ruined Sengye Dzong atop the rock. The path overlooks some dramatic sand dunes and the views from the retreat are simply stunning but the faint, sandy trail is a hard slog up and a steep scramble down. You need to scale a fence to get to the *dzong* ruins.

Dorje Drak is on the northern bank of the Yarlung Tsangpo, 18km east of the Gālá Shān tunnel and bridge leading to the airport, along a road that is currently being upgraded. Very few people still take the ferry across the Yarlung Tsangpo, which until just a few years ago was the only way to reach the monastery. Hard-core trekkers can approach Dorje Drak from Lhasa, a trek of around four days.

Drak Yangdzong སྒྲགས་ཡང་རྫོང་
扎央宗

For an adventurous off-the-beaten-track trip, pack your sleeping bag and a head torch and budget a couple of days to explore the cave complexes of the Drak Valley (Drakyul). Several sacred sites pepper the valley and all are visited by pilgrims en route to the caves. Our best advice is to try to visit the sites and caves with a band of Tibetan pilgrims.

The first stop is 4km off the main road at the Dromochen Lhakhang, from where it's another 6km to Tsogyel La-tso. The road continues a further 6km to Ngadrak village (pronounced Na-dra), which has several shops and a monastery. The dirt road then continues up the valley past Gyarong village at the base of the ruined Pema Dzong, and turns west up the valley at Ngalu village for the final climb to Chusi Nunnery.

If you arrive in Chusi Nunnery by lunchtime you can visit Drak Yangdzong in the afternoon and Dzong Kumbum the next morning, before heading off after a late lunch.

⊙ Sights

Dromochen Lhakhang
BUDDHIST, CHAPEL

A small chapel commemorates the birthplace of Nubchen Sangye Yeshe, a 9th-century Tantric master who was one of the 25 disciples of Guru Rinpoche.

Tsogyel La-tso
BUDDHIST, TEMPLE

This small pond marks the birthplace and spirit lake of Guru Rinpoche's consort Yeshe Tsogyal. The golden-roofed chapel at the north end of the lake has a statue of Tsogyel, as well as her stone foot- and hand-prints and a breast-shaped piece of sandalwood said to have travelled from the subterranean world of the *naga* (snake spirits). Look for the photo of her previous reincarnation, who lived in Amdo.

Ngadrak Monastery
BUDDHIST, MONASTERY

Ngadrak is the main Karma Kagyu monastery in the valley. Look for the stone footprint of Yeshe Tsogyal beside one of the assembly-hall pillars. Pilgrims are blessed with the tiny shoe worn by Powa Rinpoche when he was four years old.

Chusi (Tsetsep) Nunnery
BUDDHIST, NUNNERY

This 17th-century nunnery was largely left in ruins after the Cultural Revolution but has since been rebuilt and is now home to about 14 nuns.

★ Drak Yangdzong Caves
CAVES

(Zhāyángzōng; guide ¥5) From Chusi Nunnery it's a tough 1½-hour climb up to the Drak Yangdzong caves. Access to the upper caves is via a 10m ladder secured with strips of yak hide. Note that the caves are very narrow and slippery in places and are absolutely no place for those with claustrophobia, vertigo or a tendency to eat too many doughnuts. The spiritual and physical heart of the complex is a tiny Guru Rinpoche cave. It's great fun – or terrifying, depending on how you feel about caving.

The large cave below the main entrance has a chapel with an interesting side mural of Mindroling Monastery and a couple of resident nuns, who will act as your guide through the caves.

Back into the daylight (and after a quick round of butter tea) pilgrims continue to a side cave, which is smaller but leads down to a subterranean pool (the spirit lake of a *dakini*). A trail continues for 10 minutes to the ruins of a monastery on a spur.

Dzong Kumbum Caves
CAVES

(guide ¥5) To visit the separate Dzong Kumbum cave complex you really need to spend the night in the valley. Make your way back to Ngadrak village and drive 6km to a parking lot, from where it's an hour's walk (gaining 400m) to the main cave entrance. There are four main caves here.

The main cave is much larger than Drak Yangdzong and winds for several hundred metres to a large Guru Rinpoche cave and shrine. A side shaft leads to an underground stream and pool. Exit the cave and climb up the hillside with the aid of ropes to the shallow but wide third cave before scrambling up to the narrow fourth cave, where you'll have to crawl on your belly to make much progress.

🛌 Sleeping

Chusi Nunnery Guesthouse
GUESTHOUSE $

(☑133 9803 6553; dm ¥20-30, d ¥100) Cosy, clean rooms and a Tibetan-style restaurant make this a fine place to base yourself for a night or two. The upper-floor, five-bed rooms are the best option; the pricier prefab doubles have better beds but are noisy and charmless. There are communal squat toilets but no showers.

Kimzang Dromkhang
GUESTHOUSE $

(家庭旅馆, Jiātíng Lǚguǎn; ☑139 8903 7035; Ngadrak village; dm ¥30) The Karthok family runs this charming homestay, one of several pilgrim guesthouses in Ngadrak run by local families. It's at the south end of town and is a good base for a visit to Dzong Kumbum. It's clean and well kept, with a sunny balcony.

❶ Getting There & Away

Drak village is 18km east of Dorje Drak and marks the entry to the Drak Valley. (Note that the Drak Valley is not the same as the valley behind Dorje Drak Monastery.) From Drak village it's a further 28km east to Samye Monastery.

Trekkers can access the Drak Yangdzong cave complex on foot from the Dorje Drak Valley over the Gur-la.

Samye Monastery

བསམ་ཡས་དགོན་པ་ 桑耶寺

📷 0893 / ELEV 3630M

Beautiful **Samye Monastery** (Sāngyē Sì) is deservedly the most popular destination for travellers in the Ü region. Surrounded by barren mountains and rolling sand dunes, the monastery has a magic about it that causes many travellers to rate it as the highlight of Ü.

As Tibet's first monastery and the place where Buddhism was established, the monastery is also of major historical and religious importance. No journey in Ü is complete without a visit to Samye.

Permits

Your guide will need to arrange an alien's travel permit to visit Samye. Many agencies do this on the spot in Tsetang, but if you are approaching Samye from Dorje Drak you'll need to make sure they get this done beforehand in Lhasa.

History

Samye was Tibet's very first monastery and has a history that spans more than 1200 years. It was founded in the reign of King Trisong Detsen, who was born close by, though the exact date is subject to some debate – probably between 765 and 780. Whatever the case, Samye represents the Tibetan state's first efforts to allow the Buddhist faith to set down roots in the country. The Bön majority at court, whose religion prevailed in Tibet prior to Buddhism, were not at all pleased with this development.

The victory of Buddhism over the Bön-dominated establishment was symbolised by Guru Rinpoche's triumph over the massed demons of Tibet at Hepo Ri, to the east of Samye. It was this act that paved the way for the introduction of Buddhism to Tibet.

Shortly after the founding of the monastery, Tibet's first seven monks (the 'seven examined men') were ordained here by the monastery's first abbot, Indian Shantarakshita (Kende Shewa), and Indian and Chinese scholars were invited to assist in the translation of Buddhist texts into Tibetan.

Before long, disputes broke out between followers of Indian and Chinese scholarship. The disputes culminated in the Great Debate of Samye, an event that is regarded by Tibetan historians as a crucial juncture in the course of Tibetan Buddhism. The debate, which probably took place in the early 790s, was essentially an argument between the Indian approach to bodhisattvahood via textual study and scholarship, and the more immediate Chan (Zen) influenced approach of the Chinese masters, who decried scholarly study in favour of contemplation on the absolute nature of buddhahood. The debates came out on the side of the Indian scholars.

Samye has never been truly the preserve of any one of Tibetan Buddhism's different orders. However, the influence of Guru Rinpoche in establishing the monastery has meant that the Nyingmapa order has been most closely associated with Samye. When the Sakyapa order came to power in the 15th century it took control of Samye, and the Nyingmapa influence declined, though not completely.

Samye's most common icons are of the Khenlop Chösum – the trinity of Guru Rinpoche, King Trisong Detsen and Shantarakshita.

Samye has been damaged and restored many times over the last 1000 years. The most recent assault on its antiquity was by the Chinese during the Cultural Revolution. Extensive renovation work has been going on since the mid-1980s and there are now 190 monks at Samye.

◉ Sights

★ **Ütse**   BUDDHIST, TEMPLE

(admission ¥40; ⊙ 8am-5.30pm) The central building of Samye, the Ütse, comprises a unique synthesis of architectural styles.

THE SAMYE MANDALA

Samye's overall design was based on that of the Odantapur Temple of Bihar in India, and is a highly symbolic mandalic representation of the universe. The central Ütse temple represents Mt Meru (or Sumeru; Rirab in Tibetan), and the temples around it in two concentric circles represent the oceans, continents and subcontinents that ring the mountain in Buddhist cosmology. The complex originally had 108 buildings (an auspicious number to Tibetans). The 1008 chörtens on the circular wall that rings the monastery represent Chakravala, the ring of mountains that surrounds the universe.

Samye Monastery

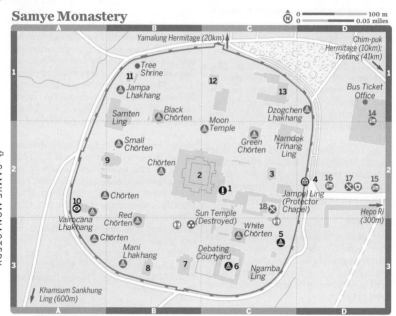

0 — 100 m
0 — 0.05 miles

Samye Monastery

⊙ Sights

🛏 Sleeping

✗ Eating

The ground and 1st floors were originally Tibetan in style, the 2nd floor was Chinese and the 3rd floor Khotanese. The corner parapets with green and gold *dorje* designs are also unique. There's a lot to see here, so budget a couple of hours.

Just to the left of the main entrance is a **stele** dating from 779. The elegant Tibetan script carved on its surface proclaims Buddhism as the state religion of Tibet by order of King Trisong Detsen. The entryways are flanked by two ancient stone lions and two elephants.

From here the entrance leads into the first of the ground-floor chambers: the **assembly hall**. As you enter the hall look for the mural of a white chicken that is said to have once saved the monastery by waking up its monks during a fire. You pass statues of Tangtong Gyelpo and the writers Buton Rinchen Drup and Longchen Rabjampa to the left, before a row of figures greet you straight ahead: the translator Vairocana, Shantarakshita, Guru Rinpoche, Trisong Detsen and Songtsen Gampo (with an extra head in his turban). The photo below the Guru Rinpoche statue is of the famous original statue (now destroyed), which was a likeness of the guru and allegedly had the power of speech.

To the rear of the assembly hall are steps leading into Samye's most revered chapel, the **Jowo Khang**. You enter the inner chapel via three painted doors – an unusual feature. They symbolise the Three Doors of Liberation: those of emptiness, signlessness and wishlessness. A circumambulation of the inner chapel follows at this point (take a torch).

The centrepiece of the inner chapel is a 4m statue of Sakyamuni. Ten bodhisattvas and two protective deities line the heavy side walls of the chapel, which are decorated with ancient murals. Look also for the blackened Tantric mandalas on the ceiling.

As you leave the inner chapel look for a hole in the wooden panelling; steps lead up from inside the false wall to a secret room with statues of Vairocana, Trisong Detsen and Guru Rinpoche.

Back in the main assembly hall, on the right are two groups of three statues: the first group is associated with the Kadampa order (Dromtompa and Atisha); the second group is multidenominational and includes lamas from the Nyingmapa, Sakyapa and Gelugpa orders.

To the right of the hall is a *gönkhang,* reeking of *chang,* with statues of deities so terrible that they must be masked. A stuffed snake lurks over the blocked exit.

Before ascending to the 1st floor, take a look at the **Chenresig Chapel**, outside and to the left of the main assembly hall, which features a dramatic 1000-armed statue of Chenresig.

The structure of the 2nd floor echoes the inner chapel and houses an image of Guru Rinpoche in a semiwrathful aspect, flanked by Tsepame and Sakyamuni, with Shantarakshita and Trisong Detsen flanking them. Look up to see the Chinese-influenced bracketing on the beams. There is an inner kora around the hall.

Some of the murals outside this hall are very impressive; those on the southern wall depict Guru Rinpoche, while those to the left of the main door show the fifth Dalai Lama with the Mongol Gushri Khan and various ambassadors offering their respects. The Dalai Lama's quarters are just behind you at the southeast corner of this floor, featuring fine murals depicting Samye.

The 3rd floor is a recent addition to the Ütse. It holds statues of four of the five Dhyani Buddhas, with a mandala of the fifth (Namse) on the ceiling.

Walk around the back to a ladder leading up to the 4th floor. This chapel holds the sacred core of the temple, as well as an image of Dukhor (Kalachakra), a Tantric deity, but it is generally locked. As you descend from the 3rd floor look for a rare mural of the 14th (current) Dalai Lama at the top of the stairwell.

As you head back downstairs, stop at the 1st-floor relic chamber. Among the sacred objects on display are the staff of Vairocana, the stone skull of Shantarakshita, a *dorje* made from meteorite and a turquoise amulet containing a lock of Guru Rinpoche's hair.

Back on the ground floor you can follow the prayer-wheel circuit of the Ütse, and look at the interesting murals showing the founding of the monastery. You can also ascend to the outer roof for views over the complex.

Ling Chapels
Walking Circuit   BUDDHIST, CHAPEL
(མགོན་ཁང་དང་མཆོད་རྟེན་) As renovation work continues at Samye, the original *ling* (royal) chapels – lesser, outlying chapels that surround the Ütse – are slowly being restored. Wander around and see which are open. Following is a clockwise tour of the major chapels open at the time of research.

The square in front of the Ütse has some interesting elements, including a *gönkhang* just inside the eastern gate. The ruined seven-storey **geku** (tower) that used to display festival thangkas has been rebuilt in recent years.

From the **east gate** *(gegyu shar)* follow the prayer wheels south to the **Tsengmang Ling**, once the monastery printing press, and look for the sacred stone in the centre of the chapel.

If you pass the yellow-walled residential college of the **Shetekhang** between 11am and noon, or between 5.30pm and 7pm, listen for the sounds of debating in the attached courtyard.

The restored **Aryapalo Ling** was Samye's first building and has a lovely ancient feel. The statue of Arya Lokeshvara is similar to one seen in the Potala Palace. A small door allows pilgrims to inch around the base of the protector Tamdrin.

The **Drayur Gyagar Ling** was originally the centre for the translation of texts, as depicted on the wall murals. There's an inner kora here. The main statue on the upper floor is of Sakyamuni, flanked by his Indian and Chinese translators.

WORTH A TRIP

HEPO RI

Hepo Ri (ཧེ་པོ་རི; 哈不日神山; Hābùrì Shénshān) is the hill some 400m east of Samye, where Guru Rinpoche vanquished the demons of Tibet. King Trisong Detsen later established a palace here. Pilgrims honour it as one of the four sacred hills of Tibet (the others being Gangpo Ri at Tsetang, Chagpo Ri in Lhasa and Chuwo Ri at Chushul). Even for the nonreligious, it's worth coming up here for the views of Samye. Paths wind up the side of the hill from the road leading from Samye's east gate. A 30-minute climb up the side ridge takes you to an incense burner, festooned with prayer flags and with great views of Samye below. Head south along the ridge and descend along the paved path. Early morning is the best time for photography.

The **Jampa Ling** on the west side is where Samye's Great Debate was held. On the right as you go in, look out for the mural depicting the original design of Samye with zigzagging walls. There is an unusual semicircular inner kora here that is decorated with images of Jampa. Just south of here is a chörten that pilgrims circumambulate and a **sacred tree** to which pilgrims tie stones. The **triple Mani Lhakhang** to the north has lovely murals.

The green-roofed, Chinese-style **Jangchub Semkye Ling** to the east houses a host of bodhisattvas around a statue of Marmedze on a lotus plinth, with a 3D wooden mandala to the side. Look for the sacred stone to the left. Take a torch to see the Central Asian–style murals.

East of here is the **Kordzo Pehar Ling**, the home of the oracle Pehar until he moved to Nechung Monastery outside Lhasa. It's currently under renovation. Pilgrims stick passport photos of themselves onto the locked entrance of the ground-floor chapel, which is flanked by two ancient-looking leather bags. The upstairs portico has some old cane helmets. The inner chapel reeks of alcohol, hooks hang from the ceiling and demons' hands reach out from their cases, as if trying to grab you.

It is also possible to enter the four reconstructed concrete chörtens (white, red, green and black), though there is little of interest inside.

If you exit the southern gate and walk for 10 minutes you get to the **Khamsum Sankhung Ling**, a smaller version of the Ütse which once functioned as Samye's debating centre. It's currently closed but there are plans to reopen it soon.

🛏 Sleeping

Outside of the monastery's eastern gates are a line of almost identical restaurant-guesthouses. None offer showers.

Snowland Yungdruk Restaurant   GUESTHOUSE $
(雪域玉龙饭馆, Xuěyù Yùlóng Fànguǎn, Kangchen Yungdruk Sarkhang; ☏133 9803 5171; dm ¥40-60) This Tibetan restaurant has a couple of dorm rooms in the back, behind a small courtyard garden. You can take tea in the sunny atrium if it's not full of locals playing dice. The staff are friendly and the bedding appears to be washed regularly. It was formerly known as the Dawa Guesthouse.

Friendship Snowland Hotel   GUESTHOUSE $
(雪域同胞旅馆, Xuěyù Tóngbāo Lûguǎn, Gangjong Pönda Sarkhang; ☏136 1893 2819; dm ¥50) Proper mattresses (not just foam) are on offer, in concrete triples out back or above the cosy restaurant of the same name.

Tashi Guesthouse   GUESTHOUSE $
(扎西旅馆, Zhāxī Lûguǎn; ☏189 8993 7883; dm/r ¥50) Pleasant two-, four- and five-bed dorms with clean foam beds, above a shop by the east gate. If things are busy you may have to pay for all beds in a room.

Samye Monastery Guesthouse   HOTEL $$
(桑耶寺宾馆, Sāngyésì Bīnguǎn; ☏783 6666; d without bathroom ¥140, d/tr ¥220/280) This huge modern hotel is located outside the monastery walls in its own compound. Although devoid of monastic charm, the carpeted double rooms are comfortable (check for barking dogs when choosing your room). Standard rooms come with a hot-water shower while the cheaper doubles share a bathroom down the hall (no showers).

Don't confuse this with the Monastery Guesthouse annexe, located outside the monastery's eastern gate, which is worth avoiding.

Eating

Friendship Snowland
Restaurant CHINESE $
(雪域同胞旅馆, Xuěyù Tóngbāo Lǚguǎn, Gangjong Pönda Sarkhang; meals ¥14-40; ⊙8am-midnight; 🖥) The backpacker-inspired menu at this pleasant Tibetan-style restaurant includes banana pancakes, hash browns and omelettes, making this your best breakfast bet. Decent Chinese and Tibetan dishes are also available (yak steak, fried mushrooms).

Monastery Restaurant TIBETAN $
(dishes ¥10-35; ⊙8am-9pm) Loads of atmosphere, sunny outdoor seating and pilgrims galore at this recently improved place within the monastery compound.

❶ Getting There & Away

Samye is a three-hour drive from Lhasa, either along the southern bank of the river via Tsetang, or along the northern bank via Dorje Drak Monastery. From the south bank most groups take the bridge from Tsetang, though a new bridge across the Yarlung Tsangpo 17km west of Samye will soon offer a short cut.

Once the only way to get to Samye, the old ferry across the Yarlung Tsangpo was not running at the time of research.

A pilgrim bus runs daily between Lhasa's Barkhor Sq and Samye but foreigners are currently not allowed to take it.

Around Samye

Chim-puk Hermitage HERMITAGE
(青朴寺, Qīngpò Sí) Chim-puk Hermitage is a collection of cave shrines northeast of Samye that grew up over the centuries around the meditation retreat of Guru Rinpoche. Chim-puk's Tantric practitioners were once famed for their ability to protect fields from hailstorms. It is a popular hiking excursion for travellers spending two days at Samye. Make sure your agency knows in advance that you want to visit or you'll have to haggle over the return 20km trip.

From the impressive new nunnery at the base of the hill, trails lead up for about an hour past dozens of cave shrines to the *lhakhang* built around Guru Rinpoche's original **meditation cave** halfway up the hill. Painted numbers mark the most important hillside shrines, most of which are still inhabited by practitioners.

If you are feeling fit and acclimatised, it is possible to climb to the top of the peak above Chim-puk. To make this climb from the Guru Rinpoche cave follow the left-hand valley behind the caves and slog it uphill for 1½ hours to prayer flags on the top of the ridge, from where a path leads for another 1½ hours to the top of the conical peak, where there are a couple of meditation retreats and fine views of the Yarlung Tsangpo Valley.

Yamalung Hermitage HERMITAGE
(聂玛隆圣洞, Nièmǎlóng Shèngdòng) It is possible to head up the valley directly behind Samye to the Yamalung Hermitage, around 20km from Samye along a dirt road. Prearrange this in your tour itinerary otherwise your driver will object to the extra mileage.

Ön Valley

This historic but little-visited valley is a surprisingly easy detour between Samye and Tsetang. The main Keru Lhakhang here dates back to the first half of the 8th century, and so represents one of the very first attempts to plant Buddhism in Tibet.

The valley essentially starts at the crossroad ruins of Ngari Dratsang monastery 40km east of Samye. From here roads lead east to Densatil Monastery (21km), south to Tsetang (8km) and north to Keru Lhakhang (11km). As you head north up the valley you pass the turn-off to Tashi Doka Monastery after 6km.

Further north the valley swings to the left, eventually arriving at the Önphu Taktsang, a Guru Rinpoche cave high on the hillside. There is no road here; the best way to visit is on the five-day trek from Tashigang on the Lhasa–Rutok road.

As you head back to Tsetang over the modern bridge look for the ruined base of the old Tangtong Gyelpo iron link bridge of Nyango Druka.

Keru Lhakhang BUDDHIST, TEMPLE
(吉如拉康, Jírú Lākāng; ⊙dawn-dusk) The main chapel of Keru (or Drakmar Keru) is one of Tibet's oldest temples, dating from the mid-8th century, before Samye Monastery was even a glimmer in Songtsen Gampo's eye. The main draws are the original statues, possibly the oldest left in Tibet.

The temple was used to store salt during the Cultural Revolution.

The main 3m-tall statue in the inner sanctum is of Jowo Sakyamuni and was crafted by Khotanese artists. Experts trace a Central Asian influence in the image's full face and barrelled chest. To the side are a set of 9th-century bodhisattvas and a statue of Tamdrin (Hayagriva), considered to be the first such statue in Tibet; pilgrims drag their children here for a blessing. The massive tree-trunk pillars date back to the chapel's construction. The two statues facing the Jowo are of Chinese Princess Jincheng and Tibet's 37th king Tride Tsugtsen (705–755; the father of Trisong Detsen), during whose reign the temple was constructed.

Follow the door to the right past a protector chapel to the rebuilt Namla (or Namdung) Lhakhang, where Atisha is said to have stayed in 1047. The attendant monk will thump you on the back with a stone footprint of Guru Rinpoche. Before they exit, pilgrims buy sacred seeds and a *kathak* (ceremonial scarf) printed with the image of Tamdrin.

Chodung Monastery
RUINS

A rewarding 90-minute hike, gaining 400m, leads from Chode Ön village just north of Keru Lhakhang to the impressive, sprawling ruins of 12th-century Chodung Monastery. En route you pass the ruins of Samtenling Nunnery. Return to the village by following the main valley, stopping en route at the ruins of a *dzong* just above the village. To get to Chode Ön, drive north from Keru to Gyelzang and cross the river.

Tashi Doka Monastery
MONASTERY

Tashi Dhoka is famed as a meditation retreat of Tsongkhapa. You can visit the meditation caves of Tsongkhapa and his student Genden Drup (who later became the first Dalai Lama) before checking out the largest Drölma statue in Tibet. The monastery of 60 monks has a reputation for scholarship, as evident during the afternoon debating between 3pm and 6pm. Tashi Doka is 2km off the main road to Keru.

Tsetang
ইন্দ'অন্দ 泽当

☑ 0893 / POP 52,000 / ELEV 3515M

An important Chinese administrative centre and army base, Tsetang (Zédāng) is the fourth-largest city in Tibet and the capital of huge Shānnán (Lhoka) prefecture.

The centre of town is a modern, thoroughly Chinese city where you'll find decent restaurants, midrange accommodation and a couple of internet cafes. The more interesting area is the small traditional Tibetan town, clustered to the east around Gangpo Ri, one of Ü's four sacred mountains.

Most travellers use Tsetang as a base to visit outlying sites of the Yarlung Valley. The PSB has a strong presence here so your guide will probably disappear for a few minutes to register your passport and pick up an alien's travel permit for outlying sights (including Samye Monastery).

⊙ Sights

Ganden Chökhorling Monastery
BUDDHIST, MONASTERY

This 14th-century monastery was originally a Kagyu institution, but by the 18th century the Gelugpas had taken it over, which is why the large central statue is of Tsongkhapa. Look for the weird model of Yumbulagong made from animal bone. During the Cultural Revolution the building was used as an army hospital.

Ngamchö Monastery
BUDDHIST, MONASTERY

On the top floor is the bedroom and throne of the Dalai Lama. A side chapel is devoted to medicine, with images of the eight medicine buddhas. The protector chapel displays fine festival masks, representing snow lions, stags and demons.

Sang-ngag Zimchen Nunnery
BUDDHIST, NUNNERY

(桑阿赛津尼姑寺, Sāng'āsàijīn Nígū Sì; admission ¥10) The principal image is of a 1000-armed Chenresig, dating back to the time of King Songtsen Gampo. According to some accounts, the statue was fashioned by the king himself. There are around 20 resident nuns.

Gangpo Ri
MOUNTAIN

(ঐহঐহ, 贡不日神山) Gangpo Ri (4130m) is of special significance for Tibetans as the legendary birthplace of the Tibetan people, where Chenresig in the form of a monkey mated with the white demon Sinmo to produce the beginnings of the Tibetan race. The Monkey Cave, where all this took place, can be visited near the summit of the mountain. Do it in the spirit of a demanding half-day walk in the hills, as the cave itself is somewhat uninspiring.

The most direct trail leads up from the Sang-ngag Zimche Nunnery, climbing about

Tsetang

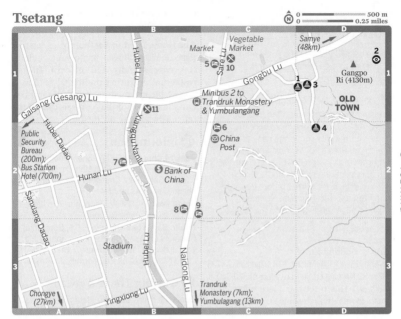

Ü TSETANG

550m to the cave. The walk up will take about two hours – bring plenty of water. The walk up Gangpo Ri is a part of a long pilgrim route, which local Tibetans make each year on the 15th day of the 4th lunar month.

🛏 Sleeping

Finding good budget accommodation is a problem in Tsetang. The town's cheaper hotels are prevented from accepting foreigners by a strong PSB presence, and those that will accept you will notify the PSB within minutes of you checking in.

Dragon Horse Hotel HOTEL $$
(龙马宾馆, Lóngmǎ Bīnguǎn; ☑ 782 3335; 5 Sare Lu; standard/superior d ¥180/260; ✳ @ ☎) A good first choice, whose best rooms are in the quiet block in a courtyard off the main street. Rooms come with modern furnishings and air-con, while superior rooms come with their own computer.

Bus Station Hotel HOTEL $
(客运宾馆, Kèyùn Bīnguǎn; ☑782 6660; Gesang Lu; d¥150-200, tr¥300; ✳☎) This new Tibetan-run place currently offers the best-value rooms in town. The location next to the bus station certainly isn't great but a ¥10 taxi ride (or minibus 3 or 5) takes you to the centre in five minutes. The superior rooms on the top

floors are fresh, spacious and surprisingly quiet.

Snow Pigeon Hotel HOTEL $$
(雪鸽宾馆, Xuěgē Bīnguǎn; ☑ 751 0111; cnr Xiangqu Nanlu & Hunan Lu; d/tr ¥260/300; ✳☎) This place has old-fashioned rooms replete with 1970s wallpaper and a smoky residue but it's acceptable. You might need to leave the shower running for 10 minutes to get any hot water. The location off the main drag means that most of the rooms are reasonably quiet.

ⓘ TSETANG'S OLD-TOWN KORA

The best way to visit the small monasteries in the Tibetan quarter is to join the pilgrims on the clockwise kora circuit.

From Ganden Chökhorling Monastery swing north and then east to Ngamchö Monastery. From here the kora path winds round the base of Gangpo Ri to a holy spring where pilgrims wash their hair. The trail climbs to a bundle of prayer flags and a throne-shaped incense burner before descending to Sang-ngag Zimche Nunnery. A side trail ascends the hill to the Monkey Cave.

Yulong Holiday Hotel   HOTEL $$
(裕砻假日大酒店, Yùlóng Jiàrì Dàjiǔdiàn; ☑783 2888; 30 Naidong Lu; incl breakfast r ¥320-340, tr ¥480; ❄) This three-star place offers clean plush rooms, though some streetside rooms are noisy. You can even listen to your favourite Chinese pop tunes in the power shower, if you can figure out how the damn thing works. The lack of wi-fi is a drag.

Shannan Post Hotel   HOTEL $$
(山南邮政大酒店, Shānnán Yóuzhèng Dàjiǔdiàn; ☑782 1888; 12 Naidong Lu; d ordinary/standard ¥220/260, tr ¥320; ☎) Standard rooms in the main building are decorated with Tibetan motifs but are quite small. The cheaper rooms in the back are bigger and almost as good.

Tsetang Hotel   HOTEL $$$
(泽当饭店, Zédāng Fàndiàn; ☑782 5555; www. tsetanghotel.com; 19 Naidong Lu; d ¥400-500; ❄@☎) Tsetang's premier tour-group lodging has small but comfortable four-star rooms behind a cheesy faux-European exterior. The cheaper three-star rooms are of similar size but lack lift access.

✕ Eating

Tashi Restaurant   RESTAURANT $
(扎西餐厅, Zhāxī Cāntīng; ☑783 1958; Gaisang Lu; mains ¥20-35; ⊙8am-10.30pm; 🍴) Branch of the Tashi Restaurant in Shigatse (not Tashi 1 in Lhasa) that offers Nepali-style Western goodies, such as pizza, curry and good breakfasts, in a nice Tibetan-style hall.

Check to see that the Nepali chef is in the kitchen before ordering.

Aba Home Tibetan Restaurant   TIBETAN $
(Sare Lu; dishes ¥15-35) Invite your guide to this cosy, friendly and modern Tibetan restaurant, featuring traditional seating, a partial picture menu and lots of local colour. Choose one of the set meals that all the other Tibetans are diving into.

ⓘ Information

Bank of China (中国银行, Zhōngguó Yínháng; Hunan Lu; ⊙9.30am-6pm Mon-Fri, 10.30am-4.30pm Sat & Sun) Changes cash and travellers cheques and has an ATM.

China Post (中国邮政, Zhōngguó Yóuzhèng; 12 Naidong Lu; ⊙9am-6.30pm)

Public Security Bureau (公安局, Gōng'ānjú; Gaisang Lu; ⊙9am-12.30pm & 3-6pm) Time your arrival in Tsetang to ensure that your guide has time to pick up permits if necessary.

ⓘ Getting There & Away

Buses run hourly between Tsetang and Lhasa's main Western Bus Station (2½ hours) until around 6pm, passing Dranang and Gongkar airport en route. Private cars also do the run at dangerous speeds.

Yarlung Valley   ཡར་ཀླུང་གཙང།
雅鲁流域

The Yarlung Valley (Yǎlǔ Liúyù) is considered the cradle of Tibetan civilisation. Tibetan creation myths tell of how the first Tibetan people evolved here from the union of a monkey and an ogre, and early histories state that the first kings descended from heaven on a sky cord at Mt Yarlha Shanpo on the western edge of the valley. The early Tibetan kings unified Tibet from their base here in the 7th century and their massive burial mounds still dominate the area around Chongye. Yumbulagang, perched on a crag like a medieval European castle, is the alleged site of Tibet's oldest building, while Tibet's first cultivated field is said to lie nearby.

The major attractions of the Yarlung Valley can just about be seen in a day.

★ Trandruk Monastery   MONASTERY
(ཁྲ་འབྲུག་དགོན་པ་, 昌珠寺, Chāngzhū Sì; admission ¥35, photos ¥75; ⊙dawn-dusk) Dating back to the 7th-century reign of Songtsen Gampo,

Trandruk is one of the earliest Buddhist temples in Tibet. It was founded at the same time as Lhasa's Jokhang and Ramoche to act as one of Tibet's demoness-subduing temples (Trandruk pins down the demoness' left shoulder). In order to build the monastery here, Songtsen Gampo had first to take the form of a *tra* (hawk) in order to overcome a local *druk* (dragon), a miracle that is commemorated in the monastery's name.

Trandruk was significantly enlarged in the 14th century and again under the auspices of the fifth and seventh Dalai Lamas. The monastery was badly desecrated by Red Guards during the Cultural Revolution.

The entrance of the monastery opens into a courtyard area ringed by cloisters. The building to the rear of the courtyard has a ground plan similar to that of the Jokhang, and shares the same Tibetan name, Tsuglhakhang. Like the Jokhang, there is both an outer and inner kora path.

The principal chapel, to the rear centre, holds a statue of white Tara known as Drölma Sheshema (under a parasol), in front of what remains of five stone Dhyani Buddhas. The statue of Jampelyang (Manjushri) in the corner allegedly swam to the monastery during a flood.

To the left is the Choegyel Lhakhang, with statues of Songtsen Gampo and his wives and ministers, next to original fragments of stone statuary from next door's stone Dhyani Buddhas.

The Tuje Lhakhang to the right has statues of Chenresig, Jampelyang and Chana Dorje, who form the Tibetan trinity known as the Rigsum Gonpo. The stove to the right is said to have belonged to Princess Wencheng (Wencheng Konjo), the Chinese consort of Songtsen Gampo.

Upstairs and to the rear is a central chapel containing a famous thangka of Chenresig (known as Padmapani) made up of 29,000 pearls, as well as an ancient appliqué thangka depicting Sakyamuni. A protector chapel to the side has an unusual statue of the Hindu god Brahma.

Trandruk is around 7km south of the Tsetang Hotel.

Yumbulagang   HISTORIC BUILDING
(ཡུམ་བུ་བླ་སྒང་, 雍布拉康, Yōngbùlākāng; ⏱7am-7pm)
A fine, tapering finger of a structure that sprouts from a craggy ridge overlooking

the patchwork fields of the Yarlung Valley, Yumbulagang is considered the oldest building in Tibet. At least that is the claim for the original structure – most of what can be seen today dates from 1982. It is still a remarkably impressive sight, with a lovely setting.

The founding of Yumbulagang stretches back into legend and myth. The standard line is that it was built for King Nyentri Tsenpo, a historic figure who has long since blurred into mythology. Legend has him descending from the heavens and being received as a king by the people of the Yarlung Valley. More than 400 Buddhist holy texts (known collectively as the 'Awesome Secret') are said to have fallen from the heavens at Yumbulagang in the 5th century. Murals at Yumbulagang depict the magical arrival of the texts.

There has been no conclusive dating of the original Yumbulagang, although some

Yarlung & Chongye Valleys

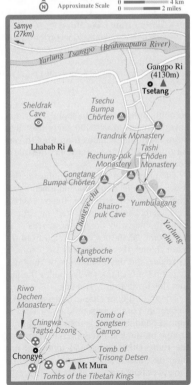

WORTH A TRIP

LHAMO LA-TSO ৰ্ম্ঝ্ৰ্সৰ্ঞ 拉姆拉措

One of Ü's most important pilgrimage destinations, Lhamo La-tso (Lāmǔ Lācuò) has been revered for centuries as an oracle lake.

The Dalai Lamas have traditionally made pilgrimages to Lhamo La-tso to seek visions that appear on its surface. The Tibetan regent journeyed to the lake in 1933 after the death of the 13th Dalai Lama and had a vision of a monastery in Amdo that led to the discovery of the present Dalai Lama. The lake is considered the home of the protector Palden Lhamo.

The gateway to Lhamo La-tso is the dramatic, but mostly ruined, **Chökorgye Monastery** (琼果杰寺; Qióngguǒjié Sì; 4500m). Founded in 1509 by the second Dalai Lama, Gendun Gyatso (1476–1542), the monastery served later Dalai Lamas and regents as a staging post for visits to the lake. On the nearby slope is a mani wall that consecrates a footprint stone of the second Dalai Lama.

From the monastery, 4WD vehicles can drive 12km (about 40 minutes) up a twisting mountain road to the *shökde*, a ritual throne built for the Dalai Lamas just short of the mountain pass that overlooks Lhamo La-tso. It is now buried under a mound of *kathak* (silk scarves). It's a 90-minute walk to get down to the lake (roughly 3.5km in total), which is encircled by a kora. The lake is a perfect place to camp.

A visit to Lhamo La-tso requires five permits (seven to 15 days to process), which are only available with the help of a tourist company in Lhasa. The village has a checkpoint where you'll need to buy a ticket (¥100) for the area.

The nearest accommodation to Lhamo La-tso is **Chökorgye Monastery** (dm ¥50), with a few basic dorm rooms. You are technically not allowed to stay here so check with your guide. Camping spots are possible behind the temple walls.

Gyatsa Holy Lake Hotel (加查神湖宾馆, Jiāchá Shénhú Bīnguǎn; d ¥160) is the best of several hotels in Gyatsa Xian, on the eastern edge of town.

The drive from Tsetang to Chökorgye Monastery via Gyatsa Xian currently takes six hours, though things should speed up when road construction is completed in 2015. The most interesting way to reach the lake is to trek from Olkhar or Dzingchi via the Gyelung-la (three to four days).

accounts indicate that the foundations may have been laid over 2000 years ago. It is more likely that it dates from the 7th century, when Tibet first came under the rule of Songtsen Gampo.

The plan of Yumbulagang indicates that it was originally a fortress and much larger than the present structure. Today it serves as a chapel and is inhabited by around eight monks who double as guards – in 1999 some 30 statues were stolen from the main chapel. Its most impressive feature is its **tower**, and the prominence of Yumbulagang on the Yarlung skyline belies the fact that this tower is only 11m tall.

The ground-floor **chapel** (admission ¥60) is consecrated to the ancient kings of Tibet. A central buddha image is flanked by Nyentri Tsenpo on the left and Songtsen Gampo on the right. Other kings and ministers line the side walls. There is another chapel on the upper floor with an image of Chenresig, similar to the one found in the Potala. There

are some excellent murals by the door that depict, among other things, Nyentri Tsenpo descending from heaven, Trandruk Monastery, and Guru Rinpoche arriving at the Sheldrak meditation cave (in the mountains west of Tsetang).

Perhaps the best part is a walk up along the ridge above the building, if only to get some peace from the syrupy Chinese pop music blasting from the car park below. There are fabulous views from a promontory topped with prayer flags. It's an easy five-minute climb and no entry fee is needed.

Across the valley from Yumbulagang is an incredibly fertile and verdant crop field known as **zortang**, said to be the first cultivated field in Tibet. Farmers who visit the valley will often scoop up a handful of earth to sprinkle on their own fields when they return home, thereby ensuring a good crop. Yumbulagang is 6km south of Trandruk Monastery.

Rechung-puk Monastery   MONASTERY

(རས་ཆུང་ཕུག, 日琼布寺, Rìqióngbù Sì) A popular pilgrimage site associated with the illustrious Milarepa (1040–1123), the remains of Rechung-puk Monastery are set high on a dramatic escarpment that divides the two branches of the Yarlung Valley.

Milarepa, founder of the Kagyupa order, is revered by many as Tibet's greatest songwriter and poet. It was his foremost disciple, Rechungpa (1083–1161), who founded Rechung-puk as a *puk* (cave) retreat. Later a monastery was established at the site, eventually housing up to 1000 monks. This now lies in ruins.

For pilgrims, the draw of the monastery is the atmospheric **cave of Black Heruka**, draped with hundreds of bracelets; the pilgrims are thumped on the back with Milarepa's walking stick and the stone footprint of Rechungpa.

Bhairo-puk   BUDDHIST, CHAPEL

Hidden in a cleft in the rock a couple of kilometres south of Rechung-puk is the Bhairo-puk. The tiny cave is home to a nun who spends her days and nights in a meditation box. The site is named after the stone handprint of the translator Vairocana.

Gongtang
Bumpa Chörten   BUDDHIST, CHÖRTEN

The large Gongtang Bumpa chörten was allegedly commissioned by Vairocana as a way to resolve a border dispute between rival kings. It's just off the main Tsetang-Chongye road and marks the turn-off to Bhairo-puk.

Tangboche Monastery   MONASTERY

(ཏང་བོ་ཆེ, 唐布齐寺, Tángbùqí Sì; admission ¥10) A minor site thought to date back to 1017, Tangboche Monastery is about 15km southwest of Tsetang on the way to Chongye. Atisha, the renowned Bengali scholar, stayed here in a meditation retreat. The monastery's murals, which for most visitors with an interest in things Tibetan are the main attraction, were commissioned by the 13th Dalai Lama in 1913. They can be seen in the monastery's main hall – one of the few monastic structures in this region that was not destroyed by Red Guards.

One thing to look out for are the unusual long side chapels lined with protector puppets dressed in monk's robes. The assembly hall is home to local protector Yongsten Gyelpo and a heart-shaped stone made of meteorite.

Chongye Valley   འཕྱོང་རྒྱས་གཞུང
琼结山谷

The Chongye Valley (Qióngjié Shāngǔ) holds a special place in the heart of every Tibetan, for it was here that the first great Tibetan monarchs forged an empire on the world's highest plateau. The capital eventually moved to Lhasa but the valley remained hallowed ground and the favoured place of burial for Tibetan kings. Rugged cliffs surround the scenic burial ground on all sides.

Chongye town (population 3000) is a small and slow-paced spot where you'll see as many yaks as people. The burial mounds, fort and Riwo Dechen Monastery are all with 2km of town.

Most visitors to the Chongye Valley go as a day trip from Tsetang and combine it with attractions in the Yarlung Valley.

Chongye Burial Mounds   TOMBS

(འཕྱོང་ རྒྱ་ ས་ས་ བཙན་པོ་རབས, 臧王墓群, Zāngwáng Mùqún; admission ¥30) The tombs of the Tibetan kings at Chongye represent one of the few historical sites in the country that give any evidence of a pre-Buddhist culture in Tibet. Accounts of the location and number of the heavily eroded mounds differ. All said and done, the faint mounds of earth are somewhat underwhelming, but the views back towards Chongye are impressive.

Most of the kings interred here are now firmly associated with the rise of Buddhism on the high plateau, but the methods of their interment point to the Bön faith. It is thought that the burials were probably officiated by Bön priests and accompanied by sacrificial offerings. Archaeological evidence suggests that earth burial, not sky burial, might have been widespread in the time of the Yarlung kings, and may not have been limited to royalty.

The most revered of the 10 burial mounds, and the closest to the main road, is the 130m-long **Tomb of Songtsen Gampo**. It has a small Nyingmapa temple atop its 13m-high summit, which isn't worth the entry fee. The furthest of the group of mounds, high on the slopes of Mt Mura, is the **Tomb of Trisong Detsen**.

Riwo Dechen Monastery MONASTERY
(འོད་རྒྱས་རི་བོ་བདེ་ཆེན་, 日乌德庆寺, Rìwū Déqìng Sì)
The large, active, Gelugpa-sect Riwo Dech-
en Monastery sprawls above Chongye's old
town across the lower slopes of Mt Chingwa below the fort. The main assembly hall
has a statue and throne of the 5th Dalai
Lama. Just below the monastery is a grand
new chörten.

Chingwa Tagtse Dzong FORT
(འཕྱིང་བ་སྟག་རྩེ་རྫོང་, 青瓦达孜宫, Qīngwǎ Dázī Gōng)
This *dzong* can be seen clearly from
Chongye town and from the burial mounds,
its crumbling ramparts straddling a ridge
of Mt Chingwa. Once one of the most powerful forts in central Tibet, it dates back to
the time of the early Yarlung kings. The
dzong is also celebrated as the birthplace
of the great fifth Dalai Lama. There is
nothing to see in the fort itself, but again
you are rewarded with some great views
if you hike up from the reconstructed red
chapel near Riwo Dechen Monastery.

Tsang ག་ཙང་

Best off the Beaten Track

➡ Shegar Dzong (p150)

➡ Samding Monastery (p127)

➡ Tsechen Monastery (p132)

Best Hikes

➡ Rongphu (p153) to Rong Chong ruins, Everest region

➡ Tashilhunpo kora (p137), Shigatse

➡ Ridge behind Samding Monastery (p127)

Why Go?

The great overland trip across Tibet – from Lhasa to the Nepali border via Gyantse, Shigatse and Mt Everest Base Camp – goes straight through Tsang, passing most of the highlights of the region along the Friendship Hwy. Along the way are fantastic day walks, several multiday treks, an adventurous detour to the base of Mt Everest and a scattering of ancient Tibetan monasteries and historic towns. Dozens of smaller monasteries away from the highway offer adventurers plenty of scope to go exploring off the beaten track. For most travellers, Tsang is either the first or last place they experience in Tibet, and the setting for two of Asia's great mountain drives: out to far western Tibet and across the Himalayas to Nepal.

When to Go

➡ The best time of year to visit Tsang is from May to June: views of Mt Everest are usually clear before the monsoon brings cloud cover and this is an excellent time for trekking. Travel along the Friendship Hwy is possible year-round.

➡ The colourful three-day monastery festival at Tashilhunpo takes place in June or July (specific dates change each year) and culminates in the unrolling of a massive thangka. Visit Gyantse for the Dhama horse racing and archery festival (from 20 June), which includes traditional games, folk singing, picnics and much swilling of barley beer.

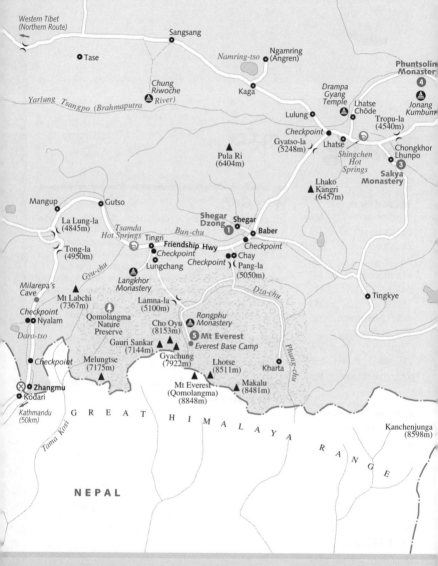

Tsang Highlights

1 Scaling the walled ruins and mighty cliffs of **Shegar Dzong** (p150), a fort and monastery on an improbably picturesque crag.

2 Winding through the inside of the dazzling **Gyantse Kumbum** (p129), a monumental chörten with mural-filled chapels.

3 Soaking up the holy atmosphere and towering gilded statues inside impressive **Sakya Monastery** (p147).

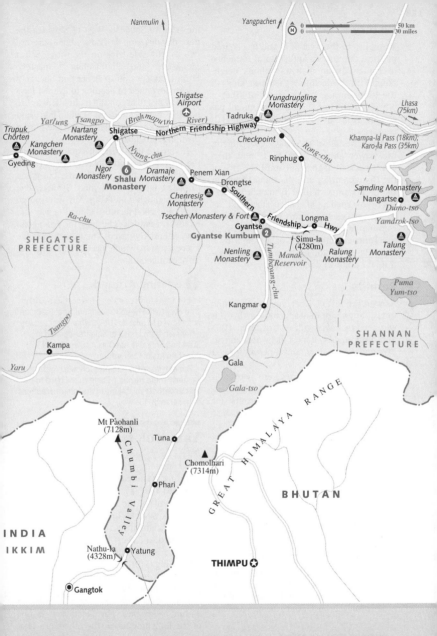

4 Getting off the beaten track at photogenic **Phuntsoling Monastery** (p146), set at the base of a monstrous sand dune.

5 Hiking past ruined retreats to gaze upon the unparalleled north face of Mt Everest from **Everest Base Camp** (p153).

6 Looking out for flying monks at the artistic treasure of **Shalu Monastery** (p142).

History

Tsang lies to the west of Ü and has shared political dominance and cultural influence over the Tibetan plateau with its neighbour. With the decline of the Lhasa kings in the 10th century, the epicentre of Tibetan power moved to Sakya, under Mongol patronage from the mid-13th to the mid-14th centuries.

After the fall of the Sakya government, the power shifted back to Ü and then again back to Tsang. But until the rise of the Gelugpa order and the Dalai Lamas in the 17th century, neither Tsang nor Ü effectively governed all of central Tibet, and the two provinces were rivals for power. Some commentators see the rivalry between the Panchen Lama and Dalai Lama as a latter-day extension of this provincial wrestling for political dominance.

Permits

As with the rest of Tibet, you need permits to visit anywhere in Tsang and for this you will need to travel with an organised 4WD tour. Your guide will most likely need to register and get an alien's travel permit for you while in Shigatse.

Special trekking permits are needed if you plan to trek in the Everest region beyond Base Camp. Trekking permits for Camp III (also known as Advanced Base Camp or ABC) are issued by the China Tibet Mountain Association. Trekkers will need help from an agency to get the permits.

Itineraries

For most travellers, visiting Tsang means a straight shot from Lhasa to the Nepali border, with stops at Gyantse, Shigatse, Sakya Monastery and Mt Everest. The 865km journey takes about eight days if done at a reasonable pace.

From Lhasa, head out on the southern Friendship Hwy, which takes you over the Kamba-la pass to the shores of Yamdrok-tso, then on to Nangartse and Gyantse. You'll need a full day in Gyantse before you can

PUBLIC TRANSPORT

At the time of research, foreigners were not allowed to travel on public transport in Tibet. Basic information is included here in case the situation changes.

move on to Shigatse. West of Shigatse the next obvious stop is Lhatse, but there are two worthy side trips on the way – Sakya Monastery and Phuntsoling Monastery. From Lhatse it's on to Baber and Shegar, a key stopover before heading to Everest Base Camp (EBC). Back on the main highway are possible overnight stops at old Tingri and Nyalam before you finally reach the border town of Zhāngmù.

If you are in a hurry, it's quicker to take the northern Friendship Hwy when travelling between Lhasa and Shigatse but going this way means you'll miss Gyantse, one of the highlights of Tsang. Any way you go you'll find good facilities along the way and relatively easy drives because the Friendship Hwy is entirely paved. The exception is the Everest region, which has dirt roads and basic accommodation.

ⓘ Getting Around

Public transport runs along the northern Friendship Hwy to the Nepali border but foreigners are not allowed to take it. The Qīnghǎi–Tibet railway extension from Lhasa to Shigatse opened in 2014 and Shigatse now has its own airport with direct flights to Chéngdū.

The entries in this chapter follow a southwesterly route through Tsang from Lhasa to the border with Nepal, taking in the main attractions of the area on the way.

Yamdrok-tso ཡར་འབྲོག་མཚོ 羊卓雍措

ELEV 4441M

Dazzling **Yamdrok-tso** (Yángzhuō Yōngcuò; admission ¥40) is normally first seen from the summit of the Kamba-la (4700m). The lake lies several hundred metres below the road, and in clear weather is a fabulous shade of deep turquoise. Far in the distance is the huge massif of Mt Nojin Kangtsang (7191m).

Yamdrok-tso is shaped like a coiling scorpion. It doubles back on itself on the western side, effectively creating a large island within its reaches. For Tibetans it is one of the four holy lakes (the others are Lhamo La-tso, Nam-tso and Manasarovar) and home to wrathful deities. Devout Tibetan pilgrims circumambulate the lake in around seven days.

Most Western travellers are content with views of the lake from the Kamba-la and drive to Nangartse. For an easy pleasant walk offering superb lake views, take the trail that leads downhill from the Kamba-la to the mobile-phone tower and then meet your vehicle on the main road.

Nangartse ཕ་དཀར་རྫེ 浪卡子

☏ 0893 / ELEV 4400M

Nangartse (Làngkǎzi) is the largest town on the lake and a popular lunch spot for groups headed to Gyantse. It's not particularly attractive but there's a small monastery in the south of town, an old Tibetan quarter and a small *dzong* (fort) to the north (famed as the birthplace of the mother of the fifth Dalai Lama). In the summer months birdwatchers will have a field day in the surrounding lake shore and marshlands.

◎ Sights & Activities

Samding Monastery   BUDDHIST, MONASTERY

(桑丁寺, Sāngdīng Sì; admission ¥20) Located near the shores of Yamdrok-tso, about 10km east of Nangartse, Samding Monastery is situated on a ridge that separates two smaller lakes that are encircled by the northern and southern arms of Yamdrok-tso. It's a great detour off the southern Friendship Hwy and a nice place to overnight, offering good hikes and excellent views of Dumo-tso and the snowcapped mountains to the south.

Samding is noted for the unusual fact that it is traditionally headed by a female incarnate lama named Dorje Phagmo (Diamond Sow). When the Mongolian armies invaded Samding in 1716, Dorje Phagmo changed her nuns into pigs to help them escape. Her current incarnation works for the government in Lhasa.

It's possible to visit the main *dukhang* (assembly hall), to the right of the courtyard, which is dominated by a statue of Sakyamuni (Sakya Thukpa). There are also photos, a statue and a footprint of the ninth Dorje Phagmo here, plus an eerie protector chapel and several chapels upstairs. The Sangok Phodrang to the left has a library, a central chörten and a fine thangka depicting five manifestations of Jampelyang (Manjushri). There are 30 monks in residence.

For dramatic views over the surrounding three lakes of Gongmo-tso, Drumo-tso and Yamdrok-tso, hike for 45 minutes up to the ridge-top cairns behind the monastery.

The snowcapped Himalayan giants to the south are Kula Kangri (7538m) and Gangkhar Phuensum (7570m), both bordering Bhutan.

🛌 Sleeping

★ Samding Monastery Guesthouse   GUESTHOUSE $

(桑丁寺招待所, Sāngdīng Sì Zhāodàisuǒ; ☏ 139 8993 3664; dm ¥40) The accommodation is quite simple, in dorms of four or five beds with a clean pit toilet down the hall, but the reception is warm, the Tibetan-style restaurant is cosy and the views over the valley are superb. It's attached to the monastery, 10km outside Nangartse.

Sheep Lake Hotel   HOTEL $$

(羊湖宾馆, Yánghú Bīnguǎn; ☏ 152 0803 1939; r ¥250-280, tr ¥350-380) This Chinese-run pile of concrete is the most comfortable place in Nangartse town. Hot showers are available (the only running water available in town), along with relatively clean and comfortable rooms. It's located on the main highway, just at the end of Yangzhuo Lu.

🍴 Eating

Lhodrak Lianzum Sarkhang   TIBETAN $

(洛扎聚缘餐馆, Luòzhā Jùlù Cānguǎn; ☏ 135 4908 6394; mains ¥15) Avoid the tour-group lunch crowd at this pleasant Tibetan teahouse-style restaurant serving good portions of Chinese and Tibetan dishes at a fraction of the tourist restaurants. The Chinese dishes with rice (盖浇饭, *gàijiāofàn*) are particularly good value.

Lhasa Restaurant   CHINESE, INTERNATIONAL $$

(拉萨餐厅, Lāsà Cāntīng; ☏ 738 2298; Yangzhuo Lu; dishes ¥25-60, buffet ¥40; ☺ 8am-10pm) This well-established restaurant has a colourful dining hall with old photos of Lhasa and is popular with tour groups for its lunchtime buffets (11am to 3pm) and big portions. It's a tad overpriced.

Yamdrok Yak Restaurant   INTERNATIONAL $$

(羊卓亚餐厅, Yángzhuō Yà Cāntīng; ☏ 139 8993 0717; dishes ¥15-40, buffet with drink ¥45; ☺ 7am-11pm) Similar to the Lhasa Restaurant, this place serves credible Western, Indian and Chinese dishes, including French toast and bacon sandwiches, as well as a lunch buffet. The restaurant is located on the road into town, just after you turn off the highway when coming from Lhasa.

❶ Getting There & Away

The main road from Lhasa climbs from the Yarlung Valley to the 4794m Khamba-la, before dropping to Yamdrok-tso. Lhasa to Nangartse is around 150km.

From Nangartse the highway climbs again to the dramatic roadside glaciers of the 5050m Karo-la. Avoid the ridiculous 'entry fee' (¥50) by parking 200m further along the road. About 60km before Gyantse you will pass a viewpoint over scenic Manak Reservoir, and 11km before Gyantse is a passport check at Niandui. From Nangartse to Gyantse it's around 95km.

Gyantse རྒྱལ་རྩེ 江孜
📞 0892 / POP 15,000 / ELEV 3980M

Lying on a historic trade route between India and Tibet, Gyantse (Jiāngzī) has long been a crucial link for traders and pilgrims journeying across the Himalayan plateau. It was once considered Tibet's third city, behind Lhasa and Shigatse, but in recent decades has been eclipsed in size and importance by fast-growing Chinese-dominated towns like Bāyī and Tsetang. Perhaps that's a good thing, as Gyantse has managed to hang onto its small-town charm and laid-back atmosphere.

Gyantse's greatest sight is the Gyantse Kumbum, the largest chörten in Tibet and one of its architectural wonders. The white chörten contains a seemingly endless series of mural-filled chapels and offers outstanding views from its upper levels.

Those with more time can take some pleasant day trips to little-visited monasteries in the vicinity. But no matter what your schedule is, try to find a little time to wander the backstreets of town: the mix of pilgrims, children, pop music, cows, motorcycles and mud is as true a picture of contemporary Tibetan life as you'll find.

If you happen to be in Tibet 20–23 June, you can catch Gyantse's three-day **Dhama Festival**, featuring 19 local villages trying to outdo each other in horse races, yak races, wrestling and traditional dances. Accommodation is tight in Gyantse during the festival but you could easily commute from Shigatse, 90 minutes away.

History

Between the 14th and 15th centuries, Gyantse emerged as the centre of a fiefdom with powerful connections to the Sakyapa order. By 1440 Gyantse's most impressive architectural achievements – the *kumbum* and the *dzong* – had been completed. The Pelkor Chöde Monastery also dates from this period.

Gyantse's historical importance declined from the end of the 15th century, although the town continued to be a major centre for the trade of wood and wool between India and Tibet. Gyantse carpets, considered the finest in Tibet, were exported by yak cart to Gangtok, Kalimpong and beyond. In 1904 it became the site of a major battle during Younghusband's advance on Lhasa.

[side margin] TSANG GYANTSE

WORTH A TRIP

RALUNG MONASTERY

If you want to get off the beaten track, make an 8km detour south across the huge, sweeping plain to **Ralung Monastery** (རྭ་ལུང་དགོན་པ་ 热龙寺, Rèlóng Sì; admission ¥15) from the road between Nangartse and Gyantse. Ralung (4750m) was founded in 1180 and gets its name from the 'self-arising' image of a *ra* (goat) that spurred the monastery's construction. It was from Ralung that the religious leader Nawang Namgyel (1594–1651) fled Tibet, finally arriving in Bhutan in 1616 to reshape that country's identity as its top religious leader, the Zhabdrung.

The original *tsuglhakhang* (great temple) stands in ruins, as does a multistoried, multichambered chörten (stupa) visible from the roof. As you wander around, look for images of the yellow-hatted founder, Tsanpa Gyare, and the Drukpa Rinpoche (head of the monastery's Drukpa Kagyud school), who resides in India. In the far left corner is the local protector Ralung Gyelpo riding a snow lion, beside the mountain deity Nojin Gangtsang, who rides a blue mule.

The monastery is home to 12 monks. Ask one of them to point out the meaning of the mountains behind the monastery; each one stands for one of the eight auspicious symbols. The dramatic snowcapped peak to the northeast is 7191m-high Nojin Gangtsang. There are *cham* dances here between the 13th and 15th of the sixth Tibetan month.

☉ Sights

★ **Gyantse Kumbum** BUDDHIST, CHÖRTEN

(ཨུང་རྩེ་སྐུ་འབུམ་, 江孜千佛塔, Jiāngzī Qiānfótǎ; admission incl in entry to Pelkor Chöde) Commissioned by a Gyantse prince in 1427 and sitting inside the Pelkor Chöde complex, the Gyantse Kumbum is the town's foremost attraction. The 32m-high chörten, with its white layers trimmed with decorative stripes and its crown-like golden dome, is awe-inspiring. But the inside is no less impressive, and in what seems an endless series of tiny chapels you'll find painting after exquisite painting (*kumbum* means '100,000 images').

The Gyantse Kumbum has been described as the most important of its kind in Tibet. There are only two contemporaries, ruined and remote, in the Buddhist world: Jonang Kumbum, 60km northeast of Lhatse, and the even more remote Chung Riwoche, in the west of Tsang. However, it is commonly held that neither could ever compare with the style and grandeur of the Gyantse Kumbum.

You can enter the *kumbum* and follow a clockwise route that leads murmuring pilgrims up through the six floors, taking in the dozens of rather tiny chapels that recede into the walls along the way. Much of the statuary in the chapels was damaged during the Cultural Revolution but the murals have weathered well. They date back to the 14th century, and if they were not created by Newari (Nepali) artisans then they were obviously influenced by Newari forms. Experts also see evidence of Chinese influence and, in the fusion of these Newari and Chinese forms with Tibetan sensibilities, the emergence of a syncretic but distinctly Tibetan style of painting.

There is a charge of ¥10 for interior photography, which is worth it. Bring a torch (flashlight).

➡ First Floor

This floor has four main chapels, two storeys high, oriented according to the cardinal points. The four chapels are dedicated to: Sakyamuni (Sakya Thukpa; along with two disciples, medicine buddhas and Guru Rinpoche) in the south; Sukhavati, the 'pure land of the west' and home of red Öpagme (Amitabha) in the west; Marmedze (Dipamkara, the Past Buddha) in the north; and Tushita, another 'pure land' and home of Jampa (Maitreya), in the east. In between

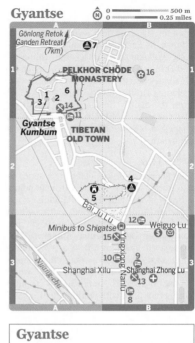

Gyantse

are some excellent murals depicting minor Tantric and protector deities. Statues of the Four Guardian Kings in the east mark the way to the upper floors.

➜ Second Floor

The first four chapels in clockwise order from the stairs are dedicated to Jampelyang (known in Sanskrit as Manjushri), Chenresig (Avalokiteshvara), Tsepame (Amitayus) and Drölma (Tara). Most of the other chapels are devoted to wrathful protector deities, including Drölkar (White Tara; 12th chapel from the stairs), Chana Dorje (Vajrapani; 14th chapel) and Mikyöba (Akshobhya; 15th chapel), a blue buddha who holds a *dorje* (thunderbolt).

➜ Third Floor

This floor is also dominated by a series of two-storey chapels at the cardinal points portraying the four Dhyani Buddhas: red Öpagme (Amitabha) in the south; orange Rinchen Jungne (Ratnasambhava) in the west; green Donyo Drupa (Amoghasiddhi) in the north; and blue Mikyöba (Akshobhya) in the east. There are several other chapels devoted to the fifth Dhyani Buddha, white Namse (Vairocana). Again, most of the other chapels are filled with wrathful deities.

➜ Fourth Floor

The 11 chapels on this floor are dedicated to teachers, interpreters and translators of obscure orders of Tibetan Buddhism. Exceptions are the Three Kings of Tibet on the north side (eighth chapel clockwise from the steps) and Guru Rinpoche (10th chapel).

➜ Upper Floors

The 5th floor, which is also known as the Bumpa, has four chapels and gives access to the roof of the *kumbum*. Hidden steps behind a statue on the western side lead to the 6th floor and take you onto the verandah at the level of the eyes painted on the wall (closed for renovation in 2014). There is also a series of murals painted around a central cube, but most people are taken in by the outstanding views, especially looking south over the old town where, in the background, the white-walled Gyantse Dzong is perched atop a colossal outcrop.

The top floor of the *kumbum* portrays a Tantric manifestation of Sakyamuni (Sakya Thukpa), but you will likely find the way up locked.

Pelkhor Chöde
Monastery
BUDDHIST, MONASTERY

(白居寺, Báijū Sì; admission ¥60; ☺9am-6.30pm, some chapels closed 1-3pm) The high red-walled compound in the far north of town houses Pelkor Chöde Monastery, founded in 1418. The main assembly hall is the main attraction but there are several other chapels to see. There's a small but visible population of 80 monks and a steady stream of prostrating, praying, donation-offering pilgrims doing the rounds almost any time of the day.

The red-walled Pelkor Chöde was once a compound of 15 monasteries that brought together three different orders of Tibetan Buddhism – a rare instance of multidenominational tolerance. Nine of the monasteries were Gelugpa, three were Sakyapa and three belonged to the obscure Büton suborder whose head monastery was Shalu near Shigatse. A climb up the nearby Gyantse Dzong will give you a clear bird's-eye view of the original extent of the complex.

The **assembly hall** is straight ahead as you walk into the compound, and is where most people begin their explorations. The entrance is decorated with statues of the Four Guardian Kings, instead of the usual paintings, and a large Wheel of Life mural. Just by the entrance on the left is a particularly spooky protector chapel, with masks, armour and murals depicting sky burial in fairly graphic details. Look for the huge *torma* (sculptures made out of tsampa) in a case outside the entrance.

The hall is quite dark inside and if you want a good look at the various murals and thangkas, it is a good idea to bring a torch (flashlight). The impressive main chapel is located to the rear. There is an inner route around the chapel, which is lined with fine but dusty murals. The towering central image is of Sakyamuni (Sakya Thukpa), who is flanked by the Past and Future Buddhas.

To the left of the main chapel is the Dorjeling Lhakhang, with a four-headed Nampa Namse (Vairocana) and the other four Dhyani (Wisdom) Buddhas in dark, ornate wooden frames. The big thangka wrapped in the yak-leather bag is displayed during the Saga Dawa festival on the 18th day of the fourth Tibetan month. Pilgrims put their heads in a hole underneath a set of ancient scriptures that is older than the monastery itself.

To the right of the main chapel is a lovely Jampa statue with the Rigsum Gonpo trinity behind it, along with the three kings of Tibet. The inner chörten was built by Prince Rabten Kunzang Phok. Outside the door is a large tent used during *cham* festivals.

Moving to the upper floor, the first chapel to the left is noted for a three-dimensional mandala, wall paintings of the Indian-looking *mahasiddhas* (highly accomplished Tantric practitioners) and lacquered images of key figures in the Sakyapa lineage. Each of the 84 *mahasiddhas* is unique and shown contorted in a yogic posture. Unfortunately, the room is often closed. Other chapels, which are open in the mornings, are dedicated to Jampa (Maitreya), Tsongkhapa and the 16 *arhats* (worthy ones). The far right chapel has a speaking statue of green Tara in an ornate case. Photos cost ¥10 to ¥20 per chapel.

A new and easily overlooked **Ganden Lhakhang** chapel to the left of the *kumbum* is worth a quick peek for the largest Tsong-khapa statue in Tibet. The Sakya-school Kur-ba Tratsang next to the assembly hall is also worth a visit.

Gyantse Dzong FORT

(☏817 2116; admission ¥30; ⊗9.30am-6.30pm) The main reason to make the 20-minute climb to the top of the Gyantse Dzong is for the fabulous views of the Pelkor Chöde Monastery and Gyantse's whitewashed old town below. Entry to the *dzong* is via a gate just north of the main roundabout. Vehicles can drive about halfway to the top.

Many of the 14th-century fort's buildings and rooms are open for exploration, though most are bare. There's a kitschy attempt to re-create the old tax office behind the ticket booth, and a little further to the left you'll find a dungeon, chapel and torture room with dioramas. Bring a torch to explore the spooky lower chambers beneath the chapel.

Rabse Nunnery BUDDHIST, NUNNERY

(热赛尼姑庙; Rèsài Nígū Miào) Hidden behind the hill that runs between the monastery and the *dzong*, this nunnery (*ani gompa* in Tibetan) is a delightful place decorated with prayer flags, chörtens and mani *lhakhang* (prayer wheel chapels). The 'correct' way to visit is along the clockwise pilgrim trail that goes around the back of the Pelkor Chöde Monastery.

Bring a compass for the walk back through the maze of streets in the old town; a new path that follows the contours of the hillside offers superb views of the fort in the distance.

Palha Manor MUSEUM

(帕拉庄园; Pàlā Zhuāngyuán; Penjor Lhunpo village; admission ¥30; ⊗10am-6.30pm) This im-pressive former merchant's house is now a government museum thick with political spin on the evils of feudal exploitation. Don't be put off, enough fascinating fragments remain to give a picture of upper-class Ti-betan life a century ago. Displays include bottles of imported port and Lady Florence maraschino cherries from Australia, some fine silks and furs, an HMV record player and a pair of rusty roller skates. The manor is just outside Gyantse town, on the road to Shigatse.

The servants' quarters across the road are popular with Chinese tourists learning about the horrors of preliberation Tibet.

Tsang Traditional Folk House MUSEUM

(后藏民俗风情院; Hòuzàng Mínsú Fēngqíngyuàn; ☏817 5555; Penjor Lhunpo village; admission ¥30; ⊗8am-9pm) If you have a spare 40 min-utes, this private folk museum opposite Palha Manor is worth a visit. Alongside the normal mockups of a traditional kitchen, mustard-seed oil press and *chang* (barley beer) still, are such treasures as a fish-skin saddle, a barley guillotine, and yak-skin bags used for transporting salt. Get your guide to teach you a traditional dice game such as *sho*, before you taste some traditional snacks and excellent home-brewed *chang*, all included in the admission fee.

Guru Lhakhang BUDDHIST, TEMPLE

(Yingxiong Beilu; ⊗dawn-dusk) On the walk back from the *dzong* to the centre, pop into this hugely atmospheric local temple burst-ing with local character.

🛏 Sleeping

★Yeti Hotel HOTEL $$

(雅迪花园酒店, Yǎdí Huāyuán Jiǔdiàn; ☏817 5555; www.yetihoteltibet.com; 11 Weiguo Lu; d incl breakfast ¥320; ❋@🛜) The revamped three-star Yeti is easily the best midrange option in Gyantse, offering 24-hour hot water, clean carpeted rooms, quality mattresses and reliable wi-fi, so make sure you reserve in advance. The cafe and excellent lobby res-taurant serve everything from yak steak to pizza, alongside one of Tibet's best buffet breakfasts. The manager has plans to open a four-star boutique hotel in 2016.

Jiànzàng Hotel HOTEL $$

(建藏饭店, Jiànzàng Fàndiàn; ☏817 3720; jian-zanghotel@yahoo.com.cn; 14 Yingxiong Nanlu, 英雄南路14号; q per bed ¥50-70, d ¥260; 🛜) The Jiànzàng, with English-speaking staff, offers rooms in a quiet new courtyard block with en suite rooms and 24-hour hot water. If pressed, staff will also show you the quad rooms with showers down the hall. The hotel is popular with 4WD groups and the 2nd-floor Tibetan-style restaurant is a cosy option for breakfast or a cup of tea.

Chat to the manager about his role in the BBC documentary *A Year in Tibet*.

Dhugu Hotel
HOTEL **$$**

(楚古宾馆, Chǔgǔ Bīnguǎn; ☑817 3165; Yingxiong Nanlu; d/tr ¥200/270; ☎) This courtyard hotel has 24-hour hot water, clean wood-floor rooms and lobby wi-fi, making it a decent budget choice. It lacks charm and sitting areas but it seems well maintained.

Gyantse Hotel
HOTEL **$$**

(江孜饭店, Jiāngzī Fàndiàn; ☑817 2222; 2 Shanghai Zhonglu; d ¥360; ☀☎) Despite being the largest hotel in town and popular with groups, this cavernous old-school place still feels like a Communist Party hotel from the 1980s. Rooms are plain but carpeted and there is 24-hour hot water. There's plenty of Tibetan kitsch but wi-fi is only available in the lobby. Rooms in B wing are the best.

Shambhala Serai Gyantse
BOUTIQUE HOTEL **$$$**

(www.shambhalaserai.com; r ¥400) Lhasa's Shambhala Serai team were putting the final touches on this stylish new place at the time of research. It has 10 rooms in a great location in an old merchant's house next to the Pelkhor Chöde Monastery.

✖ Eating

Monastery Restaurant
TIBETAN **$**

(Pelkhor Chöde Monastery; dishes ¥15-25; ✐▥) Perfectly positioned in the courtyard of Pelkhor Chöde, this is the place to share a bowl of *thenthuk* (noodles) or *momos* (dumplings) with your fellow pilgrims. Choose from pleasant interior and exterior seating and an extensive menu that offers far more than the normal monastery *thugpa*.

Tashi Restaurant
NEPALI, INTERNATIONAL **$$**

(扎西餐厅, Zhāxī Cāntīng; Yingxiong Nanlu; mains ¥30-40; ☻7.30am-11pm; ▥) This Nepali-run place (a branch of Tashi in Shigatse) whips up tasty and filling Indian fare. It also has the usual range of Western breakfasts, and Italian and Chinese food. The decor is Tibetan but the Indian movies and Nepali music give it a subcontinental vibe.

Gyantse Kitchen
TIBETAN **$$**

(江孜厨房, Jiāngzī Chúfáng; Shanghai Zhonglu; dishes ¥30-40; ☻7am-midnight; ▥) This local favourite serves Western, Tibetan and Indian favourites, from chicken sizzlers to breakfast pancakes, plus unique fusion dishes like yak pizza. The friendly owner, who may join you for a drink, donates a portion of his income to support poor families in Gyantse.

☆ Entertainment

Sound and Light Show
PERFORMING ARTS

(Horse-Racing Ground; tickets ¥280; ☻9.30pm Apr-Oct) New in 2014 is this ambitious new nightly song-and-dance show. It's aimed squarely at Chinese tour groups but is performed on a grand scale, using the entire old town as its backdrop. Expect plenty of happy, shiny minority dances from the all-Tibetan cast of 300.

ⓘ Information

Agricultural Bank of China (中国农业银行, Zhōngguó Nóngyè Yínháng; Weiguo Lu) At the time of research the ATM here was not accepting foreign cards or changing cash, so you'll have to go to Shigatse to access your money.

ⓘ Getting There & Away

Minibuses and taxis shuttle the 90km between Gyantse and Shigatse but don't take foreigners.

ⓘ Getting Around

All of Gyantse's sights can be reached comfortably on foot, but there are rickshaws and even taxis if you need them. Negotiate all prices before you head out.

Around Gyantse

The several excellent off-the-beaten-track sights around Gyantse could easily warrant an extra day in town.

Tsechen Monastery
BUDDHIST, MONASTERY

(རྩེ་ཆེན་དགོན་པ་, 慈青寺, Cíqīng Sì) The traditional village of Tsechen is located about 5km northwest of Gyantse and is a nice detour en route to Shigatse. A small Sakyapa-school monastery sits above the village, but the main reason to visit is to climb the ruined fortress, wander along its defensive walls and enjoy great views of the river valley below. It's a good idea to bring a picnic.

The fortress is believed to have been built as early as the 14th century and the

BAYONETS TO GYANTSE

The early-20th-century British invasion of Tibet, also known as the Younghusband expedition, began, as wars sometimes do, with unreliable intelligence. Newspapers were spreading the claim that Russia had designs on Tibet, and many were lapping it up. The British Raj feared losing a buffer state and so sent Major Francis Younghusband, an army officer with rich experience of Central Asia, on a diplomatic mission to the Tibetan border. After six months of waiting, no Chinese or Tibetans had showed up for the meetings. A stronger message had to be sent. Younghusband was instructed to advance on Lhasa with 3000 troops (plus 7000 servants and 4000 yaks) to force a treaty on the recalcitrant Tibetans.

Despite having had previous brushes with British firepower, it seems the Tibetans had little idea what they were up against. About halfway between Yatung and Gyantse, a small Tibetan army bearing a motley assortment of arms and lucky charms confronted a British force carrying light artillery, Maxim machine guns and modern rifles. The Tibetans' trump card was a charm marked with the seal of the Dalai Lama, which they were told would protect them from British bullets. It didn't. Firing began after a false alarm and the British slaughtered 700 Tibetans in four minutes.

The British buried the Tibetan dead (the Tibetans dug them up at night and carried them off for sky burial) and set up a field hospital, dumbfounding the wounded Tibetans, who could not understand why the British would try to kill them one day and save them the next. The British then continued their advance to Gyantse, but found the town's defensive fort (the Gyantse Dzong) deserted. Curiously, rather than occupy the *dzong,* the British camped on the outskirts of Gyantse and waited for officials from Lhasa to arrive. While they waited, Younghusband sped up to the Karo-la with a small contingent of troops to take on 3000 Tibetans who had dug themselves in at over 5000m. The result was the highest land-based battle in British military history and a fine example of frozen stiff upper lip.

After nearly two months of waiting for Lhasa officials, the British troops received orders to retake the Gyantse Dzong (which had been reoccupied by Tibetans) and march on Lhasa. Artillery fire breached the walls of the fort, and when one of the shells destroyed the Tibetan gunpowder supply the Tibetans were reduced to throwing rocks at their attackers. The *dzong* fell in one day, with four British casualties and more than 300 Tibetan dead.

With the fort under their command, the British now controlled the road to Lhasa. Younghusband led 2000 troops to the capital with few incidents. In fact, the greatest challenge he faced was getting all the troops across the Yarlung Tsangpo (Brahmaputra River): it took five days of continual ferrying.

Once in Lhasa, Younghusband discovered that the Dalai Lama had fled to Mongolia. After a month, Younghusband managed to get the Tibetan regent to sign an agreement allowing British trade missions at Gyantse and Gartok, near Mt Kailash. (Ironically, the troops discovered that British goods were already trickling into the bazaars – one British soldier wrote that he found a sausage machine made in Birmingham and two bottles of Bulldog stout in the Barkhor.) But the treaty and others that followed in 1906 were largely meaningless because Tibet simply had no capacity to fulfil them.

As for Younghusband himself, the most significant event of the campaign was yet to come. On the evening before his departure, as he looked out over Lhasa, he felt a great wave of emotion, insight and spiritual peace. Younghusband had always been a religious man, but this moment changed him forever. He later wrote, 'That single hour on leaving Lhasa was worth all the rest of a lifetime.'

early kings of Gyantse lived here until the 18th century. The British used the site during their 1904 invasion, although it was already partly ruined by then. Hike up to the right side of the fortress towards the rebuilt thangka wall and then cross over below the highest ramparts on the left to between the two towers. Across the highway and behind a hill are more monastic ruins.

Gönlong Retok Ganden Retreat MONASTERY
(རེ་ཐོག་དགའ་ལྡན་དགོན་པ་, 热托甘丹寺, Rètuō Gāndān
Sì) Hidden in the fold of a valley north of
town, this ruined and little-visited monastery is a 7km drive from Gyantse from a
turn-off near the Rabse Nunnery. There are
ruins all around the site, including what was
once the main Drölma Lhakhang; compare
it with the black-and-white photos taken of
the monastery before it was destroyed. Today there are six Gelugpa monks here.

The central Tsongkhapa statue has a glass
plate in his chest, which enshrines an even
older image of Tsongkhapa. Look for the old
stone carving of Jampa.

Gyantse to Shigatse

Travelling by 4WD from Gyantse to Shigatse
will lead you through the fertile Nyang-chu
Valley, a wide agricultural plain where col-
ourfully decorated yaks and horses are used
by Tibetan farmers to till the land. The red
tassels are placed on the horns of yaks as
a sort of lucky talisman before the serious
spring ploughing begins. Besides the yaks
and yak tenders there are a few sights of
note along the way.

Drongtse Monastery BUDDHIST, MONASTERY
(重孜寺, Zhòngzī Sì) On a *tse* (peak) said to
resemble a *drong* (wild yak), this monastery
was founded in 1442 and later adopted as
a branch of Tashilhunpo. In the *gönkhang*
look for the creepy mummified human skull,
as well as an old embroidery of Namtose.
The main statute is of the sixth Drongtse
Rinpoche whose tomb is on the top floor; to
the right is the founder and first Rinpoche
Lhajun Rinchen Gyatso. The monastery is
19km northwest of Gyantse.

Lhori Nunnery BUDDHIST, NUNNERY
Lhori Ani Gompa is a tiny place built around
two ancient meditation caves of Guru Rinpoche, one of which has a stone footprint
of the guru aged eight. It's an atmospheric
place attended by a couple of nuns. It's signposted 1km up a side road.

A couple of kilometres further is **Chenresig Monastery**, thought to have been
built by King Songsten Gampo.

Dramaje Monastery BUDDHIST, MONASTERY
About 41km from Gyantse is the county capital of Penem Xian and its 15th-century Dramaje (or Tramejen) Monastery. Levelled in
the Cultural Revolution, the monastery was

rebuilt in 2006 and is home to 20 monks. In
the inner chapel look for three lifelike statues: King Trisong Detsen (wearing a white
hat), Shantarakshita (wearing a red hat) and
Padmasambhava.

According to lore, it was Shantarakshita
(at the behest of Trisong Detsen) who invited Padmasambhava to Tibet in order to sub-
due Tibetan devils and demons.

Shigatse   གཞིས་ཀ་རྩེ་ 日喀则

📞 0892 / POP 80,000 / ELEV 3840M
About 250km southwest of Lhasa and 90km
northwest of Gyantse lies Shigatse (Rìkāzé),
Tibet's second-largest town and the traditional capital of Tsang province. Shigatse is
a modern, sprawling city, with wide boule-
vards humming with traffic (even in the
pedestrian-only lane). As you drive in across
the plains, the site of the Potala-lookalike
Shigatse Dzong, high on a hilltop overlooking the town, will probably fire your imagination, but the fort is empty and most of
what you see dates from a 2007 reconstruction. It is the Tashilhunpo Monastery, to the
west of town, that is the real draw. Since the
Mongol sponsorship of the Gelugpa order,
Shigatse has been the seat of the Panchen
Lama, and this seat was traditionally based
in the monastery.

The modern city is divided into a tiny old
Tibetan town huddled at the foot of the fort,
and a rapidly expanding modern Chinese
town that has all the charm of, well, every
other expanding modern Chinese town.

During the second week of the fifth lunar month (around June/July), Tashilhunpo
Monastery becomes the scene of a three-day
festival when a huge thangka is unveiled.

History

The town of Shigatse, formerly known as
Samdruptse, has long been an important
trading and administrative centre. The
Tsang kings exercised their power from the
dzong and the fort later became the residence of the governor of Tsang.

Tashilhunpo Monastery is one of the
six great Gelugpa institutions, along with
Drepung, Sera and Ganden Monasteries in
Lhasa, and Kumbum (Tǎ'ěr Sì) and Labrang
in Amdo (modern Gānsù and Qīnghǎi provinces). It was founded in 1447 by Genden
Drup, a disciple of Tsongkhapa. Genden
Drup was retroactively named the first Dalai Lama and he is enshrined within Tashil-

Shigatse

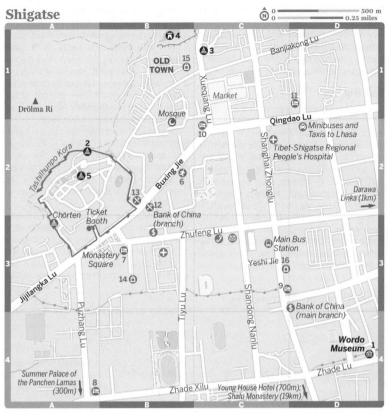

TSANG SHIGATSE

Shigatse

hunpo. Despite this important association, Tashilhunpo Monastery was initially isolated from mainstream Gelugpa affairs, which were centred in the Lhasa region.

The monastery's standing rocketed when the fifth Dalai Lama declared his teacher – then the abbot of Tashilhunpo – to be a manifestation of Öpagme (Amitabha). Thus

Tashilhunpo became the seat of an important lineage: the Panchen ('great scholar') Lamas. Unfortunately, with the establishment of this lineage of spiritual and temporal leaders – second only to the Dalai Lamas – rivalry was introduced to the Gelugpa order.

⊙ Sights

Tashilhunpo Monastery BUDDHIST, MONASTERY
(བཀྲ་ཤིས་ལྷུན་དགོན་, 扎什伦布寺, Zhāshílúnbù Sì; admission ¥80; ⊙9am-7pm) One of the few monasteries in Tibet to weather the stormy seas of the Cultural Revolution, Tashilhunpo remains relatively unscathed. It is a real pleasure to explore the busy cobbled lanes twisting around the aged buildings. Covering 70,000 sq metres, the monastery is now the largest functioning religious institution in Tibet and one of its great monastic sights. The huge golden statue of the Future Buddha is the largest gilded statue in the world.

From the entrance to the monastery, visitors get a grand view. Above the white monastic quarters is a crowd of ochre buildings topped with gold – the tombs of the past Panchen Lamas. To the right, and higher still, is the **Festival Thangka Wall**, hung with massive, colourful thangkas during festivals. Circumnavigating the exterior of the compound is a one-hour kora that takes you into the hills behind the monastery.

As you start to explore the various buildings, you'll see a lot of photos of the ninth, 10th and 11th Panchen Lamas. The ninth Panchen Lama is recognisable by his little moustache. The 11th Panchen Lama is the disputed Chinese-sponsored lama, now in his early 20s.

Morning is the best time to visit because more of the chapels are open. Monks start to lock chapels up for lunch after 12.30pm.

Severe restrictions on photography are in place inside the monastic buildings. The going cost for a photograph varies but be

Tashilhunpo Monastery

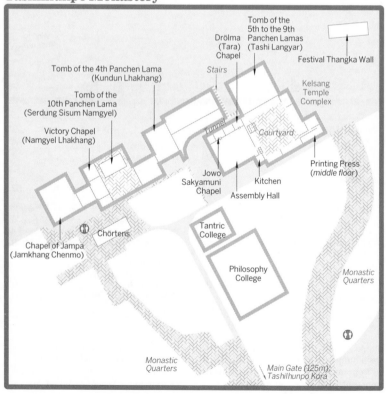

TASHILHUNPO KORA

The kora around Tashilhunpo Monastery takes about one hour to complete. From the main gate, follow the monastery walls in a clockwise direction and look for an alley on the right. The alley curves around the western wall, past *tsatsa* (clay icon) makers, stone carvers and monks reciting scripture for donations, to climb into the hills above the monastery where streams of prayer flags spread over the dry slopes like giant colourful spider limbs. The views of the compound below are wonderful.

In about 20 minutes you pass the 13-storey white tower used to hang a giant thangka at festival time. The path then splits in two: down the hill to complete the circuit of the monastery, or along the ridge to the Shigatse Dzong, a walk of around 20 minutes.

From the *dzong,* head to the old-town Tibetan market, stopping en route at the particularly charming and atmospheric roadside **mani lhakhang**.

prepared for a pricey ¥75 per chapel, and as high as ¥150 in the assembly hall. Video camera fees are an absurd ¥1000 to ¥1500 in some chapels.

➡ **Chapel of Jampa (Jamkhang Chenmo)**
Walk through the monastery and bear left for the first and probably most impressive of Tashilhunpo's sights: the Chapel of Jampa. An entire building houses a 26m figure of Jampa (Maitreya), the Future Buddha. The statue was made in 1914 under the auspices of the ninth Panchen Lama and took some 900 artisans and labourers four years to complete. The impressive, finely crafted and serene-looking statue towers high over the viewer. Each of Jampa's fingers is more than 1m long, and in excess of 300kg of gold went into his coating, much of which is also studded with precious stones. On the walls surrounding the image there are a thousand more gold paintings of Jampa set against a red background.

➡ **Victory Chapel (Namgyel Lhakhang)**
This chapel is a centre for philosophy and houses a large statue of Tsongkhapa flanked by Jampa and Jampelyang (Manjushri).

➡ **Tomb of the 10th Panchen Lama (Serdung Sisum Namgyel)**
This dazzling gold-plated funeral chörten holds the remains of the 10th Panchen Lama, who died in 1989. His image is displayed atop the tomb. The ceiling of the chapel is painted with a Kalachakra (Dukhor in Tibetan) mandala, with a mural of the deity on the left wall, and the walls are painted with gold buddhas in various *mudras* (hand gestures). From here you can normally head upstairs to proceed through a line of upper chapels.

➡ **Tomb of the Fourth Panchen Lama (Kundun Lhakhang)**
The gold-roofed chapel holds the tomb of the Fourth Panchen Lama, Lobsang Choekyi Gyeltsen (1567–1662), teacher of the fifth Dalai Lama. This was the only mausoleum at Tashilhunpo to be spared during the Cultural Revolution. The 11m-high funerary chörten is inlaid with semiprecious stones and contains 85kg of gold.

➡ **Kelsang Temple**
The centrepiece of this remarkable collection of buildings is a large courtyard, which is the focus of festival and monastic activities. It's a fascinating place to sit and watch the pilgrims and monks go about their business. Monks congregate here before lunchtime service in the main assembly hall. A huge prayer pole rears from the centre of the flagged courtyard and the surrounding walls are painted with buddhas.

The **assembly hall** is one of the oldest buildings in Tashilhunpo, dating from the 15th-century founding of the monastery. The massive throne that dominates the centre of the hall is the throne of the Panchen Lamas. The hall is a dark, moody place, with rows of mounted cushions for monks, and long thangkas, depicting the various incarnations of the Panchen Lama, suspended from the ceiling. The central inner chapel holds a wonderful statue of Sakyamuni (Sakya Thukpa), while the chapel to the right holds several images of Drölma (Tara).

You can also visit the huge new **Tomb of the Fifth to the Ninth Panchen Lamas** (Tashi Langyar), built by the 10th Panchen Lama to replace tombs destroyed in the Cultural Revolution. The central statue is of the ninth Panchen Lama. The 10th Panchen Lama returned to Shigatse from Běijīng to

TSANG SHIGATSE

dedicate the tomb in 1989. He fulfilled his prediction that he would die on Tibetan soil just three days after the ceremony.

There are a dozen other chapels in the complex on this floor. Follow the pilgrims on a clockwise circuit, ending up in a tangle of chapels above the assembly hall. Here in the far left (upper) corner chapel you'll find views of the two-storey Jampa statue below and, to the right, the tombs of the first and third Panchen Lamas and first Dalai Lama, with a fine mural of Buddha descending to earth (as celebrated in Tibet's Lhabab Dechen festival). Then descend to the middle floor and do another clockwise circuit, taking in the interesting **printing press**.

➡ **Tantric & Philosophy Colleges**

As you leave Tashilhunpo, it is also possible to visit the monastery's two remaining colleges, the Tantric College and the brown Philosophy College. They are on the left-hand side as you walk down towards the main gate. Neither is particularly interesting but you might be lucky and find yourself in time for debating, which is held in the courtyard of the Philosophy College.

Shigatse Dzong   FORT

(གཞིས་ཀ་རྩེ་རྫོང་, 日喀则宗; Rikāzé Zōng) Once the residence of the kings of Tsang and later the governor of Tsang, very little remained of this *dzong* after it was destroyed in the popular uprising of 1959. Construction on a new building began several years ago and Shigatse is now once again graced with an impressive hilltop fort that bears a close resemblance to the Potala, albeit on a smaller scale. The *dzong* was closed at the time of writing.

Summer Palace of the Panchen Lamas   PALACE

(བདེ་ཆེན་སྐལ་བཟང་ཕོ་བྲང་, 德庆格桑颇彰, Déqìng Gésāng Pōzhāng; admission ¥30; ◷ 9.30am-12pm & 3.30-6pm) Though it ranks far below Tashilhunpo, if you have extra time in Shigatse, pay a visit to this walled palace complex at the southwestern end of town. The palace was built in 1844 by the seventh Panchen Lama, Tenpei Nyima, and is a strange blend of Buddhist temple and Victorian-era mansion. It's known in Tibetan as the Dechen Gesang Podrang.

The bottom hallway has a pair of massive murals, one of which depicts the 18 levels of Buddhist hell with sadistic ingenuity, complete with humans being boiled, dismembered, speared, hacked and disembowelled – enough to keep most believers on the straight and narrow. One image is so gruesome it's covered with a scarf.

To the left of the hallway (opposite the Panchen Lama's stuffed dog) are two rooms, which an attendant monk might open for you. The first room is a *gönkhang* that features Nyeser Chöda Chenpo, the protector of Tashilunpo. The second room contains images of the 10th Panchen Lama's two *yunze* (spiritual tutors).

Walk up the grand staircase to the 2nd floor where you will find the 10th Panchen Lama's **sitting rooms**, one of which contains his desk and telephones. This floor also holds his **audience chamber**. Each room contains a *shuegje* (throne), to which pilgrims will bow. The attendant monk may even reveal one of the Panchen Lama's shoes, and proceed to bless you by rubbing the holy shoe on the back of your neck and head.

WORTH A TRIP

WORDO MUSEUM

If you plan on eating at Wordo Kitchen (p140) – or even if you don't – don't miss heading upstairs to this fascinating and totally unexpected private **museum** (☎139 8992 0067; Wordo Kitchen, Zhade Donglu; admission ¥20, for restaurant customers ¥15; ◷ 9.30am-11pm). English-speaker Kelsang does a great job of explaining the various exhibits, from the original iron links from a Tangtong Gyelpo bridge to the old English pressure cooker carried by porters over the Himalayas from Calcutta.

Look out for the Tibetan coins cut in half to provide change and the ornate saddle deconstructed during the Cultural Revolution to protect its owners. Travellers will appreciate the ancient Tibetan backpack.

Our favourites are the beauty implements designed to hang from a nomad woman's *chuba* (long-sleeved sheepskin coat), including an ear scraper and eyebrow plucker, and the karmic-related dice games that are a hit with local monks. The owner knows his stuff; he was a monk in Tashilhunpo Monastery for eight years.

The palace is about 1km south of Tashilhunpo. Follow the road to the end and turn right into the gated compound.

Darawa Linka
PARK

(སྒྲ་རྭ་གླིང་ཀ, 达热瓦林卡, Dárèwǎ Línkǎ; cnr Jilin Lu & Qingdai Lu; ⊙9am-late, summer only) FREE Locals make merry at this park on the eastern side of Shigatse. Grab a bottle of Lhasa beer and join them. There are a couple of dozen tents where people kick back, drink beer and play *sho* (a Tibetan board game) and mahjong. This is also known as the local pick-up spot so you'll see lots of eligible youngsters prowling for potential mates. On weekends it's packed with picnickers.

🏃 Activities

Tashi Dhundup Blind Massage
MASSAGE

(扎西顿株盲人按摩中心, Zhāxī Dùnzhū Mángrén Ànmó Zhōngxīn; ☑188 8909 4889; courtyard off Buxing Jie, room 102; per hour ¥120-180; ⊙11am-11pm) A graduate of the excellent Braille Without Borders training program, English-speaking Tashi offers Tibetan, Chinese and foot massages from his well-hidden office. Ring first or, even better, get your hotel to arrange for him to come to your room.

🛏 Sleeping

Shigatse has a good range of decent hotels, most with flush toilets and 24-hour hot water.

★ Gang Gyan Orchard Hotel
HOTEL $

(日喀则刚坚宾馆, Rìkāzé Gāngjiān Bīnguǎn; ☑882 0777; 77 Zhufeng Lu; dm ¥50, d with bathroom ¥180; ❄🛜) Right next to the carpet factory is this well-run hotel offering modern, recently renovated Western-style rooms with comfortable beds and clean bathrooms with hot water. Each room has its own wifi router. Dorm rooms give access to shared hot showers. Best of all is the location, less than 100m from the entrance of the Tashilhunpo Monastery and next to Shigatse's best restaurants.

Young House Hotel
HOTEL $

(康勋宾馆, Kāngxūn Bīnguǎn; ☑882 7786; 262 Shanghai Nanlu; d/tr ¥120/180) Solid upper-budget option with modern, comfortable rooms set around a sunny atrium. The small rooms don't have much natural light (corner rooms are bigger) and it's too far to walk to Tashilunpo but there's a Tibetan hot-pot

restaurant attached. This is good value for Shigatse.

Sakya Lhundup Palace Hotel
HOTEL $$

(萨迦龙珠宫廷饭店, Sàjiā Lóngzhū Gōngtíng Fàndiàn; ☑853 0558; www.yeezang.com; 24 Zhade Xilu, cnr of Puzhang Lu; d/tr ¥280/380; ❄🛜) Sakya Monastery owns this new three-star hotel but fear not, these are not your average monastery digs. Rooms are modern, fresh and spacious and there's a lovely sunny atrium bar and restaurant. It's right across from the entrance to the summer palace.

Tsampa Hotel
HOTEL $$

(糌巴大酒店, Zāngbā Dàjiǔdiàn; ☑866 7888; 9 Renbu Lu; d/tr ¥280/350; ❄🛜) This three-star Tibetan place opened in 2012 and is a good choice. The rooms are fresh, modern and carpeted with modern bathrooms and lots of Tibetan touches, including a good Tibetan restaurant.

Gesar Hotel
HOTEL $$$

(格萨尔酒店, Gésà'ěr Jiǔdiàn; ☑880 0088; Longjiang Lu; r standard/deluxe ¥380/500; ❄@🛜) This new four-star giant has clean and modern rooms, each decorated with its own thangka of Gesar Ling, and a pleasant rooftop teahouse, though the location in the southwestern suburbs is a bit of a drag. The deluxe rooms are huge but the glass-walled bathrooms won't work unless you and your room mate are very close friends. The disappointing breakfast buffet is aimed squarely at Chinese visitors (pickles and rice gruel, anyone?).

Tashi Chotar Hotel
HOTEL $$$

(扎西曲塔大酒店, Zhāxī Qūtǎ Dàjiǔdiàn; ☑883 0111; www.zxqthotel.com; 2 Xueqiang Lu; d/tr ¥780/980; ❄@🛜) A new and comfortable four-star place with Tibetan decor, internet cables, nice modern bathrooms and a good central location. Single rooms come with a computer. Rates include breakfast and can dip as low as ¥350 for a double.

Shigatse Hotel
HOTEL $$$

(日喀则饭店, Rìkāzé Fàndiàn; ☑882 2525; fax 882 1900; 12 Shanghai Zhonglu; d/tr ¥380/480; @🛜) The biggest hotel in town has a cavernous Tibetan-style lobby and even offers oxygen machines in some of the rooms, but it's really only fairly clueless tour groups that stay here. The rooms are clean but small and characterless. You can do better.

THE PANCHEN LAMAS

The second-highest-ranking lamas in Tibet, the Panchen Lamas' authority has often rivalled that of the Dalai Lamas. So great is their prestige, in fact, that the Panchen Lamas assist in the process of choosing new Dalai Lamas (and vice versa). Frequently stuck between a rock (the Dalai Lamas) and a hard place (the Chinese government), the Panchen Lamas have suffered more than most from Tibet's turbulent recent history.

The ninth Panchen Lama (1883–1937) spent his last days in the clutches of a Chinese nationalist warlord after attempting to use the Chinese as leverage in gaining greater influence in Tibet. After the ninth's death, the usual search for a replacement got underway and the Chinese forced Tibetan delegates in Běijīng to endorse their choice. The 10th Panchen Lama was initially pro-reform and pro-Chinese when he arrived at Tashilhunpo Monastery in 1951 but by his death, in 1989, he had flipped and become a hero to his people. What happened?

It seems that the Panchen Lama had a change of heart about his Chinese benefactors after the 1959 Lhasa uprising. In September 1961 the Panchen Lama presented Mao with a 70,000-character catalogue of the atrocities committed against Tibet, and a plea for increased freedoms. The answer he got was a demand that he denounce the Dalai Lama as a reactionary and take the latter's place as spiritual head of Tibet. Not only did the Panchen Lama refuse but, in 1964, with tens of thousands of Tibetans gathered in Lhasa for the Mönlam festival, he said to the crowds that he believed Tibet would one day regain its independence and the Dalai Lama would return as its leader.

It must have come as quite a shock to the Chinese to see their protégé turn on them. They responded in time-honoured fashion by throwing the 26-year-old Panchen Lama into jail, where he remained for 14 years, suffering abuse and torture. His crimes, according to the Chinese authorities, included participating in orgies, 'criticising China' and raising a private insurrectionary army. A 'smash the Panchen reactionary clique' campaign was mounted, and those close to the Panchen Lama were subject to 'struggle sessions' and imprisonment.

After emerging from prison in early 1978, the Panchen Lama rarely spoke in outright defiance of the Chinese authorities but continued to use what influence he had to press for the preservation of Tibetan cultural traditions. (He argued, for example, against the building of a hydroelectric power plant at Yamdrok-tso, one of Tibet's most sacred lakes.) In 1979 he

✖ Eating

Shigatse offers the last chance for some foreign food until you get to the Nepali border.

★ **Tibet Family Restaurant** TIBETAN $
(丰盛餐厅, Fēngshèng Cāntīng; Phuntsho Serzikhang; dishes ¥15-30; ⊙8am-10pm; 📖) This teahouse-style Tibetan place is our favourite for its excellent food, nice outdoor seating and friendly clientele of locals. It also boasts the perfect people-watching location, right at the end of the monastery kora. The food runs from simple and fresh vegetable options to more adventurous yak-meat dishes, all great value.

Sumptuous Tibetan Restaurant TIBETAN $
(丰盛臧式餐厅, Fēngshèng Zāngshì Cāntīng; Zhufeng Lu; mains ¥15-30; 📖) Another great option next to the Gang Gyen Hotel that's always buzzing and full of Tibetans. Choose from comfy Tibetan-style seats and decor inside or the pleasant back terrace. The bill is never quite what you expect but prices are reasonable, the food is good and the waiters eager to please. The menu and management is the same as the Tibet Family Restaurant.

★ **Third Eye Restaurant** NEPALI $$
(雪莲餐厅, Xuělián Cāntīng; ☎883 8898; Zhufeng Lu; dishes ¥35-50; ⊙9am-10pm; 📖) A Nepali-run place that is popular with both locals and tourists. Watch as locals sip *thugpa* while travellers treat their taste buds to the city's best Indian curries. It's upstairs, next to the Gang Gyan Shigatse Orchard Hotel.

★ **Wordo Kitchen** TIBETAN $$
(吾尔朵厨房, Wú'ěrduǒ Chúfáng; ☎882 3994; Zhade Donglu; mains ¥15-70) For something a bit special, head out to this stylish restaurant and museum in the southeast of town. The pleasant Tibetan seating is decorated with old prayer wheels and yak-butter pots.

married a Han Chinese army doctor and (uniquely for any Panchen or Dalai Lama) fathered a daughter.

It is believed that shortly before his death he again fell out with the Chinese, arguing at a high-level meeting in Běijīng that the price paid for development during the Chinese occupation was far greater than any gains. Accordingly, many Tibetans believe that the 51-year-old died not of a heart attack, as was reported, but by poisoning. Others maintain that, exhausted and perhaps despairing, the Panchen Lama came home in 1989 to die – as he always said he would – on Tibetan soil.

Of course, the story doesn't end here. In May 1995 the Dalai Lama identified Gedhun Choekyi Nyima, a six-year-old boy from Amdo, as the latest reincarnation of the Panchen Lama. Within a month the boy had been forcibly relocated to a government compound in Běijīng, causing him to be dubbed the 'world's youngest political prisoner', and an irate Chinese government had ordered the senior lamas of Tashilhunpo to come up with a second, Chinese-approved choice. Chadrel Rinpoche, the abbot who led the search that identified Gedhun, was later imprisoned for six years for 'splitting the country' and 'colluding with separatist forces abroad' (ie consulting the Dalai Lama), and Tashilhunpo was closed to tourists for a few months.

Tashilhunpo's lamas eventually settled on Gyancain Norbu, the son of Communist Party members, who was formally approved in a carefully orchestrated ceremony.

Běijīng's interest is not only in controlling the education of Tibet's number-two spiritual leader, but also influencing the boy who could later be influential in identifying the reincarnation of the Dalai Lama. Meanwhile, the Dalai Lama–appointed Panchen Lama, now in his mid-20s, remains under house arrest at an undisclosed location. In 2010 the Chinese Panchen Lama made his political debut, being named a member of the CPPCC, China's top political advisory board.

There are a number of groups campaigning to free the Panchen Lama. The organisation **Tashilhunpo Monastery in Exile** (www.tashilhunpo.org) even offers a US$33,000 reward for information on the whereabouts of Gedhun.

The Search for the Panchen Lama, by Isabel Hilton, is a look at the political intricacies of Tibet, with an emphasis on the controversial Panchen Lama and China's abduction of his current reincarnation.

Ask for Kelsang to explain the Tibetan menu and make sure you head upstairs to the museum (p138) before or after dinner. Dishes range from curried potatoes to more ambitious braised yak ribs.

Songtsen Tibetan Restaurant
INTERNATIONAL **$$**

(松赞西藏餐厅, Sōngzàn Xīzàng Cāntīng; Buxing Jie; dishes ¥30-45; ⊙9am-10pm; ▣) Popular Nepali-style place that serves hearty breakfasts, yak burgers and curries to Land Cruiser groups. It has a great location on the 'pedestrian-only' street, offering good views of the pilgrims ambling past.

🔒 Shopping

The street known as Buxing Jie (Pedestrian St) that runs northeast from Tashilunpo Monastery is the single best place for Tibetan crafts. The monastery end has a concentration of monks' supply stores, selling everything from incense and wooden tsampa bowls to bags, while further down are several souvenir, statuary and embroidery workshops.

Tibetan Market
HANDICRAFTS

(Bangjiakong Lu) The open-air market in the Tibetan old town is a good place to pick up low-grade Tibetan crafts and souvenirs, such as prayer wheels, rosaries and traditional Tibetan boots. Bargain hard. The street market just to the east is the best place to get a Tibetan *chuba* (cloak).

Tibet Gang Gyen Carpet Factory
CARPETS

(西藏刚坚地毯厂, Xīzàng Gāngjiān Dìtǎn Chǎng; www.tibetgang-gyencarpet.com; 9 Zhufeng Lu; ⊙9am-1pm & 3-7pm Mon-Sat) Beside the Gang Gyan Orchard Hotel, 100m down a side alley, this workshop hires and trains impoverished women to weave high-quality wool carpets. Upon arrival you'll be directed to the workshop, where you can watch the 80 or so women work on the carpets, singing as they weave, dye, trim and spin; you're free to take photos.

Expect to pay US$720, plus shipping if you need it, for a carpet measuring 190cm by 90cm. All the wool used is Tibetan (from Nagchu) and the vegetable dyes are natural. The factory is owned by Tashilhunpo Monastery, which takes half the profits from carpet sales. Credit cards are accepted.

Toread Outdoor Sports OUTDOOR EQUIPMENT (探路者, Tànlùzhě; ☏882 3195; 16 Shanghai Zhonglu) If you are headed off on a trek but are totally unprepared, Toread is one of several shops where you can pick up basic Chinese-made tents, sleeping bags and outdoor clothes.

ⓘ Information

MONEY

Bank of China branch (中国银行, Zhōngguó Yínháng; Zhufeng Lu; ☀9am-4pm Mon-Sat, 10am-4pm Sun) A short walk from the Gang Gyan Orchard Hotel, this useful branch changes travellers cheques and cash and has a 24-hour ATM outside.

Bank of China main branch (中国银行, Zhōngguó Yínháng; Shanghai Zhonglu) The main branch is just south of the Shigatse Hotel.

PERMITS

Public Security Bureau (公安局, PSB, Gōng'ānjú; ☏882 2240; Jilin Nanlu; ☀9.30am-12.30pm & 3.30-6.30pm Mon-Fri, 9.30am-2pm Sat & Sun) Your guide will likely have to stop here for half an hour to register and/or pick up an alien's travel permit for the Friendship Hwy or western Tibet. It's in the southeastern suburbs, near the Gesar Hotel.

POST

China Post (中国邮政, Zhōngguó Yóuzhèng; cnr Shandong Lu & Zhufeng Lu) It's possible to send international letters and postcards from here, but not international parcels.

ⓘ Getting There & Away

Tibet Airlines operates four flights a week from Shigatse's Peace Airport, 45km east of town, to Chéngdū (¥1880).

Minibuses, buses and taxis travel from Shigatse to Lhasa and run in the morning to Sakya (four hours), Lhatse (five hours) and Gyantse (1½ hours) but foreign tourists aren't allowed to take them.

The train spur line from Lhasa to Shigatse opened in late 2014 and foreigners should be able to take these trains. Train K9822 departs Shigatse daily at 5.30pm and takes 3½ hours. For ticket prices see p74. The station is about 10km south of town on the road to Gyantse.

ⓘ Getting Around

Central Shigatse can be comfortably explored on foot but many of the hotels are a short drive away. For short trips around town you might want to use a pedicab (¥5), otherwise a taxi ride anywhere in town costs ¥10.

Around Shigatse

There are several sights around Shigatse, but few are visited by Western travellers. It is possible to visit Gyantse as a day trip from Shigatse.

★**Shalu Monastery** BUDDHIST, MONASTERY (ཞ་ལུ་དགོན་པ, 夏鲁寺, Xiàlǔ Sì; admission ¥40) It's a treat for the traveller when a sight is both a pleasure to explore and of great artistic importance. Such is the Shalu Monastery which dates back to the 11th century. The monastery rose to prominence in the 14th century when its abbot, Büton Rinchen Drup, emerged as the foremost interpreter and compiler of Sanskrit Buddhist texts of the day. (A suborder, the Büton, formed around him.)

It also became a centre for training in skills such as trance walking and *thumo* (generating internal heat to survive in cold weather), feats made famous by the flying monks of Alexandra David-Neel's book *Magic and Mystery in Tibet*.

In the abstract, the design of the monastery represents the paradise of Chenresig (Avalokiteshvara), a haven from all worldly suffering. In the concrete, Shalu is the only monastery in Tibet that combines Tibetan and Chinese styles in its design. Much of the original structure was destroyed by an earthquake in the 14th century and, as this was a time of Mongol patronage, many Han artisans were employed in the reconstruction. The green-tiled Chinese-style roof, clearly visible as you approach, is one of the monastery's most easily recognisable features.

What remained of the original 11th-century Tibetan-style monastery was largely destroyed in the Cultural Revolution, but the Chinese-influenced inner Serkhang has survived reasonably well. If you enjoy looking at murals, Shalu has some fine ones from the

14th century that fuse Chinese, Mongol and Newari styles. Bring a powerful torch.

The southern chapel has particularly lovely Newari-style murals depicting the five Dhyani Buddhas. The main inner **Serkhang** has a black stone statue of Chenresig Kasrapani, the monastery's holiest relic, as well as a vase from which pilgrims receive a blessing of sacred water. The northern **Gusum Lhakhang**, so named for its three doors, has more fine murals, including one in the left corner depicting the monastery's founder. The inner kora path is currently blocked.

There are a couple of upper chapels, including the ancient-feeling **Yum Lhakhang** with its inner kora and other chapels with fine mandala murals. On the way out you can ask the ticket sellers to show you the sacred wood block which confers blessings on anyone who sees it. Monks sell block prints of the now-faded mandala.

From Shalu you can drive for 10 minutes up to **Ri-puk Hermitage**, a former meditation centre and summertime residence for Shalu's monks built around a sacred spring and destroyed chörten. There are lovely views of the Shalu Valley. The three-day trek to Nartang Monastery starts from here.

Shalu Monastery is just 4km off the Shigatse–Gyantse road. En route you can stop off at the thousand-year-old **Gyengong Lhakhang**, a small chapel that actual predates Shalu. Don't miss the sacred mushroom growing on the ground-floor pillar and the upstairs stone basin where Sakya Pandita washed his head before receiving his *gelong* monastic vows. The poster of what looks like a Chinese pop star is actually of the Panchen Lama's daughter.

The monastery restaurant at the gates sells excellent dumpling soup.

Nartang Monastery   BUDDHIST, MONASTERY

(纳唐寺, Nàtáng Sì; admission ¥15) En route to Lhatse it's worth stopping at this 12th-century Kadampa monastery, famed for wood-block printing the Nartang canon in the 18th century. Treasures in the assembly hall include small statues of Denba Tortumba said to have the power to control lightning; a mantra written in stone by the first Dalai Lama; and the self-arising stone horns and footprints of the wild yak that helped install the monastery's foundation stones.

The chapel to the left is the old *barkhang* (printing press), though printing these days takes place in the room next to the entry gate.

Kangchen Monastery   BUDDHIST, MONASTERY

(康坚寺, Kāngjiān Sì) This little-visited but interesting monastery actually consists of two separate and rival complexes. Your Tibetan guides probably won't enter the well-tended building to the left because of its statues of Dorje Shugden, the powerful Tantric protector outlawed by the Dalai Lama. Kangchen is just off the Friendship Hwy, 19km past Nartang.

Yungdrungling Monastery   BUDDHIST, MONASTERY

(雍竹林寺, Yōngzhúlín Sì) Just visible across the river from the road between Lhasa and Shigatse is the Bönpo Yungdrungling Monastery. The monastery, founded in 1834, was once the second most influential Bön monastic institution in Tibet and home to 700 monks. At first glance, Yungdrungling looks much like a Buddhist monastery, but if you look closely you'll note the swastikas and prayer wheels swirling anticlockwise. You may find your guide and driver are reluctant to enter the monastery grounds.

There are currently around 60 monks here, most of whom are from the Nagchu region of northern Tibet. If one of them can find the key, you can visit the large *dukhang*, with its impressive thrones of the monastery's two resident lamas. There are 1300 small iron statues of Tonpa Shenrab (the equivalent of Sakyamuni) along the walls. You may also be able to visit a couple of chapels behind the main hall, including the Namgyel Lhakhang and **Kudung Lhakhang**, the latter featuring the tomb of the monastery founder and Bön protector Gyachen Traksen. Remember to make the rounds in an anticlockwise direction.

The monastery is 80km east of Shigatse, on the road to Lhasa and the north bank of the Yarlung Tsangpo (Brahmaputra River), just east of where the Nangung-chu meets it. Cross the Bailey bridge and follow the dirt road north along the Nangung-chu to a road bridge. The monastery is 7km from the main road.

Phuntsoling   ཕུན་ཚོགས་གླིང་རྫོང་སྐུ། འབྲས། 平措林

If you're travelling down the paved Friendship Hwy and want to get a taste of what 'off the beaten track' looks like, consider a few hours' diversion to Phuntsoling Monastery. Not only is the drive along the winding

TSANG PHUNTSOLING

KILOMETRE MARKERS ALONG THE FRIENDSHIP HIGHWAY

The kilometre markers (signifying distance from Shànghǎi) of the following towns, geographic features and points of interest may be of help to travellers, hitchhikers and mountain bikers.

Lhasa to Shigatse

MARKER	FEATURE
4646	Lhasa's eastern crossroads to Golmud or Shigatse
4656	Blue Buddha rock painting
4661	sign to Nyetang Tashigang Monastery
4662/3	Netang village and Drölma Lhakhang
4683	bridge and tunnel to Gongkar airport
4695-7	Chushul village (Tibetan 'End of River')
4703	bridge over the Yarlung Tsangpo to Nangartse and Tsetang; shops and restaurants
4757	road to Nyemo and Yangpachen to north; restaurants; bridge
4772	passport check
4779	bridge to south side of river
4800	traffic checkpoint; turn-off to Rinphug (Rembu); old road to Gyantse
4802	remains of traditional bridge next to beach
4820	Traduka; bridge to Yungdrungling Monastery and Yangpachen; restaurants
4855	Shigatse airport
4859	Samden Ritro Monastery signed right 2km
4869	Bengon Monastery (signed Engon) on hillside 3km to south
4875	bridge north to Nanmulin
4881	Samdorje Monastery to south with large thangka wall
4900-5	Shigatse

Shigatse to Tingri

MARKER	FEATURE
4913	turn-off to Ngor Monastery (8km) and trek route to/from Shalu
4917	Nartang Monastery
4928	Jakri village
4932/3	very gentle mountain pass of Tra-la (3970m)
4936	Kangchen Monastery to right (2km)
4956/7	rebuilt Trupuk Chörten and monastery 1km to the north
4960/1	Gyeding; ruined fort; checkpoint; restaurants and shops
4972	Dilong village
4977/8	turn-off to Phuntsoling Monastery
4994	Daoban
5000	marker showing 5000km from Shànghǎi; small monastery and ruined *dzong*
5009	village and start of climb to pass
5014	Tropu-la (Tsuo-la; 4540m)
5028	Sakya bridge; turn-off to Sakya
5041	village and turn-off to Shingchen Hot Springs
5052	Lhatse
5058	checkpoint and turn-off to western Tibet

5063	start of climb to pass, with a height gain of around 1000m
5083	Gyatso-la (5248m)
5114	views of Everest and the Himalayas
5121	trail to hermitage across river
5122	Lolo Hot Springs on right side
5123	Dratsang Monastery and Lolo Dzong above
5125	Lolo (Langkhar) village across bridge, with access to ruined hermitage and caves
5126	Kawa village, fort and caves on far side of river
5133	Baber (Baipa) and turn-off to Shegar
5139	Shegar checkpoint
5144	turn-off to Everest Base Camp
5148	ruined monastery on small hill to south
5153	monastery ruins in village
5155	ruined *dzong* to left
5162	Zagor village
5165	ruins on hilltop to south
5170	village
5178	fort ruins on hilltop to right
5186	mineral-water factory
5193-4	Tingri

TSANG

Tingri to Nyalam

MARKER	FEATURE
5206	turn-off for Tsamda Hot Springs, group camping opposite turn-off
5216	two small Tibetan guesthouses in village
5221-52	various ruins by side of road
5232-3	Gutso village; guesthouse; last views of Mt Everest
5245	village and ruined monastery
5254	Menbu village traffic checkpost
5255	interesting ruins of Gongtso
5263	start climb to La Lung-la
5265	turn-off to Saga, Mt Kailash and Shishapangma Base Camp via Peiku-tso
5276	La Lung-la (4845m)
5281	bridge; road workers' hostel
5289	Tong-la (5140m) and views of Lapchi and Shishapangma
5303	roadworkers' hostel and village
5310	Yarley village, with ruins behind
5312	sacred spring said to cure eye problems
5334	Gangka village and 500m track to Milarepa's Cave
5345	Nyalam; traffic police check
5359	military checkpoint
5362	path across gorge to chörten on far hillside
5378	Zhāngmù
5386	Nepali border

Yarlung Tsangpo highly scenic, but so is the monastery itself, situated at the edge of a gargantuan sand dune. A ruined red fort, seated high above the monastery on a rocky crag, just adds to the fantastic photogenic atmosphere.

◉ Sights

Phuntsoling Monastery   BUDDHIST, MONASTERY
(平措林寺, Píngcuòlíng Sì; admission ¥35) Phuntsoling Monastery, now home to 50 monks, was once the central monastery of the Jonangpa. This Kagyu sect is especially known for the examination of the nature of emptiness undertaken at the monastery by its greatest scholar, Dolpopa Sherab Gyaltsen (1292–1361). He was one of the first proponents of the hard-to-grasp notion of *shentong*. Roughly, this is based on the idea that the buddha-mind (which transcends all forms) is not ultimately empty, even though all forms are empty illusions. (No, we don't get it either...)

Shentong has been debated among Buddhist philosophers for seven centuries. The Gelugpa school did not share Dolpopa's view, to the point where in the 17th century the fifth Dalai Lama suppressed the Jonangpa school and forcibly converted Phuntsoling into a Gelugpa institution.

The monastery was expanded by the writer and scholar Taranatha (1575–1634), whose next incarnation was the first Bogd Gegeen (spiritual leader) of Mongolia. Thereafter the monastery was closely associated with the Bogd Gegeens, which is why you will see pictures of the eighth and ninth incarnations in front of the main altar. The ninth Bogd fled to India as a young man but revisited Phuntsoling in 1986 and 1993, helping to reopen the monastery following its closure during the Cultural Revolution.

You can visit the monastery's large assembly hall, which is dominated by a statue of Chenresig (Avalokiteshvara). Other statues include those of the 10th Panchen Lama, Tsongkhapa and the fifth Dalai Lama. The inner sanctum of the hall contains a statue of Mikyöba (Akshobhya), while the murals on the roof tell the story of the life of Sakyamuni (Sakya Thukpa). Tame *ghoral* (mountain goats) wander the central courtyard.

The highlight of the monastery is a walk up to the ruined fortifications behind the monastery, which offer stunning views of the valley. Look for the ruined *dzong* on a cliff across the Yarlung Tsangpo.

A festival is held at Phuntsoling around the middle of the fourth lunar month (equivalent to June/July) every year, and sees lamas and pilgrims from all over the county gathering in the courtyard for prayers and celebrations.

Jonang Kumbum   RUINS
(觉囊千佛塔, Juénáng Qiānfó Tǎ) About 6km south of Phuntsoling are the ruins of the once-spectacular Jonang Kumbum. The former 20m-high chörten was built by Dolpopa in the 14th century and was the spiritual centre of the Jonangpas. It was said to be one of the best-preserved monuments in Tibet, resembling the Gyantse Kumbum, before it was wrecked during the Cultural Revolution. Sadly, it's currently off limits to foreigners.

❶ Getting There & Away

Phuntsoling can be visited on the way from Shigatse to Lhatse. Take the dirt-road detour north of the Friendship Hwy at kilometre marker 4977/8, from which point the monastery is 34km northwest (less than an hour's drive). After visiting the monastery you can continue 61km to rejoin the Friendship Hwy near Lhatse Chöde.

Sakya   ས་སྐྱ 萨迦
◢ 0892 / ELEV 4316M

A detour to visit the small town of Sakya (Sàjiā Sì) is pretty much de rigueur for any trip down the Friendship Hwy. The town is southeast of Shigatse, about 25km off the southern Friendship Hwy, accessed via a good dirt road through a pretty farming valley. The draw is Sakya Monastery, which ranks as one of the most atmospheric, impresive and unique monasteries in Tibet. Moreover, Sakya occupies a pivotal place in Tibetan history.

Sakya actually has two monasteries, on either side of the Trum-chu. The heavy, brooding, fortress-like monastery south of the river is the more impressive, so if you only have time to visit one, make it this. The hillside northern monastery, largely reduced to picturesque ruins, is undergoing restoration work and offers a fine kora walk.

One characteristic feature of the Sakya region is the colouring of its buildings. Unlike the standard whitewashing that you see elsewhere in Tibet, Sakya's buildings are

PRIESTS & PATRONS: THE REIGN OF THE SAKYAPAS

The 11th century was a dynamic period in the history of Tibetan Buddhism. Renewed contact with Indian Buddhists brought about a flowering of new orders and schools. During this time, the Kagyupa order was founded by Marpa and his disciple Milarepa, and in Sakya the Khon family established a school that came to be called the Sakyapa. One interesting distinction between this school and others is that the abbotship was hereditary, restricted to the sons of the aristocratic Khon family.

By the early 13th century, the Tsang town of Sakya had emerged as an important centre of scholastic study. The most famous local scholar was the fourth Khon descendent and Sakya abbot, Kunga Gyaltsen (1182–1251), who came to be known as Sakya Pandita, literally 'scholar from Sakya'.

Such was Sakya Pandita's scholastic and spiritual eminence that when the Mongols threatened to invade Tibet in the mid-13th century he represented the Tibetan people to the Mongol prince Godan (descendent of Genghis Khan). Sakya Pandita made a three-year journey to Prince Godan's camp, in modern-day Gānsù, arriving in 1247. Sakya Pandita set about instructing Godan in Buddhist philosophy and respect for human lives. Impressed by his wisdom (and the fact that he cured him of an illness), Godan made Sakya Pandita Viceroy of Tibet.

After Sakya Pandita's death, in 1251, power was transferred to his nephew Phagpa, who became a close advisor to Kublai Khan and even met Marco Polo in Běijīng. Phagpa's greatest legacy was a special script used by Kublai as the official alphabet of the Mongol court. Phagpa was named Imperial Preceptor (the highest religious title in the Mongol empire) and, thus, de facto leader of Tibet. The role of spiritual and temporal head of state became an important precedent for the Tibetan government and had far-reaching effects on the religious life of Mongolia. However, the association between Tibetan lamas and Mongol masters also set a precedent of outside rule over Tibet that the Chinese have used to justify current claims over the high plateau.

As it was, Mongol overlordship and Sakya supremacy were relatively short-lived. Mongol corruption and rivalry between the Sakyapa and Kagyupa orders led to the fall of Sakya in 1354, when power fell into the hands of the Kagyupa and the seat of government moved to Nedong, in Ü.

Sakya was to remain a powerful municipality and, like Shigatse, enjoyed a high degree of autonomy from successive central governments. Even today you can see homes across the plateau painted with the red, white and blue-black stripes associated with Sakya Monastery.

ash grey with white and red vertical stripes. The colouring symbolises the Rigsum Gonpo (the trinity of bodhisattvas) and stands as a mark of Sakya authority. Sakya literally means 'pale earth'.

In recent years Sakya village has transformed into a small town but it still feels off the grid. It's well worth spending the night here.

◉ Sights

★ **Sakya Monastery**   BUDDHIST, MONASTERY
(admission ¥45; ⊙9am-6pm) The immense, grey, thick-walled southern monastery is one of Tibet's most impressive constructed sights, and one of the largest monasteries. Established in 1268, it was designed defensively, with watchtowers on each corner of its high walls. Inside, the dimly lit hall ex-

udes a sanctity and is on a scale that few others can rival. As usual, morning is the best time to visit as more chapels are open.

Directly ahead from the east-wall main entrance is the entry to the inner courtyard and then the main **assembly hall** (Lhakhang Chenmo or Tsokchen Dukhang), a huge structure with walls 16m high and 3.5m thick.

At first glance the assembly hall may strike you as being like most others in Tibet: a dark interior illuminated with shafts of sunlight and the warm glow of butter lamps; an omnipresent smell of burning butter; and an array of gilded statues representing buddhas, bodhisattvas, Tibetan kings and lamas. But even weary tour groups seem to quickly recognise the age, beauty and sanctity of Sakya. Plan to spend time just soaking up the sacred, medieval atmosphere. You'll find few that are its equal.

A few things to look specifically for in the hall are the huge drum in the far left corner and the massive sacred pillars, some which are made of entire tree trunks and are famous throughout Tibet. One reputedly was a gift from Kublai Khan.

Another gift from Kublai to the monastery is Sakya's famous white conch shell, which currently sits in a gilded mandala. The shell is supposedly all that remains of the Buddha when in a previous incarnation he lived his life as a modest shellfish. Pilgrims queue to hear the soft, low sound of the sacred conch being blown by an attendant monk.

The walls of the assembly hall are lined with towering gilded buddhas, which are unusual in that many also serve as reliquaries for former Sakya abbots. The buddha in the far left corner holds the tooth of the past Buddha inside it. The large nearby chörten is the funeral stupa of the monastery's 40th abbot; the statue to the right of this houses the clothes and ashes of the monastery founder. The central Sakyamuni statue enshrines the clothes and relics of Sakya Pandita. To the right of the central buddha are statues of Jampelyang (Manjushri), a seated Jampa (Maitreya) and a Dorje Chang (Vajradhara).

Look for the huge animal horns, elephant tusks and tiger skin adorning the pillars alongside some lovely bodhisattva statues. Sakya's famous **library** (admission ¥10), long considered the greatest in Tibet, is also accessible from this hall and worth a visit for its floor-to-ceiling collection of texts.

As you exit the assembly hall the chapel to the right (south) is the **Purba Lhakhang**. Central images are of Sakyamuni (Sakya Thukpa) and of Jampelyang (Manjushri), while wall paintings behind depict Tsepame (Amitayus) to the left, Drölma (Tara) and white, multiarmed Namgyelma (Vijaya) to the far left, as well as a medicine buddha, two Sakyamunis and Jampa (Maitreya).

To the north of the inner courtyard is the **Nguldung Lhakhang** containing 11 gorgeous silver chörtens, which are also reliquaries for former Sakya abbots. Look to the left corner for the sand mandala inside a dirty glass case. A sometimes-locked door leads into another chapel with additional amazing chörtens and murals. Bring a torch as the room is even dimmer than others.

Next door is a new **Relic Exhibition** (admission ¥20), which contains several of the monastery's prize statues and thangkas.

As you exit the inner courtyard take the entry way left to the **Tsechu Lhakhang**, which houses a speaking statue of Guru Rinpoche and funeral chörtens from the lineage holders of Drölma Phodrang (Sakya had two ruling houses, the Drölma Phodrang and the Phutsok Phodrang).

There are a couple of chapels open outside of this central complex (but still within the walled compound), the most interesting of which is the very spooky protector chapel of the **Phakpa Lhakhang**. If the thick incense doesn't get you, the terrifying monsters, huge *cham* masks and demonic yaks that wait in the dark recesses just might.

There are several other *gönkhangs* on the top floor of the monastery, accessed by a long ladder to the side of the main entrance.

It is possible to climb up onto the outer walls of the monastery for a final kora of the monastery that takes in fine views of the surrounding valley.

Northern Monastery Ruins   RUINS

Little is left of the original monastery complex that once sprawled across the hills north of the Trum-chu, but it is still worth climbing up through the Tibetan village and wandering around what does remain. The northern monastery predates the southern monastery (the oldest temple at the northern monastery was built in 1073), and it is alleged to have contained 108 buildings, like Ganden. It may once have housed some 3000 monks who concentrated on Tantric studies.

Centred in the village is a large new **shedra** and debating courtyard. After passing through the new village, head for the white chörtens, or the ruins even further to the left. Near the chörtens are three main complexes that are open: the main **Labrang Shar**, the **Namgyel Lhakhang** to the left and the **Rinche Gang Nunnery** to the far right. Remember to walk in a clockwise fashion as this is a kora route.

🛏 Sleeping

Sakya Lowa Family Hotel   GUESTHOUSE $

(萨迦镇鲁娃家庭旅馆, Sàjiā Zhèn Lǔwā Jiātíng Lǚguǎn; ☑ 824 2156; 35 Baogang Beilu; dm ¥40, r per person ¥80, s ¥180) With its cosy teahouse, simple but clean rooms and traditional vibe, the family-run Lowa could be great. Unfortunately it's chronically overpriced, especially considering there's no running water. It's down the street on the east side of the Manasarovar Sakya Hotel.

Manasarovar Sakya Hotel   HOTEL $$
(神湖萨迦宾馆, Shénhú Sàjiā Bīnguǎn; ☑824 2555; 1 Gesang Xilu; d/tr ¥200/280) The renovated rooms at this modern hotel are spacious and comfortable, with hot-water bathrooms and electric blankets, making it the best value in town.

✖ Eating

Apart from the following, Sakya has plenty of Chinese restaurants set up by Sichuanese immigrants.

**Sakya Farmer's
Taste Restaurant**   TIBETAN $
(萨迦农民美食厅, Sàjiā Nóngmín Měishítīng; ☑824 2221; dishes ¥10-35; 🅿) Looking over the main street, this Tibetan place has a cosy atmosphere amid Tibetan decor. The green-jacketed waiters are friendly and will help explain the various Tibetan dishes available.

Sakya Monastery Restaurant   TIBETAN $
(萨迦寺餐厅, Sàjiā Sì Cāntīng; dishes ¥7-15; ⏲8am-9pm) This Tibetan joint is owned by the monastery and serves fried rice, *thugpa*, dumplings and lashings of milk tea. It's cosy and always full of characters.

**Manasarovar Sakya
Hotel Restaurant**   INTERNATIONAL $$
(神湖萨迦宾馆餐厅, Shénhú Sàjiā Bīnguǎn Cāntīng; ☑824 2222; dishes ¥25-35; ⏲breakfast, lunch & dinner; 🅿) For those who are after Western food, such as omelettes, burgers, sizzlers and pizza. There are also Tibetan, Nepalese and Indian dishes. The food is OK but the large dining hall lacks the charm of other places in town.

ⓘ Getting There & Away

Sakya is 25km off the Friendship Hwy. En route you'll pass the impressive ridgetop Tongar Choede Monastery. Just 5km before Sakya at Chonkhor Lhunpo village is the Ogyen Lhakhang, where local farmers go to get blessings from relics said to be able prevent hailstorms.

Lhatse   ཁཙ 拉孜
☑0892 / ELEV 3950M
Approximately 150km southwest of Shigatse and some 30km west of the Sakya turn-off, the bleak town of Lhatse (Lāzī) is a likely pit

stop for travellers headed to western Tibet. Lhatse is more or less a one-street town with a small square near the centre. The 3km-long main street runs east–west and used to be part of the Friendship Hwy, but this has now been diverted to the north. Passing 4WD traffic will mostly be heading to Everest Base Camp, the Tibet–Nepal border or the turn-off for Ali in western Tibet, about 6km out of town.

There's little to see in Lhatse save the renovated **Changmoche Monastery** at the western end of town.

🛏 Sleeping

Lhatse Tibetan Farmer's Hotel   HOTEL $
(拉孜农民旅馆, Lāzī Nóngmín Lǚguǎn; ☑832 2333; dm ¥25-45, d with/without bathroom ¥260/90) Located on the east side of town, this courtyard guesthouse has long been popular with 4WD drivers and guides. The older block of basic rooms with shared bathrooms offers budget travellers decent value but the back block with modern en suite rooms (solar hot water) is looking overpriced compared to the competition.

Dewang Manor   HOTEL $$
(德望庄园, Déwàng Zhuāngyuán; ☑139 8902 7775; d ¥250; ❄🅿) The old Dewang was completely rebuilt and reinvented in 2014 and the 14 spacious and modern rooms are now the most comfortable in town. There's a tea room, restaurant, ground-floor bar and lots of Tibetan decor. Back-block rooms are quietest. It's diagonally across from the Farmer's Hotel.

Yángguāng Shāngwù Bīnguǎn   HOTEL $$
(阳光商务宾馆; ☑832 2255; 32 Laozhongni Lu; r/d ¥180/220) Managed by Hui Muslims from Gānsù, this new hotel is a good-value choice. The clean and fresh carpeted rooms are small, especially the bathrooms, but the heat lamps and rain showerheads help. It's directly opposite the Farmer's Hotel in the east end of town.

Shànghǎi Hotel of Lāzī   HOTEL $$
(拉孜上海大酒店, Lāzī Shànghǎi Dàjiǔdiàn; ☑832 3786; r ¥220-260) A good value, if slightly dull, midrange option, offering decent mattresses, flush toilets and hot showers in the spacious bathrooms. The big hotel is obvious on the south side of the town square.

LOLO HOT SPRINGS

If you only stop at one hot springs in Tibet, make it this one. The clean swimming-pool-size hot pool is the perfect temperature to shake off the rigours of the road, especially after a visit to the natural steam room. The **springs** (鲁鲁温泉, Lǔlǔ Wēnquán; ☑139 8902 3494; admission ¥20) are 11km west of Baber.

Just 1km east of here is **Dratsang Monastery** and the ruins of **Lolo Dzong**, on a crag 10 minutes' climb above the monastery.

✖ Eating

Lhatse is a popular lunch stop and the main drag is lined with Chinese and Muslim restaurants.

Tibetan Farmer's Hotel Restaurant　　　INTERNATIONAL $

(mains ¥10-20; ⓘ) The guesthouse's Tibetan-style restaurant is a very cosy place, with simple but decent Tibetan and Western food, from pancakes to beef curry, at very reasonable prices.

Around Lhatse

Drampa Gyang Temple　　　MONASTERY

This small but significant monastery and ruined *dzong* is just north of Lhatse in the village of Lhatse Chöde (Lāzī Zhèn in Chinese). The temple is one of Songtsen Gampo's demoness-subduing temples; in this case it pins the troublesome demoness' left hip.

To reach the village head 1km east of Lhatse on the Friendship Hwy to the 5052km mark and then turn north. This road continues for 61km to Phuntsoling Monastery.

You need to have the actual monastery name listed on your permits to avoid a run-in with the overly sensitive local PSB.

Shingchen Hot Springs　　　HOT SPRINGS

(ⴈⴏⴑⴅⴝⴛⴗⴀ, 锡钦温泉, Xīqīn Wēnquán; ☑0892-832 3999; bath per person ¥20-40) Tibetans come from far and wide to bathe in the healing waters of these hot springs, which are said to cure everything from flatulence to skin irritations (so be careful who you share the pools with).

Choose from modern indoor pools or the smaller, cheaper and more natural looking side pool that is favoured by Tibetans. It's a pleasant enough place for a dip, especially in the cooler months or in the evenings. Bring a towel.

The hot springs are 10km east of Lhatse, 750m north of Friendship Hwy kilometre marker 5041. Hot-spring fanatics can even stay overnight in simple guest rooms and there's also a restaurant on-site.

Baber & Shegar　　　དབལ་འབར་
白坝, 协格尔

☑0892 / ELEV 4250M & 4150M

The last main stop on the way to Everest is a wind-raked truck stop called Baber (Báibà in Chinese), located at kilometre marker 5133, about 12km before the turn-off to Everest. By the time most travellers arrive from Shigatse or Sakya it's already too late to visit Everest, so most spend the night here. Baber is also the place to pick up your entry ticket to Qomolangma Nature Reserve, which includes Everest Base Camp, Rongphu Monastery and Cho Oyu Base Camp.

Shegar (Xiégé'ěr in Chinese; also known as New Tingri, but not to be confused with Tingri) is a small county town located 7km northwest of Baber, easily reached from the crossroad in the middle of Baber. If you have time it's definitely worth making the short side trip to Shegar to check out the incredible ruins of Shegar Dzong.

◉ Sights

★ **Shegar Dzong**　　　FORT

Shegar is dominated by its Crystal Fort, one of Tibet's most fantastical. Its crumbling defensive walls snake up the side of an impossibly steep mountain that looms over town; picture Mt Crumpit in *The Grinch Who Stole Christmas*. Trails allow you to clamber up from the monastery entrance to the ruined buildings, from where you can see Mt Everest in the distance. Morning light is best for taking photographs.

Shegar Chöde Monastery　　　BUDDHIST, MONASTERY

(admission ¥15) This small Gelugpa institution, built in 1269, clings like a limpet to the side of Shegar Mountain. The monastery originally followed Nyingma, Sakya, Gelug and Kagyu tradition until the fifth Dalai Lama enforced the Gelugpa doctrine. A mural by the entrance depicts the monastery at the height of its power, when it had around

800 monks. These days only 30 remain. A chörten to the right of the main assembly hall is said to enshrine the heart, eyes and tongue of a former abbot.

🛏 Sleeping & Eating

Both Shegar and Baber offer accommodation. Most groups stay in Baber and head out early to catch the dawn over the Himalayas at the Pang-la. Shegar is not a bad alternative; it has an interesting old Tibetan quarter that winds up towards the monastery.

Most guesthouses and hotels in Baber have attached restaurants.

Sunrise Hotel   HOTEL $
(阳光宾馆; Yángguāng Bīnguǎn; ☑ 139 8992 2770; Baber; d with/without bathroom ¥180/80) Located at the eastern end of town, the friendly family-run Sunrise has small but clean rooms with carpet and hot-water bathroom, making this one of the best-value options. There are also some cheaper adobe-walled rooms without bathroom.

Pentoc Guesthouse   GUESTHOUSE $
(潘多旅馆; Pānduō Lǚguǎn; ☑ 139 0891 1167; Baber; d ¥180) You'll find better value in town, but not a warmer or more authentic welcome than at this Tibetan-run guesthouse and restaurant. Rooms are spotlessly clean but a bit rough and none have attached bathrooms (there are clean sinks and squat toilets down the hallway but no showers). It's 100m west of the Kangjong, opposite the petrol station. The restaurant serves a mean yak meat and potato curry with chapatis.

Kangjong Hotel   HOTEL $$
(雪域宾馆; Xuěyù Bīnguǎn; ☑ 139 8992 3995; Baber; d ¥220-280, without bathroom ¥80; 🛜) The new blocks have good-quality carpeted rooms, clean bathrooms and hot water. Rooms in the older block above the road, with toilets down the hall (no showers), are dim and scruffy. The attached restaurant (dishes ¥20 to ¥50) is a good place to kick back with your guide over a thermos of sweet tea. The hotel is in the middle of town at the crossroads to Shegar.

Qomolangma Hotel Tingri   HOTEL $$
(定日珠峰宾馆; Dìngrì Zhūfēng Bīnguǎn; ☑ 826 2775; Baber; standard/superior d ¥300/350) Driving into this huge compound feels like entering a Peoples Liberation Army barracks circa 1956, with regimented Chinese tour groups taking the place of soldiers. Rooms are modern and clean (though not better than the

Kangjong), especially the newer and fresher superior rooms. It's on the south side of the river on the way to Shegar. You can suck on the inhouse oxygen tank for ¥70 per hour.

Dìngrì Yíng Bīnguǎn   HOTEL $$
(定日迎宾馆; ☑ 182 8909 3999; Zhufeng Nanlu, Shegar; r ¥380) Brand new, modern option, which opened in 2014, with clean, carpeted and spacious rooms with en-suite bathrooms.

Shànghǎi Dàjiǔdiàn   HOTEL $$
(上海大酒店; ☑ 826 2858; Xuebao Lu, Shegar; d/tr ¥300/390) A modern Chinese tour-group hotel with en-suite bathrooms and hot showers.

❶ Getting There & Away

Baber is around 80km from Lhatse and 60km from Tingri.

Everest Region

For foreign travellers, Everest Base Camp has become one of the most popular destinations in Tibet, offering the chance to gaze on the magnificent north face of the world's tallest peak, **Mt Everest** (珠穆朗玛峰; Zhūmùlǎngmǎ Fēng; 8848m). The Tibetan approach provides far better vistas than those on the Nepali side, and access is a lot easier as a road runs all the way to Base Camp.

Everest's Tibetan name is generally rendered as Qomolangma, and some 27,000 sq km of territory around Everest's Tibetan face have been designated as the Qomolangma Nature Reserve.

There are two roads into the Everest region: the main road from Baber via Chay

---

> ### ❶ DRIVING TO EVEREST
>
> The road to Everest Base Camp from Chay was being upgraded in 2014. Until it reopens in 2016 all road access to Everest is along the dirt road from Tingri over the Lamna-la. The impact of this is that hotels in Baber are currently much quieter than those in Tingri. You'll have to check with your agency to see if the road from Baber has reopened. If it has, it will be possible to drive into the Everest region from Chay and then drive out via Tingri, saving you some kilometres if you are headed to the Nepali border.

and the Pang-la; and from Tingri via the Lamna-la.

The main road to Everest begins around 6km west of the Shegar/Baber checkpoint. The 91km drive takes around two to three hours. About 3km from the Friendship Hwy your entry ticket will be checked at the village of Chay, from where it's a winding drive up to the Pang-la (5050m). The views here are stupendous on a clear day, and feature a huge sweep of the Himalaya range, including Makalu, Lhotse, Everest, Gyachung and Cho Oyu.

The road descends past a couple of photogenic villages and drops into the fertile Dza-ka Valley and the village of Tashi Dzom (also known as Peruche), where you can get lunch or a bed for the night. The road then runs up the wide valley to the village of Pagsum, which also offers accommodation. The next main village is Chö Dzom and from here the road turns south towards Rongphu (also Rong-puk or Rongbuk). The first views of Everest appear half an hour before you arrive at Rongphu.

The alternative driving route from Tingri is shorter at 70km but the corrugated and dusty road makes for a bumpier ride. After a permit check outside Tingri, the dirt road passes a mani *lhakhang* at Gandapa village and then branches left at the junction to Cho Oyu Base Camp. You pass the ridgetop monastery at Cholong and then Lonchung village and the ruins of Ngang Tsang Drag Dog Dzong, before climbing slowly to the

5100m Lamna-la, 27km from Tingri. The route then descends for 10km to Zombuk village to join the main valley road near the ruins of the Chö-puk hermitage across the river. From Zombuk it's 21km to Rongphu.

For an overview map of routes into the Everest region see the Trekking chapter.

Permits

Apart from the normal Tibet travel permits, you need to buy an entry ticket for Qomolangma Nature Reserve, either in Baber or in the Snow Leopard Guesthouse (p156) in Tingri. The permit costs ¥400 per vehicle plus ¥180 per passenger. Your guide will also need a ticket. Make sure you are clear with your agency about whether this cost is included in your trip (it usually isn't).

Your passport and PSB permit will be scrutinised at the major checkpoint 6km west of Shegar, where you'll have to personally walk through the passport check. The park permit is checked at the Chay checkpoint 3km after the turn-off from the Friendship Hwy, and then again just before Rongphu Monastery. If you are driving in from Tingri, you'll go to the checkpoint at Lungchang.

❶ Dangers & Annoyances

At this elevation of around 5000m it's important that you keep a close eye out for symptoms of acute mountain sickness (AMS, also known as altitude sickness). People coming from the low altitudes of the Kathmandu Valley are particularly

---

IT'S PRONOUNCED EVE-REST, DARLING

In 1856, Andrew Waugh, surveyor general of India, released the most important finding of the mapping of the 'Great Arc' of mountains from the south of India to the Himalayas: Peak XV was the highest mountain in the world and would henceforth be known as 'Mount Everest', in honour of Waugh's predecessor, Sir George Everest (actually pronounced 'eve-rest').

Waugh's proposal met with much initial opposition, including from Everest himself, who thought a local name should be used. In response Waugh claimed that there was no 'local name that we can discover'. But this was almost certainly untrue, even if Waugh himself didn't know it. Very likely there were many scholars who knew the Tibetan name for the mountain, Qomolangma, which can be interpreted as 'Goddess Mother of the Universe' or (more literally, if less poetically) 'Princess Cow'. As early as 1733, the French produced a map on which Everest is indicated as Tschoumou Lancma. In addition, on the very day that Waugh's paper on Everest was presented to the Royal Geographic Society, another was read that revealed the local Nepali name to be Deodhunga (it's currently called Sagarmatha on the Nepali side).

Still, the Everest contingent gained the upper hand (even the writer of the Nepali paper wanted the great man's name used) and in 1865 the Royal Geographic Society declared 'Mt Everest' would henceforth designate the world's highest mountain.

susceptible. Whatever you do, don't attempt to walk to Everest Base Camp directly after arriving in Tingri from Nepal. The altitude gain of over 2600m leaves most people reeling. Even those coming from Lhasa often have trouble.

It's also important to realise just how high and remote you are, and to carry warm clothing and some kind of rain gear no matter what time of year you visit and no matter how short your walk. Unlike on the Nepali side, there is no rescue service up here in the shadow of Everest. Get caught wearing shorts and a T-shirt when a sudden rain or snowfall hits and you could be in serious trouble.

The Chinese maintain a small military presence at Everest Base Camp to deal with any potential trouble, which includes attempts to camp or trek past Base Camp (you can only trek past Base Camp if you have special trekking permits). Mostly, however, they are there to jump on any Tibetan-flag-waving political activists.

◉ Sights

Rongphu Monastery BUDDHIST, MONASTERY
(admission ¥25) Although religious centres have existed in the region since around the 8th century, Rongphu Monastery (4980m) is now the main Buddhist centre in the valley. While not of great antiquity, Rongphu can at least lay claim to being the highest monastery in Tibet and, thus, the world. It's worth walking the short kora path around the monastery's exterior walls. The monastery and its large chörten make a superb photograph with Everest thrusting its head skyward in the background.

Rongphu was established with the name Dongnga Chöling in 1902 by the Nyingmapa lama Tsedru Ngawan Tenzin. It has traditionally coordinated the activities of around a dozen smaller religious institutions, all of which are now ruined. Renovation work has been ongoing since 1983, and some of the interior murals are superb. Upstairs is a large statue of Guru Rinpoche. Unusually, the 38 monks and nuns currently share the monastery, though new accommodation is being built for the nuns next to the monastery guesthouse.

For a great hike follow the walking trail south from the monastery for 30 minutes to the ruins of **Rong Chong**, Rongphu's former meditation retreat. En route you'll pass a ruined nunnery, which is still home to a couple of nuns in retreat. If in doubt about the way, follow the electricity poles. Below the ruins, next to the road, is a set of springs.

WORTH A TRIP

HIKING TO EVEREST

If you are not overly affected by the altitude, it's well worth walking the 4km from the tent camp to Everest Base Camp. The way up is gentle and the altitude gain is less than 200m: most people can cover the distance in around an hour. Along the way you pass scree slopes, jagged ridges, broad glacial valleys and stunning views of Everest. Short-cut paths avoid most of the road. Set off early as the buses start rumbling past around 9am.

Less than 10 minutes' walk from the tent camp, it's well worth visiting the **Dza Rongphu retreat**, on the left, with its photogenic collection of chörtens framed by Mt Everest. The lone resident monk will show you the trap door that drops to the atmospheric meditation cave of Guru Rinpoche (Padmasambhava).

Tent Camp CAMP
About 4km beyond Rongbuk in the direction of Base Camp is this messy corral of yak-hair tents (5050m), parked Land Cruisers and souvenir stalls. This is the furthest point vehicles can drive to; from here you'll have to walk the final 4km to Everest Base Camp or take a minibus (¥25 return). A small post office (surely the world's highest?) offers the chance to send a postcard from Everest.

Don't come expecting an isolated camp of welcoming nomads – Tibetans from Tashi Dzom and other nearby villages run the tents like small hotels. It's a scrappy location for sure but the views towards Everest's north face are amazing.

So that no one tent gets too much business, each tent is allowed a maximum of five tourists. Large groups are divided into different tents, and some groups have reported that they were not even allowed to eat together in the same tent. A few tents have beer for sale if you are in the mood to celebrate but be very circumspect about drinking at this altitude.

Everest Base Camp CAMP
(ཇོ་མོ་གླང་མའི་རིས་གའི་འོག) Endowed with springs, Everest Base Camp (5150m) was first used by the 1924 British Everest expedition. Tourists are not allowed to visit the expedition tents a few hundred metres away but you

THE ASSAULT ON EVEREST

There had been 13 attempts to climb Everest (8848m) before Edmund Hillary and Sherpa Tenzing Norgay finally reached the summit as part of John Hunt's major British expedition of 1953. Some of them verged on insanity.

In 1934 Edmund Wilson, an eccentric ex-British army captain, hatched a plan to fly himself from Hendon direct to the Himalayas, crash-land his Gypsy Moth halfway up Everest and then climb solo to the summit, despite having no previous mountaineering experience (and marginal flying expertise). Needless to say he failed spectacularly. When his plane was impounded by the British in India he trekked to Rongphu in disguise and made a solo bid for the summit. He disappeared somewhere above Camp III, and his body and diaries were later discovered by the mountaineer Eric Shipton at 6400m. A second solo effort was later attempted by a disguised Canadian from the Tibet side. It was abandoned at 7150m.

From 1921 to 1938, all expeditions to Everest were British and were attempted from the north (Tibetan) side, along a route reconnoitred by John Noel – disguised as a Tibetan – in 1913. The mountain claimed 14 lives in this period. Perhaps the most famous early-summit bid was by George Mallory and Andrew Irvine (just 22), who were last seen going strong above 7800m before clouds obscured visibility. Their deaths remained a mystery until May 1999 when an American team found Mallory's body, reigniting theories that the pair may have reached the top two decades before Norgay and Hillary. It was Mallory who, when asked why he wanted to climb Everest, famously quipped 'because it is there'.

With the conclusion of WWII and the collapse of the British Raj, the Himalayas became inaccessible. Tibet closed its doors to outsiders and, in 1951, the Chinese invasion clamped them shut even more tightly. In mountaineering terms, however, the Chinese takeover had the positive effect of shocking the hermit kingdom of Nepal into looking for powerful friends. The great peaks of the Himalayas suddenly became accessible from Nepal.

In 1951, Eric Shipton led a British reconnaissance expedition that explored the Nepali approaches to Everest and came to the conclusion that an assault via Nepal might indeed be met with success. Much to their dismay, the British found that the mountain was no longer theirs alone. In 1952 Nepal issued only one permit to climb Everest – to the Swiss, extremely able climbers who together with the British had virtually invented mountaineering as a sport. British climbers secretly feared that the Swiss might mount a successful ascent on their first attempt, when eight major British expeditions had failed. As it happened, the

can clamber up the small hill festooned with prayer flags for great views of the star attraction.

Most people have their photo taken at the 'Mt Qomolangma Base Camp' marker, which indicates that you are at 5200m above sea level. (Other measurements have it at 5020m or 5150m.) The springs are just to the left of this marker.

Note that you can get mobile-phone reception at Base Camp. Phone a friend. They'll be thrilled.

🛏 Sleeping & Eating

Rongphu Monastery

Guesthouse GUESTHOUSE $
(绒布寺招待所, Róngbù Sì Zhāodàisuǒ; ☑136 2892 1359; dm ¥60, tw without bathroom ¥200) The monastery-run guesthouse at Rong-

phu is probably the most comfortable place to stay at Everest. The private rooms with proper beds tend to be warmer than the tent camp and there's certainly more privacy. The best value is a bed in a four-bed room. All rooms share the pit toilets. Come the evenings everyone huddles around the yak-dung stove in the cosy restaurant (dishes ¥25 to ¥40).

Tent Camp TENTS $
(dm ¥60; ☺ end Mar–mid-Oct) The main alternative to staying at Rongphu is this motley collection of yak-hair tents. Don't expect much privacy: tents sleep six people (your host and perhaps one or two of their relatives will be sharing the space with you) in an open area around the central stove. Even with the fire going it's still bloody cold. Simple meals (¥25) and drinks are available.

Swiss climbed to 8595m on the southeast ridge – higher than any previous expedition – but could not reach the summit.

The next British attempt was assigned for 1953. Preparations were particularly tense. It was generally felt that if this attempt were unsuccessful, any British hopes to be the first to reach the summit would be dashed. There was considerable back-room manoeuvring before the expedition set off, which saw Eric Shipton, leader of three previous expeditions (including one in 1935), dropped as team leader. In his place was John Hunt, an army officer and keen Alpine mountaineer, though relatively unknown among British climbers.

Shipton's 1951 expedition had at the last minute accepted two New Zealand climbers. One was Edmund Hillary, professional bee-keeper and a man of enormous determination. He was invited to join Hunt's 1953 expedition, which was also joined by Tenzing Norgay, a Sherpa who had set out on his first Everest expedition in 1935, at the age of 19.

On 28 May 1953, Hillary and Norgay made a precarious camp at 8370m on a tiny platform on the southeast approach to the summit, while the other anxious members of the expedition waited below at various camps. That night the two men feasted on chicken noodle soup and dates. The pair set off early the next day (29 May) and after a five-hour final push they reached the top at 11.30am, planting the flag for Britain on the highest point on earth.

By 2014, about 4400 people had reached the peak of Everest (including George Mallory II, Mallory's grandson), while 248 climbers had died in the attempt. The first woman to reach the summit was Junko Tabei from Japan, on 16 May 1975. The youngest person was 13-year-old Jordan Romero from California, who reached the top in May 2010. The oldest person to make the climb was Yuichiro Miura of Japan, who scaled the peak in 2013 at the age of 80. Over two-thirds of the climbers who summit Everest do so from the Nepali side.

Of all the controversies that Everest generates in the world of mountaineering, its height is not one that should still be an issue. But in May 1999 an American expedition planted a global positioning system (GPS) at the top of Everest and pegged the height at a controversial 8850m – 2m higher than the 8848m accepted since 1954. The Chinese dispute this claim (and even recently lowered the height by 1.5m due to melting of the summit ice cap). Of course, plate tectonics are also at play. It is believed that the summit rises 4mm per year and is shifting 3mm to 6mm per year in a northeasterly direction.

For the latest on Everest, check out www.everestnews.com.

TSANG EVEREST REGION

Bear in mind that in July and August up to 500 people bunk down here at night, with everyone sharing the two pit toilets, so it's no surprise that they rank as some of the worst in Tibet. Be careful with your belongings as the tents are open all the time and offer no security. It's best to leave everything in your 4WD if possible. Some tents can get smoky inside.

Blankets are provided but you're better off with a subzero sleeping bag.

Chomolongma Benba
Guesthouse　　　　　　　　GUESTHOUSE **$**
(☑ 139 0892 0952; Tashi Dzom; dm/d ¥60/160) If you want to break up the drive to Everest, or want to avoid sleeping at high elevation, this family home in the village of Tashi Dzom has several rooms and a cosy restaurant. At 4150m, it's 1000m lower than Base Camp,

which will make a vital difference if you are experiencing symptoms of AMS. A large, modern hotel is due to open in the village in 2015.

Guāngjǐngtái Bīnguǎn　　　　HOTEL **$$**
(光景台宾馆; ☑ 139 0892 8499; dm/d ¥100/300) Across from the Rongphu Monastery Guesthouse, this ugly government hotel has rooms that are simple but clean. There are fine views from the comfortable restaurant and viewing terraces but, despite the price, you won't get a private bathroom or a shower.

❶ Getting There & Away

There is no public transport to Everest Base Camp. It's either trek in or come with your own 4WD. From Chay it's 91km to Base Camp; from Tingri it's around 70km.

Tingri རྡིང་རི་ 定日

ELEV 4330M

The village of Tingri (Dìngrì or Tingri Gankar), 142km from Lhatse, comprises a gritty kilometre-long strip of restaurants, guesthouses and truck-repair workshops lining the Friendship Hwy. Sometimes called Old Tingri, it overlooks a sweeping plain bordered by towering Himalayan peaks and is a usual overnight stop for tours heading to or from the Nepali border. On clear days there are stunning views of Cho Oyu from Tingri; if you can't make it to Everest Base Camp, at least pause here and take in the Himalayan eye candy. Newcomers from Kathmandu will likely experience some symptoms of altitude sickness if they have not acclimatised in Nyalam.

You can drive up the hill overlooking Tingri to the ruins that remain of **Tingri Dzong** after it was destroyed by Nepali invaders in the late 18th century. On the plains between Shegar and Tingri, dozens more ruins that shared the same fate can be seen from the Friendship Hwy.

It is possible to trek between Everest Base Camp and Tingri or vice versa, though much of the route now follows a dirt road. If you are heading to Base Camp by vehicle there is a rough 4WD track from Tingri.

In Tingri, entry tickets to Qomolangma Nature Reserve are available at an office within the compound of the **Snow Leopard Guesthouse** (☑156 9262 6148, 826 3006; r¥110).

🛏 Sleeping

Most places look like truckers' motels, which fits the mood because Tingri is little more than a truck stop en route to other places. Expect to see basic double rooms set around a dusty main courtyard with pit toilets. All are essentially overpriced.

Tingri Snowland Hotel HOTEL $
(定日雪域饭店, Dìngrì Xuěyù Fàndiàn; ☑152 0801 9009; dm/d/tr ¥35/100/120) About 800m west of the centre of town, Snowland enjoys fine Himalayan views but the rooms are poky, with cloth-covered walls and basic mattresses. The restaurant has a large menu. Showers cost ¥10.

Héhū Bīnguǎn HOTEL $$
(合呼宾馆, ☑136 4892 2335; dm ¥50-80, d with bathroom ¥260) This large hotel probably has the edge over other places in town. The ensuite rooms are clean and carpeted with a

Western toilet and hot-water shower. The price of the beds in the cheaper rooms depends on the quality of the mattresses. There are shared squat toilets but no shared hot showers.

Snow Leopard Guesthouse HOTEL $$
(雪豹客栈, Xuěbào Kèzhàn; ☑826 2711; d with/without bathroom ¥280/100) Some 4WD drivers and guides try to swing their customers here but look at a few other places in town first. Rooms come with attached bathroom. The mountain views are better here because it's out on the eastern edge of town.

🍴 Eating

★**Base Camp Restaurant** TIBETAN $$
(大本营餐厅, Dàběnyíng Cāntīng; dishes ¥20-50; 🍴) The best place in town is this pleasant Tibetan-style restaurant attached to the Héhū Bīnguǎn, boasting traditional furniture, helpful staff and tasty Chinese and Tibetan dishes. Prices are reasonable for Tingri.

Around Tingri

The odourless, iron-rich **Tsamda Hot Springs** (ཚ་མདའ་ཆུ་ཚན་; ☑139 0892 4147) 12km west of Tingri are piped directly into a tepid public pool (¥20), or you can rent a private room with simple bath (¥40) for a couple of hours. Don't expect spa treatments but it might be just the thing for cleaning yourself off after a day or two at Everest Base Camp.

Accommodation is available (dorm beds ¥35, doubles ¥280), though it's quite simple and somewhat overpriced. If you do stay there are some pleasant easy walks around the nearby hills that offer superb views of Cho Oyu. The springs are 1km off the Friendship Hwy and are signposted in English near kilometre marker 5206.

Nyalam གཉའ་ལམ་ 聂拉木

☑0892 / ELEV 3750M

Nyalam (Nièlāmù) is a one-street town with a fairly grim Chinese facade. It's about 30km from the Nepali border, 152km from Tingri, and is a usual first overnight spot for 4WD trips coming from Nepal. It's also a base for trekking in the southern Shishapangma region. Unless you are sleeping here (most people headed for Nepal will sleep in Zhāngmù) your driver will probably bomb through the town, honking and scattering locals in your wake.

There is a good (read: clean) **Internet Bar** (网吧, wǎngbā; per hr ¥10) across from the Nyalam Nga-Dhon Guesthouse.

One possible day hike from here takes you up the valley behind Nyalam to Daratso, a holy lake from which glaciers of the Langtang and Jungal Himal, and maybe even Shishapangma (the only mountain over 8000m planted squarely in Tibet), are visible on a clear day.

⊙ Sights

Milarepa's Cave   BUDDHIST, TEMPLE

(admission ¥25) The only cultural sight close to Nyalam is Milarepa's Cave. Most people can safely skip the chapel without disappointment, though the views of the surrounding valley are pleasant.

Milarepa was a famous Buddhist mystic and composer of songs who lived in the late 11th and early 12th centuries. During his time spent in long meditation in this cave he renounced all luxuries and survived on a diet of local weeds (famously turning green as a result).

A brand new assembly hall surrounds the cave, which is just below the cave of Milarepa's disciple Rechungpa. Milarepa's cave is 11km north of Nyalam, at Gangka village.

🛏 Sleeping

Between May and September Nyalam's hotels tend to get booked out with large groups of Indian pilgrims headed to Mt Kailash, so it's worth phoning ahead to secure a reservation. In general Nyalam's hotels are overpriced.

Nyalam Nga-Dhon Guesthouse   HOTEL $$

(聂拉木阿顿旅馆, Nièlāmù Ādùn Lǚguǎn; ☑827 2113; 2 Chongdui Lu; d ¥200-300, without bathroom ¥100) This well-run Tibetan place is the best bet for budget travellers, with simple Tibetan-style rooms with shared bathroom starting at ¥50 per bed. The pleasant attached restaurant has an English menu and is a good bet (mains ¥25 to ¥35).

For ¥200, you will get a dark en-suite room in the side block with a squat toilet. The best rooms overlook the main road and are clean and fresh with a Western bathroom.

New Snowlands Hotel   HOTEL $$

(雪域饭店聂拉木, Xuěyù Fàndiàn Nièlāmù; ☑136 3892 0177; r without bathroom ¥280) Prices at this modern hotel are over the top but the rooms are comfortable, with good mattresses,

and the shared sinks, Western toilets and hot showers down the hall are spotless and modern. Ask for a higher floor room. Triples and doubles are the same price.

Nyalam Hotel   HOTEL $$

(聂拉木宾馆, Nièlāmù Bīnguǎn; ☑827 9999; 28 Yantai Lu; d with/without bathroom ¥300/120) The three-star Nyalam has fresh and modern carpeted rooms in the main roadside building. The much simpler concrete rooms without bathroom in the grimmer back block are worth avoiding.

Shishapangma Hotel   HOTEL $$

(希夏邦马宾馆, Xīxiàbāngmǎ Bīnguǎn; ☑8277 2191; dm/tw ¥60/320) One of several hotels located at the southern edge of town that caters mostly to groups of Indian pilgrims. Most of the rooms are dormitory style, though there are a few doubles and triples, all of which share the clean bathroom (hot showers ¥10). It's at the top of the hill on the Zhāngmù side (just past the petrol station).

Shishapangma Hotel International   HOTEL $$$

(☑136 5892 8053; r without bathroom ¥250-400, d ¥350, ste ¥600-700) Nyalam's biggest and newest hotel is surprisingly grand and easily ranks as Tibet's best hotel west of Shigatse. The building overlooks Nyalam from the main Friendship Hwy bypass, offering fine valley views. Rooms are spacious and modern and guests are offered a free traditional dance show in the auditorium. There are also three-, four- or six-bed rooms with shared bathrooms.

✕ Eating

Snowland Restaurant   INTERNATIONAL $

(雪域餐厅, Xuěyù Cāntīng; ☑827 2111; dishes ¥20-35; 🍴) Popular with alpinists (every one of whom seems to have left a memento on the wall), the Snowland doles out a few Western dishes, including some filling pancakes, but is strongest on Tibetan and Chinese food. It's located up a rickety flight of stairs.

Tibetan Village Restaurant   TIBETAN $

(臧家乐, Zāngjiālè; dishes ¥20-30) Bright and hip, with Tibetan-style decor and friendly staff, this is the place for good Tibetan food in civilised surroundings.

Kailash Cafe   NEPALI $$

(尼泊尔风味便餐, Níbó'ěr Fēngwèi Biàncān; ☑182 8909 8771; meals ¥30) If you have a hankering for a chicken-curry set and just can't wait until you get to Nepal, this simple Nepali-run place offers a limited range of authentic home-cooked food washed down with masala chai.

ℹ Information

People's Showers (大众浴室, Dàzhòng Yùshì; shower ¥25; ☺8.30am-11pm) If your guesthouse doesn't have hot water, head to these public showers next to Nga-Dhon Guesthouse.

ℹ Getting There & Away

The only way here is by 4WD, hitching or cycling.

Nyalam to Zhāngmù

From Nyalam, the road drops like a stone off the Tibetan plateau into a deep gorge of evergreen forests, waterfalls and thundering rivers. Such noise and colour and drama after the dry, stark landscape of Tibet is a joy to the senses. Perhaps most amazing are the dozen or more waterfalls, many well over 200m tall, any one of which would be considered a great attraction anywhere else.

During the summer monsoons the road is submerged in a sea of cloud – no doubt one of the reasons why Nyalam means 'gateway to hell' in Tibetan. Temporary road blockages are common at this time.

Zhāngmù (Dram) རྫྭ་ 樟木

☑0892 / ELEV 2250M

Zhāngmù, also known as Dram in Tibetan and Khasa in Nepali, hugs the rim of what seems a never-ending succession of hairpin bends just above the border of China and Nepal. After the high plateau, it all seems incredibly green and wet.

Zhāngmù is a typical border town, much larger than Nyalam, and has a restless, reckless feel to it. There is one far-too-narrow main road through town and it gets backed up frequently. During these times the squealing of Tata truck brakes as the vehicles inch their way down will drive you insane.

All those hairpin bends can leave you spinning and upon first arrival it can be difficult to figure out where you are, relative to everything else on your map. The best way to orient yourself is to walk all the way downhill until you reach the Zhāngmù Hotel; within a few minutes' walk back uphill

you'll pass most of the hotels and restaurants reviewed by us.

Evening reveals the town's seedy side as its numerous downmarket discos, bars and brothels open for business; a sort of Tijuana-in-miniature. With its Nepali goods and thumping Bollywood soundtrack, the town feels more like a part of Nepal than anywhere else, with only a few indications that you're still in Tibet.

🛏 Sleeping

Try to get a room off the road, preferably facing the mountains, because the noise from traffic can be awful.

Jīnxīn Bīnguǎn HOTEL $
(金鑫宾馆; ☑874 3299; d¥150; 🐱) There's not much English spoken at this Chinese-run hotel but it's a good budget option if your guide doesn't mind you staying here, with comfortable rooms and attached hot-water bathrooms separated by glass walls. There's wi-fi in the lobby.

Lucien Sunny Youth Hostel HOSTEL $
(路晟阳光青年旅舍, Lùchéng Yángguāng Qīngnián Lǚshè; ☑874 2299; Sunny_guesthouse@163.com; 49 Yingbin Lu; dm ¥35-45, d ¥120) Rooms at this friendly Chinese youth hostel used to be the best value in town but at last check standards had dropped following a change of management. See if the bright rooms with homey duvets and pebble-floor showers are once again a good deal.

Gang Gyen Hotel HOTEL $
(刚坚宾馆, Gāngjiān Bīnguǎn; ☑874 2188; 2 Yingbin Lu; d with/without bathroom ¥200/130) If you're not put off by the dirty and dark stairwells then you might not mind the stained and shabby rooms at this exhausted and dingy hotel. On a positive note, it has a useful location at the bottom end of town. Consider it a backup option if others are full.

Sherpa Hotel HOTEL $$
(夏尔巴酒店, Xià'ěrbā Jiǔdiàn; ☑874 2098; d with/without bathroom ¥230/120; 🐱) The pink-painted rooms are clean (if a little small) at this friendly hotel, and hot water is available most of the time in the simple bathrooms. Back rooms are bright and sunny with valley views.

Property Hotel HOTEL $$
(财源宾馆,Cáiyuán Bīnguǎn;☑8745888; d¥360; ❋🐱) Midrange Land Cruiser groups like this

modern, new place for its clean, good-quality (but smallish) rooms, en-suite bathrooms and decent breakfasts.

Zhāngmù Hotel HOTEL **$$$**
(樟木宾馆, Zhāngmù Bīnguǎn; ☑874 2221; fax 874 2220; d without bathroom/with breakfast ¥100/400; 🛜) The modern rooms in this government-run hotel are comfortable by Tibetan standards, and back rooms have great mountain views. It's popular with Western groups. The cheaper rooms with shared bathroom are used mostly by drivers and guides. There's wi-fi but only in the lobby.

✕ Eating

Zhāngmù feels like a mini-Kathmandu, at least in its restaurant options, which offer an excellent selection of Western, Chinese, Tibetan and Nepali cuisine.

Sonam's Restaurant NEPALI, INTERNATIONAL **$$**
(索朗西餐厅, Suǒlǎng Xī Cāntīng; ☑135 4902 8933; mains ¥20-40; 🍴) The wildly ambitious menu includes pasta arrabiata and crepes with mushrooms and asparagus, but Nepali chef Sanjay claims to be able to do it all. The chicken sizzler and muesli with fruit and yoghurt may be safer bets but it all looks good and prices are reasonable. It's just uphill from the Zhāngmù Hotel.

Sherpa Tashi Restaurant INTERNATIONAL, TIBETAN **$$**
(夏尔巴餐厅, Xià'ěrbā Cāntīng; ☑874 2098; dishes ¥25-40; ⊙breakfast, lunch & dinner; 🍴) Located in the Sherpa Hotel, this Nepali-run place does everything from Tibetan *momos* to pasta and burgers, and the Nepali curries pack a punch with the spices. Service is friendly and there are sometimes baked goods available.

ℹ Information

Money changers deal openly in front of the Zhāngmù Hotel and change any combination of Chinese yuán, US dollars and Nepali rupees at substantially better rates than the bank or anywhere on the Nepali side.

Bank of China (中国银行, Zhōngguó Yínháng; ⊙9.30am-1pm & 3.30-6pm Mon-Fri, 11am-2pm Sat & Sun) This branch at the top end of town will change cash and travellers cheques into yuán and also yuán into dollars, euros or pounds, but doesn't deal in Nepali rupees. The ATM accepts Mastercard, Maestro, Cirrus, Visa and Plus cards.

Zhāngmù (Dram)

ⓞ Sights

Public Security Bureau (公安局; PSB; Gōng'ānjú; ☑874 2264; ⊙9.30am-1pm & 3.30-6.30pm Mon-Fri) If you are headed to Nyalam your guide will probably have to get a stamp at the Zhāngmù PSB. Chinese tourists also have to get stamped here if they are headed to Nepal. Beyond this, the office doesn't have much to do with tourists and cannot extend your visa. It's located between the Zhāngmù and Sherpa Hotels.

ℹ Getting There & Away

For **Chinese immigration** (⊙10am-5.30pm, sometimes closed 1.30-3.30pm) and customs you need to drive to the actual border at Kodari, around 8km below Zhāngmù. Your guide and driver will drop you off or pick you up at Kodari, although taxis also do the run.

You will need to fill in an exit form and health declaration and you may be asked for your travel permit. You will have to walk the last few metres over the Friendship Bridge.

At **Nepali immigration** (⊙8.30am-4pm) in Kodari it's possible to get a Nepali visa for the same price as in Lhasa (US$25/40/100 for up to 15/30/90 days, or the equivalent in rupees at a poor exchange rate), although it is sensible to check this in advance. You need one passport photo (or pay US$5 extra).

If you are coming from Nepal into Zhāngmù, you won't find Chinese immigration open if you leave the Nepali side after 3.30pm. Note that Nepal is an odd 2¼ hours behind Chinese time.

There are four daily buses between Kodari and Kathmandu (4½ hours), with a 1.30pm express service. Otherwise jump a local bus to Barabise (three hours) and change there. After 2pm your only option is to take a taxi for Rs 4500, or Rs 1500 per seat if shared. Jeeps cost slightly more.

Western Tibet (Ngari)
མངའ་རིས་

Best Views

➡ Humla Karnali Valley from Shepeling (Simbaling) Monastery (p185)

➡ Tagyel-tso (p168), or anywhere along the northern route

➡ Mt Kailash floating over the waters of Rakshas Tal (p175)

Best Places off the Beaten Track

➡ Gossul Monastery (p177)

➡ Ruins of Shangshung (p178) in the Khyunglung Valley

➡ Old Rutok (p184)

Why Go?

Vast, thinly populated and with an average altitude of over 4500m, Ngari is a rough and ready frontier occupying one of the remotest corners of Asia. For most travellers the main attractions of what is likely to be a two- or three-week overland trip are the almost legendary destinations of Mt Kailash and Lake Manasarovar. Indeed, many of the Tibetan and Indian pilgrims on this road have been planning a visit all their lives. For those less fussed by the spiritual significance of Mt Kailash, travelling over the Changtang (the high plateau), with its endless steppes and impossibly high snow-capped peaks, is likely to be an attraction in itself.

Freshly paved roads and a new airport are opening up the region in a way unimaginable a mere decade ago. There's no escaping mass Chinese tourism now, but the faster routes do open up all sort of possibilities for detours to still-off-the-beaten track destinations.

When to Go

➡ May to June and mid-September to early October are the best times to head to Ngari, though June and July see huge convoys of Indian pilgrims booking out entire hotels on their way to Mt Kailash.

➡ April to October is best for the Drölma-la pass on the Mt Kailash kora, as it's normally blocked with snow during other months (though you wouldn't be permitted into the region during these other months in any case).

➡ The festival of Saga Dawa in May/June is a particularly popular time to visit Mt Kailash, and hundreds of pilgrims and tourists descend on the mountain. Unfortunately, this is also a potentially sensitive time due to the Chinese government's control over the area, so the region may be closed to foreign travellers.

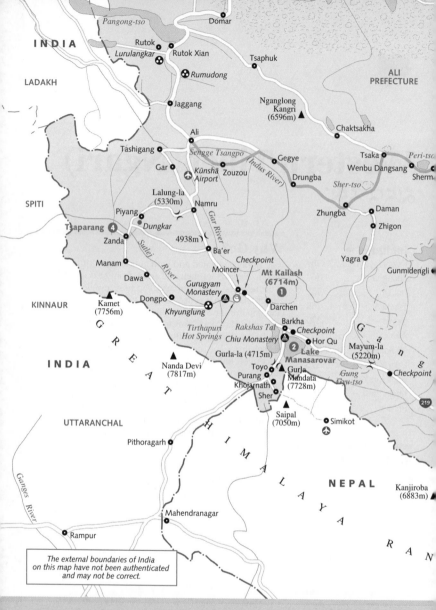

Western Tibet (Ngari) Highlights

1 Joining fellow pilgrims and erasing the sins of a lifetime on the three-day trek around sacred **Mt Kailash** (p173).

2 Hiking the sandy shores of holy **Lake Manasarovar** (p175), or just marvelling at the turquoise waters and snow-capped mountain backdrop.

3 Camping on the shores of the spectacular otherworldly lakes of **Tagyel-tso** (p169), **Dawa-tso** (p169) and **Peiku-tso** (p166).

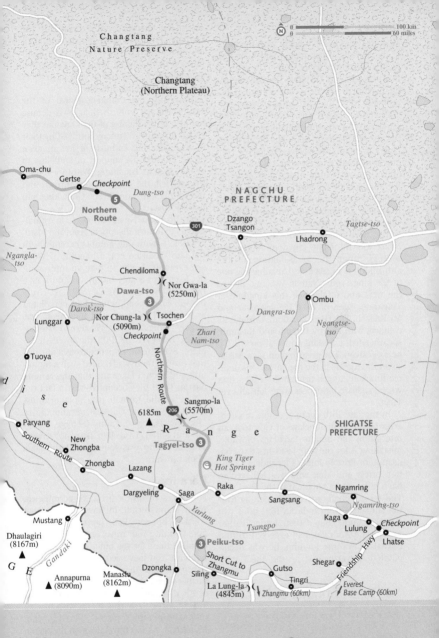

④ Scrambling through cliffside tunnels and secret passageways as you explore the ancient ruins and Kashmiri-influenced mural art of **Tsaparang** (p181), one of Asia's unknown wonders.

⑤ Spotting herds of wild asses, antelope and gazelle in the untrammelled wilderness of the Changtang, Tibet's Serengeti, along the **northern route** (p168) to Ali.

History

Most histories of Tibet begin with the kings of the Yarlung Valley region and their unification of central Tibet in the 7th century. But it is thought that the Shangshung (or Zhangzhung) kingdom of western Tibet probably ruled the Tibetan plateau for several centuries before this. According to some scholars, the Bön religion made its way into the rest of Tibet from here. The Shangshung kingdom may also have served as a conduit for Tibet's earliest contacts with Buddhism. There is little material evidence of the Shangshung kingdom in modern Tibet, though the Khyunglung Valley, on the Sutlej River near Tirthapuri hot springs, marks the site of the old kingdom.

The next regional power to emerge in Ngari was the Guge kingdom in the 9th century. After the assassination of the anti-Buddhist Lhasa king Langdharma, one of the king's sons, Namde Wosung, fled to the west and established this kingdom at Tsaparang, west of Lake Manasarovar and Mt Kailash. The Guge kingdom, through its contacts with nearby Ladakh and Kashmir, spearheaded a Buddhist revival on the Tibetan plateau. The great Indian sage Atisha spent three years in the region, and his disciple Rinchen Zangpo brought over 25 artists whose stylistic influences were felt all over Tibet.

In the late 16th century, Jesuit missionaries based in the enclave of Goa took an interest in the remote kingdom of Guge, mistaking it for the long-lost Christian civilisation of Prester John (a legendary Christian priest and king who was believed to have ruled over a kingdom in the Far East). The Jesuits finally reached Tsaparang over the Himalaya from India in 1624 after two failed attempts, but if their leader, Father Antonio de Andrade, had expected to find Christians waiting for him, he was disappointed. Nevertheless, he did meet with surprising tolerance and respect for the Christian faith. The Guge king agreed to allow de Andrade to return and set up a Jesuit mission the following year. The foundation stone of the first Christian church in Tibet was laid by the king himself.

Ironically, the evangelical zeal of the Jesuits led not only to their own demise but also to the demise of the kingdom they sought to convert. Lamas, outraged by their king's increasing enthusiasm for an alien creed, enlisted the support of Ladakhis in laying siege to Tsaparang. Within a month the city fell, the king was overthrown and the Jesuits imprisoned. The Guge kingdom never recovered.

At this point, Ngari became so marginalised as to almost disappear from the history books – with one notable exception. In the late Victorian era, a handful of Western explorers began to take an interest in the legend of a holy mountain and a lake from which four of Asia's mightiest rivers flowed. The legend, which had percolated as far afield as Japan and Indonesia, was largely ridiculed by Western cartographers. However, in 1908 the Swedish explorer Sven Hedin returned from a journey that proved there was indeed such a mountain and such a lake, and that the remote part of Tibet they occupied was in fact the source of the Karnali (the northernmost tributary of the Ganges), Brahmaputra (Yarlung Tsangpo), Indus (Sengge Tsangpo) and Sutlej (Langchen Tsangpo) Rivers. The mountain was Kailash and the lake, Manasarovar.

Permits

Foreigners require a fistful of permits: an Alien Travel Permit, military permit, Tibet Tourism Bureau (TTB) permit, foreign affairs permit... Your travel agency will organise all of these for you but give them at least a month. You may need to stop in Shigatse to process your Alien Travel Permit and may further need to get this endorsed in Darchen or Ali, depending on the direction of travel. This is particularly true if you wish to visit off-the-beaten-track places like Gurugyam Monastery. As you travel through the region your guide will need to register you with the Public Security Bureau (PSB) in some towns (such as Tsochen).

Note that Ngari is a politically sensitive area and periodically closed to foreigners: reasons include political unrest or potential

ⓘ PUBLIC TRANSPORT

At the time of research, foreigners were not allowed to travel on public transport in Tibet. The situation has been the same for years now and is not expected to change in the foreseeable future, so we do not include any public transport information within this chapter.

WHAT TO BRING

Warm clothes are essential, even in summer. The sun is strong and days can be hot, especially in a 4WD, so do bring something light to wear, ideally with SPF protection. A sleeping bag is recommended to avoid grubby truck-stop bedding. Many of the villages, towns and hotels in Ngari are dusty, dirty, depressing places so a tent gives you the flexibility to camp out in some of the most glorious scenery on the planet (assuming the PSB allow you to camp, of course). A tent is also useful (though not essential) if you are doing the Mt Kailash kora. A face-mask can be useful to keep out the copious dust.

Supplies are now easy to get in all the settlements of the west but consider bringing luxuries like instant porridge, muesli (with powdered milk), chocolate, cheese and dehydrated foods from home. A snack supply gives you the flexibility to stop for a picnic lunch somewhere beautiful (or when the car breaks down).

The only places to change money in Ngari are banks in Ali and, less reliably, Purang – it's much easier to change US dollars cash than travellers cheques. It's best to bring as much Renminbi (RMB) as you expect to spend (the chances of it being stolen if you keep it on you are very remote). There are ATMs in Ali and, less reliably, Zanda.

unrest on the Mt Kailash kora (which could simply mean the year is a popular one for mountain pilgrimages); military tension along the contested borders of China, India and Pakistan; or other reasons known only to Chinese officialdom.

In short, it's prudent to always be prepared for your trip to be cancelled, even with little to no notice. Do not blame your agency when this happens: they have no control over the situation and Tibet is not the sort of place where a few dollars can grease the wheels of bureaucracy (at least not with respect to permits).

The official announcement each year for opening Ngari is made in March or April. If your trip is cancelled you can expect a full refund from your agency though it is good to get this in writing beforehand as deposits are now quite hefty (80% in 2014). Airfares are another matter so consider cancellation insurance.

Itineraries

Most trips begin in Lhasa and take between 1½ to three weeks and are designed around a visit to Mt Kailash. Add in a spare day for delays or breakdowns and figure in some time to rest and wash up or you'll gradually get too tired to fully enjoy the trip.

➡ From Lhasa there are two approaches to Kailash: a southern route and a northern route. The southern route is the more popular one, largely because it is the fastest way to Mt Kailash. Although there are no stellar attractions on the longer northern route, the scenery is grander, traffic lighter and wildlife richer.

➡ If you're travelling to/from Kathmandu via the Friendship Hwy, a shortcut to/from Saga (via beautiful Peiku-tso) will shave a full day's travel off your trip. See p166 for more details.

➡ It is also possible to enter the region on a four-day trek from Simikot in the Humla region of western Nepal to Purang on the Chinese border near Mt Kailash. This route is open only to tour groups that trek in from Humla, which is a restricted region.

➡ Finally, there is the Xīnjiāng–Tibet Hwy, one of the highest, remotest and most spectacular roads in Asia. The route passes through the disputed Aksai Chin region; with the unpredictability of breakdowns, it can take several days or more to travel the 1350km from Kashgar to Ali. Since 2008 foreigners have not been able to take public buses. Depending on the permit situation, which varies each year, you might be able to tackle this road in a rented 4WD. See the boxed text on p172 for more.

ⓘ Dangers & Annoyances

If you've acclimatised for a few days in Lhasa, the gradual rate of gain along the southern route to Kailash shouldn't pose any serious problems, though the jump from Lhatse (3950m) to Raka (4925m) or Saga (4610m) involves a potentially dangerous jump in elevation. An overnight at Sakya (4280m) or Rongphu Monastery (4900m) en route will help your body adjust. If you're coming from Nepal you should be particularly careful as you won't be well acclimatised; an overnight in Nyalam (3750m) and either old Tingri (4250m), Baber (4250m) or Lhatse is an excellent idea.

SOUTHERN ROUTES

The upgrading of the 500km section of road from Saga to Hor Qu is now completed, which means driving times from Lhasa to Mt Kailash has been reduced to as little as three days. It is advisable that you don't rush, however, but take time to acclimate.

Saga is the last major town along the southern route and a usual overnight stop. It is at the junction of roads from Lhasa and Nepal, and the following first highlights the routes there from Lhatse (which assumes a start in Lhasa), and then also Zhangmu (which assumes a start in Nepal).

Note that even if coming from Lhatse consider taking the Friendship Hwy and joining with the road from Zhangmu as this allows for a visit to Everest Base Camp and the stunning Peiku-tso.

Lhatse to Saga (306km)

Lhatse is a usual overnight stop on the way from Lhasa to Ngari though a stay in Sakya is actually preferable as there is little to see or do in Lhatse. From Lhatse, or Sakya, to Saga, the next main town, is a full day's journey of about eight hours' driving. Just past the Lhatse checkpoint (6km after Lhatse itself), the road leaves the paved Friendship Hwy and bears northwest. After crossing the Yarlung Tsangpo the road runs for an hour through barren canyons (that swell in the summer rains) and green meadow land with scattered Tibetan villages.

Past the photogenic Lang-tso (Ox Lake) the road climbs up to the Ngamring-la (4500m), and at kilometre marker 2085, 60km from Lhatse, through the very small town of Kaga (Kajia), next to Ngamring-tso, which often appears brown because of the nearby mountains reflecting off its surface. On the other side of the lake is the army base of Ngamring (Angren), which has food and accommodation if you need it.

About 10km past Kaga you'll leave behind the last trees for many days, and soon after the last agricultural fields. Just be-

yond kilometre marker 2060, prayer flags mark the start of a path to the Dratsang Monastery, which overlooks the road from a steep fairy-tale-like crag. The road then makes a zigzag ascent past photogenic nomads' camps and their flocks to the Bang-la (4720m), then down to a valley that time forgot, and up again to the 4800m Gor-la, before dropping down over one hour to Sangsang.

Sangsang (4590m), 113km and three hours west of Lhatse, is a small grubby town with food and accommodation if you really need it.

The route then passes through a succession of wide alleys before following a gorge into the ravine of the Raka Tsangpo with its dark, craggy peaks. Emerging from this ravine the road skirts a lake, crosses a plain, and then climbs to the 4925m Jye-la, before dropping down again and passing through tiny Raka (travellers on the northern route to Mt Kailash often stay overnight here). Saga is another 60km away.

Raka

Raka (4925m, kilometre marker 1912) is a tiny settlement near the junction of the northern and southern routes, and 115km from Sangsang. If you're taking the northern route, this is pretty much the last accommodation for 240km, though you could camp at Tagyel-tso. There's decent Sichuanese food on the main street and very rustic guesthouse accommodation if you need it.

Zhangmu (Nepal Border) to Saga (280km)

The scenic short cut from Zhangmu to Saga saves 250km (at least a day of travel) and is used mostly by 4WD groups visiting Ngari directly from Nepal.

Past Nyalam the road climbs to the 4950m Tong-la and then the 4845m La Lung-la. Not long after, the short cut branches west off the Friendship Hwy (kilometre marker 5265-66; 113km from Zhangmu), rounding some hills at the entrance of a vast stony plain. From here to Saga it's about 170km or four hours of driving.

About 24km from the junction is Petse, huddled below a ruined hilltop *dzong* (fortress), and then Siling (Seylong) village, where travellers must pay ¥180 per person and ¥400 per car (your guide also must pay ¥180 so arrange beforehand who will pay this – you or the tour agency) for entry to the western section of the Qomolangma Nature Reserve.

To the south come views of sand dunes and then massive **Shishapangma** (8012m), known to the Nepalese as Gosainthan, the world's 14th-tallest peak and the only 8000m-plus mountain planted completely inside Tibet. The road provides access to the mountain's north base camp before skirting the beautiful turquoise **Peiku-tso** (4590m). This is one of Tibet's magical spots, and there's fine camping by the lakeshore, with stunning views of snow-capped Shishapangma and the Langtang Range bordering Nepal to the south. If you do plan to camp, bring your own drinking water and be well acclimatised. Also try to find a sheltered camp site as winds whip up in the afternoon.

The bumpy route then enters a side gorge before passing the turn-off to the scenic but off-limits Kyirong Valley and the border crossing with Nepal at Rasuwa (closed to foreigners). After passing small, salty Drolung-tso you climb to two passes and then drop steeply down to the bridge across the Yarlung Tsangpo. From here it's 3km to Saga, where you join the southern route.

Saga
ས་དགའ་ 萨嘎

☑ 0892 / ELEV 4610M

The sprawling truck-stop town of Saga is the last of any size on the southern route and your last chance to eat a lavish meal and enjoy 24-hour electricity. Most facilities are found on the central street, Gesang Lu, at the intersection of the roads to Zhangmu, Lhatse and Mt Kailash.

There are hot showers at a couple of **bathhouses** (淋浴; línyù) on the main street. Cash-strapped optimists could try the ATM at the Agricultural Bank by the southern square. There are well-stocked supermarkets beside the Saga and Jiling hotels.

🛏 Sleeping & Eating

For Tibetan fare, and a number of basic Tibetan guesthouses, head up the main road past the intersection with Gesang Lu, north from the Saga Hotel.

Ali Guesthouse GUESTHOUSE **$**
(阿里招待所, Ālǐ Zhāodàisuǒ; tr per bed ¥70) This is a modern concrete guesthouse at the eastern tip of Gesang Lu, opposite the Saga Hotel. The beds are comfortable and the location is central but the manager is cranky at best.

Saga Hotel HOTEL **$$$**
(萨嘎宾馆, Sàgā Bīnguǎn; ☑ 820 2888; d with bathroom ¥380-420; ❀ @) This is the only decent hotel for hundreds of kilometres, with English-speaking reception staff and clean, carpeted rooms sporting modern bathrooms, though it's well overpriced. If it's full try the affiliated and similar Jiling Hotel at the other end of the street.

Moon Star Restaurant CHINESE **$**
(dishes ¥20-40; 🍲) Attached to the Saga Hotel, this place serves decent Chinese food, but the English menu is pricier than the Chinese version.

Saga to Zhongba (145km)

There are several ruined monasteries along the 145km stretch from Saga to Zhongba, including one just 1km out of Saga. **Dargyeling Monastery**, 42km from Saga (kilometre marker 1820), sits on the hillside about 1.5km off the main road. It's the best-preserved monastery in the area and worth a visit for its fine views and unusual chörtens. From Dargyeling you cross a river and 12km further along pass the ruins of another large monastery. The road then climbs to a pass marked by hundreds of miniature chörtens, before dropping 23km to Zhongba.

With the road from Saga to Darchen now paved, and drivable in a single day, the small towns along the route are no longer necessary as overnight stops. All have accommodation if you really need it, and decent restaurants for a lunch break.

Zhongba
འབྲོང་པ་ 仲巴

'Old Zhongba' (4570m) is a tiny, dusty town on the main road with a couple of basic guesthouses, restaurants and a small monastery. ('New Zhongba', 22km northwest, is a modern Chinese military town with good restaurants but little else to recommend it.) Given the choice between overnighting here and dismal Paryang, take Old Zhongba.

The Sakayapa-school **Dradun Gompa** is worth the short stroll, especially for the remarkable Cultural Revolution–era newspapers still defacing religious murals in a side chapel of chörtens. The severed heads of goats and yaks dangle from a nearby roadside chörten.

Zhongba to Paryang པར་ཡངས་ 帕羊 (101km)

A photogenic section of sand dunes, lake and mountains kicks in 60km from Zhongba. About 23km before Paryang you crest a 4780m pass and drop past more spectacular dunes to Paryang. Photos taken along this route can often get steppes, streams, desert dunes and snow-capped mountains in the same shot.

Paryang to Hor Qu

The route is a pleasant drive along the spine of the Himalaya, passing through yellow steppes, with craggy, snow-capped peaks looming to the south when the weather is clear. At the **Mayum-la** (5220m), the road crosses from the drainage basin of the Yarlung Tsangpo to that of the Sutlej, as you cross from Shigatse to Ngari prefectures. A descent leads to the long **Gung Gyu-tso**, which nomads consider poisoned, even though it drains into Lake Manasarovar. Your first magical views of Mt Kailash come into view approximately 90km after the Mayum-la, just before the town of Hor Qu (4620m).

Hor Qu ཧོར་ཆུས་ 霍尔

Hor Qu (Huò'ěr) is another expanding village with little to recommend it but the views. However, the new eco-bus system to Darchen and Lake Manasarovar means that you will end up stopping here whether you really want to or not. The bus costs ¥150 to Darchen and the lake and is mandatory for all visitors. Your 4WD vehicle must stay in Hor Qu.

While in Hor Qu look for hulking 7728m **Gurla Mandata** to the southwest. Lake Manasarovar is also in this direction though it's a long hike away. Some trekkers walking the Lake Manasarovar kora spend the night here but most groups give it a miss and continue to Darchen or Chiu Monastery at Lake Manasarovar, both less than an hour away.

From Hor Qu it's 22km to the crossroads settlement and checkpoint of Barkha (巴嘎; Bāgā), from where it's 15km south to Chiu Monastery, or 22km west to Darchen.

NORTHERN ROUTE

The northern route is the longer of the two routes from Lhasa to Ngari, but there's a reason people put up with days of its bumpy, dusty roads. It's the landscapes, the mystical, outsized landscapes, which include huge salt lakes, multicoloured mountains, and valleys of seminomadic herders. The wildlife is also far richer than along the southern route and you are very likely to see marmots, blue sheep, wild asses, small herds of antelope and lots of yaks.

Despite the bumps, driving conditions are generally good. The first part of the route, like the southern, follows the road from Lhatse to the turn-off near Raka. If you're travelling this route by 4WD, seriously consider camping at least once or twice (though you will likely have to pay some cash for the privilege), as the towns are dismal. You need to be well acclimatised if you intend to tackle this route before the rest of Ngari (most people use this route for the return from Kailash) as the road from Raka never really drops below 4500m and is often above 5000m.

King Tiger Hot Springs & Tagyel-tso སྟག་རྒྱལ་ཚ་ཚན་

ELEV 5070M

Only 21km north of the Raka junction are the Tagyel Chutse, or **King Tiger Hot Springs**, a collection of geysers, bubbling hot springs, puffing steam outlets and smoking holes that seem to lead straight down into the bowels of the earth. The best time to visit is during the **Tibetan Bathing Festival**, or Gama Rije (early July of the lunar calendar; usually September in the Gregorian), when hundreds of nomad families, with their herds of yak, set up a colourful, lively camp around the springs. The atmosphere is convivial, making it a great time to mingle with Tibetans. The festival is associated with the re-appearance of Venus in the evening sky.

From the hot springs, the road skirts the western side of a beautiful lake, then through a wide valley, one of numerous stretches of open plateau in Ngari where you can see for many kilometres ahead of you. From a 5235m pass, the route descends to a much larger lake, **Tagyel-tso**, the waters of which are a miraculous shade of the deepest blue imaginable and ringed with snowy peaks. With luck you can spot gazelles, wild asses and even the occasional wolf, hungrily eyeing the valley's many fat marmots. This is a great place to camp but only if you're prepared for the cold and especially the altitude (around 5150m). If you've come from a night or two at Everest Base Camp you should be OK; from Lhatse this is too big a jump in altitude to be considered safe.

After Tagyel-tso the road climbs past herding camps to the 5570m Sangmo-la. About 45km after the pass the road crests a smaller pass and leads down to two conjoined lakes, past a small salt mine. Eventually you pop out into the wide sandy valley of the Yutra Tsangpo.

Not far from Tsochen a small monastery and large collection of prayer flags and mani (prayer) stones sit on a ledge above the road; 3km later is a major checkpoint where your passport and permit will be checked. The town of Tsochen is just ahead, 5km across the plains.

Tsochen མཚོ་ཆེན་ 措勤

📞 0897 / ELEV 4680M

Tsochen (Cuòqín), located 235km from the northern turn-off and 173km south of the northern road proper, is probably the most interesting town on the northern route, full of wild-haired nomads in town on a shopping trip.

The **PSB** (公安局; Gōng'ānjú) maintains a strong presence and at the time of writing all foreign travellers had to go to the station to register. The station is about halfway up the road on the left from the start of town (coming from Lhasa). They'll be waiting for you.

◉ Sights

Mendong Monastery   BUDDHIST, MONASTERY
At the east end of the 2km-long town, walk through the Tibetan quarter to reach a mass of mani stones, prayer poles and yak skulls that local pilgrims gravitate to

daily at dusk. From here you'll see a second, larger collection of prayer flags and mani stones about 1km away on the plateau to the north; just below here is the Mendong Monastery, a small but friendly place with 36 monks.

The atmospheric inner chapel of the main prayer hall holds the funeral chörten of local lama Sherab Rinpoche, plus his stone hand and footprints. The monastery belongs to the Kagyud school, so there are pictures of Milarepa, Marpa and the Karmapa here (as well as Chairman Mao!). The monastery is headed by a 91-year-old lama who fled to India in 1959 and returned in 1984 to rebuild the ruined monastery.

Zhari (Tsari) Nam-tso   LAKE
One excursion from Tsochen is to Zhari (Tsari) Nam-tso, a huge salt lake 50km east towards the town of Tseri (Tsitri). You will need to have this visit pre-arranged before leaving Lhasa or arrange extra payment for the half-day trip.

🛏 Sleeping & Eating

The main street is lined with Chinese restaurants but don't expect to find an English menu. There are several supermarkets in town.

Friendship Feria Hotel   HOTEL $
(友谊宾馆, Yǒuyì Bīnguǎn; ☑ 261 2308; tw/tr ¥120/180) The hotel is at the beginning of town on the left, before the petrol station.

Lhatse Dronkhang   HOTEL $
(家庭旅馆, Jiātíng Lüguǎn; ☑ 261 2561; s/d ¥180/200) Just past the Feria Hotel, this place has decent rooms on the 2nd floor. The walls are wood so it's potentially noisy but there are indoor toilets and showers.

Lhatse Tashi Restaurant   CHINESE, TIBETAN $
(mains ¥10-30) Opposite the Lhatse Dronkhang hotel, this restaurant is owned by the same people and offers cosy Tibetan seating and a good range of Chinese and Tibetan dishes.

Tsochen to Gertse (257km)

From Tsochen to the junction of the northern road (S301) is a journey of about 180km; Gertse is another 77km, making a total drive of around five hours. If you plan to stay in Gertse, take your time as the route is far more interesting and scenic than the town.

About 43km north of Tsochen, the road passes the 5090m **Nor Chung-la** (Small Wild Yak Pass) before descending to the dramatic turquoise waters of **Dawa-tso** (4680m), another superb camping spot. For the next 60km the route passes from one attractive valley to another, sometimes connected by the river and gorge, at other times by minor passes.

After the scenic **Nor Gwa-la** (Wild Yak Head Pass; 5250m), and for the next 50km, the road runs alongside a dramatic range of 6000m-plus glaciated mountains. After the road meets the northern road proper (linking Amdo with Ali) it's a long 15km drive in an arrow-straight line towards **Dung-tso**, with its purple mountain backdrop and salt marsh foreground looking like whitecaps on the water from a distance.

From the junction it's 90km (two hours) west to Gertse through a wide valley dotted with sheep and prayer flags. There's a checkpoint 24km before Gertse.

Gertse ঝེར་ཙེ 改则

☑ 0897 / ELEV 4445M

Gertse (Gǎizé) is the biggest town along the northern route before Ali. The main street (Luren Lu) begins from the yak statue roundabout and runs from east to west about 1.5km. Dazhong Lu is the most interesting street, lined with Tibetan teahouses and pool tables. Several shops sell colourful *chubas* (Tibetan cloaks) with fake sheepskin lining.

There are several hotels in town, though none have hot running water. If you need a shower look for the public baths or ask your guide to show you. Restaurants in town offer the usual Sichuan and Uighur fare.

Budget some time to visit the long wall of chörtens, mani stones, prayer flags and yak horns to the south of town.

Gertse to Gegye (368km)

It's a seven- to eight-hour drive from Gertse to Gegye, the next town of any size. The initial landscape is a dreamy blur of lake and sky, cut by salt rings and brooding mountains of rust, mustard, turmeric and green barley. Around **Oma-chu** (kilometre marker 982), a small village huddled beneath a rocky splinter, keep your eyes open for the round, tomb-like buildings that are actually tsampa (roasted-barley flour) storage bins.

The road passes some impressive peaks to the south and then the village of **Sherma**, squeezed between the two lakes of Rali-tso and Loma Gyari-tso. After more peaks the road drops down to large and photogenic **Peri-tso** and the nearby village of **Wenbu Dangsang**, two hours from Gertse. It's another 50km past a stony plain and a huge salt lake that looks like it's full of icebergs to ramshackle **Tsaka** (擦咔; Cākā), a small salt- and sheepskin-processing community. The centre of town has simple food and guesthouses if you need them.

From Tsaka one route continues northwest to meet the Ali–Kashgar road just north of **Pangong-tso**. The road to Ali branches south and climbs a side valley to the 4895m Gya-la, then descends past yak-hair nomads' tents to curve around salty **Sher-tso** (Bar-tso). After another pass (4855m) with a large cave on one side, the road descends to the pastures of **Zhungba** (Shungba; 雄巴; Xióngbā) via a Gobi-like stony desert. There's food here if needed.

At kilometre marker 1202, near **Drungba**, the road enters a gorge and follows the fledgling Indus River to Gegye. The Indus has its source in the northern flanks of Mt Kailash and is known here as the Sengge (or Sengye) Tsangpo, or Lion River. It's astonishing to think that this little stream continues through Ladakh and Pakistan, crossing the world's highest mountain ranges to become one of the great rivers of Asia.

Gegye དགེ་རྒྱས་ 革吉

☑ 0897 / ELEV 4520M

The mildly interesting little town of Gegye (Géjí), nestled below a ridge, is a logical overnight point, though there's little to actually do except drink beer and play pool with the local nomads. The two main streets (Hebei Lu and Yanhu Lu) join at a T-junction by the Shuǐlì Bīnguǎn. Shops on Hebei Lu offer internet access and hot showers.

🛏 Sleeping & Eating

Hebei Lu has several good supermarkets and Yanhu Lu has a number of Tibetan, Sichuan and Uighur restaurants.

Gegye Hotel HOTEL **$**

(革吉宾馆; Géjí Bīnguǎn; s/d ¥180/200) This government guesthouse is in a terminal state of decline. The carpeted rooms are OK but the bathrooms are locked, so you have to use the absolutely shocking outdoor latrines. The hotel is unsigned inside a compound with a white tiled arch.

Shuili Hotel HOTEL **$$**

(水利宾馆; Shuǐlì Bīnguǎn; ☎263 2146; cnr Yanhu Lu & Hebei Lu; r ¥240-260) Rooms are clean and comfortable with TVs and DVD players, the shared indoor squat toilets are simple but clean and there's even some running water.

Gegye to Ali (112km)

Ali is just three hours from Gegye. At first the road follows the infant Indus River, then enters a marshland rich in bird life, including golden ducks and large black-necked cranes. After passing through a canyon landscape painted in swirling desert hues of butterscotch, caramel and popcorn, you reach Zouzou village and a dramatic escarpment.

Ali gradually emerges like a desert mirage, revealing paved grids of department stores, karaoke bars and taxis. It's a surreal experience to glide smoothly into town on the tarmac after five or six days bouncing around the northern plateau.

Ali ཨ་ལི་ 阿里/狮泉河

☑ 0897 / ELEV 4280M

Ali (Ālǐ), also known as Shīquánhé (Lion Spring River) in Chinese and Sengge Khabab (Town of the Lion) in Tibetan, is the capital of the Ngari (Ali) prefecture. There's nothing much to see, but it is a good place to clean up, have some decent food, top up supplies and check your email before heading off to the real attractions of Ngari. For views of the town, climb up to the pagoda-topped hill to the north of town. Don't take pictures of the army compound to the west (recognisable by the huge '八一' army symbol painted on the hillside above).

WESTERN TIBET (NGARI) GEGYE TO ALI (112KM)

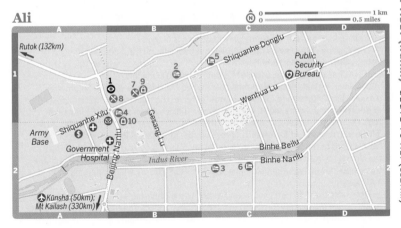

Ali

Sights
1 Viewpoint B1

Sleeping
2 Ali Hotel B1
3 Guge Dynasty Hotel C2
4 Heng Yuan Guesthouse B1
5 Shenhu Hotel C1
6 Xiangxiong Hotel C2

Eating
7 Baiyi Supermarket B1
8 Uighur Ashkhana B1

Shopping
9 Fruit & Vegetable Market B1
10 Supermarket B1

Ali is thoroughly Chinese. There are plenty of Tibetans wandering the streets but, like you, they are probably visitors from further afield. The town is expanding rapidly, especially to the south of the river, and there's a big army presence. Fleets of taxis are part of the mirage-in-the-desert shock of arriving in Ali. The centre of town is compact enough that you can walk anywhere, though.

Tibet's fourth airport, at Kūnshā (昆莎; Gunsa in Tibetan; 4274m) opened in 2010, 50km south of Ali. There are currently twice-weekly flights to Lhasa but it is very difficult to get tickets. Driving from Ali to Darchen, at the base of the Mt Kailash kora, is a day's journey of around 330km.

🛏 Sleeping

Your sleeping options are limited in Ali as many hotels are off-limits to foreigners. The better hotels fill up quickly.

Heng Yuan Guesthouse　　HOTEL **$**
(恒远宾馆; Héngyuǎn Bīnguǎn; ☑ 282 8288; cnr Beijing Nanlu & Shiquanhe Donglu; s/d with bathroom ¥140, tr without bathroom ¥180) A popular place with 4WD tours, it has decent rooms in the main building. You access the rooms through a ground-floor department store.

Shenhu Hotel　　HOTEL **$$**
(神湖宾馆, Shénhú Bīnguǎn; ☑ 136 3897 7982; s/d without bathroom ¥260, s/d with bathroom ¥280) Owned by the Yak Hotel in Lhasa, this place is an OK first choice. The cheaper

ATOP THE WORLD: THE XĪNJIĀNG–TIBET HIGHWAY

With at least two passes above 5400m, the Xīnjiāng–Tibet Hwy is the highest road in the world. Approximately 1350km from Kashgar to Ali, this is an epic journey that can form a wild extension to a trip along the Karakoram Hwy. The route can be bitterly cold, however, and closes down for the winter months from December to February.

The whole trip takes at least four days of travel. There are truck stops along the way, about a day's travel apart, but it's wise to bring food and a sleeping bag. A tent can be useful in emergencies. Coming from Kashgar, you have to be particularly careful about altitude sickness as the initial rate of altitude gain is dramatic.

The Xīnjiāng–Tibet Hwy is off limits without travel permits, but companies such as **John's Café** (www.johncafe.net), with branches in Lhasa and Kashgar, or Tibet FIT Travel (p36) in Lhasa can arrange vehicle hire (and permits) along this route.

Leaving Karghilik, the road climbs past Akmeqit village to Kudi Pass (kilometre marker 113; 3240m) then follows a narrow gorge to the truck stop and checkpost at Kudi (kilometre marker 161; 2960m). From Kudi it's 80km over the Chiragsaldi Pass (kilometre marker 217; 4960m) to the village of Mazar (kilometre marker 241; 3700m). The road turns east and climbs over the Kirgizjangal Pass (kilometre marker 09; 4930m) to the large village of Xaidulla (Sài Túlā; kilometre marker 363; 3700m), the largest town en route. The road climbs again over the 4250m Koshbel Pass to the truck stop of Dahongliutan (kilometre marker 488; 4200m), which offers basic food and lodging.

From here the road turns south, and climbs to the Khitai Pass (kilometre marker 535; 5150m), past the military base of Tianshuihai. About 100km from the pass you cross another 5180m pass (kilometre marker 670) to enter the remote region of Aksai Chin. For the next 170km road conditions are bad and progress is slow. The construction of the road here, through a triangle of territory that India claimed as part of Ladakh, was a principal cause of the border war between India and China in 1962. The fact that China managed to build this road without India even realising that it was under construction is an indication of the utter isolation of the region!

The road passes Lungma-tso, shortly afterwards entering the Changtang Nature Reserve, and 15km later reaches the small village of Sumzhi (Sōngxī; kilometre marker 720; 5200m). Finally at kilometre marker 740 you come to the edge of the Aksai Chin region and climb up to the Jieshan Daban pass (5200m). From here, Ali is around 420km away via the village of Domar (kilometre marker 828; 4440m), the eastern end of Pangong-tso (Palgon-tso; 4270m) and Rutok Xian (kilometre marker 930). From here it is 130km south to Ali.

rooms have communal squat toilets but no showers. Rooms are arranged around an inner atrium.

Ali Hotel
HOTEL $$

(狮泉河饭店, Shīquánhé Fàndiàn; ☑ 280 0004; 17 Shiquanhe Donglu; d without/with bathroom ¥250/320) This charmless two-star government hotel offers exhausted Western-style rooms with broken fixtures and small bathrooms, and very spartan rooms without.

Guge Dynasty Hotel
HOTEL $$

(古格王朝大酒店, Gǔgé Wángcháo Dà Jiǔdiàn; ☑ 266 6111; Binhe Nanlu; d/tw ¥300/320; ✲ @) The newest four-star in town with an emphasis on garish colors and faux-Tibetan stylings. Rooms have broadband internet and there is a restaurant and a bar inside the hotel.

Xiangxiong Hotel
HOTEL $$$

(象雄大酒店, Xiàngxióng Dàjiǔdiàn; ☑ 283 0888; www.xiangxionghotel.com; Binhe Nanlu; d ¥420; ✲ @) One of the best hotels in town, in the southeast suburbs.

✖ Eating

Ali has numerous Chinese restaurants south and west of the main junction and, given the town's remote location, they are surprisingly good value for money. There are also a few Tibetan places around (don't expect English menus). For supplies try the **Baiyi Supermarket** (Shiquanhe Donglu), or the supermarket next to Heng Yuan Guesthouse. For fresh produce try the **fruit & vegetable market** (Shiquanhe Donglu).

Uighur Ashkhana
UIGHUR $

(Beijing Beilu; noodles ¥12) For a taste of Central Asia head to this popular Uighur restaurant (*ashkhana* in Turkic), 100m from the main roundabout. Fresh naan bread, a bowl of *suoman* (fried noodle squares) and a couple of kebabs make for a great meal. The barbecue grill and smell of mutton are signs that you're close.

ⓘ Information

Agricultural Bank of China (中国农业银行; Zhōngguó Nóngyè Yínháng; ⊘ 10am-7pm Mon-Fri) Near the army post, west of the roundabout. Will change cash US dollars, euros and UK pounds only (no travellers cheques). There's an ATM outside on the Visa, MasterCard and Cirrus networks.

Public Security Bureau (PSB, 公安局; Gōng'ānjú; 17 Wenhua Lu; ⊘ 10am-1pm & 4-7pm Mon-Fri) Groups may need to get travel permits endorsed here if they haven't done so in Darchen. The office is in the southeast of town.

MT KAILASH & FAR WEST TIBET

Mt Kailash
གངས་རིན་པོ་ཆེ
冈仁波齐峰

Going to Ngari and not completing a kora around Mt Kailash (Kang Rinpoche, or Precious Jewel of Snow, in Tibetan) would be like visiting a great capital and stopping short outside its most famous treasure. Mt Kailash dominates the region with the sheer awesomeness of its four-sided summit, just as it dominates the mythology of a billion people.

The mountain has been a lodestone to pilgrims and adventurous travellers for centuries but until recently very few had set their eyes on it. With improved road conditions to Ngari this has changed. Large numbers of Indian pilgrims visit the mountain between June and August, as do Chinese tourists and hikers who were as rare as hen's teeth just six years ago.

Mt Kailash is accessed via the small grubby town of Darchen, the starting point of the kora. Any reasonably fit and acclimatised person should be able to complete the three-day walk, but come prepared with warm and waterproof clothing and equipment. For more information about the kora, see p223.

Note that the entrance fee to Mt Kailash has increased to ¥150 per person and in addition to this all visitors must pay another ¥150 to ride an eco-bus from Hor Qu to Darchen. Your 4WD must park in Hor Qu so there is no option to skip this fee.

History

Throughout Asia, stories exist of a great mountain, the navel of the world, from which flow four great rivers that give life to the areas they pass through. The myth originates in the Hindu epics, which speak of Mt Meru – home of the gods – as a vast column 84,000 leagues high, its summit kissing the heavens and its flanks composed of gold,

WORTH A TRIP

WARM-UP HIKES AROUND MT KAILASH

If you've got extra time at Darchen, or you want to spend a day acclimatising before setting out on the Mt Kailash kora, you can find some interesting short walks in the area. The ridge to the north of the village obscures Mt Kailash, but an hour's walk to the top offers fine views of the mountain. To the south you will be able to see the twin lakes of Manasarovar and Rakshas Tal.

A switchbacking dirt road just to the east of Darchen branches right after 1km to the **Gyangdrak Monastery**, largest of the Mt Kailash monasteries and 6km from Darchen. Like other monasteries, it was rebuilt (in 1986) after the depredations of the Cultural Revolution. The left branch of the road follows a stream west to **Selung Monastery**, where a short walk leads to a viewpoint popular with Indian pilgrims for its views of Kailash and Nandi peaks. The secret 'inner kora' of Kailash starts from here but is only open to pilgrims who have completed 13 main koras of the mountain.

For an excellent warm-up and acclimatisation hike, get dropped off at Gyangdrak and then follow the obvious path over the ridge and down to Selung (45 minutes). At the pass on the ridge a side path leads up the hillside straight towards Mt Kailash for epic views of the south face and back towards Manasarovar, Rakshas Tal and tent-shaped Gurla Mandata. From Selung you can drive back or continue over the ridges to the south to eventually drop down steeply to Darchen. Views of the Barkha plain from the ridge above Darchen are awesome but it gets very windy in the afternoons.

crystal, ruby and lapis lazuli. These Hindu accounts placed Mt Meru somewhere in the towering Himalaya but, with time, Meru increasingly came to be associated specifically with Mt Kailash. The confluence of the myth and the mountain is no coincidence. No-one has been to the summit to confirm whether the gods reside there (although some have come close), but Mt Kailash does indeed lie at the centre of an area that is the key to the drainage system of the Tibetan plateau. Four of the great rivers of the Indian subcontinent originate here: the Karnali, which feeds into the Ganges (south); Indus (north); Sutlej (west); and Brahmaputra (Yarlung Tsangpo, east).

Mt Kailash, at 6714m, is not the mightiest of the mountains in the region, but with its distinctive shape – like the handle of a millstone, according to Tibetans – and its year-round snow-capped peak, it stands apart from the pack. Its four sheer walls match the cardinal points of the compass, and its southern face is famously marked by a long vertical cleft punctuated halfway down by a horizontal line of rock strata. This scarring resembles a swastika – a Buddhist symbol of spiritual strength – and is a feature that has contributed to Mt Kailash's mythical status. Mt Kailash is actually not part of the Himalaya but rather the Kangri Tise (Gangdise) Range.

Mt Kailash has long been an object of worship. For Hindus, it is the domain of Shiva, the Destroyer and Transformer, and his consort Parvati. To the Buddhist faithful, Mt Kailash is the abode of Demchok (Sanskrit: Samvara) and Dorje Phagmo. The Jains of India also revere the mountain as the site where the first of their *tirthankara* (saints) entered Nirvana. And in the ancient Bön religion of Tibet, Mt Kailash was the sacred Yungdrung Gutseg (Nine-Stacked-Swastika Mountain) upon which the Bönpo founder Shenrab alighted from heaven.

Numerous Western explorers wanted to summit the mountain in the early 20th century but oddly ran out of time on each occasion. Reinhold Messner gained permission to scale the peak in the 1980s, but abandoned his expedition in deference to the peak's sanctity when he got to the mountain. In May 2001 Spanish climbers reportedly also gained permission to climb the peak, only to abandon their attempt in the face of international protests. Since then the Chinese government has maintained that the mountain is off limits to climbers.

Darchen   དར་ཆེན། 塔钦

☏ 0897 / ELEV 4670M

Nestled below the foothills of Mt Kailash, the small town of Darchen (Tǎqīn) is the starting point of the kora. It is a rapidly expanding settlement of hotel compounds, tourist restaurants and newly built blocks, much improved on the miserable hovel that greeted travellers to Kailash a few years ago. Most travellers make use of the town's hot showers, restaurants and supermarkets, either before or after their kora. If you need medical attention, there's a Swiss-funded traditional Tibetan clinic in the northwest of Darchen.

Darchen is 3km north of the main Ali–Saga road, about 12km from Barkha, 107km north of Purang, 330km southeast of Ali and a lonely 1200km from Lhasa.

✦ Festivals & Events

The festival of **Saga Dawa** marks the enlightenment of Sakyamuni, and occurs on the full-moon day of the fourth Tibetan month (in May or June). Saga Dawa is a particularly popular time to visit Mt Kailash, though you will have to share the Tarboche camping area with several hundred other foreigners, most of them on group tours. You can also expect that all the hotels in Darchen will be booked solid throughout this time. The presence of so many tourists and their ever-present camera lenses can spoil the occasion. Other times offer a less colourful but more personally spiritual time to make your kora.

The highlight of the festival is the raising of the Tarboche prayer pole on the morning of Saga Dawa. Monks circumambulate the pole in elaborate costumes, with horns blowing. There are plenty of stalls, a fairlike atmosphere and a nonstop tidal flow of pilgrims around the pole. After the pole is raised at about 1pm everyone sets off on their kora.

How the flagpole stands when it is re-erected is of enormous importance. If the pole stands absolutely vertical all is well, but if it leans towards Mt Kailash things are not good; if it leans away towards Lhasa, things are even worse.

⌷ Sleeping & Eating

There's not a great deal to choose from between Darchen's hotels though more are popping up, and the new **Himalaya Hotel** offers four-star comfort and occasional wifi for ¥1000 a night. Most travellers stay in rustic guesthouses that offer foam beds in clean rooms for around ¥60 per bed, with an outdoor pit toilet in the corner of a large courtyard. Bigger places like the Gandisi

Hotel are often fully booked with huge groups of Indian pilgrims.

Pilgrim Hotel   GUESTHOUSE **$**
(朝圣宾馆, Cháoshèng Bīnguǎn; ☑298 0833; dm ¥60) Turn right at the T-junction for this good place that has a cosy dining room and donates part of its profits to local monasteries.

Lhasa Holyland Guesthouse   GUESTHOUSE **$**
(拉萨圣地康桑旅馆, Lāsà Shèngdì Kāngsāng Lǔguǎn; ☑139 8907 0818; d¥70-80) This friendly place has clean rooms and an inviting Tibetan-style teahouse.

Sun & Moon Guesthouse   GUESTHOUSE **$**
(Ninda Dronkhang, 日月宾馆, Rìyuè Bīnguǎn; ☑260 7102; q per bed ¥60-70) This easily overlooked place in the far top (northwest) end of town offers the nicest accommodation, with comfortable rooms and clean communal toilets, though it's a bit out of the way. It's part of the Tibet Medical and Astrological Institute (Menkhang).

ⓘ Information

Some places have patchy internet service but it's best to use your cell phone's 3G connection to go online.

Public Security Bureau (PSB, 公安局, Gōng'ānjú) Travellers need to register and have their travel permit endorsed at the local PSB office. Your guide will arrange this.

Lake Manasarovar མ་ཕྱམ་ཡི་ཕམ་
玛旁雄错

ELEV 4560M

Lake Manasarovar, or Mapham Yum-tso (Victorious Lake) in Tibetan, is the most venerated of Tibet's many lakes and one of its most beautiful. With its sapphire-blue waters, sandy shoreline and snow-capped-mountain backdrop, Manasarovar is immediately appealing, and a welcome change of venue from the often-forbidding terrain of Mt Kailash.

Manasarovar has been circumambulated by Indian pilgrims since at least 1700 years ago when it was extolled in the sacred Sanskrit literature the *Puranas*. A Hindu interpretation has it that *manas* refers to the mind of the supreme god Brahma, the lake being its outward manifestation. Accordingly, Indian pilgrims bathe in the waters of the lake and circumambulate its shoreline. Tibetans, who are not so keen on the bathing bit, generally just walk around it. Legend

KAILASH & MANASAROVAR BOOKS

The following books about Mt Kailash, Lake Manasarovar and the surrounding area are guaranteed to whet your appetite for adventure. Charles Allen's *A Mountain in Tibet* chronicles the hunt for the sources of the region's four great rivers and is perhaps the best introduction to the region. Allen's follow up, *The Search for Shangri-La,* focuses on the region's pre-Buddhist heritage and is also a great read. *The Sacred Mountain* by John Snelling reports on early Western explorers, including those who turned up in the early 1980s when the door to China and Tibet first creaked narrowly open.

The Kailash chapters in German-born Lama Anagarika Govinda's *The Way of the White Clouds* (1966) includes a classic account of the pilgrimage during a trip to Tibet in 1948. Sven Hedin's three-volume *Trans-Himalaya: Discoveries & Adventures in Tibet* (1909–13) will keep you company for many a long night on the Changtang plateau. Hedin was the first Westerner to complete the Mt Kailash kora.

Books such as *Kailas: On Pilgrimage to the Sacred Mountain of Tibet* by Kerry Moran (with photos by Russell Johnson) and *Walking to the Mountain* by Wendy Teasdill may make you jealous that you didn't get to the mountain just a decade or two earlier. Both highlight the much greater difficulties (and, in their eyes, rewards) that one could experience on a pilgrimage as recently as the late 1980s.

The more scientifically inclined can turn to Swami Pranavananda's *Kailas Manasarovar,* an account of the author's findings over numerous stays in the region between 1928 and 1947. The book was reprinted in India in 1983 and you should be able to find a copy in a Kathmandu bookshop or online.

Most recent is Manosi Lahiri's *Here be Yaks,* an unpretentious travelogue that details a more recent Indian pilgrimage to the region, with a special focus on defining the source of the Sutlej.

has it that the mother of the Buddha, Queen Maya, was bathed at Manasarovar by the gods before giving birth to her son. It is said that some of Mahatma Gandhi's ashes were sprinkled into the lake.

The Hindi poet Kalidasa once wrote that the waters of Lake Manasarovar are 'like pearls' and that to drink them erases the 'sins of a hundred lifetimes'. Be warned, however, that the sins of a hundred lifetimes tend to make their hasty exit by way of the nearest toilet. Make sure that you thoroughly purify Manasarovar's sacred waters before you drink them, however sacrilegious that may sound.

Manasarovar is linked to a smaller lake, **Rakshas Tal** (known to Tibetans as Lhanag-tso), by the channel called Ganga-chu. Most Tibetans consider Rakshas Tal to be evil, home in Hindu minds to the demon king Ravanna, though to the secular eye it's every bit as beautiful as Manasarovar. The two bodies of water are associated with the conjoined sun and moon, a powerful symbol of Tantric Buddhism. On rare occasions, water flows through this channel from Lake Manasarovar to Rakshas Tal; this is said to augur well for the Tibetan people and most

are pleased that water has indeed been flowing between the two lakes in recent years.

Most groups and individuals base themselves at the picturesque Chiu village, site of the Chiu Monastery, on the northwestern shore of the lake. There are over a dozen simple, friendly guesthouses between the monastery and the lake, with four- or five-bed rooms charged at ¥50 to ¥60 per bed per night, and outdoor pit toilets. There's little to choose between them except perhaps the availability of food and where the big groups are staying.

The lake area has an admission fee of ¥150 per person (the Mt Kailash fee does not cover this) and 4WD vehicles are no longer permitted in the area. All visitors must leave their 4WD vehicle in Hor Qu. From Hor Qu there are eco-buses to take you to Darchen or the lake. The buses costs an additional ¥150 (one ticket covers a trip to both Darchen and the lake).

◉ Sights & Activities

Chiu Monastery　　　　BUDDHIST, MONASTERY

FREE Located 33 kilometres south of Darchen, Chiu (Sparrow) Monastery enjoys a fabulous location atop a craggy hill overlooking Lake Manasarovar. The main chapel contains the meditation cave of Guru Rinpoche, who is said to have passed away here, but most people focus on the lake views, the winding stone staircases and old wooden doorframes of this fairy-tale-like structure. A short kora path leads to a second chapel. On a clear day Mt Kailash looms dramatically to the north.

For a hike, walk along the ridge to the southeast of the monastery or make a half-day trek along part of the lake kora to the ruined chörten and prayer wall at Cherkip, returning via the shoreline cave retreats. There are fine views and lots of nesting birds along this route, but bring repellent against the annoying shoreline flies.

If you fancy a long post-hike soak, the small **hot springs** (⊙10am-8pm) beside the village pipe water into private wooden tubs.

Gossul Monastery   BUDDHIST, MONASTERY
Further south along the shore of Manasarovar, this charming monastery is part of the Manasarovar kora but can now be reached by road. The three resident monks can show you the meditation cave of Götsangpa (the ascetic who opened up the Mt Kailash kora in the 13th century) and a sacred stone conch shell, and you can buy amulets or packets of holy Manasarovar sand, incense and salt. The views of the lake are breathtaking.

The best way to reach the monastery is if you are driving from Purang; an unsigned dirt road branches off the main road 10km north of the Gurla-la (around kilometre marker 36), crosses a pass and then swings left to follow the lakeshore for 10km. From Gossul it's 7km north to the paved main road and then a further 6km to Chiu Monastery.

Tirthapuri Hot Springs & Kora   ཏེ་དྲ་པུ་རི་ཆུ་ཚན། 芝达布日寺

On the banks of the Sutlej, only a few hours' drive northwest of Darchen, the hot springs at **Tirthapuri** (admission ¥15) are the place where pilgrims traditionally bathe after completing their circuit of Mt Kailash. The one-hour kora route around the site is interesting, and 13 circumambulations are considered to bring equal merit as one Kailash kora.

Starting from the hot springs the kora trail climbs to a cremation point, an oval of rocks covered in old clothes and rags. From this point, an alternative longer kora climbs to the very top of the ridge, rejoining the trail near the long mani wall (a wall made of mani stones). The regular kora trail continues past a hole where pilgrims dig 'sour' earth for medicinal purposes. Further along, there's a 'sweet' earth hole. The trail reaches a miniature version of Mt Kailash's Drölma-la, marked with mani stones and a large collection of yak horns and skulls.

Where the trail doubles back to enter the Guru Rinpoche (Tirthapuri) Monastery, there is a rock with a hole in it right below the solitary prayer wheel, which is a handy karma-testing station. Reach into the hole and pull out two stones. If both are white your karma is excellent; one white and one black means that it's OK; and if both are

Tirthapuri Hot Springs & Kora

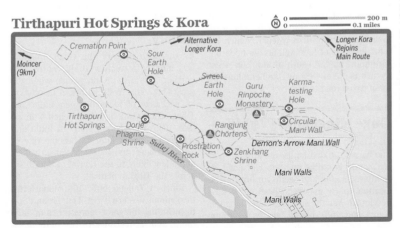

EXPLORING THE GARUDA VALLEY

Adventurers with a day up their sleeve could explore the Khyunglung (Garuda) region of the upper Sutlej Valley, southwest from Moincer. Around 16km from Moincer (8km from Tirthapuri), the Bönpo-school **Gurugyam Monastery** (གུ་རུ་རྒྱམ་དགོན་པ 故如甲木寺, Gùrújiǎmù Sì) is worth a visit, primarily for the dramatic cliffside retreat of 10th-century Bön master Drenpa Namka.

A further 14km down the Sutlej Valley, 2km past Khyunglung (曲龙; Qūlóng) village, is the extensive ruined cave city that archaeologists believe belonged to the early kingdom of **Shangshung**. The 20-minute trail to the site leads from a roadside chörten and drops past hot-spring terraces to cross the Sutlej over a bridge hung with severed animal heads. Nearby is a riverside hot-springs pool. You could easily spend a fantastic couple of hours exploring the troglodyte caves and buildings but it's dangerous to continue to the upper citadel. On the way back stop off at **Khyunglung Monastery** just above the village, which also has a couple of simple teahouses.

There are no checkpoints en route to Khyunglung though it would be prudent to have the valley added to your travel permit, either in Ali or Darchen. From Khyunglung the dirt road continues southwest to seriously remote monasteries at Dongpo, Dawa (Danba) and Manam (Malang) en route to Zanda, but also passes near several military bases so you need to bring watertight permissions and be prepared for some serious exploration.

black you have serious karma problems. Perhaps another Mt Kailash kora would help?

The monastery *dukhang* (assembly hall) has stone footprints of Guru Rinpoche and his consort Yeshe Tsogyel to the right of the altar. Outside the monastery a large circle of mani stones marks the spot where the gods danced in joy when Guru Rinpoche was enshrined at Tirthapuri. Beside it is a 200m-long mani wall, said to be the result of a demon firing an arrow at the guru (the guru stopped the arrow's flight and transformed it into this wall). Finally, the kora drops back down to the river, passing several small shrines and a series of rocky pinnacles revered as *rangjung*, or self-manifesting chörtens.

Accommodation is limited to a few simple guesthouses. If you want to stay in the area consider **Moincer** (Mensi), which has a better range of food and accommodation. Tirthapuri is 9km south of Moincer, which in turn is 65km west of Darchen along the main paved road to Ali.

Guge Kingdom གུ་གེ་རྒྱལ་རབས 古格王国

The barren, eroded landscape around modern Zanda is unlike any you will have encountered so far, and seems an improbable location for a major civilisation to have developed. Yet the ancient Guge kingdom (Gǔgé wángguó) thrived here as an impor-

tant stop on the trade route between India and Tibet. Today, the remains of Thöling Monastery, once a major centre of Tibetan Buddhism, and neighbouring Tsaparang, a 9th-century fortress etched into the very stone of a towering ridge, are two of Ngari's highlights, though few Western tourists manage to make it this far.

Tsaparang is 18km west of Zanda, while Thöling Monastery is now merely an adjunct to the town. To visit both you need to budget at least three days (two merely for getting there and back from Darchen). Both sites are in the valley of the Langchen Tsangpo (Sutlej River), the 'elephant river', which rises west of Manasarovar and continues over the border with India into Ladakh and finally Pakistan.

History

By the 10th century the Guge kingdom was already a wealthy trade centre supporting several thousand people when the great Guge king Yeshe Ö began to nurture an exchange of ideas between India and Tibet. The young monk Rinchen Zangpo (958–1055) was sent to study in India and returned 17 years later to become one of Tibet's greatest translators of Sanskrit texts and a key figure in the revival of Buddhism across the Tibetan plateau.

Rinchen Zangpo built 108 monasteries throughout western Tibet, Ladakh and Spiti, including the great monasteries of Tabo (Spiti) and Alchi (Ladakh). Two of the most important were those at Tsaparang and Thöling. He also invited Kashmiri artists to paint the murals still visible today. Their influence spread the Kashmiri tradition across Tibet.

It was partly at Rinchen Zangpo's behest that Atisha, a renowned Bengali scholar and another pivotal character in the revival of Tibetan Buddhism, was invited to Tibet. Atisha spent three years in Thöling before travelling on to central Tibet.

The kingdom fell into ruin just 50 years after the first Europeans arrived in Tibet in 1624, after a siege by the Ladakhi army. The centre of Tibet soon became the middle of nowhere.

Zanda རྩ་མདའ་ 札达

☑ 0897 / ELEV 3760M

Zanda (Zhada), or Tsamda, is the bland, one-street town that has been built up alongside Thöling Monastery. The town consists of a few hotels, restaurants, supermarkets, two army bases and some brothels.

Budget a couple of hours to visit Thöling Monastery and an hour to wander the cliffside chörtens at dusk. If you have more time the two sets of ruins south and particularly southwest of town offer amateur archaeologists plenty of scope to explore crumbling monastery walls, ruined chörtens and elaborate cave complexes.

🛏 Sleeping & Eating

The main street has at least half-a-dozen other places to eat, including generic Sichuan joints, a couple of Tibetan options and an Uighur restaurant. There are also a couple of bathhouses in town and a laundry if you need it.

Hebei Hotel HOTEL $$
(河北宾馆, Héběi Bīnguǎn; ☑ 262 2475; new block from ¥350) The old block of this hotel is grim and you may not even be allowed to stay

---

GETTING TO THE GUGE KINGDOM

There are two main roads to Zanda from the Darchen–Ali road. Both are rough and go over some very high passes. In a 4WD it's possible to make it to Zanda from either Ali or Mt Kailash in a single day.

To/From Darchen

It's about 243km from Darchen to Zanda. It's 65km along a paved road from Darchen to Moincer, which is the turn-off to Tirthapuri, and then another 50km from there to the army base at Ba'er, where the road branches south. The 122km from Ba'er to Zanda takes a few hours of winding up and down fantastically eroded gorges and gullies.

To/From Ali

Coming from Ali, the road is equally scenic and will take around five hours of driving to cover the 200km. The first hour on a paved road climbs to the 4720m Pe-la and then drops down past a great scenic viewpoint to the Gar Valley, home to Ali's new airport at Kūnshā at kilometre marker 1109. About 64km from Ali the route crosses a bridge to the western side of the valley. A further 10km and the road branches right off the main road towards Zanda. The road then climbs up to the 5330m Lalung-la (Laling Gutsa), followed by the 5390m Laochi-la before descending into a valley. About 65km from the turn-off you have to buy a ticket to the area (¥200, including Thöling and Guge).

The road branches left onto a plateau from where there are stunning 180-degree views of the Indian Himalaya, stretching from Nanda Devi in the south to the Ladakh Range in the north. Around 90km from the turn-off (36km from Zanda) look for a village surrounded by eroded cliffs with hundreds of tombs carved into the soft rock. The turn-off for Dungkar and Piyang is just before the village.

The route then drops down into deep, fantastically eroded wadi-like gullies before finally reaching the Sutlej Valley. The layers of the former sea bed are clearly visible and the scenery is a wonderland of eroded cliff faces that have taken on the most astonishing shapes. You'll swear over and over again that you're seeing the melted ruins of an ancient monastery, or the tall pillars that once held the roof of a mighty palace.

Just before reaching Zanda, 130km from the turn-off, you cross the Sutlej River on a long bridge.

here. The next-door annex has decent modern rooms that boast the town's only en suite hot showers.

Chóngqìng Hotel HOTEL $$
(重庆宾馆, Chóngqìng Bīnguǎn; ☑290 2650; d ¥300, tr without bathroom ¥350) This large, quiet compound is a favourite with overlanders but the rooms with TV and en suite squat toilet are well overpriced. Triples without bathroom are a decent deal if you bargain hard.

Transportation Hotel HOTEL $$
(交通宾馆, Jiāotōng Bīnguǎn; ☑262 2686; r ¥250-280) The spacious tiled rooms here come with attached squat toilet and sink. There's no hot water but guests can get a free hot shower next door in the attached public shower. The downside is that it always seems full.

ⓘ Information

Agricultural Bank of China (中国农业银行, Zhōngguó Nóngyè Yínháng; ☺10am-1pm & 4-7pm Mon-Fri) Has a 24-hour ATM.

Thöling Monastery མཐོ་གླིང་ 托林寺

Founded by Rinchen Zangpo in the 10th century, **Thöling Monastery** (Tuōlín Sì; joint admission ticket with Tsaparang ¥200) was once Ngari's most important monastic complex. It was still functioning in 1966 when the Red Guards shut down operations and took a sledgehammer to the chapel's magnificent interiors including the wall murals. Three main buildings survive within the monastery walls. Just north of the monastery are chörtens, mani walls and open views across the Sutlej Valley.

DON'T MISS

AN AFTERNOON STROLL

A few steps east of the monastery compound is the recently restored **Serkhang chörten**. A similar chörten stands in total isolation just to the west of the town. To the north, between the monastic compound and the cliff-face that falls away to the Sutlej River below are two long lines of miniature chörtens. The area is superbly photogenic at dusk, when locals do a kora of the complex.

◉ Sights

Main Assembly Hall (Dukhang) BUDDHIST, CHAPEL
The dimly lit chamber of the *dukhang* (assembly hall) has especially fine wall murals, showing strong Kashmiri and Nepali influences; bring a powerful torch (flashlight) to enjoy the rich detail. The Kashmiri influences are noticeable in the shading on the hands and feet, the ornate jewellery and dress, the tight stomach lines and non-Tibetan images of palm trees and *dhotis* (Indian-style loincloths). Scholarly opinion varies on whether the murals date from the 13th and 14th, or 15th and 16th centuries.

The main statues here are of the past, present and future buddhas (all of recent origin), and there's also a footprint of Rinchen Zangpo. The lower walls of the inner area have murals depicting the life of the Buddha and the founders of the monastery. Murals of the protectors Dorje Jigje (Yamantaka) and Namse (Vairocana) decorate the main entry.

White Chapel (Lhakhang Karpo) BUDDHIST, CHAPEL
The entry to this side chapel is marked by a finely carved deodar (cedar) doorframe that originated in India. Inside are detailed 15th- and 16th-century murals, somewhat affected by water damage though mostly restored with Swiss assistance. The central statue is an old Sakyamuni Buddha (his hands are new). Lining the sides are the eight medicine buddhas in various states of destruction. Male deities line the left wall; female bodhisattvas the right. The far-right-corner murals depict a gruesome sky burial.

Yeshe Ö's Mandala Chapel (Nampar Nang Lhakhang) BUDDHIST, CHAPEL
Once the main building in the Thöling complex, Yeshe Ö's Mandala Chapel was also known as the Golden Chapel. All the images have been destroyed but the four chörtens remain along with a few remaining torsos, disembodied heads and limbs, scattered around the chapel like the leftovers from a sky burial. The mood created by the senseless loss of such magnificent art hangs heavy in the air.

Before its destruction in the Cultural Revolution, the square main hall had four secondary chapels at the centre of each wall. Figures of the deities were arrayed around the wall facing towards a central image atop a lotus pedestal, in the form of a huge three-dimensional Tibetan mandala (a representation of the world of a meditational deity).

You enter the Mandala Chapel through the Gyatsa Lhakhang and finish off a visit by walking around an interior kora of chapels. Most are closed and devoid of statues but a few open to reveal broken legs and plinths.

Tsaparang ᠊ᠪᠷ 古格古城

The citadel of **Tsaparang** (Gǔgé Gǔchéng; joint admission ticket with Thöling ¥200, optional guide per person ¥10), 18km west of Zanda, has been gracefully falling into ruin ever since its slide from prominence in the 17th century. The ruins seem to grow organically out of the hills in tiers and are crowned by a red Summer Palace atop a yellow cockscomb-like outcrop. It's a photogenically surreal landscape that resembles a giant termites' nest.

The site's early Tantric-inspired murals are of particular interest to students of early Buddhist art. Even without the magnificent art, it's worth the trip for the views over the Sutlej Valley and to explore the twisting paths and secret tunnels that worm their way through the fortress.

The ruins climb up the ridge through three distinct areas. At the bottom of the hill is the monastic area with the four best-preserved buildings and their murals. From there the trail to the top climbs through former residential quarters, where monks' cells were tunnelled into the clay hillside. Finally, the route burrows straight into the hillside through a tunnel before emerging in the ruins of the palace citadel at the very top of the hill. The vast, rough-hewn landscape of the Sutlej Valley that spreads out before you is both terrifying and sublime: you can't take your eyes off its beauty, but you know you wouldn't last a day alone in it.

Early morning and evening (particularly around 8pm) offer the best light. No photography is allowed inside the chapels and guardians will watch you like a hawk. Bring a strong torch (flashlight), snacks and water, and expect to spend at least half a day exploring the ruins.

☉ Sights

★ Chapel of the Prefect BUDDHIST, CHAPEL

This small building was a private shrine for Tsaparang's prefect or regent. The care-

Tsaparang

taker has named it the 'Drölma Lhakhang' after his own sculpture of Drölma (Tara) displayed here. The exuberant wall murals date from the 16th century, by which time the style evinced in other Tsaparang murals was in decline.

The murals include fantastic multi-coloured images of elephants, Garuda-people (beside the Buddha's arms), hermits and dog-like snow lions, among others. The main mural on the back wall shows Sakyamuni flanked by Tsongkhapa and Atisha (Jowo-je). Small figures of the Buddha's disciples stand beside his throne.

Lhakhang Karpo BUDDHIST, CHAPEL

The large Lhakhang Karpo, or White Chapel, holds the oldest paintings at Tsaparang and is probably the most important chapel in all of Ngari. The murals date back to the 15th or 16th century but their influences extend back to 10th-century Kashmiri Buddhist art. Apart from at Tsaparang, very little material evidence of early Kashmiri art remains (notably at Alchi Monastery in Ladakh). Spot the Kashmiri influence in the slender torsos, thin waists and long fingers of the Hindu-inspired deities.

The ceiling of the chapel is beautifully painted, as are the many thin supporting columns made from composite pieces of wood (trees are scarcer than hen's teeth in Ngari). The carvings and paintings of Sakyamuni that top each column are particularly noteworthy. At one time, 22 life-size statues lined the walls; today only 10 remain and these are severely damaged. In the far left corner are the legs of Jampa; to the right is Yeshe Ö. Originally, each statue would have been framed by a *torana* (halo-like garland) and a Kashmiri-style plinth. Only partial sections of these remain (look in the far left corner and back recess), but you can still see the holes where these structures were once anchored to the walls.

The doors are flanked by two damaged 5m-high guardian figures, red Tamdrin (Hayagriva) and blue Chana Dorje (Vajrapani). Even armless they hint at the lost marvels of the chapel.

The huge figure of Sakyamuni that once stood in the recess, the Jowo Khang, at the back of the hall has been replaced by one of the caretaker's statues. On the side walls at the back were once row after row of smaller deities, each perched on its own small shelf.

Lhakhang Marpo
BUDDHIST, CHAPEL

Also known as the Red Chapel, this large building was constructed around 1470. The beautiful murals were repainted around 1630, shortly before the fall of the Guge kingdom. The original chapel door, with its concentric frames and carvings of bodhisattvas, elephants and the syllables of the *'Om mani padme hum'* ('hail to the jewel in the lotus') mantra in six panels, has survived and is also worth close inspection.

Inside the chapel, many thin columns support the chapel roof, similar to those of the neighbouring Lhakhang Karpo. By the main door are images of Chenresig (Avalokiteshvara), Green Tara and an angry eight-armed White Tara, with Drölma and Jampelyang (Manjushri) to the right.

The statues that once stood in the chapel were placed towards the centre of the hall, not around the edges, and although only the bases and damaged fragments remain, the crowded feel to the space, the intense colours and the eerie silence combine to create a powerful atmosphere.

Although the wall murals have been damaged by vandalism and water leakage, they remain so remarkably brilliant that it's easy to forget they are actually over 350 years

old. On the left wall are the famous murals chronicling the construction of the temple: animals haul the building's huge timber beams into place as musicians with long trumpets and dancing snow lions celebrate the completion of the temple. Officials stand in attendance (a Kashmir delegation wears turbans), followed by members of the royal family, the king and queen (under a parasol), Öpagme (Amitabha) and, finally, a line of chanting monks. The royal gifts frame the bottom of the scene.

Murals on the far right (northern) wall depict the life of the Buddha, showing him tempted by demons and protected by a naga serpent, among others. On the eastern wall are eight stylised chörtens, representing the eight events in Buddha's life.

The main deities in the chapel have very ornate *toranas*, decorated with birds and crocodiles, and topped with flying apsaras (angels). At the back of the hall, statues of the 35 confessional buddhas once sat on individual shelves; a handful of them still have bodies but all the heads have gone.

Dorje Jigje (Jikji)
Lhakhang
BUDDHIST, CHAPEL

The murals in the smaller chapel are painted red and gold, and are almost solely devoted to wrathful deities such as Demchok (Chakrasamvara), Hevajra and the buffalo-headed Dorje Jigje (Yamantaka), to whom the chapel is dedicated. On the left as you look back at the door is Namtöse (Vaishravana), the God of Wealth, who is depicted riding a snow lion and surrounded by square bands of Tibetan warriors. Beside him is a strange dog-faced protector riding a panther.

Like the Chapel of the Prefect, the paintings here are of later origin, central Tibetan in style (rather than Kashmiri-influenced) and less refined; the golden years had passed by this point. All the statues that once stood here were destroyed, including the central Dorje Jigje.

Summer Palace
BUDDHIST, CHAPEL

From the four chapels at the base of Tsaparang, the path to the top climbs up through the monastic quarters and then ascends to the palace complex atop the hill via a tunnel. The Summer Palace, at the northern end of the hilltop, is empty, with a balcony offering wonderful views. The Sutlej Valley is just to the north. Across the smaller valley to the northeast is the ruined Lotsang Lhakhang.

The small but quite well-preserved red-painted **Mandala (Demchok) Lhakhang** in the centre of the hilltop ridge once housed a wonderful three-dimensional mandala with Tantric murals, only the base of which survived the desecrations of the Cultural Revolution. It is often closed to visitors.

Winter Palace RUIN

Accessed by a steep and treacherous eroded staircase (now with an iron railing in place), the palace is an amazing ants' nest of rooms tunnelled into the clay below the Summer Palace. The rooms were built 12m underground in order to conserve warmth, and the eastern rooms have windows that open out onto the cliff-face.

There are seven dusty chambers, all empty, linked by a cramped corridor. Branching off from the stairs you will see a dim passage that provided vital access to water during sieges and served as an emergency escape route for the royal family. The easily missed stairs to the Winter Palace lead down from between the Summer Palace and the Mandala (Demchok) Lhakhang. Don't go down if you're prone to vertigo or claustrophobia.

Other Sights

North of the main entrance to Tsaparang a trail follows a green river valley down about 700m to a **cave** on the left that holds the mummified remains of several bodies. On the way back, visit the chörten and ruined chapel of the **Lotsang Lhakhang**. Only the feet of the main statue remain. Also worth a quick visit are the **caves** and **chörtens** to the west of the main site, near the public toilet behind the caretaker's compound.

Dungkar & Piyang ཌུང་དཀར

The most important monastic communities in Guge were at Thöling and Tabo (in Ladakh) but extensive cave paintings discovered in the early 1990s suggest others were of great significance as well. The 12th-century wall paintings at remote Dungkar (4250m; N 31°40.638', E 079°49.471'), approximately 40km northeast of Zanda, are possibly the oldest in Ngari. Their Kashmiri–Central Asian style ties them with the Silk Road cave murals of Kizil in China (particularly in their almost-cartoon style, and the flying apsaras, painted on a blue background). There are three main caves in a side valley before the main village, of which the best preserved is the mandala cave. Lovely nearby Dungkar village also has a ruined **monastery** above the town.

A few kilometres west, the village of **Piyang** (4180m; N 31°40.962', E 079°47.784') is also worth the small detour. It lies at the foot of a large ridge honeycombed with thousands of caves and topped with a ruined monastery and two caves with fine murals.

Entry to both Dungkar and Piyang are technically included in the ¥200 entry fee for Thöling and Tsaparang, though the Piyang caretaker charges an extra ¥30 to enter the caves there since no money from the ticket makes it to the village.

Getting to Dungkar and Piyang is not easy. Most 4WD drivers don't know the area (and may use that as an excuse not to try or to give up after a perfunctory effort) and the dirt roads are poorly signposted. If you come from the Ali–Zanda road, look for the turning east, just north of a village with caves behind it, 36km from Zanda. From here it's 9km past a stunning Himalayan viewpoint to Piyang and then another 5km to Dungkar. From Dungkar you can continue 8km to a junction, then turn right for 16km to join the main Zanda–Moincer road. From here it's 86km to the main Ali–Darchen road. This way you can get an early start and visit Piyang and Dungkar en route between Zanda and Darchen.

Rutok རུ་ཐོག 日土县

The new Chinese town of Rutok Xian (Rìtǔ Xiàn), 132km from Ali, is a modern army post, but there are a couple of great sights nearby that warrant a day trip, especially now that the upgraded road between Rutok and Ali has cut travel time down to just two hours.

Most people visit Rutok Xian as a day trip from Ali, though there are a couple of hotels in town and many restaurants. There's no accommodation or any other facilities at old Rutok.

About 8km north of Rutok Xian, the road hits the east end of turquoise **Pangong-tso** (4241m). The long lake extends 110km into

Ladakh in India. It's worth continuing here for views of the lake but beware of the tour boats; several Chinese tourists died here in 2010 when theirs capsized.

◉ Sights

Ancient Petroglyphs   PETROGLYPHS
In 1985 prehistoric rock carvings, or petroglyphs, were found at several sites in Rutok County. This was the first time such discoveries had been made in Tibet, although similar finds have since been made at numerous other sites.

➡ Rumudong
The extensive collection of rock carvings at Rumudong is right beside the road, about 36km south of the old Rutok turn-off, or about 96km north of Ali. Travelling north from Ali, start looking on the east side of the road at kilometre marker 970 (though the kilometre markers may change with the upgraded road); the petroglyphs are at around 967. There are two distinct groups on the rock face right beside the road, just before it crosses a bridge to travel along a causeway over the marshy valley floor of the Maga Zangbu-chu.

The first and more extensive group also features a number of more recent Buddhist carvings, some of them carved right over their ancient predecessors. The most impressive of the rock carvings features four extravagantly antlered deer racing across the rock and looking back at three leopards in hot pursuit. Also depicted are eagles, yaks, camels, goats, tigers, wild boars and human figures.

➡ Lurulangkar
About 12km southwest of Rutok, these relatively primitive carvings are right beside the road, up to a height of 4m above the ground, and show a variety of pre-Buddhist symbols and animals, including dogs, yaks, eagles, deer and goats. Human figures are shown standing in isolation or riding on horses. There are a number of hunting scenes showing dogs chasing deer and hunters shooting at them with bows and arrows.

Old Rutok   VILLAGE
Lovely white-painted traditional Rutok huddles at the base of a splinter of rock, atop which is **Rutok Monastery**, flanked at both ends of the hill by the crumbling, but still impressive, ruins of **Rutok Dzong**. From

here you can see the reservoir below and Pangong-tso in the distance. The surrounding villages are largely deserted in summer, as herders move to higher pastures.

The intensely atmospheric main chapel of the monastery has a large statue of Jampa (Maitreya) and a bronze Garuda to the left. Clearly, at one time the whole eastern face of the hill was covered in monastic buildings. The monastery was destroyed during the Cultural Revolution and rebuilt in 1983–84; it now has just six monks.

WESTERN NEPAL TO MT KAILASH

Fully organised trekking groups can trek to the Nepal–China border from Humla, a restricted region in the far west of Nepal. You will need a Nepali liaison officer, a specially endorsed Chinese visa and a full trek crew. See Lonely Planet's *Trekking in the Nepal Himalaya* for details of the five-day approach from Humla and the optional return via the Limi Valley.

From the Nepali border at Sher, the road makes a long descent to a stream and then follows the Humla Karnali to the village of Khojarnath, 10km north.

Khojarnath   འཁོར་ཆགས་ན
ELEV 3790M
For those travelling north from Nepal, Khojarnath, 21km south of Purang, is the first large village over the border in Tibet. It boasts the wonderful **Korjak Monastery** (admission ¥30), an important monastery of the Sakya order. The blood-red compound, which dates back to 996, escaped the worst excesses of the Cultural Revolution and the damage sustained has been repaired with financial assistance from German and Italian sponsors.

The eight-pillared Rinchen Zangpo Lhakhang adjoining the main hall is dominated by the trinity of Chenresig (Avalokiteshvara), Jampelyang (Manjushri) and Chana Dorje (Vajrapani). To the right of these statues is a small *rangjung* (self-arising) speaking Tara. The revered 2ft-high statue once warned the monastery's abbot how to prevent flooding of the local area. During the Cultural Revolution the statue was buried for safekeeping.

The atmospheric main hall is entered via an ancient wooden door with particularly fine carvings. The hall itself is presided over by a figure of Jampa (Maitreya). To the far left is a small chamber with paintings from the earliest days of the monastery. Hanging from the ceiling to the right of the entrance are the stuffed carcasses of a yak, Indian tiger, snow leopard, bear, wolverine and a wolf. The inner kora gives access to a hidden protector chapel. When you finish inside do a final kora around the compound to see the unusual *'Om mani padme hum'* mantra painted on the back wall.

Khojarnath is 130km from Darchen or about 107km from Chiu Village on Lake Manasarovar and is a worthy detour. The drive south from Lake Manasarovar is one of the most scenic in Ngari and it's easy to visit as a day trip.

Purang སྤུ་ཧྲེང་ 普兰

☎0897 / ELEV 3800M

Purang (Pǔlán to the Chinese; Taklakot to the Nepalis) is a large trading centre comprising a number of distinct settlements separated by the Humla Karnali River, known in Tibetan as Mabja Tsangpo (Peacock River). Nepali traders come up from the Humla and Darchula regions in the extreme west of Nepal to trade a variety of goods, including rice, carried up from Nepal in huge trains of goods-carrying goats. Indian consumer goods and Nepali rice are traded for Tibetan salt and wool in the **Darchula Bazaar**, a 15-minute walk south of Purang.

Purang is also the arrival point for the annual influx of Hindu pilgrims from India, intent on making a *parikrama* (the Hindu equivalent of a kora) of Mt Kailash, which devout Hindus consider the abode of Shiva. Western trekkers arriving from Nepal usually arrange to be met at the border town of Sher for the 28km drive via Khojarnath to Purang.

The road north from Purang passes the picturesque villages of Toyo and Deraling, with its unusual red chörtens on a ledge above town, en route to the Gurla-la (4715m). Though still part of Ngari, the lush terraced fields and distinct architecture feels connected to Himalayan communities of Nepal and India. Just beyond the pass, Rakshas Tal and (on a clear day) Mt Kailash come into view. Keep looking back south for dramatic views of the Himalayas.

From Purang it's 74km north to Chiu Monastery on the shores of Lake Manasarovar and another 33km from there to Darchen, the starting point for the Mt Kailash kora.

Sights

Shepeling (Simbaling) Monastery BUDDHIST, MONASTERY

This ruined monastery towers over the town from its dramatic hilltop position. In 1949 the Swami Pranavananda described this Kagyud monastery, which housed 170 monks, as the biggest in the region. The monastery's treasures allegedly included one testicle of Indian invader Zowar Singh, displayed every four years during a festival.

The Chinese army shelled the monastery during the Cultural Revolution and today only the assembly hall is partially restored. The views south over the valley and north towards a cave complex are superb but be surreptitious in taking photos. Slogans marked in stones above the military base praise Chairman Mao and the Chinese Communist Party.

Purang

N
0
0
500 m
0.25 miles
Darchen (107km)
Humla Karnali Rv (Mabja Tsangpo)
Gokung (Tsegu) Monastery & Caves
Check-point
Shepeling (Simbaling) Monastery
Mani Wall
Army Camp
Gongga Lu
Peacock Restaurant
Peacock Hotel
Deji Lu
Shepeling Monastery; Indian Border (closed to foreigners)
Darchula Bazaar (1.5km); Khojarnath (21km); Sher & Nepali Border (28km)

The hill northwest of town is the site of a huge army base said to extend far into the mountain in a series of caves. It's even rumoured there are missiles here. Be careful not to photograph – even inadvertently – this or any of the small compounds in town. It's unlawful and you or your local guide could get in serious trouble for it.

Gokung (Tsegu)
Monastery & Caves
BUDDHIST, MONASTERY

In the hills above Purang are many retreat caves formed around the cliffside Gokung (Tsegu) Monastery. A ladder leads up to a couple of upper-floor cave chapels decorated with prayer flags and impressive murals.

🛏 Sleeping & Eating

There are several hotels in town, but the PSB only allows foreigners to stay in the Peacock Hotel.

Despite the proximity to Nepal, there's little flavour of the subcontinent in Purang's restaurants.

Peacock Hotel HOTEL $$
(孔雀宾馆, Kǒngquè Bīnguǎn; ☑290 0139; Gongga Lu; s/d ¥260/280) This government hotel is actually divided into two: a rundown old block with back-breaking beds, no running water and disinterested staff, and a new block with clean bathrooms and hot water.

Peacock Restaurant CHINESE $$
(孔雀饭庄, Kǒngquè Fànzhuāng; Gongga Lu; dishes ¥20-50; ⓜ) This place has the normal range of good Chinese dishes in pleasant surroundings.

ⓘ Information

Agricultural Bank of China (中国农业银行, Zhōngguó Nóngyè Yínháng; Gongga Lu; ⓒ10am-1pm & 4-7pm Mon-Fri) Changes cash and has a 24-hour ATM.

Eastern Tibet (Kham)
ཁམས་

Best Views

➡ Draksum-tso (p193)

➡ Tashigang (p199)

➡ Ngan-tso & Rawok-tso
(p201)

Best Monasteries

➡ Lamaling Temple (p196)

➡ Tsodzong Monastery
(p193)

➡ Bakha Gompa (p199)

Why Go?

Kham is the face you never knew Tibet had: a land of raging rivers and deep gorges, immense pine forests and azalea-filled meadows, outspoken monks and rebel nomads. In Kham the Tibetan plateau begins its descent towards the subtropical Sìchuān basin, and the landscapes represent both extremes: you can drive over a scrubby high mountain pass dusted with snow and a few hours later be sliding your way through rainforest on a mud-bath road. And chances are you'll be the only foreigner in sight.

Most of Kham is off limits these days but, fortunately, the traditional territory of Kongpo, a cradle of early Tibetan civilisation, is open. In this lush, fairy-tale-like land there are intriguing distinctions in architecture, dress, food, worship (the area has a high number of Bönpo) and quirky legends regarding some of the towering figures of Tibetan history.

When to Go

➡ May and June are the best months to travel in eastern Tibet. There's less rain, temperatures are at their most comfortable and much of the landscape is covered in blankets of bright-yellow rapeseed flowers and, at higher elevations, blooming azaleas.

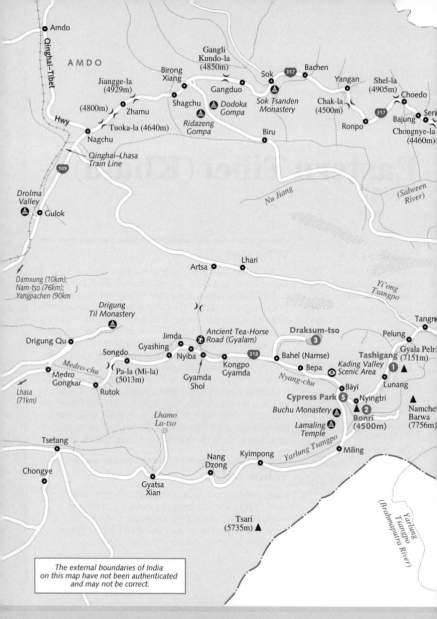

Eastern Tibet (Kham) Highlights

1 Staying with a Tibetan family in the charming village of **Tashigang** (p199).

2 Admiring the devotional spirit of pilgrims on the **Bönri kora** (p196).

3 Visiting the pilgrim power centre of **Draksum-tso** (p193) and its island monastery.

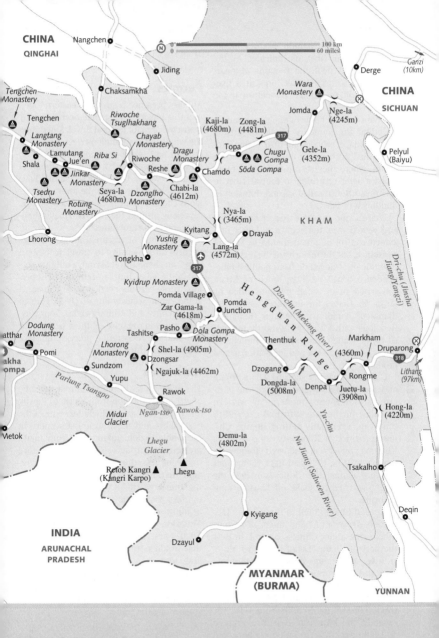

4 Learning why a monastery was built on the grave of Princess Wencheng's child at **Bakha Gompa** (p199).

5 Enjoying endless views of forested mountains, such as at **Cypress Park** (p198), and fast-flowing rivers.

History

The area around Chamdo was one of the first settled in Tibet, as indicated by the 5000-year-old neolithic remains at nearby Karo. Fossilised millet hints at a five-millennia-old tradition of agriculture in the region.

Kham was the home of many early lamas, including the founders of the Drigungpa and Karmapa schools. In 1070 many Buddhists fled persecution in central Tibet for Kham, where they set up influential monasteries, later returning to central Tibet to spearhead the so-called second diffusion of Buddhism in Tibet.

Lhasa's rule over the region has waxed and waned over the centuries. Lhasa first gained control of Kham thanks to Mongol assistance, but the majority of the region has traditionally enjoyed de facto political independence. Until recently, much of Kham comprised many small fiefdoms ruled by kings (in Derge, for instance), lamas (Lithang) or hereditary chieftains (Bathang). Relations with China were mostly restricted to the trade caravans, which brought in bricks of Chinese tea and left with pastoral products.

Chinese warlords such as Zhao Erfeng and Liu Wenhui swept through the eastern part of Kham (modern-day western Sìchuān) in the late 19th and early 20th centuries, eventually setting up the Chinese province of Xīkāng (western Kham). Khampa rebellions occurred frequently, notably in 1918, 1928 and 1932, though not all were against the Chinese; in 1933 the Khampas tried to shake off Lhasa's nominal rule.

In 1950 Chamdo fell to the People's Liberation Army (PLA) and much of eastern Tibet came under Chinese control. In 1954 the part of Kham east of the upper Yangzi River was merged into Sìchuān province and a program of land reforms was introduced, including the collectivisation of monasteries. When in 1955 the Chinese tried to disarm the Khampas and settle the nomads, the Kāngdìng Rebellion erupted and fighting spread to Lithang, Zhōngdiàn and Dàochéng. When the PLA bombed monasteries in Dàochéng and Lithang, the rebels fled to Chamdo and, later, to India and Nepal, to organise armed resistance from Mustang in Nepal with CIA assistance.

Today, eastern Tibet remains quite heavily Sinicised along the southern Sìchuān–Tibet Hwy. Off the main highways, Khampa life remains culturally strong.

Permits

Military presence is strong in eastern Tibet, and this has for a long time been a heavily restricted area for general travel. Since 2008 the whole of the Chamdo prefecture (except Rawok) and much of Nyingchi prefecture, especially along the border with Arunachel Pradesh (which the Chinese claim), have been closed to foreigners. Be aware that regions can temporarily close without notice, especially around the time of Tibetan holidays and important dates.

At the time of research, foreign visitors needed three permits to travel in eastern Tibet: an alien's travel permit, a military permit and a Tibet Tourism Bureau (TTB) permit. These permits needed to be registered at the Public Security Bureau (PSB), Foreign Affairs Office and Military Office. Your travel agency will organise all these permits for you (and the registration process), but give them at least three weeks.

Itineraries

The main route through Kham at the time of writing was a loop from Lhasa to Rawok and back. This stretch includes some of the best sights and most stunning scenery in the whole region, taking you from Lhasa prefecture, through Nyingchi prefecture (more or less the traditional Kongpo region), to the edge of Chamdo prefecture. At the time of writing it was possible to return to Lhasa via the Yarlung Tsangpo Valley by heading south from Rutok on a dirt road. This side route allows you to visit Samye, Tibet's first monastery, and other sights that would normally be covered on a separate tour.

An itinerary might include the following:

Day 1 Lhasa to Bāyī. A full day's drive so best just to include some of the minor stops along the route.

Day 2 Bāyī to Bakha Gompa with a stop in Lamaling and Buchu monasteries.

Day 3 Bakha Gompa to Rawok. Another full day's drive.

Day 4 Visit glaciers around Rawok and head back. Overnight in Tashigang.

Day 5 Full day in Tashigang.

Day 6 Tashigang to Draksum-tso. Overnight at lake.

Day 7 Draksum-tso to Samye. A long day's drive; may need to break in two.

Day 8 Explore Yarlung Tsangpo Valley on way back to Lhasa.

A separate tour of Kham goes from Lhasa to Golmud in Qīnghǎi following the same route as the Tibet–Qīnghǎi railway. Few cover this route by 4WD though some do it by cycling (see p203).

If the Chamdo prefecture ever reopens to foreign travel then the spectacular overland routes through it from Sìchuān and Yúnnán provinces should be high on your wishlist. We cover these below in the section Overland Routes from Sìchuān and Yúnnán.

HWY 318: THE SOUTHERN LOOP

This route covers an eight-day itinerary from Lhasa to Rawok Lake and back along bumpy Hwy 318. From Lhasa until Medro Gongkar the scenery looks much the same as you follow the Kyi-chu River upstream: rolling hills of scrub with patches of green.

After Medro Gongkar there is a noticeable change to a more tree-filled landscape and a more temperate climate. After climbing to the top of the near barren Pa-la pass, and descending, the trend continues with forestland predominating the further east one travels. In the approach to Bāyī, the landscape is one of thick evergreen forests and broad river valleys. A small grove just past the town contains some of the oldest cypress trees in China.

The climb to the Serkym-la pass travels through pretty undulating meadowland blooming with azaleas in spring, before the fast descent into Lunang Forest, the largest in Tibet. The road then drops to the Rong-chu Valley. Here is one of the most bucolic rural landscapes in Kham, with charming stone Tibetan villages, and fields of rapeseed, corn, potatoes and barley cleared from surrounding forests of pine and white oak.

Between Tashigang and Tangmi the road condition deteriorates as the Rong-chu Valley narrows. The hillsides here are scarred by numerous landslides and are often hidden in subtropical fog. Washouts are common on the road, and there are plenty of treacherous bends and sheer drops. But this is a spectacular route, with first the Rong-chu river and later the Parlung Tsangpo river foaming and running wild below (though, interestingly, in different directions). Just past tiny Pelung (a community of Mongpa people) the two rivers meet and turn southeast to join the Yarlung Tsangpo. This marks the lowest part of the Sìchuān–Tibet Hwy (around 1700m).

Along this section you will likely come to admire (and maybe envy) the hundreds of exhausted, wet, mud-splattered Chinese cyclists who have been on the road since Sìchuān. Give them a *jiayou* (literally 'add gas' but with the meaning of 'go, go, go!'). They've earned it.

Just before Tangmi is a one-way bridge that can take hours to cross because the Chinese military permits only a single car at a time. There's a poor-quality side road heading 23km northwest up to the Yigongtso (elevation 2150m), a stunning but hard-to-reach lake that was created by a landslide in 1900, but getting permits to the area is difficult.

Past Tangmi the tarmac returns and the road follows the bank of the ever-widening Parlung Tsangpo. By the time you reach Bakha the river is over a kilometre wide and beautified with islands and more picture-perfect villages with wattle fences on the banks. Princess Wencheng is said to have stayed in the district, known as Powo, during her journey to Lhasa in the 7th century.

The final uphill stretch from Pomi continues along the Parlung Tsangpo through a landscape of pine forests and canyons, until Rawok and its two beautiful lakes.

It's always worth asking your tour agency what additional side routes or destinations might be open or closed when you plan to visit.

Rutok & Songdo 日多，松多

Around three hours' drive from Lhasa is the one-street hot-springs town of **Rutok** (Rìduō) (elev 4300m), named after the monastery on the north hillside. On the main road you'll find rows of Chinese restaurants and Tibetan teahouses, as well as a large indoor hot-spring swimming pool (per person ¥98).

Rutok is also the trailhead for the six-day trek to Lhamo La-tso and the junction with the road heading south toward Tsetang and Samye, for those who want to finish their loop of eastern Tibet with a visit to the Yarlung Tsangpo Valley.

Not far from Rutok, after crossing the 5013m Pa-la pass, is **Songdo** (Sōngduō), which also has hot springs (though they were closed to foreigners at the time of writing) and rows of Chinese and Tibetan restaurants. Most travellers stop here for lunch on the way from Lhasa.

Gyalam: the Ancient Tea-Horse Road

Around the 4381km mark on Hwy 318, near the town of Gyamda, is a suspension bridge festooned with prayer flags. The trail that continues on the other side is part of an ancient trade route (called Gyalam in Tibetan, and the Ancient Tea-Horse Road, 茶马古道, in Chinese) linking Sìchuān, Yúnnán, Tibet and also India. It was still one of the main trade and communication routes between western China and Tibet as late as the 1940s. Today, foreign travellers can follow the trail

Kongpo Region

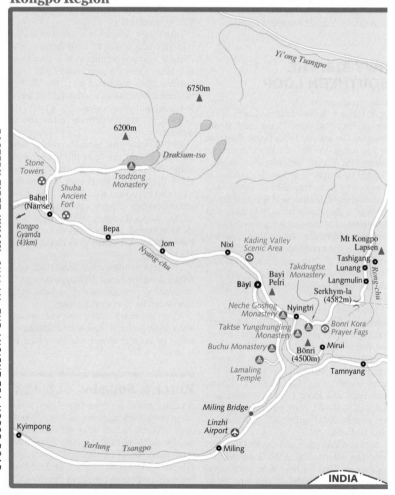

for a short distance to a lookout and some stones engraved with Buddhist mantras associated with Amitabha.

Kongpo Gyamda ཀོང་པོ་རྒྱ་མདའ

工布江达

ELEV 3200M

Unless it's getting late in the day or you are stopping for a meal (there are Chinese, Tibetan and Hui Muslim places on the main road), it's best to avoid this town. Few hotels accept foreigners, and those that do are overpriced and must be chosen carefully to avoid some shockingly sub-standard condi-

tions. The PSB are also very unwelcoming and recently seem to have made it a point to pay the very rare foreign travellers who do stay a midnight hotel-room visit.

Draksum-tso བྲག་གསུམ་མཚོ་

巴松措

☎ 0894 / ELEV 3470M

⊙ Sights

One of the east's most beautiful lakes, **Draksum-tso** (巴松措 | Bāsōngcuò; admission ¥120) is also its most sacred, with strong connections to three towering figures in Tibetan history. It's the soul-lake of Gesar of Ling, the semi-mythical king of Tibetan legends and epic poems. Gesar is said to have resided near the lake and spent years in one of the nearby monasteries. Ruins associated with the king can be found on the road up to the lake, as well as around the lake itself.

Draksum-tso was also visited by Guru Rinpoche and, as in many other places, the great sage left signs of his journey on rocks and caves. Finally, the Nyingma lama Sangye Lingpa founded the Tsodzong Monastery on a tiny islet just off the southern shore. Today, the monastery is one of Kham's most important pilgrimage sites.

The lake entrance fee is payable at a visitor centre/entrance gate about 4km before the lake. PSB officers at the ticket booth will ask to check your travel permits. A shuttle bus (¥45) then takes you to another visitor centre just above the lake. From here it's a quick walk down to the floating bridge across to Tsodzong Monastery. Note that at the time of writing visitors had a two-hour limit at the lake and monastery unless they were spending the night. If possible, try to arrive in the evening to avoid the masses of Chinese tourists.

On your way to or from Rawok Lake consider spending a night at Draksum-tso in a guesthouse rather than a second night in Bāyī.

★**Tsodzong Monastery** BUDDHIST, MONASTERY
The monastery (the Fortress on the Lake) is a small Nyingmapa chapel tucked into the forest on a tiny islet off the shore of Draksum-tso. Associated with the 8th-century king Trisong Detsen, it is also the 14th-century birthplace of Sangye Lingpa, a *terton*. *Tertons* are reincarnations of

EASTERN TIBET (KHAM) KONGPO GYAMDA

THE KONGPO REGION

Kongpo is a large traditional territory in southwestern Kham. While no longer an official administrative name (though it's more or less the same territory as Nyingtri prefecture), for Tibetans it still spells out an area that is linguistically, culturally and even ecologically distinct. A former kingdom of the early Yarlung kings and a rival to Lhasa, Kongpo has for centuries been vilified by central Tibetan rulers as a land of incest and poison, and a land where strangers are drugged so that locals can steal their souls.

The traditional Kongpo costume features a round hat with an upturned rim of golden brocade for men (known as a *gyasha*) and a pretty pillbox hat with winged edges (known as a *dieu*) for women. Men also wear brown woollen tunics, belted around the waist.

Kongpo is a stronghold for Bön, with many of the religion's most holy pilgrim sites found in the forested hills around Bāyī. Locals also revere Princess Wencheng, who is seen as having a special fondness for the region she reputedly passed through on her way to meet King Songtsen Gampo in the 7th century.

Owing to the heavy rainfall, Kongpo houses have slanted roofs, unlike the flat-tops seen in Lhasa. These days sheet metal (often coloured pink or blue) is used, but the open gables allow for ventilation of the attic space (used to store goods).

Barley, potatoes, corn and other staples are farmed all over the region, but several local foods are worth seeking out. Best in our opinion is the red chili mashed into a paste and spread on flat bread. The chili has the sweetness of a *Piment d'Espelette* and the mild kick of a jalapeño. You might be able to bring yourself to eat the adorable free-roaming pigs – they apparently live up to their Chinese name Zàng xiāng zhū, 藏香猪, fragrant Tibetan pig. In the Lunang area check out the stone-pot chicken.

Warmer, wetter and more forested than anywhere else in Tibet, Kongpo has numerous biological niches with large concentrations of rare animals and plants. In the dense forests of the subtropical regions along the southern borderlands are takins, red pandas, long-tailed monkeys, musk deer and abundant bird species. The region is also a botanical powerhouse, and attracted the attention of intrepid 19th- and 20th-century British plant hunters. From May onwards Kongpo is a riot of wildflowers, bursting with 190 species of rhododendron, 110 types of gentians, and rare flowers such as the blue poppy, which was discovered by the explorer (and spy) FM Bailey in the Rong-chu Valley in 1913. Many rhododendrons and azaleas now found in the West in fact descend from species picked in eastern Tibet. Pockets of ancient cypresses up to 2500 years old also continue to thrive, and the first week of April brings the bloom of cherry blossom trees.

Guru Rinpoche's disciples and are tasked with recovering the great spiritual leader's buried relics and texts. The monastery and surrounding kora are filled with holy relics and attract numerous pilgrims.

The main chapel has statues of Sangye Lingpa, Guru Rinpoche, Sakyamuni, Chenresig (Avalokiteshvara) and Kongtsun Demo, a local protector, on horseback. The monastery statues were actually shot and then burned by Red Guards during the Cultural Revolution, before being restored by the famous local lama Dudjom Rinpoche and his son Chuni Rinpoche (now resident at Lamaling Monastery). In the corner is a stone hoofprint of Gesar of Ling's horse. You may see Tibetans rubbing this on their backs to take advantage of its healing powers.

The short kora around the island is filled with relics and natural objects associated with Gesar, Guru Rinpoche and Sangye Lingpa (you'll need the old monk caretaker to help point these all out). On the north side look for an oriental white oak on whose leaves appear the outline of snakes and other animals of the zodiac. As with the hoofprint in the monastery, the likeness to real animals may not strike you as particularly close, but to devout pilgrims in the right visionary frame of mind, it is clear that the outer world is revealing the mythic.

After you have completed the kora head across the small pier to feed tsampa (roasted-barley flour) to the fish. Tibetans will do this when someone they love is ill or suffering.

🛏 Sleeping & Eating

If the PSB allows it, you can stay in Tibetan guesthouses in Jepa Village further up the road from the visitor centre across from Tsodzong Monastery.

ℹ Getting There & Away

Draksum-tso is about a six- or seven-hour drive from Lhasa, or two hours from Bāyī. The road to the lake branches off the Sichuān–Tibet Hwy 318 at Bahel (also known as Namse), where there's a cluster of teahouses, restaurants and lodgings. From there it's around 40km to the lake up a gorgeous farming valley dotted with Tibetan villages and intersected with deep-sided canyons.

Around Draksum-tso

About 12km from the highway junction, the road up to the lake passes tall 12-sided **stone towers** on your left. No one quite knows for what purpose they were built – they stand empty and entry-less. Locals refer to them as *dudkhang* (demons' houses) and recite legends connecting them to Gesar of Ling.

A more accessible group of relics (though largely reconstructed), known as the **Shuba Ancient Fort** (秀巴千年古堡 | Xiùbā Qiānnián Gǔbǎo; admission ¥90), stands on the main highway, 7km east of Bahel. The fort and the half-ruined towers behind it are said to date from the reign of Songtsen Gampo (r 629–49). Most people take photos from the parking lot to avoid the rather steep entrance fee.

Kading Valley Scenic Area   卡定沟风景区

About 27km before Bāyī, at the 4257km mark, is this **forested park** (卡定沟风景区, Kǎdìng Gōu Fēngjǐng Qū; admission ¥20) dominated by a thundering 200m-high waterfall. It's a beautiful area for an hour's break, with lush forests, dark cliff faces and wide views over the Ngang-chu Valley. Note the Chinese have built pathways to the falls, lined them with bamboo, and created fresh legends for the many rocks and land formations, something that does not sit right with Tibetans who consider the area sacred to Palden Lhamo.

Bāyī   བརྒྱད་གཅིག 八一

📞 0894 / POP 60,000 / ELEV 2990M

Bāyī, a recent Chinese creation close to the small county capital of Nyingtri, is the largest town along this stretch of the southern route. At a full day's drive from Lhasa (expect to arrive around 5pm or 6pm after a 7am start from Lhasa) it's an obvious choice for an overnight stay. There are plenty of hotels in town and an abundance of Chinese, Hui Muslim restaurants and some Tibetan teahouses. Locals tend to be coolly curious rather than friendly toward foreigners.

Bāyī is surrounded by forested hills and the descent into town offers fine views of the valley. Ask your guide to show you **Bayi Pelri**, on the east side of town. This holy mountain is associated with the epic battles of Guru Rinpoche against an array of evil forces. The kora around the mountain takes a few hours though it is highly unlikely you will be allowed to join it.

🛏 Sleeping

Bātáng Línqiáo Zhùsùbù   GUESTHOUSE $
(巴塘林桥住宿部; 📞136 5894 8880; 212 Guangdong Lu; dm/s/d ¥30/50/60) This is the cheapest place allowing foreigners. Rooms are pretty shabby but the common showers are hot.

Azalea Hotel   HOTEL $$
(杜鹃花酒店, Dùjuānhuā Jiǔdiàn; 📞582 3222; 408 Guangdong Lu; tw/tr ¥288/388; ❄@🛜) The hotel is ageing but is still a good first choice for clean and comfortable rooms, usually discounted 20%. There's wi-fi in the lobby.

Post Hotel   HOTEL $$
(邮政大酒店, Yóuzhèng Dàjiǔdiàn; 📞588 9666; cnr Xianggang Lu & Guangdong Lu; d/tw ¥200/298; ❄🛜) The twins are modern and comfortable with carpeted floors, TV, and piping-hot showers in admittedly slightly grubby bathrooms. Expect discounts of 20% and wi-fi in the lobby. The front of the hotel always sees a lively group of Tibetans selling medicinal herbs.

🍴 Eating

It seemed like half of Bāyī was under construction at the time of writing, and a new eating and entertainment area was being built alongside the canal in the northern

Bāyī

N 0 ——————— 500 m
  0 ——————— 0.25 miles

Bāyī

part of town. Otherwise, head to the main roads for noodle shops, and Guangdong Lu for a row of Hui Muslim restaurants. For breakfast, look for stacks of steamed dumplings (bāozi; 包子) sold in tiny shops on the main roads.

Héngyuán Xiǎochī   CHINESE $
(恒源小吃; 109 Fujian Lu; dishes ¥8-30; ◷9am-3am) This late-running establishment specialises in pigs' trotters (猪蹄; zhūtí; half a trotter ¥15) from the local free-ranging swine. It also serves decent noodles – try the spicy dàndàn miàn (担担面; ¥13/15 per small/large bowl).

ℹ Information

Bank of China (中国 银行, Zhōngguó Yínháng; Bayi Da Jie; ◷Mon-Fri 9.30am-6.30pm) Two blocks south of Ping'an Lu on the east side of Bayi Da Jie. ATM accepts foreign cards.

Around Bāyī

Bönri   MOUNTAIN
(苯日神山) Bönri (Běnrì Shénshān) is the Bön religion's most sacred mountain, a sprawling massif where Bön founder Tonpa

Shenrab fought and defeated his arch-rival Khyabpa Lagring. Bönpo pilgrims come from all over Tibet to circumambulate the mountain in an anticlockwise direction. Foreign travellers are currently not permitted to do the kora.

The full 60km kora starts and finishes in Nyingtri, 18km west of Bāyī, and takes two or three days, climbing to the 4500m Bönri-la on the second day. It passes many sites connected to Tonpa Shenrab, as well as an ancient burial tumulus, a 9th-century stele and a cemetery for babies.

It's now possible to complete the main part of the kora in around seven hours, thanks to a new road built around the back of the mountain. It's a tough trek because of the steepness of the climb, not to mention the altitude, but it's incredibly rewarding to follow pilgrims over such sacred ground and among such fabulous scenery. The forested mountainside eventually opens onto grasslands at the top where nomads graze their yaks. Azalea bushes also cover parts of the top of the mountain and in season splash the landscape with pink and violet.

The seven-hour section of the kora starts in the village of **Miru** (米瑞; Mīruì), where you can also find a local hiking guide, but it's just as easy to follow the pilgrims. In any case, prayer flags line pretty much the whole route.

The path will take you up and over Bönri-la until you eventually meet the main Sìchuān–Tibet Hwy (Hwy 318) where your driver can pick you up. Don't be persuaded by your guide or driver to either start from the highway, or to trek up and down the same side of the mountain. Doing this may be quicker, and more convenient for your driver of course, but will result in you walking part of the kora in a clockwise instead of anticlockwise direction which will be considered highly disrespectful by the Bönpo pilgrims.

★**Lamaling Temple**   BUDDHIST, TEMPLE
(喇嘛宁寺) The centrepiece of a large walled complex, the colourful Lamaling Temple (Lǎmaníng Sì) is a rare example of the Zangtok Pelri style of building. This style, which imitates the 'Glorious Copper Mountain Paradise' of Guru Rinpoche with a three-storey pagoda-like temple, is unique to the Nyingma order. As with all such temples, the ground floor has a statue of Guru Rinpoche, the second Chenresig (Avalokite-

shvara), while the top chapel is for Öpagme (Amitabha).

The Glorious Copper Mountain is Guru Rinpoche's Pureland, and has been described as a mountain on an island in the cosmic ocean. The island forms a mandala, which is represented architecturally by the Lamaling complex walls: the temple, with its golden-eaved pagoda structure rising from a square base (itself coloured differently on each side), is the mountain in the centre. Statues of Guru Rinpoche are matched with Chenresig and Öpagme to symbolise his birth legend in which Öpagme imagined a being of perfect enlightenment and compassion, and Chenresig sent a golden *vajra* into a lotus bud to give birth to the guru.

The original Lamaling Temple burned down in the 1930s and a new structure was built on the flat below. In the 1960s this too was destroyed during the Cultural Revolution. In 1989 work began on the current temple under the supervision of the daughter of Dudjom Rinpoche (1904–87), former head of the Nyingma order, who had his seat at Lamaling. The monastery is cur-

rently home to around 40 monks, 30 nuns and a number of ornery goats (be careful, they buck).

Take your shoes off before entering the temple – the floor is polished wood. On the ground floor next to the Guru Rinpoche statue look for a stone footprint of the guru on the altar. A passageway behind the altar leads to a mezzanine level with four protector chapels in each corner. Also note the giant coloured prayer beads festooned on the outer walls.

The complex's other main building, to the right, is the assembly hall, where religious services are held on the 10th, 15th and 25th days of each lunar month. The hall is dominated by a huge statue of Sakyamuni and more images of Dudjom Rinpoche wearing his characteristic sunglasses. Pilgrims circumambulate both this building and the main temple.

Lamaling is about 30km south of Bāyī.

Buchu Monastery   BUDDHIST, MONASTERY
(ঠৃ৳ঀ৾ঀৄ৾ 布久寺) FREE This small Gelugpa monastery (Bùjiŭ Sì) dates from the 7th century, when it was built at the command of King Songtsen Gampo as one of the

FOUR RIVERS, SIX RANGES: THE KHAMPA RESISTANCE

Following a failed rebellion against new Chinese rule in the late 1950s, a core of Khampa fighters managed to regroup in Lhoka, in southern Tibet, and in a rare moment of Khampa unity formed an organisation called Chizhi Gangdrung (Four Rivers, Six Ranges), the traditional local name for the Kham region. Soon 15,000 men were assembled.

The Khampa's cause attracted attention from abroad and, before long, Tibetan leaders were liaising with CIA agents in Kolkata (Calcutta), arranging secret meetings through dead letter drops. The first batch of six Khampa agents trekked over the border to India, were driven to Bangladesh and then flown to the Pacific island of Saipan, where they were trained to organise guerrilla groups. Agents were later parachuted behind enemy lines into Samye and Lithang.

In 1957, guerrilla attacks were made on Chinese garrisons and road camps, and in 1958, 700 Chinese soldiers were killed by guerrillas near Nyemo. The movement met with the Dalai Lama in southern Tibet when he fled Lhasa in 1959 as the CIA readied three planeloads of arms – enough for 2000 people. The flight of the Dalai Lama to India marked a setback for the resistance and the focus switched to a base in Mustang, an ethnically Tibetan area in Nepal, where initially at least the Nepalis turned a blind eye to the movement.

Between 1960 and 1962 more than 150 Tibetans were sent to Colorado for training. Yet the resistance was living on borrowed time. By the mid-1960s CIA funding had dried up. By 1972 the international political climate had changed; US President Richard Nixon's visit to China and the coronation of Nepal's pro-Chinese king left the Khampas out on a limb. Moreover, the resistance was riddled with feuds – most of the Khampa rebels had always been fighting more for their local valley and monastery than for any national ideal. In 1973 the Nepalis demanded the closure of the Mustang base and the Dalai Lama asked the rebels to surrender. It was the end of the Khampa rebellion and the end of Tibetan armed resistance to the Chinese.

BĀYĪ TO TASHIGANG

The 70km stretch from Bāyī to Tashigang passes over the 4582m **Serkhym-la** (色齐拉; Sèqí Lā) and is one of the most sublime sections of road in Kham. To start, the road winds around the back of the forested holy mountain Bönri (4500m), passing the point at which the Bönri kora meets the highway, marked by a flurry of prayer flags. You'll see numerous pilgrims on the highway at any point.

The slow crawl up to the Serkhym-la pass takes you through a magical landscape of rolling fields of azaleas, sharp distant peaks, and rushing streams cutting through deep gullies. You'll want to stop often, especially in June when the flowers are in bloom.

As you head down from the pass, you'll see dramatic views of shark-toothed Namche Barwa (7756m), Gyala Pelri (7151m) and Lunang Forest, the largest in Tibet. Be careful where you pull over for a look on this section as any spot that looks officially like a rest area will have an exorbitant fee.

The village of Lunang (鲁朗; Lǔlǎng), set in the valley of the Rong-chu River, makes for a good rest stop, both for the high mountain views from the grasslands, and for the numerous restaurants off the main road. The local dish is chicken served in a stone pot (shíguōjī; 石锅鸡) but there is also regular Sìchuān fare and Tibetan grub at a couple of teahouses.

At the time of writing, about 2km of land alongside the road from Lunang to Tashigang was under construction as part of what is being called the Lunang International Tourism Village. Change is coming to this area to prepare for mass tourism. How it will affect the overall rural environment is difficult to say – with any luck most tourists will stay in the new village, leaving the true homestays and countryside for the more intrepid.

Expect to take about two hours to drive this route without breaks for the scenery.

demoness-subduing temples; it pins the demoness' right elbow. Inside are a number of holy relics including a footprint of Guru Rinpoche and a *lado* (a 'life supporting' stone) in a glass case.

The monastery is recognisable by its striking golden roof. The entrance to the main chapel is flanked by murals of several protector gods, including the Kongpo local deity Kongtsun Demo (in the far right on horseback, next to the Wheel of Life). The main hall has a rare statue of the standing form of Guru Rinpoche and also a large Jampa (Maitreya).

The inner sanctum houses statues of Chenresig (Avalokiteshvara), with Songtsen Gampo in the left corner. Behind them is the trinity of Guru Rinpoche, the Indian translator Shantarakshita and King Trisong Detsen. Here also is the stone footprint of Guru Rinpoche, one of only three in all of the Kongpo region.

It's said that the monastery's outer walls survived destruction during the Cultural Revolution (as so many did not) so save time for a walk round the short kora that follows the perimeter. The monastery is about 1km before the turn for Lamaling Temple.

Neche Goshog Monastery
BUDDHIST, MONASTERY

(尼池寺) This small, golden-roofed Bön monastery was rebuilt in 2008 after being gutted in a fire. It's home to around 25 monks and is famous for a 2000-year-old juniper tree that is sacred to Bönpos. The manicured courtyard includes a small side shrine dedicated to the Bön founder Tonpa Shenrab. The monastery is about 17km east of Bāyī, on your right just before you reach the town of Nyingtri.

Cypress Park
FOREST

(世界柏树王园林, Shìjiè Bóshù Wáng Yuánlín; admission ¥30; ☺9am-5pm) A few kilometres south of Bāyī a stand of ancient cypress trees dot a steep but inviting hillside. The most venerable cypress is a reported 2500 years old, making it the oldest tree in China, and as old as the Buddha himself. This, in addition to the tree being sacred to Bön founder Tonpa Shenrab, makes the site exceptionally holy for Tibetans, and a prime pilgrim spot.

Owing to the short growing season at altitude, the trees in this park are not as thick or tall as those you find in Redwood Park in California, for example, but they are still magnificent. As with many sights in Tibet, the Chinese have built pavilions and paths around the trees (and given them new legends), though mercifully they are largely unobtrusive. Walk a few minutes up the paths from the oldest tree and you will likely be alone with the 'younger' trees and the big views across the valley.

Tashigang བཀྲ་ཤིས་སྒང་དམར་གསོལ།
གོང་ཚོ་ 扎西岗民俗村
📞 0894 / ELEV 2530M

☉ Sights & Activities

A visit to this tiny rural village, a couple of kilometres east of Lunang, is for many travellers a highlight of a trip to eastern Tibet. For here you can stay with a Tibetan family in a local house, eat home-cooked meals, and stroll through a dreamy landscape of green barley and yellow rapeseed fields, with dense, forested mountains rising across the valley. Tashigang (Zhāxīgǎng) is as pretty and bucolic a place as you could wish for.

The village is comprised of walled stone Tibetan block homes, which gives you a rare chance to examine this hardy architecture up close. Do ask if you can visit the attic of a house. While houses in Lhasa sport flat roofs, in Kongpo they are slanted with open gable ends. Food and other materials are usually stored in the well-ventilated attic space.

On a knoll above the village is a highly visible kora (look for the cluster of prayer flags). You can complete a circuit and return to your guesthouse in an hour.

🛏 Sleeping & Eating

There are 14 guesthouses in the village, all offering similar levels of accommodation and home-cooked meals. Beds might be a bit hard, but expect to be generally comfortable and to have flushing squat toilets available. If you don't like the guesthouse your guide has brought you to, by all means ask to see another.

Guests are charged per person (around ¥60 to ¥80), which includes breakfast. Other meals are extra. If you stay for dinner be sure to ask to try the local chili paste, used as a dip for bread. With the rise of mass tourism in the area and the building of the tourism village nearby we can't say how this rural experience will change in the coming years, though prices will likely rise sharply.

Bakha Monastery ས་ཁ
☉ Sights & Activities

The road from Tashigang to Bakha Gompa (ས་ཁ), or monastery, situated on an island in the Parlung Tsangpo River, is alternately one of the most dramatic and bucolic in all Kham. After Tashigang the Rong-chu river valley narrows and enters a deep canyon where road washouts are common and delays are to be expected: it could take three to four hours to drive this route, or double that.

At the village of Pelung watch for the water flow changing direction: the Parlung Tsangpo and Rong-chu rivers (coming from different directions) meet here and then continue southeast through a canyon that may be the world's deepest. After Tangmi the valley begins to widen again, the river swells to over a kilometre wide, and stonehouse villages with yellow rapeseed fields hemmed in by wattle fences appear on the banks. These achingly beautiful landscapes are backed by towering snow-capped peaks so be sure you make time for photo breaks.

At the 4036km mark look for a small bridge over to Bakha Island. Cross and head left 200m to reach Bakha Gompa, an 800-year-old Nyingma monastery which was once the seat of power in Powo (the traditional name of the formerly highly independent region bordering Kongpo). The monastery is home to 12 monks and is reputed to have been built on the grave site of the illegitimate child of Princess Wencheng and Tibetan Minister Gar Tongtsen. Gar is the man who had arranged the marriage alliance between the Tang princess and his king Songtsen Gampo, and had also accompanied her from Chang'an to Tibet.

While the stillborn child of an illicit affair might seem an odd thing to commemorate with a temple, Princess Wencheng is revered across eastern Tibet, where she is often seen more as a private missionary to the region than as part of an official exchange between Lhasa and the Tang dynasty. Numerous locations in Kham claim to be the meeting point of the princess and Songtsen Gampo, while legends claim she left the real Jowo Buddha statue, and other parts of her dowry, in Kham temples. Stories also recount the love affair with Minister Gar that tell of either a live babe abandoned to its fate in a basket sent downriver, or of the infant buried at Bakha.

EASTERN TIBET (KHAM) TASHIGANG

TIBET'S HIDDEN LANDS

The Pemako region south of Pomi is a *beyul* (or *pelyul*), one of 16 'hidden lands' scattered throughout the Himalaya that were rendered invisible by Guru Rinpoche. Guidebooks on how to get to the hidden lands were written by the guru as *terma* (concealed teachings) to be rediscovered at a suitable time by *tertons*. Tertons are reincarnations of the guru's disciples specifically tasked with recovering hidden treasures such as the guru's footprints found in many temples or, in this case, the concealed teachings.

Spiritual realisation is said to be easily attained in such places, but the *beyul* also act as sanctuaries providing protection in times of war or famine. Many Khampas fled to Pemako when the Chinese invaded eastern Tibet in the 1950s.

The Tsangpo Gorges, south of Tangmi, are a hidden land of another sort – entry is currently banned to foreign travellers. It's still worth knowing as you travel between Lunang and Tangmi that just over the mountains in the Yarlung Zangbo Grand Canyon National Park (inaugurated in 2010) is what may be the world's deepest gorge. In this region the swollen Yarlung Tsangpo makes some dramatic U-turns and crashes over a series of spectacular falls. With 7756m Namche Barwa and 7151m Gyala Pelri towering on either side, the gorge records a depth of 5382m (almost three times the depth of the Grand Canyon), with a length of 496km. At one point the river narrows to a mere 20m, before bursting into the Assamese plain as the vast Brahmaputra River.

The region remains one of the world's least explored, and is home to king cobras, leopards, red pandas, monkeys, musk deer, tigers, waterfalls and virgin forests. For a contemporary account of Tsangpo exploration, read Tom Balf's *The Last River: The Tragic Race for Shangri-la*, which details an ill-fated 1998 National Geographic–sponsored expedition in which kayaker Doug Gordon was killed.

The name Bakha in fact comes from *basa*, which means hiding place. Historically, lamas of the monastery believed themselves to be reincarnations of the dead infant, and scholar Cameron Davis Warner in his very readable essay *A Miscarriage of History* writes that their dual Chinese-Tibetan origin may have been understood by Powo rulers as justification for their independence from both China and central Tibetan authority.

While the current Bakha Monastery is small, the views of the surrounding mountains and river, to say nothing of the island itself, are near indescribably charming; this is a fairy-land landscape that is, not surprisingly, infused with connections and manifestations to Buddhist faith. Ask the monks to point out the Naga tree, as well as Elephant Mountain (unusually, not a bad likeness of a profile of an elephant with a long stretched trunk).

🛏 Sleeping & Eating

⭐ **Rinchen Family Guesthouse**   GUESTHOUSE **$**

(仁青家庭旅馆 | Rénqīng Jiātíng Lǚguǎn; ☑139 0894 0848; r from ¥180) Set on a slope above the Parlung Tsangpo, across from Bakha Gompa, this family-run guesthouse is one of the most scenically placed in all Kham.

In the handsome pine main lodge you'll find cosy wood-panelled rooms (those on the second floor are best) with large bathrooms, Tibetan details, and outstanding views from the balcony.

Room walls are a bit thin so you will hear every noise from your neighbours. Fortunately, there's plenty of land to wander about for privacy. Less fortunate is that the family hasn't decided whether they are running an intimate guesthouse or a small resort. Chinese tour groups and cultural entertainment, such as kitschy campfire dances and opportunities for tourists to dress in traditional Tibetan clothing, add nothing to the experience of staying here. Still, it is easy to get away from the tackiness, and mornings and afternoons are sublime. The **restaurant** (dishes ¥5 to ¥35, breakfast ¥10), set even higher on the slope and even more scenically placed, offers excellent Chinese and Tibetan fare including local specialities such as free-range pork and wild mushrooms.

Pomi   སྤོ་མེས། 波密

☑ 0894 / ELEV 2740M

This bustling county capital (Bōmì) has well-stocked shops and several hotels and restaurants, making it a good place to spend the night (though Bakha is better). The main street now sports wide sidewalks, and re-facaded buildings in a fake but still pleasant Tibetan style. High forested mountains provide the backdrop.

Pomi is less than an hour's drive from Bakha Gompa.

◉ Sights

Dodung Monastery   BUDDHIST, MONASTERY
This tranquil, 600-year-old Nyingma-sect monastery is set on a pine-clad hill overlooking the valley, and is home to 56 monks. The main prayer hall includes the footprint of the seventh Khamtrul Rinpoche, Sangye Tenzin (1909–29). Upstairs are murals depicting the life of two forms of Gesar, as well as Guru Rinpoche and Tsepame (Amitayus). Also look for several delightful mani lhakhangs (buildings holding prayer wheels) and a traditional woodblock printing room.

The monastery, a branch of Chayab Monastery, is around 6km west of Pomi. Cross the road bridge over the Parlung Tsangpo, opposite the Jiāotōng Lǚguǎn, and take the first right. This road continues all the way to Metok (and made Metok the last county in China to be connected by road!), but after about 3km to 4km you need to turn sharp left uphill to the monastery.

⫶ Sleeping & Eating

For Tibetan teahouses or Sìchuān fare head to Ping'an Jie, a little tree-lined street running for a block south toward the river from across the Agricultural Bank.

Jiāotōng Lǚguǎn   HOTEL $
(交通旅馆; ☏189 0894 3591, 542 2798; tw without/with bathroom ¥68/158; ☎) Rooms are basic but have 24-hour hot water and are usually discounted 20%. Wi-fi is available in the lobby. Do note that the hotel is on the north side of the main road (the river is to the south) so don't confuse it with the larger hotel of the same name just opposite.

Míngzhū Bīnguǎn   HOTEL $$
(明珠宾馆; ☏542 4688; Zhamuxi Lu, 扎木西路; tw ¥288-368; @) Among the best-quality rooms in town, these come with clean bathrooms, 24-hour hot water, ADSL and, in some cases, river views. Standard twins are usually discounted to ¥150. The hotel is at the west end of the main road, next to the petrol station.

ℹ Information

Agricultural Bank of China ATM (农业银行; Nóngyè Yínháng) On the main road; may accept foreign cards.

Rawok   ར་འོག 然乌
☏0895 / ELEV 3880M

Rawok (Ránwū) is a small ramshackle outpost off Hwy 318 on the northeast corner of Ngan-tso Lake. It's about three hours' drive from Pomi with the snow-capped forested mountains and the Rong-chu as your companion (the river drains from Ngan-tso). The town is a decent base for enjoying the lake and the nearby glaciers.

★ Ngan-tso & Rawok-tso   LAKES
Ringed by mountains, and joined by a stream so that on the map they resemble the infinity symbol, these are the largest lakes in Kham. Ngan-tso is the more westerly and so is the one seen first by travellers from Lhasa. Ask your guide to show you how to get to the old village near Rawok (on the lake's northeastern shore) to visit the large chörten and small temple nearby overlooking Ngan-tso. You need to drive another 6km southeast to visit Rawok-tso.

Píng'ān Fàndiàn   GUESTHOUSE $$
(平安饭店; ☏456 2606; dm/tw ¥30/220; ☎) A few hundred metres west of the main strip is this popular place with a lively restaurant

---

⬤ WORTH A TRIP

GLACIERS AROUND RAWOK

The most popular excursion from Rawok is to the **Lhegu Glacier**, 31km south of town, but this was off limits to foreigners at the time of research.

Midui Glacier (米堆冰川 | Mǐduī Bīngchuān; admission ¥50), about 35km west, on the road to Pomi, was open but always check before heading out as the rules can change without warning. This quiet and picturesque glacier is reached by first driving 7km off the main highway to a car park. From here it's a two-hour horse ride or walk to Midui Village (Mǐduī Cūn; 米堆村), then the glacier is a further 2km. Depending on current regulations you may be able to approach closer or you may just be permitted to view it from the village.

and ageing but decent twin rooms in the main building. There's also a romantic alternative in the form of a cabin on stilts hovering above the cool-blue waters of Ngan-tso (when the lake waters are high enough, that is). Staff are friendly and the lobby/restaurant has a cosy wood-burning stove. If you need fancier digs the owner has another hotel nearby.

Ránwū Bīnguǎn   GUESTHOUSE **$$**
(然乌宾馆; ☎ 139 8905 8387; tr ¥220; ☎) Close to town, this place has acceptable rooms and also a good restaurant with wi-fi.

OVERLAND ROUTES FROM SÌCHUĀN & YÚNNÁN

At the time of research, foreigners were forbidden from travelling overland from Sìchuān into Tibet proper (and vice versa) because Tibet's far eastern prefecture of Chamdo, which borders Sìchuān, was closed.

The two main routes start from Kanding in Sìchuān until they join with the Tibetan Autonomous Region (TAR) towns of Chamdo and Pomda. Both routes are part of the legendary Sìchuān–Tibet Hwy, which splits in two about 200km east of the TAR border to form the northern route (Hwy 317) and the southern route (Hwy 318). Both lead to Lhasa. The slightly busier and strategically more important southern route takes in the best of the alpine scenery. Here you'll see (and hear) rivers powering their way through deep gorges and subtropical forests before flowing into sublime mirror lakes overlooked by distant snow-capped peaks.

The reasons to travel these routes are many. Wild, mountainous and deliciously remote, the traditionally Tibetan areas of western Sìchuān are a cultural and geographical extension of the Tibetan plateau in all but name. This area was once part of the eastern Tibetan region of Kham, and has long been the meeting point of the Chinese and Tibetan worlds. In many ways Tibetan culture is better preserved here than in the TAR. It's certainly subject to fewer religious restrictions, and you'll see photos of the Dalai Lama displayed freely.

Unlike the TAR, western Sìchuān is permit-free, meaning foreign travellers can explore to their heart's content. May and June are the prime times for a visit. For details, including weather, and specific sleeping and eating options along the route, see Lonely Planet's *China* guidebook.

Kanding

Kanding (康定; Kāngdìng; Dardo) is the gateway into Sìchuān's Tibetan world, and has long been a trade centre between Tibetans and Han Chinese. The 'do' of Kāngdìng's Tibetan name, Dardo, means 'river confluence', and aptly this lively town is nestled in a deep river valley with distant snow-capped mountains, including the imperious Gònggā Shān (Minyak Gangkar in Tibetan; 7556m). Today, although there is a large Tibetan population, the city feels more Chinese, but you can still find elements of Tibetan culture in the food, the dress and, to a lesser extent, in the architecture.

The Northern Route (Hwy 317)

It may have only been around since 1954, but the Sìchuān–Tibet Hwy has a well-deserved reputation for being one of the highest, roughest, most dangerous and most beautiful roads in the world. Around 70km west of Kāngdìng it splits, and one branch becomes the northern route (Hwy 317).

The northern route is around 300km longer and generally less travelled than the Southern. It runs through 'big sky' country, with wide-open grasslands, soaring snow-topped mountains, and traditional Tibetan communities with their remote monasteries and motorcycle-riding yak herders. The road also crosses Tro-la (5050m), the highest pass this side of Lhasa, before descending towards the Tibet border.

You must come prepared with warm clothing; even in midsummer, it can be very cold at higher elevations once the sun goes down.

The first stop along this route is **Tăgōng** (Lhagong; 塔公; elevation 3750m), a small Tibetan village with beautiful surrounding grasslands. As well as an important monastery and a fascinating nearby nunnery to visit, there's also horse trekking (and a horse festival in July) and hiking. Travellers have given rave reviews to the Tibetan homestays here.

Next up is **Gānzī** (Garzê; 甘孜; elevation 3394m), a dusty but lively market town in a picturesque valley surrounded by snow-capped mountains. It's easy to spend a couple of days exploring the beautiful countryside, which is scattered with Tibetan villages and monasteries. Between Gānzī and Derge is the stunning turquoise **Yilhun Lha-tso** (新路海), a holy alpine lake which has great hiking and camping possibilities. The town nearest the lake is tiny Yùlóng or Mǎnígāngē, commonly referred to by its Tibetan name, Manigango.

The last town before the TAR is **Derge** (德格; elevation 3270m), cut off from the rest of western Sìchuān by the towering Chola Mountain. Derge is famous for its 18th-century monastery housing a printing press that still uses traditional wood-block printing methods. There are more than 217,000 engraved blocks of Tibetan scriptures here from all the Tibetan Buddhist orders, including Bön. These texts include ancient works about astronomy, geography, music, medicine and Buddhist classics, including two of the most important Tibetan sutras. A history of Indian Buddhism, comprising 555 wood-block plates in Hindi, Sanskrit and Tibetan, is the only surviving copy in the world. All in all the monastery holds an astonishing 70% of Tibet's literary heritage.

After Derge you cross into the TAR. Chamdo is still another 347km away.

The Southern Route (Hwy 318)

The southern section of the Sìchuān–Tibet Hwy is shorter and less remote (relatively speaking, of course), and so is more commonly used by travellers (especially cyclists, who number daily in the hundreds), young Chinese hitchhikers, and pilgrims who prostrate their way slowly along the main road, often walking as far as Lhasa.

Travel here takes you through vast grasslands dotted with Tibetan block homes and contentedly grazing yaks, while majestic peaks tower beyond. While journeying along this route is slightly easier than taking the northern route, it's still not for the faint-hearted: road conditions vary from rough to rougher and, just like on the northern route, cold weather and altitude can be an issue.

One of the major stops along the route is **Lithang** (理塘; Lǐtáng, elevation 4014m) with opportunities for getting into the surrounding mountains by horse, motorbike or simply hiking. Lithang is famed as the birthplace of the seventh and 10th Dalai Lamas, and has one of the Tibetan world's biggest and most colourful festivals: the annual Lithang Horse Festival, which includes horse racing, stunt riding, dance competitions and an arts-and-crafts fair.

Around 32km from the TAR border is **Bathang** (巴塘; Bātáng; elevation 2589m). Bathang itself has a welcoming monastery, while outside the town are lovely suburbs of ochre-coloured Tibetan houses. Bathang is much lower than surrounding areas, so when it's late winter in Lithang it's already spring here. There are some fine walks, including to a lovely Tibetan hillside village, a riverside chörten and a hilltop covered in prayer flags that offers views of the town.

From Batang it's possible to make it all the way to Pomda in one long day's drive (about eight hours), or you can stop in **Markham** (Mángkāng) which has for centuries been a strategic crossroads town on the salt- and tea-trade routes between Tibet and China. Either way the roller-coaster road crosses three high mountain passes and some stunning scenery before arriving at Pomda (Bāngdá) and the junction of Hwys 318 and 317.

Yúnnán–Tibet Highway

The Yúnnán–Tibet Hwy is a wonderful way to approach Tibet, though once again the route is officially closed. From Lijiang a road heads up to the Tibetan towns and monasteries of Zhōngdiàn (Gyeltang), Benzalin and Déqīn (Jol), and then north across the Tibetan border and up to Markham, where the road joins the Sìchuān southern route.

THE NORTHERN ROUTES OF KHAM

The remote highways running along the north of Kham can be used to exit the TAR into Qīnghǎi, Sìchuān, or as part of a long loop around Kham. At the time of writing, only one route into Qīnghǎi was open to foreign travellers: Hwy 109 (also known as the Qīnghǎi–Tibet Hwy) running from Lhasa to Xīníng. As the railway covers the same route most people do not hire private vehicles for this section. A few hardy souls make the trip by bike, crossing into Tibet over the 5180m Tangu-la pass. Under current regulations, a guide still needs to accompany you and your bicycle in a support vehicle. Check out Bike China (p305) for more.

Hwy 317, a high roller-coaster ride past Bön monasteries and herding communities, has been closed to foreign travellers for many years now. Assuming it ever reopens, the journey starts with a day's ride to **Nagchu** (Nàqū), one of the highest, coldest and most windswept towns in all of Tibet. Perched on the edge of the Changtang (northern plateau), it is an important stop on both the road and railway line between Qīnghǎi and Tibet. In fact, this is where Hwy 317 ends as it joins the Qīnghǎi–Tibet Hwy (Hwy 109) on its way to Lhasa.

On the western outskirts of the town is the large **Shabten Monastery** (founded 1814), a branch of Lhasa's Sera Monastery, with more than 90 monks. The main hall here is particularly atmospheric. Look in the back hall for the strings of dried tamarind pods, said to have been brought here from India as gifts for the Buddha.

Continuing east of Nagchu look for a turnoff, south of Hwy 317, that brings you to **Dodoka Gompa** (达木寺; Dámù Sì). This remote monastery in Biru County contains one of Tibet's strangest, creepiest and least-visited sights: the mysterious **Biru's Skull Wall** (骷髅墙, kūlóu qiáng; admission ¥10). Making up the southern part of a half-open courtyard in the monastery, the wall looks like any other Tibetan mani wall from a distance. But as you approach it you realise that instead of being made of engraved prayer stones, it's made of hundreds and hundreds of human skulls.

Further along is **Sok**, a crossroad town whose claim to fame is the impressive **Sok Tsanden Monastery** (索赞丹寺 | Suǒzàndān Sì) perched on an outcrop in the southern suburbs. Built in 1667 by the Mongol leader Gushri Khan, this Gelugpa monastery, home to 150 monks, looks like a miniature version of the Potala.

From Sok to Tengchen is a journey of 270km. There are several small towns to get

food and accommodation, and two stunning passes along the way: the 4460m-high pass **Chongnye-la** (Chuni-la) which offers fabulous views across nomad camps and yak herds to the huge range of snowy peaks to the south; and the impressive 4905m-high **Shel-la**, the highest and most dramatic pass along the northern route.

Tengchen (ༀ཈ཅ丁青, Dīngqīng), sitting at 3820m, is a largely Tibetan town and it and the surrounding area of Khyungpo are strong centres of the Bön religion. The Bön **Tengchen Monastery**, founded in 1110, sits on a hillside about 3km west of town.

The 148km stretch of Hwy 317 from Tengchen to Riwoche is littered with more monasteries, including **Tsedru Monastery** (孜珠寺 | Zīzhū Sì), at 4800m one of Tibet's highest monasteries and its largest Bön monastery. The location, strung out along a ridgeline below a series of natural cliffs and caves, is about as fantastical as you can imagine.

From the western edge of the midsize town of **Riwoche** (ར་བ་ཆེ 类乌齐县, Lèiwūqí Xiàn), a road branches northwest to Yùshù in Qīnghǎi province. Near the town is the village of Riwoche (类乌齐镇; Lèiwūqí Zhèn) and the fascinating monastery **Riwoche Tsuglhakhang** (类乌齐寺 | Lèiwūqí Sì), which towers over the village, dwarfing the circumambulating pilgrims.

Another 110km from Riwoche is **Chamdo** (ཆབ་མདོ 昌都, Chāngdū), a major stop on the northern route into Tibet from Sìchuān province. Chamdo, at the strategic river junction of the Dza-chu and the Ngon-chu, is a surprisingly pleasant town and is dominated by the hilltop **Galden Jampaling Monastery**. Over 1000km from Lhasa and 1250km from Chéngdū, the town is the major transport, administrative and trade centre of the Kham region.

From Chamdo, the road follows the **Mekong River** (Dza-chu; 澜沧江; Láncāng Jiāng) 65km to Kyitang, passing a Willy Wonka-esque landscape of spearmint green fields, raspberry purple hills and chocolate-coloured streams, as well as a number of monasteries. Leaving Kyitang, the road dramatically climbs 29km to the 4572m-high **Lang-la pass** (浪拉山; Lànglā Shān) before descending again and continuing past the turn-off for an old caravan trail to Lhasa and then on to the airport.

One site worth dropping into is **Yushig Monastery**, around 6km before the airport. The spirited debating that takes place here in the afternoons sounds more like a pub brawl than a theological discussion!

Further south about 45km is **Pomda** (སྤོམ་ མདའ་ 邦达, Bāngdá), which comes in two parts: the T-junction where Hwy 318 meets Hwy 317, and the village, about 5km north of the junction, where you'll find **Pomda Monastery** (邦达寺; Bāngdá Sì). The junction is full of restaurants, teahouses and guest-houses and makes an OK place to bunk up for the night.

Continuing south you pass the one-street town of **Pasho** (དཔའ་ཤོད་ 八宿, Bā Xiù), and then follow a dramatic 90km stretch of road to Rawok (and its two stunning lakes) which includes a climb up the 4462m-high pass **Ngajuk-la**, at which you end your time on the arid plateau and start the descent into the subtropical Parlung Tsangpo Valley.

Tibetan Treks

Best Long Trek

➜ Ganden to Samye (p213)

Best Short Trek

➜ Shalu to Nartang (p221)

Best Cultural Trek

➜ Mt Kailash Kora (p223)

Best Trek to Spot Wildlife

➜ Nyenchen Tanglha
Traverse (p229)

Why Go?

Tibet, the highest land on earth, is a trekker's dream. Its towering mountains, deep valleys and verdant forests offer unbounded opportunities for walking. On foot the joys of the Tibetan landscape are heightened and immediate, and all other modes of transport pale in comparison. The wonders of Tibet's natural environment are enhanced by the people met along the trail, heirs to an ancient and fascinating way of life. By plying the highland paths one can enter into the same solemn relationship with nature that has sustained Tibetans through the ages.

When to Trek

➜ The best time to trek in Tibet is during the warmer half of the year.

➜ May and June are excellent months without much rain or snowfall but some high alpine passes may still be closed.

➜ July and August are the warmest months of the year, but they tend to be rainy and this can make walking messy and trails harder to find.

➜ September and October are excellent months for trekking, but in high areas the nights are cold and early snow is always a possibility.

PLANNING YOUR TREK

For all its attractions, Tibet is a formidable place where even day walks involve survival skills and generous portions of determination. The remoteness of Tibet combined with its extreme climate poses special challenges for walkers – and unique rewards. As it's situated on the highest plateau on earth and crisscrossed by the world's loftiest mountains, nothing comes easily and careful preparation is all important. Even on the most popular treks high passes up to 5600m are crossed.

Cities such as Lhasa and Shigatse provide bases from which to equip and launch treks. Walking the classic treks presented here will serve you well. Should you decide to venture further afield, there are certainly many more frontiers beckoning the experienced, well-equipped trekker.

It's a good idea to budget an extra day for your trek in case you get on the road more slowly than intended. Your travel guide might also need additional time hiring local help and beasts of burden.

Trekkers must be prepared for extremes in climate, even in the middle of summer. A hot, sunny day can turn cold and miserable in a matter of minutes, especially at higher elevations. Night temperatures above 4700m routinely fall below freezing, even in July and August. At other times of year it gets even colder. In midwinter in northwestern Tibet, minimum temperatures reach minus 40°C. Yet Tibet is a study in contrasts, and in summer a scorching sun and hot, blustery winds can make even the hardiest walker scurry for any available shade. Between the two extremes, the Tibetan climate – cool and dry – is ideal for walking, but always be prepared for the worst.

Before embarking on a trek, make sure you're up to the challenge of high-altitude walking through rugged country. Test your capabilities by going on day walks in the hills around Lhasa and Shigatse. Attempt a hike to the top of a small mountain such as Bumpa Ri, the prayer-flag-draped peak on the far side of the Kyi-chu from Lhasa.

What to Bring

There is a great deal to see while trekking and you will be revitalised by the natural surroundings, but you must be prepared for extremes in weather and terrain. The time

of year and the places where you choose to walk will dictate the equipment you need.

Clothing & Footwear

As a minimum, you will need basic warm clothing, including a hat, scarf, gloves, down jacket, long underwear, warm absorbent socks, all-weather shell and sun hat, as well as comfortable and well-made pants and shirts. Women may want to add a long skirt to their clothing list. Bring loose-fitting clothes that cover your arms, legs and neck, and a wide-brimmed hat like the ones Tibetans wear.

If you attempt winter trekking, you will certainly need more substantial mountaineering clothing. Many people opt for synthetic clothing, but also consider traditional wool or sheep fleece, which have proven themselves in the mountains of Tibet for centuries. One of your most important assets will be a pair of strong, well-fitting hiking boots. And remember to break them in before starting your trekking!

Equipment

Three essential items are a tent, sleeping bag and portable stove. There are few restaurants in the remote areas of Tibet and provisions are hard to come by, so you or your support staff will end up preparing most of your meals. Expect to camp most nights – except in certain villages on the main trekking routes, it can be difficult to find places to sleep. Invest in a four-season tent that can

HEALTHY TREKKING

To maintain your health in such a difficult high-elevation environment you will need to take some special precautions. However, with a little preparation and good sense, your trekking experience will be one of the highlights of your trip to Tibet. Bring a first-aid kit with all the basics (and perhaps some extras as well). Never trek alone and ensure you have adequate health and evacuation insurance. Trekkers are particularly vulnerable to sunburn, hypothermia and acute mountain sickness (AMS): make sure you're prepared.

handle big storms and heavy winds. A warm sleeping bag is a must. Manufacturers tend to overrate the effectiveness of their bags, so always buy a warmer one than you think you'll need.

You will also need a strong, comfortable backpack or duffel bag large enough to carry all of your gear and supplies. To save a lot of misery, test the backpack on short hikes to be certain it fits and is properly adjusted. When trekking with animal transport a small knapsack is essential for your immediate daily needs.

Other basic items include water containers with at least 2L capacity, a system for water purification, a torch (flashlight), compass, pocketknife, first-aid kit, waterproof matches, sewing kit, shrill whistle and walking stick or ski pole. This last item not only acts as a walking aid, but also as a defence against dog attacks. Tibetan dogs can be particularly large and brutal, and they roam at will in nearly every village and herders' camp. Bring your walking stick or pole from home, or purchase trekking poles in Lhasa.

Petrol for camping stoves is widely available in towns and cities but is of fairly poor quality. To prevent your stove from getting gummed up you will have to clean it regularly. Kerosene (煤油; méiyóu in Chinese; sanum in Tibetan) can also be obtained in cities. At the time of research there was a ban on selling petrol in portable containers. To get around this restriction ask your tour drivers to siphon fuel for you.

Nowadays, there are scores of shops in Lhasa selling trekking equipment.

Maps

There are numerous commercially available maps covering Tibet, but very few of these maps are detailed enough to be more than a general guide for trekkers.

The Chinese government produces small-scale topographic and administrative maps, but these are not for sale to the general public. The US-based Defense Mapping Agency Aerospace Center produces a series of charts covering Tibet at scales of 1:1,000,000, 1:500,000 and 1:250,000. The most useful of the American 1:500,000 references for trekking in Tibet are H-10A (Lhasa region, Ganden to Samye, Tsurphu to Yangpachen), H-9A (Kailash and Manasarovar) and H-9B (Shigatse region, Shalu to Nartang, Everest region).

Old Soviet 1:200,000 topographic maps can be consulted in many large university library map rooms. Buying them has become easier with commercial outlets in the West stocking them. Punch 'Tibet maps' into your computer search engine to see who carries them in your area.

Digital maps are freely available at www.earth.google.com. To access them you will have to download the Google Earth installer. The images currently available vary widely in quality but many are now of a standard allowing you to closely chart your trekking routes.

The Swiss company **Gecko Maps** (www.geckomaps.com) produces a 1:50,000-scale Mt Kailash trekking map.

Trekking Agencies

The kind of trek you take will depend on your experience and the amount of time you have. Whatever your choice you must go through an offically recognised trekking agency and take a guide along with you. In this age of intense scrutiny, the good old days of going at it alone are over.

One of the main advantages of signing up with an agency is that it takes care of all the red tape and dealings with officials. Most agencies offer a full-package trek, including transport to and from the trailhead, guide, cook, yaks, horses or burros to carry the equipment, mess tent and cooking gear. The package may even include sleeping bags and tents if these are required. You can also negotiate cheaper, less inclusive packages by bringing more equipment from home and cooking yourself along the trail.

There is a plethora of private agencies that can arrange treks. Let the buyer beware though, for the standard of service fluctuates wildly and may bear little relation to what you pay. Shop around online or better yet on the ground. Competition between agencies is strong, impelling the smarter ones to up the quality of their trekking services. Be prepared to provide all your own personal equipment.

Make sure the agency spells out exactly what is included in the price it is quoting you, and insist on a written contract detailing all services that are to be provided as well as a money-back guarantee should it fail to deliver what has been agreed. For the standard contents of tour contracts, have a look at the brochures of adventure-travel companies in your home country. It is prudent to pay one-half of the total cost of a trip up front and the balance after the trek is completed. This is now more or less standard operating procedure in Tibet.

All the Lhasa-based agencies listed here have run many successful treks. Trekkers are particularly at the mercy of those driving them to and from the trailheads. To avoid problems, it is prudent to test the driver and guide on a day trip before heading off into the wilds with them. Always have the phone number of your agency so that you can contact them should something go awry. Mobile (cell) phone coverage has now been extended to all the trailheads and to many places along the trekking routes.

Prices vary according to group size, ranging from US$170 to US$300 per person per day. For treks in remote and border areas, your agency will need up to three weeks to sort out the permits. If you feel you have been cheated by your agent, you may find help with the marketing and promotion department of the **Tibet Tourism Bureau** (☑0891-683 4315; fax 683 4632) in Lhasa. This government organisation is in charge of training tour guides and monitoring the performance of all trekking and tour companies.

The agencies listed below tend to be tucked away in hard-to-find spots. If you are in Lhasa call first and ask the staff to come and pick you up.

Lhasa Agencies

Higher Ground Treks & Tours   TOUR
(☑0891-686 5352; higherground_treks_tours@yahoo.com; 75 Beijing Middle Rd) The head of this agency, Karma Khampa, was once a manager at Tibet International Sports Travel.

Tibet International Sports Travel   TOUR
(Xīzàng Shèngdì Guójì Lǚxíngshè;   Map p44; ☑0891-633 4082; www.sdtist.com; 6 Lingkhor Shar Lam) The oldest agency specialising in trekking. Located next to the Himalaya Hotel, it has been managed for many years by Peldon.

Tibet Wind Horse Adventure   TOUR
(☑0891-683 3009; www.windhorsetibet.com; B32 Shenzheng Huayuan, Sera Beilu) One of the best-managed agencies in town. The running of treks and white-water rafting trips is handled by Jampa, the general manager.

Tibet Songtsan International Travel Company   TRAVEL AGENCY
(☑136 3890 1182; www.songtsantravel.com; 2nd fl next to Dico's restaurant, Jokhang Temple Sq; ☏) Run by Tenzin, this up-and-coming outfit is eager to serve new clients.

Tibet Yongdru International Travel Service   TRAVEL AGENCY
(☑0891-683 5813; info@tibet-yongdrutravel.com; No 5 Bldg, 1st fl, New Shol Village) A main focus of the sales director Thupden is trekking in the more remote regions of Tibet.

SAFETY GUIDELINES FOR WALKING

Before embarking on a walking trip, consider the following points to ensure a safe and enjoyable experience:

➡ Be sure you are healthy and feel comfortable walking for a sustained period.

➡ Only undertake treks that are well within your physical capacity and level of experience.

➡ Obtain reliable information about the terrain and current conditions along your intended route from local inhabitants.

➡ Be aware of local laws, regulations and customs about wildlife and the environment.

RESPONSIBLE TREKKING

With average temperatures increasing more rapidly than almost any other place on earth, the environment of Tibet is under unprecedented pressure. It is imperative that trekkers make their way lightly and leave nothing behind but their proverbial footprints. Tibet's beautiful but vulnerable landscape deserves the utmost respect. A fire, for instance, can scar the landscape for centuries. Stay off fragile slopes and do not tread on delicate plants or sensitive breeding grounds. Follow the Tibetan ethos, killing not even the smallest of insects. This approach guarantees that later visitors get to enjoy the same pristine environment as you.

Rubbish

➡ Carry out every piece of your rubbish including toilet paper, sanitary napkins, tampons and condoms.

➡ Have a dedicated rubbish bag and minimise packaging materials.

➡ Do not burn plastic and other garbage as this is believed to irritate the Tibetan divinities.

Human Waste Disposal

➡ Where there is a toilet, use it.

➡ Where there is none, human waste should be left on the surface of the ground away from trails, water and habitations to decompose. If you are in a large trekking group, dig a privy pit. Be sure to build it far from any water source or marshy ground and carefully rehabilitate the area when you leave camp. Ensure it's not near shrines or any other sacred structures.

Washing

➡ Don't use detergents or toothpaste in or near watercourses, even if they are biodegradable.

➡ For all washing use biodegradable soap and a lightweight, portable basin at least 50m away from the water source.

➡ Try using a scourer, sand or snow instead of detergent. Widely disperse the waste water to allow the soil to filter it.

Kathmandu Agencies

If you want to organise your Tibet trek from Kathmandu in Nepal, here are some of the most qualified agencies.

Dharma Adventures TOUR
(☑01 4430499; www.dharma.com.np; GPO Box 5385, 205 Tangal Marg, Tangal)

Sunny Treks and Expeditions TOUR
(☑01 4432190; www.sunnytravel.com.np; PO 7823, Baluwatar)

Tibet International Travels and Tours TOUR
(☑01 4444339; www.tibetintl.com; 29 Tridevi Marg, Thamel)

Miteri Nepal International Trekking TOUR
(☑01 4437163; www.miterinepaltrekking.com; Bhagwatisthan 29, Thamel)

Western Agencies

A few Western companies organise fixed-departure treks in Tibet. These tours can be joined in your home country or abroad, usually in Chéngdū or Kathmandu. Prices are higher than treks arranged directly in Tibet or Kathmandu, but they save you a lot of effort and are useful if you have the money but only a couple of weeks to spend.

A trek organised at home includes a Western leader, a local guide, porters, a cook and so on. All your practical needs will be taken care of, freeing you up to enjoy the walking.

Erosion

➡ Hillsides and mountain slopes are prone to erosion, so stick to existing tracks and avoid short cuts.

➡ Do not trench around tents.

➡ Never remove the plant life that keeps topsoil in place.

Fires & Low-Impact Cooking

➡ Building fires is not an option. Wood is nonexistent in much of Tibet and where there are trees and bushes they are desperately needed by locals.

➡ Cook on a lightweight kerosene, petrol, alcohol or multifuel stove and avoid those powered by disposable butane gas canisters.

➡ Make sure your guide and porters have stoves.

➡ Ensure that all members are outfitted with adequate clothing so that fires are not needed for warmth.

Good Trekking Partnerships

➡ Monitor all your staff members closely and make it clear that any gratuities will hinge upon good stewardship of the environment.

➡ Stress to your agency that you will not tolerate rubbish being thrown along the trail or at the trailheads.

➡ Explain to your drivers that rubbish should not be thrown out the windows (a common practice in Tibet).

Wildlife Conservation

➡ Do not engage in or encourage illegal hunting.

➡ Don't buy items or medicines made from endangered wild species.

➡ Discourage the presence of wildlife by cleaning up your food scraps.

Camping

➡ Seek permission to camp from local villagers or shepherds. They will usually be happy to grant permission.

Permits

Individuals are not permitted to trek independently in Tibet and must join an organised group. Trekking, as with all travel in Tibet apart from Lhasa city, requires travel permits.

ON THE TREK

Trekking trails in Tibet are not marked and in many places there are no people to ask for directions. Paths regularly merge, divide and peter out, making route-finding inherently difficult. If you're not good at trailblazing, this is another good reason to have a registered guide provided by a travel agency.

Guides & Pack Animals

The rugged terrain, long distances and high elevations of Tibet make most people think twice about carrying their own gear. In villages and nomad camps along the main trekking routes it's often possible to hire yaks or horses to do the heavy work for you.

Your guide will negotiate what you need in the way of pack animals. A mule skinner, horseman or yak driver will also serve as a local guide; they are an important asset on the unmarked trails of Tibet. Local guides can also share their knowledge of the natural history and culture of the place, greatly adding to your experience.

The rates for pack animals vary widely according to the time of the year and location.

Horses and yaks are pricey at Mt Kailash, costing upwards of ¥250 per animal. In most other places burros and horses can be had for ¥120 to ¥200 per head. Local guides and livestock handlers usually command ¥150 to ¥200 per day. Remember that your hired help are also paid for the time it takes them to return home.

Food

You should be self-sufficient with food since there isn't much to eat along the trail. Bring anything you can't live without from home, such as high-energy bars and your favourite chocolates. In Lhasa there are thousands of stalls and shops selling a huge variety of foodstuffs, making well-balanced, tasty meals possible on the trail. Even in Shigatse and the smaller cities there are many foods suitable for trekking.

Vacuum-packed red meat and poultry, as well as packaged dried meat, fish and tofu, are readily found in Lhasa. Varieties of packaged and bulk dried fruits are sold around the city. You can even find almonds and pistachios imported from the USA.

Dairy- and soybean-milk powders can be used with several kinds of prepackaged cereals. Oatmeal and instant barley porridge are widely available in the supermarkets. Pickled and dried vegetables are good for dressing up soups and stir-fries. For an added touch, Indian pickles and curry powders are available in shops near the Barkhor. Lightweight vegetables such as seaweed and dried mushrooms can do wonders for macaroni and instant noodles. Wholemeal Chinese noodles made of various grains are now on the supermarket shelves as well.

Cooking mediums include butter, margarine, vegetable oil and sesame oil. Butter can be preserved for long treks or old butter made more palatable by turning it into ghee

(boil for about 20 minutes and then strain). All kinds of biscuits and sweets are sold in Lhasa and the larger regional towns, while decent-quality Chinese and Western chocolate is available in Lhasa.

Drink

As wonderfully cold and clear as much of the water in Tibet is, do not assume that it's safe to drink. Livestock contaminate many of the water sources and Tibetans do not always live up to their cultural ideals. Follow Tibetan tradition and eliminate the monotony of drinking plain water by downing as much tea as you can. You can buy Chinese green tea in all its varieties in every city and town in Tibet. If you're offered Tibetan yak-butter tea, have it served in your own cup as per tradition – this eliminates the risk associated with drinking from used cups. More like a soup than a tea, it helps fortify you against the cold and replenishes the body's salts.

TREKKING ROUTES

Detailed descriptions of several popular treks are given here. They offer fantastic walking, superb scenery and, with the exception of Lake Manasarovar and Mt Kailash, are close to Lhasa or the main highways. Walking times given are just that: they don't include breaks, nature stops or any other off-your-feet activities. On average, plan to walk five to seven hours per day, interspersed with frequent short rests. You will also need time for setting up camp, cooking and eating, and for the plain enjoyment of being there.

The trek stages can be used as a daily itinerary, but plan ahead to avoid spending the night at the highest point reached in the day.

SOCIAL TREKKING

In most out-of-the-way places trekkers can quickly become the centre of attention, and sometimes just a smile may lead to dinner invitations and offers of a place to stay. If you really detest being the star of the show, don't camp in villages. If you do, don't expect Western notions of privacy to prevail.

If you have any religious sentiments, your trek probably qualifies as a pilgrimage, in which case you will generally receive better treatment than if you are 'just going someplace'. Another helpful hint: if all else fails try a song and dance. Even the most amateur of efforts is met with great approval. For other cultural considerations, see the boxed text on p276.

Tibetan Treks

0 — 400 km
0 — 200 miles

The external boundaries of India on this map have not been authenticated and may not be correct.

1. Ganden to Samye Map (p215)
2. Tsurphu to Yangpachen Map (p219)
3. Shalu to Nartang Map (p222)
4. Mt Kailash Kora Map (p224)
5. Nyenchen Tanglha Traverse Map (p230)
6. Lake Manasarovar Kora Map (p233)

CHINA

CHINA

Sumzhi

Nganglong Kangri

Tangu-la

Ali   Tsaka   Dzango   Amdo
Tsaparang   Tsangon

Mt Kailash   Tsochen   Mt   Nagchu   Riwoche
Darchen   Nyenchen   Kongpo   Tangmi
   Tanglha   Gyamda   Rawok
Paryang   Lhasa   Bayi
Zhongba   Shigatse   Namche   Yanjing
   Sakya   Gyantse   Barwa
Dzongka   Tingri
   Tsona

NEPAL   Mt   BHUTAN   INDIA
KATHMANDU   Everest   THIMPHU

INDIA

Ganden to Samye

This trek has much to offer: lakes, beautiful alpine landscapes, herders' camps and sacred sites, as well as two of Tibet's greatest centres of religious culture. With so much to offer, its popularity is understandable, but you should not underestimate this walk.

The best time for the trek is from mid-May to mid-October. Summer can be wet but the mountains are at their greenest and wildflowers spangle the alpine meadows. Barring heavy snow, it's also possible for those with a lot of trekking experience and the right gear to do this trek in the colder months. If you're coming straight from Lhasa, you should spend at least one night at Ganden Monastery (4190m) to acclimatise.

If you're fit, acclimatised and have a pack animal to carry your bags, it's not difficult to do the trek in 3½ days, overnighting in Hepu/Yama Do, Tsotup-chu and Yamalung, though some groups take the full five days. You'll experience at least three seasons on this trek, probably in the same day! From the wintry feel of the Chitu-la you rapidly descend to the springtime rhododendron blooms of the middle valley until the summer heat hits you on the final approach to Samye. Pack accordingly.

Guides and pack animals can be procured in the villages of Trubshi and Hepu, situated in the Tashi-chu Valley near Ganden. An improved road now connects these villages to the Kyi-chu Valley.

Stage 1: Ganden to Yama Do

5-6 HOURS / 17KM / 300M ASCENT/450M DESCENT

The trek begins from the car park at the base of Ganden Monastery. It may be possible to find a pack animal or porter here to help carry your bags to Hepu or beyond; ask among the incense and prayer-flag sellers near the car park.

Leave the car park and look for the well-trodden trail heading south along the side of Angkor Ri, the highest point on the Ganden kora. After 20 minutes the Ganden kora branches off to the right (4360m; N 29°44.891', E 091°28.788'); keep ascending to the south for another 30 minutes. You quickly lose sight of Ganden but gain views of Samadro village below you, before reaching a **saddle**, marked by a large *lapse* or cairn (4530m; N 29°44.130', E 091°29.729').

From the saddle, look south to open the approach to the Shuga-la in the distance. Traversing the west side of the ridge from the saddle, you briefly get views of Trubshi village below and the Kyi-chu Valley to the west. After 45 minutes the trail descends towards Hepu village. About 20 minutes from the spur is a spring. From here it's a further 30 minutes to the village, 2½ hours or so from Ganden.

There are around 30 houses in the village of **Hepu** (4240m; N 29°42.387, E 091°31.442') and it's possible for trekkers to camp or find accommodation among the friendly locals. There's good camping to the south and west of the village. Look for a red-and-yellow masonry structure and white incense hearths at the southeastern edge of the village. This is the **shrine** of Hepu's *yul lha* (local protecting deity), the Divine White Yak.

From Hepu the trail climbs towards the Shuga-la, 3½ hours away. Walk west downhill from the village towards a bridge crossing the Tashi-chu, near the confluence with another stream. Round the inner side of the confluence and head south upstream along the east bank. You are now following the watercourse originating from the Shuga-la. Near the confluence are good camp sites.

One hour from Hepu you reach **Ani Pagong**, a narrow, craggy bottleneck in the valley. A small nunnery used to be above the trail. Across the valley is the seasonal herders' camp of Choden. From Ani Pagong, the trail steadily climbs for one hour through marshy meadows to **Yama Do** (4490m; N 29°40.511', E 091°30.918').

Yama Do offers extensive camp sites suitable for larger groups. Consider spending the night here as it's still a long climb to the pass and there are few other camping places along the way.

Stage 2: Yama Do to Tsotup-chu Valley

5-7 HOURS / 10KM / 1000M ASCENT/450M DESCENT

Above Yama Do the valley's watercourse splits into three branches. Follow the central (southern) branch, not the southeast or southwest branches. The route leaves the flank of the valley and follows the valley bottom. The trail becomes indistinct but it's a straight shot up to the pass. About 30 minutes from Yama Do are two single-tent camp sites, the last good ones until the other side of the pass, at least five hours away. One hour past Yama Do leave the valley floor and ascend a shelf on the east side of the valley to avoid a steep gully that forms around the stream. In another 45 minutes you enter a wet alpine basin studded with tussock grass.

The **Shuga-la** is at least 1¼ hours from the basin. Remain on the east side of the valley as it bends to the left. You have to negotiate boulders and lumpy ground along the final steep climb to the pass. The Shuga-la (5250m; N 29°38.472', E 091°32.015') cannot be seen until you're virtually on top of it. It's marked by a large cairn covered in prayer flags and yak horns, and is the highest point of the trek.

The route continues over the Shuga-la and then descends sharply through a boulder field. Be on the lookout for a clear trail marked by cairns on the left side of the boulder field. This trail traverses the ridge in a southeasterly direction, paralleling the valley below. Do not head directly down to the valley floor from the pass unless you have good reason. It's a long, steep descent and once at the bottom you have to go back up

---

GANDEN TO SAMYE AT A GLANCE

Duration 4–5 days

Distance 80km

Difficulty medium to difficult

Start Ganden Monastery

Finish Samye Monastery

Highest Point Shuga-la (5250m)

Nearest Large Towns Lhasa and Tsetang

Accommodation camping

Best Time to Trek mid-May to mid-October

Summary This demanding trek crosses two passes over 5000m, connects two of Tibet's most important monasteries and begins less than 50km from Lhasa. It has emerged as the most popular trek in the Ü region.

the valley to complete the trek. In case of emergency, retreat down the valley for a bolt back to the Lhasa–Ganden Hwy, a long day of walking away.

The trail gradually descends to the valley floor, 1½ hours from the pass and 200m below it. The views of the valley and the lake at its head are one of the highlights of the trek. Cross the large **Tsotup-chu** (4980m; N 29°37.366', E 091°33.288'), which flows through the valley, and keep an eye out for the herders' dogs. During heavy summer rains take special care to find a safe ford. The pastures in the area support large herds of yaks, goats and sheep, and during the trekking season herders are normally camped here. Known as Tsogo Numa, this is an ideal place to camp and meet the *drokpas* (nomads).

An alternative route to Samye via the **Gampa-la** (5050m) follows the main branch of the Tsotup-chu past a couple of lakes to the pass. South of the Gampa-la the trail plunges into a gorge, crisscrossing the stream that flows down from it. These fords may pose problems during summer rains or when completely frozen. See Gary McCue's *Trekking in Tibet – A Traveler's Guide* for details of this route.

Stage 3: Tsotup-chu Valley to Herders' Camps

5 HOURS / 14KM / 300M ASCENT/400M DESCENT

From the Tsotup-chu ford, the main watercourse flows from the southeast and a minor tributary enters from the southwest. Follow this tributary (which quickly disappears underground) steeply up for about 30 minutes until you reach a large basin and a cairn that offers fine views down onto Palang Tsodü lake. Stay on the west side of the basin and turn into the first side valley opening on the right. A couple of minutes into the valley you'll pass a large group **camp site** (5079m; N 29°36.604', E 091°33.544'). This is a good alternative camp site to the Tsotup-chu, but only if you're acclimatised as it's 100m higher.

Follow this broad valley, which soon arcs south to the Chitu-la. The pass can be seen in the distance, a rocky rampart at the head of the valley. At first, stay on the west side of the valley; there is a small trail. As you approach the pass, the trail switches to the east side of the valley. If you miss the trail just look for the easiest route up: the terrain is not particularly difficult.

Ganden to Samye

Approximate Scale

The **Chitu-la** (5210m; N 29°34.810', E 091°33.160') is topped by several cairns and a small glacial tarn. Move to the west side of the pass to find the trail down and to circumvent a sheer rock wall on its south flank. A short descent will bring you into a basin with three small lakes. The trail skirts the west side of the first lake and then crosses to the eastern shores of the second two. It takes 45 minutes to reach the south end of the basin. Drop down from the basin on the west side of the stream and in 30 minutes you'll pass a collection of **cairns** (5077m; N 29°33.924', E 091°32.790') to the right. A further 20 minutes brings you to the stone walls of a camp where herders have carved out level places for their tents.

Below the herders' highest camp, the valley is squeezed in by vertical rock walls, forcing you to pick your way through the rock-strewn valley floor. Pass a side stream after 15 minutes and then cross over to the west side of the widening valley to recover the trail. In 20 more minutes you will come to a flat and a seasonal **herders' camp** on the east side of the valley, which is good for camping. At the lower end of the flat, return to the west side of the valley. The trail again disappears as it enters a scrub willow and rosebush forest, but there is only one way to go to get to Samye and that is downstream.

In 30 minutes, when a tributary valley enters from the right, cross to the east side of the valley. After 10 minutes more you will reach another seasonal **herders' camp**, inhabited for only a short time each year. Another 20 minutes beyond this camp, hop back to the west bank to avoid a cliff hugging the opposite side of the stream. Pass through a large meadow and ford the stream back to the east bank. From this point the trail remains on the east side of the valley for several hours.

Camp sites are numerous here. Soon you'll pass herders' tents near the spot where the side valley coming from the Gampa-la joins the main valley. Descend the finger of land formed by the river junction and then cross the **stream** (4460m; N 29°31.603', E 091°32.980'). Unless an impromptu wooden bridge has been erected by the herders, during heavy summer rain you might have to wait for the water to subside in order to cross safely.

Stages 4 & 5: Herders' Camps to Samye Monastery

10 HOURS / 39KM / 1200M DESCENT

The trail is now wide and easy to follow as it traces a course down the east side of the valley. Walk through the thickening scrub forest for one hour and you will come to another stream entering from the east side of the main valley. Look for the wood-and-stone **Diwaka Zampa bridge** (4335m; N 29°30.439', E 091°33.165') 50m above the confluence. The valley now bends to the right (west) and the trail enters the thickest and tallest part of the scrub forest. The right combination of elevation, moisture and aspect create a verdant environment, while just a few kilometres away desert conditions prevail.

The next two-hour stretch of the trail is among the most delightful of the entire trek. According to local woodcutters more than 15 types of trees and shrubs are found here, some growing to as high as 6m. Fragrant junipers grow on exposed south-facing slopes, while rhododendrons prefer the shadier slopes. The rhododendrons start to bloom in early May and by the end of the month the forest is ablaze with pink and white blossoms.

The trail winds through a series of meadows. After 40 minutes the stony flood plain of a tributary joins the river from the north. In another 30 minutes look for a mass of prayer flags and an ancient juniper tree at a place known as Gen Do. This is a **shrine** (4165m; N 29°29.525', E 091°31.805') to the protector of the area, the goddess Dorje Yudronma. Just past the shrine, cross a small tributary stream. In one hour the forest

---

TREKKING TIBETAN STYLE

Given the chance, many Tibetans would rather ride or drive than go on foot, but there are also great trekkers among them. The ubiquitous shepherds traipse around on a daily basis searching out pasture for their sheep and goats. Typically they set out early in the morning and cover up to 40km before returning to camp in the evening with their herds. Then there are the pilgrims who visit temples, monasteries and holy mountains on foot. Pilgrimages can last two or three years and stretch from one end of the vast Tibetan plateau to the other. The greatest Tibetan trekkers though are the 'swift foot', mystic athletes reputed to move many leagues in a single day. Imagine leaving London in the morning and arriving in Edinburgh in the evening without ever taking your feet off the ground! It is said that years of special physical training and esoteric initiation are required to accomplish the amazing feats of the swift foot.

While few trekkers visiting Tibet are likely to attain swift foot status, there is still much to be gained by emulating the native people. When walking long distances they breathe slowly and deeply, filling their lungs completely. Tibetan walkers inhale and exhale exclusively through the nose, conditioning the cold, dry air before it reaches the lungs. Like the proverbial turtle they tread slowly and steadily, avoiding excess rest stops. Being immersed in prayer is also traditionally thought to aid trekkers. At the very least it helps keep the mind off the minor discomforts that inevitably come from moving a long time under one's own steam. For a bit of a challenge try imitating the rolling gait of Tibetans, but be forewarned: you may need to spend a few years on horseback before perfecting this technique!

rapidly thins and **Changtang**, the first permanent village since Hepu, pops up. There's good camping just before the village. From Changtang the walking trail becomes a full-fledged motorable road.

Look south to the distant mountains; this is the range on the far side of the Yarlung Tsangpo Valley. About 45 minutes down the valley at a prominent bend in the valley is the turn-off for the **Yamalung Hermitage**, visible on the cliff-face high above the valley. A small shop run by the nuns of Yamalung sells soft drinks, beer and instant noodles. There's fine camping across the bridge; the path to Yamalung also leads up from here. It's a 45-minute steep climb to the hermitage. Yamalung (also called Emalung) is where the Tibetan wonder-worker Guru Rinpoche is said to have meditated and received empowerment from the long-life deity Tsepame (Amitayus).

From the turn-off to Yamalung the valley is much wider. Nowadays many groups opt to end their trek at Yamalung, but if the weather is good and you want a taste of southern Tibetan cultural life, consider carrying on. In 15 minutes you will reach a bridge; the road now sticks to the west side of the valley all the way to Samye, a 3½-hour walk away. Some 20 minutes from the bridge you will come to the village of **Nyango**, with its substantially built stone houses. A big tributary stream, entering from the northwest, joins the Samye Valley here. The old trade route from Lhasa to Samye via the Gokar-la follows this valley.

A 30-minute walk past Nyango is the village of **Wango** and, an hour beyond here, the hamlet of **Pisha**. From the lower end of Pisha, a hill can be seen in the middle of the mouth of the Samye Valley. This is **Hepo Ri**, one of Tibet's most sacred mountains. The entire lower Samye Valley – a tapestry of fields, woods and villages – can be seen from Pisha. Pisha is the last place where water can be conveniently drawn from the river. From here on, the trail only intersects irrigation ditches.

Around 15 minutes past Pisha a ridge spur called **Dragmar** meets the trail. On the ridge is the partially rebuilt palace where King Trisong Detsen is said to have been born. Formerly a lavish temple, it now stands forlorn. Below, just off the road, is a small red-and-white **temple** (3687m; N 29°22.802', E 091°30.399'), which is often locked and enshrines the stump of an ancient tree. Legend

PASS HEIGHTS

Elevations in Tibet, especially for passes, are notoriously inconsistent, with maps and road signs rarely agreeing over the correct elevation. In this guide we have tried to use composite measurements, incorporating the most accurate maps, the most consistently agreed on figures and on-the-spot GPS readings (which have their own inconsistencies and inaccuracies). Most figures should be accurate within 100m or so, but use the elevations here as a guide only.

has it that a red-and-white sandalwood tree grew here, nourished by the buried placenta of Trisong Detsen. During the Cultural Revolution the tree was chopped down.

A further 20 minutes down the trail is **Sangbu** village, from where there are good views of the golden spires of Samye. The route follows the road direct to Samye along the margin of woods and desert: it takes about one hour. The closer you get to Samye the hotter the valley can become; in May and June it can be fiery hot. You finally enter the perimeter wall of **Samye** (3630m), about three hours from Nyango.

Tsurphu to Yangpachen

Beginning at Tsurphu Monastery, this rugged walk crosses several high valleys before emerging into the broad and windswept Yangpachen Valley. Combining alpine tundra and sweeping mountain panoramas with visits to monasteries, this trek nicely balances cultural and wilderness activities.

The best time for this walk is from mid-April to mid-October. Summer can be rainy but be prepared for snow at any time. As you will be in nomad country, beware of vicious dogs, some of which take a sadistic pride in chasing hapless foreigners. Fuel and food are not available, so come prepared. There are few permanent settlements along the way and the inhabitants are often away from home. Your only option on this trek is to be fully self-sufficient.

Tsurphu Monastery (4500m) is a good place to spend a night acclimatising. The area around the Karmapa's former *lingka* (garden), 10 minutes' walk upstream from the monastery, is ideal for camping. Villagers in Tsurphu ask around ¥2000 for a guide and two yaks for a five-day return trip to Yangpachen.

If you're well acclimatised, it's possible to do this trek in three days by continuing on to Tajung on day two and finishing at the Dorje Ling Nunnery or continuing all the way to Yangpachen on day three.

Stage 1: Tsurphu Monastery to Leten
3½-4 HOURS / 11KM / 500M ASCENT

The trek begins by heading west or up the valley. Follow the kora trail 10 minutes west to the lingka (4550m; N 29°43.436', E 090°34.128'), a walled copse of old trees with a brook. This garden-like wood has been established as a trekkers' camp free of charge by the monks of Tsurphu. The trees here are the last you will see until after finishing the trek. Consider spending two nights at this leafy location to give your body a chance to acclimatise. Just above the copse, the valley splits: follow the northwest branch and remain on the north side of the stream. There is now a narrow dirt road all the way to Leten.

Walking through a rocky gorge along a well-graded trail for 45 minutes brings you to Shupshading (4700m; N 29°43.574', E 090°32.876'), a seasonal herders' camp on an easily missed shelf above the trail. After 40 minutes look for a line of ruined red chörtens to your right. After a further 15 minutes the valley looks like it splits; follow the main river valley (to the left) and cross the stream on a small concrete bridge (4890m; N 29°43.396', E 090°31.859'). Above the north side of the bridge is the permanent pastoral village of Sercha Sumdo, but the trail now continues on the south side of the valley. In another 20 minutes you'll pass a popular camping spot. Look out for small herds of na (blue sheep) on the slopes to the north.

About 25 minutes further on, by a mani wall (N 29°43.373', E 090°30.856'), the road climbs up over a high saddle while the trail splits off and follows the valley floor. From the mani wall Leten is about an hour away. This trail passes to the right of a large cliff, past the remains of winter ice, before swinging to the left up into the natural bowl of Leten.

Several families live year-round in the drokpa settlement of Leten (5090m; N 29°43.557, E 090°30.094'), braving the severe climate with their livestock. Leten is the last chance to find yaks. Camping spots are limited by the lumpy terrain and places already staked out by the nomads. If you value your peace and quiet, consider camping in the valley below Leten.

Spend at least one night (and preferably two) in Leten acclimatising.

Stage 2: Leten to Bartso
5-6 HOURS / 15KM / 300M ASCENT/600M DESCENT

It's about a three-hour walk from Leten to the Lasar-la. Head for the northern half of the settlement (assuming you aren't already there). The route climbs steeply up a short ridge, reaching the highest house. Bear northwest into a steep side valley. As you ascend, a reddish knob of rock looms up ahead. Angle to the north, or right, of this formation, past a mani (prayer) wall in the centre of the bowl, and leave the valley by climbing to the top of a spur marked

---

TSURPHU TO YANGPACHEN AT A GLANCE

Duration 3 days

Distance 45km

Difficulty medium to difficult

Start Tsurphu Monastery

Finish Dorje Ling Nunnery or Yangpachen Monastery

Highest Point Lasar-la (5400m)

Nearest Large Town Lhasa

Accommodation camping

Best Time to Trek mid-April to mid-October

Summary An excellent choice for those who want to get a close look at the lifestyle of the drokpas (nomads). You need to be well acclimatised for this high-elevation trek, which never dips below 4400m.

by three **cairns** (5270m; N 29°43.973′, E 090°29.869′). It's a 45-minute walk to here from Leten. The peak attached to this spur is called **Damchen Nyingtri** and is holy to the god ruling the environs.

As per Buddhist tradition, stay to the left of the three cairns and descend sharply into a narrow valley. As you look into the curved valley ahead you'll notice a round, bald, red peak called **Tamdrim Dora**; the main trail you'll be following for the next hour or so keeps to the right of that.

Once on the valley bottom, stay on the west side of the stream and strike out north (up the valley). In 15 minutes a side-stream enters from the west: keep following the main north branch. In another 10 minutes you'll see **O-Lha** peak, the prominent jagged mountain to the northeast. Walk up the widening valley through arctic-like mounds of tundra for 40 minutes, following a minor trail. Then, as the valley floor veers west, look for a **cairn** (5310m; N 29°45.631′, E 090°29.813′) on the opposite bank of the stream.

Using this cairn as a marker, bear northwest over an inclined plain. This plain parallels the valley floor before the two merge. Continue ascending as the plain opens wider in the direction of the pass. The **Lasar-la** (5400m; N 29°46.165′, E 090°29.600′) is a broad gap at the highest point in the plain, and is only heralded by small cairns and few prayer flags. (A separate pass to the northwest, the Tigu-la, also descends towards Yangpachen, but this is not the route described here.)

From the Lasar-la the descent is gradual. A faint trail can be found on the east side of the stream that forms below the pass. About 30 minutes from the pass the trail passes a decent camp site, just before descending into a short gully. A side valley joins from the right, offering fine views of the back side of **O-Lha**. When this side-stream joins the main stream, cross over to the west side of the main watercourse. The way to the valley bottom is now much steeper but the broad slopes make walking relatively easy. In 20 minutes you'll reach the valley floor. There are many possible camp sites along this next stretch, as well as views of the snowcapped **Nyenchen Tanglha Range** to the north. Gravitate to the west side of the valley.

The valley is covered with hummocks, but a trail avoids the ups and downs of these mounds of turf and earth. About 60

Tsurphu to Yangpachen

minutes along the valley bottom, just past a large corral, you meet a large westward bend in the valley. If water levels are high, you should ford the river here and continue on the north side of the valley. In early summer when water levels are lower you can simply follow the valley as it bends to the west and ford the river further downstream.

As you now head westwards, along the north side of the river, there are superb views of the surrounding mountains. In the north is **Brize**, which is a heavily glaciated peak enclosing the south side of the Yangpachen Valley, and towards the west is a distinctive pinnacle named **Tarze**. Brize, the 'female-yak herder', and Tarze, the 'horse keeper', are just two of many topographical features in a mythical society ruled by the great mountain god Nyenchen Tanglha. These two mountains make convenient landmarks for trekkers further along the route as you go against the grain by heading north over a series of drainage systems that run from east to west.

Around 40 minutes after the big bend the trail hits **Bartso** (4950m; N 29°48.962′, E 090°28.091′). If you have not already crossed back to the right side of the valley there is a concrete footbridge just below this settlement. This *drokpa* village is now

PUBLIC TRANSPORT

At the time of research, foreigners were not allowed to travel on public transport in Tibet.

devoid of permanent dwellings but is still used as a summer camp. There are decent places to camp in the vicinity. The hills around Bartso are still dotted with juniper. In the 1960s and '70s huge amounts of this valuable bush were extracted from the region and trucked to Lhasa to feed the hearths of the new provincial city.

Stage 3: Bartso to Dorje Ling Nunnery

4-5 HOURS / 15KM / 150M ASCENT/150M DESCENT

Look northwest from Bartso to the far end of the valley. A clearly visible trail winds up from the valley to the top of the ridge. Make for this trail, 25 minutes' walk over marshy ground from Bartso, following the fence line. It's another half-hour to the summit of the ridge. A trail leads up to a saddle north of the valley for fine views of Nyenchen Tanglha. However, the more straightforward main path continues down into a gully heading westward. It's about 40 minutes to the village of **Tajung** (4660m; N 29°50.286′, E 090°25.116′), a walk of around 90 minutes from Bartso. Tajung is a decent alternative spot to end the second stage, though the insatiably curious villagers can be demanding of your time and supplies.

Stay to the left of the 14 whitewashed houses and ford the stream below the village. Bear northeast-wards into the parting in the ridge and, after a few minutes, cross a low saddle. Continue going northeast in the direction of Brize until a large dip appears in the ridgeline to the west, 40 minutes from Tajung. Reaching a dirt road going towards Brize head cross-country between the ridgeline and a large hill to the right, using a **cairn** (4630m; N 29°51.353′, E 090°25.740′) on the saddle as your marker. If you have gained enough height as you head north, you will be able to see a group of white houses at the base of a hill to the far northwest. The Dorje Ling Nunnery is just downstream from here.

One excellent possible side trip from here is the 20-minute climb to the top of the hill to the right (east), known as **Nyinga Ri** (4800m; N 29°51.688′, E 090°25.990′). Views of the Nyenchen Tanglha Range, and the dis-

tinctive flat-topped 7111m massif that gives its name to the entire range, are fantastic from here. Nyenchen Tanglha is the holiest mountain in central Tibet, the haunt of a divine white warrior on a white horse. The range is part of the trans-Himalaya, which circumscribes the plateau, dividing southern Tibet from the Changtang.

A steep descent from the saddle of Nyinga Ri brings you to a stream at the base of a ridge, aligned east to west. Ford the stream and look for the uppermost house in a group of seven dwellings. A trail from this house climbs to the ridge top in just a few minutes. From the top of the ridge the terrain gradually falls away to the north. Here you have good views of the village just upstream of Dorje Ling Nunnery. The nunnery, which is out of view, sits at the bottom of a rock outcrop visible from the ridge top.

Strike out directly across the plain in a northwesterly direction for the village, taking in the awesome views of the glaciers tumbling off Brize and the fertile flood plain below. After dipping briefly into a dry gully you crest a small ridge and see **Dorje Ling** (4474m; N 29°53.600′, E 090°24.782′); the nunnery is less than one hour away (two to three hours from Tajung).

The centrepiece of this friendly nunnery is the red *dukhang* (assembly hall). Camping is found in the meadow to the southwest of the nunnery, but cleaner camps can be found upstream of Dorje Ling.

Most treks now end at Dorje Ling. In recent years a concrete road link has been constructed to Dorje Ling and places further up the valley. If you are hardcore it is still possible, however, to trek the 14km from the nunnery via Tsaburing Valley to the monastery of Yangpachen.

Perched on top of a ridge, the 15th-century **Yangpachen Monastery** overlooks a broad sweep of trans-Himalaya peaks. The monastery was once home to 115 monks, but many of them have fled to Rumtek Monastery in Sikkim, and less than half remain behind. Yangpachen is headed by Shamar Rinpoche (also known as the Sharmapa), a leading lama of the Kagyupa order, whose 14th incarnation is based in India. You'll see images here of the important fourth Sharmapa (wearing a red hat), the 16th Karmapa (a black hat) and the 'alternative' rival Karmapa, who is supported by the Sharmapa in India.

From Yangpachen Monastery it's an 18km road journey to Yangpachen town. About halfway there look out for **Galo Nunnery**, nestled in the hills to the left after about 7km.

For a post-trek treat, the swimming-pool-sized **hot-springs complex** (Yangbajian Wenchuan; admission ¥120; ⊙ 7am-9pm), located 7km west of Yangpachen town, is great for easing your aching limbs. This entire region has undergone rapid development in recent years.

Shalu to Nartang

This trek follows the old trade route between the great Buddhist centres of Shalu and Nartang, marking a glorious chapter in Tibetan history. Treading the ancient trail you can almost feel the caravans laden with scriptures and treasures that once passed this way.

The trek begins at the historic Shalu Monastery and traverses west over a couple of small ranges to Ngor Monastery. From Ngor it's a downhill roll to Nartang Monastery. The route passes through several villages as well as uninhabited dry canyons. It's about a 10-hour walk to Ngor from Shalu, which is best divided into two days and, if you chose to walk the road, another five hours from there to Nartang. Finding guides and burros to carry your gear in Shalu is usually not difficult. Expect to pay ¥120 to ¥160 for each. Having local support is a good thing because the route is not always easy to discern – the trail tends to vanish in the canyons.

The optimal walking season is from the beginning of April to the end of October. In summer the trail can be sizzling hot, and in other months cold and windy, so be prepared.

Stage 1: Shalu Monastery to Upper Lungsang

5½-6½ HOURS / 19KM / 420M ASCENT/240M DESCENT

From **Shalu Monastery** (3980m; N 29°07.625', E 088°59.590') walk the motorable road south (up the valley). After 30 minutes from Shalu you will pass by the **Ri-puk Hermitage**, set on a hillside on the west side of the valley. If you wish to visit, cut across the fields and head directly up to the hermitage – the way is not difficult and there are several trails leading up to it.

About 45 minutes from Shalu the road forks: take the south fork. In the south, a conical-shaped hill and a village at its base can be made out. If you struck out in Shalu, stay on the road to this village, called **Phun-up**, about a one-hour walk away – you may also find a guide and pack animals here. Otherwise, there is a short cut that saves 2km of walking. A few minutes from the fork in the road, look for the base of a long red ridge. Leave the road and skirt the base of this ridge, going in a southerly direction. First cross a flood plain to reach a rectangular red shrine and, beyond it, enter a plain bounded in the south by the red ridge.

Gradually the trail climbs to a small white ridge blocking the route to the south. As you approach you will see a line of white cairns marking its **summit** (4030m; N 29°06.011', E 088°59.590'). Look for the trail that ascends to the cairns, a one-hour walk from

---

SHALU TO NARTANG AT A GLANCE

Duration 2 days

Distance 27km

Difficulty medium

Start Shalu Monastery

Finish Ngor Monastery or Nartang Monastery

Highest Point Char-la (4550m)

Nearest Large Town Shigatse

Accommodation camping

Best Time to Trek early April to late October

Summary This walk will give you a good feel for trekking in Tibet. The trail and passes are not particularly high or difficult and the trailheads are easily accessible from Shigatse.

Shalu to Nartang

N Approximate Scale

0 ———— 5 km
0 ———— 3 miles

the fork in the road. From the ridge's summit, Phunup village is to the south and the Showa-la is to the west. The pass is the obvious low point in the range at least one hour away. The trail descends gradually to enter the stream bed coming from the Showa-la, 30 minutes from the cairns. If you came via Phunup, your route will converge with the main trail here.

The climb up to the pass and the descent on the other side is through some heavily eroded, waterless ravines and slopes. Bring plenty of drinking water from the trailhead. From the stream bed the trail soon climbs back up the right side of the valley only to drop back in and out of the stream bed in quick succession. Don't make the mistake of walking up the stream bed as you will encounter ledges and other difficult terrain. After twice briefly dropping into the narrow stream bed, be alert for a trail carving a route up the right slope. It's situated just a few metres before a fork in the stream bed. The trail climbs steeply to a group of ruins and then winds around to the pass in 30 minutes. The top is marked by white cairns.

From the **Showa-la** (4170m; N 29°06.371′, E 088°56.939′), the second pass, the Char-la, can be seen in the range of hills west of an intervening valley. It is the dip in the crest of the range. The easy-to-follow trail descends from the pass along the south side of a ravine. In one hour you will reach the valley floor. Leave the trail just before it crosses a small rise marked with cairns and continue west towards a distant group of trees. Cross over the sandy north–south valley, intersect-

ing a road. Shigatse is about three hours north along this road.

The valley watercourse is dry except during summer flash floods. West of it is a **poplar and willow copse** (3950m; N 29°06.572′, E 088°54.093′), the only bit of shade in the area. Consider stopping here for lunch and a rest. From the copse, you enter a side valley, continuing in a westerly direction towards the Char-la. There are places suitable for camping along the length of this valley and water is available in the villages. In a few minutes you will reach the village of **Manitinge**, on the southern margin of the valley, and pick up the main cart track going up the valley. The track passes through the village of Siphu and, one hour from the copse, crosses to the south side of the valley. You can glimpse the Char-la from here, which for most of the trek is hidden behind folds in the mountains.

In 30 minutes you will reach **Lower Lungsang** (4060m; N 29°06.265′, E 088°51.824′); a few minutes later **Upper Lungsang**. There is a fine old wood here ideal for camping and resting.

Stage 2: Upper Lungsang to Ngor Monastery

3½-4 HOURS / 8KM / 550M ASCENT/240M DESCENT

From Upper Lungsang the trail cuts across the valley floor, gradually making its way back to the northern side of the valley. The cart track does not extend past the village and the trail up to the pass may be difficult to find in places. It is at least three hours from Upper Lungsang to the Char-la. At first, the trail skirts the edge of a gravel wash. However, in 15 minutes a series of livestock tracks climbs out of the stream bed and onto an eroded shelf that forms above it. Observe the old agricultural fields here, many of which have been long abandoned due to a lack of water.

The terrain becomes more rugged and a gorge forms below the trail. There is a side-stream and small **reservoir** (4190m; N 29°06.619', E 088°50.763') 45 minutes above Upper Lungsang. This is the last convenient place to collect water until over the pass. From the reservoir, the trail descends back to the stream bed but quickly exits the opposite side of the valley.

Look for a series of switchbacks on the southern side of the gorge and then follow them up. A further 15 minutes on, the trail crosses a gully and then another gully in 15 more minutes. The final leg to the pass is pretty much cross-country over a steep slope of raw expanses of rock. From the second gully, the Char-la can be reached in 45 minutes of steep uphill walking. At one time this trail was well maintained and formed a main trade link between Shalu and Sakya Monasteries, but it has fallen into disrepair.

Eventually, the white cairns along the summit ridge come into focus. The pass is the obvious notch in the ridge line. From the **Char-la** (4550m; N 29°07.000', E 088°49.850'), mountain ranges stretch to the west across the horizon and Ngor Monastery is visible directly below. Ngor is a 45-minute steep descent from the pass. The route from the Char-la descends the south side of a ravine that forms below it. Several trails cross the stream that flows from the pass and provide access to Ngor, but the

first trail is the quickest route – it climbs the right side of the ravine and traverses directly to the monastery. Consider camping near Ngor or staying in the monastery's little guesthouse and save the last five hours of walking for the next day, when you're rested.

Sakya master Ngorchen Kunga Sangpo founded **Ngor Monastery** in 1429, giving rise to the Ngorpa suborder, a distinctive school of Buddhist thought. Once an important centre of learning, Ngor used to boast four monastic estates and 18 residential units inhabited by about 340 monks. Only a portion of the monastery has been rebuilt, but what has is pleasing to behold. The largest structure is the assembly hall, called the Gonshung. The outer walls of its gallery are painted in vertical red, white and blue stripes, a characteristic decorative technique used by the Sakya order. The three colours represent the Rigsum Gonpo, the three most important bodhisattvas. The present head of Ngor, Luding Khenpo, resides in northern India.

Most trekkers end their walk at Ngor. A new improved road now connects Ngor to the Nartang Monastery 19km away. Once reaching the Lhatse–Shigatse Hwy just east of the 4914 road marker head in the direction of Shigatse. **Nartang Monastery** and its huge perimeter walls are just 3km away.

Mt Kailash Kora

The age-old path around Mt Kailash is one of the world's great pilgrimage routes and completely encircles Asia's holiest mountain. With a 5630m pass to conquer, this kora is a test of both the mind and the spirit.

MT KAILASH KORA AT A GLANCE

Duration 3 days

Distance 52km

Difficulty medium to difficult

Start/Finish Darchen

Highest Point Drölma-la (5630m)

Nearest Large Town Ali

Accommodation camping or monastery guesthouses

Best Time to Trek mid-May until mid-October

Summary The circuit, or kora, of Mt Kailash (6714m) is one of the most important pilgrimages in Asia. It's been a religious sanctuary since pre-Buddhist times, and a trek here wonderfully integrates the spiritual, cultural and physical dimensions of a trip to Tibet. Being able to meet pilgrims from across Tibet and other countries is another allure.

There's some gorgeous mountain scenery along this trek, including close-ups of the majestic pyramidal Mt Kailash, but just as rewarding is the chance to see and meet your fellow pilgrims, many of whom have travelled hundreds of kilometres on foot to get here. Apart from local Tibetans, there are normally dozens of Hindus on the kora during the main pilgrim season (June to September). Most ride horses, with yak teams carrying their supplies. Of course these days, there are also plenty of Chinese tourists.

The route around Mt Kailash is a simple one: you start by crossing a plain, then head up a wide river valley, climb up and over the 5630m Drölma-la, head down another river valley, and finally cross the original plain to the starting point. It's so straightforward and so perfect a natural circuit, it's easy to see how it has been a pilgrim's favourite for thousands of years.

The Mt Kailash trekking season runs from mid-May until mid-October but trekkers should always be prepared for changeable weather. Snow may be encountered on the Drölma-la at any time of year and the temperature will often drop well below freezing at night. The pass tends to be snowed in from early November to early April.

The kora is getting more and more popular (and there's litter everywhere to prove it). A tent and your own food are recommended, although there is now accommodation and simple food at Dira-puk and Zutul-puk. Bottled water, instant noodles and snacks are available every few hours at nomad tents. Natural water sources abound.

Horses, yaks and porters are all available for hire in Darchen, the gateway town to the kora. Big groups often hire yaks to carry their supplies so yaks will only travel in pairs or herds, so you have to hire at least two. Horses are an easier option but are surprisingly expensive because they are in great

Mt Kailash Kora

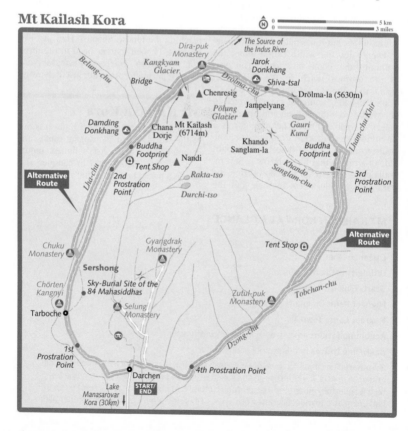

ESSENTIAL CONSIDERATIONS FOR WALKING AROUND MT KAILASH

There are several important questions to consider when planning to walk the 52km Mt Kailash circuit. Firstly, will you be walking the mountain in a clockwise or anticlockwise direction? Hindus, Jains and Buddhists go clockwise, but followers of Bön go anticlockwise.

If you're a Tibetan, you'll probably plan to complete the circuit in one hard day's slog. Achieving this feat requires a predawn start and a late-afternoon return to Darchen. Otherwise plan on a comfortable three days around the holy mountain. Some very devout Tibetans make the round much more difficult by prostrating themselves the entire way. Count on around three weeks to complete a kora in this manner and be sure to wear knee padding and thick gloves.

It is said by Tibetans that circling the mountain once will wipe out the sins of a lifetime, while 108 circuits guarantees instant nirvana. Cost-cutters should note that koras completed during a full moon or in the Tibetan Year of the Horse are more beneficial than ordinary ones.

Assuming you're not a Buddhist, Bönpo or Hindu, the promise of liberation may not grab you no matter how caught up in the moment you are. And yet, many foreigners go truly expecting to experience something holy or profound. This is a little like wanting to fall in love. But why not?

demand by Indian pilgrims. Most hikers carry their own gear or get by with the services of a local porter for ¥100 to ¥120 a day. Guesthouse owners can normally help put you in touch with porters and guides.

Stage 1: Darchen to Dira-puk Monastery

6 HOURS / 20KM / 200M ASCENT

The kora path begins rather obviously on the western edge of Darchen. Quickly leaving all traces of the village behind, you head westward across the Barkha plain, a sandy expanse speckled with greenery like a massive camouflage jacket. To the north, the east–west ridge blocks your view of Mt Kailash, but to the southeast are clear views of huge **Gurla Mandata** (7728m). Api and other peaks in Nepal are visible to the south, while look to the southwest for the twin, sharp humps of **Kamet** (7756m) in India.

Only 4km from Darchen the trail climbs up over the southwest end of the ridge to reach a **cairn** at 4790m. The cairn is bedecked with prayer flags and marks the first views of Mt Kailash's southern and lapis lazuli face and a *chaktsal gang,* the first of the kora's four prostration points.

Very quickly the trail bends round to the north and enters the barren Lha-chu Valley. From here on, the narrow Lha-chu River provides a steady supply of water all the way to Dira-puk Monastery. For the best water, however, look for the occasional side-stream flowing down from the cliffs.

The valley is so open at this point you can see ahead to the tall Tarboche flagpole (4750m) in the distance. The Tarboche area is one of the most significant sites for Tibet's most important festival, Saga Dawa, when hundreds of pilgrims clamour to watch the annual raising of the flagpole. The pole was first erected in 1681 during the reign of the fifth Dalai Lama to commemorate a military victory over Ladakh.

Just west of Tarboche is the 'two-legged' **Chörten Kangnyi**. It's an auspicious act for pilgrims to walk through the small chörten's archway. A short climb above Tarboche to the east is the sky-burial site of the 84 *mahasiddhas* (Tantric practitioners who reached a high level of awareness). The site is revered, as it was once reserved for monks and lamas, but is no longer used: too few birds these days and too many wild dogs (it's wise not to hike alone). The first of the kora's three Buddha footprints is here, but it's hard to find. The views of the valley in this section are superb.

Beyond Tarboche the valley narrows dramatically at an area called Sershong. You can begin to get clear views of Mt Kailash now, standing to attention above the eastern ridge. After passing a series of ruined chörtens and a number of long mani (prayer) walls, the trail reaches a small bridge across the Lha-chu at 4710m. The bridge is less than an hour's walk from Tarboche, about 2½ hours from Darchen, and is directly below Chuku Monastery. Most Indian pilgrims begin their kora here.

Chuku Monastery (4820m), founded in the 13th century by Götsangpa Gompo

MILAREPA VERSUS NARO BÖNCHUNG

All around Mt Kailash there are signs of a legendary contest for control that involved Milarepa, the Buddhist poet-saint, and Naro Bönchung, the Bön master. According to the Buddhists, Milarepa came out the victor in all the various challenges, but despite this Naro Bönchung still argued for a final, winner-takes-all duel: a straightforward race to the top of the mountain.

Mounting his magic drum, Naro Bönchung immediately set out to fly to the summit. Unperturbed by the progress made by his rival, Milarepa rose from his bed at dawn and was carried by a ray of light directly to the summit. Shocked by this feat, Naro Bönchung tumbled off his drum, which skittered down the south face of the mountain, gouging the long slash marking Mt Kailash to this day. Gracious in victory, Milarepa decreed that Bön followers could continue to make their customary anticlockwise circuits of Mt Kailash, and awarded them Bönri as their own holy mountain.

Pel, a Kagyupa-order master, is perched high above the valley floor on the hillside to the west. It blends so secretively into its rocky background you may not even notice it's there. All Mt Kailash monasteries were wrecked during the Cultural Revolution and the Chuku (or Nyenri) Monastery was the first to be rebuilt. Inside look for a glass case over the altar: there's a highly revered marble statue called Chuku Opame (originally from India and reputed to talk) inside and a conch shell inlaid with silver. Beside the altar there's a copper pot and elephant tusks, the latter a leftover from when Bhutan exerted religious control over the monasteries around Kailash.

From the Chuku bridge there are alternative trails along the east and west banks of the river. Either way it's about three hours to Dira-puk Monastery. The trail along the eastern bank is the regular pilgrim route, but on the western trail there are some fine grassy camp sites at Damding Donkhang (4890m), about an hour before the monastery. The west or ruby face of Mt Kailash makes a dramatic backdrop to this camp site and in the early morning Tibetan pilgrims can be seen striding past on the other side of the river, already well into their one-day circuit.

Be aware, though, that walking on the western side may require crossing the sidestreams that flow into the Lha-chu. Even in early summer these can be waist high. Wear socks or rubber sandals when you cross; it helps on the slippery rocks.

Take your time between Chuku Monastery and Dira-puk Monastery as this stretch has some of the best scenery of the entire kora. High sedimentary faces, wonderfully puckered and dented, and chiselled into shapes that seem alive, hem you in on both sides. When the weather is warmer there's even the occasional ribbon of water tumbling down the slopes from hundreds of metres high.

Many of the formations along the way have mythical connections, with a number of them related to Tibet's legendary hero Gesar of Ling – but you're unlikely to find them without a guide. Along the eastern route, however, you will have no problem finding the **second prostration point** (N 31°04.430′, E 081°16.942′), with its prayer flags and clear view of the east side of Mt Kailash. Around 30 minutes later, just past a tea tent selling the usual drinks and snacks, look for the second Buddha footprint, and a **carving** (N 31°05.126′, E 081°17.264′) of the god Tamdrin, a wrathful horse-headed deity, on a black stone smeared with aeons of yak butter.

From the rock, the trail starts to climb and heads northeast towards Dira-puk Monastery. Cross the bridge to head directly to the monastery or continue straight ahead for the main trail. Eventually you'll spot a couple of buildings. To the right is the old **Indian guesthouse** (dm ¥60-70), a series of simple stone dormitory rooms with a cosy tented teahouse and several shops. Below and to the left is the huge new **Shishapangma Guesthouse** (西夏邦马宾馆, Xīxiàbāngmǎ Bīnguǎn; per bed ¥60-70), a two-storey concrete guesthouse boasting real beds and real toilets. The third and quietest option is a bed in the **Monastery Guesthouse** (dm ¥60-70), though food here is limited to instant noodles.

If you're camping, head for the grassy flats below the monastery or the northern valley (leading to the source of the Indus River) east of the monastery.

Dira-puk (Lhalung Dira) Monastery (5080m) sits in a superb location on the hillside north of the Lha-chu across from the Shishapangma Guesthouse. It directly faces the astonishing north face of Mt Kailash, which from this angle appears as a massive, jet-black slab of granite ornamented with alabaster-white stripes of snow. Three lesser mountains are arrayed in front of Mt Kailash: Chana Dorje (Vajrapani) to the west, Jampelyang (Manjushri) to the east and Chenresig (Avalokiteshvara) in the centre, but there's no doubting who is the superstar in this band.

Dira-puk Monastery takes its name from the words *dira* (female yak horn) and *puk* (cave) – this is where the Bön warrior god king Gekho tossed boulders around with his horns. The great saint Götsangpa, who opened up the kora route around Mt Kailash, was led this far by a yak that turned out to be the lion-faced goddess Dakini (Khandroma), who guards the Khando Sanglam-la. Colourful murals mark the entry to Götsangpa's atmospheric meditation cave. The monastery was rebuilt in 1985.

To get to the monastery, cross the bridge just north of the Shishapangma Guesthouse and then cross the river on stones or head to the bridge further upstream – a trying ordeal at the end of a long day.

If you have the time, consider walking up to the **Kangkyam Glacier** that descends from the sheer north face of Mt Kailash. It takes about two hours there and back and you'll feel you're getting so close to the peak that you could touch it.

Stage 2: Dira-puk Monastery to Zutul-puk Monastery

7-8 HOURS / 18KM / 550M ASCENT/600M DESCENT

No doubt when you wake in the morning and step outside you'll want to revel in the glory of your surroundings. Mt Kailash's dramatic black face dominates the skyline, while the middle slopes echo with the moans of yak teams complaining as drivers load them with the day's supplies.

The main kora path heads off to the east, crossing the Lha-chu by bridge and then climbs on to a moraine to meet the trail on the east bank. The long ascent up the Drölma-chu Valley that will eventually lead to the Drölma-la has begun. Bring water to last a few hours.

Less than an hour along is the meadow at **Jarok Donkhang** (5210m), where some trekking groups set up camp. It's not wise to camp any higher up than here because of the risks associated with altitude.

Near Jarok Donkhang a trail branches off to the southeast, leading over the snow-covered Khando Sanglam-la. This shortcut to the east side of Mt Kailash bypasses the normal route over the Drölma-la, but only those on their auspicious 13th kora may use it. That lion-faced goddess Dakini, who led Götsangpa to Dira-puk, makes sure of that.

Also nearby, another **glacier** descends from the east ridge off the north face of Mt Kailash, down through the Pölung Valley between Chenresig (Avalokiteshvara) and Jampelyang (Manjushri). This glacier can be reached in a return trip of a couple of hours from Jarok Donkhang. You can follow the glacial stream that runs down the middle of the valley to merge with the Drölma-chu, or you can avoid losing altitude from Jarok

TIBETAN TREKS MT KAILASH KORA

THE FACES & RIVERS OF MT KAILASH

On a mystical level, Tibetans identify Mt Kailash with the mythical world mountain known as Meru, which reaches from the lowest hell to the highest heaven. According to ancient tradition, four rivers flow down the flanks of Mt Kailash. While no major river really issues from this mountain, four do begin within just 100km of it.

DIRECTION	FACE	MYTHICAL RIVER	REAL RIVER
south	lapis lazuli	Mabja Kambab (Peacock Fountain)	Karnali
west	ruby	Langchen Kambab (Elephant Fountain)	Sutlej
north	gold	Sengge Kambab (Lion Fountain)	Indus
east	crystal	Tamchog Kambab (Horse Fountain)	Yarlung Tsangpo (Brahmaputra)

Donkhang by terracing around the side of Jampelyang.

Only a short distance above Jarok Donkhang, about two hours from the day's starting point, is the rocky expanse of **Shiva-tsal** (5330m; N 31°05.795', E 081°20.856'). Pilgrims are supposed to undergo a symbolic death at this point, entering in the realm of the Lord of the Dead, until they reach the top of the Drölma-la and are reborn again. It is customary to leave something behind at Shiva-tsal – an item of clothing, a drop of blood or a lock of hair – to represent the act of leaving this life behind.

After Shiva-tsal the trail mercifully flattens for a time and proceeds along a glacial ridge. There are a number of interesting sights ahead, such as the sin-testing stone of **Bardo Trang** (a flat boulder that pilgrims are supposed to squeeze under to measure their sinfulness), but even your guide may not know where they are.

About 30 minutes from Shiva-tsal the trail turns eastward for the final ascent. The saddle is fairly dull looking, just a long slope of boulders and scree, but there are some stark, jagged peaks to the right. Look south for your last glimpse of the north face of Mt Kailash, since there are no views of the mountain from the pass.

Allow around an hour for the 200m climb to the top of the **Drölma-la** (5630m; N 31°05.719', E 081°22.204'). The trail disappears at times, merging with glacial streams in summer, but the way up, up, up is obvious. Take your time. Let the children and old women pass you, and if you can't go more than a few metres at a time, then don't.

After a few false summits, the rocky pass is reached. The great cubic **Drölma Do** (Drölma's Rock) that marks the top is barely visible behind an enormous number of prayer flags. Pilgrims perform a circumambulation nonetheless, pasting money onto the rock with yak butter, and stooping to pass under the lines of prayer flags and add a new string or two to the collection. They also chant the Tibetan pass-crossing mantra, '*ki ki so so, lha gyalo*' ('*ki ki so so*' being the empowerment and happiness invocation, '*lha gyalo*' meaning 'the gods are victorious'). They have now been reborn, and, by the mercy and compassion of Drölma, their sins have been forgiven.

The tale associated with the revered Drölma Do is worth telling. When Götsangpa pioneered the kora and wandered into the valley of Dakini (Khandroma), he was led back to the correct route by 21 wolves that were, of course, merely 21 emanations of Drölma (Tara), the goddess of mercy and protector of the pass. Reaching the pass, the 21 wolves merged into one and then merged again into the great boulder. To this day Drölma helps worthy pilgrims on the difficult ascent.

Weather permitting, most pilgrims and trekkers pause at the pass for a rest and refreshments before starting the steep descent. Almost immediately, **Gauri Kund** (5608m; the Tibetan name Tukje Chenpo translates as 'Lake of Compassion') comes into view below. Hindu pilgrims are supposed to immerse themselves in the lake's green waters, breaking the ice if necessary, but few actually do.

It takes approximately an hour to make the long and steep 400m descent to the grassy banks of the Lham-chu Khir. You may have to cross snowfields at first, sometimes leaping across streams that have cut through the valley floor, but later the trail turns dry and rocky. Walking sticks are useful here.

En route there is a much-revered footprint of Milarepa, though again, spotting it on your own is difficult. When the trail reaches the valley, you may find nomad tents and a teahouse selling drinks and noodles. A huge rock topped by the kora's third **Buddha footprint** stands nearby (5245m).

As with the Lha-chu Valley on the western side of Mt Kailash, there are routes that follow both sides of the river. The eastern bank trail presents better views and there's less marshy ground, but it requires crossing the river by boulder hopping, and later recrossing by wading into the river itself (which may be quite deep during the wetter months).

About 30 minutes south, a valley comes down from the Khando Sanglam-la to join the western trail. This valley provides the only glimpse of Mt Kailash's eastern or crystal face. The kora's third prostration point is at the valley mouth, but it's easy to miss this point if you're walking on the eastern bank.

Grassy fields start to appear alongside the river, affording those with tents endless spots to set up camp. A couple of hours from the third Buddha footprint a side valley enters from the left. From here on the river changes name to the Dzong-chu, translated as 'Fortress River'. Soon afterwards you'll likely see a neat line of tents set up for one of the Indian pilgrim groups. Trekkers can often stay here if there's space.

Zutul-puk Monastery (4820m) is 10 minutes from the Indian camp. The *zutul phuk* (miracle cave) that gives the monastery its name is at the back of the main hall. As the story goes, Milarepa and Naro Bönchung were looking for shelter from the rain. They decided to build a cave together, but Milarepa put the roof in place without waiting for Naro Bönchung to make the walls (thus once again showing the supremacy of Buddhism). Milarepa then made a couple adjustments to the cave, which left a footprint and handprint that can still be seen today.

The monastery has a simple guesthouse (beds ¥70-80), but the half-dozen rooms sometimes get booked out by Indian groups. The area around the monastery is also littered with rubbish mounting with every pilgrim season.

Stage 3: Zutul-puk Monastery to Darchen

3-4 HOURS / 14KM / 150M DESCENT

From the monastery the trail follows the river closely for an hour or so then climbs above the river and enters the lovely Gold & Red Cliffs, a narrow canyon whose walls are stained purple, cobalt and rust.

When the canyon narrows look for holes gouged into the cliff walls. These are not natural but made by pilgrims looking for holy stones. Also look for prayer flags festooned across the river, and in the far distance the blue waters of the lake Rakshas Tal.

Where the trail emerges onto the Barkha plain, close to the fourth prostration point (4700m), Gurla Mandata is again visible in the distance. It's now an easy one-hour walk back to Darchen along a dirt road. While not a very scenic stretch of the kora, the steady ground below does allow you to drift off and reflect on the past three days.

Nyenchen Tanglha Traverse

This is a fabulous trek for those who want to see the ecological mosaic of northern Tibet in all its splendour. Close encounters with the *drokpa,* the seminomadic shepherds of the region with their ancient customs and traditions, enliven the trail. Herds of blue sheep live in the crags, and in the woodlands the endangered musk deer makes its home.

The trek begins at Kyang-rag Monastery just off the main road to the Nam-tso, 7km beyond the Damxung–Lhasa Hwy turn-off. The trail cuts across the mighty Nyenchen Tanglha Range and heads directly for Tashi Dor, the celebrated headland on the southeast shore of Nam-tso.

The route leaves the Damxung Valley and wends its way through a rocky defile, the gateway to a high-elevation forest in which dwarf willow and rhododendron are dominant species. A number of stream crossings await you. A tundra-filled upper valley gradually climbs to the Kyang-la (On-ager pass), followed by a steep descent onto the Changtang plains. Fantastic views of sparkling Nam-tso and Tashi Dor are visible

---

NYENCHEN TANGLHA TRAVERSE AT A GLANCE

Duration 3 days

Distance 60km

Difficulty moderate to demanding

Start Kyang-rag Monastery

Finish Tashi Dor (Buildings Complex)

Highest Point Kyang-la (5330m)

Nearest Large Town Damxung

Accommodation camping

Best Time to Trek May to October

Summary Passing through gorges, forested slopes, alpine meadows and the plains of the Changtang, this is a great walk for those interested in the ecological diversity of northern Tibet.

Nyenchen Tanglha Traverse

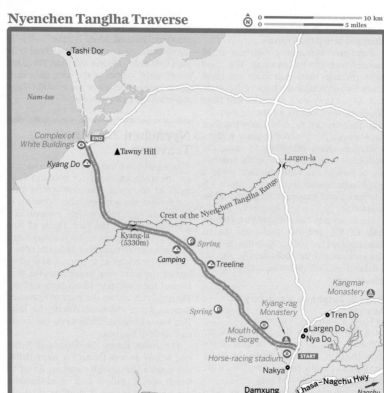

from many vantage points on the trail, and colourful *drokpa* camps dot the way.

The best time to make the Nyenchen Tanglha traverse is from May to October. A winter crossing is also sometimes possible but don't attempt one unless you have the green light from local residents. This is a very high elevation trek with a 5330m pass and minimum elevations of 4320m, so factor in plenty of time for acclimatising. It's prudent to spend two nights in Damxung before setting out. You will have to be fully equipped with a tent and stove and enough food to reach Tashi Dor, three days away. Temperatures even in summer regularly dip below freezing and gale force winds are common.

Horses and guides should be available in the villages near the trailhead for ¥150 to ¥200 apiece per day. In June, when locals are out collecting caterpillar fungus, horses may be hard to get. If you're not successful in the nearby villages of Nakya or Baga Ara, try Nya Do, Largen Do or Tren Do, which are a little further afield but larger in size.

Stage 1: Nakya to the Treeline

5 HOURS / 18KM / 480M ASCENT

This trail sets off from Kyang-rag Monastery and pushes up through the Kyang Valley. From the turn-off for Nam-tso at Damxung proceed along the black-top road for 6km passing the large **horseracing stadium** to the left. Turn left onto the narrow concrete road about 1km beyond the stadium. From this turnoff the white Kyang-rag Monastery, a white beacon on the slopes, is seemingly a stone's throw away. Reach **Kyang-rag Monastery** (4370m; N 30°31.694', E 091°05.759') perched above the northeast side of the valley in 2km.

All the way to the Kyang-la the valley runs in a northwest direction. From Kyang-rag Monastery remain on the east side of the valley heading upstream. Along the narrow valley floor are plenty of small places to camp. About one hour from Kyang-rag Monastery ford the crystal waters of the Kyang-chu to the west side of the valley and enter a narrow **rocky gorge**. The gorge coincides with the high mountains that close in around the Kyang-chu. Five more fords await, so it's a good idea to bring canvas tennis shoes or rubber sandals especially dedicated to this purpose. A walking stick is also very helpful. The Kyang-chu is a fairly shallow stream but it has a swift current, so make sure your legs are up to the task.

The trail is clear and easy to follow. In 10 minutes it crosses to the east side of the valley. There are rocks popping up out of the water but these may be slippery and it's safer to get your feet wet. Within half an hour the trail crosses the river four more times, breaking out of the gorge at the last ford and landing on the east side of the valley.

The valley is now a little more open and the west slopes quite heavily forested. The trail remains in the valley bottom or along the east edge of the slope. There are a number of places to camp provided they are not already occupied by the *drokpa* shepherds. In two or 2½ hours, reaching the treeline, the trail skips over stones to the west side of the valley (4790m; N 30°34.662', E 91°02.350'). There are a number of excellent camp sites in the vicinity.

Stage 2: Treeline to Kyang Do
8-9 HOURS / 25KM / 540M ASCENT/490M DESCENT

About 20 minutes up the valley **springs** gush out of the base of a cliff. In 200m the trail returns to the east side of the valley where it remains until the pass crossing. There are good camp sites on both sides of the stream ford. Now the valley becomes more sinuous and somewhat steeper. The trail enters the tundra zone and becomes faint in places. Stay in the valley floor and head upstream. After around 45 minutes enter a long, wide section of the valley gravitating towards its east flank. You will need at least 1½ hours to trek over this stretch of the valley. High peaks of the Nyenchen Tanglha Range tower above your line of travel.

Above this point you're not likely to find any more *drokpa* camps until well after the Kyang-la, but there are quite a few places to set up your tent should you decide to tarry in the flower-spangled meadows. Further up the valley narrows a little and becomes steeper. The trail is still near the east edge of the valley but hardly visible in places. In 1½ hours ascend the broad shelf east of the valley. It's only about 10m higher than the valley floor. In the vicinity the Kyang-chu forks: the larger branch flows down from the southwest originating in a group of dark-coloured rocky peaks. The smaller branch cascades down from the pass in the northwest. This is the last place to collect water until after the pass. Paralleling the smaller branch of the stream the trail heads in a northwest and then westerly direction to meet the Kyang-la's base (5240m; N 30°37.522', E 090°58.080') in about 45 minutes.

Climb up to a higher and narrower bench continuing in a westerly direction. The way is moderately steep. Soon a line of brown cairns comes into view. These cairns mark the broad saddle rising to the Kyang-la. Continue walking up parallel to these cairns. The high point is **Kyang-la** (5330m; N 30°37.700', E 090°57.320'), about a 45-minute hike from the base of the pass.

It's only about a 30m descent to the head of the valley on the Changtang side of the

---

KYANG-RAG

It is said that the sixth Panchen Lama, Palden Yeshe (1738–80), and his retinue once camped along the Kyang-chu. One day a *kyang* (wild ass) wandered into camp and entered the tent used by him in his religious practice. The Panchen Lama tossed a sack containing sacrificial cakes on the back of the wild ass. The *kyang* exited the tent, wandered to the other side of the river and disappeared into a cliff. Curious, Palden Yeshe went in pursuit of the *kyang* and reached the cliff where it was last seen. Here he found an old monk who had covered the very spot with his cloak. The Panchen Lama demanded to know what was going on and pulled off the cloak. Immediately his nose began to bleed. Taking this as a mystic sign, he used the blood to paint an image of Palden Lhamo on the rocks. This site became the inner sanctum of Kyang-rag Monastery. As it turned out the *kyang* was no ordinary animal but a local deity and the mount of the great goddess Palden Lhamo. For that reason the place became known as Kyang-rag (Wild Ass Beheld).

pass. This valley is also known as Kyang. Good drinking water is had here – fill up because water can be scarce down the valley. The valley now bends to the north, the direction it takes all the way down to the Nam-tso basin. Soon the great lake in all its glory comes into view. The eastern tip of Tashi Dor and a long headland jutting deep into the lake, bright gems on a scintillating cobalt-blue surface, are clearly visible.

Stay on the east side of the valley. In a few minutes the trail leaves the valley and steeply descends through rocky slopes, followed by grassy slopes. In about 45 minutes you'll reach the **valley floor** (5120m; N 30°38.505', E 090°56.954'). Note that the Kyang-chu on this side of the pass is much smaller and prone to disappear underground in places.

The trail soon crosses to the west side of the valley before returning to the east side in only five minutes. The trail traces the east edge of the valley. In 45 minutes the magnificent Tashi Dor comes into full view. In 20 minutes recross to the west side of the stream and point your feet downstream. The terrain is quite gentle and Nam-tso is your constant companion, so going cross-country is easy and fun. The valley is wide open and in 30 minutes there are many excellent camps by the stream at **Kyang Do**.

Stage 3: Kyang Do to Tashi Dor
4-5 HOURS / 17KM / 80M DESCENT

A tawny-coloured hill appears in the distance. Leave the valley and skirt its west side by walking across the plain. The base of this hill is reached in approximately one hour. Do not make the mistake of staying in the valley floor, although this may seem the best route – further down swampy ground would come between you and Tashi Dor. After walking around the base of the tawny hill look for a complex of mainly white buildings to the north. Hike directly to the buildings in about an hour, slipping through the wires of a fence enclosing the range. Otherwise go around the enclosure in a clockwise direction, adding about 20 minutes to your walk. This complex at the base of the Tashi Dor headland is part of its management apparatus.

The tourist centre of **Tashi Dor** (4730m; N 30°46.652', E 090°52.243') is still 8km away on a black-top road. It should be easy should you want to hitch a ride from there.

MORE TREKS

Lake Manasarovar Kora

Although there is now a road all the way around Lake Manasarovar (4575m), this is still a very lovely walk. Fortunately, the road can be avoided for much of the mostly level 110km route. Lake Manasarovar reflects the most lucid shades of blue imaginable. It represents the female or wisdom aspect of enlightenment and is a symbol of good fortune and fertility, explaining why Tibetans are always very eager to circumambulate it. There are five Buddhist monasteries along the way. Horses and guides (both cost at least ¥180 per day) can be hired in Hor Qu, the town on the northeastern side of the lake, and at Chiu Monastery.

Due to the elevation (averaging 4600m) this is a moderately difficult trek. May, June and September are the best months for the four- or five-day trek; July and August are also good, save for the hordes of gnats that infest the shores. A tent and stove are required and you should be prepared for any kind of weather at any time.

The best place to start the walk is at **Chiu Monastery** on the northwest corner of the lake. Go in either a clockwise or counterclockwise direction, depending on whether you more closely relate to the Buddhists and Hindus or the Bönpos. If walking in a clockwise direction you will reach **Langbona Monastery** in about four hours. From Langbona, the pilgrims trail cuts inland to avoid lagoons that form along the north shore of Manasarovar. Look for cairns, prayer flags and other signs of pilgrim activity that herald the way. Do not make the mistake of hugging the lakeshore unless you are up for an icy-cold swim or have a raft in tow. It's about four hours from Langbona to Hor Qu.

Seralung Monastery, on the east side of Lake Manasarovar, is approximately three hours beyond Hor Qu and a good place to camp and experience Tibetan religious life. Four or five more hours brings you to **Trugo Monastery** on the southern flank of the lake. Camp well away from the monastery to avoid the hordes of Indian pilgrims that have become a regular feature of the travel scene in recent years. You can make it back to Chiu Monastery via Gossul Monastery in nine to 10 hours of walking from Trugo

Lake Manasarovar Kora

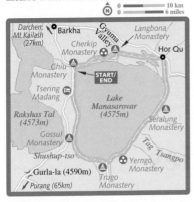

Monastery. On either side of Gossul Monastery are caves where one can shelter and get a feel for the meditator's way of life that once ruled in Tibet.

Everest Advance Base Camps

Walking in the shadow of iconic Mt Everest is mentally exhilarating and physically challenging. By following in the footsteps of great explorers one also gets a feeling for the history of the region. Underlying this more recent history is the mountain's primordial aspect, a holy land sheltering the powerful long-life goddess, Miyo Langsangma. Now that the track to Tingri has become a major traffic artery, the focus of trekking in the region has switched to the advance base camps of Mt Everest.

The trekking season in the Everest region extends from April to late October. The trek up from Everest Base Camp to more advanced camps at the foot of the mountain requires much time for acclimatisation. This is a very difficult high-elevation region with al-

titudes ranging between 5400m and 6400m. Subfreezing temperatures occur all year round in this rarified world of ice and hoar.

Expeditions beyond Base Camp are only for those very experienced in trekking and mountaineering. Being highly fit combined with careful preparation and the right gear are imperative. It's all too easy, once you have reached Base Camp, to succumb to the temptation to push further up the mountains. Do not do so without spending a couple of days acclimatising in the Rongphu area and doing day hikes to higher altitudes.

For properly prepared groups, with the right permits from Lhasa, it's possible to trek beyond Base Camp as far as **Camp III**. Including time for acclimatising, you would need to allow at least one week for this trek. The route skirts the Rongphu Glacier until **Camp I** and then meets the East Rongphu Glacier at **Camp II**. This glacier must be crossed in order to reach Camp III (6340m). Those reaching Camp III stand before the north face of Mt Everest, a close encounter between the stupendous and the seemingly insignificant. For detailed information on reaching the advanced base camps, see Gary McCue's *Trekking in Tibet*.

Everest East Face

Follow a river conduit breaching the Himalaya to the spectacular forested east flank of Mt Everest. Small lakes and fantastic camping make this a most attractive trek. Drive to **Kharta**, with its alpine hamlets, some 90km from Shegar on the Friendship Hwy. Budget at least 10 days for the trek. There are two main passes accessing the east or Kangshung side of Everest: **Langma-la** (5330m) and **Shao-la** (5030m). The huge **Kangchung Glacier** reposes on the west end of the Karma Valley. For detailed information, see *Tibet Handbook* by Victor Chan and *Trekking in Tibet* by Gary McCue.

Gateway Cities

Best Places to Stay Kathmandu

➡ Hotel Ganesh Himal (p237)

➡ Kantipur Temple House (p238)

➡ Kathmandu Guest House (p238)

Best Places to Stay Chéngdū

➡ Hello Chéngdū International Youth Hostel (p240)

➡ BuddhaZen Hotel (p241)

➡ Loft Design Hostel (p240)

Which City?

Given the complicated logistics of getting into Tibet, it's advisable to at least stay overnight in a gateway city en route to Lhasa, either to pick up your Tibet Tourism Bureau (TTB) permit, meet up with your fellow travellers or to buffer potential delays in your international flights. Most travellers reach Lhasa from Chéngdū or Kathmandu, though it's equally feasible to fly or train in from Běijīng, Xīníng, Guǎngzhōu or a half-dozen other Chinese cities.

Kathmandu

Crowded, colourful and chaotic Kathmandu has been a popular destination for travellers since the Hippy Trail in the '60s and '70s, but there are a couple of drawbacks to entering Tibet from here. Prime among these is the time needed to get a Chinese visa (group visas only) and the hassle that this group visa brings if you plan to travel further inside China. However, if you want to get a taste of both sides of the Himalaya and plan to return to Nepal, it's an interesting choice. It's also an extremely satisfying way to end an overland trip through China and Tibet.

Chéngdū

Sìchuān's huge capital city has long been the main logistical gateway to Tibet. With ever-increasing international air connections and excellent hostels that are very much used to helping travellers headed to Tibet, it's still a logical choice (unless you want to travel by train, then Xīníng is better). It's also a great starting point for exploring the ethnically Tibetan areas of western Sìchuān.

KATHMANDU

🎵 01 / POP 1 MILLION / ELEV 1300M

Kathmandu is an endlessly interesting, and sometimes maddening, city that seems to straddle both the 15th and 20th centuries. Most people head straight for the Thamel district, a travellers' mecca and the place to get a yak steak, a cut-price down jacket, buddhas and hard-to-find books on Tibet. But it's also a bit of a tourist zoo, with too many vehicles, Tiger-balm pedlars and trekking touts all sharing the same narrow, footpath-less roads. A few days here is plenty. For full details, see Lonely Planet's *Nepal* guide.

During the June to August monsoon season (when most visitors travel to or from Tibet) it is usually humid and rainy in Kathmandu, with average highs peaking at 28°C .

ⓘ Dangers & Annoyances

There are far fewer political demonstrations and strikes in Nepal than there were a few years ago but it's still possible that you might be affected by a disturbance. Check news reports and your own country's travel warnings for the current situation.

During the monsoon months landslides can affect travel from Tibet; in 2014 a massive landslide blocked the Kathmandu–Tibet road for days.

Kathmandu is plagued by power strikes lasting up to 16 hours a day – choose a hotel with a generator (and a room at the other end of the building). Congestion and pollution are crippling problems in Kathmandu and many people wear a face mask when moving around town.

⊙ Sights

★**Durbar Square**   HISTORIC SITE
(Royal Square; foreigner/SAARC Rs 750/150, no student tickets; ⊙ticket office 7am-7pm) Kathmandu's Durbar Sq was where the city's kings were once crowned and legitimised, and from where they ruled ('durbar' means palace). As such, the square remains the traditional heart of the old town and Kathmandu's most spectacular legacy of traditional architecture.

It's easy to spend hours wandering around the square and watching the world go by from the terraced platforms of the towering **Maju Deval**; it's a wonderful way to get a feel for the city. Although most of the square dates from the 17th and 18th centuries (many of the original buildings are much older), a great deal of rebuilding happened after the great earthquake of 1934. The entire square was designated a Unesco World Heritage Site in 1979.

The Durbar Sq area is actually made up of three loosely linked squares. To the south is the open Basantapur Sq area, a former royal elephant stables that now houses souvenir stalls and off which runs Freak St. The main Durbar Sq area, with its popular watch-the-world-go-by temples, is to the west. Running northeast is a second part of Durbar Sq, which contains the entrance to the **Hanuman Dhoka** and an assortment of temples. From this open area **Makhan Tole**, at one time the main road in Kathmandu and still the most interesting street to walk down, continues northeast.

A good place to start an exploration of the square is with what may well be the oldest building in the valley, the unprepossessing **Kasthamandap**.

Durbar Square (Patan)   HISTORIC SITE
(foreigner/SAARC Rs 500/150) The ancient Royal Palace of Patan faces on to a magnificent Durbar Square. This concentrated mass of temples is perhaps the most visually stunning display of Newari architecture to be seen in Nepal. Temple construction in the square went into overdrive during the Malla period (14th to 18th centuries), particularly during the reign of King Siddhi Narsingh Malla (1619–60).

Swayambhunath Stupa   BUDDHIST STUPA
(foreigner/SAARC Rs 200/50) The Swayambhunath stupa is of the crowning glories of Kathmandu Valley architecture. This perfectly proportioned monument rises through a whitewashed dome to a gilded spire, from where four faces of the Buddha stare out across the valley in the cardinal directions. The nose-like squiggle below the piercing eyes is actually the Nepali number *ek* (one), signifying unity, and above is a third eye signifying the all-seeing insight of the Buddha.

Bodhnath Stupa   BUDDHIST STUPA
(foreigner/SAARC Rs 150/40) The first stupa at Bodhnath was built sometime after AD 600, when the Tibetan king, Songtsen Gampo, converted to Buddhism. In terms of grace and purity of line, no other stupa in Nepal comes close to Bodhnath. From its whitewashed dome to its gilded tower painted with the all-seeing eyes of the Buddha, the monument is perfectly proportioned.

Central Kathmandu

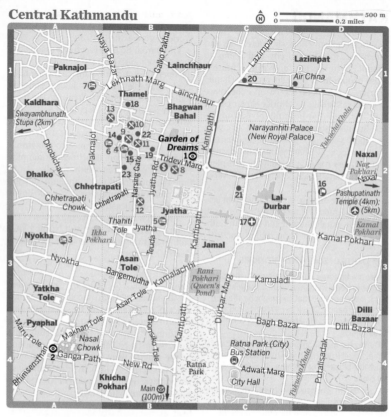

| | | 0 | 500 m |
| | | 0 | 0.2 miles |

GATEWAY CITIES KATHMANDU

Central Kathmandu

Pashupatinath Temple   HINDU TEMPLE
(admission Rs 1000, child under 10yr free; ⊙ 24hr)
The pagoda-style temple was constructed in

1696 but Pashupatinath has been a site of Hindu and Buddhist worship for far longer. Only Hindus are allowed to enter the compound of the famous main temple, but you can catch tantalising glimpses of what is going on inside from several points around the perimeter wall.

Garden of Dreams GARDENS
(☑ 4425340; www.gardenofdreams.org.np; Swapna Bagaicha; adult/child Rs 200/100; ⊙ 9am-10pm) The beautifully restored Swapna Bagaicha, or Garden of Dreams, is one of the most serene and beautiful enclaves in Kathmandu. Bring a book. It's two minutes' walk and one million miles from central Thamel.

☞ Tours

Several agencies in Thamel offer fixed-departure tours to Tibet twice a week, though these days they aren't much cheaper than arranging a tour yourself through an agency in Lhasa. Regardless of who you book with, at the border everyone ends up on the same bus. The following agencies offer tours to Tibet, including fly-in and fly-out tours to Lhasa. For more on the logistical details involved in visiting Tibet from Nepal see p35.

Adventure Greenhill TOUR AGENCY
(☑ 4700803; www.advgreenhill.com; Thamel) A travel and trekking agency that can book overland trips to Tibet.

Adventure Silk Road TOUR AGENCY
(☑ 4700275; www.silkroadgroup.com; Narsingh Chowk, Thamel)

Earthbound Expeditions TOUR AGENCY
(☑ 4701041; www.enepaltrekking.com; Thamel)

Eco Trek TOUR AGENCY
(☑ 4423207; www.ecotrek.com.np; Thamel) Seven-day overland trips, plus tours to Mt Kailash, the latter in conjunction with Indian pilgrim groups.

Royal Mount Trekking TOUR AGENCY
(☑ 4241452; www.royaltibet.com; Durbar Marg)

Tashi Delek Nepal Treks & Expeditions TOUR AGENCY
(☑ 4410746; www.tashidelektreks.com.np; Thamel)

🛏 Sleeping

There are dozens of places to stay in the tourist ghetto of Thamel; here are just a few. Discounts of 30% are commonplace, especially in the low season (May to September). Prices are quoted in US dollars but you can pay in Nepali rupees. Midrange and top-end places add 23% government tax.

KATHMANDU PRICES

For Kathmandu we have used the following price indicators:

Sleeping (Double Room)

$ less than US$20

$$ US$20–60

$$$ over US$60

Eating (Per Dish)

$ less than Rs 300

$$ Rs 300–600

$$$ over Rs 600

Tibet Peace Guest House GUESTHOUSE **$**
(☑ 4381026; www.tibetpeace.com; Sorakhutte; r Rs 800-1200, s/d Rs 1300/1600) Friendly and family-run, this is a quiet and mellow hang-out with a very nice back garden and a small restaurant. There's a wide range of rooms, some ramshackle and others with private balconies, so have a dig around before committing.

Hotel Potala GUESTHOUSE **$**
(☑ 4700159; www.potalahotel.com; s/d US$8/12, without bathroom US$5/8, deluxe US$10/15; @) Bang in the beating heart of Thamel, this small backpacker place is a good option, and has free internet, a nice rooftop area and a convenient restaurant overlooking Thamel's main drag. Rooms are simple but clean and decent, with sunny corner deluxe rooms the best. It's down an alleyway near the Maya Cocktail Bar. Rates include taxes. Don't confuse it with Potala Guest House.

★ **Hotel Ganesh Himal** HOTEL **$$**
(☑ 4263598; www.ganeshhimal.com; standard s/d US$20/25, deluxe US$30/35, super deluxe r US$45; ❄@☎) Our pick for comfort on a budget is this well-run and friendly place, located a 10-minute walk southwest of Thamel – far enough to be out of range of the tiger-balm salesmen but close enough to restaurants for dinner. The rooms are among the best value in Kathmandu, with endless hot water, satellite TV and lots of balcony and garden seating, plus a sunny rooftop. The deluxe rooms are more spacious and a little quieter and the new super-deluxe rooms have brick floors. The best standard rooms are in the new block. Throw in free internet access, a good-value garden restaurant and free

airport pick-up and this place is hard to beat, even if the reception gets a bit overwhelmed at times. Here's a tip: bring earplugs, as the residential neighbourhood can be noisy.

Kathmandu Guest House HOTEL $$

(☑4700800; www.ktmgh.com; r US$40-60, without bathroom US$2-16, deluxe US$60-180; ✳@☎) The KGH is an institution. A former Rana palace, it was the first hotel to open in Thamel and still serves as the central landmark. Everyone from Jeremy Irons to Ricky Martin has stayed here. In strictly dollar terms you can get better rooms elsewhere, but most people enjoy the atmosphere here and it's often booked out weeks in advance.

Kantipur Temple House BOUTIQUE HOTEL $$$

(☑4250131; www.kantipurtemplehouse.com; s/d US$70/80, deluxe US$110/140) ✿ Hidden down an alley on the edge of the old town, at the southern end of Jyatha, this Newari-temple-style hotel has been built with meticulous attention to detail. The spacious rooms are tastefully decorated, with traditional carved wood, window seats and specially commissioned fair-trade dhaka (hand-woven) cloth bedspreads. Due to the traditional nature of the building, rooms tend to be a little dark. This place is doing its best to be eco-friendly – guests are given cloth bags to use when shopping and bulk mineral water is available free of charge in bronze pitchers (in fact, there's no plastic anywhere in the hotel). The new block encircles a traditional brick courtyard and there's garden and rooftop seating. The old-town location is close to almost anywhere in town, but taxi drivers might have a hard time finding it.

✖ Eating

Central Thamel offers an amazing range of food, with dozens of backpacker-friendly cafes, bakeries and restaurants. Most places add 13% tax and 10% service onto listed prices. Bakeries offer a useful 50% discount after 9pm. All places are open lunch and dinner and menus are in English.

★ Or2k MIDDLE EASTERN $

(www.or2k.net; mains Rs 200-350; ☑) This bright, buzzy and popular Israeli-run vegetarian restaurant is our favourite for fresh and light Middle Eastern dishes. The menu spreads to crêpes, soups, zucchini pie, coco-

nut tofu and ziva (pastry fingers filled with cheese), as well as a great meze sampler of hummus, felafel and labane (sour cream cheese) served in neat little brass bowls. The fresh mint lemonade is a lifesaver on a hot day. All seating is on cushions on the floor; you have to take your shoes off so make sure you're wearing your clean pair of socks. A small stand at street level serves takeaway felafel wraps (Rs 155).

Yangling Tibetan Restaurant MOMOS $

(Saatghumti Chowk; momos Rs 150-200; ☻closed Sat) Both locals and tourists flock to this unpretentious family-run place for possibly the best momos (dumplings) in town (try the chicken ones). The kitchen here is a nonstop momo production line. You can also get soupy Tibetan butter tea and tasty thenthuk (noodle soup).

Utse Restaurant TIBETAN $

(Jyatha Rd; mains Rs 170-350) In the hotel of the same name, this is one of the longest-running restaurants in Thamel and it turns out excellent Tibetan dishes, including unusual Tibetan desserts such as dhayshi (sweet rice, curd and raisins) that you won't find anywhere else. The traditional decor feels lifted straight from an old Lhasa backstreet. For a group blowout, gacok (also spelt gyakok) is a form of hotpot named after the brass tureen that is heated at the table (Rs 780 for two). The set meals are a worthy extravagance.

Yak Restaurant TIBETAN $

(Narsingh Gate; mains Rs 155-250) We always find ourselves returning to this unpretentious and reliable Tibetan-run place at the southern end of Thamel. The booths give it a 'Tibetan diner' vibe and the clientele is a mix of trekkers, Sherpa guides and local Tibetans who come to shoot the breeze over a tube of tongba (hot millet beer). The menu includes Tibetan dishes, with good kothey (fried momos), and some Indian dishes, at unbeatable prices. It feels just like a trekking lodge, down to that familiar electronic sound of a chicken being strangled every time a dish leaves the kitchen.

Third Eye INDIAN $$

(☑4260160; www.thirdeyerestaurant.com; JP School Rd; mains Rs 475-675) Next door to Yin Yang, and run by the same people, this is another long-running favourite, popular with well-heeled tourists. Book a window seat at the sit-down section at the front or try the more informal section with low tables and cushions at the back; both are candlelit to create an intimate vibe. Indian food is the speciality and the tandoori dishes are especially good, even if the portions are a bit small. Spice levels are set at 'tourist' so let the efficient (if not friendly) suited waitstaff know if you'd like extra heat.

La Dolce Vita   ITALIAN **$$**
(☑ 4700612; pastas Rs 310-385, mains Rs 450-550, house wine per glass Rs 375) Life is indeed sweet at Thamel's best Italian bistro, offering up delights such as parmesan gnocchi; excellent antipasti; goat's cheese, spinach and walnut ravioli; sinfully rich chocolate torte; gelato; and wines by the glass. The pastas are better than the pizzas. Choose between the rustic red-and-white tablecloths and terracotta tiles of the main restaurant, a rooftop garden, the yummy-smelling espresso bar or sunny lounge space; either way the atmosphere and food are excellent. It's right on the corner opposite Kathmandu Guest House.

New Orleans Cafe   INTERNATIONAL **$$**
(☑ 4700736; mains Rs 370-550; ☑) Hidden down an alley opposite Pilgrims Book House, New Orleans boasts a relaxed and intimate candlelit vibe and a great selection of music, live on Wednesdays. It's a popular spot for a drink but the menu also ranges far and wide, from Thai curries and good burgers to Creole jambalaya and oven-roasted vegies, plus good breakfasts.

Fire & Ice Pizzeria   PIZZA **$$**
(☑ 4250210; www.fireandicepizzeria.com; Sanchaya Kosh Bhawan, Tridevi Marg; pizzas Rs 475-725; ⊙ 8am-11pm) This is an excellent and informal Italian place, serving some of the best pizzas in Kathmandu (wholewheat crusts available), as well as breakfasts, smoothies, seriously good Illy espresso and rousing opera – Italian, of course. It's very popular so make a reservation and expect to share one of the tavern-style tables.

🔒 Shopping

The Thamel area is crammed with shops selling trekking gear and outdoor clothing. What you purchase probably won't be genuine, but it should last at least one trip through Tibet. Other great buys include books, tea, Buddhist statuary and paper products.

ℹ Information

MONEY

The many licensed moneychangers are the easiest places to change cash; all offer the same rate. At the time of writing US$1 dollar got you around Nepali Rs 100.

Himalayan Bank (☑ 4250208; www.himalayanbank.com; Tridevi Marg; ⊙ 10am-8pm Sun-Fri, 9am-noon Sat) Close to Thamel, changes travellers cheques, has an ATM and gives cash advances on Visa cards.

Standard Chartered Bank Has two ATMs in Thamel, with one inside the grounds of the Kathmandu Guest House.

TRAVEL AGENCIES

Wayfarers (☑ 4266010; www.wayfarers.com. np; JP School Rd, Thamel; ⊙ 9am-6pm Mon-Fri, to 5pm Sat & Sun) For straight-talking ticketing, bespoke tours and Kathmandu Valley walking trips.

ℹ Getting There & Away

Air China operates flights between Kathmandu and Lhasa three times a week for around US$550 one-way, or between US$420 and US$460 from Lhasa.

Visas are available on arrival at the airport or Nepal–China border at Kodari for US$25/40/100 for up to 15/30/90 days. You'll need to fill out a visa form and arrival form and give one photo.

ℹ Getting Around

TAXI & RICKSHAW

Taxis are reasonably priced and most drivers will use the meter for short trips around town, which rarely come to more than Rs 150. Note that in the evening you may have to negotiate a fare.

Cycle rickshaws cost Rs 50 for short rides around town but require considerably more bargaining. Always agree on a price before you get in.

TO/FROM THE AIRPORT

Kathmandu's **Tribhuvan International Airport** (www.tiairport.com.np) is about 3km east of the centre. International airport departure tax is included in the price of air tickets.

You'll find a **pre-paid taxi service** (☑ 4112521) in the ground-floor foyer area immediately after you leave the baggage collection area. The fixed fare to Thamel is currently Rs 700, plus a surcharge after 9pm. A taxi to the airport costs around Rs 500.

Hotel touts outside the international terminal will offer you a free lift to their hotel, but you are less likely to get a discounted room rate after the tout gets their hefty commission.

CHÉNGDŪ 成都

🔲 28 / POP 5.3 MILLION / ELEV 500M

The modern, surprisingly laid-back city of Chéngdū is the largest and most important in China's southwest. With excellent (and spicy!) regional food, charming teahouses, good accommodation and iconic pandas, you could easily fill a few enjoyable days here. Temperatures can hit an uncomfortable 35°C during muggy July and August. For details on the city see Lonely Planet's *China* guide.

⊙ Sights

Giant Panda Breeding Research Base
WILDLIFE RESERVE

(大熊猫繁育基地, Dàxióngmāo Fányù Jīdì; 🔲 8351 0033; www.panda.org.cn; 1375 Xiongmao Dadao; adult/student ¥58/29; ⊙ 8am-5.30pm) One of Chéngdū's most popular attractions, this reserve, 18km north of the city centre, is the easiest way to glimpse Sìchuān's famous residents outside of a zoo. The enclosures here are large and well maintained. Home to nearly 120 giant and 76 red pandas, the base focuses on getting these shy creatures to breed.

Wénshū Temple
BUDDHIST TEMPLE

(文殊院, Wénshū Yuàn; Renmin Zhonglu; ⊙ 8am-10.50pm; M 1) FREE This Tang-dynasty monastery is dedicated to Wénshū (Manjushri), the Bodhisattva of Wisdom, and is Chéngdū's largest and best-preserved Buddhist temple. The air is heavy with incense and the low murmur of chanting; despite frequent crowds of worshippers, there's still a sense of serenity and solitude.

Jīnshā Site Museum
MUSEUM

(金沙遗址博物馆, Jīnshā Yízhī Bówùguǎn; www. jinshasitemuseum.com; 227 Qingyang Dadao; admission ¥80; ⊙ 8am-5.30pm) In 2001 archaeologists made a historic discovery in Chéngdū's western suburbs: they unearthed a major site containing ruins of the 3000-year-old Shu kingdom. This excellent, expansive museum includes the excavation site and beautiful displays of many of the uncovered objects, which were created between 1200 and 600 BC.

People's Park
PARK

(人民公园, Rénmín Gōngyuán; ⊙ 6.30am-10.30pm, to 10pm winter; M 2) FREE On weekends, locals fill this park with dancing, song and taichi. There's a small, willow-tree-lined boating lake and a number of teahouses:

Hè Míng Teahouse (鹤鸣茶馆, Hèmíng Cháguǎn; tea ¥12-30; ⊙ 6am-9pm) is the most popular.

Wǔhóu Temple
TEMPLE

(武侯祠, Wǔhóu Cí; 231 Wuhouci Dajie; admission ¥60; ⊙ 8am-6pm; 🔲 1, 21, 26) Located adjacent to **Nánjiāo Park** (南郊公园, Nánjiāo Gōngyuán; 235 Wuhouci Dajie; ⊙ 6am-7.30pm) FREE and surrounded by mossy cypresses, this temple (rebuilt in 1672) honours several figures from the Three Kingdoms period, namely legendary military strategist Zhuge Liang and Emperor Liu Bei (his tomb is here). Both were immortalised in the Chinese literature classic, *Romance of the Three Kingdoms (Sān Guó Yǎnyì)*.

🛏 Sleeping

Hello Chéngdū International Youth Hostel
HOSTEL $

(老宋青年旅舍, Lǎosòng Qīngnián Lüshě; 🔲 8196 7573, 8335 5322; www.gogosc.com; 211 Huanlu Bei 4 Duan, 一环路北四段211号; dm from ¥40, s without/with bathroom ¥90/120, d from ¥140, ste ¥210; ⊛✴@🛜; 🔲 28, 34) Once one of the best hostels in China, nevermind Chéngdū, this place has lost some of its finesse in recent years. It's still a nice space, though, sprawled around two garden courtyards, good for kids and adults to laze about. Rooms are clean and simple, and facilities are what you'd expect from a top-class hostel.

There's a solid bar and cafe, bike rental (from ¥10), a DVD library, and ready travel advice.

Loft Design Hostel
HOSTEL $

(四号工厂青年旅馆, Sìhào Gōngchǎng Qīngnián Lüguǎn; 🔲 8626 5770; www.lofthostel.com; 4 Xiaotong Xiang off Zhongtongren Lu, 中通仁路, 小桶巷4号; dm ¥50-60, s/d from ¥180/300; ✴@🛜; 🔲 48, 54, 341) Chic boutique meets trendy hostel in this converted printing factory, with its pretty cafe and bar, exposed brick, and arty vibe. The front desk at this hostel for grown-ups offers solid travel advice plus a decent cocktail selection. Dorms are small but the deluxe private rooms are spacious. The main downfall: wi-fi is only in the common spaces.

Holly's Hostel
HOSTEL $$

(九龙鼎青年客栈, Jiǔlóngdǐng Qīngnián Kèzhàn; 🔲 8555 7349, 8554 8131; hollyhostelcn@ yahoo.com; 246 Wuhouci Dajie, 武侯祠大街246号; dm ¥40-55, d ¥260-280; ✴@🛜; 🔲 27, 45) Prepare for trips out west by plugging yourself in to Chéngdū's small Tibetan district, which surrounds this cute and friendly hostel. Holly's has clean, basic rooms plus wi-fi, bike rentals (¥20) and a nice rooftop cafe (Western and Chinese mains ¥10 to ¥50). They can also help with permits to Lhasa. Discounted doubles go for as low as ¥120.

BuddhaZen Hotel
BOUTIQUE HOTEL **$$**

(圆和圆佛禅客栈, Yuán Hé Yuán Fú Chán Kèzhàn, O和O; ☑8692 9898; www.buddhazenhotel.com; B6-6 Wenshufang, 青羊区文殊坊B6-6号, near Wénshū Temple; incl breakfast s & d from ¥495, ste from ¥788; ❄@✿; Ⓜ1) Set in a tranquil courtyard building, this boutique hotel blends traditional decor with modern comforts and a taste of Buddhist philosophy. You can ponder life sipping tea on your private balcony, circling the sand garden, or soaking in a wooden tub at the spa.

Jǐnlǐ Hotel
HOTEL **$$**

(锦里客栈, Jǐnlǐ Kèzhàn; ☑6631 1335; www.cdjinli.com; 231 Wuhouci Dajie, 11 Zhangwu Jie, 武侯祠大街章武街11号; s/d/ste ¥398/518/618; ❄✿; ⬚1, 21, 26) If you don't mind the tourists swarming Jǐnlǐ Gǔjiē by Wǔhóu Temple, this upmarket inn set in two courtyard-style buildings, is a nice place to stay. Rooms mix traditional Chinese wooden furnishings with modern touches such as puffy white duvets and wide-screen TVs. The two standard rooms do not have wi-fi.

Jǐnjiāng Hotel
HOTEL **$$$**

(锦江宾馆, Jǐnjiāng Bīnguǎn; ☑8550 6550; www.jjhotel.com; 80 Renmin Nanlu, 2nd Section, 人民南路二段80号; r from ¥1099; ❄@✿➹; ⬚1, 57, Ⓜ1) At nine storeys, Jǐnjiāng was Sìchuān's first five-star hotel and the tallest building in Chéngdū until the late 1970s. There are more luxurious options now, but this one retains a charm that the chains lack, from the courteous and polished bell hops to the Michelin-level chef helming Jinyue French Restaurant.

✗ Eating

Arè Tibetan Restaurant
TIBETAN **$**

(啊热藏餐老店, Arè Zángcān Lǎo Diàn; ☑8551 0112; 3 Wuhouci Dongjie; mains from ¥13; ✿8.30am-10pm; ▣) Choose from a delicious array of Tibetan staples from tsampa (roasted barley flour, ¥20) to *thugpa* (noodles in soup; ¥13 to ¥16), *momo* (dumplings; ¥20), and yak-butter tea (¥18 to ¥25). Their newer, less quaint location (啊热藏餐店,

Arè Zángcān Diàn; ☑8557 0877; 234 Wuhouci Dajie; ✿8.30am-10pm), just across from Wǔhóu Temple, has fast counter service and a dining rooms upstairs. English, picture menus.

★ Yùlín Chuànchuàn Xiāng
HOTPOT **$$**

(玉林串串香; 2-3 Kehua Jie, 科华街2附3号; broth ¥20-25, skewers short/long ¥0.20/¥1.50, sauce from ¥2; ✿10.30am-2am) Sìchuān University's hungry students crowd this lively branch of the popular chain, which specialises in *chuànchuàn xiāng* (串串香), Chéngdū's version of the Chóngqìng hotpot. Pick your broth, then load up on skewers from the refrigerated back room to cook up at your table. Staff will tally the damage at the end of your meal.

Chén Mápó Dòufu
SICHUANESE **$$**

(陈麻婆豆腐; ☑8674 3889; 197 Xi Yulong Jie, 西玉龙街197号; mains ¥22-58; ✿11.30am-2.30pm & 5.30-9pm; ▣) The plush flagship of this famous chain is a great place to experience *mápó dòufu* (麻婆豆腐; small/large ¥12/20) – soft, house bean curd with a fiery sauce of garlic, minced beef, fermented soybean, chilli oil and Sìchuān pepper. It's one of Sìchuān's most famous dishes and is this restaurant's speciality. Non-spicy choices, too.

Yu Family Kitchen
MODERN CHINESE **$$$**

(喻家厨房; Yù Jiā Chúfáng; ☑8669 1975; 43 Zhai Xiangzi near Xia Tongren Lu, 下同仁路, 窄巷子43号; set menu per person ¥660, with four or more guests ¥330; ✿noon-2pm, 5-9pm) Pioneering the next phase of Chinese cuisine, Chef Yu Bo dazzles and delights with a set menu that begins with 16 intricate cold

Chéngdū

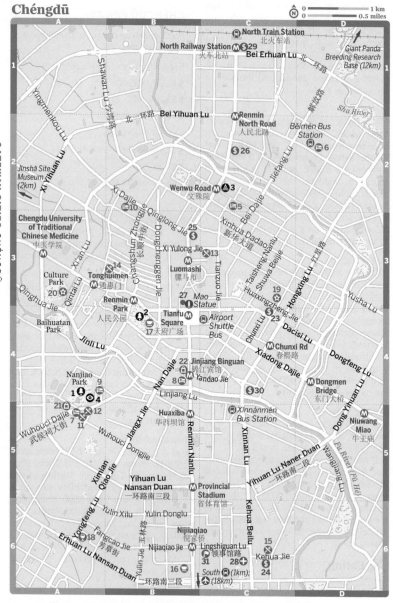

0 ____ 1 km
0 ____ 0.5 miles

North Train Station
北火车站
North Railway Station 29
火车北站　Bei Erhuan Lu 北一环路
Giant Panda
Breeding Research
Base (12km)

Sha River

Bei Yihuan Lu 北一环路

Renmin
North Road
人民北路

Běimén Bus
Station
6

26

Xi Dajie 西大街 Qinglong Jie
Wenwu Road 3
文殊院

Xinhua Dadao 新华大道

Jinsha Site
Museum
(2km)

Chengdu University
of Traditional
Chinese Medicine
中医学院

10

5

25

Xi Yulong Jie 13

Luomashi
骡马市

Culture
Park
20

Tonghuimen
通惠门

14

27 Mao
Statue

Tianfu
Square
17 天府广场

Airport
Shuttle
Bus

19

23

Chunxi Rd
春熙路

Dacisi Lu

Renmin
Park
人民公园

2

Qinghua Jie

Baihuatan
Park

Jinli Lu

Jiangxi Jie

Nan Dajie

22 Jinjiang Binguan
锦江宾馆
8 Yandao Jie

Linjiang Lu

Xiadong Dajie

Dongmen
Bridge
东门大桥

Niuwang
Miao
牛王庙

Nanjiao
Park

1

9

4

21

12

7

11

Wuhouci Dajie
武侯祠大街

Wuhouci Dongjie

Huaxiba
华西坝馆

Renmin Nanlu

Xinnánmén
Bus Station

30

Dongfeng Lu

Ximian
Qiao Jie

Yihuan Lu
Nansan Duan
一环路南三段

Yihuan Lu Naner Duan
一环路南二段

Provincial
Stadium
省体育馆

Kehua Beilu

Yongfeng Lu

18

Yulin Xilu

Yulin Donglu

Fangcao Jie

Nijiaqiao
倪家桥

Nijiaqiao jie

Lingshiguan Lu
领事馆路

31

15

28

Kehua Jie

24

16

South (1km);
(18km)

Erhuan Lu Nansan Duan 二环路南三段

dishes followed by many more courses of ever-changing, meticulously prepared seasonal dishes – some traditional and many you've never seen before. By reservation only. With all the acclaim and just six private rooms, call early.

🍷 Drinking

Bookworm
CAFE

(老书虫, Lǎo Shūchóng; ☎8552 0177; www.cheng-dubookworm.com; 2-7 Yujie Dongjie, 28 Renmin Nanlu, 人民南路28号、玉洁东街2-7号; ⓘ9am-1am) This hopping bookstore-cafe, like its

Chéngdū

⊙ Sights

🛏 Sleeping

✖ Eating

🍷 Drinking & Nightlife

✪ Entertainment

🛍 Shopping

ℹ Information

branches in Běijīng and Sūzhōu, is a gathering place for expats and a pleasant spot for a beer or coffee (from ¥25). It also serves decent Western food. You can buy or borrow from the English-language section, or stop by for author talks, live music and other events. Check the website for the schedule.

New Little Bar   LIVE MUSIC
(小酒馆(芳沁店), Xiǎo Jiǔguǎn (Fāngqìn Diàn); ☑8515 8790; site.douban.com/littlebar; 47 Yongfeng Lu & Fangqin Jie, 永丰路47号丰尚玉林商务港1楼附5号, 芳沁街; beer from ¥15, cocktails from ¥25; ⊙6pm-2am) This small pub-like venue is *the* place in Chéngdū to catch live local bands. Bands play most Fridays and Saturdays, and occasional weekdays, usually from 8pm. Live music carries a cover charge of around ¥15, depending on who's playing. Check online for the schedule.

☆ Entertainment

A night out at the Sichuanese opera is a must-do in Chéngdū. Most of the budget guesthouses run tours and some can even get you backstage.

Shǔfēng Yǎyùn Teahouse   SÌCHUĀN OPERA
(蜀风雅韵, Shǔfēng Yǎyùn; ☑8776 4530; www.shufengyayun.net; inside Culture Park; tickets ¥140-320; ⊙ticket office 3-9.30pm, nightly shows at 8pm) This famous century-old theatre and teahouse puts on excellent 1½ hour shows that include music, puppetry and Sìchuān opera's famed fire breathing and face changing. Come at around 7.30pm to watch performers putting on their elaborate make-up and costumes. For ¥50 to ¥100, kids (and adults) can try on garb and have a costume artist paint their face.

Jǐnjiāng Theatre   SÌCHUĀN OPERA
(锦江剧场, Jǐnjiāng Jùchǎng; ☑8666 6891; 54 Huaxingzheng Jie, 华兴正街54号; tickets ¥150-280; ⊙8pm-9.10pm) Mixed-performance shows are held daily at this renowned opera theatre. The adjoining **Yuèlái Teahouse** (悦来茶楼, Yuèlái Chálóu; 54 Huaxingzheng Jie, 华兴正街54号; tea from ¥12, tickets for shows ¥20-40; ⊙8.30am-5pm), a local favourite, holds wonderfully informal performances on its small stage on Saturdays from 2pm to 4.30pm.

🛍 Shopping

Sanfo   OUTDOOR EQUIPMENT
(三夫户外, Sānfū Hùwài; www.sanfo.com; 243 Wuhouci Dajie, 武侯祠大街243号; ⊙10am-8.30pm) Outdoor clothing and camping equipment are a brisk business in Chéngdū, as many people head to Tibet or the western mountains. Quality varies and fakes abound, but this place has good-quality gear. Another large **branch** (32 Renmin Nanlu, 人民南路32号) is by Nijiaqiao metro station.

ℹ Information

Best sources for restaurant, bar and entertainment listings are the websites **GoChengdoo** (www.gochengdoo.com), **Chéngdū Living**

GATEWAY CITIES CHÉNGDŪ

(www.chengduliving.com) and **Chengdu Places** (www.chengduplaces.com).

Bank of China (中国银行, Zhōngguó Yínháng; 35 Renmin Zhonglu, 2nd Section, 人民中路二段35号; ⊙8.30am-5.30pm Mon-Fri, to 5pm Sat & Sun) Changes money and travellers cheques, and offers cash advances on credit cards.

Global Doctor Chéngdū Clinic (环球医生, Huánqiú Yīshēng; ☎8528 3660, 24hr helpline 139 8225 6966; www.globaldoctor.com.au; 2nd fl, 9-11 Lippo Tower, 62 Kehua Beilu, 科华北路62号力宝大厦2层9-11号; consultation ¥840, after-hours visit ¥1050, house call ¥1700; ⊙9am-6pm Mon-Fri) English- and Chinese-speaking doctors and a 24-hour emergency line.

Chéngdū Entry & Exit Service Centre (成都市出入境接待中心, Chéngdūshì Chūrùjìng Jiēdài Zhōngxīn; ☎8640 7067; www.chengdu.gov.cn; 2 Renmin Xilu, 人民西路2号; ⊙9am-noon & 1-5pm Mon-Fri, to 4pm Sat) Visa extensions (five working days), residence permits, and paperwork for lost passports on the third floor. In the building behind the Mao statue's right hand.

❶ Getting There & Away

There are flights and trains to Chéngdū from every city in China. Multiple flights per day depart for Lhasa (¥1670, discounts of 30% common) and there are three flights a week to Shigatse (¥1880).

❶ Getting Around

The most useful bus is route 16 (¥2), which connects the north and south train stations along Renmin Nanlu.

Taxis have a flag fall of ¥8 (¥1 extra at night) for the first 2km.

Most hostels rent bikes for ¥20 per day.

TRAIN

Chéngdū's shiny new metro currently has two lines. Useful Line 1 links the North and South Train Stations along the length of Renmin Lu. East–west Line 2 meets Line 1 at Tianfu Sq before continuing west to Chádiànzì Bus Station. Line 3, which will run to the Panda Breeding Base and Xīnnánmén bus station, and Line 4, for the new Chéngdū West Train Station, are due to be completed by 2015. Rides cost ¥2 to ¥6 depending on distance.

TO/FROM THE AIRPORT

Shuāngliú airport (双流飞机场; Shuāngliú Fēijīchǎng) is 18km west of the city. **Airport shuttle buses** (机场大巴; Jīchǎng Dàbā; www.cdairport.com; ¥10; ⊙6am-10pm, varies by route) run into town; take route 1 for the city centre or route 2 for the South and North Train Stations via Renmin Lu.

A taxi costs around ¥70, depending on the traffic, or arrange a pickup through one of the hostels for around ¥90.

Understand Tibet

Tibet Today

Change is afoot in Tibet. The economy is booming at the fastest rate in China; extended train, air and road links are revolutionising life across the plateau; and Tibet's urban areas are modernising and expanding at an unprecedented rate. As the face of Tibet changes beyond recognition, many Tibetans feel they are becoming increasingly marginalised in their own land. With every expression of Tibetan discontent, Běijīng simply tightens its political and religious controls.

Best in Print

The Open Road: The Global Journey of the Fourteenth Dalai Lama (Pico Iyer) An engaging look at the warmth and contradictions of the 14th Dalai Lama.

Fire Under the Snow (Palden Gyatso) A moving autobiography of a Buddhist monk imprisoned in Tibet for 33 years.

Tears of Blood (Mary Craig) A riveting and distressing account of the Tibetan experience since the Chinese takeover.

Tibet, Tibet (Patrick French) A nuanced look beyond the propaganda and myth surrounding Tibet.

Trespassers on the Roof of the World (Peter Hopkirk) Chronicles European explorers' early attempts to enter forbidden Tibet. Superbly readable.

Best on Film

Kundun (1997) Martin Scorsese's beautifully shot depiction of the life of the Dalai Lama.

Vajra Sky Over Tibet (2006) John Bush's Buddhist-inspired cinematic pilgrimage to the principal sites of central Tibet.

Seven Years in Tibet (1997) Yes, it's a bit silly, and, no, it's not the greatest film but it's still great inspiration before a trip to Tibet.

Modernisation, But At What Cost?

As part of its 'great leap west', the Chinese government has poured US$45 billion into Tibet's infrastructure. It has resettled 1.3 million Tibetans in new housing and created a domestic tourist boom that is spurring hotel and restaurant construction across the plateau. The speed of modernisation is breathtaking.

In most parts of the world this would all be good news, but herein lies Tibet and China's conundrum. Alongside the short-term tourists has come a flood of Chinese immigrants, whom Tibetans claim are the real beneficiaries of Tibet's economic boom.

As the Tibetan people bristle under a lack of control over their own communities and religion, China reminds the Tibetans that it has brought in education, health and infrastructure to the plateau, and spent millions renovating monasteries. Tibetan groups maintain that it is mostly Chinese immigrants who run Tibet's businesses, and that monasteries remain under tight political control and exist largely for tourism. The Chinese counter that they are just trying to bring economic prosperity to one of its most backward provinces, at a large financial loss. (At this point, everyone storms out of the room.)

Environmental Challenges

Perhaps the greatest loser in Tibet's race towards economic development has been its once-pristine environment. Urbanisation projects, hydroelectric dams and urban expansion are rapidly changing the face of Tibet. In the last few years alone hundreds of thousands of Tibetan nomads have been resettled into modern housing communities, effectively bringing an end to a traditional way of life. China says it is protecting the grasslands from overgrazing, protesters (often jailed) say it is a cynical move by the government to gain access to mining and drilling rights. A short drive around Tibet will reveal dozens of new mines and quarries, dug by outside entrepreneurs racing to capitalise on local resources in an atmosphere of economic free-for-all. On the high plateau short-term economic gains are starting to leave long-term environmental scars.

Dark Days

Tibet's long-simmering tensions boiled over on 10 March 2008, the anniversary of the Dalai Lama's flight into exile, kicking off several days of protests by monks from Lhasa's big monasteries. As protest turned to violence, at least 19 people, mostly Han Chinese, were killed and disturbances quickly spread to Tibetan towns in Gānsù, western Sìchuān and Qīnghǎi, marking the worst political unrest in Tibet for 20 years.

In the wake of the riots Tibet remains a tightly controlled place, with armed riot police posted on every street corner in Lhasa's old town. Basic religious and political freedoms are lacking and political propaganda campaigns and surveillance programs are pervasive. Monastery populations are tightly limited by the government, which forces monks to undergo frequent 'patriotic education' and 'civilising atheism' campaigns. In recent years political management teams and security personnel have set up barracks in hundreds of monasteries. To show support for the Dalai Lama continues to result in long jail sentences. Even tourism regulations have been tightened, limiting the contact foreign tourists have with Tibetans.

Cosmetic changes and tightened political controls are unlikely to solve the frustration and resentment that runs deep in Tibet. As Tibetans increasingly feel their culture is under threat and lack channels to air their grievances, their frustration and despair are being reflected in ever more desperate acts. The horrific series of recent Tibetan self-immolations (more than 130 at the time of writing) demonstrates the hopelessness felt by many Tibetans. The root causes remain unaddressed. The longest-lasting result of Tibet's economic boom is clear though: the ties that bind China and Tibet are stronger than ever.

POPULATION: **3 MILLION (2011)**

AREA: **1.23 MILLION SQ KM**

GDP: **US$13.2 BILLION (2013)**

GDP GROWTH: **12% (2013)**

PER CAPITA DISPOSABLE INCOME: **RURAL/URBAN US$1060/3630 (2013)**

NUMBER OF MOBILE PHONES PER 100 PEOPLE: **7**

where Tibetans live (%)

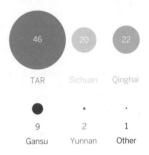

46 TAR
20 Sichuan
22 Qinghai

9 Gansu
2 Yunnan
1 Other

population per sq km

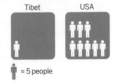

Tibet　　USA

≈ 5 people

History

Tibet's history has been a heady mixture of invasion and intrigue, of soaring religious debate and of reincarnation, miracles and murders, all taking place under the backdrop of one of the world's most extreme environments. If one event has defined Tibet, it has been the nation's remarkable transformation from warring expansionist empire to non-violent Buddhist nation. Running alongside Tibet's history has been its knotty, intertwined relationship with its giant neighbour China.

Murky Origins

The best single-volume introduction to Tibetan history is Sam van Schaik's *Tibet: A History*. It's even-handed, engrossing and highly recommended as a key to understanding the region.

The origins of the Tibetan people are not clearly known. Today, Chinese historians claim the Tibetan people originally migrated from the present-day areas of the Qīnghǎi–Gānsù plains and were descended from people known as Qiang. Although there is evidence of westward migration, it is not possible to trace a single origin of the Tibetan people.

The Tibetan people have their own mythic stories explaining their origins. According to legend, the earth was covered in a vast sea; eventually the water receded and land appeared in the present-day Tsetang area in central Tibet. In a curious paralleling of evolution theory, the first humans were descendants of the union between a monkey and ogress (later identified as the emanations of Chenresig, the Bodhisattva of Compassion, and the goddess Drolma). The half-simian offspring eventually evolved into six families known as Se, Mu, Dong, Tong, Wra and Dru, who became the six clans of the Tibetan people.

Kings, Warriors & the Tibetan Empire

As early myths of the origin of the Tibetan people suggest, the Yarlung Valley was the cradle of central Tibetan civilisation. The early Yarlung kings, although glorified in legend, were probably no more than chieftains whose domains extended not much further than the Yarlung Valley itself. A reconstruction of Tibet's first fortress, Yumbulagang, can still be seen in the Yarlung Valley, and it is here that the 28th king of Tibet is said to have received Tibet's first Buddhist scriptures in the 5th century AD, when they fell from heaven onto the roof of Yumbulagang.

TIMELINE	28,000 BC	300 BC	c 600
	The Tibetan plateau is covered in ice. It's cold. Very cold. But there are people living there. Tools, stone blades and hunting instruments are in use in Chupsang, 85km from Lhasa.	Throughout the plateau people are building stone dwellings and producing fine pottery; petroglyphs indicate that Buddhism may have started to spread by this time.	Nyatri Tsenpo, the first king of Tibet, founds the Yarlung dynasty and unifies the people and the land; according to legend he is responsible for the first building in Tibet.

By the 6th century the Yarlung kings, through conquest and alliances, had made significant headway in unifying much of central Tibet. Namri Songtsen (c 570–619), the 32nd Tibetan king, continued this trend and extended Tibetan influence into inner Asia, defeating the Qiang tribes on China's borders. But the true flowering of Tibet as an important regional power came about with the accession to rule of Namri Songtsen's son, Songtsen Gampo (r 629–49).

Under Songtsen Gampo the armies of Tibet ranged as far afield as northern India and threatened even the great Tang dynasty in China. Both Nepal and China reacted to the Tibetan incursions by reluctantly agreeing to alliances through marriage. Princess Wencheng, Songtsen Gampo's Chinese bride, and Princess Bhrikuti, his Nepali bride, became important historical figures, as it was through their influence that Buddhism first gained royal patronage and a foothold on the Tibetan plateau.

Contact with the Chinese led to the introduction of astronomy and medicine, while a delegation sent to India brought back the basis for a Tibetan script. It was used in the first translations of Buddhist scriptures, in drafting a code of law and in writing the first histories of Tibet.

For two centuries after the reign of Songtsen Gampo, Tibet continued to grow in power and influence. By the time of King Trisong Detsen's reign (r 755–97), Tibetan influence extended over Turkestan (modern-day Xīnjiāng), northern Pakistan, Nepal and India. In China,

The Snow Lion and the Dragon by Melvyn C Goldstein is worth wading through if you want an unsentimental analysis of the historically complex issue of China's claims to Tibet, and the Dalai Lama's options in dealing with the current Chinese leadership.

HISTORY KINGS, WARRIORS & THE TIBETAN EMPIRE

SHANGRI-LA

The slippery notion of Shangri-la has been captivating foreigners for over 80 years now, but mention the phrase to a Tibetan and you'll likely get little more than a blank stare. The origins of Shangri-la lie in James Hilton's novel *Lost Horizon,* a post-WWI fable of a lost Himalayan utopia, where people live in harmony and never age. Hilton's inspiration may well have been National Geographic articles on the remote kingdom of Muli in Kham, and may have even adapted the idea from Tibetan tradition.

Tibetan texts talk of Shambhala, a hidden land to the north whose king will eventually intervene to stop the world from destroying itself. The notion of Shangri-la also bears strong similarities to the Tibetan tradition of *beyul,* hidden lands visible only to the pure of heart that act as refuges in times of great crisis. Tibetan Buddhism also refers directly to various heavenly lands, from the western paradise of Ganden to Guru Rinpoche's paradise of Zangtok Pelri.

Whatever the origins, Shangri-la is firmly lodged in the Western psyche. The name has been adopted as a hotel chain and even as a US presidential retreat. In 2001 the Chinese county of Zhōngdiàn upped the ante by renaming itself 'Shanggelila' in a blatant ploy to boost local tourism. Shangri-la is probably best filed under 'M' for the mythologising of Tibet, on the shelf in between levitating monks and yetis.

608	629	640s	7th century
The first mission is sent to the court of Chinese Emperor Yangdi. This brings Tibet in direct contact with China and sees increasing Tibetan interest in the frontier of China.	Namri Songtsen is assassinated and his son, Songtsen Gampo, aged 13, inherits the throne. He will be regarded as the founder of the Tibetan empire and a cultural hero for the Tibetan people.	Songtsen Gampo marries Chinese Princess Wencheng and Nepalese Princess Bhrikuti. They are credited with bringing Buddhism, silk weaving and new methods of agriculture to Tibet.	The Tibetan empire stretches to include north Pakistan and the Silk Road cities of Khotan and Dūnhuáng.

Tibetan armies conquered Gānsù and Sìchuān and gained brief control over the Silk Road, including the great Buddhist cave complex of Dūnhuáng.

Traces of the Yarlung Kings

Yumbulagang (Yarlung Valley), the first building in Tibet

Tombs of the early Tibetan kings, Chongye

Zortang (Yarlung Valley), the first field in Tibet

Introduction of Buddhism

By the time Buddhism arrived in Tibet during the reign of Songtsen Gampo, it had already flourished for around 1100 years and had become the principal faith of all Tibet's neighbouring countries. But it was slow to take hold in Tibet.

Early Indian missionaries, such as the famous Shantarakshita, faced great hostility from the Bön-dominated court. The influence of Songtsen Gampo's Buddhist Chinese and Nepali wives was almost certainly limited to the royal court, and priests of the time were probably Indian and Chinese, not Tibetan.

It was not until King Trisong Detsen's reign that Buddhism began to take root. Trisong Detsen was responsible for founding Samye Monastery, the first institution to carry out the crucial systematic translation of Buddhist scriptures and the training of Tibetan monks.

Contention over the path that Buddhism was to take in Tibet culminated in the Great Debate of Samye, in which King Trisong Detsen is said to have adjudicated in favour of Indian teachers over the Chan (Zen) approach of Chinese advocates. There was, however, considerable opposition to this institutionalised, clerical form of Buddhism, largely from supporters of the Bön faith. The next Tibetan king, Tritsug Detsen Ralpachen, was assassinated by his brother, Langdharma, who launched an attack on Buddhism. In 842 Langdharma was himself assassinated – by a Buddhist monk – and the Tibetan state soon collapsed into a number of warring principalities. In the confusion that followed, support for Buddhism dwindled and clerical monastic Buddhism experienced a 150-year hiatus.

Famous Early Monasteries

Trandruk (7th–8th century)

Keru (8th century)

Samye (765)

Thöling (996)

Second Diffusion of Buddhism

Overwhelmed initially by local power struggles, Buddhism gradually began to exert its influence again. As the tide of Buddhist faith receded in India, Nepal and China, Tibet slowly emerged as the most devoutly Buddhist nation in the world. Never again was Tibet to rise to arms.

The so-called second diffusion of Buddhism corresponded with two developments. First, Tibetan teachers who had taken refuge in Kham, to the east, returned to central Tibet in the late 10th century and established new monasteries. The second great catalyst was the arrival of two figures in far western Tibet: the Bengali Buddhist scholar Atisha (Jowoje in Tibetan; 982–1054), whom the kings of Guge in far western Tibet invited to Tibet in the mid-11th century; and the great translator Rinchen

763	790s	822	842
Trisong Detsen attacks the Chinese capital Chang'an (Xi'ān) after a Chinese tribute of 50,000 bolts of silk is late.	Samye's Great Debate takes place, as Tibet chooses between the Indian and Chinese schools of Buddhist teachings.	The Sino-Tibetan treaty is signed, defining China's and Tibet's boundaries on largely Tibetan terms. The bilingual inscription of the treaty is erected on a stele outside the Jokhang.	Monk Lhalung Palgye Dorje assassinates anti-Buddhist king Langdharma in disguise. The event is still commemorated by the Black Hat Dance, performed during monastic festivals.

Zangpo (958–1055), who after travelling to India brought back Buddhist texts and founded dozens of monasteries in the far West. Travellers can still get a sense of the glory years of the kingdom of Guge at the spectacular site of Tsaparang (p181) and at Thöling Monastery (p180).

Back in central Tibet disciples of Atisha, chiefly Dromtönpa, were instrumental in establishing the Kadampa order and such early monasteries as Reting.

The Sakyas & the Mongols

With the assassination of Tritsug Detsen Ralpachen and the collapse of a central Tibetan state, Tibet's contacts with China withered. By the time the Tang dynasty collapsed in 907, China had already recovered almost all the territory it had previously lost to the Tibetans. Throughout the Song dynasty (960–1276) the two nations had virtually no contact with each other, and Tibet's sole foreign contacts were with its southern Buddhist neighbours.

This was all to change when Genghis (Chinggis) Khan launched a series of conquests in 1206 that led to a vast Mongol empire that straddled Central Asia and China. By 1239 the Mongols started to send raiding parties onto the Tibetan plateau. Numerous monasteries were razed and the Mongols almost reached Lhasa, before turning back.

Tibetan accounts have it that returning Mongol troops related the spiritual eminence of the Tibetan lamas to Godan Khan, grandson of Genghis Khan and ruler of the Kokonor region (which means 'Blue Sea' in Mongolian) in modern-day Qīnghǎi. In response, Godan summoned Sakya Pandita, the head of Sakya Monastery, to his court. The outcome of this meeting was the beginning of a blurry priest-patron (*cho-yon*) relationship that has come to dog the definitions of Tibetan independence and its relationship to China. Tibetan Buddhism became the state religion of the Mongol empire in east Asia, and the head Sakya lama became

The Tibetan Lama Phagpa, nephew of Kunga Gyaltsen, enjoyed a close relationship with the Mongol leader Kublai Khan, likely met Marco Polo in Běijīng and even helped create a new Mongol script.

Songtsen Gampo went as far as passing a law making it illegal *not* to be a Buddhist.

WRITTEN IN STONE

A Sino-Tibetan treaty was signed in 822 during the reign of King Tritsug Detsen Ralpachen (r 817–36), heralding an era in which 'Tibetans shall be happy in Tibet and Chinese shall be happy in China'. It was immortalised in stone on three steles: one in Lhasa, outside the Jokhang; one in the Chinese capital of Chang'an; and one on the border of Tibet and China. Only the Lhasa stele still stands, in Barkhor Square (p43).

Signatories to the treaty swore that '...the whole region to the east...being the country of Great China and the whole region to the west being assuredly that of the country of Great Tibet, from either side of that frontier there shall be no warfare, no hostile invasions, and no seizure of territory...'.

996	1042	1073	1110–1193
Thöling Monastery is founded in far western Tibet and becomes the main centre of Buddhist activities in Tibet, translating large numbers of Buddhist texts from Kashmir.	Atisha, the Bengali Buddhist scholar and abbot, arrives in Tibet. With his disciple Dromtönpa (1004–64) he is credited with founding the Kadampa, the first distinctive Tibetan Buddhist School.	The Khon family, which traces its lineage from the nobility of the Yarlung dynasty, founds the Sakya school of Tibetan Buddhism. The family remains the hereditary head of Sakya tradition to this day.	The first Karmapa introduces the concept of reincarnation, which eventually spreads to other schools of Tibetan Buddhism and to the institution of the Dalai Lamas.

its spiritual leader, a position that also entailed temporal authority over Tibet. The Sakyapa ascendancy lasted less than 100 years but its ties to the Mongol Yuan dynasty was to have profound effects on Tibet's future.

Tibetan Independence (Part I)

The process of reincarnation has been likened to a flame that passes from candle to candle, yet remains the same flame.

Certain Chinese claims on Tibet have looked to the Mongol Yuan dynasty overlordship of the high plateau, and the priest-patron relationship existing at the time, as setting a precedent for Chinese sovereignty over Tibet. The Yuan dynasty may have claimed sovereignty over Tibet, yet this 'Chinese' dynasty was itself governed by the invading Mongols and their ruler Kublai Khan. Pro-independence supporters state that this is like India claiming sovereignty over Myanmar (Burma) because both were ruled by the British.

In reality, Tibetan submission was offered to the Mongols before they conquered China and it ended when the Mongols fell from power in that country. When the Mongol empire disintegrated, both China and Tibet regained their independence. Due to the initial weakness of the Ming dynasty, Sino-Tibetan relations effectively took on the form of exchanges of diplomatic courtesies by two independent governments.

The Tibetans undertook to remove all traces of the Mongol administration, drawing on the traditions of the former Yarlung kings. Officials were required to dress in the manner of the former royal court, a revised version of King Songtsen Gampo's code of law was enacted, a new taxation system was enforced, and scrolls depicting the glories of the Yarlung dynasty were commissioned. The movement was a declaration of Tibet's independence from foreign interference and a search for national identity.

Rise of the Gelugpa & the Dalai Lamas

In 1374, a young man named Lobsang, later known as Tsongkhapa, set out from his home near Kokonor in Amdo to central Tibet, where he undertook training with all the major schools of Tibetan Buddhism. By the time he was 25 he had already gained a reputation as a teacher and a writer.

TANGTONG GYELPO

Tangtong Gyelpo (1385–1464) was Tibet's Renaissance man *par excellence*. Nyingmapa yogi, treasure finder, engineer, medic and inventor of Tibetan opera, Tangtong formed a song-and-dance troupe of seven sisters to raise money for his other passion, bridge building. He eventually built 108 bridges in Tibet, the most famous of which was over the Yarlung Tsangpo near modern-day Chushul. Tangtong is often depicted in monastery murals with long white hair and a beard, and is usually holding a section of chain links from one of his bridges.

1201	**1240**	**1249**	**1260**
Sakya Pandita (1182–1251) travels to India, studying under Indian gurus. He becomes a great religious and cultural figure, creating a Tibetan literary tradition inspired by Sanskrit poetry.	The grandson of Genghis Khan, Godan Khan, invades central Tibet with 30,000 troops, ransacking the monastery of Reting.	Sakya Pandita becomes the spiritual advisor to Godon Khan and converts the Mongols to Buddhism. Godon invests Sakya Pandita as the secular ruler of Tibet.	Kublai Khan appoints Phagpa as an imperial preceptor. This ushers in what the Tibetans call the priest–patron relationship between Mongol Khans, later Chinese emperors and Tibetan lamas.

Tsongkhapa established a monastery at Ganden, near Lhasa, where he refined his thinking, steering clear of political intrigue, and espousing doctrinal purity and monastic discipline. Although it seems unlikely that Tsongkhapa intended to found another school of Buddhism, his teachings attracted many disciples, who found his return to the original teachings of Atisha an exciting alternative to the politically tainted Sakyapa and Kagyupa orders. Tsongkhapa's movement became known as the Gelugpa (Virtuous) order, which today remains the dominant school in Tibet.

By the time of the third reincarnated head of the Gelugpa, Sonam Gyatso (1543–88), the Mongols began to take a renewed interest in Tibet's new and increasingly powerful order. In a move that mirrored the 13th-century Sakyapa entrance into the political arena, Sonam Gyatso accepted an invitation to meet with Altyn Khan near Kokonor in 1578. At the meeting, Sonam Gyatso received the title of *dalai,* meaning 'ocean', and implying 'ocean of wisdom'. The title was retrospectively bestowed on his previous two reincarnations, and so Sonam Gyatso became the third Dalai Lama.

Their relationship with the Mongols marked the Gelugpa's entry into the turbulent waters of worldly affairs. It is no surprise that the Tsang kings and the Karmapa of Tsurphu Monastery saw this Gelugpa-Mongol alliance as a direct threat to their power. Bickering ensued, and in 1611 the Tsang king attacked Drepung and Sera Monasteries as the country slid into civil war. The fourth (Mongolian) Dalai Lama fled central Tibet and died at the age of 25 in 1616.

The Great Fifth Dalai Lama

A successor to the fourth Dalai Lama was soon discovered, and the boy was brought to Lhasa, again under Mongol escort. In the meantime, Mongol intervention in Tibetan affairs continued in the guise of support for the embattled Gelugpa order.

Unlike the Sakya-Mongol domination of Tibet, under which the head Sakya lama was required to reside in the Mongol court, the fifth Dalai Lama was able to rule from within Tibet. With the backing of the Mongol Gushri Khan, all of Tibet was pacified by 1656, and the Dalai Lama's control ranged from Mt Kailash in the west to Kham in the east. Ngawang Lobsang Gyatso, the fifth Dalai Lama, had become both the spiritual and temporal sovereign of a unified Tibet.

The fifth Dalai Lama is remembered as having ushered in a great new age for Tibet. He made a tour of Tibet's monasteries, and although he stripped most Kadampa monasteries – his chief rivals for power – of their riches, he allowed them to re-establish. A new flurry of monastic construction began, the major achievement being Labrang Monastery

The Dalai Lamas are depicted in wall paintings holding the Wheel of Law (Wheel of Dharma) as a symbol of the political power gained under the Great Fifth Dalai Lama.

The concept of reincarnation was first introduced by the Karmapa and adopted in the 15th century by the Gelugpa order and the Dalai Lamas.

The fifth Dalai Lama wrote a detailed history of Tibet and his autobiography is regarded as a literary treasure of Tibet.

1268	1290	1357–1419	1368
The first census of central Tibet counts some 40,000 households. Basic taxation and a new administrative system is established in Tibet.	Kublai Khan's army supports the Sakya and destroys the main centres of the Kagyud school. With the death of Kublai Khan in 1294, the power of the Sakya school begins to wane.	Tsongkhapa establishes himself as a reformer, founds the reformist Gelugpa school, writes the influential Lamrin Chenpo and introduces the popular Mönlam festival.	The Mongol Yuan dynasty in China ends, and the Ming dynasty begins. This coincides with the final demise of Sakya rule in Tibet.

REINCARNATION LINEAGES

There are thought to be several thousand *trulku* (also spelt *tulku;* 'incarnate lamas') in contemporary Tibet. The abbots of many monasteries are *trulku,* and thus abbotship can be traced back through a lineage of rebirths to the original founder of a monastery. The honorific title *rinpoche,* meaning 'very precious', is a mark of respect and does not necessarily imply that the holder is a *trulku.* The Chinese use the confused translation 'Living Buddha' for *trulku.*

A *trulku* can also be a manifestation of a bodhisattva that repeatedly expresses itself through a series of rebirths. The most famous manifestation of a deity is, of course, the Dalai Lama lineage. The Dalai Lamas are manifestations of Chenresig (Avalokiteshvara), the Bodhisattva of Compassion. The Panchen Lama is a manifestation of Jampelyang (Manjushri), the Bodhisattva of Insight. There is no exclusivity in such a manifestation: Tsongkhapa, founder of the Gelugpa order, was also a manifestation of Jampelyang (Manjushri), as traditionally were the abbots of Sakya Monastery.

Lamas approaching death often leave behind clues pointing to the location of their reincarnation. Potential reincarnations are often further tested by being required to pick out the former lama's possessions from a collection of objects. Disputes over *trulku* status are not uncommon. A family's fortunes are likely to drastically improve if an incarnate lama is discovered among the children; this creates an incentive for fraud.

It is possible to see in the *trulku* system a substitute for the system of hereditary power (as in Western royal lineages) in a society where, historically, many of the major players were celibate and unable to produce their own heirs. Not that celibacy was exclusively the case. The abbots of Sakya took wives to produce their own *trulku* reincarnations, and it is not uncommon for rural *trulkus* to do the same.

The major flaw in the system is the time needed for the reincarnation to reach adulthood. Regents have traditionally been appointed to run the country during the minority of a Dalai Lama but this tradition takes on an added dimension under modern political circumstances. The current Dalai Lama has made it clear that he will not be reincarnated in Chinese-occupied Tibet and may even be the last Dalai Lama.

(in what is now Gānsù province). In Lhasa, work began on a fitting residence for the head of the Tibetan state: the Potala.

Manchus, Mongols & Murder

With the death of the fifth Dalai Lama in 1682, the weakness of reincarnation as a system of succession became apparent. The Tibetan government was confronted with the prospect of finding his reincarnation and then waiting 18 years until the boy came of age. The great personal prestige and authority of the fifth Dalai Lama had played no small part in holding together a newly unified Tibet. The Dalai Lama's

1565	1578	1588	1601
The kings of Tsang became secular rulers of Tibet from Shigatse. Spiritual authority at this time is vested in the Karmapa, head of a Kagyupa suborder at Tsurphu Monastery.	Mongolian Altyn (Altan) Khan converts to Buddhism and bestows the title 'Dalai Lama' to Sonam Gyatso, who becomes the third Dalai Lama (the first two are honoured retroactively).	The third Dalai Lama dies en route to Tibet, aged 45, after a visit to the Ming court at Běijīng.	The Mongolian great-grandson of Altyn Khan is recognised by the Panchen Lama as the fourth Dalai Lama. This establishes the tradition of the Dalai Lamas being recognised by the Panchen.

regent decided to shroud the Dalai Lama's death in secrecy, announcing that the fifth lama had entered a long period of meditation (over 10 years!).

In 1695 the secret was leaked and the regent was forced to hastily enthrone the sixth Dalai Lama, a boy of his own choosing. The choice was an unfortunate one and could not have come at a worse time.

Tibet's dealings with the new Qing government went awry from the start. Kangxi, the second Qing emperor, took offence when the death of the fifth Dalai Lama was concealed from him. At the same time, an ambitious Mongol prince named Lhabzang Khan came to the conclusion that earlier Mongol leaders had taken too much of a back-seat position in their relations with the Tibetans and appealed to Emperor Kangxi for support. It was granted and, in 1705, Mongol forces descended on Lhasa, deposing the sixth Dalai Lama. Depending on your source, he either died at Lithang (where he was probably murdered), or he lived to a ripe old age in Amdo. The seventh Dalai Lama was subsequently found in Lithang, fulfilling a famous poem written by the sixth.

In 1717 the Dzungar Mongols from Central Asia attacked and occupied Lhasa for three years, killing Lhabzang Khan and deposing the seventh Dalai Lama. The resulting confusion in Tibet was the opportunity for which Emperor Kangxi had been waiting. He responded by sending a military expedition to Lhasa. The Chinese troops drove out the Dzungar Mongols and were received by the Tibetans as liberators. They were unlikely to have been received any other way: with them, they brought the seventh Dalai Lama, who had been languishing in Kumbum Monastery under Chinese 'protection'.

Emperor Kangxi wasted no time in declaring Tibet a protectorate of China. Two Chinese representatives, known as *ambans* (a Manchurian word), were installed at Lhasa, along with a garrison of Chinese troops. It was just a beginning, leading to two centuries of Manchu overlordship and serving as a convenient historical precedent for the communist take-over nearly 250 years later.

Manchu Overlordship

The seventh Dalai Lama ruled until his death in 1757. However, at this point it became clear that another ruler would have to be appointed until the next Dalai Lama reached adulthood. The post of regent (*gyeltshab*) was created.

It is perhaps a poor reflection on the spiritual attainment of the lamas appointed as regents that few were willing to relinquish the reins once they were in the saddle. In the 120 years between the death of the seventh Dalai Lama and the adulthood of the 13th, actual power was wielded by the Dalai Lamas for only seven years. Three of them died

Kate Teltscher's *The High Road to China* details the 1774–45 journey of 27-year-old George Bogle to Shigatse and his fascinating relationship with the Panchen Lama.

Charles Allen's *Duel in the Snows* brings to life the 1903–4 Younghusband expedition to Tibet through the letters and accounts of its main protagonists.

1624	1640–42	1652	1695
Jesuits open their first mission at Tsaparang in far western Tibet after an epic journey across the Himalaya from bases in Goa.	Mongolian Gushri Khan executes the King of Tsang and hands over religious and secular power to the fifth Dalai Lama. Lhasa becomes the capital and construction begins on the Potala.	The Manchu Emperor Shunzhi invites the fifth Dalai Lama to China; to mark the occasion the Yellow Temple is built on the outskirts of Běijīng.	Completion of Potala Palace. The death of the fifth Dalai Lama is announced the following year, though in reality he had died 15 years previously.

THE PLAYBOY LAMA

Tsangyang Gyatso (1683–1706), the young man chosen as the sixth Dalai Lama, was, shall we say, unconventional. A sensual youth with long hair and a penchant for erotic verse, he soon proved himself to be far more interested in wine and women than meditation and study. He refused to take his final vows as a monk and he would often sneak out of the Potala at night to raise hell in the inns and brothels of Lhasa, under the pseudonym Norsang Wangpo. A resident Jesuit monk described him as a 'dissolute youth' and 'quite depraved', noting that 'no good-looking person of either sex was safe from his unbridled licentiousness'.

very young and under suspicious circumstances. Only the eighth Dalai Lama survived into his adulthood, living a quiet, contemplative life until the age of 45.

Barbarians at the Doorstep

Early contact between Britain and Tibet commenced with a mission to Shigatse headed by a Scotsman, George Bogle, in 1774. Bogle soon ingratiated himself with the Panchen Lama – to the extent of marrying one of his sisters. With the death of the third Panchen Lama in 1780 and the ban on foreign contact that came after the Gurkha invasion of Tibet in 1788, Britain lost all official contact with Tibet.

The Younghusband invasion of Tibet included 10,091 porters, 7096 mules, 2668 ponies, 4466 yaks and six camels in a train that stretched for 7km!

Meanwhile, Britain watched nervously as the Russian empire swallowed up Central Asia, pushing its borders 1000km further towards India. The reported arrival of Russian 'adviser' Agvan Dorjieff in Lhasa exacerbated fears that Russia had military designs on British India, the 'jewel in the crown' of the empire.

When Dorjieff led an envoy from the Dalai Lama to Tsar Nicholas II in 1898, 1900 and 1901, and when British intelligence confirmed that Lhasa had received Russian missions (while similar British advances had been refused), the Raj broke into a cold sweat. There was even wild conjecture that the tsar was poised to convert to Buddhism.

It was against this background that Russophobe Lord Curzon, viceroy of India, decided to nip Russian designs in the bud. In late 1903 a British military expedition led by Colonel Francis Younghusband entered Tibet via Sikkim. After several months waiting for a Tibetan delegation, the British moved on to Lhasa, where it was discovered that the Dalai Lama had fled to Mongolia with Dorjieff. However, an Anglo-Tibetan convention was signed following negotiations with Tri Rinpoche, the abbot of Ganden whom the Dalai Lama had appointed as regent in his absence. British forces withdrew after spending just two months in Lhasa.

1706	1716–21	1724	1774
Lhabzang Khan's army marches into Lhasa, deposes (and likely poisons) the sixth Dalai Lama and installs Yeshi Gyatso, who is not accepted by Tibetans as a Dalai Lama.	Italian priest Ippolito Desideri travels to the Guge Kingdom and Lhasa, where he lives for five years, trying to convert Tibetans to Catholicism. He is the first Westerner to see Mt Kailash.	The Manchu Qing dynasty appoints a resident Chinese *amban* to run Tibet.	Scotsman George Bogle, aged 27, travels to Tibet to investigate the opening of trade and spends the winter at Tashilhunpo Monastery in Shigatse.

The missing link in the Anglo-Tibetan accord was a Manchu signature. In effect, the accord implied that Tibet was a sovereign power and therefore had the right to make treaties of its own. The Manchus objected and, in 1906, the British signed a second accord with the Manchus, one that recognised China's suzerainty over Tibet. In 1910, with the Manchu Qing dynasty teetering on collapse, the Manchus made good on the accord and invaded Tibet, forcing the Dalai Lama once again into flight – this time into the arms of the British in India.

Tibetan Independence Revisited

In 1911 a revolution finally toppled the decadent Qing dynasty in China, and by the end of 1912 the last of the occupying Manchu forces were escorted out of Tibet. In January 1913 the 13th Dalai Lama returned to Lhasa from Sikkim.

In reply to overtures from the government of the new Chinese republic, the Dalai Lama replied that he was uninterested in ranks bestowed by the Chinese and that he was assuming temporal and spiritual leadership of his country.

Tibetans have since read this reply as a formal declaration of independence. As for the Chinese, they chose to ignore it, reporting that the Dalai Lama had responded with a letter expressing his great love for the motherland. Whatever the case, Tibet was to enjoy 30 years free of interference from China. What is more, Tibet was suddenly presented with an opportunity to create a state that was ready to rise to the challenge of the modern world. The opportunity foundered on Tibet's entrenched theocratic institutions, and Tibetan independence was a short-lived affair.

Attempts to Modernise

During the period of his flight to India, the 13th Dalai Lama had become friends with Sir Charles Bell, a Tibetan scholar and political officer in Sikkim. The relationship was to initiate a warming in Anglo-Tibetan affairs and to see the British playing an increasingly important role as mediators between Tibet and China.

In 1920 Bell was dispatched on a mission to Lhasa, where he renewed his friendship with the Dalai Lama. It was agreed that the British would supply the Tibetans with modern arms, providing they agreed to use them only for self-defence. Tibetan military officers were trained in Gyantse and India, and a telegraph line was set up linking Lhasa and Shigatse. Other developments included the construction of a small hydroelectric station near Lhasa and the establishment of an English school at Gyantse. Four Tibetan boys were even sent to public school at Rugby in England. At the invitation of the Dalai Lama, British

Fans of Great Game history can visit Gyantse Dzong and nearby Tsechen Dzong, both of which were taken by Younghusband in 1904, as well as the Karo-la, scene of the highest battle in British Imperial history.

HISTORY TIBETAN INDEPENDENCE REVISITED

Scott Berry's *A Stranger in Tibet* tells the fascinating story of Ekai Kawaguchi, a young Japanese monk, who was one of the first foreigners to reach Lhasa in 1900 and who managed to stay over a year in the capital before his identity was discovered and he was forced to flee the country.

1788	1879	1893	1904
Chinese troops expel Nepali invaders from Tibet. Three years later the Nepali troops return and are beaten back again.	The 13th Dalai Lama is enthroned. In 1895 he takes his final ordination and becomes the secular and spiritual ruler of Tibet.	Tibet cedes Sikkim and opens the Chumbi Valley to trade with British India.	The British mobilise over 8000 soldiers and launch an invasion of Tibet from the Sikkim frontier. The ill-equipped Tibetan army is no match. The 13th Dalai Lama escapes to Mongolia.

experts conducted geological surveys of parts of Tibet with a view to gauging mining potential.

It is highly likely that the 13th Dalai Lama's trips away from his country had made him realise that it was imperative that Tibet begin to modernise. At the same time he must also have been aware that the road to modernisation was fraught with obstacles, foremost of which was the entrenched Tibetan social order.

Since the rise of the Gelugpa order, Tibet had been ruled as a (some would say feudal) theocracy. Monks, particularly those in the huge monastic complexes of Drepung and Sera in Lhasa, were accustomed to a high degree of influence in the Tibetan government. And the attempts to modernise were met with intense opposition.

Before too long, the 13th Dalai Lama's innovations fell victim to a conservative backlash. Newly trained Tibetan officers were reassigned to nonmilitary jobs, causing a rapid deterioration of military discipline; a newly established police force was left to its own devices and soon became ineffective; the English school at Gyantse was closed down; and a mail service set up by the British was stopped.

While lying in state the head of the 13th Dalai Lama's corpse allegedly turned repeatedly towards the northeast, indicating that the 14th Dalai Lama would be born in Amdo.

However, Tibet's brief period of independence was troubled by more than just an inability to modernise. Conflict sprang up between the Panchen Lama and the Dalai Lama over the autonomy of Tashilhunpo Monastery and its estates. The Panchen Lama, after appealing to the British to mediate, fled to China, where he stayed for 14 years until his death.

In 1933 the 13th Dalai Lama died, leaving the running of the country to the regent of Reting. The present (14th) Dalai Lama was discovered in Amdo but was brought to Lhasa only after the local Chinese commander had been paid off with a huge 'fee' of 300,000 Chinese dollars. The boy was renamed Tenzin Gyatso and he was installed as the Dalai Lama on 22 February 1940, aged 4½.

In 1947 an attempted coup d'état, known as the Reting Conspiracy, rocked Lhasa. Lhasa came close to civil war, with 200 monks killed in gunfights at Sera Monastery. Reting Rinpoche was thrown into jail for his part in the rebellion and was later found dead in his cell, though it remains unclear whether he was set up or not.

It was not a good time for Tibet to be weakened by internal disputes. By 1949 the Chinese Nationalist government had fled to Taiwan and Mao Zedong and his Red Army had taken control of China. Big changes were looming.

Liberation

Unknown to the Tibetans, the communist takeover of China was to open what is probably the saddest chapter in Tibetan history. The ensuing Chinese 'liberation' of Tibet eventually led to the deaths of hundreds of thou-

1907	1909	1910	1913
Britain and Russia acknowledge Chinese suzerainty over Tibet in a resolution of Great Game tensions.	The 13th Dalai Lama returns to Lhasa after an absence of five years.	Chinese resident in Tibet, Zhao Erfeng, attempts to re-establish Qing authority and storms Lhasa. The Dalai Lama escapes again, this time to India. On his return he declares Tibet independent.	The Simla Convention between Britain, China and Tibet is held in India. The main agenda for the conference is to delimit and define the boundary between Tibet and China.

sands of Tibetans, an assault on the Tibetan traditional way of life, the flight of the Dalai Lama to India and the destruction of almost every historical structure on the plateau. The chief culprits were Chinese ethnic chauvinism and an epidemic of social anarchy known as the Cultural Revolution.

On 7 October 1950, just a year after the communist takeover of China, 40,000 battle-hardened Chinese troops attacked central Tibet from six different directions. The Tibetan army, a poorly equipped force of around 4000 men, stood little chance of resisting, and any attempt at defence soon collapsed. In Lhasa the Tibetan government reacted by enthroning the 15-year-old 14th Dalai Lama, an action that brought jubilation and dancing on the streets but did little to protect Tibet from advancing Chinese troops.

Presented with a seemingly hopeless situation, the Dalai Lama dispatched a mission to Běijīng with orders that it refer all decisions to Lhasa. As it turned out, there were no decisions to be made. The Chinese had already drafted an agreement. The Tibetans had two choices: sign on the dotted line or face further military action.

The 17-Point *Agreement on Measures for the Peaceful Liberation of Tibet* promised a one-country-two-systems structure much like that offered later to Hong Kong and Macau, but provided little in the way of guarantees. The Tibetan delegates protested that they were unauthorised to sign such an agreement but were strongarmed and the agreement was ratified.

Initially, the Chinese occupation of central Tibet was carried out in an orderly way, with few obvious changes or reforms, but tensions inevitably mounted. The presence of 8000 Chinese troops in Lhasa (doubling the city's population) soon affected food stores and gave rise to high inflation. Rumours of political indoctrination, massacres and attacks on monasteries in Kham (far eastern Tibet) slowly began to filter back to Lhasa.

In 1956 uprisings broke out in eastern Tibet in reaction to enforced land reform, and in 1957 and 1958 protests and armed guerrilla revolt spread to central Tibet (with covert CIA assistance). With a heavy heart, the Dalai Lama returned to Lhasa in March 1957 from a trip to India to celebrate the 2500th anniversary of the birth of the Buddha. It seemed inevitable that Tibet would explode in revolt and equally inevitable that it would be suppressed by China.

Marco Polo and Alexandra David-Neel both wrote about the magical powers of Tibetan monks, including the ability to move cups with their minds, travel cross-country while levitating or keep warm in subzero temperatures simply through the power of their minds.

Uprising & Bloodshed

The Tibetan New Year of 1959, like all the New Year celebrations before it, attracted huge crowds to Lhasa, doubling the city's population. In addition to the standard festival activities, the Chinese had added a highlight of their own – a performance by a Chinese dance group at the Lhasa military base. The invitation to the Dalai Lama came in the form of a thinly veiled command. The Dalai Lama, wishing to avoid offence, accepted.

1923	1933	1935	1950
A clash with Lhasa sends the Panchen Lama into exile in China. This is to have disastrous consequences for Tibet: he comes under Chinese influence and never returns.	The 13th Dalai Lama dies, and secular authority is passed to Reting Rinpoche, who rules as regent until 1947. He is an eminent Gelugpa Lama, but young and inexperienced in state affairs.	Birth of the present 14th Dalai Lama in Taktser village, Amdo, just outside Xīníng in present Qīnghǎi; his younger and older brothers are also *trulkus* (reincarnated lamas).	China attacks Chamdo; the Tibetan army is greatly outnumbered and defeat is swift. The Tibetan government in Lhasa reacts by enthroning the 15-year-old 14th Dalai Lama. There is jubilation in the streets.

THE FALL OF CHAMDO

In spring 1950, Chamdo in eastern Tibet was in real trouble. Although pockets of resistance remained at Derge and Markham, the communist Chinese had taken control of most of Kham without a fight. Chinese armies were quickly tightening the noose around Tibet, moving in from Xīnjiāng and Xikang (now Sìchuān) provinces in a pincer movement masterminded by, among others, Deng Xiaoping.

The first skirmish between Chinese and Tibetan troops took place in May 1950 when the People's Liberation Army (PLA) attacked Dengo on the Dri-chu (Yangzi River). Then on 7 October 1950 the PLA moved in earnest, as 40,000 troops crossed the Dri-chu and attacked Chamdo from three directions: Jyekundo to the north, Derge to the east and Markham to the south.

As panic swept through Chamdo, the city responded to the military threat in characteristic Tibetan fashion – with a frenzy of prayer and religious ritual. When the local Tibetan leader radioed the Tibetan government in Lhasa to warn of the Chinese invasion, he was coolly told that the government members couldn't be disturbed because they were 'on a picnic'. To this the Chamdo radio operator is said to have replied *'skyag pa'i gling kha!'* or 'shit the picnic!'. It was to be the last ever communication between the Chamdo and Lhasa branches of the Tibetan government.

The city was evacuated but the PLA was one step ahead. Chinese leaders knew that speed was of the essence (the Chinese described the military operation as 'like a tiger trying to catch a fly') and had already cut the Tibetans off by taking Riwoche. The Tibetans surrendered without a shot on 19 October. The Tibetan troops were disarmed, given lectures on the benefits of socialism, and then given money and sent home. The British radio operator Robert Ford, who was based in Chamdo, was less lucky. He was arrested, subjected to thought reform and held in jail for five years. It was the beginning of the end of an independent Tibet.

As preparations for the performance drew near, however, the Dalai Lama's security chief was surprised to hear that the Dalai Lama was expected to attend in secrecy and without his customary contingent of 25 bodyguards. Despite the Dalai Lama's agreement to these conditions, news of them soon leaked, and in no time simmering frustration at Chinese rule came to the boil among the crowds on the streets. It seemed obvious to the Tibetans that the Chinese were about to kidnap the Dalai Lama. A huge crowd (witnesses claim 30,000 people) gathered around the Norbulingka (the Dalai Lama's summer palace) and swore to protect him with their lives.

The Dalai Lama had no choice but to cancel his appointment at the military base. In the meantime, the crowds on the streets were swollen by Tibetan soldiers, who changed out of their People's Liberation Army

1950	1951	1954	1955
El Salvador sponsors a UN motion to condemn Chinese aggression in Tibet. Britain and India, traditional friends of Tibet, convince the UN not to debate the issue.	The 17-Point Agreement is signed by the Governor of Kham, acknowledging Tibet's autonomy as a part of the People's Republic of China. Chairman Mao's first remark is 'Welcome Back to the Motherland'.	In 1954 the Dalai Lama spends almost a year in Běijīng, where, amid cordial discussions with Mao Zedong, he is told that 'religion is poison'.	Xikang province is absorbed into Sichuān province, eating up a large chunk of the traditional Tibetan province of Kham.

(PLA) uniforms and started to hand out weapons. A group of government ministers announced that the 17-Point Agreement was null and void, and that Tibet renounced the authority of China.

The Dalai Lama was powerless to intervene, managing only to pen some conciliatory letters to the Chinese as his people prepared for battle on Lhasa's streets. In a last-ditch effort to prevent bloodshed, the Dalai Lama even offered himself to the Chinese. The reply came in the sound of two mortar shells exploding in the gardens of the Norbulingka. The attack made it obvious that the only option remaining to the Dalai Lama was flight (a measure the Nechung oracle agreed with). On 17 March, he left the Norbulingka disguised as a soldier and surrounded by Khampa bodyguards; 14 days later he was in India. The Dalai Lama was 24 years old.

With both the Chinese and the Tibetans unaware of the Dalai Lama's departure, tensions continued to mount in Lhasa. On 20 March, Chinese troops began to shell the Norbulingka and the crowds surrounding it, killing hundreds of people. Artillery bombed the Potala, Sera Monastery and the medical college on Chagpo Ri. Tibetans armed with petrol bombs were picked off by Chinese snipers, and when a crowd of 10,000 Tibetans retreated into the sacred precincts of the Jokhang, that too was bombed. It is thought that after three days of violence, hundreds of Tibetans lay dead in Lhasa's streets. Some estimates put the numbers of those killed far higher.

Socialist Paradise on the Roof of the World

The Chinese quickly consolidated their quelling of the Lhasa uprising by taking control of all the high passes between Tibet and India and disarming the Khampa guerrillas. As the Chinese themselves put it, they were liberating Tibet from reactionary forces, freeing serfs from the yoke of monastic oppression and ushering in a new equitable socialist society, whether the Tibetans liked it or not.

The Chinese abolished the Tibetan government and set about re-ordering Tibetan society in accordance with their Marxist principles. The monks and the aristocratic were put to work on menial jobs and subjected to violent ideological struggle sessions, known as *thamzing*, which sometimes resulted in death. A ferment of class struggle was whipped up and former feudal exploiters – towards some of whom Tibet's poor may have harboured genuine resentment – were subjected to cruel punishments.

The Chinese also turned their attention to Tibet's several thousand 'feudal' monasteries, lhakhangs and shrines. Tibetans were refused permission to donate food to the monasteries, and monks were compelled to join struggle sessions, discard their robes and marry. Monasteries

Education was once under the exclusive control of the monasteries, and the introduction of a secular education system has been a major goal of the communist government. These days most education is in the Chinese language.

HISTORY SOCIALIST PARADISE ON THE ROOF OF THE WORLD

1956	late 1950s	1962	1964
Rebellions break out in monasteries in Kham (modern-day western Sìchuān). The siege of Lithang lasts 67 days and ends in aerial bombardment of the monastery.	The Khampas found the resistance group Four Rivers, Six Ranges. The Tibetan exile groups in India make contact with the CIA; Tibetans are sent for training to the Pacific island of Saipan.	The Indo-Chinese war ends in defeat for India, but territorial disputes over Arunachal Pradesh and Aksai Chin continue to this day between the two rising giants.	Three years after writing a 70,000-character petition, accusing China of committing genocide, the Panchen Lama is arrested and charged with instigating rebellion.

were stripped of their riches, Buddhist scriptures were burnt and used as toilet paper. The wholesale destruction of Tibet's monastic heritage began in earnest.

Neither Mao Zedong nor Deng Xiaoping ever visited Tibet.

Notable in this litany of disasters was the Chinese decision to alter Tibetan farming practices, as part of an economic 'Great Leap Forward'. Instead of barley, the Tibetan staple, farmers were instructed to grow wheat and rice. Tibetans protested that these crops were unsuited to Tibet's high altitude. They were right, and mass starvation resulted. It is estimated that by late 1961, 70,000 Tibetans had died or were dying of starvation. Across China it is estimated that up to 35 million people died.

By September 1961, even the Chinese-groomed Panchen Lama began to have a change of heart. He presented Mao Zedong with a 70,000-character report on the hardships his people were suffering and also requested, among other things, religious freedom and an end to the sacking of Tibetan monasteries. Four years later he was to disappear into a high-security prison for a 14-year stay. Many more would soon join him.

Around 2500 monasteries existed in Tibet in 1959. By 1962 only 70 remained.

The Cultural Revolution

Among the writings of Mao Zedong is a piece entitled 'On Going Too Far'. It is a subject on which he was particularly well qualified to write. What started as a power struggle between Mao and Liu Shaoqi in 1965 had morphed by August 1966 into the Great Proletarian Cultural Revolution, an anarchic movement that was to shake China to its core, trample its traditions underfoot, cause countless deaths and turn the running of the country over to rival mobs of Red Guards. All of China suffered in Mao's bold experiment in creating a new socialist paradise, but Tibet suffered more than most.

The first Red Guards arrived in Lhasa in July 1966. Two months later, the first rally was organised and Chinese-educated Tibetan youths raided the Jokhang, smashing statues and burning thangkas. It was the beginning of the large-scale destruction of virtually every religious monument in Tibet, and was carried out in the spirit of destroying the 'Four Olds': old thinking, old culture, old habits and old customs. Images of Chairman Mao were plastered over those of Buddha, as Buddhist mantras were replaced by communist slogans. The Buddha himself was accused of being a 'reactionary'.

Cultural Revolution– Era Ruins

Jampaling Kumbum, Tsangpo Valley

Thöling Monastery, Zanda

Tibetan farmers were forced to collectivise into communes and were told what to grow and when to grow it. Anyone who objected was arrested and subjected to struggle sessions, during which Tibetans were forced to denounce the Dalai Lama as a parasite and traitor.

1 September 1965	**1967–76**	**1975**	**1979–85**
The Tibetan Autonomous Region (TAR) is formally brought into being with much fanfare and Chinese talk of happy Tibetans fighting back tears of gratitude at becoming one with the great motherland.	The Cultural Revolution sweeps China and Tibet. Ideological frenzy results in the destruction of monasteries, shrines and libraries and the imprisonment of thousands of Tibetans.	The last CIA-funded Tibetan guerrilla bases in Mustang, northern Nepal, are closed down, bringing an end to armed rebellion and CIA involvement in the Tibetan resistance movement.	China enters a period of liberalisation and reform and limited religious freedoms are restored in Tibet. Out of a pre-1950 total of around 2000 monasteries, only 45 are reopened.

The Dust Settles

By the time of Mao's death in 1976 even the Chinese had begun to realise that their rule in Tibet had taken a wrong turn. Mao's chosen successor, Hua Guofeng, decided to soften the government's line on Tibet and called for a revival of Tibetan customs. In mid-1977 China announced that it would welcome the return of the Dalai Lama and other Tibetan refugees, and shortly afterwards the Panchen Lama was released from 14 years of imprisonment.

The Tibetan government-in-exile received cautiously the invitation to return to Tibet, and the Dalai Lama suggested that he be allowed to send a fact-finding mission to Tibet first. To the surprise of all involved, the Chinese agreed. As the Dalai Lama remarked in his autobiography, *Freedom in Exile*, it seemed that the Chinese were of the opinion that the mission members would find such happiness in their homeland that 'they would see no point in remaining in exile'. In fact, the results of the mission were so damning that the Dalai Lama decided not to publish them. Nevertheless, two more missions followed. They claimed up to 1.2 million deaths (one in six Tibetans, according to the disputed report), the destruction of 6254 monasteries and nunneries (also disputed), the absorption of two-thirds of Tibet into China, 100,000 Tibetans in labour camps and extensive deforestation.

In China, Hua Guofeng's short-lived political ascendancy had been eclipsed by Deng Xiaoping's rise to power. In 1980 Deng sent Hu Yaobang on a Chinese fact-finding mission that coincided with the visits of those sent by the Tibetan government-in-exile. Hu's conclusions, while not as damning as those of the Tibetans, painted a grim picture of life on the roof of the world. A six-point plan to improve the living conditions and freedoms of the Tibetans was drawn up, taxes were dropped for two years and limited private enterprise was allowed. The Jokhang was reopened for two days a month in 1978; the Potala opened in 1980. As in the rest of China, the government embarked on a program of extended personal and economic freedoms in concert with authoritarian one-party rule.

Reforms & Riots

The early 1980s saw the return of limited religious freedoms. Monasteries that had not been reduced to piles of rubble began to reopen and some religious artefacts were returned to Tibet from China.

Importantly, there was also a relaxation of the Chinese proscription on pilgrimage. Pictures of the Dalai Lama began to reappear on the streets of Lhasa. Talks aimed at bringing the Dalai Lama back into the ambit of Chinese influence continued, but with little result. Tibet, according to

Over the centuries Tibet has suffered from ill-defined borders and a lack of internal unity, with large parts of Amdo, Kham and Ngari and independent tribes like the Goloks only nominally ruled by Lhasa.

An illuminating glimpse of the Tibetan experience is provided by *Freedom in Exile: The Autobiography of the Dalai Lama*. With great humility the Dalai Lama outlines his personal philosophy, his hope to be reunited with his homeland and the story of his life. *Kundun* by Mary Craig is a biography of the Dalai Lama's family.

1982	1987–89	1989	2006
A three-person team sent to Běijīng from Dharamsala is told Tibet is part of China and that the Dalai Lama would be given a desk job in Běijīng on his return. By 1983 talks had broken down.	Pro-independence demonstrations take place in Lhasa; the response is violent, several tourists are injured and martial law is declared.	The Dalai Lama's efforts to achieve peace and freedom for his people are recognised when he is awarded the Nobel Peace Prize.	Western climbers on Mt Cho Oyu film Chinese border guards shooting unarmed nuns as they flee China over the Nangpa-la to Nepal.

Sorrow Mountain: The Journey of a Tibetan Warrior Nun by Ani Pachen and Adelaide Donnelley is the story of a nun who became a resistance leader and was imprisoned by the Chinese for 21 years before escaping to India.

the Chinese government, became the 'front line of the struggle against splittism', a line that continues to be the official government position to this day.

In 1986 a new influx of foreigners arrived in Tibet, with the Chinese beginning to loosen restrictions on tourism. The trickle of tour groups and individual travellers soon became a flood. For the first time since the Chinese takeover, visitors from the West were given the opportunity to see the results of Chinese rule in Tibet.

When in September 1987 a group of 30 monks from Sera Monastery began circumambulating the Jokhang and crying out 'Independence for Tibet' and 'Long live his Holiness the Dalai Lama', their ranks were swollen by bystanders and arrests followed. Four days later, another group of monks repeated their actions, this time brandishing Tibetan flags. The monks were beaten and arrested. With Western tourists looking on, a crowd of 2000 to 3000 angry Tibetans gathered. Police vehicles were overturned and Chinese police began firing on the crowd.

The Chinese response was swift. Communications with the outside world were broken but this failed to prevent further protests in the following months. The Mönlam festival of March 1988 saw shooting in the streets of Lhasa, and that December a Dutch traveller was shot in the shoulder; 18 Tibetans died and 150 were wounded in the disturbances.

The Dalai Lama & the Search for Settlement

By the mid-1970s the Dalai Lama had become a prominent international figure, working tirelessly from his government-in-exile in Dharamsala to make the world more aware of his people's plight. In 1987 he addressed the US Congress and outlined a five-point peace plan.

The journalist Harrison Salisbury referred to Tibet in the mid-1980s as a 'dark and sorrowing land'.

The plan called for Tibet to be established as a 'zone of peace'; for the policy of Han immigration to Tibet to be abandoned; for a return to basic human rights and democratic freedoms; for the protection of Tibet's natural heritage and an end to the dumping of nuclear waste on the high plateau; and for joint discussions between the Chinese and the Tibetans on the future of Tibet. The Chinese denounced the plan as an example of 'splittism'. They gave the same response when, a year later, the Dalai Lama elaborated on the speech before the European Parliament in Strasbourg, France, dropping demands for full independence in favour of a form of autonomy and offering the Chinese the right to govern Tibet's foreign and military affairs.

On 5 March 1989, three months before the student demonstrations in Běijīng's Tiān'ānmén Square, Lhasa erupted in the largest anti-Chinese demonstration since 1959. Běijīng reacted strongly, declaring martial law

2006	2007	2008	2008
The 4310m Nathu-la pass with Sikkim opens to local traders for the first time in 44 years, hinting at warmer ties between India and China.	The Chinese government passes a new law requiring all incarnate lamas to be approved by the government, part of an attempt to increase political control over Tibet's religious hierarchy.	In the run-up to the Olympic Games in Běijīng, the worst riots for 20 years hit Lhasa, southern Gānsù and western Sìchuān; 19 people are killed and thousands are subsequently arrested.	The British government recognises China's direct rule over Tibet for the first time, shifting the language from 'suzerainty' to 'sovereignty'.

in Tibet, which lasted for more than a year. Despairing elements in the exiled Tibetan community began to talk of the need to take up arms. It was an option that the Dalai Lama had consistently opposed. His efforts to achieve peace and freedom for his people were recognised on 4 October 1989, when he was awarded the Nobel Peace Prize.

In January 1989, after denouncing the Communist Party's policies in Tibet and while visiting Tashilhunpo, the traditional seat of all the Panchen Lamas, the 10th Panchen Lama died, triggering a succession crisis that remains unresolved. The Dalai Lama identified the 11th Panchen Lama in 1995, whereupon the Chinese authorities detained the boy and his family (who have not been seen since) and orchestrated the choice of their own preferred candidate. The Chinese began to toughen their policy towards the Dalai Lama and launched the anti-Dalai Lama campaign inside Tibet, compelling all government officials and monks to denounce the Dalai Lama.

The Chinese authorities believe that one of the reasons for continuing separatist sentiments and opposition is Tibet's lack of integration with China. The solution since the mid-1980s has been to encourage Han immigration to the high plateau, a policy already successfully carried out in Xīnjiāng, Inner Mongolia and Qīnghǎi. As Běijīng attempts to shift the economic gains of the east coast to its underdeveloped hinterland, hundreds of thousands of Han Chinese have taken advantage of attractive salaries and interest-free loans to 'modernise' the backward province of Tibet. By the end of the millennium Tibetans were facing the fastest and deepest-reaching changes in their history.

John Avedon's *In Exile from the Land of Snows* is largely an account of the Tibetan community in Dharamsala, and is an excellent and informative read.

The definitive (but weighty) account of Tibetan history since 1947 is *The Dragon in the Land of Snows* by Tsering Shakya.

HISTORY THE DALAI LAMA & THE SEARCH FOR SETTLEMENT

2010	**2010**	**2011**	**2012**
The Dalai Lama celebrates his 75th birthday.	A huge 6.9 scale earthquake devastates the Tibetan town of Jyekundo (Yùshù) in Amdo (southeast Qīnghǎi), killing over 1700 people and leaving tens of thousands homeless.	The Dalai Lama cedes political control as head of the Tibetan government-in-exile to former Harvard academic and lawyer Lobsang Sangay.	Two Tibetans set themselves on fire in the Barkhor Circuit, joining the over 130 Tibetans who have committed self-immolation since 2011 in protest against Chinese rule.

Tibetan Landscapes

It's hard to overstate the global significance of the Tibetan plateau. Not only is it the earth's highest ecosystem and one of its last remaining great wildernesses, but it also contains the headwaters of Asia's greatest rivers; rivers that deliver water to half the world's population! How the Chinese government harnesses these resources, particularly Tibet's water, without harming their long-term sustainability will shape the future of half the planet.

Tibet has several thousand lakes (*tso* in Tibetan), of which the largest are Namtso, Yamdrok-tso, Manasarovar (Mapham Yumtso), Siling-tso and Pangong-tso, the last crossing the Indian border into Ladakh.

The Roof of the World

The Tibetan plateau is one of the most isolated regions in the world, bound to the south by the 2500km-long Himalayan arc, to the west by the Karakoram and to the north by the Kunlun and Altyn Tagh ranges, two of the least explored ranges on earth. The northwest in particular is bound by the most remote wilderness left on earth, outside the polar regions. Four of the world's 10 highest mountains straddle Tibet's southern border with Nepal.

The plateau is also home to the world's highest number of glaciers outside the poles, making it the source of Asia's greatest rivers. Furthermore, it is thought that the high plateau affects global jet streams and even influences the Indian monsoon. With an average altitude of 4000m and large swaths of the country well above 5000m, the Tibetan plateau aptly deserves the title the 'roof of the world'.

Much of Tibet is a harsh and uncompromising landscape, best described as a high-altitude desert. Little of the Indian monsoon makes it over the Himalayan watershed, which is one reason why there is surprisingly little snow in the 'Land of Snows'! Shifting sand dunes are a common sight along the Samye Valley and the road to Mt Kailash.

The plateau's regions are surprisingly diverse and can be loosely divided into four major regions.

Ütsang

Made up of the combined regions of Ü and Tsang, which constitute central Tibet, Ütsang is the political, historical and agricultural heartland of Tibet. Its relatively fertile valleys enjoy a mild climate and are irrigated by wide rivers such as the Yarlung Tsangpo and the Kyi-chu.

Changtang

Towards the north of Ütsang are the harsh, high-altitude plains of the Changtang (northern plateau), the highest and largest plateau in the world, occupying an area of more than one million sq km (think France, the UK and Germany). The dead lakes of the Changtang are the brackish remnants of the Tethys Sea that found no run-off when the plateau started its skyward ascent.

Ngari

Ngari (western Tibet) is similarly barren, although here river valleys provide grassy tracts that support nomads and their grazing animals. Indeed, the Kailash range in the far west of Tibet is the source of the subcontinent's four greatest rivers: the Ganges, Indus, Sutlej and Brahmaputra. The Ganges, Indus and Sutlej Rivers all cascade out of Tibet in its far west. The Brahmaputra (known in Tibet as Yarlung Tsangpo) meanders along the northern spine of the Himalaya for 2000km, searching for a way south, before draining into India not far from the Myanmar border.

Kham

Eastern Tibet marks a tempestuous drop in elevation down to the Sìchuān plain. The concertina landscape produces some of the most spectacular roller-coaster roads in Asia, as Himalayan extensions such as the Héngduàn Mountains are sliced by the deep gorges of the Yangzi (Dri-chu in Tibetan; Jīnshā Jiāng in Chinese), Salween (Gyalmo Ngulchu in Tibetan; Nù Jiāng in Chinese) and Mekong (Dza-chu in Tibetan; Láncáng Jiāng in Chinese) headwaters.

The Yarlung Tsangpo crashes through an incredible 5km-deep gorge here (often described as the world's deepest) as it swings violently around 7756m Namche Barwa. Many parts of this alpine region are lushly forested and support abundant wildlife, largely thanks to the lower altitudes and effects of the Indian monsoon.

The Chinese province commonly referred to as Tibet is officially called the Tibetan Autonomous Region (TAR) and has an area of 1.23 million sq km; bigger than the combined area of France, Spain and Portugal.

TIBETAN LANDSCAPES THE ROOF OF THE WORLD

FROM SEABED TO SNOW CAPS: THE RISE OF TIBET

Some 50 million years ago, the Indian and Eurasian plates collided. What happened next in the long development of the Tibetan plateau is the subject of much debate.

'There are several different ideas,' says geologist Kristen Cook, who has been studying the plateau for the past 11 years. 'One possibility is that large chunks of Eurasia were just pushed out of the way towards what is now southeast Asia. Another is that the Eurasian crust just piled up in front of India, crumpling up in folds and faults until it became extremely thick. It's also possible that, rather than a simple collision, the lower part of the Indian crust was shoved underneath the Eurasian crust and kept moving northwards; this would mean that there could be bits of India sitting below central Tibet today. Most likely, a combination of these things happened, but we need more evidence to know for sure. There is even renewed debate in the past year or two about the timing of the India-Asia collision, which was one of the few things we thought was pretty settled.'

Of course 'settled' is not a word usually associated with the plateau. India moves toward the rest of Asia at a rate of about 4cm each year; the plateau is actually spreading out rather than getting higher, and devastating earthquakes such as the one that rocked Yùshù (Jyekundo) in Amdo in 2010 killing 2700 people testify to the powerful tectonic forces still at play.

For those interested in the geological history of Tibet, the boundary between India and Eurasia can still be seen in the geology around the Yarlung Tsangpo River. 'You'll find rocks here,' says Cook, 'that came from deep below the floor of the ocean that used to separate the two plates. Visiting Everest Base Camp on a clear day you may be able to see horizontal layering on the very top of Mount Everest. That's because it's made of limestone – former ocean floor – that was thrust on top of the rocks above and then lifted all the way up to the top of the world.'

Indeed, visitors to Shegar may well find locals selling ancient fossils of marine animals – at 4000m above sea level!

How much Tibetans understand from experience or traditional teachings about their geology is hard to say, but in Cook's experience, people learn fast and have a lot of natural curiosity. 'My favourite encounter was with a Tibetan boy who played hooky from his shepherd duties to come with us as we walked up a river valley in search of some particular rocks. He was fascinated by our geologic map, soon had it completely figured out, and then took over and started leading the way, asking questions about the geology of his valley the whole time. We've also made pretty good geologists out of some of our regular drivers – they sometimes know what we want to stop and look at before we do.'

The Struggle for Life

The vast differences in altitude in Tibet give rise to a spread of ecosystems from alpine to subtropical, but generally speaking life on the Tibetan Plateau is a harsh one and travellers are unlikely to encounter too much in the way of wildlife. Nevertheless, for those that have the time to get off the beaten track – particularly in western Tibet – or to go trekking in more remote areas, there are some unusual and understandably hardened species out there.

Tibet Wild by George Schaller describes the eminent field biologist's three decades of travel and research on the remote Changtang plateau.

What Will I See?

On the road out to Mt Kailash, it is not unusual to see herds of fleet-footed Tibetan gazelles *(gowa* in Tibetan)*, antelope *(tso)* and wild asses *(kyang)*, particularly along the northern route. During the breeding season antelope converge in groups numbering several hundred.

Trekkers might conceivably see the Himalayan black bear or, if they're exceeding lucky, the giant Tibetan blue bear searching for food in the alpine meadows. Herds of blue sheep, also known as bharal *(nawa na)*, are frequently spied on rocky slopes and outcrops (although the dwarf bharal is much rarer), but the argali, the largest species of wild sheep in the world, now only survives in the most remote mountain fastnesses of western Tibet.

Wolves of various colours can be seen all over the Tibetan plateau. Much rarer than the all-black wolf is the white wolf, one of the sacred animals of Tibet. Smaller carnivores include the lynx, marten and fox.

Marmots *(chiwa* or *piya)* are very common and can often be seen perched up on their hind legs sniffing the air curiously outside their burrows – they make a strange birdlike sound when distressed. The pika *(chipi)*, or Himalayan mouse-hare, a relative of the rabbit, is also common. Pikas have been observed at 5250m on Mt Everest, thus earning the distinction of having the highest habitat of any mammal.

Geographically speaking, the Tibetan plateau makes up almost 25% of China's total landmass, spread over five provinces.

A surprising number of migratory birds make their way up to the lakes of the Tibetan plateau through spring and summer. Tibet has over 30 endemic birds, and 480 species have been recorded on the plateau. Birds include the black-necked crane (whose numbers in Tibet have doubled over the last decade), bar-headed goose and lammergeier, as well as grebes, pheasants, snowcocks and partridges. Watching a pair of black-necked cranes, loyal mates for life, is one of the joys of traipsing near

---

FLORA OR FAUNA?

In early summer (May and June) you will see nomads and entrepreneurs camped in the high passes of eastern Tibet, digging for a strange root known as *yartsa gunbu (Cordiceps sinensis)* that locals say is half vegetable, half caterpillar. It is actually a fusion of a caterpillar and the parasitic fungus that mummifies it and then grows Alien-like out of the dead caterpillar's head. The Chinese name for the root is *dōngchóng xiàcǎo* (冬虫夏草; 'winter-worm, summer-grass'), a direct translation of the Tibetan name. Used by long-distance Chinese runners, it's also nicknamed 'Himalayan Viagra', and is highly prized in Tibetan and Chinese medicine as an aphrodisiac and tonic similar to ginseng.

Fetching around ¥20,000 (US$3200) per kilo, it's one of the most expensive commodities in Tibet and is fast being harvested to extinction. The business is most lucrative in Tengchen county, where amazingly it accounts for more than 60% of the local GDP. Entire tent villages spring up on the grasslands during harvest time, equipped with restaurants and shops, causing great environmental damage, and it's not unusual for turf wars to erupt between local communities and outside speculators. The economic boom in Tibet and China has caused *yartsa gunbu* fever to spread over the Himalayas, with the Himalayan gold rush revolutionising local economies as far away as Bhutan, Dolpo and Ladakh.

THE IMPORTANCE OF YAKS

Only 50 years ago an estimated one million wild yaks roamed the Tibetan plateau. Now it is a rare treat to catch a glimpse of one of these huge creatures, which weigh up to a tonne and can reach 1.8m at the shoulder. Wild yaks have diminished in number to 15,000 as a result of the increased demand for yak meat and a rise in illegal hunting.

Few, if any, of the yaks that travellers see are *drong* (wild yaks). In fact, most are not even yaks at all but rather dzo, a cross between a yak and a cow. A domestic yak rarely exceeds 1.5m in height. Unlike its wild relative, which is almost always black, the dzo varies in shade from black to grey and, primarily around Kokonor in Qīnghǎi, white.

With three times more red blood cells than the average cow, the yak thrives in the oxygen-depleted high altitudes. Its curious lung formation, surrounded by 14 or 15 pairs of ribs rather than the 13 typical of cattle, allows a large capacity for inhaling and expelling air (one reason why its Latin name *Bos grunniens* means 'grunting ox'). In fact, a descent below 3000m may impair the reproductive cycle and expose the yak to parasites and disease.

Tibetans rely on yak milk for cheese, as well as for butter for the ubiquitous butter tea and offerings to butter lamps in monasteries. The outer hair of the yak is woven into tent fabric and rope, and the soft inner wool is spun into *chara* (a type of felt) and used to make bags, blankets and tents. Tails are used in both Buddhist and Hindu religious practices. Yak hide is used for the soles of boots and the yak's heart is used in Tibetan medicine. In the nomadic tradition, no part of the animal is wasted and even yak dung is required as a fundamental fuel, left to dry in little cakes on the walls of most Tibetan houses. In fact, so important are yaks to the Tibetans that the animals are individually named, like children.

the wetlands of northern and western Tibet. Flocks of huge vultures can often be seen circling monasteries looking for a sky burial.

On the Brink

About 80 species of animal that are threatened with extinction have been listed as protected by the Chinese government. These include the almost-mythical snow leopard *(gang-zig)* as well as the wild yak *(drong)*.

The Tibetan red deer was recently 'discovered' only 75km from Lhasa after a 50-year hiatus, as was a hitherto unknown breed of ancient wild horse in the Riwoche region of eastern Tibet.

Wild yaks are mostly encountered in the far northern region of Changtang. The biggest bull yaks are reputed to be as large as a 4WD. Even rarer is the divine giant white yak, thought by Tibetans to inhabit the higher reaches of sacred mountains.

The *chiru,* a rare breed of antelope, was recently placed on the Red List (www.redlist.org), a list of threatened species maintained by the World Conservation Union. Numbers in Tibet dropped from over a million *chiru* 50 years ago to around 100,000 today. Poachers kill the animal for its *shatoosh* wool (wool from the animal's undercoat).

The illegal trade in antelope cashmere, musk, bear paws and gall bladders, deer antlers, and other body parts and bones remains a problem. You can often see Tibetan traders huddled on street corners in major Chinese cities selling these and other medicinal cures.

Tibet in Bloom

Juniper trees and willows are common in the valleys of central Tibet and it is possible to come across wildflowers such as the pansy and the oleander, as well as unique indigenous flowers such as the tsi-tog (a light-pink, high-altitude bloom).

Yak-tail hair was the main material used to produce Father Christmas (Santa Claus) beards in 1950s America!

Two of the best places to go birdwatching are Yamdrok-tso and Nam-tso; a section of the latter has been designated a bird preserve, at least on paper. April and November are the best times.

Eastern Tibet, which sees higher rainfall, has an amazing range of flora, from oak, elm and birch forests to bamboo, subtropical plants and flowers, including rhododendrons, azaleas and magnolias. It was from here that intrepid 19th-century plant hunters FM Bailey, Frank Kingdon-Ward and Frank Ludlow took the seeds and cuttings of species that would eventually become staples in English gardening.

In the arid climate of much of Tibet, water takes on a special significance. The *lu* (water spirits) guard the wellbeing of the community and are thought to be very dangerous if angered.

A Fragile Ecosystem

Tibet has an abundance of natural resources: many types of minerals, strong sunlight, fierce winds and raging rivers that supply water to an estimated 50% of the world's population.

The Tibetan Buddhist view of the environment has long stressed the intricate and interconnected relationship between the natural world and human beings. Buddhist practice in general stands for moderation and is against overconsumption, and tries to avoid wherever possible hunting, fishing and the taking of animal life. Tibetan nomads, in particular, have traditionally lived in a fine balance with their harsh environment.

Modern communist experiments, such as collectivisation and the changing of century-old farming patterns (for example, from barley to wheat and rice), upset the fragile balance in Tibet and resulted in a series of great disasters and famines in the 1960s (as, indeed, they did in the rest of China). By the mid-1970s, the failure of collectivisation was widely recognised and Tibetans have since been allowed to return to traditional methods of working the land.

As early as 1642, the fifth Dalai Lama issued an edict protecting animals and the environment.

The Tibetan plateau has rich deposits of gold, zinc, chromium, silver, boron, uranium and other metals. The plateau is home to most of China's huge copper reserves. A single mine in northern Tibet is said to hold over half the world's total deposits of lithium, while the Changtang holds five billion tonnes of oil and gas. Reports indicate mining now accounts for one-third of Tibet's industrial output. Mining has long been traditionally inimical to Tibetans, who believe it disturbs the sacred essence of the soil. The Chinese name for Tibet, Xīzàng – the Western Treasure House – now has a ring of prophetic irony.

Rapid modernisation threatens to bring industrial pollution, a hitherto almost unknown problem, onto the high plateau. Mass domestic tourism is also beginning to take its toll, with litter and unsustainable waste management a major problem in areas like Nam-tso and the Everest region.

TIBET'S ENDANGERED SPECIES

SPECIES	ESTIMATED WORLD POPULATION	ESTIMATED TIBETAN POPULATION	CURRENT STATUS
snow leopard (*gang-zig*)	6500	2000	endangered
Tibetan antelope (*chiru*)	75,000–150,000	75,000–150,000	endangered
white-lipped deer (*shawa chukar*)	7000	5000	endangered
dwarf blue sheep, or dwarf bharal (*nawa na*)	7000	7000	endangered
Tibetan blue bear (*dom gyamuk*)	a few hundred	a few hundred	endangered
wild yak (*drong*)	15,000	8500	vulnerable
black-necked crane	11,000	7000	vulnerable
Tibetan gazelle (*gowa*)	100,000	100,000	near threatened
argali, or wild sheep	150,000	7000	near threatened
Tibetan wild ass (*kyang*)	60,000-70,000	37,000–48,000	least concern

PROTECTING THE PLATEAU

Nature reserves officially protect over 20% of the Tibetan Autonomous Region (TAR), although many exist on paper only. The reserve with the highest profile is the Qomolangma National Park, a 34,000-sq-km protected area straddling the 'third pole' of the Everest region. The park promotes the involvement of the local population, which is essential as around 67,000 people live within the park.

Tibet's newest reserve is the Changtang Nature Reserve, set up in 1993 with the assistance of famous animal behaviourist George Schaller. At 247,120 sq km (larger than Arizona), this is the largest nature reserve in the world after Greenland National Park. Endangered species in the park include bharal, argali sheep, wolves, lynxes, gazelles, snow leopards, wild yaks, antelopes, brown bears and wild asses.

Other protected areas include the Nam-tso National Park, the Great Canyon of the Yarlung Tsangpo Nature Reserve (formerly the Metok reserve) to the south of Namche Barwa, the Dzayul (Zayu) Reserve along the far southeast border with Assam, and the Kyirong and Nyalam Reserves near the Nepali border. Unfortunately, these reserves enjoy little protection or policing.

Sustainable Energy

Tibet has abundant supplies of geothermal energy thanks to its turbulent geological history. The Yangpachen Geothermal Plant already supplies Lhasa with much of its electricity. Portable solar panelling has also enjoyed some success; the plateau has some of the longest and strongest sunlight outside the Saharan region. And experimental wind-power stations have been set up in northern Tibet.

But, much to the dismay of worried environmental groups worldwide, it's Tibet's enormous potential for hydroelectricity that has been the focus of the Chinese government in recent years. The undisputed heavyweight champion of dam building, China has 24 dams up and running on the Tibetan plateau and a further 76 in the pipeline. One particularly sensitive hydroelectric project has been draining water from sacred Yamdrok-tso for years now.

Plans to construct a so-called 'super-dam' (which could generate twice as much electricity as the Three Gorges Dam) on the Yarlung Tsangpo (Brahmaputra River) in the remote southeast of Tibet still seem to be on the table, and have the Indians and Bangladeshis downstream deeply concerned. Five dams are currently under construction on the Yarlung Tsangpo further upstream near Gyatsa.

The Future

In the long term, climate change is expected to affect Tibet as much as the earth's low-lying regions. The rate of temperature rise in Tibet is around double the average global level and over the last 30 years Tibet's glaciers have shrunk by 15% – around 8000 sq km. Chinese scientists believe that 40% of the plateau's glaciers could disappear by 2050 if current trends hold. Considering that the Tibetan plateau is the source of Asia's greatest rivers, this is of profound importance to China and the Indian subcontinent.

The results of glacial melting are likely to include initial flooding and erosion, followed by a long-term drought that may turn Tibet into a desert wasteland and the rest of Asia into a region desperately searching for new supplies of water.

The mythical *sengye*, or snow lion, is one of Tibet's four sacred animals and acts as a mount for many Tibetan protector deities. The other three animals are the garuda (*khyung*), dragon (*druk*) and tiger (*dak*).

For more on environmental issues in Tibet, visit Tibet Environmental Watch at www.tew.org.

The People of Tibet

Tibetans have a unique identity that mixes influences from their Himalayan neigh-bours, extreme mountain environment and war-like past. In terms of language, script, food, temperament and above all religion, they are poles apart from their Han Chinese neighbours. Where the Chinese drink their tea green, Tibetans take theirs with yak butter; when the rest of China eats rice and drinks rice wine, Tibetans eat tsampa (roasted-barley flour) washed down with barley beer.

Traditional Lifestyle

When going over a pass, Tibetans say, 'Ki ki so so, lha gyalo!' ('May the gods be victorious!'), which may have its origins in an ancient battle cry.

Tibetans are such a deeply religious people that a basic knowledge of Buddhism is essential in understanding their world view. Buddhism per-meates most facets of Tibetan daily life and shapes aspirations in ways that are often quite alien to the Western frame of mind. The ideas of accumulating merit, of sending sons to be monks, of undertaking pil-grimages, and of devotion to the sanctity and power of natural places are all elements of the unique fusion between Buddhism and the older shamanistic Bön faith.

Traditionally there have been at least three distinct segments of Tibet-an society: the *drokpa* (nomads); *rongpa* (farmers); and *sangha* (com-munities of monks and nuns). All lead very different lives but share a deep faith in Buddhism.

These communities have also shared a remarkable resistance to change. Until the early 20th century Tibet was a land in which virtu-ally the only use for the wheel was as a device for activating mantras. Tibet has changed more in the past 50 years than in the previous 500, although many traditional social structures have endured Chinese at-tempts at iconoclasm.

Nomads' marriage customs differ from those of farming communities. When a child reaches a marriageable age, enquiries are made, and when a suitable match is found the two people meet and exchange gifts. If they like each other, these informal meetings may go on for some time. The date for a marriage is decided by an astrologer, and when the date arrives the family of the son rides to the camp of the prospective daughter-in-law to collect her. On arrival there is a custom of feigned mutual abuse that appears to verge on giving way to violence at any moment. This may continue for several days before the son's family finally carry off the daughter to their camp and she enters a new life.

GOOD GENES

In case you're wondering why your Tibetan guide can run up the side of a 4500m hill with ease, while you collapse gasping in the thin air after less than one minute, recent DNA research has shown that the Tibetan people are genetically adapted to living at high altitudes. In fact, the 3000 years it took Tibetans to change their genes is considered the fastest genetic change ever observed in humans. You never stood a chance.

CULTURAL DOS & DONT'S

Tibetans are some of the most tolerant and easy-going people you will meet, but you can avoid potential misunderstandings or offence by bearing in mind the following guidelines:

➡ In general negotiations it is a good idea to ensure that the person you are dealing with does not lose face, does not appear to be wrong and is not forced to back down in front of others. A negotiated settlement is always preferable and outright confrontation is a last resort.

➡ Tibetans show respect to an honoured guest or a lama by placing a *kathak* (prayer scarf) around their neck. When reciprocating, hold the scarf out in both hands with palms turned upwards.

➡ Don't wear short skirts or shorts, especially at religious sites.

➡ Don't point at people or statues with your finger, use your full upturned hand.

➡ Don't pat children on the head, as the head is considered sacred.

➡ Always circle a Buddhist monastery building or chörten clockwise.

As in most societies, there is some generational divide among Tibetans. The younger generation (in Lhasa and the main towns at least) is as enamoured with pop music, karaoke, mobile phones and the internet as most young people are around the world and most know little about 'old' Tibet, having often grown up in a Chinese-language environment. That said, young Tibetans still have a remarkably strong sense of Tibetan identity and you'll still see many young Tibetans visiting monasteries, wearing traditional dress and making pilgrimages to holy sites.

Farming & Trading

Farming communities in Tibet usually comprise a cluster of homes surrounded by agricultural lands that were once owned by the nearest large monastery and protected by a *dzong* (fort). The farming itself is carried out with the assistance of a dzo, a breed of cattle where bulls have been crossbred with yaks. Some wealthier farmers own a small 'walking tractor' (a very simple tractor engine that can pull a plough or a trailer). Harvested grain is carried by donkeys to a threshing ground where it is trampled by cattle or threshed with poles. The grain is then cast into the air from a basket and the task of winnowing carried out by the breeze. Animal husbandry is still extremely important in Tibet, and there are around 21 million head of livestock in the country.

Until recently such communities were effectively self-sufficient in their needs and, although theirs was a hard life, it could not be described as abject poverty. Plots of land were usually graded in terms of quality and then distributed so that the land of any one family included both better- and poorer-quality land. This is changing rapidly as many regions become more economically developed.

Imports such as tea, porcelain, copper and iron from China were traditionally exchanged for exports of wool and skins. Trading was usually carried out by nomads or in combination with pilgrimage. Most villages now have at least one entrepreneur who has set up a shop and begun to ship in Chinese goods from the nearest urban centre.

One significant change to rural life has been the government-sponsored construction of over 230,000 new houses across Tibet, providing new housing for some 1.3 million Tibetan farmers and herders. Families are given around ¥10,000 to ¥15,000 as a base subsidy to construct a home. A typical house might cost around ¥33,000 to ¥44,000 so farmers usually take out a loan (interest-free for three years) to cover the

Older country folk may stick out their tongue when they meet you, a very traditional form of respect that greeted the very first travellers to Tibet centuries ago. Some sources say that this is done to prove that the person is not a devil, since devils have green tongues, even when they take human form.

PILGRIM MAGNETS

In Tibet there are countless sacred destinations, ranging from lakes and mountains to monasteries and caves that once served as meditation retreats for important yogis. Specific pilgrimages are often prescribed for specific ills; certain mountains, for example, expiate certain sins. A circumambulation of Mt Kailash offers the possibility of liberation within three lifetimes, while a circuit of Lake Manasarovar can result in spontaneous buddhahood. Pilgrimage is also more powerful in certain auspicious months and years.

Pilgrims often organise themselves into large groups, hire a truck and travel around the country visiting all the major sacred places in one go. Pilgrim guidebooks have existed for centuries to help travellers interpret the 24 'power places' of Tibet. Such guides even specify locations where you can urinate or fart without offending local spirits (and probably your fellow pilgrims).

Making a pilgrimage is not just a matter of walking to a sacred place and then going home. There are a number of activities that help focus the concentration of the pilgrim. The act of kora (circumambulating the object of devotion) is chief among these. Circuits of three, 13 or 108 koras are especially auspicious, with sunrise and sunset the most auspicious hours. The particularly devout prostrate their way along entire pilgrimages, stepping forward the length of their body after each prostration and starting all over again. The hardcore even do their koras sideways, advancing one side-step at a time!

Most pilgrims make offerings during the course of a pilgrimage. *Kathaks* (white ceremonial scarves) are offered to lamas or holy statues as a token of respect (and then often returned by the lama as a blessing). Offerings of yak butter or oil, fruit, tsampa, seeds and money are all left at altars, and bottles of *chang* (barley beer) and rice wine are donated to protector chapels.

Outside chapels, at holy mountain peaks, passes and bridges, you will see pilgrims throwing offerings of tsampa or printed prayers into the air. Pilgrims also collect sacred rocks, herbs, earth and water from a holy site to take back home to those who couldn't make the pilgrimage, and leave behind personal items as a break from the past, often leaving them hanging in a tree. Other activities in this spiritual assault course include adding stones to cairns, rubbing special healing rocks, and squeezing through narrow gaps in rocks as a method of sin detection.

Koras usually include stops that are of particular spiritual significance, such as rock-carved syllables or painted buddha images. Many of these carvings are said to be 'self-arising', meaning that they haven't been carved by a human hand. The Mt Kailash kora is a treasure trove of these, encompassing sky-burial sites, stones that have 'flown' from India, monasteries, bodhisattva footprints and even a *lingham* (phallic image).

Other pilgrimages are carried out to visit a renowned holy man or teacher. Blessings or *tsering rilbu* (long-life pills) from holy men, *trulkus* (reincarnated lamas) or *rinpoches* (highly esteemed lamas) are particularly valued, as are the possessions of famous holy men. According to Keith Dowman in his book *The Sacred Life of Tibet*, the underpants of one revered lama were cut up and then distributed amongst his eager followers!

Pilgrimage Sites

MOUNTAINS	LAKES	CAVES
Mt Kailash, western Tibet	Manasarovar, western Tibet	Drak Yerpa, outside Lhasa
Bönri, eastern Tibet	Nam-tso, northern Ü	Chim-puk, near Samye
Tsari, southern Tibet	Yamdrok-tso, Tsang	Sheldrak, Yarlung Valley
Mt Labchi, east of Nyalam	Lhamo La-tso, eastern Ü	Drakyul, Yarlung Tsangpo Valley

remaining costs. Critics of the scheme claim that many of the new home-owners then have to rent out their farmland to Chinese immigrants in order to pay off the loans.

Individual households normally have a shrine in the home and some religious texts, held in a place of honour, which are reserved for occasions when a monk or holy man visits the village. Ceremonies for blessing yaks and other livestock to ensure a productive year are still held. One of the highlights of the year for rural Tibetans is visiting nearby monasteries at festival times or making a pilgrimage to a holy site.

As traditional life reasserts itself after 50 years of communist dogma and the disastrous Cultural Revolution, many of these traditions are slowly making a comeback.

Pilgrimage

Pilgrimage is practised throughout the world, although as a devotional exercise it has been raised to a level of particular importance in Tibet. This may be because of the nomadic element in Tibetan society; it may also be that in a mountainous country with no roads and no wheeled vehicles, walking long distances became a fact of life, and by visiting sacred places en route pilgrims could combine walking with accumulating merit. To most Tibetans their natural landscape is imbued with a series of sacred visions and holy 'power places': mountains can be perceived as mandala images, rocks assume spiritual dimensions and the earth is imbued with healing powers.

The motivations for pilgrimage are many, but for the ordinary Tibetan it amounts to a means of accumulating *sonam* (merit) or *tashi* (good fortune). The lay practitioner might go on pilgrimage in the hope of winning a better rebirth, to cure an illness, end a spate of bad luck or as thanks for an answered prayer.

Death

Although the early kings of Tibet were buried in tomb mounds with complex funerary rites (the tombs are still visible in Chongye), ordinary Tibetans have not traditionally been buried. The dead bodies of the very poor were usually dumped in a river and the bodies of the very holy were cremated and their ashes enshrined in a chörten (or their bodies dried in salt). But in a land where soil is at a premium and wood for cremation is scarcer still, most bodies were, and still are, disposed of by sky burial.

After death, the body is kept for 24 hours in a sitting position while a lama recites prayers from *The Tibetan Book of the Dead* to help the soul on its journey through the 49 levels of Bardo, the state between death and rebirth. Three days after death, the body is blessed and early-morning prayers and offerings are made to the monastery. The body is folded up (the spine is broken and the body itself is folded into a surprisingly small package) and carried on the back of a close friend to the *dürtro* (burial site). Here, special body-breakers known as *rogyapas* cut off the deceased's hair, chop up the body and pound the bones together with tsampa for vultures to eat.

There is little overt sadness at a sky burial: the soul is considered to have already departed and the burial itself is considered to be mere disposal, or rather a final act of compassion to the birds. Sky burial is, however, very much a time to reflect on the impermanence of life. Death is seen as a powerful agent of transformation and spiritual progress.

Tibetans often gesture with their lips to indicate a particular direction, so if a member of the opposite sex pouts at you, they are just showing you where to go. Also, if a road worker looks like he's blowing you kisses, he probably just wants a cigarette. Then again, maybe he's just blowing you kisses...

Torma (or *towa*) are small offerings made of yak butter and tsampa adorned with coloured medallions of butter. They probably developed as a Buddhist substitute for animal sacrifice. Most are made during the Shötun festival and remain on display throughout the year.

THE PEOPLE OF TIBET TRADITIONAL LIFESTYLE

TOURISTS & SKY BURIALS

Sky burials are funeral services and, naturally, Tibetans are often very unhappy about camera-toting foreigners heading up to sky-burial sites. The Chinese authorities do not like it either and may fine foreigners who attend a burial. You should never pay to see a sky burial and you should *never* take photos. Even if Tibetans offer to take you up to a sky-burial site, it is unlikely that other Tibetans present will be very happy about it. As tempting as it may be, if nobody has invited you, don't go.

RESPONSIBLE TOURISM

Tourism has already affected many areas in Tibet. Most children will automatically stick their hand out for a sweet, a pen or anything. In some regions, locals have become frustrated at seeing a stream of rich tourist groups but few tangible economic results. Please try to bear the following in mind as you travel through Tibet:

➡ Try to patronise as many small local Tibetan businesses (including your tour agent), restaurants and guesthouses as possible. Revenues created by organised group tourism go largely into the pockets of the Chinese authorities.

➡ Doling out medicines can encourage people not to seek proper medical advice, while handing out sweets or pens to children encourages begging. If you wish to contribute something constructive, it's better to give pens directly to schools and medicines to rural clinics, or make a donation to an established charity.

➡ Monastery admission fees go largely to local authorities, so if you want to donate to the monastery, leave your offering on the altar.

➡ Don't buy skins or hats made from endangered animals such as snow leopards.

➡ Don't pay to take a photograph of someone, and don't photograph someone if they don't want you to. If you agree to send a photograph of someone, ensure you follow through on this.

➡ If you have any pro-Tibetan sympathies, be very careful with whom you discuss them. Don't put Tibetans in a politically difficult or even potentially dangerous situation. This includes handing out photos of the Dalai Lama (these are illegal in Tibet) and politically sensitive materials.

➡ Try to buy locally made souvenirs and handicrafts, especially authentic and traditionally made products whose profits go directly to artisans, such as at Dropenling (p71).

➡ If you have a guide, try to ensure that he or she is a Tibetan, as Chinese guides invariably know little about Tibetan Buddhism or monastery history.

Tibetans are encouraged to witness the disposal of the body and to confront death openly and without fear. This is one reason that Tantric ritual objects such as trumpets and bowls are often made from human bone.

Dress

Traditional dress is still the norm among Tibetans in the countryside. The Tibetan national dress is a *chuba* (long-sleeved sheepskin cloak), tied around the waist with a sash and worn off the shoulder with great bravado by nomads and Khampas (people from Kham). An inner pouch is often used to store money belts, amulets, lunch and even small livestock. Most women wear a long dress, topped with a colourful striped apron known as a *pangden*. Traditional Tibetan boots have turned-up toes, so as to kill fewer bugs when walking (or so it is said).

From Ütsang (central Tibet) comes the best religion, from Amdo the best horses, from Kham the best men.
Traditional Tibetan saying

Women generally set great store in jewellery and invest their personal wealth and dowry in it. Coral is particularly valued (as Tibet is so far from the sea), as are Baltic amber, Indian ivory, Afghan turquoise and silver of all kinds. The Tibetan *zee*, a unique elongated agate stone with black and white markings, is highly prized for its protective qualities and can fetch tens of thousands of US dollars. Earrings are common in both men and women and they are normally tied on with a piece of cord. You'll see visiting Tibetans shopping for all these goodies around the Barkhor in Lhasa.

Tibetan women, especially those from Amdo (northeastern Tibet and Qīnghǎi), wear their hair in 108 braids, an auspicious number in Buddhism. Khampa men plait their hair with red or black tassels and wind the lot around their head. Cowboy hats are popular in summer and fur hats are common in winter. Most pilgrims carry a *thogcha* (good luck charm) or *gau* (amulet), with perhaps a picture of the owner's personal deity or the Dalai Lama inside.

The Politics of People

Modern political boundaries and history have led to the fracture of the Tibetan nation. Large areas of historical and ethnic Tibet are now incorporated into the Chinese provinces of Qīnghǎi and Gānsù (traditionally known as Amdo), and Sìchuān and Yúnnán (traditionally known as Kham). More Tibetans now live outside the Tibetan Autonomous Region (TAR) than inside it.

Tibetan babies are considered to be one year old at the time of birth, since reincarnation took place nine months previously upon conception.

Population Control

Population control is a cornerstone of Chinese government policy, but the regulations are generally less strictly enforced in Tibet. 'Minority nationalities' such as the Tibetans are allowed two children before they lose certain stipends and housing allowances. Ironically, the most effective form of birth control in modern Tibet still seems to be to join a monastery.

Ethnic Groups

There are considerable variations between regional groups of Tibetans. The most recognisable are the Khampas of eastern Tibet, who are generally larger and a bit more rough-and-ready than other Tibetans and who wear red or black tassels in their long hair. Women from Amdo are especially conspicuous because of their elaborate braided hairstyles and jewellery.

Ethnic Tibetan Regions of China (Greater Tibet)

TAP Tibetan Autonomous Prefecture

The people of Kongpo in eastern Tibet have a distinctive traditional dress that features a round hat with an upturned rim of golden brocade for men (known as a *gyasha*) and a pretty pillbox hat with winged edges for women. Men and women wear brown woollen tunics, belted around the waist. The former kingdom of Kongpo has for centuries been vilified by central Tibetan rulers as a land of incest and poison, whose inhabitants would routinely drug unsuspecting strangers to steal their souls.

There are pockets of other minority groups, such as the Lhopa (Lhoba) and Monpa in the southeast of Tibet, but these make up less than 1% of the total population and only very remote pockets remain. A more visible ethnic group are the Hui Muslims. Tibet's original Muslim inhabitants were largely traders or butchers (a profession that most Buddhists abhor), although the majority of recent migrants are traders and restaurant owners from southern Gānsù province. Tibetans are also closely related to the Qiang people of northern Sìchuān, the Sherpas of Nepal and the Ladakhis of India.

> Tibetans are often named after the day of week they were born on; thus you'll meet Nyima (Sunday), Dawa (Monday), Mingmar (Tuesday), Lhakpa (Wednesday), Phurba (Thursday), Pasang (Friday) and Pemba (Saturday). Popular names such as Sonam (merit) and Tashi (good fortune) carry religious connotations.

Han Migration

Official statistics claim 93% of the TAR's population is Tibetan, a figure that is hotly contested by almost everyone except the government. Chinese figures for the population of Lhasa, for example, suggest it is just over 87% Tibetan and just under 12% Han Chinese, a ratio that stretches the credulity of anyone who has visited the city in recent years. It is more likely that well over 50% of Lhasa's population is Han Chinese.

The current flood of Chinese immigrants into Tibet has been termed China's 'second invasion'. The Chinese government is very coy about releasing figures that would make it clear just how many Chinese there are in Tibet, but for visitors who have made repeated trips to Tibet the increased numbers of Han Chinese are undeniable.

Perhaps unsurprisingly, there's an endemic mistrust between the Tibetans and Chinese and ethnic tensions bubble just under the surface. Many Tibetans see the Han Chinese as land-hungry outsiders, while the Chinese often complain that the Tibetans are ungrateful and slow to adjust to economic opportunities. Actual violence between the two communities is rare, but it's quickly apparent to visitors that most towns have quite separate Chinese and Tibetan (and in some cases also Hui Muslim) quarters.

TIBET IN EXILE

About 120,000 Tibetans live in exile, mostly in India and Nepal but also in the United States, Canada and Switzerland. Hundreds of refugees a year continue to brave high passes and border guards to get to Kathmandu, paying as much as ¥2000 for a guide to help them across. The trek takes several days, with no supplies other than all the dried yak meat and tsampa (roasted-barley flour) they can carry, and no equipment except canvas shoes to help them get over the 6000m passes. Most make the crossing these days as educational refugees, travelling to Dharamsala to get a traditional education, learn Tibetan and English language and to study Tibetan arts and history.

Dharamsala in India's Himachal Pradesh has become a de facto Tibetan town, although the Dalai Lama, after personally meeting each refugee, actively encourages many of them to return to Tibet. The great monasteries of Tibet have also relocated, many to the sweltering heat of South India, where you can find replicas of the Sera, Ganden and Drepung Monasteries.

With exile has come an unexpected flowering of Tibetan Buddhism abroad; you can now find prayer flags gracing the Scottish glens of Samye Ling Monastery in Dumfriesshire and huge chörtens decorating the countryside of California.

GUCCI GUCHI

Being a devout Buddhist region, Tibet has a long tradition of begging for alms. Generally, beggars will approach you with thumbs up and mumble *'guchi, guchi'* – 'please, please' (not a request for Italian designer clothes).

Tibetans tend to be generous with beggars and usually hand out a couple of máo to anyone deserving. Banks and monasteries will swap a ¥10 note for a wad of one-máo notes, which go a long way.

If you do give (and the choice is entirely yours), give the same amount Tibetans do; don't encourage the beggars to make foreigners a special target by handing out large denominations. It's worth keeping all your small change in one pocket – there's nothing worse than pulling out a ¥100!

Women in Tibet

Women have traditionally occupied a strong position in Tibetan society, often holding the family purse strings and running businesses like shops and guesthouses. Several of Tibet's most famous Buddhist practitioners, such as Yeshe Tsogyel and Machik Labdronma, were women, and Tibet's nuns remain at the vanguard of political dissent. Most of the road workers you see across the plateau are women!

Up until the Chinese invasion many Tibetan farming villages practised polyandry. When a woman married the eldest son of a family she also married his younger brothers (providing they did not become monks). The children of such marriages referred to all the brothers as their father. The practice was aimed at easing the inheritance of family property (mainly the farming land) and avoiding the break-up of small plots.

Tibetan Buddhism

A basic understanding of Buddhism is essential to getting beneath the skin of things in Tibet. Exploring the monasteries and temples of Tibet and mixing with its people, yet knowing nothing of Buddhism, is like visiting the Vatican and knowing nothing of Roman Catholicism. To be sure, it's an awe-inspiring experience, but much will remain hidden and indecipherable. A little studying here will give you a far deeper connection to Tibet and its people.

The Roots of Religion in Tibet

Since the 1959 departure of the Dalai Lama, Tibet has been largely cut off from its Buddhist teachers and lineage masters, most of whom remain in exile.

For those who already know something of Zen Buddhism, Tibet can seem baffling. The grandeur of the temples, the worship of images and the bloodthirsty protective deities that stand in doorways all seem to belie the basic tenets of an ascetic faith that is basically about renouncing the self and following a path of moderation.

One reason for this is that in Tibet the establishment of Buddhism was heavily marked by its interaction with the native religion Bön. This animist or shamanistic faith – which encompassed gods and spirits, exorcism, spells, talismans, ritual drumming, sacrifices and the cult of dead kings, among other things – had a major influence on the direction Buddhism took in Tibet. Many popular Buddhist symbols and practices, such as prayer flags, sky burial, the rubbing of holy rocks, the tying of bits of cloth to trees and the construction of spirit traps, all have their roots deep in Bön tradition.

Tibetan Buddhism's interaction with both Bön spirit worship and the Hindu pantheon, as well as Tibet's affinity for the Tantric side of Buddhist thought, has resulted in a huge range of deities, both wrathful and benign. Grafted onto these have been the scholastic tradition of the Indian Buddhist universities and the ascetic, meditative traditions of the Himalayan religion. Yet for all its confusing iconography and philosophy, the basic tenets of Buddhism are very much rooted in daily experience. Even high lamas and monks come across as surprisingly down to earth.

The Buddha

What Makes You Not a Buddhist by Dzongsar Jamyang Khyentse is an illuminating introduction to Buddhism from the Bhutanese reincarnate lama and film director.

Buddhism originated in the northeast of India around the 5th century BC, at a time when the local religion was Brahmanism. Some brahman, in preparation for presiding over offerings to their gods, partook of an asceticism that transported them to remote places where they fasted, meditated and practised yogic techniques.

Many of the fundamental concepts of Buddhism find their origin in the brahman society of this time. The Buddha (c 480–400 BC), born Siddhartha Gautama, was one of many wandering ascetics whose teachings led to the establishment of rival religious schools. Jainism was one of these schools; Buddhism was another.

Little is known about the life of Siddhartha. It was probably not until some 200 years after his death that biographies were compiled, and by that time many of the circumstances of his life had merged with legend. It is known that he was born in Lumbini (modern-day Nepal) of a noble family and that he married and had a son before renouncing a life of privilege and embarking on a quest to make sense of the suffering in the world.

After studying with many of the masters of his day he embarked on a course of intense asceticism, before concluding that such a path was too extreme. Finally, in the place that is now known as Bodhgaya in India, Siddhartha meditated beneath a *bo* (pipal) tree. At the break of dawn at the end of his third night of meditation he became a buddha (awakened one).

You'll see many famous stories from Buddha's life painted on monastery murals, from his birth (his mother Maya is depicted holding on to a tree) and his first seven steps (lotus flowers sprouted from the ground) to his skeletal ascetic phase and temptation by the demon Mara.

Buddhist Concepts

Buddhism's early teachings are based on the insights of the Buddha, known in Mahayana tradition as Sakyamuni (Sakya Thukpa in Tibetan), and form the basis of all further Buddhist thought. Buddhism is not based on any revealed prophecy or divine revelation but rather is firmly rooted in human experience. The later Mahayana school (to which Tibetan Buddhism belongs) diverged from these early teachings in some respects, but not in its fundamentals.

The Buddha commenced his teachings by explaining that there was a Middle Way that steered a course between sensual indulgence and ascetic self-torment – a way of moderation rather than renunciation. This Middle Way could be pursued by following the Noble Eightfold Path. The philosophical underpinnings of this path were the Four Noble Truths, which addressed the problems of karma and rebirth. These basic concepts are the kernel of early Buddhist thought.

The lotus (*padma* in Sanskrit, *metok* in Tibetan) is an important Buddhist symbol and the thrones of many deities are made from a lotus leaf. The leaf symbolises purity and transcendence, in the world but not of it, rising as it does from muddy waters to become a flower of great beauty.

TIBETAN BUDDHISM BUDDHIST CONCEPTS

WHEEL OF LIFE

The Wheel of Life (Sipa Khorlo in Tibetan), depicted in the entryway to most monasteries, is an aid to realising the delusion of the mind. It's a complex pictorial representation of how desire chains us to samsara, the endless cycle of birth, death and rebirth.

The wheel is held in the mouth of Yama, the Lord of Death. The inner circle of interdependent desire shows a cockerel (representing desire or attachment) biting a pig (ignorance or delusion) biting a snake (hatred or anger). A second ring is divided into figures ascending through the realms on the left and descending on the right.

The six inner sectors of the wheel symbolise the six realms of rebirth: gods, battling demigods and humans (the upper realms); and hungry ghosts, hell and animals (the lower realms). All beings are reborn through this cycle dependent upon their karma. The Buddha is depicted outside the wheel, symbolising his release into a state of nirvana.

At the bottom of the wheel are hot and cold hells, where Yama holds a mirror that reflects one's lifetime. A demon to the side holds a scale with black and white pebbles, weighing up the good and bad deeds of one's lifetime.

The *pretas* (hungry spirits) are recognisable by their huge stomachs, thin needle-like necks and tiny mouths, which cause them insatiable hunger and thirst. In each realm the Buddha attempts to convey his teachings (the dharma), offering hope to each realm.

The 12 outer segments depict the so-called '12 links of dependent origination', and the 12 interlinked, codependent and causal experiences of life that perpetuate the cycle of samsara. The 12 images (whose order may vary) are of a blind woman (representing ignorance), a potter (unconscious will), a monkey (consciousness), men in a boat (self-consciousness), a house (the five senses), lovers (contact), a man with an arrow in his eye (feeling), a drinking scene (desire), a figure grasping fruit from a tree (attachment), pregnancy, birth and death (a man carrying a corpse to a sky burial).

FOLK RELIGION

Closely linked to both Bön and Buddhism is the folk religion of Tibet, known as *mi chös* (the dharma of man), which is primarily concerned with the appeasement of spirits. These spirits include *nyen,* which reside in rocks and trees; *lu* or *naga,* snake-bodied spirits, which live at the bottom of lakes, rivers and wells; *sadok,* lords of the earth, which are connected with agriculture; *tsen,* air or mountain spirits, which shoot arrows of illness and death at humans; and *dud,* demons linked to the Buddhist demon Mara. Into this stew are thrown the spirits of the hearth, roof and kitchen that inhabit every Tibetan house, and a collection of local deities, border gods and pilgrimage-site protectors. Like most Himalayan people, the religious beliefs of the average Tibetan are a fascinating melange of Buddhism, Bön and folk religion.

In modern terms, Buddhist thought stresses nonviolence, compassion, equanimity (evenness of mind), mindfulness (awareness of the present moment) and nonattachment.

Rebirth

Life is a cycle of endless rebirths. The Sanskrit word 'samsara' (Tibetan: *khorwa*), literally 'wandering on', is used to describe this cycle, and life is seen as wandering on limitlessly through time, and through the birth, extinction and rebirth of galaxies and worlds. There are six levels of rebirth or realms of existence, as depicted in the Wheel of Life. It is important to accumulate enough merit to avoid the three lower realms, although in the long cycle of rebirth, all beings pass through them at some point. All beings are fated to tread this wheel continuously until they make a commitment to enlightenment.

Karma

All beings pass through the same cycle of rebirths. Their enemy may once have been their mother, and like all beings they have lived as an insect and as a god, and suffered in one of the hell realms. Movement within this cycle, though, is not haphazard. It is governed by karma.

Prayer flags are strung up to purify the air and pacify the mountain gods. All feature a *longta* (windhorse), which carries the prayers up into the heavens. The colours are highly symbolic – red, green, yellow, blue and white represent fire, wood, earth, water and iron.

Karma (*las* in Tibetan) is a slippery concept. It is sometimes translated simply as 'action', but it also implies the consequences of action. Karma might be thought of as an overarching condition of life. Every action in life leaves a psychic trace that carries over into the next rebirth. It should not be thought of as a reward or punishment, but simply as a result. In Buddhist thought karma is frequently likened to a seed that ripens into a fruit: thus a human reborn as an insect is harvesting the fruits of a previous immoral existence.

Merit

Given that karma is a kind of accumulated psychic baggage that we must lug through countless rebirths, it is the aim of all practising Buddhists to try to accumulate as much 'good karma' – merit – as possible. Merit is best achieved through the act of rejoicing in giving. The giving of alms to the needy and to monks, the relinquishing of a son to monkhood, and acts of compassion and understanding are all meritorious and have a positive karmic outcome.

The Four Noble Truths

If belief in rebirth, karma and merit are the basis of lay-followers' faith in Buddhism, the Four Noble Truths (Tibetan: *phakpay denpa shi*) might be thought of as its philosophical underpinning.

Dukkha (Suffering)

The first of the Four Noble Truths is that life is suffering. This suffering extends through all the countless rebirths of beings, and finds its origin in the imperfection of life. Every rebirth brings with it the pain of birth, the pain of ageing, the pain of death, the pain of association with unpleasant things, the loss of things we are attached to and the failure to achieve the things we desire.

Tanha (Desire)

The reason for this suffering is the second Noble Truth, and lies in our dissatisfaction with imperfection, in our desire for things to be other than they are. What is more, this dissatisfaction leads to actions and karmic consequences that prolong the cycle of rebirths and may lead to even more suffering, much like a mouse running endlessly in a wheel.

Nibbana (Cessation of Desire)

Known in English as nirvana, *nibbana* (Tibetan: *namtrol*) is the cessation of all desire; an end to attachment. With the cessation of desire comes an end to suffering, the achievement of complete nonattachment and an end to the cycle of rebirth. Nirvana is the ultimate goal of Buddhism. Nitpickers might point out that the will to achieve nirvana is a desire in itself. Buddhists answer that this desire is tolerated as a useful means to an end, but it is only when this desire, too, is extinguished that nirvana is truly achieved.

Noble Eightfold Path

The fourth of the Noble Truths prescribes a course that for the lay practitioner will lead to the accumulation of merit, and for the serious devotee may lead to nirvana. The components of this path are (1) right understanding, (2) right thought, (3) right speech, (4) right action, (5) right

Whether hand-held or building-sized, prayer wheels are always filled with prayers which are 'activated' with each revolution of the wheel. Pilgrims spin the wheels to gain merit and to concentrate the mind on the mantras they are reciting.

RELIGIOUS FREEDOM IN TIBET

Religious freedoms in Tibet have certainly increased since the 1980s, though any form of nationalist or political protest is still quickly crushed. Monks and nuns, who have traditionally been at the vanguard of protests and Tibetan aspirations for independence, are regarded with particular suspicion by the authorities. The demonstrations of 2008 were initially led by monks from Sera, Drepung and Ramoche Monasteries and turned to riots after police beat a line of monks from Ramoche. Nuns, in particular, considering their small numbers, have been very politically active, accounting for 55 of the 126 independence protests in the mid-1990s. Regulations make it impossible for nuns, once arrested and imprisoned, to return to their nunneries.

Political-indoctrination or 'patriotic education' teams are frequent visitors to (or residents in) most monasteries, as are the recurring campaigns to denounce the Dalai Lama. Images of the current Dalai Lama are illegal, which is why you'll see pictures of the 13th Dalai Lama on most monastery thrones, as a symbolic stand-in. Since 2008 most monasteries now have a police station or army post on-site and the numbers of resident monks are strictly controlled. The friendly orange-clad Chinese fire-prevention teams you may see in larger monasteries are actually there to keep an eye on the monks (to prevent self-immolations), not potential arsonists. While many monasteries now gleam after million-dollar renovations and are bustling with monks and tourists, the authorities are also there in the background, keeping a close eye open for the first sign of dissent.

According to the US government's 2012 International Religious Freedom Report, recent years have seen 'a prolonged period of progressively more repressive government actions and religious policies in Tibetan areas, including intense official crackdowns at monasteries and nunneries resulting in the loss of life, arbitrary detentions, and torture.'

livelihood, (6) right effort, (7) right mindfulness and (8) right concentration. Needless to say, each of these has a 'wrong' corollary.

Schools of Buddhism

If you see a collection of spider-web-like coloured threads woven around a wooden frame, this is a *dzoe* (spirit trap), designed to catch and then get rid of troublesome evil spirits.

Not long after the death of Sakyamuni, disagreements began to arise among his followers – as they tend to do in all religious movements – over whose interpretations best captured the true spirit of his teachings. The result was the development of numerous schools of thought and, eventually, a schism that saw the emergence of two principal schools: Hinayana and Mahayana.

Hinayana, also known as Theravada, encouraged scholasticism and close attention to what were considered the original teachings of Sakyamuni. Mahayana, on the other hand, with its elevation of compassion *(nyingje)* as an all-important idea, took Buddhism in a new direction. It was the Mahayana school that made its way up to the high plateau and took root there, at the same time travelling to China, Korea and Japan. Hinayana retreated into southern India and took root in Sri Lanka and Thailand.

Buddhism is perhaps the most tolerant of the world's religions. Wherever it has gone it has adapted to local conditions, like a dividing cell, creating countless new schools of thought. Its basic tenets have remained very much the same and all schools are bound together in their faith in the original teachings of Sakyamuni (Sakya Thukpa), the Historical Buddha. The Chinese invasion has ironically caused a flowering of Tibetan Buddhism abroad and you can now find Tibetan monasteries around the world.

Mahayana

The claims that Mahayanists made for their faith were many, but the central issue was a change in orientation from individual pursuit of enlightenment to bodhisattvahood. Rather than striving for complete non-attachment, the bodhisattva aims, through compassion and self-sacrifice, to achieve enlightenment for the sake of all beings.

THE WORLD OF A MONK

The Western term 'monk' is slightly misleading when used in the context of Tibetan Buddhism. The Tibetan equivalent would probably be *trapa,* which means literally 'scholar' or 'student', and is an inclusive term that covers the three main categories of monastic inmates. Monks in these categories should also be distinguished from lamas who, as spiritual luminaries, have a privileged position in the monastic hierarchy, may have considerable wealth and, outside the Gelugpa order, are not necessarily celibate.

The first step for a monk, usually after completing some prior study, is to take one of two lesser vows, the *genyen* or *getsul* ordination – a renunciation of secular life that includes a vow of celibacy. This marks the beginning of a long course of study that is expected to lead to the full *gelong* vows of ordination. These vows are also supplemented by higher courses of study, which are rewarded in the Gelugpa order by the title *geshe*.

These three categories do not encompass all the monks in a monastery. There are usually specific monastic posts associated with administrative duties, with ritual and with teaching. Before land reform in the 1950s, Tibet's monasteries owned as much as half of Tibet's farmland, and received taxes from local farmers in the form of money or grain. In premodern Tibet the larger monasteries also had divisions of so-called 'fighting monks', or monastic militias who acted as an internal police force or, at times, even a private monastic army.

In 1950, on the eve of the Chinese invasion, it was estimated that as much as a quarter of the entire population of Tibet were monks, the highest in the Buddhist world. Today there are around 47,000 monks in the Tibetan Autonomous Region.

In the meantime, Sakyamuni slowly began to change shape. Mahayanists maintained that Sakyamuni had already attained buddhahood many aeons ago and that there were now many such transcendent beings living in heavens or 'pure lands'. The revolutionary concept had the effect of producing a pantheon of bodhisattvas, a feature that made Mahayana more palatable to cultures that already had gods of their own. In Tibet, China, Korea and Japan, the Mahayana pantheon came to be identified with local gods as their Mahayana equivalents replaced them.

Tantrism (Vajrayana)

A further Mahayana development that is particularly relevant to Tibet is Tantrism. The words of Sakyamuni were recorded in sutras and studied by students of both Hinayana and Mahayana, but according to the followers of Tantrism, a school that emerged from around AD 600, Sakyamuni left a corpus of esoteric instructions to a select few of his disciples. These were known as Tantra (*Gyü*).

Tantric adepts claimed that through the use of unconventional techniques they could jolt themselves towards enlightenment, and shorten the long road to bodhisattvahood. The process involved identification with a tutelary deity invoked through deep meditation and recitation of the deity's mantra. The most famous of these mantras is the *'Om mani padme hum'* ('hail to the jewel in the lotus') mantra of Chenresig (Avalokiteshvara). Tantric practice also employs Indian yogic techniques to channel energy towards the transformation to enlightenment. Such yogic techniques might even include sexual practices. Tantric techniques are rarely written down, but rather are passed down verbally from tutor to student, increasing their secret allure.

From ritual thigh bones and skull cups to images of deities in *yab-yum* sexual union, many of the ritual objects and images in Tibetan monasteries are Tantric in nature. Together they show the many facets of enlightenment – at times kindly, at times wrathful.

Buddhism in Tibet

The story of the introduction of Buddhism to Tibet is attended by legends of the taming of local gods and spirits and their conversion to Buddhism as protective deities. This magnificent array of buddhas, bodhisattvas and sages occupies a mythical world in the Tibetan imagination. Chenresig is perhaps chief among them, manifesting himself in the early Tibetan kings and later the Dalai Lamas. Guru Rinpoche, the Indian sage and Tantric magician who bound the native spirits and gods of Tibet into the service of Buddhism, is another, and there are countless others, including saints and protector gods. While the clerical side of Buddhism concerns itself largely with textual study and analysis, the Tantric shamanistic-based side seeks revelation through identification with these deified beings and through their *terma* ('revealed' words or writings).

It is useful to consider the various schools of Tibetan Buddhism as revealing something of a struggle between these two orientations: shamanism and clericalism. Each school finds its own resolution to the problem. In the case of the last major school to arise, the Gelugpa order, there was a search for a return to the doctrinal purity of clerical Buddhism. But even here, the Tantric forms were not completely discarded; it was merely felt that many years of scholarly work and preparation should precede the more esoteric Tantric practices.

The clerical and shamanistic traditions can also be explained as the difference between state-sponsored and popular Buddhism, respectively. There was always a tendency for the state to emphasise monastic Buddhism, with its communities of rule-abiding monks. Popular Buddhism, on the other hand, with its long-haired, wild-eyed ascetic recluses capable

The *chokyi khorlo* (dharma wheel) symbolises the Buddha's first sermon at Sarnath. The eight spokes recall the Eightfold Path. The wheel was the earliest symbol of Buddhism, used for centuries before images of the Buddha became popular.

Chömay (butter lamps) are kept lit continuously in all monasteries and many private homes, and are topped up continuously by visiting pilgrims equipped with a tub of butter and a spoon.

TIBETAN BUDDHISM BUDDHISM IN TIBET

EIGHT AUSPICIOUS SYMBOLS

The Eight Auspicious Symbols *(tashi targyel)* are associated with gifts made to Sakyamuni (Sakya Thukpa) upon his enlightenment and appear as protective motifs across Tibet.

Knot of eternity Representing the entwined, never-ending passage of time, harmony and love and the unity of all things, the knot of eternity is commonly seen on embroidery and tents.

Lotus flower The *padma* (lotus flower) stands for the purity and compassion of Sakyamuni and has become a symbol of Buddhism.

Pair of golden fishes Shown leaping from the waters of captivity, they represent liberation from the Wheel of Life (for years they were the logo of Lhasa Beer!).

Precious umbrella Usually placed over buddha images to protect them from evil influences, the precious umbrella is a common Buddhist motif also seen in Thailand and Japan.

Vase of treasure The vase is a sacred repository of the jewels of enlightenment or the water of eternity.

Victory banner Heralding the triumph of Buddhist wisdom over ignorance.

Wheel of Law Representing the Noble Eightfold Path to salvation, the wheel is also referred to as the Wheel of Dharma. The wheel turns 12 times, three times for each of the Four Noble Truths.

White conch shell Blown in celebration of the enlightenment of Sakyamuni and the potential of all beings to be awakened by the sound of dharma, the shell is often used to signal prayer time.

Knot of eternity

of performing great feats of magic, had a great appeal to ordinary Tibetans, for whom ghosts, demons and sorcerers were a daily reality.

Nyingmapa Order

➡ **Main monasteries** Mindroling (p108), Dorje Drak (p109)

➡ **Also known as** Red Hats

The Nyingmapa order is the Old School, and traces its origins back to the teachings and practices of the 8th- or 9th-century Indian master Guru Rinpoche. Over the centuries the Nyingmapa failed to develop as a powerful, centralised school, and for the most part prospered in villages throughout rural Tibet, where it was administered by local shamanlike figures.

Lotus flower

The Nyingma school was revitalised through the 'discovery' of hidden texts in the 'power places' of Tibet visited by Guru Rinpoche. In many cases these *terma* (revealed texts) were discovered through yogic-inspired visions by spiritually advanced Nyingmapa practitioners, rather than found under a pile of rocks or in a cave. Out of these *terma* arose the Dzogchen (Great Perfection) teachings, an appealing Tantric short cut to nirvana that teaches that enlightenment can come in a single lifetime. Today the Nyingmapa have a particularly strong presence in western Sìchuān.

Kagyupa Order

➡ **Main monastery** Tsurphu (p94)

➡ **Subschools** Drigungpa (Drigung Til Monastery, p104); Taglungpa (Talung, p100); Drukpa (Ralung, p128); Karma Kagyu (Tsurphu)

➡ **Founder** Milarepa

➡ **Also known as** Black Hats

Pair of golden fishes

The resurgence of Buddhist influence in the 11th century led to many Tibetans travelling to India to study. The new ideas they brought back with them had a revitalising effect on Tibetan thought and produced other new schools of Tibetan Buddhism. Among them was the Kagyupa order, established by Milarepa (1040–1123), who was the disciple of Marpa the translator (1012–93).

Precious umbrella

The establishment of monasteries eventually overshadowed the ascetic-yogi origins of the Kagyupa. The yogi tradition did not die out completely, however, and Kagyupa monasteries also became important centres for synthesising the clerical and shamanistic orientations of Tibetan Buddhism.

In time, several suborders of the Kagyupa sprang up, the most prominent of which was the Karma Kagyu, also known as the Karmapa. The practice of reincarnation originated with this suborder, when the abbot of Tsurphu Monastery, Dusum Khyenpa (1110–93), announced that he would be reincarnated as his own successor. The 16th Karmapa died in 1981, and his disputed successor fled to India in 1999.

Vase of treasure

Sakyapa Order

→ **Main monasteries** Sakya (p147)

→ **Subschools** Tsarpa, Ngorpa

→ **Founder** Kongchog Gyelpo

From the 11th century many Tibetan monasteries became centres for the textual study and translation of Indian Buddhist texts. One of the earliest major figures in this movement was Kunga Gyaltsen (1182–1251), known as Sakya Pandita (literally 'scholar from Sakya').

Victory banner

Sakya Pandita's renown as a scholar led to him, and subsequent abbots of Sakya, being recognised as a manifestation of Jampelyang (Manjushri), the Bodhisattva of Insight. Sakya Pandita travelled to the Mongolian court in China, with the result that his heir became the spiritual tutor of Kublai Khan. In the 13th and 14th centuries, the Sakyapa order became embroiled in politics and implicated in the Mongol overlordship of Tibet.

Many Sakyapa monasteries contain images of the Sakyapa protector deity Gompo Gur and photographs of the school's four head lamas: the Sakya Trizin (in exile in the US), Ngawang Kunga (head of the Sakyapa order), Chogye Trichen Rinpoche (head of the Tsarpa subschool) and Ludhing Khenpo Rinpoche (head of the Ngorpa subschool). You can easily recognise Sakyapa monasteries from the three stripes painted on the generally grey walls.

Wheel of Law

Gelugpa Order

→ **Main monasteries** Ganden (p85), Sera (p80), Drepung (p75), Tashilhunpo (p136)

→ **Founder** Tsongkhapa

→ **Also known as** Yellow Hats

It may not have been his intention, but Tsongkhapa (1357–1419), a monk who left his home in Amdo (Qīnghǎi) at the age of 17 to study in central Tibet, is regarded as the founder of the Gelugpa (Virtuous School) order, which came to dominate political and religious affairs in Tibet.

Tsongkhapa studied with all the major schools of his day, but was particularly influenced by the Sakyapa and the Kadampa orders, the latter based on the teachings of 11th-century Bengali sage Atisha. After experiencing a vision of Atisha, Tsongkhapa elaborated on the Bengali sage's clerical-Tantric synthesis in a doctrine that is known as *lamrim*

White conch shell

TIBETAN BUDDHISM BUDDHISM IN TIBET

(the graduated path). The Gelugpa school eventually subsumed the Kadampa school.

Tsongkhapa basically advocated a return to doctrinal purity and stressed the structure of the monastic body and monastic discipline as prerequisites to advanced Tantric studies. Tsongkhapa established Ganden Monastery, which became the head of the Gelugpa order. The Ganden Tripa is actually the titular head of the order, but it was the Dalai Lamas who came to be increasingly identified with the order's growing political and spiritual prestige.

Despite its connotations abroad, the swastika is an ancient Indian religious symbol that was later adopted by Buddhism and is often found painted on Tibetan houses to bring good luck. Swastikas that point clockwise are Buddhist; those that point anticlockwise are Bön.

Bön

➜ **Main monasteries**: Yungdrungling (p143), Gurugyam (p178)

➜ **Founder** Shenrab Miwoche

The word 'Bön' today has three main connotations. The first relates to the pre-Buddhist religion of Tibet, suppressed and supplanted by Buddhism in the 8th and 9th centuries. The second is the form of 'organised' Bön (Gyur Bön) systematised along Buddhist lines, which arose in the 11th century. Third, and linked to this, is a body of popular beliefs that involves the worship of local deities and spirit protectors.

The earliest form of Bön, sometimes referred to as Black Bön, also Dud Bön (the Bön of Devils) or Tsan Bön (the Bön of Spirits), was concerned with countering the effects of evil spirits through magical practices. Bönpo priests were entrusted with the wellbeing and fertility of the living, as well as curing sicknesses, affecting the weather and mediating between humans and the spirit world. A core component was control of the spirits, to ensure the safe passage of the soul into the next world. For centuries Bönpo priests controlled the complex burial rites of the Yar-

BÖN MONASTERIES

As a result of the historical predominance of Buddhism in Tibet, the Bön religion has been suppressed for centuries and has only recently started to attract the attention of scholars. Many Tibetans remain quite ignorant of Bön beliefs and your guide might refuse to even set foot in a Bön monastery. Yet Bön and Buddhism have influenced and interacted with each other for centuries, exchanging texts, traditions and rituals. In the words of Tibet scholar David Snellgrove, 'every Tibetan is a Bönpo at heart'.

To the casual observer it's often hard to differentiate between Bönpo and Buddhist practice. Shared concepts include those of samsara, karma and rebirth in the six states of existence. Even Bön monasteries, rituals and meditation practice are almost identical to Buddhist versions.

Still, there are obvious differences. Bön has its own Kangyur, a canon made up of texts translated from the Shang-Shung language, and Bönpos turn prayer wheels and circumambulate monasteries anticlockwise. The main difference comes down to the source of religious authority: Bönpos see the arrival of Buddhism as a catastrophe – the supplanting of the truth by a false religion.

Bön iconography is unique. Tonpa Shenrab is the most common central image, and is depicted as either a monk or a deity. He shares Sakyamuni's *mudra* (hand gesture) of 'enlightenment' but normally holds the Bön sceptre, which consists of two swastikas joined together by a column. Other gods of Bönpo include Satrid Ergang, who holds a swastika and mirror; Shenrab Wokar and his main emanation, Kuntu Zangpo, with a hooklike wand; and Sangpo Bumptri.

Complementing these gods is a large number of local deities – these are potentially harmful male spirits known as *gekho* (the protectors of Bön) and their female counterparts, *drapla*. Welchen Gekho is the king of the harmful *gekho*, and his consort Logbar Tsame is the queen of the *dralpa*.

lung kings. Bön was the state religion of Tibet until the reign of Songtsen Gampo (r 629–49).

Bön is thought to have its geographical roots in the kingdom of Shang-Shung (which is located in western Tibet), and its capital at Kyunglung (Valley of the Garuda). Bön's founding father was Shenrab Miwoche, also known as Tonpa Shenrab, the Teacher of Knowledge, who was born in the second millennium BC in the mystical land of Olma Lungring in Tajik (thought to be possibly the Mt Kailash area or even Persia). Buddhists often claim that Shenrab is merely a carbon copy of Sakyamuni (Sakya Thukpa), and certainly there are similarities to be found. Biographies state that he was born a royal prince and ruled for 30 years before becoming an ascetic. His 10 wives bore him 10 children who formed the core of his religious disciples. Many of the tales of Shenrab Miwoche deal with his protracted struggles with the demon king Khyabpa Lagring.

Bön was first suppressed by the eighth Yarlung king, Drigum Tsenpo, and subsequently by King Trisong Detsen. The Bön master Gyerpung Drenpa Namkha (a *gyerpung* is the Bön equivalent of a lama or guru) struggled with Trisong Detsen to protect the Bön faith until the king finally broke Shang-Shung's political power. Following the founding of Samye Monastery, many Bön priests went into exile or converted to Buddhism, and many of the Bön texts were hidden.

The modern Bön religion is known as Yungdrung (Eternal Bön). A *yungdrung* is a swastika, Bön's most important symbol. (Yungdrungling means 'swastika park' and is a common name for Bön monasteries.) *The Nine Ways of Bön* is the religion's major text. Bönpos still refer to Mt Kailash as Yungdrung Gutseg (Nine-Stacked-Swastika Mountain).

The Bön order, as it survives today, is to all intents and purposes the fifth school of Tibetan Buddhism. Pockets of Bön exist in the Changtang region of northern Tibet and the Aba region of northern Sìchuān (Kham).

The *dorje* (thunderbolt) and *drilbu* (bell) are ritual objects symbolising male and female aspects used in Tantric rites. They are held in the right and left hands respectively. The indestructible thunderbolt cuts through ignorance.

Important Figures of Tibetan Buddhism

This is a brief iconographical guide to some of the gods and goddesses of the vast Tibetan Buddhist pantheon, as well as to important historical figures. It is neither exhaustive nor scholarly, but it may help you to recognise a few of the statues and murals you encounter during your trip. Tibetan names are given first, with Sanskrit names provided in parentheses. (The exception is Sakya Thukpa, who is generally known by his Sanskrit name, Sakyamuni.) See also the Who's Who section on p338.

Buddhas

Sakyamuni (Sakya Thukpa)

Sakyamuni is the Historical Buddha (the Buddha of the Present Age), whose teachings set in motion the Buddhist faith. In Tibetan-style representations he is always pictured sitting cross-legged on a lotus-flower throne. His tight curled hair is dark blue and there is a halo of enlightenment around his head. The Buddha is recognised by 32 marks on his body, including a dot between his eyes, a bump on the top of his head, three folds of skin on his neck and the Wheel of Law on the soles of his feet. In his left hand he holds a begging bowl, and his right hand touches the earth in the 'witness' *mudra* (hand gesture). He is often flanked by his two principal disciples Sariputra and Maudgalyana.

Marmedze (Dipamkara)

The Past Buddha, Marmedze, came immediately before Sakyamuni and spent 100,000 years on earth. His hands are shown in the 'protection' *mudra* and he is often depicted in a trinity with the Present and Future Buddhas, known as the *dusum sangay*.

Sakyamuni (Sakya Thukpa)

Tsepame (Amitayus)

Jampa (Maitreya)

Öpagme (Amitabha)

The Buddha of Infinite Light resides in the 'pure land of the west' (Dewachen in Tibetan, or Sukhavati in Sanskrit). The Panchen Lama is considered a reincarnation of this buddha. He is red, his hands are held together in his lap in a 'meditation' *mudra* and he holds a begging bowl.

The Ten Meritorious Deeds in Buddhism are to refrain from killing, stealing, inappropriate sexual activity, lying, gossiping, cursing, sowing discord, envy, malice and opinionatedness.

Tsepame (Amitayus)

The Buddha of Longevity, like Öpagme, is red and holds his hands in a meditation gesture, but he holds a vase containing the nectar of immortality. He is often seen in groups of nine.

Medicine Buddhas (Menlha)

The medicine buddha holds a medicine bowl in his left hand and herbs in his right, while rays of healing light emanate from his blue body. He is often depicted in a group of eight.

Dhyani Buddhas (Gyalwa Ri Nga)

Each of the five Dhyani buddhas is a different colour, and each of them has different *mudras,* symbols and attributes. They are Öpagme, Nampar Namse (Vairocana), Mikyöba (or Mitrukpa; Akhshobya), Rinchen Jungne (Ratnasambhava) and Donyo Drupa (Amoghasiddhi).

Jampa (Maitreya)

Jampa, the Future Buddha, is passing the life of a bodhisattva until it is time to return to earth in human form 4000 years after the disappearance of Sakyamuni. He is normally seated in European fashion, with a scarf around his waist, often with a white stupa in his hair and his hands by his chest in the *mudra* of turning the Wheel of Law. Jampa is much larger than the average human and so statues of Jampa are often several storeys high.

Chenresig
(Avalokiteshvara)

Bodhisattvas

These are beings who have reached the state of enlightenment but work for the salvation of other beings before they themselves enter nirvana. Unlike buddhas, they are often shown decorated with crowns and princely jewels.

Chenresig (Avalokiteshvara)

Jampelyang
(Manjushri)

The 'glorious gentle one', Chenresig (Guānyīn to the Chinese) is the Bodhisattva of Compassion. His name means 'he who gazes upon the world with suffering in his eyes'. The Dalai Lamas are considered to be reincarnations of Chenresig (as is King Songtsen Gampo), and pictures of the Dalai Lama and Chenresig are interchangeable, depending on the political climate.

In the four-armed version (known more specifically in Tibetan as Tonje Chenpo), his body is white and he sits on a lotus blossom. He holds crystal rosary beads and a lotus, and clutches to his heart a jewel that fulfils all wishes. A deer skin is draped over his left shoulder.

Found on all altars and replenished twice a day, the seven bowls of water symbolise either the 'Seven Examined Men' (the first seven monks in Tibet) or the seven first steps of Buddha.

There is also a powerful 11-headed, 1000-armed version, known as Chaktong Chentong. The head of this version is said to have exploded when confronted with the myriad problems of the world. One of his heads is that of wrathful Chana Dorje (Vajrapani), and another (the top one) is that of Öpagme (Amitabha), who is said to have reassembled Chenresig's body after it exploded. Each of the 1000 arms has an eye in the palm. His eight main arms hold a bow and an arrow, lotus, rosary, vase, wheel, staff and a wish-fulfilling jewel.

Jampelyang (Manjushri)

The Bodhisattva of Wisdom, Jampelyang is regarded as the first divine teacher of Buddhist doctrine. He is connected to science and agriculture and school children; architects and astrologers often offer prayers to him. His right hand holds the flaming sword of awareness, which cuts through delusion. His left arm cradles a scripture on a half-opened lotus blossom and his left hand is in the 'teaching' *mudra*. He is often yellow and may have blue hair or an elaborate crown. He is sometimes called Manjughosa.

Drölma (Tara)

A female bodhisattva with 21 different manifestations or aspects, Drölma is also known as the saviouress. She was born from a tear of compassion that fell from the eyes of Chenresig and is thus considered the female version of Chenresig and a protector of the Tibetan people. She also symbolises purity and fertility and is believed to be able to fulfil wishes. Images usually represent Dröljang (Green Tara), who is associated with night, or Drölkar (White Tara), who is associated with day (and also Songtsen Gampo's Chinese wife). She is often seen as part of the Tsela Nam Sum longevity triad, along with red Tsepame (Amitayus) and three-faced, eight-armed female Namgyelma (Vijaya).

Drölma (Tara)

Protector Deities

Protectors are easily recognised by their fierce expressions, bulging eyes, warrior stance (with one leg outstretched in a fencer's pose), halo of flames and Tantric implements. They either stand trampling on the human ego or sit astride an animal mount, dressed in military regalia and flayed animal or human skins. They represent on various levels the transformed original demons of Tibet, the wrathful aspects of other deities and, on one level at least, humankind's inner psychological demons.

Nagpo Chenpo
(Mahakala)

Four Guardian Kings (Chökyong)

The four Chökyong (Lokapalas in Sanskrit) are normally seen at the entrance hallway of monasteries and are possibly of Mongol origin. They are the protectors of the four cardinal directions: the eastern chief is white with a lute; the southern is green with a red beard and holds a sword; and the western is red and holds a green *naga*. Namtöse (Vaishravana), the protector of the north, doubles as the god of wealth (Zhambhala or Jambhala) and can be seen with an orange body (the colour of 100,000 suns) and clumpy beard, riding a snow lion and holding a banner of victory, a jewel-spitting mongoose and a lemon.

Dorje Jigje (Yamantaka)

Dorje Jigje is a favourite protector of the Gelugpa order. A wrathful form of Jampelyang, he is also known as the destroyer of Yama (the Lord of Death). He is blue with eight heads, the main one of which is the head of a bull. He wears a garland of skulls around his neck and a belt of skulls around his waist, and holds a skull cup, butchers' chopper and a flaying knife in his 34 arms. He tramples on eight Hindu gods, eight mammals and eight birds with his 16 feet.

Nagpo Chenpo (Mahakala)

A wrathful Tantric deity and manifestation of Chenresig, Nagpo Chenpo (Great Black One) has connections to the Hindu god Shiva. He can be seen in many varieties with anything from two to six arms. He is black ('as a water-laden cloud') with fanged teeth, wears a cloak of elephant

The Buddhist parable of the Four Harmonious Brothers is painted on walls at the entrance to many monasteries. The image is of a bird picking a treetop fruit, while standing atop a hare, who is atop a monkey, who is atop an elephant. On its most basic level the image symbolises cooperation and harmony with the environment.

skin and a tiara of skulls, carries a trident and skull cup, and has flaming hair. In a form known as Gompo (or Yeshe Gompo), he is believed by nomads to be the guardian of the tent.

Tamdrin
(Hayagriva)

Tamdrin (Hayagriva)

Another wrathful manifestation of Chenresig, Tamdrin (the 'horse necked') has a red body. His right face is white, his left face is green and he has a horse's head in his hair. He wears a tiara of skulls, a garland of 52 severed heads and a tiger skin around his waist. His six hands hold a skull cup, a lotus, a sword, a snare, an axe and a club, and his four legs stand on a sun disc, trampling corpses. On his back are the outspread wings of Garuda and the skins of a human and an elephant. He has close connections to the Hindu god Vishnu and is popular among herders and nomads.

Chana Dorje
(Vajrapani)

Chana Dorje (Vajrapani)

The name of the wrathful Bodhisattva of Energy means 'thunderbolt in hand'. In his right hand Chana Dorje holds a thunderbolt *(dorje* or *vajra),* and so is often prayed to during times of droughts or floods. He is blue with a tiger skin around his waist and a snake around his neck. Together with Chenresig and Jampelyang, he forms part of the trinity known as the Rigsum Gonpo.

Palden Lhamo (Shri Devi)

The special protector of Lhasa, the Dalai Lama and the Gelugpa order, Palden Lhamo is a female counterpart of Nagpo Chenpo and closely connected with divination. Her origins probably lie in the Hindu goddess Kali. She is blue, wears clothes of tiger skin, rides on a saddle of human skin, and has earrings made of a snake. She uses the black and white dice around her waist (tied to a bag of diseases) to determine people's fates. She holds the moon in her hair, the sun in her belly and a corpse in her mouth, and rides a wild ass with reins of poisonous snakes and an eye in its rump.

Palden Lhamo
(Shri Devi)

Historical Figures

Guru Rinpoche (Padmasambhava)

The 'lotus-born' 8th-century Tantric master and magician from modern-day Swat in Pakistan, Guru Rinpoche subdued Tibet's evil spirits and helped to establish Buddhism in Tibet. He is regarded by followers of Nyingmapa Buddhism as the 'second Buddha'. His domain is the copper-coloured mountain called Zangdok Pelri. He has bug eyes and a curly moustache and holds a thunderbolt in his right hand, a skull cup in his left hand and a *katvanga* (staff) topped with three heads – one shrunken, one severed and one skull – in the crook of his left arm. He has a *phurbu* (ritual dagger) in his belt. Guru Rinpoche has eight manifestations, known collectively as the Guru Tsengye, which correspond to different stages of his life. He is often flanked by his consorts Mandarava (Indian) and Yeshe Tsogyel (Tibetan).

Guru Rinpoche
(Padmasambhava)

Tsongkhapa

Founder of the Gelugpa order and a manifestation of Jampelyang, Tsongkhapa (1357-1419) wears the yellow hat of the Gelugpas. Also known as Je Rinpoche, he is normally portrayed in the *yab-se sum* trinity with his two main disciples, Kedrub Je (later recognised as the first Panchen Lama) and Gyaltsab Je. His hands are in the 'teaching' *mudra* and he holds two lotuses.

Tsongkhapa

Fifth Dalai Lama

The greatest of all the Dalai Lamas, the fifth (Ngawang Lobsang Gyatso; 1617–82) unified Tibet and built the bulk of the Potala. He was born at Chongye (in the Yarlung Valley) and was the first Dalai Lama to exercise temporal power. He wears the Gelugpa yellow hat and holds a flower or thunderbolt in his right hand and a bell *(drilbu)* in his left. He may also be depicted holding the Wheel of Law (symbolising the beginning of political control of the Dalai Lamas) and a lotus flower or other sacred objects.

Fifth Dalai Lama

King Songtsen Gampo

Tibet was unified under Songtsen Gampo (r 629–49). Together with his two wives, he is credited with introducing Buddhism to the country early in the 7th century. He has a moustache and wears a white turban with a tiny red Öpagme poking out of the top. He is flanked by Princess Wencheng Konjo, his Chinese wife, on the left, and Princess Bhrikuti, his Nepali wife, on his right.

King Songtsen Gampo

King Trisong Detsen

The founder of Samye Monastery (r 755–97) is normally seen in a trio of kings with Songtsen Gampo and King Ralpachen (r 817–35). He is regarded as a manifestation of Jampelyang and so holds a scripture on a lotus in the crook of his left arm and a sword of wisdom in his right. He resembles Songtsen Gampo but without the buddha in his turban.

Milarepa

A great 11th-century Tibetan magician and poet, Milarepa (c 1040–1123) is believed to have attained enlightenment in the course of one lifetime. He became an alchemist in order to poison an uncle who had stolen his family's lands and then spent six years meditating in a cave in repentance. During this time he wore nothing but a cotton robe and so became known as Milarepa (Cotton-Clad Mila). Most images of Milarepa depict him smiling, sitting on an antelope skin, wearing a red meditation belt and holding his hand to his ear as he sings. He may also be depicted as green because he lived for many years on a diet of nettles.

Milarepa

TIBETAN BUDDHISM IMPORTANT FIGURES OF TIBETAN BUDDHISM

Tibetan Art

It is Buddhism that inspires almost all Tibetan art. Paintings, architecture, literature, even dance, all in some way or another attest to its influence. Perhaps more unexpected is that, despite the harshness of their surroundings, Tibetans have great aesthetic taste, from stylish traditional carpets and painted furniture to jewellery and traditional dress.

Tibetan Art Websites

....

www.asianart.com
– general

....

www.mechakgal-lery.com –
contemporary art

....

www.himalayanart.
org – online
collections

Art & History

The arts of Tibet represent the synthesis of many influences. The Buddhist art and architecture of the Pala and Newari kingdoms of India and Nepal were an important early influence in central Tibet, and the Buddhist cultures of Khotan and Kashmir spilled over the mountains into western Tibet. Newari influence is clearly visible in the early woodcarvings of the Jokhang, and Kashmiri influence is particularly strong in the murals of Tsaparang in western Tibet. Chinese influences, too, were assimilated, as is clear at Shalu Monastery near Shigatse and in the Karma Gadri style prevalent in eastern Kham. A later, clearly Tibetan style known as Menri was perfected in the monasteries of Drepung, Ganden and Sera.

Tibetan art is deeply conservative and conventional. Personal expression and innovation are not greatly valued, indeed individual interpretation is actually seen as an obstacle to Tibetan art's main purpose, which is to represent the path to enlightenment. The creation of religious art is seen primarily as an act of merit and the artist generally remains anonymous.

Much of Tibet's artistic heritage fell victim to the Cultural Revolution. What was not destroyed was, in many cases, ferreted away to China or onto the Hong Kong art market. Over 13,500 images have since been returned to Tibet but this is still just a fraction of the number stolen. Many of Tibet's traditional artisans were persecuted or fled Tibet. It is only in recent years that remaining artists have again been able to return to their work and start to train young Tibetans in skills that faced the threat of extinction. New but traditional handicraft workshops are popping up all the time in Lhasa's old town.

Dance & Drama

Anyone who is lucky enough to attend a Tibetan festival should have the opportunity to see performances of *cham,* a ritual masked dance performed over several days by monks and lamas. Although every movement and gesture of *cham* has significance, it is no doubt the spectacle of the colourful masked dancers that awes the average pilgrim.

Cham is all about the suppression of malevolent spirits and is a clear throwback to the pre-Buddhist Bön faith. The chief officiant is an unmasked Black Hat lama who is surrounded by a mandalic grouping of masked monks representing manifestations of various protective deities. The act of exorcism – it might be considered as such – is focused on a human effigy made of dough or perhaps wax or paper, through which the evil spirits are channelled.

The proceedings of *cham* can be interpreted on a number of levels. The Black Hat lama is sometimes identified with the monk who slew Langdharma, the anti-Buddhist king of the Yarlung era, and the dance is seen as echoing the suppression of malevolent forces inimical to the establishment of Buddhism in Tibet. Some anthropologists, on the other hand, have also seen in *cham* a metaphor for the gradual conquering of the ego, which is the ultimate aim of Buddhism. The ultimate destruction of the effigy that ends the dance might represent the destruction of the ego itself. Whatever the case, *cham* is a splendid, dramatic performance that marks the cultural highlight of the year for most Tibetans.

Lhamo Opera

Lighter forms of entertainment usually accompany performances of *cham*. *Lhamo*, not to be confused with *cham*, is Tibetan opera. A largely secular art form, it portrays the heroics of kings and the villainy of demons, and recounts events in the lives of historical figures. *Lhamo* was developed in the 14th century by Tangtong Gyelpo, known as Tibet's Leonardo da Vinci because he was also an engineer, a major bridge builder and a physician. Authentic performances still include a statue of Tangtong on the otherwise bare stage. After the stage has been purified, the narrator gives a plot summary in verse and the performers enter, each with his or her distinct step and dressed in the bright and colourful silks of the aristocracy.

Music

Music is one aspect of Tibetan cultural life in which there is a strong secular heritage. In the urban centres, songs were an important vent for social criticism, news and political lampooning. In Tibetan social life, both work and play are seen as occasions for singing. Even today it is not uncommon to see the monastery reconstruction squads pounding on the roofs of buildings and singing in unison. Where there are groups of men and women, the singing alternates between the two groups in the form of rhythmic refrains.

The ultimate night out in Lhasa is to a *nangma* venue, where house dancers and singers perform traditional songs and dances as part of a stage show, with members of the audience often joining in at smaller venues.

Tibet also has a secular tradition of wandering minstrels. It's still possible to see minstrels performing in Lhasa and Shigatse, where they play on the streets and occasionally (when they are not chased out by the owners) in restaurants. Generally, groups of two or three singers perform heroic epics and short songs to the accompaniment of a four-stringed guitar and a nifty little shuffle, before moving around tables soliciting donations with a grin. In times past, groups of such performers travelled around Tibet, providing entertainment for villagers who had few distractions from the constant round of daily chores.

While the secular music of Tibet has an instant appeal for foreign listeners, the liturgical chants of Buddhist monks and the music that accompanies *cham* dances is a lot less accessible. Buddhist chanting creates an eerie haunting effect, but can soon become very monotonous. The music of *cham* is a discordant cacophony of trumpet blasts and boom-crash drums – atmospheric as an accompaniment to the dancing but not necessarily the kind of thing you would want to put on an MP3 player.

Tibetan religious rituals use *rolmo* and *silnyen* (cymbals), *nga* (suspended drums), *damaru* (hand drums), *drilbu* (bells), *drungchen* (long trumpets), *kangling* (conical oboes; formerly made from human thighbones)

If you are interested in actually creating, not just understanding Tibetan art, look for the master work on the subject, *Tibetan Thangka Painting: Methods & Materials* by David P Jackson and Janice A Jackson.

and *dungkhar* (conch shells). Secular instruments include the *dramnyen* (a six-stringed lute), *piwang* (two-stringed fiddle), *lingbu* (flute) and *gyumang* (Chinese-style zither).

Recordings

See traditional craftsmen at the Ancient Art Restoration Centre (AARC) in Lhasa, next to Dropenling. The AARC managed the restoration of the Potala, and Sera and Drepung Monasteries; craftsmen here include thangka painters, metal workers, woodcarvers and dye makers.

Most recordings of traditional Tibetan music have been made in Dharamsala or Dalhousie in India. The country's biggest musical export (or rather exile) is Yungchen Lhamo, who fled Tibet in 1989 and has since released several excellent world-music recordings. She also appeared on Natalie Merchant's *Ophelia* album. Other Tibetan singers based abroad include Dadon Dawa Dolma and Kelsang Chukie Tethong (whose release *Voice from Tara* is worth checking out).

➡ *Chö* by Choying Drolma and Steve Tibbetts (Hannibal, 1997) – a deeply beautiful and highly recommended recording of chants and songs by the Nepali-based Tibetan nun; the follow-up, *Selwa* (Six Degrees Records), is also wonderful.

➡ *Coming Home* by Yungchen Lhamo (Real World, 1998) – Tibetan world music with modern production; try also *Ama* (2006), which features a duet with Annie Lennox, or the earlier *Tibet, Tibet* if you prefer something more traditional.

➡ *Sacred Tibetan Chant* – even the monks of Sherab Ling Monastery in northern India were surprised when they won the 2003 Grammy for Best Traditional World Music Recording; the traditional chants are deep and guttural, and similar to what you'll hear in prayer halls across Tibet (Naxos, 2003).

Literature

The development of a Tibetan written script is credited to a monk by the name of Tonmi Sambhota and corresponded with the early introduction of Buddhism during the reign of King Songtsen Gampo. Before this, pre-Buddhist traditions were passed down as oral histories that told of the exploits of early kings, the spirits and the origins of the Tibetan people. Some of these oral traditions were later recorded using the Tibetan script.

Two years after killing off his main character, Arthur Conan Doyle explained the resurrection of Sherlock Holmes by saying that he had spent two years wandering in Tibet. Tibetan writer Jamyang Norbu cleverly conjectures on what Holmes may have been up to in his 2003 novel *The Mandala of Sherlock Holmes*.

But for the most part, literature in Tibet was dominated by Buddhism, first as a means of translating Buddhist scriptures from Sanskrit into Tibetan and second, as time went by, in association with the development of Tibetan Buddhist thought. There is nothing in the nature of a secular literary tradition – least of all novels – such as can be found in China or Japan.

One of the great achievements of Tibetan culture was the development of a literary language that could, with remarkable faithfulness, reproduce the concepts of Sanskrit Buddhist texts. The compilation of Tibetan-Sanskrit dictionaries in the early 9th century ensured consistency in all subsequent translations.

Through the 12th and 13th centuries, Tibetan literary endeavour was almost entirely consumed by the monumental task of translating the complete Buddhist canon into Tibetan. The result was the 108 volumes of canonical texts (Kangyur), which record the words of the Historical Buddha, Sakyamuni, and 208 volumes of commentary (Tengyur) by Indian masters that make up the basic Buddhist scriptures shared by all Tibetan religious orders. What time remained was used in the compilation of biographies and the collection of songs of revered lamas. Perhaps most famous among these is the *Hundred Thousand Songs of Milarepa*. Milarepa was an ascetic to whom many songs and poems concerning the quest for buddhahood are attributed.

Alongside Buddhist scriptures exists an ancient tradition of storytelling, usually concerning the taming of Tibet's malevolent spirits to allow the introduction of Buddhism. Many of these stories were passed from generation to generation orally, but some were recorded. Examples include the epic *Gesar of Ling* and the biography of Guru Rinpoche, whose countless tales of miracles and battles with demons are known to peoples across the entire Himalayan region. The oral poetry of the Gesar epic is particularly popular in eastern Tibet, where a tiny number of age-ing bards just keep alive a tradition that dates back to the 10th century.

Wood-block printing has been in use for centuries and is still the most common form of printing in monasteries. Blocks are carved in mirror image; printers then work in pairs putting strips of paper over the inky block and shuttling an ink roll over it. The pages of the text are kept loose, wrapped in cloth and stored along the walls of monasteries. Tibet's most famous printing presses were in Derge in modern-day Sìchuān, at Nartang Monastery and at the Potala. You can see traditional block printing at Drepung, Ganden and Sera monasteries outside Lhasa. Sakya Monastery has a particularly impressive Tibetan library.

Very little of the Tibetan literary tradition has been translated into English. Translations that may be of interest include the *Bardo Thödol*, or *Tibetan Book of the Dead*, a mysterious but fascinating account of the stages and visions that occur between death and rebirth. The book gained a certain cult status in the late 1960s thanks to the interest of such luminaries as Carl Jung and Timothy Leary.

Architecture

Most early religious architecture – the Jokhang in Lhasa for example – owed much to Pala (Indian) and especially Newari (Nepali) influences. A distinctively Tibetan style of architectural design gradually emerged, and found its expression in huge chörtens (stupas), hilltop *dzongs* (forts) and the great Gelugpa monastic complexes, as well as the lesser-known stone towers of Kongpo and the Qiang regions of western Sìchuān. The great American architect Frank Lloyd Wright is said to have had a picture of the Potala on the wall of his office.

Chörtens

Probably the most prominent Tibetan architectural motif is the chörten. Chörtens were originally built to house the cremated relics of the Histor-ical Buddha and as such have become a powerful symbol of the Buddha and his teachings. Later, chörtens also served as reliquaries for lamas and holy men and monumental versions would often encase whole mummified bodies, as is the case with the tombs of the Dalai Lamas in the Potala. The tradition is very much alive: a stunning gold reliquary chörten was constructed in 1989 at Tashilhunpo Monastery to hold the body of the 10th Panchen Lama.

In the early stages of Buddhism, images of the Buddha did not exist and chörtens served as the major symbol of the new faith. Over the next two millennia, chörtens took many different forms across the Buddhist world, from the sensuous stupas of Burma to the pagodas of China and Japan. Most elaborate of all are the *kumbums* (100,000 Buddha imag-es), of which the best remaining example in Tibet is at Gyantse. Many chörtens were built to hold ancient relics and sacred texts and have been plundered over the years by treasure seekers and vandals.

Chörtens are highly symbolic. The five levels represent the four ele-ments, plus eternal space: the square base symbolises earth, the dome is water, the spire is fire, and the top moon and sun are air and space. The 13 discs of the ceremonial umbrella can represent the branches of the tree of life or the 10 powers and three mindfulnesses of the Buddha. The top seed-shaped pinnacle symbolises enlightenment. The chörten as a whole can therefore be seen as a representation of the path to enlight-enment. The construction can also physically represent the Buddha, with the base as his seat and the dome as his body.

The Tibetan epic *Gesar of Ling* is the world's long-est epic poem, 25 times as long as *The Iliad*, and takes years to recite in full!

Tales of Tibet: Sky Burials, Prayer Wheels & Wind Horses, edited by Herbert J Batt, gathers contem-porary fiction by Tibetan and Chinese writers. The scholarly introduction explains how the nationality of the authors influences this sometimes elegiac, some-times confronting collection.

Tibet's Archi-tectural Highlights

Kumbum, Gyantse

Potala Palace, Lhasa

Tashilhunpo Mon-astery, Shigatse

Samye Monastery, Yarlung Tsangpo Valley

MONASTERY LAYOUT

Tibetan monasteries are based on a conservative design and share a remarkable continuity of layout. Many are built in spectacular high locations above villages. Most were originally surrounded by an outer wall, built to defend the treasures of the monastery from bands of brigands, Mongolian hordes or even attacks from rival monasteries. Most monasteries have a kora (pilgrimage path) around the complex, replete with holy rocks and meditation retreats high on the hillside behind. A few monasteries have a sky-burial site and most are still surrounded by ruins dating from the Cultural Revolution.

Main Buildings Inside the gates there is usually a central courtyard used for special ceremonies and festivals and a *darchen* (flag pole). Surrounding buildings usually include a *dukhang* (main assembly or prayer hall) with *gönkhang* (protector chapels) and *lhakhang* (subsidiary chapels), as well as monks' quarters, a *kangyur lhakhang* (library) and, in the case of larger monasteries, *tratsang* (colleges), *kangtsang* (halls of residence), kitchens and a *barkhang* (printing press). At the entrance to most buildings are murals of the Four Guardian Kings and perhaps a Wheel of Life or a mandala mural.

Main Prayer Hall The *dukhang* consists of rows of low seats and tables, often strewn with cloaks, hats, ritual instruments, drums and huge telescopic horns. There is a small altar with seven bowls of water, butter lamps and offerings of mandalas made from seeds. The main altar houses the most significant statues, often Sakyamuni, Jampa (Maitreya) or a trinity of the Past, Present and Future Buddhas and perhaps the founder of the monastery or past lamas. Larger monasteries contain funeral chörtens of important lamas, as well as special relics such as 'self-arising' (ie not human-made) footprints or handprints made from stone. There may be a *tsangkhang* (inner sanctum) behind the main hall, the entrance of which is flanked by protector gods, often one blue, Chana Dorje (Vajrapani) and the other red, Tamdrin (Hayagriva). There may well be an inner kora (*korlam*) of prayer wheels. Back at the entrance side stairs lead to higher floors.

Protector Chapels *Gönkhang* are dark and spooky protector chapels that hold wrathful manifestations of deities, frequently covered with a cloth because of their terrible appearance. Murals here are often traced against a black background and walls are decorated with Tantric deities, grinning skeletons or even dismembered bodies. The altars often have grain, dice or mirrors, used for divination, and the pillars are decorated with festival masks, antique weapons and sometimes stuffed snakes and wolves. Deep Tantric drumming often pulsates through the room. Women are often not allowed into protector chapels.

Roof Stairs lead up to subsidiary chapels and monk accommodation. The roof usually has excellent views as well as vases of immortality, victory banners, dragons and copper symbols of the Wheel of Law flanked by two deer, recalling the Buddha's first sermon at the deer park of Sarnath.

Houses & Homes

Typical features of Tibetan secular architecture, which are also used to a certain extent in religious architecture, are buildings with inward-sloping walls made of large, tightly fitting stones or sun-baked bricks. Below the roof is a layer of twigs, squashed tight by the roof and painted to give Tibetan houses their characteristic brown band. Roofs are flat, as there is little rain or snow, made from pounded earth and edged with walls. You may well see singing bands of men and women pounding a new roof with sticks weighted with large stones. In the larger structures wooden pillars support the roof inside. The exteriors are generally whitewashed brick, although in some areas, such as Sakya in Tsang, other colours may be used. In rural Tibet, homes are often surrounded by walled compounds, and in some areas entrances are protected by painted scorpions and swastikas.

For an in-depth look at Lhasa's traditional Tibetan architecture and interactive maps of Lhasa, check out www.tibetheritagefund.org.

Nomads, who take their homes with them, live in *bar* (yak-hair tents), which are normally roomy and can accommodate a whole family. An opening at the top of the tent lets out smoke from the fire.

Painting

As with other types of Tibetan art, painting is very symbolic and can be interpreted on many different levels. It is almost exclusively devotional in nature.

Tibetan mural painting was strongly influenced by Indian, Newari and, in the far West, Kashmiri painting styles, with later influence coming from China. Paintings usually followed stereotypical forms with a central Buddhist deity surrounded by smaller, lesser deities and emanations. The use of colour and proportion is decided purely by convention and rigid symbolism. Later came depictions of revered Tibetan lamas or Indian spiritual teachers, often surrounded by lineage lines or incidents from the lama's life.

Chinese influence began to manifest itself more frequently in Tibetan painting from around the 15th century. The freer approach of Chinese landscape painting allowed some Tibetan artists to break free from some of the more formalised aspects of Tibetan religious art and employ landscape as a decorative motif. Painting in Tibet was passed on from artisan to apprentice in much the same way that monastic communities maintained lineages of teaching.

Thangkas

Religious paintings mounted on brocade and rolled up between two sticks are called thangkas. Their eminent portability was essential in a land of nomads, as mendicant preachers and doctors often used them as a visual learning aid. Not so portable are the huge thangkas known as *gheku* or *koku*, the size of large buildings, that are unfurled every year during festivals.

The production of a thangka is an act of devotion and the process is carefully formalised. Linen (or now more commonly cotton) is stretched on a wooden frame, stiffened with glue and coated with a mix of chalk

Art of Tibet by Robert Fisher is a portable colour guide to all the arts of Tibet, from the iconography of thangkas to statuary.

TIBETAN ART PAINTING

Best Monastery Murals
....
Shalu, near Shigatse
....
Gongkar Chöde, Yarlung Valley
....
Thöling, Zanda

MANDALAS

The mandala (*kyilkhor*, literally 'circle') is more than a beautiful artistic creation, it's also a three-dimensional meditational map. What on the surface appears to be a plain two-dimensional design emerges, with the right visual approach, as a three-dimensional picture. Mandalas can take the form of paintings, patterns of sand, three-dimensional models or even whole monastic structures, as at Samye. In the case of the two-dimensional mandala, the correct visual approach can be achieved only through meditation. The painstakingly created sand mandalas also perform the duty of illustrating the impermanence of life (they are generally swept away after a few days).

A typical mandala features a central deity surrounded by four or eight other deities who are aspects of the central figure. These surrounding deities are often accompanied by a consort. There may be several circles of these deities, totalling several hundred deities. These deities and all other elements of the mandala have to be visualised as the three-dimensional world of the central deity and even as a representation of the universe.

The mandala is associated with Tantric Buddhism and is chiefly used in a ritual known as *sadhana* (means for attainment). According to this ritual, the adept meditates on, invokes and identifies with a specific deity, before dissolving into emptiness and re-emerging as the deity itself. The process, in so far as it uses the mandala as an aid, involves a remarkable feat of imaginative concentration. One ritual calls for the adept to visualise 722 deities with enough clarity to be able to see the whites of their eyes and hold this visualisation for four hours.

and lime called *gesso*. Iconography is bound by strict mathematical measurements. A grid is drawn onto the thangka before outlines are sketched in charcoal, starting with the main central deity and moving outwards.

Colours are added one at a time, starting with the background and ending with shading. Pigments were traditionally natural: blue from lapis, red from cinnabar and yellow from sulphur. Most thangkas are burnished with at least a little gold. The last part of the thangka to be painted is the eyes, which are filled in during a special 'opening the eyes' ceremony. Finally a brocade backing of three colours and a protective 'curtain' are added, the latter to protect the thangka.

Lhasa's old town is stuffed with traditional workshops. Dropenling runs a two-hour walking tour of several old town artisans.

Statuary & Sculpture

Tibetan statuary, like Tibetan painting, is almost exclusively religious in nature. Ranging in height from several centimetres to several metres, statues usually depict deities and revered lamas. Most of the smaller statues are hollow and are stuffed with paper texts, prayers, amulets and juniper when consecrated. Very few clay or metal sculptures remaining in Tibet date from before 1959.

Metal statues are traditionally sculpted in wax and then covered in clay. When the clay is dry it is heated. The wax melts and is removed, leaving a mould that can be filled with molten metal. Statues are generally then gilded and painted.

Sculptures are most commonly made from bronze or stucco mixed with straw, but can even be made out of butter and tsampa, mounted on a wooden frame.

Handicrafts

A burgeoning economy in Lhasa has fuelled a real growth in traditional crafts in recent years, though these are partially for the Chinese tourist market.

Tibet has a 1000-year history of carpet making; the carpets are mostly used as seat covers, bed covers and saddle blankets. Knots are double tied (the best carpets have 100 knots per square inch), which results in a particularly thick pile. Tibet's secret carpet ingredient is its particularly high-quality sheep wool, which is hand spun and coloured with natural dyes such as indigo, walnut, madder and rhubarb. Tibetan cashmere goat's wool and antelope wool are also in great demand. Gyantse and Shigatse were the traditional centres of carpet production, although the modern industry is based almost exclusively in Tibetan exile communities in Nepal.

To see a selection of Tibetan carpets visit the Gang Gyen Carpet Factory in Shigatse or check out the Wangden-style carpets at Dropenling.

Inlaid handicrafts are common, particularly in the form of prayer wheels, daggers, butter lamps and bowls, although most of what you see these days in Lhasa is made by Tibetan communities in Nepal. Nomads in particular wear stunning silver jewellery; you may also see silver flints, horse tack, amulets known as *gau*, and ornate chopstick and knife sets.

Tibetan singing bowls, made from a secret mix of seven different metals, are a meditation device that originated from pre-Buddhist Bön practices. The bowls produce a 'disassociated' mystic hum when a playing stick is rotated around the outer edge of the bowl.

Woodcarving is another valued handicraft, used in the production of brightly coloured Tibetan furniture and window panels, not to mention wood-print blocks.

The Future of Tibet

China is playing the long game in Tibet. It is betting that over time economic advancement will win over Tibetan hearts and minds and compensate for the lack of religious and political freedoms; it's certainly a payoff that seems to be working in the rest of China. As Tibetans struggle with the perceived lack of control over their land, religion and resources, many reply that they are not so easily bought. Alienation and tension looks set to remain high on the plateau.

Full Speed Ahead

As ground is broken on airports and a new series of rail links, China's future policy in Tibet is clear: invest billions on massive economic development to improve the lives of hundreds of thousands of Tibetans.

Unfortunately, the modernisation is squarely on China's terms. Questions over the suitability and sustainability of hydroelectric projects, mining and mass tourism look set to dominate the next decade, as environmental problems intensify alongside exploitation. Moreover, with a transient migrant Chinese population spearheading the economic growth, the bulk of the profits from mining, tourism and other industries in Tibet are flowing straight out of the plateau back into China. It's a bittersweet boom that looks set only to accelerate.

> Encouragingly, Tibet is now seriously cool among Chinese backpackers from Běijīng to Guǎngzhōu, many of whom are as enamoured with Tibet as their Western counterparts.

The International Area

The more things change in Tibet, the more they stay the same outside. Talks between the Chinese and the Dharamsala-based Tibetan government in exile remain stalled, with the Chinese taking every opportunity to denounce the Nobel Peace Prize–winning Dalai Lama for being a 'wolf in sheep's clothing' or trying to 'split the motherland'. The Dalai Lama himself has abandoned any hope of nationhood, opting to push for cultural, religious and linguistic autonomy within the Chinese state, yet even this 'middle path' of conciliation has yielded nothing. Fearful of upsetting their trade balance with China, foreign governments will continue to be careful not to receive the Dalai Lama in any way that recognises his political status as the head of an exiled government.

In an age of terrorism and rising religious extremism it is perhaps surprising how little attention the Dalai Lama's remarkable insistence on non-violence gets from the world community. As years pass with no discernable progress, tensions inside the Tibetan community are becoming apparent, with younger Tibetans increasingly pushing for direct, perhaps even violent, action.

> 'The empire long divided, must unite; long united it must divide. Thus has it ever been.' *Romance of the Three Kingdoms*, 14th century

For its part China seems incapable of seeing Tibetan dissent in any terms other than 'separatism' and 'splittism'. The fear in Běijīng is that continued unrest or concessions made to the Tibetans will cause a domino effect with other restive nationalities like the Uighurs of Xīnjiāng, a stand largely backed by an increasingly nationalist Chinese public. Until that changes, a political settlement will remain elusive. The political reality is that Tibet is firmly a part of China. No one expects that to change any time soon.

As modern Tibet teeters on the edge of losing its cultural identity, some observers look to the cyclical nature of Chinese history. Over the centuries China has grown, cracked and collapsed. If that happens again, or if fundamental changes occur in Chinese domestic politics, Tibet may perhaps once again have a say in its own affairs.

The Politics of Reincarnation

In 2014 the Dharamsala-backed 11th Panchen Lama turned 25 in his 19th year of house arrest.

Only in Tibet could the 13th-century practice of reincarnation become a 21st-century political hot potato. Recent disputes between Dharamsala and Běijīng over the selection of various lamas, most notably the Panchen Lama, have spotlighted how religious decisions are becoming increasingly politicised, a trend that will doubtless only intensify as the Dalai Lama heads into his 80s.

Both sides have their eyes firmly on the future here, for it is the Panchen Lama who traditionally assists in choosing the next Dalai Lama. The Chinese government knows that the struggle to control future reincarnations is fundamental to controlling Tibet; the rather bizarre result being that the avowedly atheist Chinese Communist Party is now in charge of choosing incarnate lamas for a religion it doesn't believe in. For his part, the Dalai Lama has made it clear that he will only be reborn in Tibet if he is allowed to return there as part of a political settlement.

The spectre of the death of the Dalai Lama haunts the entire Tibetan world. More than just 'a simple monk' or even a god-king, the Dalai Lama has become a shining symbol of Tibetan identity. When he dies, Tibet will have lost something essential to its modern identity. Some commentators even believe that the death of the Dalai Lama may herald the death of the Tibetan cause, one reason why both sides are laying the ground for future rebirth.

Cultural Survival

Tragedy in Crimson: How the Dalai Lama Conquered the World but Lost the Battle with China, by former Běijīng-based journalist Tim Johnson, examines the current state of Tibet, its political status and possible future.

The greatest threat to Tibetan cultural life comes from indiscriminate economic change and Chinese migration, as government subsidies and huge infrastructure projects change the face and ethnic make-up of cities across the breadth of Tibet. As Tibetan culture becomes diluted, there is a fear that Tibetans will become a minority in their own country, a situation the Dalai Lama has described as 'cultural genocide'. Tibetans point to Amdo in Qīnghǎi, once a Tibetan-dominated area that now has three Han Chinese to every Tibetan.

Education is another sore point that has long-term cultural consequences. An education system that exclusively uses the (Mandarin) Chinese language reinforces the fact that only Sinicised Tibetans are able to actively participate in Tibet's economic advances. Parents face the unenviable balancing act of preserving Tibetan language and tradition (often sending their children to Dharamsala for a Tibetan education), while preparing the coming generation for the realities of life in a Chinese-language-dominated economy.

And yet for all the new supermarkets, karaoke joints, brothels and mobile phones, Tibet's traditional and religious values remain at the core of most Tibetans' identities, and the quintessence of rural Tibet remains remarkably intact. Some 50 years of political indoctrination and religious control has failed to dull the devotion of most Tibetans to either Buddhism or the Dalai Lama and there's little sign of this changing.

It's hard to separate myth from reality in Tibet. The half-truths and propaganda from all sides can be so enticing, so pervasive and so entrenched that it's hard to see the place through balanced eyes. The reality is that Tibet is no fragile Shangri-la but a resilient land underpinned by a unique culture and a deep faith, and it is perhaps this above all that offers Tibet's best hope for its future.

Survival Guide

Directory A–Z

Accommodation

Most towns in Tibet offer a decent range of hotels, many with hot showers and some three- or four-star options. In smaller towns you may be limited to rooms with a shared bathroom, while in the countryside electricity and running water are luxuries that cannot be relied on. Hotels are divided into *bīnguǎn* (宾馆), *fàndiàn* (饭店) or *dàjiǔdiàn* (大酒店; hotels), *zhāodàisuǒ* (招待所; guesthouses) and *lǚguǎn* (旅馆; simple hostels). The Tibetan terms are *drukhang* (hotel) and *dronkhang* (guesthouse).

Budget accommodation generally means a room without a bathroom or, at the top end of the scale, a simple room with a hot-water bathroom. Lhasa in particular has many budget guesthouses and youth hostels. Midrange hotels generally have rooms with a private bathroom and hot-water showers, at least for part of the day. Top-end hotels are limited to the main cities and Lhasa now boasts several luxury and boutique hotels.

Hot water is provided everywhere in thermoses and even in the simplest places a basin and drum of cold water is usually provided for washing. Bedding is provided, but in the cheapest places it's often not that clean and a sleeping bag is a nice luxury.

In some towns (such as Tsetang, Ali and Purang), and in most of Eastern Tibet, the local Public Security Bureau (PSB) keeps a frustratingly tight lid on which places can and cannot accept foreigners, and budget hotels are often not permitted to accept foreigners.

Groups are sometimes expected to share rooms at remote truck-stop places, since many only have four- or five-bed rooms. If you want your own room, you may be able to either pay for only the number of beds you require, or for all the beds in a room.

Midrange and top-end hotels in Lhasa are more expensive than elsewhere, though standards are higher. You can sometimes get good deals on midrange and top-end hotels in China at booking sites such as **Ctrip** (www.english. ctrip.com) and **Elong** (www. elong.com), though many of the Lhasa hotels listed on these sites are dull Chinese places in poor locations. You can also ask your tour agency to book for you as they are often able to get deals on the type of hotels and guesthouses foreign travellers like to stay in.

Camping

Camping out is well understood by Tibetans, many of whom still spend their summers herding livestock in mountain valleys. Always ask permission if camping near a settlement or encampment, watch out for the dogs and expect an audience.

Guesthouses & Hotels

Lhasa is full of clean, well-run Tibetan-style guesthouses and hostels, many of which are aimed at Chinese backpackers. Similar set-ups can be found in Shigatse, Sakya and Tingri.

Monasteries such as Samye, Ganden, Drigung Til, Dorje Drak, Mindroling, Tidrum and Reting have their own pilgrim guesthouses – normally a bank of carpeted seats that double as beds –

SLEEPING PRICE RANGES

The following price ranges refer to a standard double room before discounts. Unless otherwise stated, breakfast is not included.

$ less than ¥200

$$ ¥200 to ¥400

$$$ more than ¥400

and a night here can be a magical experience. Your guide may be reluctant for you to overnight at a monastery guesthouse, however.

Most of the larger hotels are anonymous Chinese-style places that share several traits: the plumbing is often dodgy, the toilets stinky, the carpets dotted with a mosaic of cigarette burns and the light bulbs too dim to read by. The one thing that will always work is the TV.

Rooms are generally divided into *biāozhǔn* (标准; standard), which come with a bathroom, and *pǔtōng* (普通; ordinary), which don't. Standard rooms are often divided into *jīngjì* (经济; economy) and *háohuá* (豪华; deluxe) rooms. Both standard and ordinary rooms can be either twins (two beds) or doubles (one large bed), though twins are far more common. Sometimes each twin bed is large enough for two (so couples don't always have to search for a double room), but in a triple room the beds are always just large enough for a single person.

Some hotels (generally the cheaper ones) also price their *pǔtōng* accommodation per bed rather than per room, which can work out well for solo travellers. To guarantee that you have the room to yourself, you would theoretically have to pay for all beds (and a few hotel owners will try to force you to do so), but usually that's not necessary.

Single rooms are normally the same price (or even more expensive!) as a double room. Where they are cheaper they are generally much smaller than a twin/double. Twins and doubles are usually priced the same.

Activities

Tibet offers the type of topography to delight horse riders, mountaineers, white-water rafters and others, though the problem, as always, is the confusing travel permit system, which many authorities manipulate to their own financial advantage.

Cycling

Tibet offers some of the most extreme and exhilarating mountain biking in the world. Unfortunately the current permit system means that independent tours on bikes are effectively impossible, or at least much more expensive than a few years ago, since cyclists require a guide and vehicle support like everyone else.

If things change and if you are fit and well equipped, it's possible to visit most places in this guide by bike, although the most popular route is the paved roller-coaster ride along the Friendship Hwy from Lhasa down to Kathmandu. Mountain bikes can be hired in Lhasa for short trips around the city and surrounding valley.

For a double shot of inspiration, check out the home page of Martin Adserballe (www.adserballe.com).

US-based **Bike China** (☑1-800-818 1778; www.bike-china.com) is a good resource and offers organised supported bike rides including tours from Golmud (in Qīnghǎi) to Lhasa.

Horse Riding

There's something romantic about travelling across Tibet on horseback. The easiest place to arrange this is in the Kham region of western Sìchuān, where it's just a matter of coming to an agreement with local herdsmen. A kora (ritual circumambulation circuit) of Lake Manasarovar on horseback is a great idea and a few travellers have managed to arrange this. You may also be able to arrange day horse rental in villages in eastern Tibet.

Tibet Wind Horse Adventure (☑0891 683 3009; www.windhorsetibet.com; B32 Shenzheng Huayuan, Sera Beilu) offers one- and two-day trips on horseback in the Dechen Valley near Lhasa and can customise longer adventures.

Mountaineering

There are some huge peaks in Tibet, including the 8000m-plus giants of Cho Oyu, Shishapangma and, of course, Everest, which are enough to send a quiver of excitement through vertically inclined explorers. Unfortunately, the Chinese government charges exorbitant fees for mountaineering permits, which puts mountaineering in

Tibet out of the range of most individuals or groups devoid of commercial sponsorship.

Foreign travel companies, such as **Alpine Ascents** (www.alpineascents.com) and **Jagged Globe** (www.jagged-globe.co.uk) can arrange mountaineering trips in Tibet.

Rafting

Tibet Wind Horse Adventure (☏0891 683 3009; www.windhorsetibet.com; B32 Shenzheng Huayuan, Sera Beilu) offers rafting trips between June and October, either a half-day on the Tolung-chu, one or two days on the Drigung-chu or ambitious four- to 21-day trips on the Reting Tsangpo. Prices depend on group size.

Bathhouses

Cheap hotels often don't have hot showers, but staff can normally direct you to a simple bathhouse (淋浴; línyù; sugpo truya in Tibetan), where you can get a hot shower for ¥10 to ¥20. These are purely functional places, and sometimes a bit grotty, but after a few days on the road you'll be glad for the chance to wash. Bring your own towel and flip-flops.

Children

Children can be a great ice-breaker in Tibet and generally generate a lot of interest.

Many hotels offer family rooms, which normally have three or four beds arranged in two connected rooms. On the down side, children don't get on with Tibetan food or toilets any better than grown-ups. They also tire more easily from an endless round of visiting monasteries. Bring along a copy of Tintin in Tibet for when morale flags. In Kathmandu several bookshops sell Tibetan thangka (religious paintings) and mandala colouring books. Children under 1.5m (5ft) or under a certain age (the definition depends on the site) get in free at most sights in Tibet.

Tibet is probably not a great place to bring a very small child. You should bring all supplies (including nappies and medicines) with you. Small spoons can be useful as most places have only chopsticks. There's plenty of boiling water to sterilise bottles etc. It's possible to make a cot from the copious numbers of duvets

supplied with most hotel rooms.

Be especially careful with children and altitude sickness, as they won't be on the lookout for signs.

Customs Regulations

➡ Chinese border crossings have gone from being severely traumatic to exceedingly easy for travellers. You are unlikely to even be checked when flying in or out of the country.

➡ You can legally bring in or take out ¥20,000 in Chinese currency and must declare any cash amount exceeding US$5000 or its equivalent.

➡ It is illegal to import any printed material, film, tapes etc 'detrimental to China's politics, economy, culture and ethics'. This is a particularly sensitive subject in Tibet, but even here it is highly unusual to have Chinese customs officials grilling travellers about their reading matter. Maps and political books printed in Dharamsala, India, could cause a problem.

➡ It is currently illegal to bring into China pictures, books, videos or speeches of or by the Dalai Lama. Moreover, you may be placing the recipient of these in danger of a fine or jail sentence from the Chinese authorities. Images of the Tibetan national flag are even 'more' illegal.

Climate

Lhasa

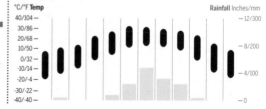

→ If travelling from Nepal to Tibet by air or overland it's a good idea to bury this guide deep in your pack or sleeping bag (and have a backup on your laptop or mobile phone), as overzealous customs officials have been known to confiscate Lonely Planet *Tibet* guides.

→ Be very circumspect if you are asked to take any packages, letters or photos out of Tibet for anyone else, including monks. If caught, you'll most likely be detained, interrogated and then probably expelled.

→ Anything made in China before 1949 is considered an antique and needs a certificate to take it out of the country. If it was made before 1795, it cannot legally be taken out of the country.

Electricity

→ Electricity is 220V, 50 cycles AC. Note that electronics such as laptops and iPods (anything with a hard drive) are often affected by altitudes above 4500m and may stop working.

→ There are at least five plug designs: three-pronged angled pins (like in Australia);

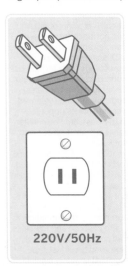

220V/50Hz

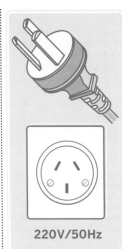

220V/50Hz

three-pronged round pins (like in Hong Kong); two flat pins (US style but without the ground wire); two narrow round pins (European style); and three rectangular pins (British style).

Embassies & Consulates

For Chinese embassies abroad, consult the Chinese Foreign Ministry website at www.fmprc.gov.cn.

Consulates in Tibet

The only diplomatic representation in Tibet is the **Nepali Consulate-General** (尼泊尔领事馆, Níbó'ěr Lǐngshìguǎn; Map p44; ☑0891 681 3965; www.nepalembassy.org.cn; 13 Luobulingka Beilu; ☉10am-noon Mon-Fri) in Lhasa. Visas are issued the next day at 4.30pm, though you can sometimes get your passport back the same day. It's located on a side street between the Lhasa Hotel and the Norbulingka.

Visa fees change frequently, but at the time of research 15-/30-/90-day multiple entry visas cost ¥175/280/700. All visas are valid for six months from the

date of issue. Bring one visa photo.

It should also be possible to obtain the same Nepali visas at Kodari, the Nepali border town, although it would be sensible to check first that this has not changed.

Consulates in Chéngdū

French Consulate (☑028-6666 6060; 30th fl, Times Plaza, 2 Zongfu Lu)

US Consulate (Map p242; ☑028-8558 3992; 4 Lingshiguan Lu)

Embassies in Běijīng

In case of emergency in Tibet, your nearest embassy is most likely in Běijīng:

Australian Embassy (☑010-5140 4111; www.china.embassy.gov.au)

Canadian Embassy (☑010-5139 4000; www.canadaint-ernational.gc.ca/china-chine/offices-bureaux/index.aspx?lang=eng)

French Embassy (☑010-8531 2000; www.amba-france-cn.org)

German Embassy (☑8532 9000; www.china.diplo.de)

Irish Embassy (☑010-6531 6200; www.embassyofireland.cn)

Netherlands Embassy (☑010-8532 0200; http://china.nlambassade.org/organization/peking)

New Zealand Embassy (☑010-8531 2700; www.nzembassy.com/china)

UK Embassy (☑010-5192 4000; www.ukinchina.fco.gov.uk)

US Embassy (☑010-8531-3000; http://beijing.usembassy-china.org.cn)

Food & Drink

Though you won't starve, food will probably not be a highlight of your trip to Tibet. A few restaurants in Lhasa and some guesthouses in the countryside have begun to elevate a subsistence diet into the beginnings of a

EATING PRICE RANGES

The following price ranges refer to a standard dish in Chinese restaurants or main course in Western restaurants. There are no additional taxes though some higher-end places may add a service charge.

$ less than ¥30

$$ ¥30 to ¥80

$$$ more than ¥80

cuisine, but Tibetan food is usually more about survival than pleasure. On the plus side, fresh vegetables and packaged goods are now widely available and you are never far away from a good Chinese *fànguǎn* (饭馆) or *cāntīng* (餐厅) restaurant. In eastern Tibet look for the local chilli (made into a paste and served on bread) and free-range pig.

Staples & Specialities

TIBETAN

The basic Tibetan meal is a kind of dough made with tsampa (roasted-barley flour) and yak butter mixed with something wet – water, tea or beer. Tibetans skilfully knead and mix the paste by hand into dough-like balls, which is not as easy as it looks! Tsampa with milk powder and sugar makes a pretty good porridge and is a fine trekking staple, but only a Tibetan can eat it every day and still look forward to the next meal.

Some common Tibetan dishes include *momos* and *thugpa*. *Momos* are small dumplings filled with meat or vegetables or both. They are normally steamed but can be fried and are pretty good. More common is *thugpa*, a noodle soup with meat or vegetables or both. Variations on the theme include *hipthuk* (squares of noodles and yak meat in a soup) and *thenthuk* (more noodles). Glass noodles known as *phing* are also sometimes used.

The other main option is *shemdre* (sometimes called curried beef), a stew of potatoes and yak meat on a bed of rice. In smarter restaurants in Lhasa or Shigatse you can try dishes such as *damje* or *shomday* (butter fried rice with raisins and yoghurt), *droma desi* (wild ginseng with raisins, sugar, butter and rice) and *shya vale* (fried pancake-style pasties with a yak-meat filling). Formal Tibetan restaurants (*sakhang* in Tibetan) in particular are very big on yak offal, with large sections of menus sumptuously detailing the various ways of serving up yak tongues, stomachs and lungs.

In rural areas and markets you might see strings of little white lumps drying in the sun that even the flies leave alone – this is dried yak cheese and it's eaten like a boiled sweet. For the first half-hour it is like having a small rock in your mouth, but eventually it starts to soften up and taste like old, dried yak cheese.

Also popular among nomads is *yak sha* (dried yak jerky). It is normally cut into strips and left to dry on tent lines and is pretty chewy stuff.

See also the Eating Tibetan box on p343.

CHINESE

Chinese restaurants can be found in every settlement in Tibet these days, but are around 50% more expensive than elsewhere in China.

Chinese food in Tibet is almost exclusively Sichuanese,

the spiciest of China's regional cuisines. One popular Sichuanese sauce is *yúxiāng* (鱼香), a spicy, piquant sauce of garlic, vinegar and chilli that is supposed to resemble the taste of fish (though it's more like a sweet and tangy marinade). You'll also taste *huājiāo* (花椒; Sichuan pepper), a curious mouth-numbing spice popular in Sichuanese food.

Outside of Lhasa, few Chinese restaurants have menus in English and when they do the prices are often marked up by as much as 50%. We indicate restaurants with English menus by the icon 🅼. In most restaurants you can simply wander out into the kitchen and point to the vegetables and meats you want fried up, but you'll miss out on many of the most interesting sauces and styles this way.

Chinese snacks are excellent and make for a fine light meal. The most common are *shuǐjiǎo* (ravioli-like dumplings), ordered by the bowl or weight (half a *jin*, or 250g, is enough for one person), and *bāozi* (thicker steamed dumplings), which are similar to *momos* and are normally ordered by the steamer, and are a common breakfast food. Both are dipped in soy sauce, vinegar or chilli (or a mix of all). You can normally get a bowl of noodles anywhere for around ¥10; *shāguō mǐxiàn* is a particularly tasty form of rice noodles cooked in a clay pot. *Chǎomiàn* (fried noodles) and *dàn chǎofàn* (egg fried rice) are not as popular as in the West, but you can get them in many Chinese and backpacker restaurants.

You can get decent breakfasts of yoghurt, muesli and toast at backpacker hotels in Lhasa, Gyantse and Shigatse, but elsewhere you are more likely to find Chinese-style dumplings, fried bread sticks (油条; *yóutiáo*) and tasteless rice porridge (稀饭; *xīfàn*). One good breakfast-type food that is widely available is scrambled eggs and tomato (*fānqié chǎodàn*).

See the Chinese Menu Reader on p342 for more details.

MUSLIM

The Muslim restaurants found in almost all urban centres in Tibet are an interesting alternative to Chinese or Tibetan food. They are normally recognisable by a green flag hanging outside or Arabic script on the restaurant sign. Most chefs come from the Línxià area of Gānsù. The food is based on noodles, and, of course, there's no pork.

Dishes worth trying include *gānbànmiàn,* a kind of stir-fried spaghetti bolognaise made with beef (or yak) and sometimes green peppers; and *chǎomiànpiàn,* fried noodle squares with meat and vegetables. *Xīnjiāng bànmiàn* (Xīnjiāng noodles) are similar, but the sauce comes in a separate bowl, to be poured over the noodles. It's fun to go into the kitchen and see your noodles being handmade on the spot.

Muslim restaurants also offer good breads and excellent *bā bǎo chá* (eight treasure tea), which is made with dried raisins, plums and rock sugar, and only releases its true flavour after several cups.

SELF-CATERING

There will likely be a time somewhere on your trip when you'll need to be self-sufficient, whether you're staying overnight at a monastery or are caught between towns on an overland trip. Unless you have a stove, your main saviour will be instant noodles. Vegetables such as onions, carrots and bok choy (even seaweed and pickled vegetables) can save even the cheapest pack of noodles from culinary oblivion, as can a packet of mixed spices brought from home.

It's a good idea to stock up on instant coffee (or ground coffee and a French press), tea, oats, hot chocolate and dried soups, as flasks of boiling water are offered in every hotel and restaurant.

Drinks

NONALCOHOLIC DRINKS

The local beverage that every traveller ends up trying at least once is yak-butter tea. Modern Tibetans these days use an electric blender to mix their yak-butter tea.

The more palatable alternative to yak-butter tea is sweet, milky tea, or *cha ngamo*. It is similar to the tea drunk in neighbouring Nepal or Pakistan. Soft drinks and mineral water are available everywhere.

ALCOHOLIC DRINKS

The Tibetan brew is known as *chang* (青稞酒; *qīngkèjiǔ* in Chinese), a fermented barley beer. It has a rich, fruity taste and ranges from disgusting to pretty good.

True connoisseurs serve it out of a jerry can. Those trekking in the Everest region should try the local variety (similar to Nepali *tongba*), which is served in a big pot. Hot water is poured into the fermenting barley and the liquid is drunk through a wooden straw – it is very good. Sharing *chang* is a good way to get to know local people, if drunk in small quantities. On our research trips we have never suffered any adverse effects from drinking copious amounts of *chang*. However, you should be aware that it is often made with contaminated water, and there is always some risk in drinking it.

The main brand of local beer is Lhasa Beer, now brewed in Lhasa in a joint venture with Carlsberg at the world's highest brewery.

Supermarkets in Lhasa stock several types of (usually awful) Chinese red

---

YAK-BUTTER TEA

Bö cha, literally 'Tibetan tea', is unlikely to be a highlight of your trip to Tibet. Made from yak butter mixed with salt, milk, soda, tea leaves and hot water all churned up in a wooden tube, the soupy mixture has more the consistency of bouillon than of tea (one traveller described it as 'a cross between brewed old socks and sump oil'). When mixed with tsampa (roasted barley flour) and yak butter it becomes the staple meal of most Tibetans, and you may well be offered it at monasteries, people's houses and even while waiting for a bus by the side of the road.

At most restaurants you mercifully have the option of drinking *cha ngamo* (sweet, milky tea), but there will be times when you just have to be polite and down a cupful of *bö cha* (without gagging). Most nomads think nothing of drinking up to 40 cups of the stuff a day. On the plus side it does replenish your body's lost salts and prevents your lips from cracking. As one reader told us, 'Personally we like yak-butter tea, not so much for the taste as the view'.

Most distressing for those not sold on the delights of yak-butter tea is the fact that your cup will be refilled every time you take even the smallest sip, as a mark of the host's respect. There's a pragmatic reason for this as well; there's only one thing worse than hot yak-butter tea – cold yak-butter tea.

DHARMA FOOD

Need to cook dinner for a visiting *rinpoche*? Try *Tibetan Cooking: Recipes for Daily Living, Celebration, and Ceremony* by Elizabeth Kelly or *The Lhasa Moon Tibetan Cookbook* by Tsering Wangmo. Both books offer recipes for everything from *momos* (dumplings) to Milarepa-style nettle soup.

wine, including Shangri-La, produced in the Tibetan areas of northeast Yúnnán using methods handed down by French missionaries at the beginning of the 19th century.

Gay & Lesbian Travellers

Homosexuality has historical precedents in Tibet, especially in Tibetan monasteries, where a male lover was known as *trap'i kedmen*, or 'monk's wife'. The Dalai Lama has sent mixed signals about homosexuality, describing gay sex as 'sexual misconduct', 'improper' and 'inappropriate', but also by saying, 'There are no acts of love between adults that one can or should condemn'.

The official attitude to gays and lesbians in China is also ambiguous, with responses ranging from draconian penalties to tacit acceptance. Travellers are advised to act with discretion. Chinese men routinely hold hands and drape their arms around each other without anyone inferring any sexual overtones.

Hanns Ebensten Travel
(☎800-825 9766; www.hetravel.com) This US-based company has organised gay and lesbian group trips to Tibet in the past.

Out Adventures (☎866-360 1152; www.out-adventures.com) A Canada-based company that can organise tailor-made tours to Tibet.

Utopia (www.utopia-asia.com/tipschin.htm) Has a good website and publishes a guide to gay travel in China, though with little specific to Tibet.

Insurance

Travel insurance is particularly recommended in a remote and wild region like Tibet. Make sure that the policy covers ambulances or an emergency flight home, which is essential in the case of altitude sickness. Some policies specifically exclude 'dangerous activities' such as rafting and even trekking.

You may prefer a policy that pays doctors or hospitals directly rather than you having to pay on the spot and claim later. If you have to claim later, make sure you keep all documentation. Some policies ask you to call to a centre in your home country where an immediate assessment of your problem is made. Note that reverse charge (collect) calls are not possible in Tibet.

It is very useful to have trip and flight cancellation insurance if you are heading to western or eastern Tibet as these regions are frequently closed with little to no warning. The announcement for opening is made in March or April each year but some years the region closes again suddenly after a brief opening, or opens later in the season after a prolonged closure.

Worldwide travel insurance is available at www.lonelyplanet.com/travel-insurance. You can buy, extend and claim online any time – even if you're already on the road.

Internet Access

Internet cafes (网吧; *wǎngbā* in Chinese) are in almost every town in Tibet, but few allow foreigners to use the computers so we generally do not mention them in the guide.

Some social networking sites (such as YouTube and Blogspot) and websites (eg those of the Dalai Lama) have been blacklisted by the Chinese government and are unavailable inside China unless you use a VPN (virtual private network), which is essentially an easy-to-use piece of software for a laptop computer or an app for a smart phone. Gmail and Google searches can also be spotty but again usually work well with a VPN.

Many hotels and restaurants now offer free wi-fi access (无线网; *wúxiàn wǎng*). Sometimes hotels will only offer it in the lobby. Connecting to the internet through a smart phone's 3G service is often more reliable.

In this guide 🛜 means that a hotel or cafe provides either wi-fi or a LAN cable in the room (normally free), and @ means that an internet-connected computer is available for guests (normally for a fee).

Language Courses

It is possible to enrol in a Tibetan-language course at Lhasa's Tibet University. There are two semesters a year, but international students can only begin studies in autumn and must register by 31 March. Beginner up to advanced level language classes are available as well as cultural classes on such topics as calligraphy, history, and painting. For an application form contact the **Foreign Affairs Office** (☎0891-634 3254; www.utibet.edu.cn; Tibet University, Lhasa 850000, Tibetan Autonomous Region).

Once you are accepted, the university will help arrange a student ('X') visa and, after three months, residency status in Lhasa. Students have to stay in campus accommodation. It should also be possible to hire a private tutor from the university.

Many travellers find it more convenient to study at Dharamsala or Kathmandu, although students say that the mix of dialects and high levels of English make them less effective places to study. Courses offered there include Tibetan Buddhist philosophy, Tibetan language and Tibetan performing arts.

Many universities in the West also have Tibetan language courses and it's also possible to take classes just about anywhere with a private teacher via Skype.

Legal Matters

Most crimes arle handled administratively by the Public Security Bureau (PSB; 公安局; Gōng'ānjú), which acts as police, judge and executioner.

China takes a particularly dim view of opium and all its derivatives. Foreigners have been executed for drug offences (trafficking in more than 50g of heroin can result in the death penalty). It's difficult to say what attitude the Chinese police will take towards foreigners caught using marijuana – they often don't care what foreigners do if it's not political, and if Chinese or Tibetans aren't involved. Then again the Chinese are fond of making examples of wrongdoings and you don't want to be the example. If arrested you should immediately contact your nearest embassy, which is probably in Běijīng.

In general, as you must travel throughout Tibet with guides, refrain from doing anything that would get them in trouble, such as visiting monasteries alone in Lhasa, photographing riot police or military installa-

tions, talking politics openly or even visiting private Tibetan homes without special permission.

Public Security Bureau (PSB)

The PSB is the name given to China's police, both uniformed and plain clothed. The foreign affairs branch of the PSB deals with foreigners. This branch (also known as the 'entry-exit branch') is responsible for issuing visa extensions and Alien Travel Permits.

In Tibet it is fairly unusual for foreigners to have problems with the PSB, though making an obvious display of pro-Tibetan political sympathies is guaranteed to lead to problems. Photographing Tibetan protests or military sites will lead to the confiscation of your camera or memory card and possibly a brief detention.

Attempting to travel into, through or out of Tibet without a travel permit is likely to end in an encounter somewhere en route, most likely when checking into a hotel in a closed area, or trying to board public transport at the bus station. If you are caught in a closed area without a permit, you face a fine. Make sure you are friendly and repentant: the only times things get nasty is if you (or the police) lose your cool. Get a receipt to make sure you don't get fined a second time during your return to where you came from.

If you do have a serious run-in with the PSB, you may have to write a confession of guilt. In the most serious cases, you can be expelled from China (at your own expense).

Maps

Good mapping for Tibet is not easy to come by, especially inside China, so stock up on maps before you leave. Good online map shops include Stanfords (www.stanfords.co.uk), Map Shop (www.

themapshop.co.uk) and Map Link (www.maplink.com).

For information on trekking-specific maps, see p208.

Maps of Tibet

Chinese provincial atlases to Tibet are available in bookshops throughout China. They show the most detail, but are of little use if you or the person you are asking doesn't read Chinese characters. Most locals know place names in Tibetan only, not Chinese.

Road maps available in Kathmandu include *Tibet – South-Central* by Nepa Maps, *Latest Map of Kathmandu to Tibet* by Mandala Maps, the *Namaste Trekking Map* and *Lhasa to Kathmandu,* which is a mountain-biking map, by Himalayan Map House. They are marginally better than Chinese-produced maps, but still aren't up to scratch.

Amnye Machen Institute in Dharamsala (www.amnyemachen.org) The *Tibet and Adjacent Areas under Chinese Communist Occupation* is an unusual map that covers the entire Tibetan world. It uses traditional Tibetan place names, which not everyone in Tibet (certainly not the many Chinese immigrants) will know.

Gecko Maps (www.geckomaps.com, in German; formerly Karto Atelier) Produces an excellent general *Himalaya-Tibet* map, as well as trekking and panoramic maps of Mt Kailash. Also has a 1:50,000 *Kailash Tibet* map and a 1:600,000 *East Tibet* map covering Lhasa to Chéngdū. Website is in German but English maps are available from outlets such as Amazon.com.

Google Earth (www.google.com/earth) Offers fascinating detail on Tibet, including many monasteries and several treks. However, road names and even town names are often incorrect.

ITMB (www.itmb.com) Publishes a good and (usefully) waterproof *Tibet* map (1:1,850,000; 2006).

Reise Know-How (www.reise-know-how.de, in German) Perhaps the best overview is this 1:1,500,000 scale *Tibet* map. Website is in German so order from Amazon.com.

TerraQuest (www.terraquest.eu/en/Maps) TerraQuest do a useful laminated 1:400,000 *Tibet* map, with inserts covering the Friendship Hwy, Nam-tso and Central Tibet.

Tibet Map Institute (www.tibetmap.com) Try this website for detailed and downloadable online maps of Tibet.

Maps of Lhasa

Gecko Maps produces *The Lhasa Map*. The map has architectural detail of the old town, which helps identify which buildings are genuinely old and which are merely facades, but it's getting a bit dated. More offbeat, and also dated these days (published in 1995), is the Amnye Machen Institute *Lhasa City* (1:12,500).

On This Spot – Lhasa, published by the **International Campaign for Tibet** (ICT; www.savetibet.org) in 2001, is a unique political map of the Lhasa region, pinpointing the locations of prisons, demonstrations, human-rights abuses and more. It's a really fascinating read, but it's too politically subversive to take into Tibet.

Money

The Chinese currency is known as Renminbi (RMB) or 'people's money'. The basic unit of this currency is the yuán, and is designated by a '¥'. In spoken Chinese, the word 'kuài' is almost always substituted for the yuán. Ten jiǎo (commonly known as máo) make up one yuán.

A reserve of travellers cheques (and US dollars) are useful to carry with you in Tibet and can be exchanged at the Bank of China in Lhasa, Shigaste and Ali.

ATMs

Several ATMs (自动取款机; *zìdòng qǔkuǎnjī*) in Lhasa and Shigatse and even as far afield as Ali accept foreign cards. The Bank of China accepts Visa, MasterCard, Diners Club, American Express, Maestro, Cirrus and Plus. Check before trying your card as many ATMs can only be used by domestic account holders.

In Lhasa, the Bank of China also has currency exchange ATMs that will change the currency of the US, UK, Eurozone, Hong Kong and Japan.

The maximum amount you can withdraw per transaction is around ¥2400 with the Bank of China. ATMs at the Construction Bank and Agricultural Bank also sometimes take foreign cards; the former is usually more reliable these days. Cards are occasionally eaten by machines, so try to make your transaction during bank hours.

Credit Cards

You'll get very few opportunities to splurge on the plastic in Tibet, unless you spend a few nights in a top-end hotel. Most local tours, train tickets and even flights out of Lhasa still can't be paid for using a credit card (unless purchased online). The few shops that do accept credit cards often have a 4% surcharge.

The Lhasa central branch of the Bank of China is the only place in Tibet that provides cash advances on a credit card. A 3% commission is deducted.

Exchanging Money

In Tibet, the main place to change foreign currency is the Bank of China or at the new currency exchange ATMs. Top-end hotels in Lhasa have exchange services, but only for guests. Outside of Lhasa the only other locations to change money are in Shigatse, Zhangmu, Purang (cash only), Ali, and at the airport. If you are travelling upcountry, try to get your cash in small denominations: ¥100 and ¥50 bills are sometimes difficult to get rid of in rural Tibet.

The currencies of Australia, Canada, the US, the UK, Hong Kong, Japan, and the Eurozone are acceptable at the Lhasa Bank of China. ATM currency exchange machines accept the currency of the US, UK, Eurozone, Hong Kong and Japan. There is a ¥2400 transaction limit but no daily limit.

The official rate is given at all banks and most hotels, so there is little need to shop around for the best deal. There's generally no commission to change cash.

The only place in Tibet to officially change yuán back into foreign currency is the central Lhasa branch of the Bank of China. You'll need your original exchange receipts.

Moneychangers at Zhangmu (by the Nepal border) will change yuán into Nepali rupees and vice versa. Yuán can also easily be reconverted in Hong Kong and, increasingly, in many Southeast Asian countries.

China has a problem with counterfeit notes. Very few Tibetans or Chinese will accept a ¥100 or ¥50 note without first subjecting it to intense scrutiny, and many will not accept old, tattered notes or coins. Check the watermark when receiving any ¥100 note.

International Transfers

Getting money sent to you in Lhasa is possible, but it can be a drag. One option is to use the Bank of China's central office in Lhasa.

The second option is via **Western Union** (www.westernunion.com), which can wire money to one of several Postal Savings Bank of China outlets in Lhasa.

Taxes

Although big hotels may add a tax or 'service charge' of 10% to 15%, all other taxes are included in prices, including airline departure tax.

Tipping & Bargaining

Tibet is one of those wonderful places where tipping is generally not done or asked for. If you go on a long organised trip out to eastern or western Tibet, however, your guide and driver will probably expect a tip at the end, assuming all went well. ¥30 to ¥40 per day for the guide and ¥20 per day for the driver is considered usual.

Basic bargaining skills are essential for travel in Tibet. You can bargain in shops, hotels, street stalls and travel agencies, and with pedicab drivers and most people – but not everywhere. In small shops and street stalls, bargaining is expected, but there is one important rule to follow: be polite.

Tibetans are no less adept at driving a hard deal than the Chinese and, like when dealing with the Chinese, aggressive bargaining will usually only serve to firm their conviction that the original asking price is the one they want. Try to keep smiling and firmly whittle away at the price. If this does not work, try walking away. They might call you back, and if they don't there is always somewhere else.

Travellers Cheques

Besides the advantage of safety, travellers cheques are useful to carry in Tibet because the exchange rate is higher than it is for cash. Cheques from the major companies such as Thomas Cook, Visa and American Express are accepted. US dollar denomination cheques are best.

Opening Hours

Standard opening hours for banks, government offices and PSB offices are 9.30am to 1pm and 3pm to 6.30pm Monday to Friday, and sometimes 10am to 1pm Saturday.

Hours for shops and restaurants vary considerably, but generally shops open from 10am to 9pm and restaurants 10.30am to 11pm. Bars may close at 8pm or 2am, depending on their location and clientele.

Opening hours listed in this guide are for summer; winter hours generally start half an hour later and finish half an hour earlier.

Many smaller monasteries have no set opening hours and will open up chapels once you've tracked down the right monk. Others, such as Samye, are notorious for only opening certain rooms at certain times. In general it's best to try to tag along with pilgrims or a tour group.

Photography

Batteries & Memory Cards

Shops in Lhasa stock a decent range of memory cards and rechargeable batteries (though don't expect to find every camera model's type). Battery life plummets at Tibet's higher elevations and lower temperatures. Keep your batteries warm and separate from your camera overnight and during cold weather. Just heating up batteries in your pocket or the sun can draw some extra juice from them.

Restrictions

Photographs of airports and military installations are prohibited, and bridges are also a touchy subject. Don't take any photos or especially video footage of civil unrest or public demonstrations. Chinese authorities are paranoid about foreign TV crews filming unauthorised documentaries on Tibet.

Restrictions on photography are also imposed at most monasteries and museums. This is partly an attempt to stop the trade of antiquities out of Tibet (statues are often stolen to order from photos taken by seemingly innocuous 'tourists'). In the case of flash photography, such restrictions protect wall murals from damage. Inside the larger monasteries, a fee of ¥20 to ¥50 is often imposed in each chapel for taking a photograph. Video fees can be up to ¥800 (US$100) in some monasteries. You are free, however, to take any photos of the exteriors of monasteries.

Technical Tips

➡ Dust gets into everything in Tibet, so make a point of carefully cleaning your lenses as often as possible.

➡ Take photographs early in the morning and late in the afternoon, to cope with the harsh light conditions.

➡ Use a polarising filter to deepen contrast and blue skies.

Lonely Planet's full-colour *Travel Photography: A Guide to Taking Better Pictures*, written by internationally renowned travel photographer Richard I'Anson, is full of handy hints and is designed to be taken on the road.

Post

China's post service is generally inexpensive and efficient: airmail letters and postcards take around a week to 10 days to reach most destinations. Writing the country of destination in Chinese can speed up the delivery. Domestic post is very swift, often reaching the destination in one or two days. Lhasa is the only place in Tibet from which it's possible to send international parcels whether by air or surface mail.

Post offices are very picky about how you pack things; do not finalise your packing until the parcel has its last customs clearance. If you have a receipt for the goods, then put it in the box when you are mailing it, since it may be opened again by customs further down the line.

China Post operates an express mail service (EMS) – a worldwide priority mail service – that is fast and reliable. Documents to most foreign countries arrive in around five days.

Public Holidays

China has several traditional and modern national holidays. These are mainly Chinese holidays and mean little to many Tibetans, but government offices and banks will be closed on many of these dates. Note the length of holidays is subject to change.

New Year's Day 1 January

Chinese New Year 19 February 2015, 8 February 2016, 28 January 2017; one-week holiday for most

Serf Emancipation Day 28 March

Qing Ming Jie (Tomb Sweeping Day) 4/5 April; a three-day holiday, not really observed in Tibet

Labour Day 1 May; a three-day holiday

Dragon Boat Festival 20 June 2015, 9 June 2016, 30 May 2017

Mid-Autumn Festival 27 September 2015, 15 September 2016, 4 October 2017

National Day 1 October; a week-long holiday

Chinese New Year, otherwise known as the Spring Festival, is definitely not the time to travel around China, cross borders (especially the Hong Kong one) or to be caught short of money.

Serf Emancipation Day was introduced as a public holiday in Tibet in 2009 to commemorate 50 years of Communist Chinese control in Tibet and what China says was the freeing of one million Tibetan 'serfs'. Don't expect much in the way of celebration among the ex-serfs.

Many Tibetan businesses, restaurants, shops and travel agencies are closed on the days of Losar and Saga Dawa. Tibetan festivals like these are held according to the Tibetan lunar calendar, which usually lags at least a month behind the Gregorian calendar. Ask around for the exact dates of religious festivals because monasteries often only fix these a few months in advance. Check Tibetan lunar dates against Gregorian dates at www.kalachakranet.org/ta_tibetan_calendar.html.

The following are politically sensitive dates, as are 5 March, 27 September, 10 December and 1 October, which mark past political protests. It may be difficult for travellers to fly into Tibet for a few days before these dates.

10 March Anniversary of the 1959 Tibetan uprising and flight of the Dalai Lama

23 May Anniversary of the signing of the Agreement on Measures for the Peaceful Liberation of Tibet

1 September Anniversary of the founding of the Tibetan Autonomous Region (TAR)

Safe Travel

Dogs

If you are exploring remote monasteries or villages on foot, keep an eye open for dogs, especially at remote homesteads or nomad encampments, where the powerful and aggressive mastiffs should be given a very wide berth. Travelling with a walking pole or stick is recommended. Keep this between you and the dog should one come near and remain calm, speaking in a normal voice and avoiding direct eye contact. Using pepper spray or Chinese fireworks to scare dogs may backfire by making them even more aggressive in the future.

Political Disturbances

Tourists can be caught up in Tibet's political violence and backpackers have even been injured in crossfire in the past. If a demonstration or full-blown riot breaks out (as it did in 2008) it's safest to stay in your hotel. If things get really bad local authorities or your embassy may organise emergency flights out of Lhasa.

Staring Squads

It is very unusual to be surrounded by staring Tibetans and Chinese in Lhasa, but visiting upcountry is another matter. Trekkers will soon discover that it is not a good idea to set up camp beside Tibetan villages. The spectacle of a few foreigners putting up tents is probably the closest some villagers will ever come to TV.

GOVERNMENT TRAVEL ADVICE

The following government websites offer travel advisories and information on current hot spots.

Australian Department of Foreign Affairs & Trade (www.smarttraveller.gov.au)

British Foreign Office (www.fco.gov.uk/travel)

Canadian Department of Foreign Affairs (www.voyage.gc.ca)

New Zealand Ministry of Foreign Affairs & Trade (www.safetravel.govt.nz)

US State Department (http://travel.state.gov)

Theft

Theft is rare in Tibet, which is generally safer than other provinces of China. Trekkers in the Everest region have reported problems with petty theft, and pickpockets work parts of Lhasa.

Small padlocks are useful for backpacks and some dodgy hotel rooms. Bicycle chain locks come in handy not only for hired bikes but also for attaching backpacks to railings or luggage racks.

If something of yours is stolen, you should report it immediately to the nearest foreign affairs branch of the PSB. They will ask you to fill in a loss report, which you will also need to claim the loss on your travel insurance.

Telephone

The cheapest way to make an international call is via Skype or some other voice-over-IP service with your laptop or mobile device (either using wi-fi or 3G). Mobile phone coverage is generally good, even in far western Tibet and at Everest Base Camp! You can purchase a local SIM card in Lhasa from China Mobile (¥60 to ¥100, which gives you around 200 minutes of local calls plus 300MB of data, easily enough for 2 weeks of emails and internet usage for most). You can add credit with a credit-charging card (充值卡; *chōngzhí kǎ*) for ¥50 or ¥100 of credit. It's best to take your guide with you to purchase a card as there are many options.

If you are without a mobile phone or laptop, look around for public use telephones in small shops (your guide will know where these are). Be sure to purchase a local internet phone (IP) card.

Most hotels in Lhasa have International Direct Dial (IDD) telephones, but levy a hefty surcharge on calls.

It is still impossible to make reverse-charge (collect) calls or to use foreign telephone debit cards. The best you can do is give someone your number and get them to call you back.

The China country code is ☑86. Local area codes are given at the start of each town's entry within this guidebook.

Time

Time throughout China – including Tibet – is set to Běijīng time, which is eight hours ahead of GMT/UTC. When it is noon in Běijīng it is also noon in far-off Lhasa, even if the sun only indicates around 9am or 10am.

Toilets

Chinese toilets might be fairly dismal, but Tibetan toilets make them look like little bowers of heaven. The standard model is a deep hole in the ground, often without partitions, that bubbles and gives off noxious vapours. Many Tibetans (including women with long skirts) prefer to urinate in the street.

On the plus side there are some fabulous 'toilets with a view'. Honours go to the Samye Monastery Guesthouse, the Sakya Guesthouse, the public toilets in the Potala and the small village of Pasum on the way to Everest Base Camp.

With the exception of midrange and top-end hotels, hotel toilets in Tibet are of the squat variety – as the clichés go, good for the digestion and character building, too. *Always* carry an emergency stash of toilet paper or tissues with you.

Tourist Information

Tibet is officially a province of China and does not have tourist offices as such. Similarly, the Tibetan government-in-exile does not provide information specifically relating to travel in Tibet. Several of the pro-Tibetan organisations abroad offer travel advice (see the box, p316).

Travellers with Disabilities

High altitudes, rough roads and lack of access make Tibet a hard place for people with mobility difficulties. Monasteries in particular often involve a hike up a hillside or steep, very narrow steps. Few hotels offer any facilities for the disabled.

Braille Without Borders (www.braillewithoutborders. org) Blind visitors can contact this excellent organisation based in Lhasa. It developed the first Tibetan Braille system and runs a school for blind Tibetan kids, as well as supporting a blind massage clinic in Lhasa. The co-founder, Sabriye Tenberken, is the author of the book *My Path Leads to Tibet: The Inspiring Story of How One Young Blind Woman Brought Hope to the Blind Children of Tibet*, and stars alongside blind climber Erik Weihenmayer in the moving documentary film *Blindsight*.

Navyo Nepal (☑01-691 6359; www.navyonepal.com; Kathmandu, Nepal) This Nepal-based company has some experience in running tours for the disabled to Tibet and Nepal.

Visas

Visa regulations for China are subject to change so treat the following as general guidelines. In 2013, the visa system had a major overhaul and there are now 13 categories of visas.

Apart from citizens of Brunei, Japan and Singapore, all visitors to Tibet require a valid China visa. Visas for individual travel in China are usually easy to get from most Chinese embassies, or their associated visa centres.

FINDING OUT MORE

The following organisations do excellent work to help the people of the Tibetan plateau.

Braille Without Borders www.braillewithoutborders.org

Kham Aid Foundation www.khamaid.org

Seva www.seva.ca/sevaintibet.htm

Tibet Foundation www.tibet-foundation.org

Tibet Fund www.tibetfund.org

Tibet Poverty Alleviation Fund www.tpaf.org

Tibetan Village Project www.tibetanvillageproject.org

Pro-Tibetan organisations abroad have good news services and some cultural coverage. The ICT website includes an interesting guide for tourists visiting Tibet. The Tibet Support Group (www.tibet.org) offers online links to most pro-Tibet organisations.

Australia Tibet Council www.atc.org.au

Canada Tibet Committee www.tibet.ca

International Campaign for Tibet (ICT) www.savetibet.org

Students for a Free Tibet www.studentsforafreetibet.org

Tibet House www.tibethouse.org

Tibet Information Network www.tibetinfonet.net

Tibet Society www.tibetsociety.com

Tibetan Centre for Human Rights and Democracy www.tchrd.org

Most visa offices will issue a standard 30-day (sometimes 60- or 90-day) single-entry tourist (an 'L' category) visa in three to five working days. The 'L' means *lüxing* (travel). Fees vary: UK citizens pay £30 for a single entry L visa, Americans US$140 (Americans always pay dramatically more for China visas), while most other countries' citizens pay US$30. In many countries the visa service has been outsourced to a **China Visa Application Service Centre** (www.visaforchina.org) which levies additional charges that can effectively double the price.

The visa application form asks you a lot of questions (your entry and exit points, travel itinerary, means of transport etc), but once in China you can deviate from this as much as you like. When listing your itinerary, pick the obvious contenders: Běijīng, Shànghǎi and so on.

Don't mention Tibet and don't list your occupation as 'journalist'. You may need to show proof of a return air ticket, hotel bookings and photocopies of previous Chinese visas. You must also have one entire blank page in your passport for the visa, as well as a passport valid for at least six months.

Note that you must be physically present in the country you apply in (ie. you cannot send your passport back to your home country if you are staying somewhere else).

Some embassies offer a postal service (for an additional fee), which takes around three weeks. In the US and Canada mailed visa applications have to go via a visa agent, at extra cost. In the US many people use **China Visa Service Center** (www.mychinavisa.com). Express services are available for a premium.

Hong Kong is usually a reliable place to pick up visas, often with next day service, but confirm with the companies listed below before you decide this is the route you will take to obtain a visa.

A standard single-entry visa must be used within three months from the date of issue and is activated on the date you enter China. There is some confusion over the validity of Chinese visas. Most Chinese officials look at the 'valid until' date, but on most 30-day visas this is actually the date by which you must have *entered* the country, not the visa's expiry date. Longer-stay visas are often activated on the day of issue, not the day you enter the country, so there's no point in getting one too far in advance of your planned entry date. Check with the embassy if you are unsure.

It's possible to travel in Tibet with a visitor (L), student (X), resident (D) or business (M, F or Z) visa, but not on a journalist (J) visa. For an M, F or Z visa the agency handling your Tibet Tourism Bureau (TTB) permit may ask you to provide documentation showing your place of work in China, or a letter of invitation.

Hong Kong

Single-, double-, multiple-entry and business visas are usually available at the following places in Hong Kong. For reference, a single entry L visa costs HK$350 for four-day service, HK$650 for next-day service.

China Travel Service (CTS; ☑852-2315 7171; www.ctshk.com; 1st fl, Alpha House, 27-33 Nathan Rd, Tsim Sha Tsui, enter from Peking Rd)

Forever Bright Trading Limited (☑852-2369 3188; www.fbt-chinavisa.com.hk; Rm 916-917, Tower B, New Mandarin Plaza, 14 Science Museum Rd, Tsim Sha Tsui East, Kowloon)

Kathmandu

For the last few years the Chinese embassy in Kathmandu has not been issuing visas to individual travellers, only to those booked on a tour and then only group visas. If you turn up with a Chinese visa in your passport, it will be cancelled.

Nepali agencies currently charge US$58 per person for a visa. US citizens pay US$142. Allow at least three days to process; faster service is available for a premium.

The visa office at Nepal's **Chinese Embassy** (☑444 0286; http://np.china-embassy.org/eng; Hattisar, Kathmandu) accepts applications from 9.45am to 11am Monday to Friday. Note that the main embassy is in Baluwatar but the separate visa office is in Hattisar.

If you are flying from Kathmandu directly to Chinese cities outside Tibet (ie. Chéngdū or Shànghǎi), you can enter China on an individual tourist visa issued from abroad. Thus if you want to continue travelling in China after your Tibet trip the easiest thing is to fly from Kathmandu to Chéngdū (the plane stops in Lhasa but TTB permits are not required for transfer) and then fly back to Lhasa with your TTB permit and on your normal China visa.

Visa Extensions

The *waishike* (foreign affairs) section of the local PSB handles visa extensions. Extensions are difficult in Tibet (and only likely in Lhasa) so don't count on one. It is far easier to extend your visa in other areas of China such as Chéngdū, Xīníng or Xī'ān, where a 30-day extension is commonplace.

Volunteering

There are limited opportunities for volunteer work in the TAR. There are considerably more opportunities outside the TAR, in Tibetan areas of Sìchuān and Qīnghǎi, and especially in Dharamsala (see www.volunteertibet.org.in).

Conscious Journeys (www.consciousjourneys.org) Runs medical 'voluntourism' trips to Tibetan areas of Sìchuān, as well as responsibly run tours in Tibet.

Rokpa (www.rokpauk.org/volunteering.html) Volunteer teaching positions in the Jyekundo (Yùshù) region of Qīnghǎi.

United Planet (www.unitedplanet.org) Also in the Jyekundo (Yùshù) region of Qīnghǎi.

Weights & Measures

The metric system is used, though traders measure fruit and vegetables by the *jin* (500g).

Women Travellers

Sexual harassment is extremely rare in Tibet and foreign women seem to be able to travel here with few problems. Naturally, it's worth noticing what local women are wearing and how they are behaving, and making a bit of an effort to fit in, as you would in any other foreign country. Probably because of the harsh climate, Tibetan women dress in bulky layers of clothing. It would be wise to follow their example and dress modestly, especially when visiting a monastery. Several women have written of the favourable reactions they have received from Tibetan women when wearing Tibetan dress; you can get one made in Lhasa.

Women are generally not permitted to enter the *gönkhang* (protector chapel) in a monastery, ostensibly for fear of upsetting the powerful protector deities inside.

Transport

For most international travellers, getting to Tibet will involve at least two legs: first to a gateway city such as Kathmandu (Nepal) or Chéngdū (China) and then into Tibet.

From within Asia, the most popular options into Tibet are as follows: flights from Kathmandu, Chéngdū, Kūnmíng, Xī'ān or Běijīng; the train link from Qīnghǎi to Lhasa; or the overland drive from Kathmandu to Lhasa along the Friendship Hwy.

At the time of writing, bureaucratic obstacles to entering Tibet from China were tight and involved signing up for a preplanned and prepaid tour. The situation from Nepal is even trickier because of ever-changing visa requirements. Political events, both domestic and international, can mean the regulations for entry into Tibet change overnight. It would be wise to check on the latest developments before setting out.

It can be very hard to get hold of air and train tickets to Lhasa around the Chinese New Year and the week-long holidays around 1 May and 1 October.

Flights, hotels and tours can be booked online at www.lonelyplanet.com/bookings.

GETTING THERE & AWAY – GATEWAY CITIES

Entering the Country

Arriving in China is pretty painless these days. All travellers fill in a health declaration form on arrival in the country. Expect closer scrutiny of your group documents and luggage when crossing into Tibet from Nepal at Zhāngmù, where some travellers have on occasion had Tibet-related books and images confiscated.

Chinese embassies will not issue a visa if your passport has less than six months' validity remaining.

Air

There are no direct long-haul flights to Tibet. You will probably have to stop over in Kathmandu, Chéngdū or Běijīng, even if you are making a beeline for Lhasa.

Airports & Airlines

For China, you generally have the choice of flying first to Běijīng, Shànghǎi or Hong Kong, although there is a small but growing number of flights direct to Chéngdū or Kūnmíng. There's little difference in fares to these airports though fares can fluctuate by the day (Monday and Tuesday flights are generally cheaper than Friday and Saturday flights). There are now direct flights from Běijīng

---

CLIMATE CHANGE & TRAVEL

Every form of transport that relies on carbon-based fuel generates CO_2, the main cause of human-induced climate change. Modern travel is dependent on aeroplanes, which might use less fuel per kilometre per person than most cars but travel much greater distances. The altitude at which aircraft emit gases (including CO_2) and particles also contributes to their climate change impact. Many websites offer 'carbon calculators' that allow people to estimate the carbon emissions generated by their journey and, for those who wish to do so, to offset the impact of the greenhouse gases emitted with contributions to portfolios of climate-friendly initiatives throughout the world. Lonely Planet offsets the carbon footprint of all staff and author travel.

and Shànghǎi to Lhasa so it is no longer necessary to first fly into Chéngdū.

TO/FROM KATHMANDU

Generally speaking, fares to/from Kathmandu are not all that cheap as there is a limited number of carriers operating out of the Nepali capital. The national carrier, Nepal Airlines, is to be avoided if possible. Depending on where you are coming from, it may be cheaper to fly to Delhi and make your way overland. International airlines flying in and out of Kathmandu include the following:

Air Asia (www.airasia.com) Low-cost carrier from Malaysia. Direct flights from Kuala Lumpur.

China Southern (www.flychinasouthern.com)

Dragonair (www.dragonair.com) Hong Kong hub.

Jet Airways (www.jetairways.com) Currently, the best connections to Delhi are with Jet Airways.

Nepal Airlines Corporation (www.nepalairlines.com.np) The flagship carrier of Nepal, formerly called Royal Nepal Airlines (RNAC). As airlines go, this is a shoestring operation. It has only two aircraft for international flights and services are notoriously unreliable, though its safety record is comparable with other regional carriers. There are flights to Delhi, Dubai, Hong Kong, Bangkok and Kuala Lumpur.

TO/FROM CHÉNGDŪ

Chéngdū's Shuangliu International Airport is well connected to other cities in China, with daily flights arriving from Běijīng, Shànghǎi, Guǎngzhōu, Kūnmíng and Hong Kong, among others. There is also a handful of international carriers making nonstop flights into Chéngdū, mainly from Southeast Asian hubs like Bangkok, Kuala Lumpur and Singapore. It's also possible to reach Chéngdū nonstop from Amsterdam or the UK and there are direct flights from the Middle East. Arriving from other international destinations will likely require a layover in a mainland Chinese hub.

Chéngdū is well connected by rail, so if you want to see a bit of China, fly into a major city and spend a few days travelling by train to Chéngdū. Lonely Planet's *China* guide has more on getting around China by train.

International airlines flying in and out of Chéngdū include **Air Asia** (www.airasia.com), **British Airways** (www.britishairways.com) and **KLM** (www.klm.com).

Tickets

If you want to get to Tibet as quickly as possible (perhaps to get the maximum use from your visa), consider buying a domestic Air China ticket as part of your international ticket. Some Air China offices will give you a discount on the domestic leg if you buy the long-haul leg through them. Airfares to China peak between June and September.

The cheapest tickets to China are available on the various international ticket and price comparison websites such as Skyscanner (www.skyscanner.com), Expedia (www.expedia.com) or Travelocity (www.travelocity.com). You can buy discounted domestic tickets to Chéngdū from online Chinese ticket agencies such as Elong (www.elong.net) and Ctrip (http://english.ctrip.com). However, these latter sites will not sell you a ticket from Chéngdū to Tibet without Chinese ID. International online ticket sites do not have this stipulation. Your best best is usually to ask your tour agency to handle domestic tickets to Lhasa.

GETTING THERE & AWAY – TIBET

This section has detailed information about getting directly into Tibet from Nepal or China.

Air

Within China there are flight connections (direct or with a stopover but no change of planes) to Lhasa from a dozen cities (and growing), including direct flights from Běijīng with Air China. Most travellers still fly in from Chéngdū. Permits are checked on arrival at Lhasa's Gongkar airport, as well as when checking in for your flight to Lhasa.

Note that flights to and from Lhasa are sometimes cancelled or delayed in the winter months, so if you are flying at this time give yourself a couple of days' leeway if you have a connecting flight.

Baggage allowance on flights to Lhasa is 20kg in economy class and 40kg in 1st class, so you'll have to limit your gear to avoid penalties, regardless of what you are allowed to bring on your international flight into China.

Nepal

Flights between Kathmandu and Lhasa run three to four times a week in the high summer season. From April to October flights are organised by demand only, usually operating once or twice a week.

Individual travellers can't buy air tickets from the Air China office in Kathmandu without a Tibet Tourism Bureau (TTB) permit. To get a ticket you'll have to purchase a multi-day package tour through a travel agency. This includes the flight ticket, airport transfers, TTB permit and accommodation.

It is possible to buy air tickets from Kathmandu to other destinations in China; you don't need a TTB permit to take these flights.

Chéngdū

Flights into Lhasa are shared by Air China (CA; www.airchina.com.cn), China Southern (CZ; www.csair.com), Sichuan Airlines (3U; www.scal.com.cn), Hainan Airlines (HU; www.hnair.com) and China Eastern (MU; www.ce-air.com). Note that on many online booking sites you need to spell Lhasa as Lasa.

Flights between Chéngdū and Lhasa cost around ¥1600 to ¥2000 one way. You can buy them online or through an agent (the agency that is handling your TTB permit and tour is usually best). You will not be able to book through a Chinese booking website without Chinese ID. Overseas booking sites don't seem to have this problem.

If you are coming to Tibet from somewhere outside China, have your agency mail your permit to a hotel in Chéngdū where you can pick it up and fly out the next day. Make sure the permit is sent a few days before you arrive and that you confirm its arrival.

Chéngdū has long been the main gateway to Lhasa for travellers coming by air, and multiple flights a day go to Lhasa in the height of summer. Try to book the first flight of the day because weather conditions and visibility will be optimal in the morning. On a clear day the views from the plane are stupendous, so try to get a window seat. In general the best views are from the left side of the plane from Chéngdū to Lhasa and the right side from Lhasa to Chéngdū. Getting into Lhasa early also gives you a little more time to acclimatise if you are on a short tour.

Zhōngdiàn & Kūnmíng

China Eastern (www.flychinaeastern.com) operates two daily flights from Kūnmíng to Lhasa via Zhōngdiàn (aka Shangri-la) in northwest Yún-nán. China Southern (www.csair.com) also flies from Lhasa to Zhōngdiàn en route to Guǎngzhōu. As with other flights to Lhasa, foreigners won't be allowed on board without a TTB permit.

Land

Many individual travellers make their way to Tibet as part of a grand overland trip through China, Nepal, India and onwards. In many ways, land travel to Tibet is the best way to go, not only for the scenery en route but also because it can help spread the altitude gain over a few days.

Road

In theory there are several land routes into Tibet. The bulk of overland travellers take the Friendship Hwy between Kathmandu and Lhasa.

In the current climate it's most unwise to try any route on your own (ie not in a 4WD or cycling tour) – you have a very good chance of being caught and fined and dragging any Tibetan who has helped you into your troubles.

Other possible routes (though in recent years these have been officially closed to foreign travellers) are the Sìchuān–Tibet Hwy and the Yúnnán–Tibet Hwy (see Overland Routes From Sichuan & Yunnan, p202). The Qīnghǎi–Tibet Hwy (see Northern Routes of Kham, p203) and the Xīnjiāng–Tibet Hwy (see the Atop the World: Xīnjiāng–Tibet Highway box, p172) are possible on a 4WD tour with all the proper permits. The Qīnghǎi–Tibet Hwy is also possible on an organised cycling tour.

(see Overland Routes From Sichuan & Yunnan, p202)

FRIENDSHIP HIGHWAY (NEPAL TO TIBET)

The 865km stretch of road between Kathmandu and Lhasa is known as the Friendship Hwy. The journey is without a doubt one of the most spectacular in the world.

From Kathmandu (elevation 1300m) the road travels gently up to Kodari (1873m), before leaving Nepal to make a steep switchback ascent to Zhāngmù (2250m), the Tibetan border town, and then Nyalam (3750m), where most people spend their first night. The road then climbs to the top of the Tong-la (4950m), continuing to Tingri (4250m) for the second night. The road is paved the whole way.

It is essential to watch out for the effects of altitude sickness during the early stages of this trip. If you intend to head up to Everest Base Camp (5150m) you really need to slip in a rest day at Tingri or Nyalam.

China is 2¼ hours ahead of Nepali time.

OTHER ROUTES INTO TIBET

Another route into Tibet, for trekking groups only, passes through Purang (Taklakot in Nepali). Special visas are required for this trip. Trekkers start by travelling by road or flying from Kathmandu to Nepalganj, then flying from there to Simikot in the far west of Nepal. From Simikot it's a five- or six-day walk to the Tibetan border, crossing the Humla Karnali. You can then drive the 28km to Purang and the further 107km to the Mt Kailash area via Lake Manasarovar. See Lonely Planet's *Trekking in the Nepal Himalaya* for details of the trek.

Tibetan, Chinese and Hong Kong travellers can cross into Tibet's Yadong region from Gangtok in Sikkim via the 4310m Nathu-la, tracing the former trading routes between Lhasa, Kalimpong and Calcutta, and the path taken by Younghusband's invasion of Tibet in 1903. The route is not yet open to foreign travellers though both India and China are planning rail service to the regions in the coming years.

There is talk of opening the Kyirong-la (Kerong-la) to organised tour groups headed to/from the Langtang region of Nepal, but there are no definite plans as yet. Roads are in place on both sides of the border.

Indian pilgrims on a quota system travel to Purang via the Lipu Lekh pass from Pithoragarh.

Train

Trains to Lhasa leave from Běijīng, Chéngdū, Shànghǎi, Xīníng and Guǎngzhōu daily and every other day from Chóngqìng (via Xī'ān) and Lánzhōu, which link with the Chéngdū and Xīníng trains, respectively. In 2014 a new route began operating from Shíjiāzhuāng, Héběi Province, and a new daily train service from Lhasa to Shigatse started in late 2014. Future extensions will include lines from Lhasa to Zhangmu on the Nepal border and Golmud to Dūnhuáng in Gānsù Province.

All current trains cross the Tibetan plateau during daylight, guaranteeing great views. From Golmud the train climbs through desert into the jagged caramel-coloured mountains of Nanshankou (Southern Pass), passing what feels like a stone's throw from the impressive glaciers beside Yuzhu Feng (Jade Pearl Peak; 6178m). Other highlights include the tunnel through the 4776m Kunlun Pass, where you can see the prayer flags at the top of the pass, and Tsonak Lake (4608m), 9½ hours from Golmud near Amdo, claimed to be the highest freshwater lake in the world. Keep your eyes peeled throughout the journey for antelope, foxes and wild asses, plus the occasional nomad. The train crosses into Tibet over the 5072m Tangu-la (Tanggula Shankou) Pass, the line's high point.

SCHEDULES & SERVICES

China Highlights (www.chinahighlights.com) Searchable timetables.

China Tibet Train (www.chinatibettrain.com) The official website. Good background info.

Railway Customer Service Centre (www.12306.cn) If you can read Chinese, you might be able to purchase tickets up to 20 days in advance.

Seat 61 (www.seat61.com/China.htm) General info on trains in China.

Travel China Guide (www.travelchinaguide.com/china-trains) Searchable timetables.

PRACTICALITIES

At the time of writing, foreigners needed a TTB permit to buy a ticket and board the train. Most travellers ask the same tour agency handling their TTB permits to secure tickets. However, be aware that tickets can be purchased only 10 to 20 days in advance (fewer during major long holidays) and there is no guarantee of getting one. If you are lucky enough you might have to pay a premium because agencies must often buy through scalpers.

The lack of certainty around the train makes it difficult to coordinate plans so it's a good idea to also have a flight ticket booked (especially in summer) just in case you do not get train tickets. Make sure you are aware of the airline's flight cancellation policy.

If you want to try to secure a ticket on your own you can try to find a scalper, or purchase through www.china-train-tickets.com, www.12306.cn or www.piao.com/train. Again, there is no guarantee.

Train carriages are much better than your average Chinese train and are more like the express trains that link Běijīng with Shànghǎi. All passengers have access to piped-in oxygen through a special socket beside each

TRAIN SCHEDULES TO LHASA

TRAIN NO	TO/FROM	DEPARTURE	DISTANCE (KM)	DURATION (HR)	HARD SLEEPER/ SOFT SLEEPER
T27/8	Běijīng (west)	8pm	3753	44	¥742/1186
T22/3	Chéngdū	8.55pm	3360	43	¥689/1101
T222/3	Chóngqìng	7.37pm every 2nd day	3641	45	¥730/1165
T264/5	Guǎngzhōu	12.19pm	4980	55	¥892/1526
T164/5	Shànghǎi	7.36pm	4373	52	¥818/1311
**	Xīníng	various	1960	23	¥497/794

NB Sleeper fares are for lower berth. Unless noted, services run every day.

** Multiple train options

THE WORLD'S HIGHEST TRAIN RIDE

There's no doubt the new Qīnghǎi–Tibet train line is an engineering marvel. Topping out at 5072m, it is the world's highest railway, snatching the title from a Peruvian line. The statistics speak for themselves: 86% of the line is above 4000m, and half the track lies on permafrost, requiring a cooling system of pipes driven into the ground to keep it frozen year-round to avoid a rail-buckling summer thaw. Construction of the line involved building 160km of bridges and elevated track, seven tunnels (including the world's highest) and 24 hyperbaric chambers, the latter to treat altitude-sick workers.

Aside from environmental concerns, Tibetans are deeply worried about the cultural and political impact of the train. The trains unload thousands of Chinese tourists and immigrants into Lhasa every day, and connecting China's rail network to the only province in China lacking a rail link has forged Tibet and China in an iron grip. A similar thing happened with the 1999 railway line to Kashgar in Xīnjiāng.

The authorities stress the economic benefits of the line: highly subsidised, it has decreased transport costs for imports by up to 75%. But Tibetans remain economically marginalised. More than 90% of the 100,000 workers employed to build the line came from other provinces and few, if any, Tibetan staff work on the trains. The US$4.1 billion cost of building the line is greater than the amount Běijīng has spent on hospitals and schools in Tibet over the last 50 years.

As ambitious as the current line is, connecting Lhasa with the rest of China was only the beginning. An extension to Shigatse opened in 2014, and plans are in place to continue this line with routes to the Nepal border and west to the India and Bhutan borders by 2020. Another line will connect Golmud to Dūnhuáng in Gānsù Province.

seat or berth and all carriages are nonsmoking after Golmud. There are power sockets by the window seats, though be aware that laptops and MP3 players often stop working at points during the trip, due to the altitude. Each train has a small but decent dining car (mains ¥15 to ¥25).

Hard-sleeper (硬卧; yìng wò) carriages are made up of doorless six-berth compartments with bunks in three tiers, with sheets, pillows and blankets provided. There is a small price difference between berths, with the lowest bunk the most expensive and the top-most bunk the cheapest. Four-bed soft-sleeper (软卧; ruǎn wò) berths come with individual TVs and doors that close and lock. Hard seats (硬座; yìng zuò) are just that.

Sleeper tickets to Lhasa sell out quickly. Getting a ticket for a train out of Lhasa is easier than getting a ticket into Lhasa.

GETTING AROUND

Tibet's transport infrastructure has developed rapidly in recent years. While some areas are still a patchwork of rough roads, most of the main highways are now paved. Airports are springing up on the plateau and the railway line is extending beyond Lhasa. Tibet's Metok country was the very last of China's 2100 counties to be connected by road, completed in 2011 via a 3km tunnel.

Air

Tibet is one of China's biggest provinces, but flights within the Tibetan Autonomous Region are few and far between and tickets can be hard to secure. There are airports for Lhasa, Nyingtri and Chamdo, Ali and Shigatse. Outside of Lhasa, these are of limited use to tourists, and most are not open to foreign travellers. Shigatse's

Peace Airport has flights to Chéngdū with Tibet Airlines (www.tibetairlines.com.cn). Tibet Airlines also has flights between Lhasa and Ali's Ngari Gunsa Airport.

An airport in Nagchu is slated to open in 2014. It will be the highest civilian airport in the world.

Bicycle

Long-distance cyclists, the majority of whom are Chinese, are an increasingly frequent sight on the roads of Tibet, especially along the Friendship Hwy and Hwy 318 in eastern Tibet. For foreign travellers, cycling is no longer a free and easy adventure in Tibet; like everyone else, you'll need a guide, who will likely follow you in a support vehicle.

Most long-distance cyclists bring their own bikes to Tibet, though a few buy mountain bikes in China or Lhasa. Nowadays it is possible to buy a Chinese-made or (better) Taiwanese-made mountain bike in the capital.

Standards aren't all that bad, although you should check the gears and brakes in particular and do not expect the quality of these bikes to be equal to those you might buy at home – bring plenty of spare parts. Bikes have a relatively high resale value in Kathmandu and you might even make a profit if the bike is in good shape (unlikely after a trip across Tibet!).

Tibet poses unique challenges to individual cyclists. The good news is that the main roads are in surprisingly good condition (the Friendship Hwy was recently upgraded and roads everywhere are under improvement) and the traffic is fairly light. The main physical challenges come from the climate, terrain and altitude: wind squalls and dust storms can make your work particularly arduous; the warm summer months can bring flash flooding; and then there is the question of your fitness in the face of Tibet's high-altitude mountainous terrain.

A full bicycle-repair kit, several spare inner tubes, and a spare tyre and chain are essential. Preferably bring an extra rim and some spare spokes. Extra brake wire and brake pads are useful (you'll be descending 3000m from Lhasa to Kathmandu!). Other useful equipment includes reflective clothing, a helmet, a dust mask, goggles, gloves and padded trousers.

If going solo, you will also need to be prepared with supplies such as food, water-purifying tablets and camping equipment, just as if you were trekking. Most long-distance cyclists will probably find formal accommodation and restaurants only available at two- or three-day intervals. It may be possible to stay with road repair camps (known as *daoban* in Chinese) in remote places.

The Trailblazer guidebook *Tibet Overland: A Route and Planning Guide for Mountain Bikers and Other Overlanders*, by Kym McConnell, has useful route plans and gradient charts aimed at mountain bikers, with a notice board at www.tibetoverland.com. The website www.bikechina.com is another good resource.

Obviously, you need to be physically fit to undertake road touring in Tibet. Spend some time acclimatising to the altitude and taking leisurely rides around Lhasa (for example) before setting off on a long trip.

On the plus side, although Tibet has some of the highest-altitude roads in the world (be aware that official pass altitudes are often off by hundreds of meters), gradients are usually quite manageable. The Tibetan roads are designed for low-powered Chinese trucks, which tackle the many high passes of the region via its low-gradient switchback roads. And apart from the military convoys, which can include a hundred or more trucks, you rarely have to put up with much traffic.

Touring Routes
The most popular touring route at present is Lhasa to Kathmandu along the Friendship Hwy. It is an ideal route in that it takes in most of Tibet's main sights, offers superb scenery and (for those leaving from Lhasa) features a spectacular rollercoaster ride down from the heights of the La Lung-la

into the Kathmandu Valley. The trip will take a minimum of two weeks, although to do it justice and include stopovers at Gyantse, Shigatse and Sakya, budget 20 days. The entire trip is just over 940km, though most people start from Shigatse. The roadside kilometre markers are a useful way of knowing exactly how far you have gone and how far you still have to go.

If you are travelling via Kathmandu, Nepali mountain-bike agencies such as **Dawn Till Dusk** (www.nepalbiking.com) can offer tips, equipment and organised biking tours in Tibet.

Keen cyclists with good mountain bikes might want to consider the detour to Everest Base Camp as a side trip on the Lhasa–Kathmandu route. The 108km one-way trip starts from the Shegar turn-off, and it takes around two days to get to Rongphu Monastery.

Other possibilities are endless. Tsurphu, Ganden and Drigung Til Monasteries are relatively easy trips and good for acclimatisation (though the road to Tsurphu is rough and Ganden has a fierce final 10km uphill section). The Gyama Valley is an easy detour on a bike if you are headed to Ganden. Cycling in the Yarlung Valley region is another fine option. Some cyclists even tackle the paved road to Nam-tso, although the nomads' dogs can be a problem here.

Bike China (www.bike-china.com) offers tours from Golmud to Lhasa.

Permits

It's currently not possible to cycle anywhere in Tibet independently. You must sign up for a 'tour', which essentially means being followed by a support vehicle and guide. There are no specific permits for cycling but you will need all the usual permits as if you were travelling by 4WD.

Hazards

Cycling in Tibet is not to be taken lightly. Dogs are a major problem, especially in more remote areas. Children have been known to throw stones at cyclists. Erratic driving is another serious concern.

Wear a cycling helmet and lightweight leather gloves and, weather permitting, try to keep as much of your body covered with protective clothing as possible. It goes without saying that cyclists should also be prepared with a comprehensive medical kit.

Hitching

Hitching is never entirely safe in any country, and we don't necessarily recommend it. Travellers who decide to hitch should understand that they are taking a small but potentially serious risk.

It goes without saying that if you are hitching in Tibet you are doing so because you decided to forgo the permit-and-tour route (tsk! tsk!) and risk fines or expulsion by the Public Security Bureau (PSB). At the moment, one of the biggest hurdles to hitching is simply getting a ride. Drivers will be reluctant to pick you up because the authorities impose heavy fines on anyone transporting foreign travellers and may even confiscate their licence.

If things do change, sometimes you can get a lift on a pilgrim truck or an organised passenger truck. If you are headed out to fairly remote destinations you should be equipped to camp out for the night if you don't get a ride. There are also plenty of half-empty 4WDs heading down the Friendship Hwy to pick up a group, or returning after having dropped one off.

Normally you will be expected to pay for your lift. The amount is entirely negotiable, but in areas where traffic is minimal, drivers will often demand quite large sums.

It's a good idea to start hitching a few kilometres out of town because then you know that traffic is going in your direction and is not about to turn off after 400m.

The most common hitching gesture is to stick out one or two fingers towards the ground and wave them up or down, though the thumbs-up gesture is increasingly popular with young Chinese hitchhikers.

Local Transport

Local city transport only really operates in Lhasa and Shigatse. Buses run on set routes and charge a fixed fare of ¥1.

Pedicabs (pedal-operated tricycles transporting passengers) are available in Lhasa, Gyantse, Shigatse and Bāyī, but require extensive haggling and are often as expensive, if not more, than a taxi.

One result of China's economic infusion into Tibet is the large number of taxis now available in most towns, even Ali in western Tibet. In Lhasa most fares are ¥10, more for a trip outside town to Drepung Monastery, for example. Fixed-route passenger taxis (which you can pay for by the seat) run between several cities, including Lhasa and Tsetang.

Tractors can be an option for short trips in rural areas, especially in the Yarlung Valley. For a few yuan, drivers are normally quite happy to have some passengers in the back. Rides of anything over 10 minutes quickly become seriously uncomfortable unless on a tarmac road.

Health

Tibet poses some unique and particular risks to your health, mostly associated with altitude. There is no need to be overly worried: very few travellers are adversely affected by altitude for very long, and greater risks are present in the form of road accidents and dog bites.

Sensible travellers will rely on their own medical knowledge and supplies. Outside of Lhasa there is very little in the way of expert medical care available. Make sure you travel with a well-stocked medical kit and knowledge of how to use it.

BEFORE YOU GO

Make sure you're healthy before you start travelling. If you are going on a long trip, make sure your teeth are OK. If you wear glasses, take a spare pair and your prescription.

If you require a particular medication take a good supply, as it may not be available in Tibet. Take along part of the packaging showing the generic name rather than the brand to make getting replacements easier. To avoid problems, have a legible prescription or letter from your doctor to show that you legally use the medication.

Insurance

Tibet is a remote location, and if you become seriously injured or very sick, you may need to be evacuated by air. Under these circumstances, you don't want to be without adequate health insurance. Be sure your policy covers evacuation.

Recommended Vaccinations

China doesn't officially require any immunisations for entry into the country; however, the further off the beaten track you go, the more necessary it is to take all precautions.

Plan well ahead (at least eight weeks before travel) and schedule your vaccinations – some require more than one injection, while others should not be given together. Note that some vaccinations should not be given during pregnancy or to people with allergies.

Discuss your requirements with your doctor, but vaccinations you should consider for this trip include the following:

Chickenpox (Varicella) Discuss this vaccine with your doctor if you have not had chickenpox.

Diphtheria & Tetanus Vaccinations for these two diseases are usually combined and are recommended for everyone. After an initial course of three injections (usually given in childhood), boosters are necessary every 10 years.

Hepatitis A The vaccine for Hepatitis A (eg Avaxim, Havrix 1440 or VAQTA) provides long-term immunity (at least 20 years) after an initial injection and a booster at six to 12 months. Hepatitis A vaccine is also available in a combined form, Twinrix, with hepatitis B vaccine. Three injections over a six-month period are required, the first two providing substantial protection against hepatitis A.

Hepatitis B China (although not so much Tibet) is one of the world's great reservoirs of hepatitis B infection, a disease spread by contact with blood or by sexual activity. Vaccination involves three injections, the quickest course being over three weeks with a booster at 12 months.

Influenza The flu vaccine is recommended for anyone with chronic diseases, such as diabetes, lung or heart disease. Tibet has a high rate of respiratory illness, so all travellers should consider vaccination.

Measles, mumps and rubella (MMR) All travellers should ensure they are immune to these diseases, either through infection or vaccination. Most people born before 1966 will be immune; those born after this date should have received two MMR vaccines in their lifetime.

Pneumonia A vaccine is recommended for anyone over 65 or those over 55 with certain medical conditions.

Polio Everyone should keep up to date with this vaccination, which is normally given in childhood. One adult booster is then needed (as long as the full childhood course was completed), particularly if travelling to a country with recent polio activity such as Nepal. This should be discussed with your doctor.

Rabies Rabies is the most common cause of death by infectious disease in China. Vaccination is strongly recommended for those spending more than a month in Tibet (especially if you are cycling, handling animals, caving or travelling in remote areas) and for children. Pretravel vaccination means you do not need to receive Rabies Immuno Globulin (RIG) after a bite. RIG is very unlikely to be available in Tibet. If you are prevaccinated and then bitten, you need only get two further shots of vaccine, as soon as possible, three days apart. If not prevaccinated, you require RIG plus five shots of vaccine over the course of 28 days. The full series of vaccination does not require any boosters *unless* a bite occurs.

Tuberculosis The risk of tuberculosis (TB) to travellers is usually very low, unless you'll be living with or closely associated with local people in high-risk areas. Recommendations for BCG vaccination vary considerably around the world. Discuss with your doctor if you feel you may be at risk. It is strongly recommended for children under five who are spending more than three months in a high-risk area.

Typhoid This is an important vaccination to have for Tibet, where hygiene standards are low. It is available either as an injection or oral capsules. A combined hepatitis A-typhoid vaccine was launched recently.

Yellow Fever This disease is not endemic in China or Tibet and a vaccine (proven by an International Health Certificate) is only required if you are coming from an infected area (parts of South America and Africa).

Medical Checklist

Following is a list of items you should consider including in your medical kit for travelling.

➡ Antibiotics – useful for everyone travelling to Tibet to avoid risks of receiving poorly stored local medications; see your doctor (antibiotics must be prescribed) and carry the prescription with you. Good to have two types: one for lung infections, and one for general skin and other infections.

➡ Antifungal cream or powder – for fungal skin infections and thrush

➡ Antihistamine – for allergies (eg hay fever), to ease the itch from insect bites or stings, and to prevent motion sickness

➡ Antiseptic (such as povidone-iodine) – for cuts and grazes

➡ Bandages, Band-Aids (plasters) and other wound dressings

➡ Calamine lotion, sting-relief spray or aloe vera – to ease irritation from sunburn and insect bites or stings

➡ Cold and flu tablets, throat lozenges and nasal decongestant

➡ Homeopathic medicines – including gentiana for altitude sickness, echinacea for warding off infections, and tea-tree oil for cuts and scrapes

➡ Insect repellent, sunscreen, lip balm and eye drops

➡ Loperamide or diphenoxylate – 'blockers' for diarrhoea

➡ Multivitamins – for long trips, when dietary vitamin intake may be inadequate

➡ Paracetamol (acetaminophen in the USA) – for pain or fever

➡ Prochlorperazine or metaclopramide – for nausea and vomiting

➡ Rehydration mixture – to prevent dehydration (eg during bouts of diarrhoea); particularly important when travelling with children

➡ Scissors, tweezers and a thermometer – note that mercury thermometers are prohibited by airlines

➡ Sterile kit – in case you need injections in a country with medical hygiene problems; discuss with your doctor

➡ Water purification tablets or iodine

Websites

There are a number of excellent travel-health sites on the internet. From the Lonely Planet website (lonelyplanet.com) there are links to the World Health Organization (WHO) and the US Centers for Disease Control and Prevention.

Further Reading

Lonely Planet's *Healthy Travel – Asia & India* is a handy pocket size and packed with useful information, including pretrip planning, emergency first aid, immunisation and disease information, and what to do if you get sick on the road. *Travel with Children* from Lonely Planet also includes advice on travel health for younger children.

Other detailed health guides you may find useful:

Medicine for Mountaineering by James Wilkerson is still the classic text for trekking first aid and medical advice.

Pocket First Aid and Wilderness Medicine by Jim Duff and Peter Gormly is a great pocket-sized guide that's easily carried on a trek or climb.

The High Altitude Medicine Handbook by Andrew J Pollard and David R Murdoch is a small-format guide full of valuable information on prevention and emergency care.

Travellers' Health by Richard Dawood is comprehensive, easy to read, authoritative and highly recommended, although it's rather large to lug around.

IN TIBET

Availability & Cost of Health Care

Self-diagnosis and treatment can be risky, so you should always seek medical help where possible. Although we do give drug dosages in this section, they are for emergency use only. Correct diagnosis is vital.

Top-end hotels can usually recommend a good place to go for advice. Standards of medical attention are so low in most places in Tibet that for some ailments the best advice is to go straight to Lhasa, and in extreme cases get on a plane to Kathmandu or Chéngdū:

CIWEC Clinic Travel Medicine Center (Map p236; ☑+977-1-4424111, 4435232; www.ciwec-clinic.com; ☺24h emergency, clinic 9am-noon & 1-4pm Mon-Fri) In Kathmandu. In operation since 1982 and has an international reputation for research into travellers' medical problems. Staff are mostly foreigners and a doctor is on call around the clock. A consultation costs around US$65. Credit cards are accepted and the centre is used to dealing with insurance claims.

Global Doctor Chengdu Clinic (☑8528 3638, 24hr emergency 139-8225 6966; www.globaldoctor.com.au; 62 Kehua Beilu, Lippo Tower, Section S, 2nd fl, No 9-11, Chéngdū) Offers pre-Tibet medical examinations and a Tibet Travellers Assist Package that can be useful if you are worried about an existing medical condition.

Infectious Diseases

Rabies

This fatal viral infection is found in Tibet. Many animals (such as dogs, cats, bats and monkeys) can be infected and it is their saliva that is infectious. Any bite, scratch or even lick from an animal should be cleaned immediately and thoroughly. Scrub gently with soap and running water, and then apply alcohol or iodine solution. Prompt medical help should be sought to receive a course of injections to prevent the onset of symptoms and save the patient from death.

If you have any potential exposure to rabies, seek medical advice in Lhasa (or ideally Kathmandu, Chéngdū or Běijīng) as soon as possible. Even in these centres full treatment may not be available and you may need to travel to Bangkok or Hong Kong.

Respiratory Infections

Upper respiratory tract infections (like the common cold) are frequent ailments all over China, including Tibet, where the high altitude aggravates symptoms.

Some of the symptoms of influenza include a sore throat, fever and weakness. Any upper-respiratory-tract infection, including influenza, can lead to complications such as bronchitis and pneumonia, which may need to be treated with antibiotics. Seek medical help in this situation.

No vaccine offers complete protection, but the influenza vaccine is highly recommended for travellers to China and Tibet, and is good for up to one year.

Amoebic Dysentery

Caused by the protozoan *Entamoeba histolytica*, amoebic dysentery is characterised by a gradual onset of low-grade diarrhoea, often with blood and mucus. Cramping abdominal pain and vomiting are less likely than in other types of diarrhoea, and fever may not be present. It will persist until treated and can recur and cause other health problems.

You should seek medical advice if you think you have giardiasis or amoebic dysentery, but where this is not possible, tinidazole or metronidazole are the recommended drugs. The better option of the two is tinidazole, which is not easily obtained in Tibet. If you are going to be travelling in high mountain areas, it's a good idea to keep your own stock with you.

Cholera

This is the worst of the watery diarrhoeas. Outbreaks are generally widely reported, so you can avoid problem areas. Fluid replacement is the most vital treatment: the risk of dehydration is severe, as you may lose up to 20L a day. Seek medical advice if you think you may have this disease. If there is a delay in getting to hospital, begin taking doxycycline.

Giardiasis

Known as giardia, giardiasis is a type of diarrhoea. It's relatively common in Tibet and is caused by a parasite, *Giardia lamblia*, present in contaminated water. Many kinds of mammals harbour the parasite, so you can easily get it drinking 'pure mountain water', or even brushing your teeth with contaminated water. Symptoms include stomach cramps, nausea, a bloated stomach, watery, foul-smelling diarrhoea and frequent gas. Giardiasis can appear several weeks after you have been exposed to the parasite. The symptoms may disappear for a few days and then return; this can go on for several weeks. Treatment is with tinidazole, 2g in a single dose for one to two days.

Environmental Hazards

Acute Mountain Sickness

Acute mountain sickness (AMS; also known as altitude sickness) is common at high elevations; relevant factors are the rate of ascent and individual susceptibility. The former is the major risk factor. On average, one tourist a year dies in Tibet from AMS. Any traveller who flies to where the elevation is around 3600m is likely to experience some symptoms of AMS.

AMS is a notoriously fickle affliction and can also affect trekkers and walkers accustomed to walking at high altitudes. It has been fatal at 3000m, although 3500m to 4500m is the usual range.

ACCLIMATISATION

AMS is linked to low atmospheric pressure. Those who travel up to Everest Base Camp, for instance, reach an altitude where atmospheric pressure is about half of that at sea level.

With an increase in altitude, the human body needs time to develop physiological mechanisms to cope with the decreased oxygen. This process of acclimatisation is still not fully understood, but is known to involve modifications in breathing patterns and heart rate induced by the autonomic nervous system, and an increase in the blood's oxygen-carrying capabilities. These compensatory mechanisms usually take about one to three days to develop at a particular altitude. You are unlikely to get AMS once you are acclimatised to a given height, but you can still get ill when you travel higher. If the ascent is too high and too fast, these compensatory reactions may not kick into gear fast enough.

SYMPTOMS

Mild symptoms of AMS usually develop during the first 24 hours at altitude. These will generally disappear through acclimatisation in several hours to several days.

Symptoms tend to be worse at night and include headache, dizziness, lethargy, loss of appetite, nausea, breathlessness and irritability. Difficulty sleeping is another common symptom, and many travellers have trouble for the first few days after arriving in Lhasa.

AMS may become more serious without warning and can be fatal. Symptoms are caused by the accumulation of fluid in the lungs and brain, and include breathlessness at rest, a dry irritative cough (which may progress to the production of pink, frothy sputum), severe headache, lack of coordination (typically leading to a 'drunken walk'), confusion, irrational behaviour, vomiting and eventually unconsciousness.

The symptoms of AMS, however mild, are a warning: be sure to take them seriously! Trekkers should keep an eye on each other as those experiencing symptoms, especially severe symptoms, may not be in a position to recognise them. One thing to note is that while the symptoms of mild AMS often precede those of severe AMS, this is not always the case. Severe AMS can strike with little or no warning.

PREVENTION

If you are driving up from Kathmandu, you will experience rapid altitude gain. An itinerary that takes you straight up to Everest Base Camp is unwise; plan to see it on your way back if possible. The best way to prevent AMS is to avoid rapid ascents to high altitudes. If you fly into Lhasa, take it easy for at least three days; this is enough for most travellers to get over any initial ill-effects.

To prevent acute mountain sickness:

→ Ascend slowly. Have frequent rest days, spending two to three nights at each rise of 1000m. If you reach a high altitude by trekking, acclimatisation takes place gradually and you are less likely to be affected than if you fly or drive directly to high altitude.

→ Trekkers should bear in mind the climber's adage of 'climb high, sleep low'. It is always wise to sleep at a lower altitude than the greatest height that's reached during the day.

→ Once above 3000m, care should be taken not to increase the sleeping altitude by more than 400m per day.

→ Drink extra fluids. Tibet's mountain air is cold and dry, and moisture is lost as you breathe. Evaporation of sweat may occur unnoticed and result in dehydration.

→ Avoid alcohol as it may increase the risk of dehydration, and don't smoke.

→ Avoid sedatives.

→ When trekking, take a day off to rest and acclimatise if feeling overtired. If you or anyone else in your party is having a tough time, make allowances for unscheduled stops.

→ Don't push yourself when climbing up to passes; rather, take plenty of breaks. You can usually get over the pass as easily tomorrow as you can today. Try to plan your itinerary so that long ascents can be divided into two or more days. Given the complexity and unknown variables involved with AMS and acclimatisation, trekkers should always err on the side of caution and ascend mountains slowly.

TREATMENT

Treat mild symptoms by resting at the same altitude until recovery, usually a day or two. Take paracetamol or acetaminophen for headaches. If symptoms persist or become worse, however, *immediate* descent is necessary. Even 500m can help.

The most effective treatment for severe AMS is to get down to a lower altitude as quickly as possible. In less severe cases the victim will be able to stagger down with some support; in other cases they may need to be carried down. Whatever the case, any delay could be fatal.

AMS victims may need to be flown out of Tibet as quickly as possible, so make sure you have adequate travel insurance.

The drug acetazolamide (Diamox) is recommended for the prevention of AMS – take 125mg twice a day as a preventive dose. Be aware that even when you are on Diamox, you should not ignore any symptoms of AMS. Diamox should be avoided in those with a sulphur allergy.

Drug treatments should never be used to avoid descent or to enable further ascent (although they can help get people well enough to descend).

Several hotels in Lhasa sell a Tibetan herbal medicine recommended by locals for easing the symptoms of mild altitude sickness. The medicine is known as *solomano* in Tibetan and *hóngjīngtiān* (红景天) in Chinese, though locals also recommend *gāoyuānníng* (高原宁) and *gāoyuánkāng* (高原康). A box of vials costs around ¥35 to ¥50; take three vials a day.

Food

Vegetables and fruit should be washed with purified or bottled water or peeled where possible. Beware of ice cream that is sold in the street or anywhere it might have been melted and refrozen; if there's any doubt (eg a power cut in the last day or two) steer clear. Avoid undercooked meat.

In general, places that are packed with travellers or locals will be fine, while empty restaurants are questionable. Chinese food is usually cooked over a high heat, which kills most germs.

Frostbite

This is the freezing of extremities, including fingers, toes and nose. Signs and symptoms of frostbite include a whitish or waxy cast to the skin, or even crystals on the surface, plus itching, numbness and pain. Warm the affected areas by immersing them in warm (not hot) water or with blankets or clothes, only until the skin becomes flushed. Note: frostbitten areas should only be rewarmed if there is not a likelihood they can be frostbitten again prior to reaching medical care. Frostbitten parts should not be rubbed. Pain and swelling are inevitable. Blisters should not be broken. Get medical attention right away.

Heat Exhaustion

Dehydration and salt deficiency can cause heat exhaustion. Take time to acclimatise to high temperatures, be sure to drink sufficient liquids and do not do anything too physically demanding.

Salt deficiency is characterised by fatigue, lethargy, headaches, giddiness and muscle cramps; salt tablets may help, but adding extra salt to your food is better.

Hypothermia

Tibet's cold climate must be treated with respect. Subfreezing temperatures mean there is a risk of hypothermia, even during the summer season when high areas around western Tibet and the northern Changtang can be hit without warning by sudden snow storms. Exposed plains and ridges are prone to extremely high winds and this significantly adds to the cold. For example, on a 5000m pass in central Tibet in July, the absolute minimum temperature is roughly -4°C, but regularly occurring 70km/h winds plunge the wind-chill factor or apparent temperature to -20°C.

Always be prepared for cold, wet or windy conditions, especially if you're out walking at high altitudes or even taking a long bus trip over mountains (particularly at night).

Hypothermia occurs when the body loses heat faster than it can produce it and the core temperature of the body falls. It is surprisingly easy to progress from very cold to dangerously cold through a combination of wind, wet clothing, fatigue and hunger, even if the air temperature is above freezing.

Symptoms of hypothermia are exhaustion, numb skin (particularly toes and fingers), shivering, slurred speech, irrational or violent behaviour, lethargy, stumbling, dizzy spells, muscle cramps and violent bursts of energy. Irrationality may take the form of sufferers claiming they are warm and trying to take off their clothes.

To treat mild hypothermia, first get the person out of the wind and rain, remove their clothing if it's wet and replace it with dry, warm clothing. Give them hot liquids (not alcohol) and some high-energy, easily digestible food. Do not rub victims; instead, allow them to slowly warm themselves. This should be enough to treat the early stages of hypothermia. The early recognition and treatment of mild hypothermia is the only way to prevent severe hypothermia, which is a critical condition.

Sunburn

It's very easy to get sunburnt in Tibet's high altitudes, especially if you're trekking. Wear sunglasses, loose-fitting clothes that cover your arms, legs and neck, and a wide-brimmed hat like the ones Tibetans wear (not a baseball cap).

Choose sunscreen with a high sun protection factor (SPF). Those with fair complexions should bring reflective sunscreen (containing zinc oxide or titanium oxide) with them. Apply the sunscreen to your nose and lips (and especially the tops of your ears if you are not wearing a hat).

Water

The number-one rule is don't drink the tap water, including ice. In urban centres Tibetans, like the Chinese, boil their drinking water to make it safe to drink hot or cooled. In the country and while trekking you should boil your own water or treat it with water-purification tablets, as livestock contaminate many of the water sources. Tea is always safe to drink. Locally brewed beer (chang) is another matter. It is often made with contaminated well water and there is always some risk in drinking it.

WATER PURIFICATION

The simplest way to purify water is to boil it thoroughly. At Tibet's high altitude, water boils at a lower temperature and germs are less likely to be killed, so make sure you boil water for at least 10 minutes.

Consider purchasing a water filter for a long trip (often more economical than buying bottled water). Total filters take out all parasites, bacteria and viruses, and make water safe to drink.

Chlorine tablets (eg Puritabs or Steritabs) will kill many pathogens, but not giardia and amoebic cysts.

Iodine is more effective for purifying water and is available in liquid (Lugol's solution) or tablet form (eg Potable Aqua). Follow the directions carefully and remember that too much iodine can be harmful.

Tibetan Medicine

The basic teachings of Tibetan medicine share much with those of other Asian medical traditions, which, according to some scholars, made their way to the East via India from ancient Greece. These traditions look at symptoms as indications of an imbalance in the body and seek to restore that balance.

The theory of Tibetan medicine is based on an extremely complex system of checks and balances between what can be broadly described as three 'humours' (related to state of mind), seven 'bodily sustainers' (related to the digestive tract) and three 'eliminators' (related to the elimination of bodily wastes). There is also the influence of harmful spirits to consider: 360 harmful female influences, 360 harmful male influences, 360 malevolent naga (water spirits) influences and, finally, 360 influences stemming from past karma. All these combine to produce 404 basic disorders and 84,000 illnesses!

How does a Tibetan doctor assess the condition of a patient? The most important skill is pulse diagnosis. A Tibetan doctor is attuned to 360 'subtle channels' of energy that run through the body's skin and muscle, internal organs and bone and marrow. The condition of these channels can be ascertained through six of the doctor's fingers (the first three fingers of each hand). Tibetan medicine also relies on urine analysis as an important diagnostic tool.

Yuthok Yongten Gonpo (1182–1251), the physician of King Trisong Detsen, who was born near Ralung Monastery, is credited as the founder of the Tibetan medical system. For more on Tibetan medicine see www.tibetan-medicine.org.

Lhasa's **Mentsikhang** (Traditional Tibetan Hospital, 藏医院, Zàngyīyuàn; Map p46; Yuthok Lam; ☺9.30am-12.30pm & 3.30-6pm) is located opposite the Barkhor. Two English-speaking doctors attend to foreigners on the 3rd floor.

Language

The two principal languages of Tibet are Tibetan and Mandarin Chinese. In urban Tibet (the countryside is another matter) almost all Tibetans speak Tibetan and Mandarin, and all Tibetans undertaking higher studies do so in Chinese. Linguistically, Chinese and Tibetan have little in common. They use different sentence structures, and the tones are far less crucial in Tibetan than in Chinese. Also, unlike the dialects of China, Tibetan has never used Chinese characters for its written language.

TIBETAN

Tibetan belongs to the Tibeto-Burman group of languages, and is spoken by around six million people, mainly in Tibet but also within Tibetan communities in Nepal, India, Bhutan and Pakistan. The Lhasa dialect is the standard form of Tibetan.

Most sounds in Tibetan are similar to those in English, so if you read our coloured pronunciation guides as if they were English, you'll be understood. Note that the symbol â is pronounced as the 'a' in 'ago', ö as the 'er' in 'her', and ü as the 'u' in 'flute' but with a raised tongue.

When a vowel is followed by n, m or ng, this indicates a nasalised sound (pronounced with air escaping through the nose). When a consonant is followed by h, the consonant is aspirated (ie accompanied by a puff of air).

Basics

There are no words in Tibetan that are the direct equivalents of the English 'yes' and 'no'. You'll be understood if you use *la ong* for 'yes' and *la men* for 'no'.

Hello.		ta·shi de·lek
Goodbye.		ka·lee pay
	(said when staying)	
		ka·lee shu
	(said when leaving)	

Sorry.		gong·da
Excuse me.		gong·da
Please.		tu·jay·sig
Thank you.		tu·jay·chay

How are you?
kay·râng ku·su
de·po yin·bay

Fine, and you?
de·bo·yin kay·râng·yâng
ku·su de·po yin·bay

What's your name?
kay·râng·gi tsen·lâ
kâ·ray·ray

My name is ...
ngay·ming·la ... ray

Do you speak English?
kay·râng in·ji·kay
shing·gi yö·bay

I don't understand.
ha ko ma·song

WANT MORE?

For in-depth language information and handy phrases, check out Lonely Planet's *Tibet Phrasebook* and *China Phrasebook*. You'll find them at **shop. lonelyplanet.com**, or you can buy Lonely Planet's iPhone phrasebooks at the Apple App Store.

Accommodation

I'm looking	གཅིག་མིག་	...·chig mig
for a ...	བཙ་གྱི་ཡོད།	ta·gi·yö
campsite	གུར་བརྒྱབ་ནས་	gur gyâb·nay
	སྡོད་སའི་ས་ཆ	dö·say sa·cha
guesthouse	མགྲོན་ཁང་	drön·khâng
hotel	འགྲུལ་ཁང་	drü·khâng

I'd like to book a room.

ཁང་མིག་ཅིག་གླ་དགོས་ལ་ཡོད། khâng·mi·chig la gö·yö

How much for one night?

མཚན་གཅིག་ལ་གོང་ tsen chig·la gong
ག་ཚོད་རེད། kâ·tsay ray

I'd like to stay with a Tibetan family.

དབོད་པའི་མི་ཚང་ nga bö·pay mi·tsâng
མཉམ་དུ་བསྡད་འདོད་ཡོད། nyâm·do den·dö yö

I need some hot water.

ང་ལ་ཆུ་ཚ་པོ་དགོས། nga·la chu tsa·po gö

Numbers – Tibetan		
1	༡	chig
2	༢	nyi
3	༣	soom
4	༤	shi
5	༥	nga
6	༦	doog
7	༧	dün
8	༨	gye
9	༩	gu
10	༡༠	chu
20	༢༠	nyi·shu
30	༣༠	soom·chu
40	༤༠	shib·chu
50	༥༠	ngâb·chu
60	༦༠	doog·chu
70	༧༠	dün·chu
80	༨༠	gyay·chu
90	༩༠	goob·chu
100	༡༠༠	gya
1000	༡༠༠༠	chig·tong

Directions

Where is ...?

... ག་བར་ཡོད་རེད། ... ka·bah yö·ray

Can you show me (on the map)?

(ས་ཁྲ་འདི་ནང་) (sâp·ta di·nâng)
སྟོན་གནང་དང་། tön nâng·da

Turn left/right.

གཡོན་ལ་/གཡས་ལ་ yön·la/yeh·la
སྐྱོག་གནང་། kyog·nâng

straight ahead	ཁ་ཐུག་འགྲོ།	ka·toog·do
behind ...	... རྒྱབ་ལ་	... gyâb·lâ
in front of ...	... མདུན་ལ་	... dün·lâ
near (to) ...	... འཁྲིས་ལ་	... tee·lâ
opposite ...	... ཕར་ཕྱོགས་ལ་	... pha·chog·lâ

Eating & Drinking

What do you recommend?

ཁྱེད་རང་བྱེད་ན་ག་རེ་ kay·râng chay·na kâ·ray
ཡག་གི་རེད། yâ·gi·ray

What's in that dish?

ཁ་ལག་ཕ་གིའི་ནང་ག་རེ་ kha·la pha·gi·nâng kâ·ray
ཡོད་རེད། yö·ray

I'm vegetarian.

ང་ཤ་མི་ཟ་མཁན་ཡིན། nga sha mi·sa·ken yin

That meal was delicious.

ཁ་ལག་ཞིམ་པོ་ཞེ་དྲགས་ kha·la shim·bu shay·ta
བྱུང་། choong

breakfast	ཞོགས་ཀའི་ཁ་ལག་	shog·kay kha·la
coffee	ཇ་ཀ་པི་	cha ka·bi
dinner	དགོང་དག་ཁ་ལག་	gong·da kha·la
fish	ཉ་ཤ་	nya·sha
food	ཁ་ལག་	kha·la
fruit	ཤིང་ཏོག་	shing·tog
juice	ཁུ་བ་	khu·wa
lunch	ཉིན་གུང་	nyin·goong
	ཁ་ལག་	kha·la
meat	ཤ་	sha
milk	འོ་མ་	oh·ma

Tibetan Trekking Essentials

How many hours to ...?

ང... བར་དུ་ཆུ་ཚོད་ག་ཚོད་འགོར་གི་རེད།

... bah·tu chu·tsö kâ·tsay go·gi·ray

I want to rent a yak/horse.

ངག་ཡལ་/ར་གཅིག་ག་དགོས་ཡོད།

nga yâk/ta·chig la·gö·yö

I need a porter.

ངའི་དོ་པོ་ཁུར་མཁན་གཅིག་དགོས།

nga doh·bo khu·khen·chig gö

I need a guide.

ངལ་སྐྱ་ས་བྱེད་མཁན་གཅིག་དགོས།

nga lâm·gyü chay·khen·chig gö

How much does it cost per day?

ཉིན་མ་རེ་རེ་ལ་སྐ་ཆག་ཚོ་རེད།

nyi·ma ray·ray·la la·ja kâ·tsay ray

Which way to ...?

ང... འགྲོ་ཡག་གི་ལམ་ག་ག་གི་རེད།

... doh·ya·gi lâm·ga ka·gi·ray

Is this the trail to ...?

འདི ... འགྲོ་ཡག་གི་ལམ་ག་རེད་པས།

di ... doh·ya·gi lâm·ga re·bay

What is the next village on the trail?

ལམ་ག་དེ་ནས་ཕྱིན་ན་དང་པོ་ལུང་པ་ག་རེ་སྐེབས་ཀྱི་རེད།

lâm·ga te·nay chin·na dàng·po loong·pa ka·ray leb·ki·ray

I have altitude sickness.

ངལ་དུག་ན་གིས།

nga lâ·du na·gi

I must get to low ground as quickly as possible.

ངས་དམའ་སར་གང་གྱོགས་མགྱོགས་འཕྲོ་ར་དགོས་ཀྱི་འདུག

nga sa mah·sa gâng gyok·gyok joh go·ki·du

Slowly, slowly!	ག་ལེ་ག་ལེ།	ka·lee ka·lee
Let's go!	ད་འགྲོ།	ta doh
north	བྱང་	chàng
south	ལྷོ་	lho
east	ཤར་	shâr
west	ནུབ་	noob
cave	བྲག་ཕུག	dâg·phuk
hot spring	ཆུ་ཚན་	chu·tsen
lake	མཚོ་	tso
mountain	རི	ri
pass	ལ་	la
river	གཙང་པོ་	tsàng·po
road/trail	ལམ་	lam
sleeping bag	ཉལ་ཁུག	nye·koog
tent	གུར་	gur
valley	ལུང་གཤོང་	loong shong

restaurant	ཟ་ཁང་	sa·khâng
tea	ཇ་	cha
vegetable	སྔོ་ཚལ་	ngo·tsay
(boiled) water	ཆུ་ (འཁོལ་མ་)	chu (khö·ma)

For more food terms, see the Glossary.

Emergencies

Help!	རོགས་གནང་དང་།	rog nàng·da
Go away!	ཕར་རྒྱུགས།	phâh gyook
Call ...	... སྐོད།	... kay
	གཏོང་དང་།	tong·da
a doctor	ཨེམ་ཆི	ahm·chi
the police	སྐོར་སྲུང་བ་	kor·soong·wa

I'm lost.

ངལ་ག་བརྫངས་ཤག

nga lâm·ga la·sha

I'm allergic to ...

ངར་ ... ཕོགས་ཀྱི་ཡོད།

ngah ... pho·gi·yö

Shopping & Services

Do you have any ... ?

ཁྱེད་རང་ལ་ ...

kay·râng·la ...

བཙོང་ཡག་ཡོད་པས།

tsong·ya yö·bay

How much is it?

གོང་ག་ཚོ་རེད།

gong kâ·tsay ray

It's too expensive.

གོང་ཆེ་དྲགས་ཤག

gong chay·ta·sha

Signs – Tibetan

Tibetan	English
འཛུལ་ས་	Entrance
དོན་ས་	Exit
སྒོ་ཕྱེ་	Open
སྒོ་བརྒྱབ་	Closed
པར་བརྒྱབ་མི་ཆོག	No Photographs
གསང་སྤྱོད་	Toilets

I'll give you ...

	ངས་ ... སྤྲད་དགོས།	ngay ... tay go
bank	དངུལ་ཁང་	ngü·khâng
post office	སྦྲག་ཁང་	da·khâng
tourist office	ཡུལ་སྐོར་	yu·kor
	སྒོ་འཛམས་པའི་	to·châm·pay
	ལས་ཁུངས་	lay·khoong

Time & Dates

What time it is?
དཔྱ་ཆུ་ཚོད་ག་ཚོད་རེད། — tân·da chu·tsö kâ·tsay·ray

It's half past (two).
ཆུ་ཚོད་ (གཉིས་) དང་ — chu·tsö (nyi)·dâng
ཕྱེད་ཀ་རེད། — chay·ka ray

It's (two) o'clock.
ཆུ་ཚོད་ (གཉིས་) པ་རེད། — chu·tsö (nyi)·pa ray

yesterday	ཁ་ས་	kay·sa
today	དེ་རིང་	te·ring
tomorrow	སང་ཉིན་	sa·nyin
Monday	གཟའ་ཟླ་བ་	sa da·wa
Tuesday	གཟའ་མིག་དམར་	sa mig·ma
Wednesday	གཟའ་ལྷག་པ་	sa lhâg·bâ
Thursday	གཟའ་ཕུར་བུ་	sa phu·bu
Friday	གཟའ་པ་སངས་	sa pa·sâng
Saturday	གཟའ་སྤེན་པ་	sa pem·pa
Sunday	གཟའ་ཉི་མ་	sa nyi·mâ

Transport

Where is this	... འདི་ག་པར་	... ka·bah
... going?	འགྲོ་གི་རེད་	doh·gi ray
boat	གྲུ་གཟིངས་	dru·zing
bus	སྤྱི་སྤྱོད་	chi·chö
	ལྕགས་འཁོར་	lâng·kho
plane	གནམ་གྲུ་	nâm·du
I'd like to	ང་ ... གཅིག	nga ...·chig
hire a ...	གླས་འདོད་ཡོད།	yar dhö·yö
car	མོ་ཊ་	mo·ta
donkey	བོང་གུ་	boong·gu
landcruiser	ལེན་ཀུ་རུ་ས་	len ku·ru·sa
pack animals	ཁལ་སེམས་ཅན་/	kel sem·chen/
	ཁལ་མ་	kel·ma
porter	དོ་པོ་ཁུར་མཁན་	doh·po khu·khen
yak	གཡག་	yak

How much is it daily/weekly?
ཉིན་/བདུན་ཕྲག་རེ་རེར་ — nyin/dun·tâg ray·ray
གོང་ག་ཚོད་རེད། — gong kâ·tsay ray

Does this road lead to ...?
ལམ་ག་འདི་ ... — lâm·ga·di ...
འགྲོ་ཡག་རེད་པས། — doh·ya re·bay

Can I get there on foot?
ཕ་གིར་གོམ་པ་བརྒྱབ་ནས་ — pha·gay gom·pa gyâb·nay
སླེབས་ཐུབ་ཀྱི་རེད་པས། — leb thoob·ki re·bay

MANDARIN

Pronunciation

In this section we've provided Pinyin (a system of writing Chinese using the Roman alphabet) alongside the Mandarin script.

Vowels

a	as in 'father'
ai	as in 'aisle'
ao	as the 'ow' in 'cow'
e	as in 'her', with no 'r' sound
ei	as in 'weigh'
i	as the 'ee' in 'meet' (or like a light 'r' as in 'Grrr!' after c, ch, r, s, sh, z or zh)
ian	as the word 'yen'

ie	as the English word 'yeah'
o	as in 'or', with no 'r' sound
ou	as the 'oa' in 'boat'
u	as in 'flute'
ui	as the word 'way'
uo	like a 'w' followed by 'o'
yu/ü	like 'ee' with lips pursed

Consonants

Note that in Pinyin apostrophes are sometimes used to separate syllables in order to avoid mispronunciation, eg píng'ān.

c	as the 'ts' in 'bits'
ch	as in 'chop', but with the tongue curled up and back
h	as in 'hay', but articulated from farther back in the throat
q	as the 'ch' in 'cheese'
r	as the 's' in 'pleasure'
sh	as in 'ship', but with the tongue curled up and back
x	as in 'ship'
z	as the 'dz' in 'suds'
zh	as the 'j' in 'judge' but with the tongue curled up and back

Tones

Mandarin has many words with the same pronunciation but a different meaning. What distinguishes these words is their 'tonal' quality – the raising and the lowering of pitch on certain syllables. For example, the word ma has four different meanings according to tone, as shown below. Tones are indicated in Pinyin by the following accent marks on vowels:

high tone	mā (mother)
rising tone	má (hemp, numb)
falling-rising tone	mǎ (horse)
falling tone	mà (scold, swear)

Basics

Hello.	你好。	Nǐhǎo.
Goodbye.	再见。	Zàijiàn.
How are you?	你好吗？	Nǐhǎo ma?
Fine. And you?	好。你呢？	Hǎo. Nǐ ne?
Yes./No.	是。/不是。	Shì./Bùshì.
Please ...	请……	Qǐng ...
Thank you.	谢谢你。	Xièxie nǐ.
You're welcome.	不客气。	Bù kèqi.
Excuse me.	劳驾。	Láojià.
Sorry.	对不起。	Duìbùqǐ.

What's your name?
你叫什么名字？　　　Nǐ jiào shénme míngzi?

My name is ...
我叫……　　　Wǒ jiào ...

Do you speak English?
你会说英文吗？　　　Nǐ huìshuō Yīngwén ma?

I don't understand.
我不明白。　　　Wǒ bù míngbai.

Accommodation

Do you have a single/double room?
有没有（单人/　　　Yǒuméiyǒu (dānrén/
套）房？　　　tào) fáng?

How much is it per night/person?
每天/人多少钱？　　　Měi tiān/rén duōshǎo
　　　qián?

campsite	露营地	lùyíngdì
guesthouse	宾馆	bīnguǎn
hostel	招待所	zhāodàisuǒ
hotel	酒店	jiǔdiàn
air-con	空调	kōngtiáo
bathroom	浴室	yùshì
bed	床	chuáng
window	窗	chuāng

Numbers – Mandarin

1	一	yī
2	二/两	èr/liǎng
3	三	sān
4	四	sì
5	五	wǔ
6	六	liù
7	七	qī
8	八	bā
9	九	jiǔ
10	十	shí
20	二十	èrshí
30	三十	sānshí
40	四十	sìshí
50	五十	wǔshí
60	六十	liùshí
70	七十	qīshí
80	八十	bāshí
90	九十	jiǔshí
100	一百	yībǎi
1000	一千	yīqiān

Signs – Mandarin

入口	Rùkǒu	**Entrance**
出口	Chūkǒu	**Exit**
问讯处	Wènxùnchù	**Information**
开	Kāi	**Open**
关	Guān	**Closed**
禁止	Jìnzhǐ	**Prohibited**
厕所	Cèsuǒ	**Toilets**
男	Nán	**Men**
女	Nǚ	**Women**

Directions

Where's (a bank)?
（银行）在哪儿？ (Yínháng) zài nǎr?

What is the address?
地址在哪儿？ Dìzhǐ zài nǎr?

Could you write the address, please?
能不能请你 Néngbunéng qǐng nǐ
把地址写下来？ bǎ dìzhǐ xiě xiàlái?

Can you show me where it is on the map?
请帮我找它在 Qǐng bāngwǒ zhǎo tā zài
地图上的位置。 dìtú shàng de wèizhi.

Go straight ahead.
一直走。 Yīzhí zǒu.

at the next corner
在下一个拐角 zài xià yīge guǎijiǎo

at the traffic lights
在红绿灯 zài hónglǜdēng

behind	背面	bèimiàn
far	远	yuǎn
in front of ...	……的前面	... de qiánmian
near	近	jìn
next to	旁边	pángbiān
on the corner	拐角	guǎijiǎo
opposite	对面	duìmiàn
Turn left/right.	左／右转。	Zuǒ/Yòu zhuǎn.

Eating & Drinking

What would you recommend?
有什么菜可以 Yǒu shénme cài kěyǐ
推荐的？ tuījiàn de?

What's in that dish?
这道菜用什么 Zhèdào cài yòng shénme
东西做的？ dōngxi zuòde?

That was delicious!
真好吃！ Zhēn hǎochī!

The bill, please! 买单！ Mǎidān!
Cheers! 干杯！ Gānbēi!

I don't eat ... 我不吃…… Wǒ bùchī ...
fish 鱼 yú
nuts 果仁 guǒrén
poultry 家禽 jiāqín
red meat 牛羊肉 niúyángròu

Emergencies

Help! 救命！ Jiùmìng!
I'm lost. 我迷路了。 Wǒ mílù le.
Go away! 走开！ Zǒukāi!

There's been an accident!
出事了！ Chūshì le!

Call a doctor!
请叫医生来！ Qǐng jiào yīshēng lái!

Call the police!
请叫警察！ Qǐng jiào jǐngchá!

I'm ill.
我生病了。 Wǒ shēngbìng le.

I'm allergic to (antibiotics).
我对（抗菌素） Wǒ duì (kàngjūnsù)
过敏。 guòmǐn.

Shopping & Services

I'd like to buy ...
我想买…… Wǒ xiǎng mǎi ...

Can I look at it?
我能看看吗？ Wǒ néng kànkan ma?

How much is it?
多少钱？ Duōshǎo qián?

That's too expensive!
太贵了！ Tàiguì le!

Can you lower the price?
能便宜一点吗？ Néng piányi yīdiǎn ma?

There's a mistake in the bill.
帐单上 Zhàngdān shàng
有问题。 yǒu wèntí.

internet cafe	网吧	wǎngbā
post office	邮局	yóujú
tourist office	旅行店	lǚxíng diàn

Time & Dates

What time is it?
现在几点钟？ Xiànzài jǐdiǎn zhōng?

It's (10) o'clock.
（十）点钟。 (Shí)diǎn zhōng.

Half past (10).
（十）点三十分。 (Shí)diǎn sānshífēn.

morning	早上	zǎoshang
afternoon	下午	xiàwǔ
evening	晚上	wǎnshàng
yesterday	昨天	zuótiān
today	今天	jīntiān
tomorrow	明天	míngtiān

Monday	星期一	xīngqī yī
Tuesday	星期二	xīngqī èr
Wednesday	星期三	xīngqī sān
Thursday	星期四	xīngqī sì
Friday	星期五	xīngqī wǔ
Saturday	星期六	xīngqī liù
Sunday	星期天	xīngqī tiān

Transport

boat	船	chuán
bus	长途车	chángtú chē
plane	飞机	fēijī
taxi	出租车	chūzū chē
train	火车	huǒchē

I want to go to ...
我要去……   Wǒ yào qù ...

What time does it leave?
几点钟出发？   Jǐdiǎnzhōng chūfā?

What time does it get to ...?
几点钟到……？   Jǐdiǎnzhōng dào ...?

I want to get off here.
我想这儿下车。   Wǒ xiǎng zhèr xiàchē.

When's the ... (bus)?	……（车） 几点走？	... (chē) jǐdiǎn zǒu?
first	首趟	Shǒutàng
last	末趟	Mòtàng
next	下一趟	Xià yītàng

A ... ticket to (Dalian).	一张到 （大连）的 ……票。	Yīzhāng dào (Dàlián) de ... piào.
1st-class	头等	tóuděng
2nd-class	二等	èrděng

Question Words – Mandarin

How?	怎么？	Zěnme?
What?	什么？	Shénme?
When?	什么时候	Shénme shíhòu?
Where?	哪儿	Nǎr?
Which?	哪个	Nǎge?
Who?	谁？	Shuí?
Why?	为什么？	Wèishénme?

one-way	单程	dānchéng
return	双程	shuāngchéng

cancelled	取消	qǔxiāo
delayed	晚点	wǎndiǎn
ticket office	售票处	shòupiàochù
timetable	时刻表	shíkè biǎo
I'd like to hire a ...	我要租 一辆……	Wǒ yào zū yīliàng ...
4WD	四轮驱动	sìlún qūdòng
bicycle	自行车	zìxíngchē
car	汽车	qìchē
motorcycle	摩托车	mótuochē

Does this road lead to ...?
这条路到……吗？   Zhè tiáo lù dào ... ma?

How long can I park here?
这儿可以停多久？   Zhèr kěyǐ tíng duōjiǔ?

The car has broken down (at ...).
汽车是（在……）坏的。   Qìchē shì (zài ...) huài de.

I have a flat tyre.
轮胎瘪了。   Lúntāi biě le.

I've run out of petrol.
没有汽油了。   Méiyou qìyóu le.

bicycle pump	打气筒	dǎqìtóng
child seat	婴儿座	yīng'érzuò
diesel	柴油	cháiyóu
helmet	头盔	tóukuī
gas/petrol	汽油	qìyóu
mechanic	机修工	jīxiūgōng
service station	加油站	jiāyóu zhàn

GLOSSARY

The main entries in this chapter are the Tibetan terms, unless otherwise indicated. (S) denotes Sanskrit and (M) stands for Mandarin.

Who's Who

This section presents some of the deities, historical figures and other people mentioned in this book. Many terms are of Sanskrit origin.

Akshobhya (S) – see *Mikyöba*

Amitabha (S) – see *Öpagme*

Amitayus (S) – see *Tsepame*

Atisha (S) – see *Jowo-je*

Avalokiteshvara (S) – see *Chenresig*

Bhrikuti – the Nepali consort of King Songtsen Gampo (Tibetan: Pesa Chitsun)

Büton Rinchen Drup – compiler of the Tibetan Buddhist canon; established a sub-school of Tibetan Buddhism, based in Shalu Monastery

Chana Dorje (S: Vajrapani) – the wrathful Bodhisattva of Energy whose name means 'thunderbolt in hand'

Chenresig (S: Avalokiteshvara) – an embodiment of compassionate bodhisattvahood and the patron saint of Tibet; the Dalai Lamas are considered to be manifestations of this deity

Chögyel (S: Dharmaraja) – Gelugpa protector deity; blue, with the head of a bull

Chökyong (S: Lokapalas) – the Four Guardian Kings

Citipati – dancing skeletons, often seen in protector chapels

Dalai Lama – spiritual head of the Gelugpa order, which ruled over Tibet from 1642 until 1959; the term is an honorific that means 'ocean of wisdom' and was bestowed by the Mongolian Altyn Khan; also believed to be the manifestation of Chenresig (Avalokiteshvara)

Dharmaraja (S) – see *Chögyel*

Dorje Chang (S: Vajradhara) – one of the five Dhyani buddhas, recognisable by his crossed arms holding a bell and thunderbolt

Dorje Drolo – wrathful form of Guru Rinpoche, seated on a tiger

Dorje Jigje (S: Yamantaka) – a meditational deity who comes in various aspects; the Red and Black aspects are probably the most common

Dorje Lekpa – Dzogchen deity, recognisable by his round green hat and goat mount

Dorje Shugden – controversial protector deity outlawed by the Dalai Lama

Drölma (S: Tara) – a female meditational deity who is a manifestation of the enlightened mind of all buddhas; she is sometimes referred to as the mother of all buddhas, and has many aspects, but is most often seen as Green Tara or as Drölkar (White Tara)

Dromtönpa – 11th-century disciple of Jowo-je (*Atisha*) who founded the Kadampa order and Reting Monastery

Ekajati (S) – see *Tsechigma*

Gar Tsongtsen – Prime Minister of King Songtsen Gampo who travelled to Chang'an in 641, returning with Princess Wencheng

Gesar – a legendary king and also the name of an epic concerning his fabulous exploits; the king's empire is known as Ling, and thus the stories, which are usually sung and told by professional bards, are known as the *Stories of Ling*

Gompo Gur – a form of Nagpo Chenpo (Mahakala) and protector of the Sakyapa school

Guru Rinpoche – credited with having suppressed demons and other malevolent forces in order to introduce Buddhism into Tibet during the 8th century; in the Nyingmapa order he is revered as the Second Buddha

Hayagriva (S) – see *Tamdrin*

Jamchen Chöje – disciple of Tsongkhapa and founder of Sera Monastery; also known as Sakya Yeshe

Jampa (S: Maitreya) – the Buddha of Loving Kindness; also the Future Buddha, the fifth of the 1000 buddhas who will descend to earth (Sakyamuni or Sakya Thukpa was the fourth)

Jampelyang (S: Manjushri) – the Bodhisattva of Insight; usually depicted holding a sword (which symbolises discriminative awareness) in one hand and a book (which symbolises his mastery of all knowledge) in the other

Jamyang Chöje – founder of Drepung Monastery

Je Rinpoche – see *Tsongkhapa*

Jowo Sakyamuni – the most revered image of Sakyamuni (Sakya Thukpa) in Tibet, it depicts the Historical Buddha at the age of 12 and is kept in the Jokhang in Lhasa

Jowo-je (S: Atisha) – 11th-century Buddhist scholar from contemporary Bengal whose arrival in Tibet at the invitation of the king of Guge was a catalyst for the revival of Buddhism on the high plateau

Karmapa – a lineage (17 so far) of spiritual leaders of the Karma Kagyupa; also known as the Black Hats

Khenlop Chösum – Trinity of Guru Rinpoche, Trisong Detsen and Shantarakshita, found at Samye Monastery

Kunga Gyaltsen – see *Sakya Pandita*

Langdharma – the 9th-century Tibetan king accused of having persecuted Buddhists

Lokapalas (S) – see *Chökyong*

Longchen Rabjampa – (1308–63) *Nyingmapa* and *Dzogchen* teacher and writer, revered as a manifestation of Jampelyang; also known as Longchenpa

Machik Labdronma – (1031–1129) female yogini connected to Shugsheb Nunnery

LANGUAGE GLOSSARY

Mahakala (S) – see *Nagpo Chenpo*

Maitreya (S) – see *Jampa*

Manjushri (S) – see *Jampelyang*

Marpa – 11th-century ascetic whose disciple, Milarepa, founded the Kagyupa order

Mikyöba (S: Akshobhya) – the Buddha of the State of Perfected Consciousness, or Perfect Cognition; literally 'unchanging', 'the immutable one'

Milarepa (1040–1123) disciple of Marpa and founder of the Kagyupa order; renowned for his songs

Nagpo Chenpo – The Great Black One, wrathful manifestation of Chenresig that carries echoes of the Indian god Shiva; see *Mahakala*

Namgyelma – three-faced, eight-armed female deity and one of the three deities of longevity

Namse (S: Vairocana) – Buddha of Enlightened Consciousness, generally white; also a renowned Tibetan translator

Namtöse (S: Vaishravana) – the Guardian of the North, one of the Chökyong or Four Guardian Kings

Nechung – protector deity of Tibet and the Dalai Lamas; manifested in the State Oracle, who is traditionally installed at Nechung Monastery

Nyenchen Tanglha – mountain spirit and protector deity that has its roots in Bön

Nyentri Tsenpo – legendary first king of Tibet

Öpagme (S: Amitabha) – the Buddha of Perfected Perception; literally 'infinite light'

Palden Lhamo (S: Shri Devi) – special protector of Lhasa, the Dalai Lama and the Gelugpa order; the female counterpart of Nagpo Chenpo (Mahakala)

Panchen Lama – literally 'guru and great teacher'; the lineage is associated with Tashilhunpo Monastery, Shigatse, and goes back to the 17th century; the Panchen Lama is a manifestation of Öpagme (Amitabha)

Pehar – oracle and protector of the Buddhist state, depicted with six arms, wearing a round hat and riding a snow lion

Rahulla – Dzogchen deity with nine heads, eyes all over his body, a mouth in his belly and the lower half of a serpent (coiled on the dead body of ego)

Ralpachen – 9th-century king whose assassination marked the end of the Yarlung Valley dynasty

Rigsum Gonpo – trinity of bodhisattvas consisting of Chenresig (Avalokiteshvara), Jampelyang (Manjushri) and Chana Dorje (Vajrapani)

Rinchen Zangpo – (958–1055) the Great Translator, who travelled to India for 17 years and established monasteries across Ladakh, Spiti and western Tibet

Sakya Pandita (S) – literally 'scholar from Sakya'; former abbot of Sakya Monastery who established the priest-patron system with the Mongols; also known as Kunga Gyaltsen

Sakya Thukpa – see *Sakyamuni*

Sakyamuni (S) – literally the 'sage of Sakya'; the founder of Buddhism, the Historical Buddha; known in Tibetan as Sakya Thukpa; see also *Siddhartha Gautama* and *buddha*

Samvara (S) – a wrathful multi-armed deity and manifestation of Sakyamuni (Demchok in Tibetan)

Shantarakshita – Indian scholar of the 8th century and first abbot of Samye Monastery; Kende Shewa in Tibetan

Shenrab – founder of the Bön faith

Shiromo – Bönpo deity, the equivalent of Sakyamuni

Shri Devi (S) – see *Palden Lhamo*

Siddhartha Gautama (S) – the personal name of the Historical Buddha; see also *Sakyamuni* (Sakya Thukpa)

Songtsen Gampo – the 7th-century king associated with the introduction of Buddhism to Tibet

Tamdrin (S: Hayagriva) – literally 'horse necked'; a wrathful meditational deity and manifestation of Chenresig, usually associated with the Nyingmapa order

Tangtong Gyelpo – (1385–1464) Tibetan yogi, treasure finder (*terton*), bridge builder, medic and developer of Tibetan opera; often depicted holding a chain link in his hands

Tara (S) – see *Drölma*

Tenzin Gyatso – the 14th and current Dalai Lama

Terdak Lingpa – founder of Mindroling Monastery

Trisong Detsen – 8th-century Tibetan king; founder of Samye Monastery

Tsechigma (S: Ekajati) – protectress with one eye, one tooth and one breast, associated with the Dzogchen movement

Tsepame (S: Amitayus) – a meditational deity associated with longevity; literally 'limitless life'; often featured in a trinity with Drölma (Tara) and Namgyelma (Vijaya)

Tseringma – protector goddess of Mt Everest, depicted riding a snow lion

Tsongkhapa – 14th-century founder of the Gelugpa order and Ganden Monastery, also known as 'Je Rinpoche'

Vairocana (S) – see *Namse*

Vaishravana (S) – see *Namtöse*

Vajradhara (S) – see *Dorje Chang*

Vajrapani (S) – see *Chana Dorje*

Vijaya (S) – Sanskrit name for Namgyelma

Wencheng – Chinese wife of King Songtsen Gampo; called Wencheng Konjo in Tibetan

Yama (S) – Lord of Death, who resides in sky-burial sites

Yamantaka (S) – see *Dorje Jigje*

Yeshe Tsogyel – female consort of Guru Rinpoche and one-time wife of King Trisong Detsen

General Terms

Amdo – a traditional province of Tibet, now Qīnghǎi province

AMS – acute mountain sickness; often referred to as altitude sickness

ani – Tibetan for 'nun', as in ani gompa (nunnery)

arhat (S) – literally 'worthy one'; a person who has achieved nirvana; the Tibetan term is 'neten'

Bardo – as detailed in the *Tibetan Book of the Dead*, this term refers to the intermediate stages between death and rebirth

Barkhor – an intermediate circumambulation circuit, or kora, but most often specifically the intermediate circuit around the Jokhang temple of Lhasa

bīnguǎn (M) – guesthouse or hotel

Black Hat – strictly speaking, this refers to the black hat embellished with gold that was presented to the second Karmapa of the Karma Kagyupa order of Tsurphu Monastery by a Mongol prince, and worn ceremoniously by all subsequent incarnations of the Karmapa; by extension the black hat represents the Karma Kagyupa order

Bö – Tibetans' name for their own land, sometimes written 'Bod' or 'Po'

Bodhgaya – the place in contemporary Bihar, India, where Sakyamuni, the Historical Buddha, attained enlightenment

bodhisattva (S) – literally 'enlightenment hero'; the bodhisattva chooses not to take the step to nirvana, being motivated to stay within the Wheel of Life by compassion for all sentient beings

Bön – the indigenous religion of Tibet and the Himalayan borderlands; in its ancient form its main components were royal burial rites, the cult of indigenous deities and magical practices; in the 11th century, Bön was systematised along Buddhist lines and it is this form that survives today

Bönpo – a practitioner of Bön

buddha (S) – literally 'awakened one'; a being who through spiritual training has broken free of all illusion and karmic consequences and is 'enlightened'; most often specifically the Historical Buddha, Sakyamuni

Büton – suborder of Tibetan Buddhism based on the teachings of Büton Rinchen Drup, the 14th-century compiler of the major Buddhist texts; associated with Shalu Monastery, near Shigatse

CAAC – Civil Aviation Authority of China

chakje – handprint of a deity or a religious figure made in rock

chaktsal – ritual prostration

chaktsal gang – prostration point

cham – a ritual dance carried out by monks and lamas, usually at festivals; all participants except the central lama are masked

chang – Tibetan barley beer

Changtang – vast plains of north Tibet extending into Xīnjiāng and Qīnghǎi; the world's largest and highest plateau

chö – see *dharma*

chömay – butter lamp

chörten – Tibetan for stupa; usually used as reliquary for the cremated remains of important lamas

chu – river, stream, brook etc

chuba – long-sleeved sheepskin cloak

CITS – China International Travel Service

CTS – China Travel Service

cūn (M) – village; 'tson' in Tibetan

dakini (S) – see *khandroma*

dharma (S) – 'chö' in Tibetan, and sometimes translated as 'law', this very broad term covers the truths expounded by Sakyamuni, the Buddhist teachings, the path and goal of nirvana; in effect it is the 'law' that must be understood, followed and achieved in order for one to be a Buddhist

doring – stele; carved obelisk commemorating a historic event or edict

dorje – literally 'diamond' or 'thunderbolt'; a metaphor for the indestructible, indivisible nature of buddhahood; also a Tantric hand-held sceptre symbolising 'skilful means'

drokpa – nomad

drubkhang – meditation chamber

dukhang – assembly hall

dukkha (S) – suffering, the essential condition of all life

dungkhar – conch shell

dürtro – sky-burial site

dzo – domesticated cross between a bull and a female yak

Dzogchen – the Great Perfection teachings associated with the Nyingmapa order

dzong – fort

Eightfold Path – one of the Four Noble Truths taught by Sakyamuni; the path that must be taken to achieve enlightenment and liberation from the Wheel of Life

FIT office – Family (or Foreign) and Independent Traveller office

Four Noble Truths – as stated in the first speech given by Sakyamuni after he achieved enlightenment, the Four Noble Truths are: the truth that all life is suffering; the truth that suffering originates in desire; the truth that desire may be extinguished; and the truth that there is a path to this end

Ganden (S) – the pure land of Jampa (Maitreya) and the seat of the Gelugpa order; 'Tushita' in Tibetan

garuda (S: khyung) – mythological bird associated with Hinduism; in Tibetan Tantric Buddhism it is seen as a wrathful force that transforms malevolent influences

gau – an amulet or 'portable shrine' worn around the neck, containing the image of an important spiritual figure, usually the Dalai Lama

Gelugpa – major order of Tibetan Buddhism, associated with the Dalai Lamas, the Panchen Lamas, and the Drepung, Sera,

Ganden and Tashilhunpo Monasteries; founded by Tsongkhapa in the 14th century and sometimes known as the Yellow Hats

geshe – title awarded on completion of the highest level of study (something like a doctorate) that monks may undertake after completing their full indoctrinal vows; usually associated with the Gelugpa order

gompa – monastery

gönkhang – protector chapel

Guge – a 9th-century kingdom of western Tibet

guru (S) – spiritual teacher; literally 'heavy'; the Tibetan equivalent is lama

Hinayana (S) – also called Theravada, this is a major school of Buddhism that follows the original teachings of the Historical Buddha, Sakyamuni, and places less importance on the compassionate bodhisattva ideal and more on individual enlightenment; see also *Mahayana*

Jokhang – situated in Lhasa, this is the most sacred and one of the most ancient of Tibet's temples; also known as the Tsuglhakhang

Kadampa – order of Tibetan Buddhism based on the teachings of the Indian scholar Atisha (Jowo-je); the school was a major influence on the Gelugpa order

Kagyupa – order of Tibetan Buddhism that traces its lineage back through Milarepa and Marpa and eventually to the Indian mahasiddhas; divided into numerous suborders, the most famous of which is the Karma Kagyupa, or the Karmapa; also known as Kagyud

kangtsang – monastic residential quarters

Kangyur – the Tibetan Buddhist canon; its complement is the *Tengyur*

karma (S) – action and its consequences, the psychic 'imprint' that action leaves on the mind and that continues into further rebirths; the term is found in both Hinduism and Buddhism,

and may be likened to the law of cause and effect

Karma Kagyupa – suborder of the Kagyupa order, established by Gampopa and Dusum Khyenpa in the 12th century; represented by the Black Hat

kathak – prayer scarf; used as a ritual offering or as a gift

Kham – traditional eastern Tibetan province; much of it is now part of western Sichuān and northwestern Yúnnán

Khampa – a person from Kham

khandroma (S: dakini) – literally 'sky dancer' or 'sky walker'; a flying angel-like astral being that communicates between the worlds of buddhas, humans and demons

khenpo – abbot

kora – ritual circumambulation circuit; pilgrimage circuit

kumbum – literally '100,000 images', this is a chörten that contains statuary and paintings; the most famous in Tibet is the Gyantse Kumbum in Tsang

la – mountain pass

lama – literally 'unsurpassed'; Tibetan equivalent of Sanskrit word 'guru'; a title bestowed on monks of particularly high spiritual attainment

lamaism – term used by early Western writers on the subject of Tibet to describe Tibetan Buddhism; also used by the Chinese in the term 'lamajiao', literally 'lama religion'

lamrim – the stages on the path to enlightenment; a graduated approach to enlightenment as expounded by Tsongkhapa; associated with the Gelugpa order

lapse – a cairn

lha – life spirit; it may also be present in inanimate objects such as lakes, mountains and trees

lhakhang – chapel

ling – Tibetan term meaning 'royal', usually associated with lesser, outlying temples

lingkhor – an outer pilgrimage circuit; famously, the outer pilgrimage of Lhasa

Losar – Tibetan New Year

lu (M) – road; see also *naga*

mahasiddha – literally 'of great spiritual accomplishment'; a Tantric practitioner who has reached a high level of awareness; there are 84 famous mahasiddhas; the Tibetan term is 'drubchen'

Mahayana (S) – the other major school of Buddhism along with Hinayana; this school emphasises compassion and the altruism of the bodhisattva who remains on the Wheel of Life for the sake of all sentient beings

mandala – a circular representation of the three-dimensional world of a meditational deity; used as a meditation device; the Tibetan term is 'kyilkhor'

mani – prayer

mani lhakhang – small chapel housing a single large prayer wheel

mani stone – a stone with the mantra 'Om mani padme hum' ('hail to the jewel in the lotus') carved on it

mani wall – a wall made with mani stones

mantra (S) – literally 'protection of the mind'; one of the Tantric devices used to achieve identity with a meditational deity and break through the world of illusion; a series of syllables recited as the pure sound made by an enlightened being

meditational deity – a deified manifestation of the enlightened mind with which, according to Tantric ritual, the adept seeks union and thus experience of enlightenment

momo – Tibetan dumpling

Mönlam – a major Lhasa festival established by Tsongkhapa

Mt Meru – the sacred mountain at the centre of the universe; also known as Sumeru

naga (S) – water spirits that may take the form of serpents or semi-humans; the latter can be seen in images of the *naga* kings; the Tibetan term is 'lu'

nangkhor – inner circumambulation circuit, usually within the

CHINESE MENU READER

Snacks

beef noodles in a soup	*niúròu miàn*	牛肉面
boiled dumplings	*shuǐjiǎo*	水饺
fried Muslim noodles and beef	*gānbàn miàn*	干拌面
fried noodle squares	*chǎo miànpian*	炒面片
fried noodles with vegetables	*shūcài chǎomiàn*	蔬菜炒面
fried rice with egg	*jīdàn chǎofàn*	鸡蛋炒饭
fried rice with vegetables	*shūcài chǎofàn*	蔬菜炒饭
Muslim noodles	*lāmiàn*	拉面
steamed meat buns	*bāozi*	包子
steamed white rice	*mǐfàn*	米饭
vermicelli noodles in casserole pot	*shāguō mǐixiàn*	沙锅米线
wonton (soup)	*húndùn (tāng)*	馄饨 (汤)
Xīnjiāng noodles	*Xīnjiāng lāmiàn*	新疆拉面

Top Chinese Dishes

double-cooked fatty pork	*huíguō ròu*	回锅肉
dry-fried runner beans	*gānbiān sìjìdòu*	干煸四季豆
egg and tomato	*fānqié chǎodàn*	番茄炒蛋
eggplant with garlic, ginger, vinegar and scallions	*yúxiāng qiézi*	鱼香茄子
fried green beans	*sùchǎo biǎndòu*	素炒扁豆
fried vegetables	*sùchǎo sùcài*	素炒素菜
pork and green peppers	*qīngjiāo ròupiàn*	青椒肉片
pork and sizzling rice crust	*guōbā ròupiàn*	锅巴肉片
pork in soy sauce	*jīngjiàng ròusī*	京酱肉丝
braised eggplant	*hóngshāo qiézi*	红烧茄子
spicy chicken with peanuts	*gōngbào jīdīng*	宫爆鸡丁
spicy tofu	*málà dòufu*	麻辣豆腐
stir-fried baby bok choy	*sùchǎo xiǎo báicài*	素炒小白菜
stir-fried broccoli	*sùchǎo xīlánhuā*	素炒西兰花
stir-fried greens	*sùchǎo yóucài /kòngxīncài*	素炒油菜/空心菜
stir-fried spinach	*sùchǎo bōcài*	素炒菠菜
sweet and sour pork fillets	*tángcù lǐjí*	糖醋里脊
wood mushrooms and pork	*mù'ěr ròu*	木耳肉

Drinks

beer	*píjiǔ*	啤酒
boiled water	*kāi shuǐ*	开水
hot	*rède*	热的
ice cold	*bīngde*	冰的
mineral water	*kuàngquán shuǐ*	矿泉水
Muslim tea	*bābǎo wǎnzi*	八宝琬子
tea	*chá*	茶

EATING TIBETAN

ENGLISH	TIBETAN PRONUNCIATION	TIBETAN SCRIPT	CHINESE PRONUNCIATION	CHINESE SCRIPT
Butter tea	*bo-cha*	བོད་ཇ།	*sūyóu chá*	酥油茶
Noodles	*thuk-pa*	ཐུག་པ།	*zàngmiàn*	藏面
Rice, potato and yak-meat stew	*shemdre*	ཤ་འབྲས།	*gālí niúròu fàn*	咖喱牛肉饭
Roasted barley flour	*tsampa*	ཙམ་པ།	*zānbā*	糌粑
Tibetan yoghurt	*sho*	ཞོ།	*suānnǎi*	酸奶
Vegetable dumplings	*tse-momo*	ཚལ་མོག་མོག	*sùcài bāozi*	素菜包子
Yak-meat dumplings	*sha-momo*	ཤ་མོག་མོག	*niúròu bāozi*	牛肉包子

interior of a temple or monastic assembly hall, and taking in various chapels en route

neten – see *arhat*

Newari – the people of the Nepali Buddhist kingdoms in the Kathmandu Valley

Ngari – ancient name for the province of western Tibet; later incorporated into Ütsang

Ngorpa – sub-school of the Sakyapa school of Tibetan Buddhism founded by Ngorchen Kunga Sangpo and based at Ngor Monastery in Tsang

nirvana (S) – literally 'beyond sorrow'; an end to desire and suffering, and an end to the cycle of rebirth

Norbulingka – the summer palace of the Dalai Lamas in Lhasa

Nyingmapa – the earliest order of Tibetan Buddhism, based largely on the Buddhism brought to Tibet by Guru Rinpoche

Om mani padme hum – this mantra means 'hail to the jewel in the lotus' and is associated with Chenresig, patron deity of Tibet

oracle – in Tibetan Buddhism an oracle serves as a medium for protector deities, as in the State Oracle of Nechung Monastery near Drepung, Lhasa; the State Oracle was consulted on all important matters of state

Pandita – a title conferred on great scholars of Buddhism, as in Sakya Pandita

parikrama – the Hindu equivalent of a kora

PLA – People's Liberation Army (Chinese army)

PRC – People's Republic of China

protector deities – deities who can manifest themselves in either male or female forms and serve to protect Buddhist teachings and followers; they may be either wrathful aspects of enlightened beings or worldly powers who have been tamed by *Tantric* masters; the Tibetan term is 'chojung'

PSB – Public Security Bureau

puk – cave

pure lands – otherworldly realms that are the domains of buddhas; realms completely free of suffering, and in the popular Buddhist imagination are probably something like the Christian heaven

Qiang – proto-Tibetan tribes that troubled the borders of the Chinese empire

Qomolangma – Tibetan name for Mt Everest as transliterated by the Chinese; also spelt 'Chomolangma'

Qu (M) – administrative district

rangjung – self-manifesting or self-arising; for example, a rock spire could be a rangjung chörten

rebirth – a condition of the Wheel of Life; all beings experience limitless rebirths until they achieve enlightenment

regent – a representative of an incarnate lama who presides over a monastic community during the lama's minority; regents came to play an important political role in the Gelugpa lamaist government

ri – mountain

Rinpoche – literally 'high in esteem', a title bestowed on highly revered lamas; such lamas are usually incarnate but this is not a requirement

ritrö – hermitage

RMB – acronym for Renminbi or 'people's money', the currency of China

rogyapas – the 'body breakers' who prepare bodies for sky burial

sadhu – an Indian ascetic who has renounced all attachments

Saga Dawa – festival held at the full moon of the fourth lunar month to celebrate the enlightenment of Sakyamuni

Sakyapa – Tibetan Buddhist order associated with Sakya Monastery and founded in the 11th century; also known as the Red Hats

samsara (S) – 'kyor dumi' in Tibetan; the cycle of birth, death and rebirth

Samye – the first Buddhist monastery in Tibet, founded by King Trisong Detsen in the 8th century

sang – incense

sangha (S) – community of Buddhist monks or nuns

sangkang – pot-bellied incense burners

Sanskrit – ancient language of India; a classical mode of expression with the status that Latin had in earlier Western society

self-arising – thought to have been created naturally (ie not by humans); often applied to rock carvings; see also *rangjung*

serdung – golden funeral stupa

Shambhala – the mythical great northern paradise, believed to be near the Kunlun mountains

Shangshung – ancient kingdom of western Tibet and place of origin of the Bön faith

shedra – Buddhist college

sky burial – funerary practice of chopping up the corpses of the dead in designated high places (dürtro) and leaving them for the birds

spirit trap – collection of coloured threads wrapped around a wooden frame, used to trap evil spirits

stupa – see *chörten*

sutra (S) – Buddhist scriptures that record the teachings of the Historical Buddha, Sakyamuni

suzerainty – system whereby a dominant power controls a region or country's foreign relations but allows it sovereignty in its internal affairs

Tantra – scriptures and oral lineages associated with Tantric Buddhism

Tantric – of Tantric Buddhism, a movement combining mysticism with Buddhist scripture

TAR – Tibetan Autonomous Region

Tengyur – a Tibetan Buddhist canonical text of collected commentaries on the teachings of Sakyamuni

terma – 'discovered' or 'revealed' teachings; teachings that have been hidden until the world is ready to receive them; one of the most famous *termas* is the *Tibetan Book of the Dead*

terton – discoverer of *terma*, sometimes referred to as a 'treasure finder'

thamzing (M) – 'struggle sessions', a misconceived Chinese tool for changing the ideological orientation of individuals; ultimately a coercive tool that encouraged deceit under the threat of torture

thangka – a Tibetan religious painting usually framed by a silk brocade

Theravada – see *Hinayana*

thugpa – traditional Tibetan noodle dish

torana – halo-like garland that surrounds Buddhist statues

torma – offerings of sculptured *tsampa*

trapa – Tibetan for 'monk'

tratsang – monastic college

Tripa – the post of abbot at Ganden Monastery; head of the Gelugpa order

trulku – incarnate lama, sometimes inaccurately called a 'Living Buddha' by the Chinese

tsampa – roasted-barley flour, traditional staple of the Tibetan people

tsangkhang – inner chapel

tsangpo – large river

tsatsa – stamped clay religious icons

tsenyi lhakhang – debating hall

tso – 'lake'

tsogchen – cathedral or great chapel, also an assembly hall

tsuglhakhang – literally 'grand temple', but often specifically the Jokhang of Lhasa

TTB – Tibet Tourism Bureau

Ütsang – the area comprising the provinces of Ü and Tsang, also incorporating Ngari, or western Tibet; effectively central Tibet, the political, historical and agricultural heartland of Tibet

Vajrayana (S) – literally the 'diamond vehicle', a branch of Mahayana Buddhism that finds a more direct route to bodhisattvahood through identification with meditational deities; vajrayana is the Sanskrit term for the form of Buddhism found in Tibet, known in the West as Tantrism

Wheel of Life – this term refers to the cyclical nature of existence and the six realms where rebirth takes place; often depicted in monasteries

xian (M) – country town

xiang (M) – village

yabyum – Tantric sexual union, symbolising the mental union of female insight and male compassion; fierce deities are often depicted in yabyum with their consorts

yidam – see *meditational deity*; may also have the function of being a personal protector deity that looks over an individual or family

yogin (S: yoga) – an adept of Tibetan Buddhist techniques for achieving a union with the fundamental nature of reality; the techniques include meditation and identification with a meditational deity

yuan (M) – unit of Chinese currency

zhāodàisuŏ (M) – guesthouse, usually a basic hostel

Behind the Scenes

SEND US YOUR FEEDBACK

We love to hear from travellers – your comments keep us on our toes and help make our books better. Our well-travelled team reads every word on what you loved or loathed about this book. Although we cannot reply individually to your submissions, we always guarantee that your feedback goes straight to the appropriate authors, in time for the next edition. Each person who sends us information is thanked in the next edition – the most useful submissions are rewarded with a selection of digital PDF chapters.

Visit **lonelyplanet.com/contact** to submit your updates and suggestions or to ask for help. Our award-winning website also features inspirational travel stories, news and discussions.

Note: We may edit, reproduce and incorporate your comments in Lonely Planet products such as guidebooks, websites and digital products, so let us know if you don't want your comments reproduced or your name acknowledged. For a copy of our privacy policy visit lonelyplanet.com/privacy.

OUR READERS

Many thanks to the travellers who used the last edition and wrote to us with helpful hints, useful advice and interesting anecdotes:

Friso Annema, Pippa Curtis, John Hardy, Koni Helfrich, Michele Henry, Tara Hewitt, Tuomo Huuskonen, Katerina Ioannidou, Ralpha Jacobson, Jill Kramer, Janet Ludlow, Jose Moran, Denis Morris, Catherine Murphy, Camilla Nielsen, Tatjana Pavlova, Christopher Psomadellis, Ken Pugh, Neil Small, Myat Thwin, Heather Watson, Nancy Watson, Jeffrey Wijling, Brantly Womack, Yarui Zheng

AUTHOR THANKS

Bradley Mayhew

Thanks to Kelsang at the Wordo Museum in Shigatse, and to Kelsang at the Yeti Hotel in Gyantse for showing me that city's tourism plans. Thanks to Lobsang Jigme at Shambhala Palace and greetings to Nyima Tashi at Dropenling. A big personal thanks to first-rate guide Tenzin Gelek and driver Nordrup, to Big Tenzin and Aja at Tibet Highland Tours and to Andre, Alyson and Wanda for their company on the road. Cheers to Robert and John for their fine contributions and to Megan and Joe for editorial assistance. Love as always to Kelli for doing without me for way too long this year.

John Vincent Bellezza

Travelling in Tibet for Lonely Planet is as much a social enterprise as it is a physical journey. For all those who pointed the way, offered moral support or cups of tea, I doff my cap in thanks. I especially want to express gratitude to my vermilion-clad teachers of Tibetan history and culture – individuals of the highest order.

Robert Kelly

Immense thanks are due to Chris Nelson, abandoned traveller and steadfast friend, who never gave up trying to find free wi-fi. Thanks also to Tenzin at Tibet Highland Tours for stepping in when help was needed. Lele and Ping, you know what you did. Finally, great love to Tania Simonetti, desert wanderer, and heart of my heart, for making the journey always as fascinating as the destination.

ACKNOWLEDGMENTS

Climate map data adapted from Peel MC, Finlayson BL & McMahon TA (2007) 'Updated World Map of the Köppen-Geiger Climate Classification', *Hydrology and Earth System Sciences*, 11, 163344.

Cover photograph: Monks playing music, Dennis Walton/Getty ©

THIS BOOK

This 9th edition of Lonely Planet's *Tibet* guidebook was researched and written by Bradley Mayhew and Robert Kelly. John Vincent Bellezza wrote the Tibetan Treks chapter. The 8th edition was written by Bradley Mayhew, Michael Kohn, Daniel McCrohan and John Vincent Bellezza. Xiao Bianr assisted with research. The 7th edition was written by Bradley Mayhew, John Vincent Bellezza and Robert Kelly. This guidebook was commissioned in Lonely Planet's London office, and produced by the following:

Commissioning Editor
Joe Bindloss

Destination Editor
Megan Eaves

Coordinating Editors
Carolyn Boicos, Nigel Chin

Senior Cartographer
David Kemp

Book Designer
Wendy Wright

Assisting Editors
Kate Mathews, Jenna Myers, Charlotte Orr, Kirsten Rawlings

Assisting Cartographer
Julie Dodkins

Cover Researcher
Naomi Parker

Thanks to David Carroll, Kate Chapman, Dan Corbett, Michael Essex, Ryan Evans, Larissa Frost, Noirin Hegarty, Andi Jones, Jouve India, Claire Naylor, Karyn Noble, Dianne Schallmeiner, Samantha Tyson, Lauren Wellicome

Index

Map Legend

Sights

- Beach
- Bird Sanctuary
- Buddhist
- Castle/Palace
- Christian
- Confucian
- Hindu
- Islamic
- Jain
- Jewish
- Monument
- Museum/Gallery/Historic Building
- Ruin
- Shinto
- Sikh
- Taoist
- Winery/Vineyard
- Zoo/Wildlife Sanctuary
- Other Sight

Activities, Courses & Tours

- Bodysurfing
- Diving
- Canoeing/Kayaking
- Course/Tour
- Sento Hot Baths/Onsen
- Skiing
- Snorkelling
- Surfing
- Swimming/Pool
- Walking
- Windsurfing
- Other Activity

Sleeping

- Sleeping
- Camping

Eating

- Eating

Drinking & Nightlife

- Drinking & Nightlife
- Cafe

Entertainment

- Entertainment

Shopping

- Shopping

Information

- Bank
- Embassy/Consulate
- Hospital/Medical
- Internet
- Police
- Post Office
- Telephone
- Toilet
- Tourist Information
- Other Information

Geographic

- Beach
- Hut/Shelter
- Lighthouse
- Lookout
- Mountain/Volcano
- Oasis
- Park
- Pass
- Picnic Area
- Waterfall

Population

- Capital (National)
- Capital (State/Province)
- City/Large Town
- Town/Village

Transport

- Airport
- Border crossing
- Bus
- Cable car/Funicular
- Cycling
- Ferry
- Metro/MRT/MTR station
- Monorail
- Parking
- Petrol station
- Skytrain/Subway station
- Taxi
- Train station/Railway
- Tram
- Underground station
- Other Transport

Note: Not all symbols displayed above appear on the maps in this book

Routes

- Tollway
- Freeway
- Primary
- Secondary
- Tertiary
- Lane
- Unsealed road
- Road under construction
- Plaza/Mall
- Steps
- Tunnel
- Pedestrian overpass
- Walking Tour
- Walking Tour detour
- Path/Walking Trail

Boundaries

- International
- State/Province
- Disputed
- Regional/Suburb
- Marine Park
- Cliff
- Wall

Hydrography

- River, Creek
- Intermittent River
- Canal
- Water
- Dry/Salt/Intermittent Lake
- Reef

Areas

- Airport/Runway
- Beach/Desert
- Cemetery (Christian)
- Cemetery (Other)
- Glacier
- Mudflat
- Park/Forest
- Sight (Building)
- Sportsground
- Swamp/Mangrove

OUR STORY

A beat-up old car, a few dollars in the pocket and a sense of adventure. In 1972 that's all Tony and Maureen Wheeler needed for the trip of a lifetime – across Europe and Asia overland to Australia. It took several months, and at the end – broke but inspired – they sat at their kitchen table writing and stapling together their first travel guide, *Across Asia on the Cheap*. Within a week they'd sold 1500 copies. Lonely Planet was born.

Today, Lonely Planet has offices in Franklin, London, Melbourne, Oakland, Beijing and Delhi, with more than 600 staff and writers. We share Tony's belief that 'a great guidebook should do three things: inform, educate and amuse'.

OUR WRITERS

Bradley Mayhew

Coordinating Author; Lhasa, Ü, Tsang, Gateway Cities Bradley has been visiting the Tibetan plateau for 20 years now, since studying Chinese for four long years at Oxford University. Over the years he's been horse trekking in Kham, done the Mt Kailash kora twice and clocked up around 40,000km bumping across Tibet. Bradley has coordinated the last five editions of this guide and is also the coauthor of over 25 Lonely Planet titles, including *Bhutan*, *China*, *Trekking in the Nepal Himalaya* and *Central Asia*, as well as the Odyssey guide to Uzbekistan. He has lectured on Central Asia to the Royal Geographical Society and was the subject of a five-part Arte/SWR documentary retracing the route of Marco Polo. See what he's currently up to at www.bradleymayhew.blogspot.com.

Read more about Bradley at:
lonelyplanet.com/members/nepalibrad

Robert Kelly

Western Tibet, Eastern Tibet With an equal love of nature and fine art, Robert finds Tibet to be one of his favourite destinations. On this research trip, he grew obsessed with comparing the finer points of Tibetan architecture with Chinese, as well as understanding the complex geology of Kham and Ngari. A freelance writer since the early 2000s, Robert has contributed twice to Lonely Planet's *Tibet*, as well as covered Tibetan regions in Qinghai, Sichuan and Gansu provinces for *China*. Robert also wrote the Mt Kailash Kora section in the Tibetan Treks chapter, and the Survival Guide.

Contributing Author

John Vincent Bellezza researched and wrote the Tibetan Treks chapter. John has been living and travelling in Tibet and the Himalaya since 1983. A leading authority in the pre-Buddhist civilisation of Tibet, he is a Senior Research Fellow at the Tibet Center, University of Virginia. He has been charting Zhang Zhung and Sumpa, fabled cultures of Upper Tibet that had attained a surprising level of sophistication more than 2000 years ago. See http://tibetarchaeology.com for more information about John's life and work.

Published by Lonely Planet Publications Pty Ltd
ABN 36 005 607 983
9th edition – Mar 2015
ISBN 978 1 74220 046 0
© Lonely Planet 2015   Photographs © as indicated 2015
10 9 8 7 6 5 4 3 2 1
Printed in Singapore